A Stranger in the House – the Crossroads III.

Proceedings of an International Conference on Foreigners in Ancient Egyptian and Near Eastern Societies of the Bronze Age held in Prague, September 10–13, 2018

edited by Jana Mynářová
Marwan Kilani
Sergio Alivernini

Prague
Charles University, Faculty of Arts
2019

FACULTY OF ARTS
Charles University

The book was published with support of the research project of the Czech Science Foundation GA ČR P401/12/G168 "History and Interpretation of the Bible", a non-investment subsidy No. MŠMT-906/2019-1, VEG2019/1 and The Programme for the Development of Fields of Study at Charles University, no. Q11: Complexity and Resilience: Ancient Egyptian Civilisation in Multidisciplinary and Multicultural Perspective.

Reviewed by Lena Fijałkowska and Filip Coppens.

Contributors: Sergio Alivernini, Danielle Candelora, Gaëlle Chantrain, Susan Cohen, Katrien De Graef, Elena Devecchi, Anne Goddeeris, Caleb R. Hamilton, Ann-Kathrin Jeske, Kevin McGeough, Edward Mushett Cole, Jana Mynářová, Emanuel Pfoh, Regine Pruzsinszky, Clemens Reichel, Seth Richardson, Hannah L. Ringheim, Katharina Streit, Marta Valerio, Sarah Vilain, Federico Zangani

Cover: Illustrations: Caleb R. Hamilton, Ann-Kathrin Jeske

Type-setting layout: AGAMA® poly-grafický ateliér, s.r.o., Praha
Print: TNM print, Chlumec nad Cidlinou

ISBN: 978-80-7308-928-3

Contents

Preface 12
Contributors 14
List of Abbreviations 18

Danielle Candelora
Hybrid Military Communities of Practice: The Integration of Immigrants as the Catalyst for Egyptian Social Transformation in the 2nd Millennium BC **25**

Abstract: The second millennium BC was a period of unprecedented interconnectedness, characterized by the increasing movement of people in conjunction with the transmission of technologies across the Near East. Employing a Communities of Practice approach, this paper investigates the human networks through which this specialized knowledge might have transferred, suggesting that the interaction between foreign and local military and technological specialists was the locus of this transmission. The Middle Kingdom and Second Intermediate Period were characterized by waves of West Asian immigrants moving into the Eastern Delta, bringing with them their mastery of new production processes and technologies. This period also saw the introduction of West Asian military practices and values, including a corpus of military related Semitic loan words. Therefore, this paper will propose that the mixture of immigrant and Egyptian specialists in hybrid military communities of practice played a major role in this cultural exchange. I will also explore the cultural significance behind the adoption and maintenance of these foreign technologies and military values, as well as their impact on the New Kingdom Egyptian military and conceptions of kingship.

Keywords: communities of practice – military – immigration – hybridity – Second Intermediate Period

Gaëlle Chantrain
About "Egyptianity" and "Foreignness" in Egyptian Texts. A Context-Sensitive Lexical Study **49**

Abstract: Many interesting studies have already been published about the relations between Egypt and its neighbours. I once more would like to return to this question, through a lexical study. I here propose to examine texts from the Old Kingdom until the Third Intermediate Period, with a special focus on the New Kingdom. I present a context-sensitive lexical analysis of qualifiers and expressions related to foreigners, including the distribution of the classifiers. In so doing, I situate the respective places of Asiatics, Nubians and Libyans on the Egyptian's mental world and I will retrace the chronological evolution of these connections. This study focuses on the evolutionary process of both concepts of "Egyptianity" and "foreignness", and on the economy of the continuum between these two ends. The final aim is thus to provide new elements in light of a corpus-based study in order to solve—at least partially—the dichotomy between ongoing stereotypes and actual individuals.

Keywords: lexical study – foreigners – contact – classifiers

Abstract: Egyptian official text and image traditionally described and presented the peoples of the southern Levant using specific rhetoric, hyperbolic language, and canonized visual representation designed to highlight the concept of "Asiatic" subjugation to Egyptian sovereignty. However, while the majority of public monuments and official accounts provided this formal rhetoric, excoriating the "vile Asiatic" in a manner consistent with the Egyptian worldview, other evidence suggests that the reality of Egyptian relationships with southern Levantine peoples did not always conform to the official policy of bellicosity and disdain, and further, that the nature of this relationship changed over time in keeping with contemporary geopolitical circumstances. Specifically, the inscriptions found in Sinai dating to the Old and Middle Kingdoms that provide both textual and visual description of foreigners from the southern Levant reveal significant differences in the view and treatment of "Asiatics" in each period that can be linked with changes in the southern Levant. Examination of these inscriptions from both Old and Middle Kingdoms, together with analysis of contemporary developments in the Bronze Age southern Levant, provides further insight into the interconnections between these regions.

Keywords: Sinai – Asiatic – southern Levant – inscription – Old Kingdom – Middle Kingdom

Abstract: Of old, a patchwork of different peoples and cultures existed within the territory of Western Iran, subjected to political and military dominance and/or influence from neighbouring Mesopotamia. As a result of a continuous interaction and balancing between Mesopotamian and Elamite traditions, values and influences in political, legal, economic and administrative matters, a basic duality of cultures evolved throughout the second millennium BC. This paper focusses on the legal and administrative formulas used in the documentary texts from Sukkalmaḫ Susa, which seem to be for a great part typically local: some, although written in correct Akkadian, clearly reflect local legal practices, others even include Elamite expressions. It is clear that this is neither just a question of a simple transfer of formulas nor a comparison of two legal systems. The use of Elamite phrases and expressions as well as Akkadian phrases and formulations only used in texts from Iran (but not in texts from Mesopotamia) proves we are dealing with a bilingual and bicultural society.

Keywords: Akkadian – Elamite – Sukkalmaḫ State – biculturality

Abstract: The epigraphic finds from Ugarit always represented an unvaluable source of information on the relationship between this rich Syrian kingdom and the Hittites, who ruled over it during the 14th and 13th century BC. While the interaction between Ugarit and Ḫatti seems to have been relatively easy and smooth during the first decades of Hittite dominance, the relationship between vassal and foreign overlord starts to fray towards the mid of the 13th century BC. The recently published Akkadian texts from the so-called "House of Urtenu" provide now ample new evidence about this situation, conveying the impression that the last kings of Ugarit regularly tried to shirk their obligations towards the Hittite suzerains and their representatives in Syria. This paper will offer an updated overview on this latent conflict, analysing the occasions which prompted the Hittite reprimands and discussing the geo-political background which set the scene for this quite remarkable situation.

Keywords: Ugarit – Hittites – House of Urtenu – Alalaḫ – vassal's obligations

Abstract: During the Old Babylonian period, the members of the clergy of Nippur consider themselves to be the foremost keepers of the Sumerian traditions. Fellow townsmen circulating in other professional circles, magnates from other Babylonian cities and visitors or immigrants from outside Babylonia are not allowed membership to this exclusive category. The social identity approach comprises a group of theories developed in the field of social psychology during the seventies and the eighties explaining the mechanisms of group formation, and the role outgroup bias and in-group favouritism. This approach offers a framework to describe and to understand historical processes of group formation and the mechanisms behind the constant changes in it. Although historical sources do not inform us about individual motivations and decisions, it elucidates some factors playing a role in power shifts.

Looking at the temple management in Nippur, the growing role of the palace in the temple of Nippur can be retraced. Whereas palace magnates remain at the fringes of the temple administration when they visit Nippur during the reign of Rīm-Sîn of Larsa, they are able to acquire temple offices during the reign of Samsuiluna of Babylon. At the end of Samsuiluna's rule over Nippur, the palace plays a key role in the temple management.

In this paper, the first phase in this development will be looked at more closely. The foreigners in the administrative archive will be identified and their role will be addressed.

Keywords: Old Babylonian Period – Nippur – palace – temple – social identity

Abstract: The Egyptian representation of foreigners can be traced to the earliest period of pharaonic history. During the Early Bronze Age / 0 Dynasty, there was an active intent to separate those groups or regions who did not fall within the developing ideological and iconographic ideals promulgated by the Egyptian elite. In contrast to this, with the expansion of Egyptian interests away from the Nile Valley into the neighbouring desert regions, the evidence for the Egyptians as foreigners in these geographical areas is lacking. This paper presents evidence to convey that, during the Early Dynastic Period, the Egyptians were foreigners in the Egyptian Western Desert. This case study focusses on an array of archaeological, iconographic, and ideological evidence which indicates the Egyptian did not present themselves as foreign, even though they were conducting activity in a geographical area that was not yet part of the Egyptian state.

Interactions with the indigenous peoples of the Western Desert, especially in Dakhleh Oasis, conveys the reliance the Egyptians had on others as foreigners in a non-Egyptian region. These interactions seem to have been generally symbiotic, contrasting Egyptian interactions within other regions close to the Nile Valley, such as the Sinai. As non-natives of the Western Desert, the foreignness exhibited by the Egyptians belies the true nature of their initial presence in this region, and can be linked to the articulation of the dominant ideological conventions and iconographic expressions promulgated by royalty and the elite during the Early Dynastic Period.

Keywords: Egyptians – foreigner – Early Dynastic Period – Western Desert

Abstract: Although Egypt's involvement in the Levant during the Late Bronze Age (LB) has been subject to many studies, the early phases of this period have rarely been the primary focus. Furthermore, those who researched the early 18th Dynasty relied heavily on textual sources and even drew on references from documents written in later periods due to the meagre output of information in contemporaneous texts. Since written sources tend to remain elusive regarding the activities of Egyptian functionaries in the southern Levant, it is appropriate to turn to archaeological evidence, as the leading source, to reconstruct Egypt's engagement in this region. This paper presents an approach to filter and analyse the Egyptian material culture excavated in the southern Levant by providing a method to study and interpret such evidence while disregarding texts—at least initially—as an interpretative complement. The theoretical base of the proposed approach are the three concepts object itinerary, cultural appropriation and affordance. Applied to the archaeological record of LB I, the approach suggests that Egypt's involvement was rather limited during this period. Furthermore, there is not any indication for the maintenance of Egyptian garrisons during the Tuthmosid period, except in Tell el-ʿAjjul, situated at the terminus of the Way of Horus.

Keywords: Egypt – Levant – early 18th Dynasty – material culture – military

Abstract: The Late Bronze Age city of Ugarit has long been identified as a location of ancient cosmopolitanism, where different people from around the eastern Mediterranean and Near East met and interacted. Given the longstanding excavations of the site, the voluminous textual record that has been recovered, and the long history of scholarship, the site offers a unique opportunity to explore the dynamics of "foreignness" in a Late Bronze Age context where the presence of foreigners was, if not normative, expected. Using insights from critical theory derived from the discipline of Geography, this paper explores how, in Engin Isin's terms, the city is not where difference is found but rather where difference is made (labeled and reified), especially through what Julie Young has called "spatial practices and technologies of governance". Through the examination of locations of every day encounters, this paper shall explore how foreigners are recognized as such, how their relations with non-foreigners are managed (explicitly and implicitly), how different scales of self and otherness are created and maintained, how these constructed identities are naturalized, and what modalities emerge or are imposed to mediate these relationships. Rather than seeking to identify a monolithic approach to foreignness, by examining different examples of micropublic interactions (such as in moments of palatial administration), this paper seeks to untangle some of the multi-scalar and multi-semiotic aspects of foreignness at Ugarit.

Keywords: Ugarit – ancient urbanism – ancient foreignness – Late Bronze Age – ancient administration – urban legibility

Edward Mushett Cole
Ethnic Enclaves: A Modern Understanding of How Migratory Groups Preserve Ethnic Identity as a Potential Explanation for the Libyans' Retention of a Non-Egyptian Identity in the Late New Kingdom and Third Intermediate Period 221

Abstract: It is increasingly accepted in scholarship that the Libyans who entered Egypt during the late New Kingdom and who rose to power during the Third Intermediate Period retained, at the very least, some of their original non-Egyptian ethnic identity. Despite the evidence for this, as well as that revealing the presence of foreigners generally within the Egyptian population across the dynastic era, there has been no explanation of the mechanisms by which the Libyans would have been able to retain this non-Egyptian identity. Such a lack of explanation is significant given that many of the Libyans are believed to have arrived as prisoners-of-war following the various invasions of the late 19th and early 20th Dynasties, who were supposedly "indoctrinated" in Egyptian culture.

This paper will address this gap through reference to a sociological explanation for how modern migrants often retain their ethnic identities after settling within an area with a dominant culture: "ethnic enclaves". Using the mechanism of "ethnic enclaves" this paper will seek, therefore, to provide some explanation for the Libyans' retention of a distinctly non-Egyptian identity after their arrival into Egypt.

Keywords: Libyan Period – Third Intermediate Period – Libyans – ethnicity – ethnic enclaves

Jana Mynářová
Are you an Egyptian? Are you a Stranger? Egyptians in the Levant in the Bronze Age 239

Abstract: Egypt and the Near East. Interactions between these regions are attested from the earliest days when the first political centers started to develop in both parts of the ancient world. For this period, our information on Egyptians living "abroad" is very limited. We can hardly hope to obtain a complete picture of both the daily life of an individual and the foreign policy of the Egyptian rulers based on the evidence we currently have at our disposal. The interpretation of the Egyptian policy towards the Near Eastern polities and their peoples is hence largely dependent on the interpretation of the character of the Egyptian (or Egyptianizing) objects discovered in Near Eastern sites. The same holds true for the Near Eastern perspective as well. During the third millennium BC, the picture provided by the limited number and much formalized character of the Egyptian written evidence is often supplemented by iconographic and archaeological sources. Moreover, there are practically no ancient Near Eastern records mentioning Egyptians living "abroad". It is only in the second half of the second millennium BC, when the written evidence—both Egyptian and non-Egyptian—becomes sufficient to provide a more detailed account on the Egyptians living "outside the Egyptian borders". In my paper I will address the question of evidence of Egyptians living in the Near East. The Egyptian sources provide us only with one part of the story—the Egyptian one. But I will rather pay attention to the evidence provided by Near Eastern written documents, mentioning Egypt and especially Egyptians, being part of local communities. This evidence will be set against the perspective provided by official sources, preserved on both sides.

Keywords: Egypt – Near East – foreigners – Bronze Age – written sources

Abstract: This paper explores the modes of political sociability in the Late Bronze Age Near East, focusing in particular on the political agency of foreigners in their different historical and social manifestations (notably, messengers/ambassadors, merchants) and the socio-political spheres they interacted with in local society. Sociologically speaking, insiders and outsiders to social systems and communities operate through varied and situational codes of sociability, based on and expressed by, for instance, the circumstance of belonging to a kinship group or to a concrete political body or not, which creates positive situations of assistance and reciprocity or negative situations of partial or full rejection and opposition (and the negotiated possibilities in-between these poles). During the Late Bronze Age, instances of hospitality, alliance and subordination were among the key scenarios for dealing positively with and understanding outsiders, as an integral part of the shared codes of political sociability in the East Mediterranean and in Southwest Asia of the period. In the present communication, these practices and situations are analysed after the contemporary textual evidence (mainly, letters from Amarna) from the perspective of social anthropology and sociology with the aim of contrasting the theoretical definitions of hospitality, alliance and subordination with those potentially expressed in the textual evidence from the Late Bronze Age.

Keywords: Late Bronze Age – foreigners – hospitality – reciprocity – political sociability

Abstract: Regarding the overall topic of the 3rd Crossroads conference on the understanding of foreignness in ancient societies this paper takes a closer look on the Late Bronze Age cuneiform archives from the Middle Euphrates area. Emar, the capital of Aštata served as a trading center and important communications junction and its archives attest to various forms of contacts between locals and foreigners. Given the political changes in the region of Aštata in the late 14th century BC, when Emar entered the sphere of the Hittite Empire, special attention will be given to the Hittite influence on the social, administrative, cultural and religious changes in order to identify various forms of foreignness and to detect in which contexts and how local societies interacted with foreigners.

Keywords: Emar – Mittani – Hittites – Assyrians – onomastics – scribal traditions

Abstract: This paper addresses the topic of xenophobia in ancient times and its reflection in modern day scholarship in the case of the Gutians, a population group from Western Iran that invaded the Mesopotamian lowlands during the later part of the Akkadian Dynasty (ca. 2300–2150 BC). The "Curse of Agade", a literary composition that rationalizes the fall of the Akkadian Dynasty in ideological terms, shows the Gutians as invading hoards that ravaged the cities and hinterland of Mesopotamia at the commend of its supreme god Enlil in retaliation for the destruction of the É-kur, Enlil's temple at Nippur, by Narām-Sîn, Agade's fourth and most illustrious king. Their description as quasi-beasts with animalistic features and behaviors clearly reflects some of the fears and apprehensions against foreigners that were present in ancient Mesopotamia and which this literary composition uses in highly propagandistic terms. Reviewing the available archaeological data it is clear that post-Akkadian literary and historiographic sources overstated the impact of this invasion since no widespread post-Akkadian destructions are attested at archaeological sites. As this paper will show, this did not stop notable archaeologists of the 20th century from seeking "Gutian" traits in ancient material culture, using stereotypes that very much echo ancient Mesopotamian sentiment.

Keywords: xenophobia – Gutians – archaeology – 20th century scholarship

Abstract: By looking at issues of host and guest cultures in a particular historical culture (late Middle Bronze Age Babylonia, ca. 17th century BC), this essay examines how their interactions were not only mutually reactive, but even affected categorical understandings of foreignness itself. The chapter looks at a number of arenas of activity: the international scene; differently protected classes of citizens and aliens; exiles, especially elites; foreign mercenaries; class anxiety; women without households; and the isolated and aging nobles who ran the kingdom at the end of the period. By juxtaposing the different bases on which ideas of "insiderness" and "outsiderness" were constructed, including issues of exclusivity and rank within the host culture. Final consideration is made of a possible paradigm shift in this time, when notions first arose about alienation as a personal and interior matter—about isolation as a primarily social and spiritual experience rather than an ethnocultural one.

Keywords: alienation – foreigners – social difference – Babylonia – ethno-cultural identity

Abstract: This paper addresses one of the fundamental ways in which foreigners and Egyptians interacted during the third to second millennium: as foreign soldiers in the Egyptian army. Frequently it is suggested that these are mercenaries hired by the Egyptians; however, how accurate is this identification? When does a non-local fighter become a mercenary? To approach these questions, the paper examines specific examples from tomb inscriptions that document Nubian and Egyptian interactions and the circumstances that led to Nubians in the Egyptian military. The discussion then looks at the later Shardana contingent of the so-called Sea Peoples in the 13th to 12th centuries BC and the varying types of exchanges with the Egyptians, based on wall iconography and texts. The process in which the Shardana infiltrate the Egyptian military suggests that in certain circumstances, they evince characteristics of mercenaries. The evidence exemplifies the first instances when armies relied on foreign hires, a phenomenon that then resonated throughout antiquity.

Keywords: mercenaries – Egypt – warfare – Shardana – Nubians

Abstract: According to both written sources such as the Amarna correspondence, and to archaeological excavations, Tel Lachish was a thriving city and an important part of the diplomatic network of the Late Bronze Age. However, the precise nature of its power relations remains subject to debate, and opinions are divided on whether Egyptians were actually present at the site. It is notoriously difficult to identify individuals of specific cultural groups in the archaeological record. This is due to the complexity of such identities, and the difficulties to distinguish e.g. ethnic and economic factors in past populations. This is further complicated when different variations e.g. of ethnicities well research in anthropological literature are considered, such as "fluid", "acquired", "segmentary", and "situational" ethnicities. These can only be discerned with the help of informants. Nevertheless, indications of cultural background can be observed in how it shapes material culture. In this paper two different modes, "embodied cultural automatism" and "conscious cultural choice", are distinguished and applied to material culture from Lachish, including architecture, burial practice, the ceramic assemblage, and epigraphic finds. It is concluded that while the ruling elite appear to have been local Canaanites, at least some individuals of Egyptian origin, probably engaged in administrative tasks, seem to have been present at the site.

Keywords: cultural identity – Late Bronze Age – southern Levant – Egypt – Tel Lachish

Marta Valerio

The Egyptians' Ambivalent Relationship with Foreigners: The Case of the Prisoners of War in the New Kingdom 371

Abstract: This paper will suggest that there was a stark difference in the ways in which Egyptians described the foreigner outside or within Egypt. In the first case, the foreigner was at best a stranger element and often an enemy to be fought, in the second case it was an integral part of the society. The "external" foreigner is represented according to precise iconographic codes and epithets that make it easily recognizable in contrast to "the Egyptian being". But beyond the propagandistic proclamations, what information on the presence of foreigners in Egypt are provided by sources? In the Pharaonic ideology, foreigners represented the Nine Bows against which the Egyptians fought to maintain the order of the *Maat*, a mission that the deity attributed to the Pharaoh. The relationship between Egyptians and foreigners was thus regulated by a dualism that Antonio Loprieno has synthetized using two antithetical concepts: *topos* and *mimesis*. The *topos* considers the Egyptians as superior to "others", while the *mimesis* expresses the daily practice of relations with foreigners that goes beyond the violent relations underlying the *topos*. Referring to this theory, and using prisoners of war as a case study, this paper will investigate Egyptians' ambivalent relationship with foreigners.

Keywords: Foreigners – Egypt – prisoners of war – Egyptianisation – otherness

Sarah Vilain

The Foreign Trade of Tell el-Dabʿa during the Second Intermediate Period: Another Glance at Imported Ceramics under Hyksos Rule 387

Abstract: The extensive exploration of the archaeological site of Tell el-Dabʿa highlighted that ancient Avaris was an active trading centre, as testified by the discovery of large amounts of imported goods from the Middle Kingdom onwards. This paper presents an overview of the evolution of trade at Tell el-Dabʿa during the Second Intermediate Period through the study of foreign ceramics discovered at the site. The examination of the distribution of Levantine, Cypriot and Nubian imports is used to pinpoint periods of disturbances or ruptures in the flux of exchanges. Specific attention is given to the takeover of the Hyksos and how this event could have affected the already existing trading connections with other parts of Egypt and the Eastern Mediterranean. Finally, this article concludes with some observations about how these trading connections are closely linked to political and cultural developments that occurred in Egypt during the Second Intermediate Period.

Keywords: Egypt – Cyprus – Levant – Nubia – Trade – Second Intermediate Period

Federico Zangani
Foreign-Indigenous Interactions in the Late Bronze Age Levant: Tuthmosid Imperialism and the Origin of the Amarna Diplomatic System **405**

Abstract: This paper proposes new avenues of research to investigate foreign-indigenous interactions within 18th Dynasty Egyptian imperialism by charting the evolution of the Egyptian political and economic engagement with the northern Levant, from the phase of territorial expansionism under the Tuthmosids to the development of the diplomatic system of the Amarna archive under Amenhotep III. More specifically, it has never been questioned how the world of the Amarna letters originated in the first place, but it is likely, as I will argue, that this world did not exist at the time of Tuthmose III. In fact, the geopolitical situation in the Levant in the 15th century BC was radically different from a century later: while Tuthmose III campaigned systematically between Canaan and northern Syria, Amenhotep III no longer had this necessity, and military activity was limited to a few, targeted operations. This paper suggests that the analysis of the evidence should include not only the Egyptian royal inscriptions and the Amarna letters, but also contemporary archives from the Egyptian provincial centre in Lebanon at Kāmid el-Lōz and from the Syrian kingdom of Qaṭna, which could elucidate how 18th Dynasty Egypt coerced and / or negotiated with the indigenous realities in order to attain its own political and economic interests, and at the same time maintain regional stability. Moreover, it seems quite plausible that Egyptian territorial expansionism in the New Kingdom originated as pre-emptive warfare after the Hyksos rule, similarly to the development of Roman imperialism following Hannibal's invasion of Italy in the second Punic war. Finally, principles of political realism in the writings of Thucydides and Machiavelli will be discussed, with a view to demonstrating their profound applicability to the geopolitical systems of the Late Bronze Age.

Keywords: Egyptian imperialism – Amarna letters – pre-emptive warfare – Thucydides – Machiavelli

Preface

"The Crossroads III – A Stranger in the House. Foreigners in Ancient Egyptian and Near Eastern Societies of the Bronze Age", has been held at the Faculty of Arts, Charles University (Prague) between September 10 and 13, 2018.

The main objective of the conference was to enhance our understanding of "foreignness" in ancient societies of the Near East and Egypt between the end of the Chalcolithic period and the end of the Late Bronze Age.

Our goal, while organizing the conference, was to bring together archaeologists, philologists, as well as historians to obtain a balanced insight into the historical, social, cultural and economic aspects of "foreignness" of the respective regions (Mesopotamia, Anatolia, Levant, Egypt) at this particular moment in time. We are firmly convinced that the dialogue between experts of various disciplines is not only highly desirable, but it is also a necessity for gaining a deeper and meaningful understanding of complex social dynamics.

We thus tried to collect papers that treated the topic of "foreignness" from archaeological, historical, iconographic and philological points of view, suggesting to the contributor a series of possible research questions: Who is a foreigner, and how do we recognise foreigners in ancient societies? What is the role of foreigners and how did foreigners and indigenous population(s) interact? What can be said about foreigners as enemies of the state, and about foreigners as allies? What did it mean to be a "foreigner" in an ancient Near Eastern society? And what were the ways of communicating of individuals and societies?

The number of papers we have received, and their quality showed that this topic is very relevant in the contemporary academic discourse, and that there is a widespread desire to explore and discuss it.

This desire was well reflected already in the paper of the keynote speakers that opened the conference. In particular, Clemens Reichel discussed the characterization of the Gutians as attested in the sources of the later third and early second millennium BC, and he reassessed the scale and impact of the "Gutian invasion" taking into consideration more recent historical and archaeological evidence. Seth Richardson reviewed the terminology attested in Old Babylonian texts to refer to social roles that may have been at least in part associated with foreigners, and then discussed the general conceptual construction of "strangers/strangeness" in the Old Babylonian period. Regine Pruzsinsky, instead, explored how one can identify foreigners in the Late Bronze texts from Emar, and what such texts tell us about their interactions with the local societies. Elena Devecchi offered a reassessment of the latent conflict between the Ugaritic elite and their Hittite suzerains in the final phase of the Late Bronze Age on the basis of the documents found in the "House of Urtenu". Kevin McGeough used insights from critical theory derived from the discipline of geography to explore "foreignness" and foreign identity, by examining examples of micropublic interactions in a urban reality like that of Ugarit. Finally, Jana Mynářová reassessed the evidence for the presence of Egyptians living in the Near East during the Bronze Age, with special attention given to the Late Bronze Age sources, discussing it in relation with both Egyptian and Near Eastern official documents.

The 26 papers and 6 posters that were presented at the conference declined these topics in multiple different ways. Some decided to approach the discussion from a theoretical perspective, or to present and discuss theoretical frameworks that could be used to explore at least some of elements underlying the concept of "foreignness". Others investigated sociocultural dimension involved in the presence of foreigners, or in their interactions with local communities. Some papers focused on specific case studies, some looked for foreigners in archaeological evidence or written sources, while others turned to languages and linguistics, exploring the social interactions hidden behind the spread and circulation of loanwords and *wanderworts*, or assessing the meanings and connotations of terms used to refer to various foreign groups. Cases from Egypt, Mesopotamia, Anatolia and the Levant, covering the whole of the Bronze Age have been discussed. The wide range of perspectives, and their combination within the frame of the conference often stimulated that multidisciplinary dialogue that was the primary aim of this third edition of *Crossroads*.

This book collects some of the twenty most significant contributions presented at the conference. The contributions are here presented in alphabetic order, as the numbers of interconnections that could be highlighted among them makes any attempt to group them somehow limiting and counterproductive: we, as the editors, believe that all these papers are part of a single coherent ensemble, and we wish to present them here as such.

In Prague on July 21, 2019

Jana Mynářová, Marwan Kilani,
and Sergio Alivernini

Contributors

Danielle Candelora is an Egyptian archaeologist and Ph.D. Candidate in the Department of Near Eastern Languages and Cultures at the University of California, Los Angeles. Her research investigates the multivariate processes of identity negotiation in the Middle to Late Bronze Ages, focusing on theoretical approaches to immigration and the influence of immigrants on their host culture. In particular she examines the Eastern Nile Delta during the Second Intermediate Period, specifically the Hyksos and their impact on later Egyptian culture and especially the Ramesside conception of kingship. She has excavated a Revolutionary War battlefield in New Jersey, a Roman fortress in Spain, a Crusader site in Israel, as well as a Karanis, a Greco-Roman settlement in Egypt. She is currently co-editing a volume on the social history of ancient Egypt, and is a member of the UCLA Coffins Project directed by Kara Cooney.

Gaëlle Chantrain is a postdoctoral associate and lecturer in Egyptology at the department of Near Eastern Languages and Civilization of Yale University and Postdoctoral researcher *in absentia* at the Belgian National Fund for Scientific Research (FNRS). She did her master at the University of Liege (Belgium), where she was also collaborator in the Ramses Project. She completed her Ph.D. at the University of Louvain (Belgium), with a research fellowship from FNRS. During her Ph.D., she worked as an invited research associate at the Humboldt University in Berlin and then obtained a postdoc at the Czech Institute of Egyptology of the Charles University in Prague. Her work lays at the intersection between Egyptology and linguistics. Her main research interests are Egyptian philology, lexical semantics, classifiers studies, cognitive linguistics and semantic typology. She is also very interested in the development of digital humanities and is involved in several collaborative projects both in Egyptology and linguistics.

Susan Cohen received her Ph.D. in Syro-Palestinian Archaeology and Hebrew Bible from the Department of Near Eastern Languages and Civilizations at Harvard University in 2000. She directed the excavations at the Middle Bronze Age cemetery at Gesher, and the small rural multi-period site of Tel Zahara, both in the Jordan Valley. She is currently Chair of the Department of History and Philosophy at Montana State University.

Katrien De Graef obtained her Ph.D. in Assyriology from Ghent University, Belgium in 2004. She is currently Associate Professor of Assyriology and History of the Ancient Near East at Ghent University. Her research focuses primarily on the socio-economic history of the Old Babylonian period in general, and that of the cities of Sippar and Susa in particular, including gender studies and sealing praxis, and the relation between Babylonia and Elam in the third and second millennium BC. She published 2 monographs and more than 50 articles and book chapters and was epigraphist during the Belgo-Syrian excavations at Chagar Bazar (Syria).

Elena Devecchi is Researcher in History of the Ancient Near East at the Department of Historical Studies of the University of Turin. After receiving her Ph.D. at the University of Venice, she worked in Germany (Ludwig-Maximilians-Universität, München and Julius-Maximilians-Universität, Würzburg), Belgium (KU Leuven) and Austria (University of Innsbruck), where she carried out postdoctoral projects and taught classes on Akkadian and Hittite. Her scientific interests focus on the Near East during the Late Bronze Age, in particular on historical and diplomatic texts from Anatolia and Syria (see *Trattati internazionali ittiti*, Brescia 2015), and on the economic and administrative institutions of Kassite Babylonia. She is epigraphist of the archaeological mission conducted by the University and by the "Centro Ricerche Archeologiche e Scavi" of Turin at the site of Tulūl al-Baqarat (Iraq).

Anne Goddeeris teaches cuneiform languages and courses on the history of the Ancient Near East at Ghent University. Her research is centered around Old Babylonian society. Her publications include a monograph on the early Old Babylonian economy and society and publications of cuneiform archival documents in various collections (SANTAG 9, TMH 10).

Caleb R. Hamilton completed his Ph.D. at Monash University in 2016, graduating in 2017. His recent research centres on evidence from the Early Dynastic period in the desert margins of the Nile Valley, and also the nature of Egyptian interactions in Western Desert, including a reassessment of evidence for an unnamed king. He has also begun to assist with research on an ARC Discovery Project, exploring the archaeological nature of the cult of Seth in Egypt, under the direction of Colin Hope (Monash University), Gill Bowen (Monash University), and Iain Gardner (University of Sydney). He is also completing several edited volumes, as well as a monograph based on his doctoral dissertation.

Ann-Kathrin Jeske is a Ph.D. student and uni:docs fellow at the Institute of Egyptology, University of Vienna, studying the activities of Egyptian officials and soldiers in the southern Levant from the Protodynastic to the 18th Dynasty. Ann-Kathrin received her BA in "Ancien Cultures in the Eastern Mediterranean" at Georg August-Universität Göttingen and finished her MA studies in "Egyptology" at Johannes Gutenberg-University Mainz.

Kevin McGeough is Professor of Archaeology in the Department of Geography at the University of Lethbridge in Canada and holds a Board of Governor's Research Chair in Archaeological Theory and Reception. He has been the editor of the *Annual of the American Schools of Oriental Research*, ASOR's *Archaeological Report Series*, and is currently co-editor of the *Alberta Archaeological Review*. McGeough is the author of a three-volume series on the reception of archaeology, called *The Ancient Near East in the Nineteenth Century*. McGeough has also written extensively on economic issues at the Late Bronze Age site of Ugarit, including two books, *Exchange Relationships at Ugarit* and *Ugaritic Economic Tablets: Text, Translations, and Notes*.

Edward Mushett Cole graduated with a Ph.D. from the University of Birmingham in 2017 entitled *Decline in Ancient Egypt? A reassessment of the late New King-*

dom and Third Intermediate Period. He currently works as the Postgraduate Student Experience Officer in the College of Arts and Law at the University of Birmingham and has published several papers, most recently "'The year of hyenas when there was a famine': An assessment of environmental causes for the events of the Twentieth Dynasty" in C. Langer's *Global Egyptology* (London 2017).

Jana Mynářová is Associate Professor of Egyptology at the Czech Institute of Egyptology, Charles University. She obtained her Ph.D. in Philology – Languages of Asia and Africa in 2004. Her research focuses on various aspects of the relations between Egypt and the Ancient Near East in the second millennium BC, with special attention given to documents in Peripheral Akkadian. She is the author and co-author of several books and studies on the topic (*Language of Amarna – Language of Diplomacy. Perspectives on the Amarna Letters*, Prague 2007). Presently, she carries a research project devoted to the study of Amarna cuneiform palaeography and she is a member of a multidisciplinary research project dealing with the collection of the Old Assyrian tablets held at Charles University. She is the main organiser of the Crossroads conferences devoted to study of interrelations among the ANE societies in the Bronze Age.

Emanuel Pfoh is Researcher at the National Research Council (CONICET) and Assistant Professor in the Department of History of the National University of La Plata, Argentina. He is author of *The Emergence of Israel in Ancient Palestine: Historical and Anthropological Perspectives* (2009), *Anthropology and the Bible* (ed. 2010), *The Politics of Israel's Past* (co-edited with K.W. Whitelam, 2013) and *Syria-Palestine in the Late Bronze Age: An Anthropology of Politics and Power* (2016).

Regine Pruzsinszky is an Assyriologist at the Institute of Archaeological Studies at the University of Freiburg. Her research interests focus on cuneiform records from the Late Bronze Age, the chronology of Mesopotamia, Ancient Near Eastern onomastic and musicians. She is the author of *Die Personennamen der Texte aus Emar* (Bethesda, 2003), and *Mesopotamian Chronology of the 2nd Millennium BCE. An Introduction to the Textual Evidence and Related Chronological Issues* (Vienna, 2009). Among other edited books she has edited a volume on *Policies of Exchange, Political Systems and Modes of Interaction in the Aegean and the Near East in the 2nd Millennium B.C.E.* (Vienna, 2015) together with Birgitta Eder.

Clemens Reichel is Associate Professor for Mesopotamian Archaeology at the University of Toronto's Department of Near and Middle Eastern Civilizations and an Associate Curator for the Ancient Near East at the Royal Ontario Museum (*Mesopotamia: Inventing our World*, 2013). His research focuses predominantly on problems of complex societies, state formation, evolution of urbanism, bureaucracy, social and art history, and history of conflict and warfare. He has excavated and surveyed extensively on sites in Turkey, Syria, Jordan, and Egypt. Since 1999 he has been the director of the Diayala Project, aiming to publish an extensive collection of objects from the excavations of the Oriental Institute (University of Chicago) in the Diyala Region during the 1930's in an online database. Since 2004 he has been directing the Hamoukar Expedition in a joint project between the University of Chicago's Oriental Institute and the Syrian Department of Antiquities.

Seth Richardson is an Assyriologist and historian of the ancient world. He took his degree at Columbia University in 2002, and currently works at the University of Chicago as Managing Editor for the Journal of Near Eastern Studies and an Associate of the Oriental Institute. He works on historical topics related to state society and subjectivity, the politics of the body, the collapse of the First Dynasty of Babylon, as well as issues related to slaves, women, and political theory.

Hannah L. Ringheim is a fellow in Greek Archaeology at the University of Edinburgh. She has worked on excavations in Greece, Israel, Turkey, and Cyprus and is currently part of two projects in Egypt. Her main research interests include trade networks and interconnections between the Aegean and the Eastern Mediterranean. She is currently writing a book on mercenary warfare in the Eastern Mediterranean.

Katharina Streit is a specialist in the archaeology of the southern Levant and her research covers the Pottery Neolithic to Iron Age in this region. She is currently a postdoctoral researcher at the Martin Buber Society of Fellows of the Hebrew University of Jerusalem, Israel. Her main research interests include material culture and symbolic behaviour, chronological issues and radiocarbon dating as well as transregional exchange. She directed her first excavation at the Chalcolithic site of Ein el-Jarba, funded by the Fritz Thyssen foundation, which was completed in 2016. Since 2017, she has been the co-director (together with Felix Höflmayer) of the current Tel Lachish excavations.

Marta Valerio is currently chercheur associé at the Université Paul Valéry-Montpellier 3. In December 2017 she completed her Ph.D. at the Université Paul Valéry-Montpellier 3 and the Università degli Studi di Torino with a dissertation on the treatment of prisoners of war during the New Kingdom. Her research interests include social organization, work organization, condition of foreigners in Ancient Egypt, especially in the New Kingdom.

Sarah Vilain is currently a post-doctoral fellow at the Austrian Academy of Sciences, Vienna, for the ERC Advanced Grant Project "The Enigma of the Hyksos". She studied both Greek and Oriental Archaeology at the University Rennes 2 (France) before starting a Ph.D. at the University of Strasbourg (France). During this time, she benefited from a scholarship of the French Institute for the Near East (IFPO) and participated in archaeological excavations in Syria and Lebanon. Her dissertation, titled "Pour une archéologie des échanges en Méditerranée orientale, la céramique chypriote au Levant nord aux âges du Bronze moyen et du Bronze récent" investigated the distribution and circulation of Cypriot pottery in the Northern Levant in the Middle and Late Bronze Ages. Her main research interest concerns trading connections between Cyprus, the Levant and Egypt in the second millennium BC.

Federico Zangani received a BA in Egyptology and Ancient Near Eastern Studies in 2014 from the University of Oxford, where he studied both Egyptology and Assyriology, and is now a Ph.D. candidate in Egyptology at Brown University. His main research interests include Near Eastern languages, philology, the cultural and political history of Egypt's New Kingdom and Late Bronze Age Syria, and the interconnectedness of the Near East and the Mediterranean.

Abbreviations

ÄA	Ägyptologische Abhandlungen (Wiesbaden)
AAPSS	The Annals of the American Academy of Political and Social Science (Thousand Oaks, CA)
AAR	African Archaeological Review (Cambridge)
AAS	Annales Archéologiques de la Syrie (Damascus)
AASOR	Annual of the American Schools of Oriental Research (New Haven – Cambridge)
ÄAT	Ägypten und Altes Testament. Studien zur Geschichte, Kultur und Religion Ägyptens und des Alten Testaments (Wiesbaden)
AbB	Altbabylonische Briefe im Umschrift und Übersetzung (Leiden)
ABBWLS	Alternative Broad Band and Wavy Line Style
ABSA	Annual of the British School at Athens (London)
Ad	Ammiditana
ADAIK	Abhandlungen des Deutschen Archäologischen Instituts Kairo (Glückstadt – Mainz – Berlin)
AE	American Ethnologist (Washington, DC)
Ae	Abi-ešuḫ
AfO	Archiv für Orientforschung (Berlin – Wien)
AHw	W. von Soden, *Akkadisches Handwörterbuch*. I–III. Wiesbaden: Otto Harrassowitz 1959–1981.
AIIN	*Annali dell'Istituto Italiano di Numismatica* (Roma)
AJA	American Journal of Archaeology (Princeton – Baltimore)
AJP	American Journal of Philology (Baltimore)
AJSL	American Journal of Semitic Languages and Literatures (Chicago)
ALASP(M)	Abhandlungen zur Literatur Alt-Syrien-Palästinas (Münster)
Am. J. Sociol.	American Journal of Sociology (Chicago)
Am. Sociol. Rev.	American Sociological Review (New York)
AMD	Ancient magic and divination (Leiden – Boston)
ANESS	Ancient Near Eastern Studies Supplement Series (Louvain)
ANET^3	J.B. Pritchard, *Ancient Near Eastern Texts Relating to the Old Testament*. Princeton: Princeton University Press 1969 (3rd edition).
AOAT	Alter Orient und Altes Testament (Kevelaer – Neukirchen-Vluyn)
AnSt	Anatolian Studies (Ankara)
AoF	Altorientalische Forschungen (Berlin)
ARCANE	Associated Regional Chronologies for the Ancient Near East and the Eastern Mediterranean (Turnhout)
ArchAnz	Archäologischer Anzeiger (Berlin)
ArOr	Archiv Orientální (Praha)
ARWAW	Abhandlungen der Rheinisch-Westfalischen Akademie der Wissenschaften (Opladen)

As.	Tell Asmar *sigla*
ASAE	Annales du Service des Antiquités de l'Égypte (Le Caire)
ASE	Archaeological Survey of Egypt (London)
ASJ	Acta Sumeriologica (Hiroshima)
ASR	*American Sociological Review* (New York)
Aṣ	Ammiṣaduqa
ÄuL	Ägypten und Levante (Wien)
AuOr	Aula Orientalis (Barcelona)
AV	Archäologische Veröffentlichungen (Berlin – Mainz am Rhein)
BA	The Biblical Archaeologist (New Haven)
BaM	Baghdader Mitteilungen (Berlin)
BAP	B. Meissner, *Beiträge zum altbabylonischen Privatrecht*. Leipzig: J.C. Hinrichs 1893.
BASOR	Bulletin of the American Schools of Oriental Research (New Haven)
BBS	Broad Band Style
BdÉ	Bibliothèque d'étude (Paris)
BES	Bulletin of the Egyptological Seminar (New York)
BES	Brown Egyptological studies (Oxford – Providence)
BiAeg	Bibliotheca Aegyptiaca (Bruxelles)
BIFAO	Bulletin de l'Institut français d'archéologie orientale (Le Caire)
BiMes	Bibliotheca Mesopotamica (Malibu)
BiOr	Bibliotheca Orientalis (Leiden)
BM	Museum siglum of the British Museum, London
BMPES	British Museum Publications on Egypt and Sudan (London)
BMSAES	British Museum Studies in Ancient Egypt and Sudan (London)
BN	Biblische Notizen. Beiträge zur exegetischen Diskussion (Bamberg).
BOQ	W.G. Lambert, *Babylonian Oracle Questions*. MC 13. Winona Lake, IN: Eisenbrauns 2007.
BTM	B. Foster, *Before the Muses: An Anthology of Akkadian Literature*. Winona Lake, IN: Eisenbrauns 1996.
BS res.	Black Slip / Reserved Slip
BSOAS	Bulletin of the School of Oriental (and African) Studies (London)
BZAW	Beihefte zur Zeitschrift für alttestamentliche Wissenschaft (Berlin)
BzN	Beiträge zur Namenforschung (Heidelberg)
CA	Colloquia Antiqua (Leuven)
CAD	*The Assyrian Dictionary of the University of Chicago* (Chicago)
CahDAFI	Cahiers de la Délégation archéologique française en Iran (Paris)
CAJ	Cambridge Archaeological Journal (Cambridge)
CASAE	Cahiers supplémentaires des ASAE (Le Caire)
CBS	Museum siglum of the University Museum, Philadelphia (Catalogue of the Babylonian Section)
CCÉ	Cahier de la céramique égyptienne (Le Caire)
CChEM	Contributions to the Chronology of the Eastern Mediterranean (Wien)

CdÉ	Chronique d'Égypte (Bruxelles)
CDLI	Cuneiform Digital Library Initiative (Los Angeles – Berlin)
CDLN	*Cuneiform Digital Library Notes* (Los Angeles – Berlin)
CHANE	Culture and History of the Ancient Near East (Leiden – Boston)
CIS	Copenhagen International Seminar (London – New York)
CLS	Cross Line Style
CM	Cuneiform Monographs (Groningen)
CNIP	Carsten Niebuhr Institute Publications (Copenhagen)
CRAIBL	Comptes rendus des séances de l'Académie des Inscriptions et Belles-Lettres (Paris)
CSSH	Comparative Studies in Society and History (New York)
CT	Cuneiform Texts from Babylonian Tablets in the British Museum (London)
CTH	L. Laroche, *Catalogue des textes hittites*. Paris: Klincksieck 1971.
CUSAS	Cornell University Studies in Assyriology and Sumerology (Bethesda, MD)
DB Suppl.	L.Pirot – A. Robert – H. Cazelles – A. Feuillet, eds., *Supplément au Dictionnaire de la Bible*. I–VIII. Paris: Letouzey & Ané 1938–1972.
DN	Divine name
E	texts from Emar, see D. Arnaud, *Recherches au pays d'Aštata. Emar 6/1–4*. Paris: ÉRC 1986.
EA	J.A. Knudtzon, *Die El-Amarna-Tafeln*. VB2. Aalen: Zeller 1964 (2nd edition); A.F. Rainey, *El Amarna Tablets 359-379. Supplement to J.A. Knudtzon, Die El-Amarna-Tafeln*. AOAT 8. Kevelaer – Neukirchen-Vluyn: Butzon & Bercker – Neukirchener Verlag 1970.
EA	Egyptian Archaeology (London)
ÉAO	Égypte Afrique & Orient (Montségur)
EB	Early Bronze (Age)
EES EM	EES Excavation Memoirs (London)
ElW	W. Hinz – H. Koch, *Elamisches Wörterbuch*. Berlin: Dietrich Reimer Verlag 1987.
Ethn. Racial Stud.	Ethnic and Racial Studies (Abingdon)
ETCSL	Electronic Text Corpus of Sumerian Literature (Oxford)
EU	Egyptologische Uitgaven (Leiden – Leuven)
GM	Göttinger Miszellen (Göttingen)
GN	Geographical name
GOF	Göttinger Orientforschungen IV. Reihe: Ägypten (Wiesbaden)
HÄB	Hildesheimer Ägyptologische Beiträge (Hildesheim)
HANE/M	History of the Ancient Near East. Monographs (Padova)
HANE/S	History of the Ancient Near East. Studies (Padova)
Haradum II	F. Joannès – Ch. Kepiski-Lecomte – C. Colbow, *Haradum II. Les textes de la période paléo-babylonienne, Samsu-iluma – Ammi-ṣaduqa*. Paris: ÉRC 2006.
HdO	Handbuch der Orientalistik (Leiden – Boston)
Hdt.	Herodotus, *Histories*
HPA	High Priest of Amun
HSM	Harvard Semitic Monographs (Atlanta, GA)

HSS	Harvard Semitic Series (Cambridge, MA – Winona Lake, IN)
IJMES	International Journal of Middle East Studies (Cambridge)
IrAnt	Iranica Antiqua (Leiden)
J. Anthropol. Archaeol.	Journal of Anthropological Archaeology (New York)
JA	Journal asiatique (Paris)
JAEI	Journal of Ancient Egyptian Interconnections (Tucson, AZ)
JANER	Journal of Ancient Near Eastern Religions (Leiden – Boston)
JAOS	Journal of the American Oriental Society (Baltimore – Boston – New Haven)
JARCE	*Journal of the American Research Center in Egypt* (Baltimore – Boston – Princeton – New Haven)
JAS	Journal of Archaeological Science (London – New York)
JCS	Journal of Cuneiform Studies (New Haven – Baltimore)
JEA	Journal of Egyptian Archaeology (London)
JEH	Journal of Egyptian History (Swansea)
JEOL	Jaarbericht van het Voor-Aziatisch-Egyptisch-Genootschap Ex Oriente Lux (Leiden)
JESHO	Journal of the Economic and Social History of the Orient (Leiden)
JGA	Journal of Greek Archaeology (Oxford)
JNES	Journal of Near Eastern Studies (Chicago)
J. Popul. Econ.	Journal of Population Economics (New York)
JRAI (N.S.)	Journal of the Royal Anthropological Institute of Great Britain and Ireland (London)
JSA	Journal of Social Archaeology (London)
JSOT	Journal for the Study of the Old Testament (Sheffield)
JSS	Journal of the Semitic Studies (Manchester)
JSSEA	Journal of the Society for the Study of Egyptian Antiquities (Toronto)
KBo	Keilschrifttexte aus Boghazköi (Leipzig – Berlin)
KRI	K.A. Kitchen, *Ramesside Inscriptions. Historical and Biographical.* I–VIII. Oxford: Blackwell 1975–1990.
KRITANC	K.A. Kitchen, *Ramesside Inscriptions. Translated and Annotated. Notes and Comments.* I–VII. Chichester: Wiley-Blackwell 1995–2014.
KSG	Königtum, Staat und Gesellschaft früher Hochkulturen (Wiesbaden)
KTU	M. Dietrich – O. Loretz – J. Sanmartín, *Die keilalphabetischen Texte aus Ugarit.* AOAT 24/1. Kevelaer – Neukirchen-Vluyn: Butzon & Bercker – Neukirchener Verlag 1976; M. Dietrich – O. Loretz – J. Sanmartín, *Die keilalphabetischen Texte aus Ugarit.* ALASP(M) 8. Münster: Ugarit-Verlag 1995 (2nd edition).
KUB	Keilschrifturkunden aus Boghazköi (Berlin)
LAPO	Littératures anciennes du Proche-Orient (Paris)
LE	Codex Eshnunna
LH	Codex Hammurabi
LingAeg	Lingua Aegyptia (Göttingen)
MB	Middle Bronze (Age)

MC	Mesopotamian Civilizations (Winona Lake, IN)
MDAIK	Mitteilungen des Deutschen Archäologischen Instituts, Abteilung Kairo (Mainz – Cairo – Berlin – Wiesbaden)
MDP	Mémoires de la Délégation en Perse (Paris)
MH	Medinet Habu texts
MHET	Mesopotamian History and Environment (Ghent)
MHET I	K. Van Lerberghe – G. Voet, *Sippar-Amnānum: the Ur-utu archive.* MHET 3/I. Ghent: University of Ghent 1991.
MHET II	L. Dekiere, *Old Babylonian Real Estate Documents*, Parts 1–6. MHET 3/II. Ghent: University of Ghent 1994–1997.
MHR	Mediterranean Historical Review (London)
MIE	Mémoires de l'Institut Égyptien (Le Caire)
MIFAO	Mémoires publiés par les membres de l'Institut français d'archéologie orientale du Caire (Le Caire)
MonAeg	Monumenta Aegyptiaca (Bruxelles)
MRS	Mission des Ras Shamra (Paris)
MVS	Münchner Vorderasiatische Studien (München)
N.A.B.U.	Nouvelles Assyriologiques Brèves et Utilitaires (Paris)
NEA	Near Eastern Archaeology (Atlanta, GA)
OA	Oriens Antiquus (Roma)
OAC	Orientis Antiqvi Collectio (Roma)
OB	Old Babylonian
OBO	Orbis Biblicus et Orientalis (Fribourg)
OBO SA	Orbis Biblicus et Orientalis. Series Archeologica (Fribourg)
OIP	Oriental Institute Publications (Chicago)
OIS	Oriental Institute Seminars (Chicago)
OLA	Orientalia Lovaniensia Analecta (Leuven)
Or NS	Orientalia, Nova Series (Roma)
PdÄ	Probleme der Ägyptologie (Leiden – Boston – Köln)
PEQ	Palestine Exploration Quarterly (London)
PIHANS	Publications de l'Institut historique-archéologique néerlandais de Stamboul (Leiden)
PIOL	Publications de l'Institut Orientaliste de Leuven (Louvain)
PLS	Pendent Line Style
PM	B. Porter – R. Moss, *Topographical Bibliography of Ancient Egyptian Hieroglyphic Texts, Reliefs and Paintings.* I–VII. Oxford: Clarendon Press 1927–1951; Oxford: Griffith Institute 1960– (2nd edition).
PMMAEE	Publications of the Metropolitan Museum of Art Egyptian Expedition (New York)
PN	Personal name
PRU	Le palais royal d'Ugarit (Paris)
PSBA	Proceedings of the Society of Biblical Archaeology (London)
PW	Plain White Hand-made Ware
PWS	Proto White Slip
QS	Qaṭna Studien (Wiesbaden)
RA	*Revue d'assyriologie et d'archéologie orientale* (Paris)
RANT	Res Antiquae (Bruxelles)

RdÉ	*Revue d'Égyptologie* (Leuven)
RIK	*Reliefs and Inscriptions at Karnak*. Chicago: University of Chicago Press 1936–.
RIME	Royal Inscriptions of Mesopotamia. Early Periods (Toronto)
RlA	E. Ebelling – B. Meissner – E. Weidner – W. von Soden – D.O. Edzard, eds., *Reallexikon der Assyriologie und Vorderasiatischen Archäologie*. 1–15. Berlin – New York: De Gruyter 1928–2018.
RoB	Red-on-Black
RS	Ras Shamra *siglum*; or Red Slip pottery
RSO	Rivista degli Studi Orientali (Roma)
RSO	Ras Shamra – Ougarit (Paris)
SAHL	Studies in the Archaeology and History of the Levant (Winona Lake, IN)
SAK	Studien zur altägyptischen Kultur (Hamburg)
SANER	Studies in Ancient Near Eastern Records (Berlin – Boston)
SAOC	Studies in Ancient Oriental Civilization (Chicago)
SBA	Saarbrücker Beiträge zur Altertumskunde (Bonn)
SCCNH	Studies on the Civilization and Culture of Nuzi and the Hurrians (Bethesda, MD)
Sd	Samsuditana
SDAIK	Sonderschrift des Deutschen Archäologischen Institut, Abteilung Kairo (Wiesbaden)
SEL	Studi Epigrafici e Linguistici sul Vicino Oriente Antico (Verona)
Si	Field numbers of tablets from Sippar, held in the collections of the Archaeological Museum, Istanbul
SSLL	Studies in Semitic Languages and Linguistics (Leiden – Boston)
StBoT	Studien zu den Boghazköy-Texten (Wiesbaden)
StMed	Studia Mediterranea (Pavia)
StOr	Studia Orientalia. Edidit Societas Orientalis Fennica (Helsinki)
SVJAD	A.P. Riftin, *Staro-vavilonskije juridičeskije i administrativnye dokumenty v sobranijach SSSR*. Moscow: Izd. AN SSSR 1937.
TA	Tel Aviv (Tel Aviv)
TLOB 1	S. Richardson, *Texts from the Late Old Babylonian Period*. Journal of Cuneiform Studies Supplemental Series 2. Boston: ASOR 2010.
TLOB 2	S. Richardson, A *Texts from the Late Old Babylonian Period* 2.1: Sales of Slaves and Cattle. In prep.
TLS	Tangent Line Style
TMH	Texte und Materialien der Frau Professor Hilprecht Collection, Jena (Leipzig – Berlin)
TUAT N.F.	Texte aus der Umwelt des Alten Testaments. Neue Folge (Gütersloh)
TVOA	Testi del Vicino Oriente antico (Brescia)
OREA	Oriental and European Archaeology (Vienna)
UAVA	Untersuchungen zur Assyriologie und vorderasiatischen Archäologie (Berlin)
Ug.	Ugaritica (Paris)
UF	Ugarit-Forschungen (Münster)

UM	*Sigla* in the collections of the University Museum, University of Pennsylvania, Philadelphia
UMM	University Museum Monograph (Philadelphia)
Urk. I	K. Sethe, *Urkunden des ägyptischen Altertums I. Urkunden des alten Reiches*. Lepizig: J. C. Hinrichs 1903.
Urk. IV	K. Sethe, *Urkunden des ägyptischen Altertums IV. Urkunden der 18. Dynastie*, Heft 1–16, Leipzig: J. C. Hinrichs 1906–1909; W. Helck, *Urkunden des ägyptischen Altertums IV. Urkunden der 18. Dynastie*, Heft 17–22. Berlin: Akademie-Verlag 1955–1958.
VB	Vorderasitische Bibliothek (Leipzig)
VS	Vorderasiatische Schriftdenkmäler der Königlichen Museen zu Berlin (Berlin)
WA	World Archaeology (London)
Wb.	A. Erman – W. Grapow, *Wörterbuch der ägyptischen Sprache*. I–VII. Leipzig: Hinrichs'sche Buchhandlung 1926–1931.
WAW	Writings from the Ancient World (Atlanta, GA)
WdO	Die Welt des Orients (Wuppertal – Göttingen)
WP	White Painted
WPWM	White Painted Wheel-made
YES	Yale Egyptological Studies (New Haven)
YOS	Yale Oriental Series (New Haven)
ZA	Zeitschrift für Assyriologie und Vorderasiatische Archäologie (Leipzig – Berlin)
ZAR	Zeitschrift für altorientalische und biblische Rechtsgeschichte (Wiesbaden)
ZAW	Zeitschrift für alttestamentliche Wissenschaft (Berlin)
ZDPV	Zeitschrift des Deutschen Palästina-Vereins (Stuttgart – Wiesbaden)

HYBRID MILITARY COMMUNITIES OF PRACTICE: THE INTEGRATION OF IMMIGRANTS AS THE CATALYST FOR EGYPTIAN SOCIAL TRANSFORMATION IN THE 2ND MILLENNIUM BC

Danielle Candelora (University of California, Los Angeles)*

Despite the breakdown of the central state, the Second Intermediate Period ranks among Egypt's most innovative eras. Intense international interaction and exchange resulted in the introduction of new ideas and traditions that would persist in Egypt for millennia. One of the most striking examples of this development is the influx of numerous foreign technologies imported from the Near East, including both domestic and luxury, but most especially martial, technologies. Prior to the Second Intermediate Period, both raw and finished products were traded internationally, resulting in new designs or exposure to previously unavailable material. However, it is only in this period that the actual technical processes, the means of manufacture, were also exchanged *en masse*, as well as the cultural significance embedded within them. The major catalyst in the transfer and transformation of these martial technologies and their associated social meaning was the incorporation of immigrants within hybrid military communities of practice.

Scholarship treating the flood of foreign technology into Egypt largely focuses on demonstrating the first attested occurrence thereof in Egypt (Shaw 2012: 10). While valuable, these studies ignore the potential of such cultural exchange to illuminate the movement and integration of actual people in the ancient world, as well as the influence of this transmission on Egypt. The site of Tell el-Dabʿa undoubtedly served as the main entry point for these new technologies. The site was home to a multi-ethnic population from the late 12th Dynasty,[1] when several waves of West Asian immigrants began relocating to Northeastern Egypt. These individuals served as crucial vectors for the transmission and development of these new technologies, exposing Egyptians on their own soil to such innovations and their accompanying social structures, which would forever alter the fabric of Egyptian society.

In order to better understand the on-the-ground interaction by which these new elements were incorporated into Egyptian culture, I apply a Communities of Practice approach. The process by which once-foreign practices and technology are negotiated, blended, and reified as part of Egyptian elite identities, I argue, is

---

* A preliminary version of this paper was co-presented at the Crossroads III workshop with Nadia Ben-Marzouk.

[1] See Bietak 1996 for overview; Bietak 2010 with references; Bader 2011 for evidence of cultural mixing; Forstner-Müller 2010 for burials; see also Redmount 1995 for Asiatic population at Tell el-Maskhuta.

actually rooted in late Middle Kingdom and Second Intermediate Period immigration and the formation of new military communities. It was the interaction between these immigrants and their Egyptian neighbors that fostered the adaptation and reimagining of such innovations, as well as the development of new communal identities that had a significant impact on the Egyptian New Kingdom.

Communities of Practice

Communities of practice is a term first developed by anthropologist Jean Lave and educational theorist Etienne Wenger in a study of learning through participation. They argue that participatory learning is an inherent aspect of any social activity or engagement in social practice (Lave – Wenger 1991: 29–35). Each social engagement, and the learning embedded within it, then occurs within the context of a particular community which has its own unique practice. The members of these communities of practice are united by mutual engagement in a joint enterprise, as well as a shared repertoire (Wenger 1998: 73).

Communities of practice work towards a common goal, e.g., producing a certain type of craft, winning a sports match, or auditing a large corporation. Mutual accountability is key to the pursuit of this joint enterprise, as community members rely upon one another to fulfill their individual tasks (Wenger 1998: 81). Mutual accountability is especially intense in the military, as the community members are either training for or involved in combat situations. Communities of practice can be extended to include the artisans that produce the weapons and armor that the soldiers use, as the soldiers and those that manufacture their arms are united in a single shared enterprise (Wenger 1998: 127). For the purposes of this paper, the infantry, the chariot corps and other specialized branches of the soldiery, as well as military craftsmen, metal smiths, and even horse trainers all constitute a constellation of communities of practice united by their joint enterprise.

Wenger defines mutual engagement as "people engaged in actions whose meaning they negotiate with one another" (Wenger 1998: 73), and emphasizes the crucial role which diversity plays within such interactions. Communities of practice bring together diverse individuals, often of varying age and gender and each with their own experiences and approach that may influence their practice. In the case of the Middle Kingdom and Second Intermediate Period military communities, diversity is heightened due to the inclusion of members of different cultural backgrounds: native Egyptians, West Asian immigrants, likely immigrants from other neighboring regions, as well as individuals from hybrid backgrounds (cf. Bader 2011; Bietak 2018). During the negotiation process outlined by Wenger, individual identities are mutually transformed, resulting in the constitution of a new identity for the group as a whole. That communal identity then constantly changes, adapting to incorporate the influences of new comers to the group (Wenger 1998: 75–76).

The members of these communities also share a common repertoire of both material and non-material elements. The physical aspects include finished products, tools, artifacts, etc., while the more cerebral features consist of shared discourse and jargon, styles, stories, values, concepts, and ways of doing (Wenger 1998: 73, 125–126; Lave – Wenger 1991: 95, 109). These various elements of the shared repertoire then embody not only the practice itself and its cultural history, but also the identity of the community to which they belong.

Military Communities of Practice

The notion of mutual engagement in a joint enterprise is heightened to its most extreme degree in military communities of practice, in which participants are reliant upon one another for their very lives and personal safety. Members are not only engaged in trying to survive a battle, but are also united by patriotism or loyalty to a leader or homeland. In fact, a report on modern militaries[2] suggests that when these armed forces shift from being invasion defense forces to expeditionary forces, more emphasis is placed on the communal values and identity that will be fought for abroad (Sookermany 2011: 625). This is precisely the shift that is underway at the start of the New Kingdom. These military communities of practice also forge strongly shared identities through living and training together, learning specific jargon, or even by being required to wear uniforms and receive standardized haircuts. Hints of this can be seen in some ancient evidence, including tomb paintings in the 18th Dynasty tomb of Userhat (TT56), showing the drilling of new recruits (Fig. 1), as well as recruits receiving their regulation haircuts (Fig. 2). Indeed, the military in the modern world is still a "highly assimilative context" (Ben Shalom – Horenczyk 2004: 461; see also Sookermany 2011: 624), and "participation in military operations thus means gaining access to both formal and informal parts of various military communities of practice, as soldiers are quartered in a common camp area in which they eat, sleep, work and spend their 'free time' together" (Sookermany 2011: 621). Combined, these aspects of the military contribute to individual soldiers' development of a stout affiliation to the unit, as well as a new martial identity reflecting the attitudes and values of their military community of practice (Sookermany 2011: 623).

A study on the British military interviewed multiple soldiers who stated that the most important quality of military life was "the sense of belonging that the military personnel have to their team" (Hale 2012: 709). One individual said that this bond was heightened by intense combat situations, which as they said, "is a good thing because you have got to trust each other with your life at the end of the day" (Hale 2012: 713). Merely by participating in their daily practice, these communities form robust military identities that trend towards a "cultural ethos" on a large scale (Hale 2012: 710). These same ideas are reflected in studies of individuals from the former Soviet Union serving in the Israel Defense Forces, reinforcing the uniqueness of the military context and its tendency to produce strong communal identities (Eisikovits 2006: 293; Ben Shalom – Horenczyk 2004: 461–464).

---

[2] While a direct parallel should not be drawn between ancient and modern militaries, there is something to be gained through such a comparison. The unique general characteristics of a military context remain similar across cultures or time, and a study of the ancient evidence can be further illuminated through a critical evaluation of the modern. See for example the comparative work done by Ellen Morris on imperialism (Morris 2017; Morris 2018).

Fig. 1.
Drilling of new recruits, Tomb of Userhat (TT56), 18th Dynasty, © Nicholas R. Brown.

The military is one of the most common ways that immigrants enter the host society (Ben Shalom – Horenczyk 2004: 464), consequently incorporating them into this assimilative context that promotes a shared identity. Immigrants are often sought out by armed forces in need of extra man power, whether due to heavy losses sustained in war or because native-born citizens are unwilling to perform military service (Ford 1997: 36). Immigrants themselves are incentivized to join the military, as this service is usually accompanied by "citizenship and such fundamental social benefits as education, vocational training and upward mobility" (Ben Shalom – Horenczyk 2004: 464 and references therein). In the context of ancient Egypt, foreign soldiers were often given land, perhaps servants, and social mobility in exchange for their military service (Kemp 2006: 31–33).

Studies particularly focused on immigrants serving in modern militaries, such as the armed forces of Great Britain, The United States, Israel, and Norway, all found these military communities of practice to be unique contexts of mutual acculturation, in which the communal reliance and shared identity of the members

Fig. 2.
Recruits receiving regulation haircuts, Tomb of Userhat (TT56), 18th Dynasty, © Nicholas R. Brown.

heightened cross-cultural awareness and the adoption of "foreign" words, foods, religions, and even values into the host culture. Many of these studies actually focus on assessing the psychological effects of dealing with acculturation, and applied a framework proposed by Berry. First, Berry crucially recognizes that an immigrant can adapt to their host society while simultaneously preserving their own heritage culture, and the extent to which an individual chooses to do either of these can vary independently. In fact, many immigrants develop strategies to judge this "acculturative balance" by considering whether it is of value to maintain their culture of origin, blend more with the host culture, or find a middle ground (Berry 1997: 9; Phinney et al. 2001: 495). Berry then outlines four general acculturation strategies and identifies "integration", basically a balance between old and new cultural traditions, as the most beneficial to immigrant psychological health (Berry 1997: 9, 29). Most of the military studies concluded that the immigrant soldiers had pursued integration strategies, helped to adapt by the highly cohesive context of the military, yet also actively maintaining elements of their culture of origin. These blended immigrant identities then exposed their entire military community to their cultural traditions, making the military a unique context of mutual acculturation.

For example, the United States Army drafted over 500,000 immigrants in World War I, yet purposefully promoted dual identities for these men. They were kept in "smaller ethnic-specific platoons" while serving within larger native-born companies, and all were encouraged to "show off" their specific skills or capabilities to one another (Ford 1997: 35–40). In more contemporary studies of the United States military, research has shown that cross-cultural awareness, learning, and even comfort with other ethnicities is heightened through military service (Leal 2003: 206). Latino and Anglo veterans had more friendships with one another after their service, and there was even an "increased Anglo awareness of Cesar Chavez", suggesting that the draft military allowed both parties to engage in cross-cultural learning in "a forum that may not have been commonly available elsewhere in society" (Leal 2003: 220). Similar cross-cultural friendships developed amongst Israelis and immigrants from the former Soviet Union in the Israel Defense Forces. Even in this loaded context, in which national identity is arguably most intense, immigrants were encouraged to establish a multiculturalism and preserve their heritage (Eisikovits 2006: 299–301; Ben Shalom – Horenczyk 2004: 475–476).

One particular study on Russian soldiers in the Nineteenth century Iranian military especially mirrors the situation that begins at Tell el-Dabʿa. In this case, ethnically mixed regiments were formed which exchanged and adapted elements of one another's cultures—Russians dyed their hair with henna, took local wives, and many converted to Islam, while Iranians took up portions of the Cossack uniform, culturally specific weapons, terminology, and battle tactics (Cronin 2012: 149–158). Indeed, Russians returning home were even recorded employing forms of guerilla warfare typical of small scale Iranian tribal societies (Cronin 2012: 160). Essentially, informal situated learning had occurred among these soldiers in a community of practice, resulting in bidirectional transmission and new negotiated identities—both for the individuals and their broader societies (Iran for example adopted Russian tactics and regimentation [Cronin 2012: 150]). This process emulates the military communities of the Middle Kingdom and Second Intermediate Period, incorporating both West Asian immigrant specialists and Egyptian soldiers and having similar transformative effects on Egyptian identity.

Specialist Foreign Labor

As in the modern examples discussed above, multitudes of immigrants (whether they had relocated to Egypt willingly or not) were incorporated into the Egyptian military and its constellation of communities of practice. For instance, the Egyptian use of foreign mercenaries can be documented at least as early as the Old Kingdom, and was a continuous practice throughout the remainder of pharaonic history (see discussion in Bietak 2010a; Kemp 2006: 26–33 with references). Specialist foreign craftsmen related to military production also moved to Egypt, as evidenced by the 13th Dynasty metalworking workshop uncovered at Tell el-Dabʿa (Philip 2006: 204). This workshop seems to have produced not only standard tools, but also particular forms of West Asian weapons that were cast in bivalve molds, a technique which was also a new import to Egypt (Philip 2006: 196), brought by these immigrant craftsmen.

On the less voluntary end of the relocation scale, Moorey outlines three categories of expatriate labor which derive from the foreign prisoners captured on campaign and forcibly relocated to their new host country (also see discussion in Morris 2014). Two of these are particularly relevant to this discussion, namely the specialist craftsmen attached to the military while on campaign, and actual soldiers captured and incorporated into their captor's forces (Moorey 2001: 6–9). The first is represented in the text of Seti I's Libyan Campaign at Karnak, where he boasted that he intended "to fill every workshop" (Kitchen 2003a: 31) with prisoners of war. Their specific relocation into workshop contexts indicates that some were skilled military craftspeople who had been serving the enemy forces on campaign. Indeed, Morris notes that "virtually every known ruler from the Eighteenth and Nineteenth Dynasties claims to have offered the gods—and especially Amun—this type of simultaneously pious and warlike gift" (Morris 2014: 368). Furthermore, the six earliest (dating from the reign of Hatshepsut through Tuthmose IV) tomb depictions of chariot production workshops are labeled as being located in Karnak temple. This is likely due to the fact that Karnak was the recipient of many spoils of war, including the foreign wood required to build the chariots (Drenkhahn 1976: 170), but also West Asian craftsmen, captured as prisoners of war, who had the specialized knowledge required to construct them. In fact, Morris observes that many of these chariot workshop scenes, which also show the fashioning of composite bows and arrows, display foreign craftsmen at work (for example the tomb of Menkheperrasoneb TT86, see Morris 2014: 368, 367–371 for general discussion of the types of labor these prisoners performed).

Moorey's final category of foreign captive labor is that of captured soldiers or mercenaries. A clear example of the "re-appropriation" of enemy forces can be found in the poetical version of the Battle of Qadesh. The author writes, "So now his Majesty issued supplies to his infantry and chariotry, (and the) Sherden-warriors that his Majesty had captured, when he brought them in by the triumph of his strong arm; they being kitted-out with all their weapons, and the plan of campaign given to them" (Kitchen 2003b: 33). It is evident from this text that Ramesses II had taken foreign Sherden soldiers as prisoners of war, subsequently incorporating them into his own forces to the extent that they were armed and entrusted with the battle plan. Yet the individuals who are most pertinent to this discussion are the *maryannu*, who also fall into Moorey's final category.

The *maryannu*, or charioteers, were an elite group of specialized warriors trained specifically in chariot warfare and strategy, and likely included archers and drivers (see Shaw 2001; 2012 for broad discussion; see Raulwing 2013: 257, fig. 2 for a list of attestations of the term in Egyptian sources). The capture of these *maryannu* is documented throughout the military texts and booty lists of the New Kingdom, but are most evident during the Tuthmoside Period. One of the earliest examples comes from the Autobiography of Ahmose, son of Ibana, during Tuthmose I's campaign to Retjenu. The text states, "I brought a chariot, its horse, and him who was on it as a living captive. When they were presented to his majesty, I was rewarded with gold once again" (Lichtheim 1976: 14). While the term *maryannu* is not expressly used, it is clear that Ahmose had captured a live charioteer. He also emphasized the fact that the captive was taken alive, perhaps indicating the future potential of this West Asian individual as a member of the Egyptian military. In the Annals of Tuthmose III, the Battle of Megiddo booty list records the capture of 43 *maryannu*. Significantly, the *maryannu* are carefully tallied, and usually listed first (perhaps emphasizing their importance), in categories distinct from other groups of prisoners of war (Lichtheim 1976: 33–34). On the Memphis and Karnak Stelae of Amenhotep II, a total of 646 *maryannu* were recorded as captured during his Levantine campaigns. Again, there is significant emphasis placed on the fact that they were taken alive, and were considered a distinct category of skilled captive (Fig. 3). In fact, in one case the stelae report the capturing of "550 Maryannu and 240 of their wives" (Hoffmeier 2003: 20–23),

Fig. 3.
Captured enemy charioteer, Abydos Temple of Ramesses II, 19th Dynasty, © Danielle Candelora.

which may have created added incentive for these West Asian charioteers to resettle in Egypt and serve the Egyptian crown. These *maryannu* warriors were elites in their own right, wealthy men of Syria-Palestine who had the means to own and keep up a chariot, a team of horses, and sundry equipment. These men were therefore treated differently than common infantrymen when captured, as befitted both their specialized skills and their social status. While most of the textual sources recording the seizure of *maryannu* date to the New Kingdom, the continuous capture and integration of foreigners into military contexts served to constantly refresh the hybrid nature of these communities of practice which were originally formed by the mostly voluntary immigration of West Asian individuals in the late Middle Kingdom and Second Intermediate Period.

This association between particularly West Asian warriors and chariotry skill continued well beyond the early 18th Dynasty, as did the connection between West Asian craftsmen and specific trades. Indeed, it seems in many cases that individuals of West Asian origin may have intentionally emphasized their backgrounds as a strategy to not only legitimize, but advertise, the extent of their skills.

Maintenance and Advertisement of Foreign Identity

Further in keeping with the notion of communities of practice and integration is the idea that the maintenance and advertisement of foreign identity could be seen as beneficial to these immigrants and their descendants. If in-demand skills and knowledge are known to have west-Asian origins, then it stands to reason that emphasizing such descent—whether recent or many generations removed—would be in the best interest of individuals in certain professions. For instance, Egyptians seemed to have prized wine imported from Syria-Palestine, and when they could not access these imported wines, they frequented vineyards overseen by those of West Asian descent. These same immigrant vintners were even sent to Nubia to help establish vineyards near the new urban centers (Morris 2014: 371). A more martial case is the well-known stele now in Berlin (ÄM 14122) depicting an elite man with a foreign name, who was clearly and intentionally shown simultaneously as an Asiatic and a soldier, with his dagger prominently displayed on his belt and his spear behind him. Perhaps this individual was one of the resettled *maryannu*, now doing quite well for himself in service to the Egyptian king. Indeed, although garbed as an Egyptian, his wife also bears a foreign name, a further correlation to the practice of relocating these elite mercenaries and their wives to Egypt together.

Another example would be the connection between West Asians and seafaring skills, especially boat building. In the records of Tuthmose III regarding the port of Memphis, the "chief craftsman of the king", or royal boat builder, bore the foreign name Humasha. His son Iuna (also a foreign name) continued the family trade in a slightly different context—he was the "chief craftsman of boats of all the gods of Upper and Lower Egypt" (Glanville 1932: 39–41). Christopher Eyre argues that the particular foreign names of these two craftsmen indicate that "their family originated in Syria, whether its founder came to Egypt as a captive or a free immigrant" (Eyre 1987: 194). Whether the initial move was voluntary or not, this family of skilled West Asian craftsmen continued to pass on their trade from father to son, simultaneously maintaining that "foreign" identity and (implicitly or explicitly) advertising their particularly appropriate origins through conscious naming practices. The choice of Syrian names would have highlighted to all that these men hailed from a longstanding skilled tradition of boat building. Examples of this type of advertisement can even be found for craftsmen whose family had been in Egypt for multiple generations. Dedia, the chief draughtsman of Amun, was commissioned in the 19th Dynasty to restore several monuments in Western Thebes. In his tomb, he carefully recorded that he was the seventh generation in his family to hold this title, making certain to link the origins of the post to an ancestor with the West Asian name Pt-Baʿl (Eyre 1987: 194–195, see also Lowie 1976).

The General's Charioteer Iotefamun demonstrates the longevity of the association between West Asian origins and chariotry skill. His burial was discovered during the Metropolitan Museum of Art's early 1920's excavations in Western Thebes, specifically in a reused tomb in South Asasif. While at least the inner coffin (MMA 26.3.2a, b) and mummy board (MMA 26.3.3) were also reused, the outer coffin (MMA 26.3.1a, b) is typical of the early 21st Dynasty. Hayes identifies Iotefamun by saying he was, "to judge from his full and bushy beard, an Asiatic" (Hayes 1959: 407), presumably referring to the mummy itself. Within the coffin was also placed a ritually "killed" charioteer's whip (MMA 22.3.15), clearly marking him as a charioteer by trade. Interestingly, while Iotefamun himself had a beard, his reused coffin set did not. Perhaps he was just working with what he could find to reuse in a period of relative economic decline, but it is also possible he was exploiting multiple aspects of his identity to get the best of both of his worlds: appearing stereotypically Egyptian on his coffin in order to pursue a traditional Egyptian afterlife, yet displaying a beard in life to advantageously project a possible West Asian heritage for his profession. While a beard in and of itself of course does not mean that Iotefamun had any West Asian ancestry, at the very least this choice of facial hair allowed him to outwardly mark himself as belonging to that identity group and their martial traditions.

Like the burial of Iotefamun demonstrates, the presence in Egypt of West Asians with specialized knowledge continued throughout the New Kingdom. In the Eastern Delta specifically, there is not only consistent archaeological evidence of a West Asian population, but of a continuous tradition of the employment of foreign craftsmen (Bietak 2010b: 170). At the Tuthmoside harbor of Peru-nefer, now associated with the site of Tell el-Dabʿa, remains were found of a palatial complex that included workshops for weapons and military production (Bietak 2010b: 165). Among the West Asian population remaining in the Delta after the Hyksos expulsion, Bietak lists not only craftsmen, but also metal workers, vintners, grooms, soldiers, charioteers, sailors and shipbuilders (Bietak 2010b: 170). Still, the presence of West Asian craftsmen extended through the Ramesside Period in the same region at Piramesse/Qantir. Excavations at the Ramesside capital and military base have uncovered two quasi-industrial, state run workshops for the production of metal objects and chariots (Pusch – Tasiaux 1990; Pusch – Herold 1999). The bronze workshop of a late 18th–19th Dynasty stratum spans an area of approximately 30,000 square meters, including large melting channels and furnaces, as well as enormous amounts of bronze by-product, and fragments of crucibles, tuyeres, and casting molds (Pusch – Tasiaux 1990; Pusch – Herold 1999: 789; Rehren – Pusch 2012: 215).

In the stratum just above this industrial foundry, excavators uncovered a chariot complex containing an exercise court, multi-functional workshops for chariot production and repair, as well as a massive stable[3] (Pusch – Herold 1999: 788). Most interestingly, within the chariot complex workshops, excavators discovered stone molds for the production of "metal applications for shield rims, such as those carried by Hittite troops in the Battle of Qadesh" (Pusch – Herold 1999: 788). Using this evidence, excavators argue that Hittite craftsmen and soldiers were in residence at Piramesse following the peace treaty of Ramesses II and attusili III (Pusch – Herold 1999). It is significant that the continued presence of West Asian warriors and craftsmen in the Delta is still closely associated with both chariots and metal molds (see below), even into the Ramesside Period. Potentially, some of these Ramesside West Asian craftsmen may be the descendants[4] of those from the Second Intermediate Period or early New Kingdom production centers at Avaris and Peru-nefer, having helped to maintain a West Asian crafting tradition and a conduit for technological transmission in the Eastern Delta.

[3] The stables are actually located in a slightly separate area of the site, but belong to the same stratum (Pusch – Herold 1999).

[4] While this is admittedly a hypothetical conclusion, the Stela of Irtysen, as well as the Satire of the Trades and the hereditary succession of Deir el-Medina positions, indicate that specialized knowledge of craftsmen and scribes may have been passed down from father to son (Badawy 1961; Lichtheim 1974: 185–191). Further, in archaeological studies of apprenticeship, young sons are often instructed in family trades by their fathers (see for example Wendrich 2012, who discusses apprenticeship as preserved in the archaeological and ethnographic record all over the world).

Material Elements of Shared Repertoire

It is through the elements of the shared repertoire, from artifacts to language, that archaeologists and historians can begin to access these ancient communities of practice, as well as the integration of newcomers within them. The shared repertoire of the Middle Kingdom and Second Intermediate Period military communities of practice are represented by numerous artifact forms related to military endeavors and associated crafts with clear West Asian origins. For example, as discussed briefly above, metal working debris and several steatite bivalve mold fragments were found at Tell el-Dabʿa in the area of the 13th Dynasty "palace". Philip notes that both bivalve molds, and the products which bivalve casting must be used to produce, appear first in this context at Tell el-Dabʿa, and only in Upper Egyptian contexts in the New Kingdom (Philip 2006: 196; Scheel 1987: 259). He suggests that this collection of metalworking evidence may be indicative of an institutional workshop, staffed with at least some West Asian smiths, associated with the palace itself (Philip 2006: 197, 204). The majority of the West Asian style weapons cast in these molds were discovered in "warrior burials" in areas F/1, A/II and A/IV, some of which even included associated equid burials (see discussions in Bietak 1996; Bader 2011; Forstner-Müller 2008; Forstner-Müller 2010). At this period just at the turn of the Second Intermediate Period, a large proportion of the men at the site were buried with whole assemblages of these stylistically foreign weapon types, including ribbed daggers, fenestrated axes, socketed spear heads, a sickle sword or *khepesh*, and a duckbill axe (Philip 2006: 31–82). Consequently, excavators suggest that many of these immigrants may have served as soldiers or sea-faring sailors, or specifically as caravaneers or armed guards attached to the Sinai mining expeditions (Bietak 2006: 285–287). Thus, both the weapon forms and the process of bivalve casting were new imports, brought to Tell el-Dabʿa by West Asian immigrant craftsmen and at least initially utilized by immigrant military specialists.

Apparently, the situated learning done by local Egyptians in these mixed communities influenced broader Egyptian practice. Bivalve casting technology continued in use in Egypt beyond its initial introduction at Tell el-Dabʿa, appearing in New Kingdom contexts in Upper Egypt (Philip 2006: 196; Scheel 1987: 259). The sole depiction of the use of a bivalve mold comes from the 18th Dynasty Theban tomb of Rekhmire (TT100), in a scene in which a team of metalworkers are both heating and pouring metal into an enormous bivalve mold for the production of metal doors for Karnak temple (Scheel 1987: 259; Scheel 1989: 24–25). His access to this new technology acted as a manufacturer of social value for Rekhmire, hence the incorporation of this scene in his tomb. In archaeological contexts, 18th Dynasty examples of bivalve molds were uncovered during the Metropolitan Museum of Art's early 1900's expedition to Western Thebes. In the region of Deir el-Bahri, the Lansing expedition discovered half of a limestone bivalve mold for casting a miniature goddess amulet, as well as an openwork pendant. They also excavated half of a gabbro mold for a "knob shaped rod object", complete with a preserved pouring channel and peg holes (Hayes 1959: 218). Furthermore, some of the West Asian style weapons first seen at Tell el-Dabʿa also caught on more widely in the

Egyptian military. The *khepesh*, or sickle sword, especially becomes a standard-issue weapon in the Ramesside period, and is shown being distributed to troops from the armory at the temple of Ramesses III at Medinet Habu (Murnane 1980: 13–14, fig. 9), more than half a millennium after it entered the shared repertoire of the late Middle Kingdom hybrid military communities of practice.

Immigrant specialists also introduced the horse and chariot to Egypt in associated constellations of military practice and craft. Shaw posits that while Egyptian craftsmen were equipped with the skills and techniques required to produce the chariot by the Middle Kingdom, major elements were lacking: most importantly, the specialized knowledge needed to assemble a functioning chariot, and crucially, the horse (Shaw 2012: 99–101). To this list must be added skilled personnel to care for, breed, and train the horses, as well as warriors proficient in the use of the finished products—including knowledge of chariotry tactics and composite bow mastery on a moving platform. Furthermore, the chariot was one small part of an integrated technological system, and required the import of several other related technologies into Egypt. The introduction of the horse mandated the importation of new bits and harnesses. The transmission of the chariot was also accompanied by the introduction of composite bow technology, as well as related leather arm guards and new types of quivers that could be mounted to the chariot. Finally, the deadliness of the new bows inspired new scale armor and smaller, more mobile shields (Shaw 2001: 66–68; for a broad discussion of chariot technology and construction, see Veldmeijer – Ikram 2013; Veldmeijer – Ikram 2018). All of these elements, previously unknown in Egypt, initially required the expertise of immigrant specialists to both produce and use. As discussed above, the ongoing capture and integration of West Asian *maryannu* into the Egyptian chariot corps acted to constantly refresh the hybrid negotiated identities of these military communities of practice. The chariot, another manufacturer of social value, was also consciously depicted in the tomb scenes of elite Egyptians as part of inter-elite competition and a display of status (Morris 2014: 373). Consequently, the chariot is perhaps the most pervasive and publicized material element of these communities' shared repertoires, yet along with it came non-physical aspects, embedded traditions and even military values which had enormous influence on New Kingdom society and kingship.

Non-material Elements of Shared Repertoire

Loan Words

Several categories of evidence represent the non-material elements of these mixed military communities' shared repertoires. Most often discussed are the Semitic loan words that manifest in Late Egyptian. Terms relating to the military, the chariot, horse, weapons, etc. account for approximately 18% of the corpus of Semitic loan words in Late Egyptian (Winand 2017: 488; see also Hoch 1994: 462–470; Redford 1992: 236). While much time has been devoted to debating the etymology of these loan words, or to the unique nature of their source texts (see discussion in Winand 2017: 485–486), such as the Ramesside Poem to the King's Chariot, less has been done to understand the social context of their transmission. Redford for example explains this profusion of loan words as the result of a simple "need for terms for new techniques, manufactures, and material" (Redford 1992: 236). Thomas Schneider elucidates the social environment of these loan words by differentiating between "Militärsprache" and "Soldatensprache". The first category represents the standardized institutional language of the military, while the second, "soldier's slang" is relegated more to the colloquial language or sociolect of the soldiers themselves. While he notes that foreign terms fall more frequently into the Militärsprache category (Schneider 2008: 182–184), many such terms would also occur within the daily use of soldiers—for example weapons terminology.

Although much more needs to be done to study the sociolinguistic aspects of New Kingdom language exchange, the clustering of foreign terms around military items could be suggestive of two related communities of practice, one involving military craftsmen responsible for the production of the chariot and its technical package, and the other featuring general military specialists such as soldiers, mercenaries, and prisoners of war. In both cases, knowledge transfer between the West Asian and Egyptian members would have included technical jargon and specialized vocabulary that persisted in the Egyptian language. Winand notes that cultural words, which "express entities that are new to the culture of the recipient language", i.e. these specialized military terms, "have the highest degree of borrowability" (Winand 2017: 488, 507).[5] General studies of communities of practice have noted how specialized terminology, "jargon and shortcuts to communication" are a crucial element of the shared repertoire that is "imported, adopted, and adapted" by the community (Wenger 1998: 125–126). Lave and Wenger describe how language is central to how people learn and that members can pick up language simply by participating in these communities of practice (Lave – Wenger 1991: 85).

Much work has been done on the transfer of jargon within particularly craft and technologically oriented community of practice contexts, typically featuring apprenticeship relationships. Wendrich states that "each craft has its own specialized vocabulary" that distinguishes materials, techniques, products, etc., which are learned via situated learning during apprenticeships (Wendrich 2012: 13). Jørgensen nuances this further, arguing that specialized craft knowledge requires an immense amount of vocabulary to provide for minute distinctions in related parts of technical systems or production techniques. For example, he cites that textile experts and weavers have numerous words for "fibers, yarns, weaves, tools, and such features as drape, handle, flexibility, and surface texture" (Jørgensen 2012: 243).

In keeping with the jargon expectations provided by Jørgensen, Hoch identifies more than thirty foreign words from New Kingdom sources specifically for

[5] Whether these terms should be considered proper loan words in that they were permanently incorporated into the Egyptian language, simply cultural terms adopted alongside new entities like the chariot, or as Winand argues examples of code-switching to mark elements as foreign (Winand 2017: 508), are important distinctions that require further investigation.

the chariot and various equipment, parts, and associated weapons, as well as more for the horse[6] (Hoch 1994: 462–470). These chariot-related words are likely indicative of situated learning in workshops producing the chariot technical package under the instruction—at least initially—of West Asian craftsmen. The foreign terms were engrained in these communities as part of their shared repertoire, learned by the community members in their original linguistic forms. Eventually it is feasible that trained Egyptians may have taken over these workshops (but see above), especially as Thebans gained the technology, but the technical jargon remained etymologically foreign.[7]

The broader foreign military words found in Late Egyptian sources included weapons terminology, defensive architecture, military occupations and specific troop categories, as well as action terms (Hoch 1994: 462–470). It is possible that some of these were used within hybrid communities of military specialists, including soldiers, foreign mercenaries, and prisoners of war,[8] in keeping with Cooney's (2012: 147) conception of a diffuse network of knowledge transfer among specialists, not requiring direct apprenticeship. Several studies of modern military communities demonstrate this jargon acquisition through daily practice, or sometimes, in the case of ethnically mixed regiments, the gaining of non-specialized terms in another language (Sookermany 2011: 617–619; Leal 2003: 218–220; Eisikovits 2006: 299–301; Ben Shalon – Horenczyk 2004: 475–476; Ford 1997: 35; Hale 2012: 717). Such situated language learning occurs purely through living and training together, as well as through live operations in the field (Lave – Wenger 1991: 109). Since it is also understood that situated learning is firmly rooted in a social context (Wendrich 2012: 4), and the learning process actively constructs the character of the apprentice (Høgseth 2012: 65), the existence of these military communities also explains the broader shifts seen in the New Kingdom military.

Taking Battlefield Trophies and Receiving Gold of Valor

Along with the loan words, foreign military values and practices were introduced, mixed with local versions, and transformed in these communities of practice, eventually manifesting in the late Second Intermediate Period and early New Kingdom. Egyptian terms and phrases appeared in tomb autobiographies and military texts at the turn of the New Kingdom, used in new contexts to describe captives taken in battle, or the severing of enemy hands as trophies (Lorton 1974:

[6] This mirrors evidence found in textual sources at the Hittite capital at Ḫattuša, where a series of cuneiform tablets inscribed with a horse training manual (now in Berlin, VAT 6693) was found. The text is riddled with foreign loan words in an Indic dialect, which Beckman attributes to the Mittani origin of the supposed author of the text, a Mittani horse training expert named Kikkuli. The loan words are technical terms relating to specific training practices (Beckman 2008: 158), similarly to the technical nature of the Semitic chariot and horse terms in Late Egyptian.

[7] No conclusions can yet be drawn on the question of how such terms were perceived (as native or still foreign) by Egyptian speakers after their integration into Late Egyptian.

[8] Although these words come mainly from scribal and royal sources, rather than daily writings such as letters, receipts, etc. written by these community members—such sources would of course more directly reflect the linguistic reality within such military communities.

67–68). These texts, such as the autobiographies of Ahmose, son of Ibana, Ahmose Pennekhbet, and Amenemheb, as well as the Annals of Tuthmose III and other sources, describe the capture of living prisoners on the battlefield and their presentation to the king. The severed hands of slain enemies were also brought to the king, and the monarch would then redistribute the captives or provide gold as a reward. Lorton observes that there is no evidence for this kind of martial reward system in Egypt prior to these texts, and proposes that the system was introduced during the Hyksos period. As further support for this argument, he demonstrates that a similar system was recorded in the Mari letters. In these texts, booty and spoils, including captives, "legally reverted to the king" and while some was kept, much was later redistributed to the soldiers (Lorton 1974: 57, especially n. 16). The Mari letters thus preserve evidence of a martial reward system in place amongst the Middle Bronze Age kingdoms across Mesopotamia and Levant, a category to which the Hyksos and their domain also belonged (see Candelora *forthcoming*). The West Asian military specialists in these Delta communities of practice likely brought this system with them, as well as the values it espoused. Such a system heavily promoted, and literally rewarded, individual military prowess and acts of bravery on the battlefield, values which quickly became fundamental to New Kingdom Egyptian identity.

The collecting of severed enemy hands is well known from later Ramesside battle reliefs, for example the famous scenes at Medinet Habu (Fig. 4) (Murnane 1980: 12–13). Yet the earliest archaeological evidence known for the practice in Egypt is the cache of severed hands uncovered in the Hyksos Palace in Area F/II at Tell el-Dabʿa. The hands were discovered in four separate pits located in two phases of this palace complex, and the second phase featured two pits containing 14 severed right hands (Bietak 2012: 42–43). As mentioned above, the earliest textual evidence for this practice is found in the autobiography of Ahmose, son of Ibana as well as Ahmose Pennekhbet, who receive the "gold of valor" for these trophies (Lorton 1974: 53–60). Steven Harvey also reports evidence of what may be the earliest artistic depiction of this practice amongst the relief fragments from the mortuary temple of Ahmose I at Abydos.[9] Strikingly, the dating of all three pieces of evidence strongly indicates that these practices were reified in Egypt in the Second Intermediate Period, possibly via the integration of immigrants in military communities of practice.

Impact on the New Kingdom Military and Kingship

Alba and Nee have written about the process through which minority ethnic cultural traits become part of the mainstream host culture. They distinguish between two separate but related processes, the first of which is that the influence of the minority group serves to expand "the range of the what is considered normative behavior within the mainstream" (Alba – Nee 1997: 834). The second process in-

[9] S.P. Harvey, Representations of Foreigners in the Battle Reliefs of King Ahmose at Abydos, an unpublished talk presented on September 11, 2018 at the Crossroads III conference.

Fig. 4.
Scribes counting severed hands, Medinet Habu Temple of Ramesses III, 19th Dynasty, © Danielle Candelora.

volves the cultural trait's gradual loss of connection to the minority group. Overtime, the trait ceases to be ethnically labeled, and members of the majority group take it on, weakening the "empirical connection" between the trait and the original minority group (Alba – Nee 1997: 834). When these processes are considered in combination with communities of practice, which encourage the incorporation of new members, traits, and the corresponding negotiation of group identity, it clarifies how many of the elements discussed above became so fundamental to the mainstream cultural repertoire of New Kingdom Egypt. Lave and Wenger even stress the connection of "sociocultural transformations with the changing relations between newcomers and old-timers in the context of a changing shared practice" (Lave – Wenger 1991: 49). The hybrid military communities of practice of the Middle Kingdom and Second Intermediate Period served to mutually transform various traditions into a blended military identity, which gradually spread from within these localized communal contexts to Egyptian society as a whole.

This negotiated military identity manifested in the New Kingdom in numerous associated sociocultural transformations. Within the military itself, the reward system became fundamental to the expression of valor by elites, who were literally eternalized either receiving gold necklace rewards in tomb reliefs, such as in

Fig. 5.
Sherden mercenary and Egyptian soldier severing hands of defeated Hittites, Abydos Temple of Ramesses II, 19th Dynasty, © Danielle Candelora.

Horemheb's tomb at Saqqara, or bedecked in them in statue form like Maya in Berlin (ÄM 19286). Even the severing of enemy hands became a standard Egyptian military practice, famously depicted on temple walls half a millennium after the practice first appears in Egypt. In fact, on the rear wall of the temple of Ramesses II at Abydos, decorated with scenes from the Battle of Qadesh, is an image of soldiers in the midst of the act itself (Fig. 5). In the scene, a Sherden mercenary is shown fighting alongside an Egyptian soldier, identifiable respectively via the Egyptian style haircut and the typical Sherden horned-helmet and round shield. The Egyptian soldier to the right appears just about to sever the hand from a still-living Hittite, while the Sherden warrior simultaneously removes the hand of a slain enemy. Even this Ramesside foreign mercenary had clearly been initiated into this (by this point) longstanding *Egyptian* military tradition, through training and fighting with fellow soldiers in a military community of practice.

Also reflecting the new military identity of the New Kingdom, the language itself accommodated new foreign vocabulary. Further, scribes composed previously unattested types of literature that focused on the more martial aspects of society, including texts such as the Qadesh Battle Poem, Poem to the King's Chariot, the Tale of the Taking of Joppa, and satirical works like Papyrus Anastasi I. In fact, the heroic bravery exhibited by Tuthmose III at Megiddo, or Ramesses II in the Qadesh Battle Poem are striking examples of the stark change in the very understanding and iconography of Egyptian kingship in the New Kingdom. The very fact that these New Kingdom kings felt the need to legitimize themselves in this way is a remarkable divergence from what was previously considered necessary in images of kingship. In the Old Kingdom, kings featured in martial stock scenes such as the smiting of enemies, but there was no clear indication that they led their troops into battle. Many scholars have credited the 17th Dynasty kings with the emergence of this warrior ethos, but Spalinger argues that the "local war leaders" of the First Intermediate Period were the real model for 12th Dynasty

Fig. 6.
Stela of Amenhotep II, Luxor Museum, 18th Dynasty, © Jordan Galczynski.

kings to lead their soldiers on campaign in Nubia, the true context in which this kingly warrior ideology crystallized (Spalinger 2017: 109–110). Yet the celebration of specific and particularly brave martial exploits of the king is only attested in the New Kingdom, and has more in common with the champion-duel scene in the Story of Sinuhe (a tradition that was clearly rooted in the tale's Levantine context), than earlier Egyptian records of the king in battle.

Not only did the textual representation of kingship shift toward their martial feats, but the associated royal iconography also underwent a major shift. Another hallmark of the New Kingdom was that royal princes by default underwent extensive martial training, and served as high-ranking military officers (Spalinger 2017: 110–111). This is most famously depicted on a stela of Amenhotep II, now in the Luxor Museum, which shows the king astride his chariot shooting arrows through a copper oxhide ingot (Fig. 6). This unique iconography demonstrates not just his military prowess, but his technical knowledge of the capacity of the chariot and composite bow. Indeed, prior to this period one would be hard-pressed to find an image of an Egyptian king using a bow, but as the composite bow is inextricably linked to the chariot package (Shaw 2001: 66–68), it got incorporated in the iconography as well.

Alongside the traditional Egyptian smiting scene, the "image of a warrior king fighting alone in a chariot quickly became the visual and literary trope of the New Kingdom" (Spalinger 2017: 100), and these scenes covered temple facades across the New Kingdom monumental landscape (Sabbahy 2013; Sacco 2013). Yet another stock scene of these temple facades is the ritual presentation of a weapon from a deity, usually the head of the pantheon Amun, to the king in celebration of his military victories. This vignette appears on the first pylon at Medinet Habu (Fig. 7), and the weapon at the center of the scene is not a traditional Egyptian mace or axe, but a *khepesh*. Originally a West Asian weapon, the khepesh also became so central to the core of New Kingdom Egyptian militarism that it is the

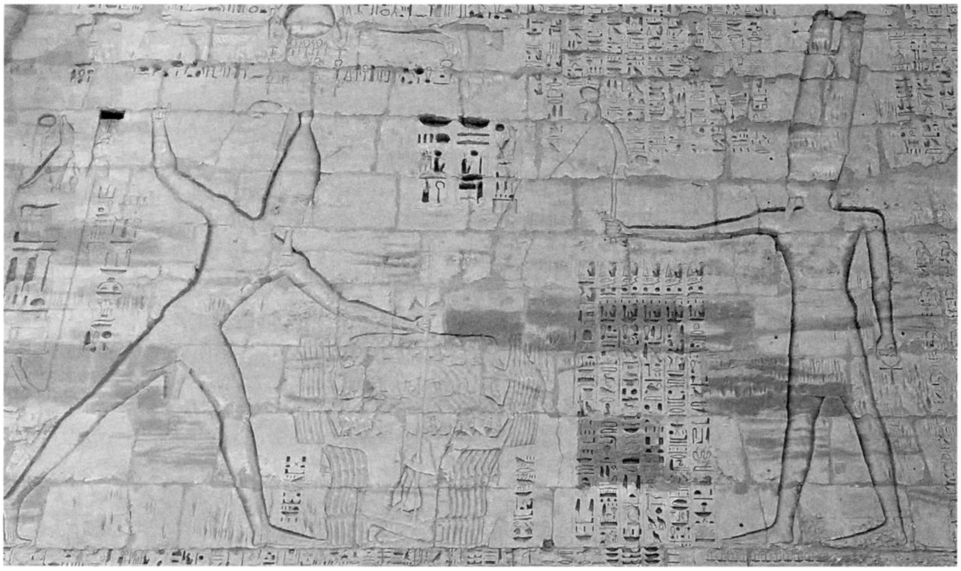

Fig. 7.
First Pylon, Medinet Habu Temple of Ramesses III, 19th Dynasty, © Danielle Candelora.

weapon of choice for these ritual scenes, and kings like Tutankhamun are referred to as "Lord of the Khepesh". In fact, the inscription on Tutankhamun's bow case encompassed all of these new martial values:

"The Good God, courageous one, son of Amun, champion, lord of the khepesh, protector of his troops, victorious *kꜣ*-bull among the multitude, who breaks a coalition, being firm on his chariot like the Lord of Thebes, strong fighter, who knows the place of his hand, who shoots with a bow, victorious one, strong authority" (Galán 1994:95).

Conclusion

New Kingdom imperialism and the military iconography and technology it inspired have long been considered an Egyptian cooption of foreign culture. Yet in reality, Egyptians had to join immigrants in communities of practice, which then negotiated between Egyptian and West Asian traditions to produce the marked social transformations of the New Kingdom. Indeed, it is striking that so many examples of this influence can be found in the Ramesside Period in particular, as these kings themselves hailed from the same hybrid military communities of the Eastern Delta. The inscription on Tutankhamun's bow case encapsulated what it meant to be an ideal Egyptian king, an ideal which was the result of the new negotiated martial identities and values developed originally in Middle Kingdom and Second Intermediate Period blended military communities. The members of such communities mutually transformed their collective self-representation—and even that of the Egyptian king himself—through daily practice alongside West Asian immigrant group members.

References

Alba, R. – V. Nee, 1997. Rethinking Assimilation Theory for a New Era of Immigration. *International Migration Review* 31(4), 826–874.

Badawy, A., 1961. The Stela of Irtysen. *CdÉ* 36(72), 269–276.

Bader, B., 2011 Contacts between Egypt and Syria-Palestine as Seen in a Grown Settlement of the Late Middle Kingdom at Tell el-Dabʿa/Egypt. In J. Mynářová, ed., *Egypt and the Near East – The Crossroads. Proceedings of the International Workshop on the Relations between Egypt and the Near East in the Bronze Age*. Prague: Charles University in Prague, 41–72.

Beckman, G., 2008. Horse Training Manual. In J. Aruz – K. Benzel – J.M. Evans, eds., *Beyond Babylon: Art, Trade, and Diplomacy in the Second Millennium B.C.* New York: Metropolitan Museum of Art, 158.

Ben Shalom, U. – G. Horenczyk, 2004. Cultural Identity and Adaptation in an Assimilative Setting: Immigrant Soldiers from the Former Soviet Union in Israel. *International Journal of Intercultural Relations* 8, 461–479.

Berry, J.W., 1997. Immigration, Acculturation, and Adaptation. *Applied Psychology: An International Review* 46(1), 5–34.

Bietak, M., 1996. *Avaris, the Capital of the Hyksos: Recent Excavations at Tell el- Dabʿa.* London: British Museum Press.

Bietak, M., 2006. The Predecessors of the Hyksos. In S. Gitin, S. – J.E.Wright – J.P. Dessel, eds., *Confronting the Past: Archaeological and Historical Essays on Ancient Israel in Honor of William G. Dever*. Winona Lake, IN: Eisenbrauns, 285–293.

Bietak, M., 2010. Where Did the Hyksos Come from and Where Did They Go? In M. Marée, ed., *The Second Intermediate Period (Thirteenth-Seventeenth Dynasties). Current Research, Future Prospects.* OLA 192. Leuven: Peeters, 139–181.

Bietak, M., 2012. The Archaeology of the "Gold of Valour". *EA* 4, 32–33.

Bietak, M., 2018. The Many Ethnicities of Avaris: Evidence from the northern borderland of Egypt. In J. Budka – J. Auenmüller, eds., *From Microcosm to Macrocosm: Individual Households and Cities in Ancient Egypt and Nubia.* Leiden: Sidestone Press, 73–92.

Candelora, D., forthcoming. Hyksos Identity Negotiation in an Eastern Delta Middle Ground. *MDAIK* 75.

Cooney, K., 2012. Apprenticeship and Figured Ostraca from the Ancient Egyptian Village of Deir El-Medina. In W. Wendrich, ed., *Archaeology and Apprenticeship: Body Knowledge, Identity, and Communities of Practice.* Tucson, AZ: University of Arizona Press, 145–170.

Cronin, S., 2012. Deserters, Converts, Cossacks and Revolutionaries: Russians in Iranian Military Service 1800–1920. *Middle Eastern Studies* 48(2), 147–182.

Drenkhahn, R., 1976. *Die Handwerker und ihre Tätigkeiten im alter Ägypten.* ÄA 31. Wiesbaden: Harrassowitz.

Eisikovits, R.A., 2006. Intercultural Learning among Russian Immigrant Recruits in the Israeli Army. *Armed Forces & Society* 32(2), 292–306.

Eyre, C.J., 1987. Work and the Organisation of Work in the New Kingdom. In M.A. Powell, ed., *Labor in the Ancient Near East.* American Oriental Series 68. New Haven: American Oriental Society, 167–222.

Ford, N.G., 1997. "Mindful of the Traditions of His Race:" Dual Identity and Foreign-Born Soldiers in the First World War American Army. *Journal of American Ethnic History* 16(2), 35–57.

Forstner-Müller, I., 2008. *Tell el-Dab'a XVI. Die Gräber des Areals A/II von Tell el-Dab'a.* Untersuchungen der Zweigstelle Kairo des Österreichischen Archäologischen Instituts 28. Wien: Verlag der Österreichischen Akademie der Wissenschaften.

Forstner-Müller, I., 2010. Tombs and Burial Customs at Tell el-Dab'a during the Late Middle Kingdom and the Second Intermediate Period. In M. Marée, ed., *The Second Intermediate Period (Thirteenth-Seventeenth Dynasties). Current Research, Future Prospects.* OLA 192. Leuven: Peeters, 127–138.

Galán, J., 1994. Bullfight Scenes in Ancient Egyptian Tombs. *JEA* 80, 81–96.

Glanville, S.R.K., 1932. Records of a Royal Dockyard of the Time of Thutmosis III: Papyrus British Museum 10056, Part II. *ZÄS* 68, 7–41.

Hale, H.C., 2012. The Role of Practice in the Development of Military Masculinities. *Gender, Work and Organization* 19(6), 699–722.

Hayes, W.C., 1959. *The Scepter of Egypt: A Background for the Study of the Egyptian Antiquities in the Metropolitan Museum of Art. Part II: The Hyksos Period and the New Kingdom (1675–1080 BC).* New York: Platin Press.

Hoch, J.E., 1994. *Semitic Words in Egyptian Texts of the New Kingdom and Third Intermediate Period.* Princeton, NJ: Princeton University Press.

Hoffmeier, J.K., 2003. The Memphis and Karnak Stelae of Amenhotep II (2.3). In W.W. Hallo – K. Lawson, Jr., eds., *Context of Scripture Vol. II: Monumental Inscriptions from the Biblical World.* Leiden – Boston: Brill, 19–23.

Høgseth, H.B., 2012. Knowledge Transfer: The Craftmen's Abstraction. In W. Wendrich, ed., *Archaeology and Apprenticeship: Body Knowledge, Identity, and Communities of Practice.* Tucson, AZ: University of Arizona Press, 61–78.

Jørgensen, L.B., 2012. Writing Craftsmanship? Vocabularies and Notation Systems in the Transmission of Craft Knowledge. In W. Wendrich, ed., *Archaeology and Apprenticeship: Body Knowledge, Identity, and Communities of Practice.* Tucson, AZ: University of Arizona Press, 240–254.

Kemp, B.J., 2006. *Ancient Egypt: Anatomy of a Civilization.* London: Routledge (2nd edition).

Kitchen, K.A., 2003a. Karnak, Campaign Against the Libyans (2.4F). In W.W. Hallo – K. Lawson, Jr., eds., *Context of Scripture Vol. II: Monumental Inscriptions from the Biblical World.* Leiden – Boston: Brill, 30–31.

Kitchen, K.A., 2003b. The Battle of Qadesh – The Poem, or Literary Record (2.5A). In W.W. Hallo – K. Lawson, Jr., eds., *Context of Scripture Vol. II: Monumental Inscriptions from the Biblical World.* Leiden – Boston: Brill, 32–38.

Lave, J. – E. Wenger, 1991. *Situated Learning: Legitimate Peripheral Participation.* Cambridge: Cambridge University Press.

Leal, D.L., 2003. The Multicultural Military: Military Service and the Acculturation of Latinos and Anglos. *Armed Forces & Society* 29(2), 205–226.

Lichtheim, M., 1974. *Ancient Egyptian Literature: Volume I, The Old and Middle Kingdoms.* Berkeley, CA: University of California Press (2006 edition).

Lichtheim, M., 1976. *Ancient Egyptian Literature: Volume II, The New Kingdom.* Berkeley, CA: University of California Press (2006 edition).

Lorton, D., 1974. Terminology Related to the Laws of Warfare in Dyn. XVIII. *JARCE* 11, 53–68.

Lowie, D.A., 1976. A Remarkable Family of Draughtsmen-Painters from Early Nineteenth-Dynasty Thebes. *OA* 15, 91–106.

Moorey, P.R.S., 2001. The Mobility of Artisans and Opportunities for Technology Transfer between Western Asia and Egypt in the Late Bronze Age. In A.J. Shortland, ed., *The Social Context of Technological Change: Egypt and the Near East, 1650-1550 BC*. Oxford: Oxbow Books, 1–14.

Morris, E., 2014. Mitanni Enslaved: Prisoners of War, Pride, and Productivity in a New Imperial Regime. In J. Galán – B. Bryan – P. Dorman, eds., *Creativity and Innovation in the Reign of Hatshepsut*. SAOC 69. Chicago: The Oriental Institute of the University of Chicago, 361–380.

Morris, E., 2017. Prevention Through Deterrence along Egypt's Northeastern Border: Or the Politics of a Weaponized Desert. *Journal of Eastern Mediterranean Archaeology & Heritage Studies* 5(2), 133–147.

Morris, E., 2018. *Ancient Egyptian Imperialism*. Hoboken, NJ: Wiley-Blackwell.

Murnane, W.J., 1980. *United with Eternity: A Concise Guide to the Monuments of Medinet Habu*. Chicago: The Oriental Institute of the University of Chicago.

Philip, G., 2006. *Tell el-Dabʿa XV: Metalwork and Metalworking Evidence of the Late Middle Kingdom and Second Intermediate Period*. Untersuchungen der Zweigstelle Kairo des Österreichischen Archäologischen Instituts 26. Vienna: Verlag der Österreichischen Akademie der Wissenschaften.

Phinney, J.S. – G. Horenczyk – K. Liebkind – P. Vedder, 2001. Ethnic Identity, Immigration, and Well-Being: An Interactional Perspective. *Journal of Social Issues* 57(3), 493–510.

Pusch, E.B. – A. Herold, 1999. Qantir/Pi-Ramesses. In K.A. Bard, ed., *Encyclopedia of the Archaeology of Ancient Egypt*. New York: Routledge, 787–790.

Pusch, E.B. – Ch. Tasiaux, 1990. Metallverarbeitende Werkstätten der frühen Ramessidenzeit in Qantir-Piramesse/Nord. *ÄuL* 1, 75–113.

Raulwing, P., 2013. Manfred Mayrhofer's Studies on Indo-Aryan and the Indo-Aryans in the Ancient Near East: A Retrospective and Outlook on Future Research. In T. Schneider – P. Raulwing, eds., *Egyptology from the First World War to the Third Reich: Ideology, Scholarship, and Individual Biographies*. Leiden: Brill, 248–285.

Redford, D.B., 1992. *Egypt, Canaan, and Israel in Ancient Times*. Princeton, NJ: Princeton University Press.

Rehren, T. – E.B. Pusch, 2012. Alloying and Resource Management in New Kingdom Egypt: The Bronze Industry at Qantir – Pi-Ramesse and Its Relationship to Egyptian Copper Sources. In V. Kassianidou – G. Papasavvas, eds., *Eastern Mediterranean Metallurgy and Metalwork in the Second Millennium BC. A Conference in Honour of James D. Muhly, Nicosia, 10th–11th October 2009*. Oxford: Oxbow Books, 215–221.

Sabbahy, L., 2013. Depictional Study of Chariot Use in New Kingdom Egypt. In A.J. Veldmeijer – S. Ikram, eds., *Chasing Chariots: Proceedings of the First International Chariot Conference (Cairo [30 November to 2 December] 2012)*. Leiden: Sidestone Press, 191–202.

Sacco, A., 2013. Art and Imperial Ideology: Remarks on the Depiction of Royal Chariots on Wall Reliefs in New Kingdom Egypt and the Neo-Assyrian Empire. In A.J. Veldmeijer – S. Ikram, eds., *Chasing Chariots: Proceedings of the First International Chariot Conference (Cairo [30 November to 2 December] 2012)*. Leiden: Sidestone Press, 203–216.

Scheel, B., 1987. Studien zum Metallhandwerk im alten Ägypten III. Handlungen und Beischriften in den Bildprogrammen der Gräber des Neuen Reiches und der Spätzeit. *SAK* 14, 248–264.

Scheel, B., 1989. *Egyptian Metalworking and Tools*. Aylesbury, UK: Shire Publications Ltd.

Schneider, T., 2008. Fremdwörter in der ägyptischen Militärsprache des Neuen Reiches und ein Bravourstück des Elitesoldaten (Pap. Anastasi I 23, 2-7). *JSSEA* 35, 181–205.

Shaw, I., 2001. Egyptians, Hyksos, and Military Hardware: Causes, Effects, or Catalysts? In A.J. Shortland, ed., *The Social Context of Technological Change: Egypt and the Near East, 1650-1550 BC*. Oxford: Oxbow Books, 59–72.

Shaw, I., ed., 2012. *Ancient Egyptian Technology and Innovation: Transformations in Pharaonic Material Culture*. London: Bloomsbury.

Sookermany, A. Mcd., 2011. Learning in Doing – Skills Acquisition in [Post-] Modernised Military Communities of Practice. *Defence Studies* 11(4), 615–635.

Spalinger, A., 2017. The Armies of Re. In P.P. Creasman – R.H. Wilkinson, eds., *Pharaoh's Land and Beyond: Ancient Egypt and Its Neighbors*. New York: Oxford University Press, 93–114.

Veldmeijer, A.J. – S. Ikram, eds., 2013. *Chasing Chariots: Proceedings of the First International Chariot Conference (Cairo [30 November to 2 December] 2012)*. Leiden: Sidestone Press.

Veldmeijer, A.J. – S. Ikram, eds., 2018. *Chariots in Ancient Egypt. The Tano Chariot, A Case Study*. Leiden: Sidestone Press.

Wendrich, W., ed., 2012. *Archaeology and Apprenticeship: Body Knowledge, Identity, and Communities of Practice*. Tucson, AZ: University of Arizona Press.

Wenger, E., 1998. *Communities of Practice: Learning, Meaning, and Identity*. Cambridge: Cambridge University Press.

Winand, J., 2017. Identifying Semitic Loanwords in Late Egyptian. In E. Grossman – P. Dils – T.S. Richter – W. Schenkel, eds., *Greek Influence on Egyptian-Coptic: Contact-Induced Change in Ancient African Language*. Hamburg: Widmaier Verlag, 481–511.

ABOUT "EGYPTIANITY" AND "FOREIGNNESS" IN EGYPTIAN TEXTS. A CONTEXT-SENSITIVE LEXICAL STUDY

Gaëlle Chantrain (Charles University – Yale University)

Introduction

In this article, I consider the role of some ethnonyms naming neighbours of Egypt as elements of the Egyptian texts and the role of the people they name in the Egyptian conception of the world. The article is not meant as an historical study: it rather aims at providing a complement of information to the data already discussed and analysed in archaeology and history.

My purpose is to show the importance of a contextualised lexical analysis for a better understanding of a broad phenomenon like the relations between Egyptians and foreigners. I hope that this study can help to trace a continuum between two poles: on the one hand a stereotyped ideological vision of Egypt *vs.* "the abroad" and, on the other hand, some elements of the actual practical situation described in everyday life texts.

The article is structured in two parts. The first part is made of seven short lexical studies through which we will see what can be inferred about the respective status of the different foreigners in the Egyptian texts and mental world.

The second part explores some links that can be drawn between the specific elements of the narrative frame and the ratio of power between protagonists marked as [+ Egyptian] and [- Egyptian] / [+ foreigner].

Corpus

The lexemes taken into consideration in this study are: *nḥsy* (Nubian), *sty.w* (Nubians), *ṯḥnw/ṯmḥw* (Libya, Libyans), *mšwš* (Libyans), *ḫ3rw* (Syro-Palestinian, Levantine) and *ꜥ3m* (Asiatic). This list is of course not exhaustive. It constitutes the first set of a series of terms to be analysed in forthcoming articles. These terms have been chosen because they work together as elements of a system and each of them has a sufficient number of attestations to highlight significant distinctive features.

The corpus is made of the texts from the Old Kingdom until the Third Intermediate period encoded into the *Thesaurus Linguae Aegyptiae*[1] and the *Ramsès*[2]

---

[1] http://aaew.bbaw.de/tla/index.html (accessed on 15 December 2018).

[2] I would like to sincerely thank St. Polis and J. Winand for giving me access to the complete corpus of the database. The beta version of *Ramses Online* is available here: http://ramses.ulg.ac.be (accessed on 15 December 2018).

database. The distribution of the texts according to the diachrony and the source corpora is organised as follows:

Tab. 1.
Distribution of the texts according to the diachrony and the source corpora.

Period	*Thesaurus Linguae Aegyptiae*	*Ramsès*
Old Kingdom	+	-
First Intermediate Period	+	-
Middle Kingdom	+	-
Second Intermediate Period	+	+
New Kingdom	+	+
Third Intermediate Period	+	+

The most represented period (that is, with the biggest amount of texts and of attestations) is the New Kingdom, which is *de facto* the main core of my study. The amount of data coming from the other periods are however sufficient to allow for an accurate diachronic perspective.

Structure of the analysis: semasiology and onomasiology

The structure of the lexical analysis is also divided in two parts. First, each lexeme is submitted to an individual (semasiological) study. The results obtained for all of them are then compared in an onomasiological study, which allows to stress the differences and common points between the lexemes.

The criteria taken into consideration in the semasiological analysis of each lexeme are the following ones:

1) Distribution of the attestations:
   - in diachrony,
   - by textual genre: all terms are not attested in the same kind of texts;

2) Classifiers (determinatives) usage and its evolution in diachrony.

The next criteria depend on the cotext analysis, performed through the use of a distributional semantic model.

3) Individuality criterion: is the term associated to the feature [+ individuality] or [- individuality]? Several clues can be checked in order to answer this question:
   a. Use of the singular *vs.* systematic use of the collective: Among the words naming the neighbours of Egypt, some of them can be used in the plural/collective as well as in the singular. Others on the other hand cannot designate a single person, but only a group.
   b. The attestation of a derived feminine noun is an element to mark the lexeme with the feature [+ individuality].
   c. The attestation of a derived personal name is another element pointing in this direction.

4) [+/- foreignness] criterion: is the foreigner named *rmṯ*?

The fact of designating some foreigners as *rmṯ* shows an acknowledgment of their individuality and a higher degree of integration within the Egyptian mental world. Indeed, as already stressed by Loprieno (1988), *rmṯ* works in complementary opposition with *ḫ3s.ti*. These terms correspond to the two ends of a continuum between [+ Egyptian] and [+ foreigner].

5) Agentivity criterion: definition of the grammatical function of the term in the clause and of its semantic role. One can notice differences in the grammatical functions and semantic roles that the lexemes predominantly (or exclusively) fulfil. The choice of using these terms as agent, experiencer or patient of an action can be directly linked to the two former criteria: higher degrees of individuality and of integration goes together with a higher degree of agentivity.

6) How much do the cotextual features point or not towards the "enemy prototype"?

7) Specific cotextual features: this category gathers relevant elements which are not included in the aforementioned categories.

Lexical Studies: Semasiology

The Nubians

nḥsy

Distribution and classifiers

The lexeme *nḥsy*[3] is attested from the Old Kingdom and refers to the inhabitants of Nubia. It is usually written with the classifiers 𓌙 and 𓈉, and with the group of classifiers  in the hieratic texts from the 19th Dynasty. The group  can also be found for the plural[4].

When looking at the distribution by textual genres, two observations can be made. The first one is that *nḥsy* is present in almost all of them, with the exception of the literary fictional texts (tales). The second one is that most of the attestations come from royal texts. These observations show that the term *nḥsy* is quite well-spread and is mainly—but not exclusively—a feature of the ideological discourse. The fact that the *nḥsy* people are not attested in tales suggests that they do not seem to be given an important role in the fictional world of the Egyptians. They are also very scarcely represented in the literary texts in general, since they are attested only one time in both poetry (love songs) and wisdom texts (Teaching of Ani).

Individuality and foreignness

A feminine form *nḥsy(.t)* is well attested from the Middle Kingdom. It is found in oracular and legal texts as well as in poetry. In Love Songs, only the *nḥsy*-woman is actually mentioned. The feminine of *nḥsy* is often written without the ending *-t*,

[3] Wb. 2: 303, 3–11 (including fem. *nḥsy.t*); Hannig 1997: 424; *TLA*: lemma no. 86650; *Ramsès*: nHsy_1006_17854.

[4] The detail of the main classifiers used for each lexeme can be found *infra*, Tab. 9.

especially in New Kingdom hieratic texts. The distinction is then made with the masculine by using the feminine classifier  and/or of the article *tꜣ* or the possessive pronoun *tꜣy.f*.

Ex. 1. *iw.n (r) šd.f r pꜣ bik <n> nḫn tꜣ{y} nḥsy(.t)*  *<n> nḫb*

"We will protect him from the falcon of Nekhen and the Nubian woman of Nekheb" (P. Turin 1985, 48–49)[5]

22nd Dynasty; amuletic

Ex. 2. *ḥꜣ n.i tꜣy.s nḥsy.t* 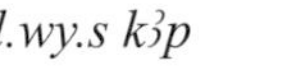 *nty m iry-rd.wy.s kꜣp*

"Ah, if I were her Nubian, who is her confidant" (O. DeM 1266 + O. CG 25218, l. 18)[6]

19th Dynasty; poetry

The lexeme *nḥsy* can be used as a singular, which shows that the Nubians *nḥsy* can be considered both as plural entity and as individuals. On a continuum between [+ individuality] and [- individuality] (= collective, undifferentiated), they were thus closer to the first end. Moreover, there is a personal name derived from *nḥsy*, which reinforces this statement.

The *nḥsy*-people are also designated as *rmṯ*. This allows to think that they rather work as intermediary members on the continuum between [+ Egyptian] and [+ foreigner]. The use of *rmṯ* indeed shows a certain degree of integration in the Egyptian society and it does not apply to all the foreigners, as we shall see[7].

Ex. 3. *pr n mniw imn-ḥtp sꜣ nḥsy* 

"House of the shepherd *imn-ḥtp*, son of *nḥsy*" (P. BM 10068, v. 8, 9 = KRI VI, 755, 1)[8]

Ramesses XI; legal

Ex. 4. *m nꜥi.t n nḥsy.w*  *m-kfꜣ sꜣw tw r nꜣy.sn rmṯ.w ḥnꜥ nꜣy.sn ḥkꜣw.w*

"Do not be complaisant at all with the Nubians, and be careful with their people and their magicians" (St. Boston MFA 25.362, 10 = Urk. IV, 1344,12)[9]

Amenhotep II; royal

Agentivity

The lexeme *nḥsy* often fulfils the grammatical function of subject in a clause, with the semantic role of experiencer or of agent. The term *nḥsy* is consequently rather high on the scale of agentivity. More specifically, *nḥsy* is mainly used as subject of verbs expressing physical activity (e.g. *sḫsḫ* "to run", *fꜣi* "to carry", …).

[5] Edwards 1960: I, 73–76; *Ramsès* text ID 1105.

[6] *Ramsès* text ID 1128.

[7] Cf. also Loprieno 1988.

[8] *Ramsès* text ID 269.

[9] *Ramsès* text ID 1128.

Ex. 5. *nꜣ nḥsy.w*  *m sẖsẖ r-ḥꜣ.t.k m sḫpr i.ir.k*

"The Nubians who are running before you are an acquisition that you made" (P. Anastasi 4, 3, 5–6 = LEM 37, 13–14)
Seti II; miscellanies

It is indeed interesting to note the fact that the emphasis is often put on the physical dimension (appearance or activities) when Nubians are mentioned in the texts. They are usually described as good-looking and active/strong people while Libyans and people from the Syro-Palestinian region are rather qualified as coward and scheming.

Ex. 6. *ḥm.w knꜥn n ḫꜣrw mnḥ.w nfr.w nḥsy.w*  *nfr.w n kš šꜥw ḥbs bh.t*

"The Cananaean servants of Syria, the beautiful young men, the beautiful Nubians from Kush, as dignified fan-bearers" (P. Anastasi 3A, 6 = LEM 33, 8–9)[10]
19th Dynasty; miscellanies

Enemy?

The term *nḥsy*, when used in the ideological discourse of royal texts, shows cotextual features corresponding to the description of a stereotyped enemy. The *nḥsy* people fulfil this role mainly before the Ramesside period (beside one example from Medinet Habu). The magic of the Nubians is also particularly feared and constitutes a recurring topic (cf. *supra*, ex. 4). However, a close look at the cotextual environment of the attestations of *nḥsy* in other textual genres reveals that the Nubians-*nḥsy* became lower on the scale [+/- enemy] than Libyans and Asiatics after the 18th Dynasty. In the New Kingdom, they indeed tend to be qualified in less pejorative terms than the latter, and this even in the ideological discourse.

Specific cotextual features

In the examples below, *nḥsy* is used in a complementary opposition with *ḫꜣrw* "Syrian". This association is very recurrent, to the point that it becomes a systemic opposition from the end of the New Kingdom to express the idea of "any kind of foreigner", "all the foreigners". It is used particularly often in the amuletic texts. The complete system is built around three terms: *nḥsy*, *ḫꜣrw* and *rmṯ n km.t*. On the level of the toponyms, a similar system of opposition exists between the terms *(tꜣ n) ḫꜣrw* "(the land of) Kharu", *(tꜣ n) kš* "(the land of) Kush" and *(tꜣ n) km.t* (the land of) Egypt. It encompasses thus the Egyptians and their two main categories of traditional enemies: the people from the South (Nubians) and the ones from the Levant (Syro-Palestinians). Other ethnonyms or toponyms (for example, *pi.t* "Libya", cf. first example *infra*) can of course be added to this picture. These three elements however remain the stable basic ones.

[10] *Ramsès* text ID 204.

Ex. 7. *iw.n (r) šd.s r ḥkꜣ n ḫꜣrw r ḥkꜣ n nḥsy r ḥkꜣ n pi.t r ḥkꜣ n rmṯ n km.t (…)*

"We will protect her from the magic of a Syrian, the magic of a Nubian, the magic from Libya, the magic of people from Egypt (…)" (P. BM 10083 [OAD L.1], v. 36)[11]
22nd Dynasty; amuletic

Ex. 8. *twtw (ḥr) sbꜣ nḥsy.w md.t rmṯ.w n km.t ḫꜣrw.w ḫꜣsty nb m-mitt*

"One teaches the language of the people of Egypt to the Nubians, the Syrians and also to every foreigner" (Ani, P. Boulaq 4, 23, 5–6)[12]
21st Dynasty; wisdom

Ex. 9. *iw.i (r) šd.s r ḥkꜣ n km.t r ḥkꜣ n ḫꜣrw r ḥkꜣ n kš*

"I will protect her from the magic of Egypt, from the magic of Syria and from the magic of Kush" (P. Berlin 10462, r. 61–62)[13]
22nd Dynasty; amuletic

The same complementary opposition is also found with the feminine counterparts of both terms:

Ex. 10. *iw ḫꜣ[rw(.t)] nḥsy.t iw mr.f sy iw.f (ḥr) di.t n.s ḫ.wt.f*

"(Even if it is not his own wife), but a Syrian woman or a Nubian woman he loves and to whom he bequeaths his goods (…)" (P. Turin 2021 + P. Genève D. 409, r. 3,11 = KRI IV, 741, 9–10)
Ramesses XI; legal

Summary of the highlighted semantic features:

nḥsy
+ individuality
+ agentivity
+/- enemy[14]
+/- foreigner

Tab. 2.
Semantic features highlighted for *nḥsy*.

***sty* "Nubian" and *tꜣ-sty* "Nubia"**

Distribution and classifiers

Another term used to name the Nubians is *sty*[15], usually found in the plural form *sty.w*. This ethnonym is attested from the Middle Kingdom, while the corresponding toponym, *tꜣ-sty*, is already attested in the Old Kingdom. When classifiers are

[11] Edwards 1960: I, 1–12; *Ramsès* text ID 1041.
[12] Quack 1994; *Ramsès* text ID 450.
[13] Edwards 1960: I, 113–117; *Ramsès* text ID 1149.
[14] The symbol +/- corresponds to the status of "intermediary member" on the scale of reference.
[15] Wb. 3: 488, 11–12; Hannig 1997: 777; *TLA*: lemma no. 147780; *Ramsès*: ID sty_1006_16403.

used, one can find mainly the following ones: , and . The two last groups are the recurrent ones in hieratic texts from the 19th Dynasty.

sty is attested in royal texts, autobiographies, funerary and magical texts, literary fictional texts and miscellanea. It does not seem to be used in documentary texts and oracular/amuletic texts. Principally attested in texts from the ideology, the *sty.w* are described as a stereotype of foreigners and enemies.

Ex. 11. *iw [mi sšm-rswt] mi gmḥ sw dḥ m ꜣbw z n ẖꜣ.t m tꜣ-sty*

"it was like a dream, like an inhabitant of the Delta seeing himself in Elephantine, a man of the marshes in the land of the Nubians" (Sinuhe [R], 65)[16]
19th–20th Dynasty (text: 12th Dynasty); fiction

Individuality and foreignness

The *sty.w* are very rarely referred to as singular individuals: the plural/collective is almost always used. There are no feminine and no personal name derived from this term, and they are not qualified as *rmṯ*. The term *sty.w* is thus low on the individuality scale and high on the foreignness scale.

Agentivity

The lexeme *sty(.w)* can fulfil all functions within the clause and can assume the semantic roles of agent, experiencer and patient. It shares its agentivity features with *nḥsy*. The only notable difference is that the actions of the *sty.w* are usually collective and come within an ideological context, while the *nḥsy* acts as a free-willing individual.

Ex. 12. *bꜣk.w in sty.w* *m ꜣbw hbny*

"the artefacts brought by the Nubians, in ivory and ebony" (Stele Boston MFA 23733, Urk. IV, 1237, 3)[17]
18th Dynasty; royal

Enemy?

In the New Kingdom, the cotextual environment associated to the lexeme *sty.w* tends however to become less negatively connoted, in comparison with terms naming Libyans, Syrians or Asiatics. Even if the term *sty.w* is part of the "ideological vocabulary" it begins to work more as intermediary member on a bipolar scale between [+ enemy] and [- enemy]. In the example below, we can note that *sty.w* is used in a complementary opposition with *rṯnw*, as representative elements of the two main geographical areas that have to be under the domination of the Pharaoh. This prefigures the similar situation that we will find later between *ẖꜣrw*, *nḥsy* and *rmṯ n km.t*.

16 Koch 1990.

17 *Ramsès* text ID 991.

Ex. 13. *wꜥf.n ḥm.i tꜣ nb rṯnw ẖr ṯb.ty.i sty.w*  *m nḏ.wt nw.t ḥm.i*

"My Majesty dominated every country: the retjenou is under my sandals and the Nubians are as subjects of my Majesty" (Stele Boston MFA 23733, Urk. IV, 1236,15)[18]

Tuthmose III; royal

Summary of the highlighted semantic features:

sty
- individuality
+ agentivity
+/- enemy
+ foreigner

Tab. 3.
Semantic features highlighted for *sty*.

sty
- individuality
+ agentivity
+/- enemy
+ foreignerTab. 3. Semantic features highlighted for *sty*.

The Libyans

mšwš*: *"Libyans"

Distribution and classifiers

The lexeme *msws*[19] is attested from the 18th Dynasty and names a Libyan tribe. This term is attested in the following textual genres: royal texts, literary satirical, letters, legal and administrative texts.

The usual group of classifiers for *mšwš* is . In rare examples (2 in total in this corpus), the classifier  is added.

Individuality and foreignness

The term *mšwš* is only used as a plural/collective. There is no personal name derived from this lexeme and no feminine counterpart either. Furthermore, the *mšwš*-people are not qualified as *rmṯ*, which situates them low on the individuality scale and high on the foreignness scale.

Agentivity

The lexeme *mšwš* can fulfil all grammatical functions in the clause and all semantic roles, including the one of agent. This term is thus rather high on the agentivity scale.

[18] Klug 2002: 193–208.
[19] Wb 2: 157, 3; Hannig 1997: 368; *TLA*: lemma no. 76410; *Ramsès*: ID mSwS_1002_11835.

Ex. 14. *iw ini.w šꜥ.t n ṯꜣty <ḥnꜥ> pꜣ sš n tmꜣ r-ḏd*
nꜣ mšwš  *m iy.t r niw.t*
"After that a letter from the vizier and the scribe of the *tmꜣ*-mat has been brought saying: the *mšwš* are coming to the city' (P. Milan E 0.9.40127 + P. Turin cat. 2074, r. 2, 9 = KRI VI, 609, 6)[20]
Ramesses IX; administrative

Enemy?

The *mšwš*-people are explicitly qualified as enemies (*ḫrw.w*) whose attacks are recurrent and feared. In the Tomb Journals, for example, raids of the *mšwš* tribes are recorded, since they prevented the workers from doing their job. These attacks became more and more widespread at the end of the 20th Dynasty, before the *mšwš* started to settle in the Western Delta, prefiguring the Libyan domination under the 22th Dynasty. Later, the king Sheshonk I was called "great chief of the Meshuesh", as a reference to his Libyan origins (cf. Stele of Sheshonk (Cairo JE 66285), 3).

Ex. 15. *n sw 21: mšwš*
(not working) on day 21: *mšwš*  (O. Cairo CG 25243, r. 21 = KRI VI, 871, 4)[21]
Ramesses XI; administrative

Ex. 16. *bw rḫ.t tw pḥ n nꜣ mšwš r-minꜣ* 
"One does not know yet attacks of *mšwš* here" (P. Berlin P 10494, v. 5 = LRL 24, 7)[22]
Ramesses XI; letter

In a general way, the Libyans-*mšwš* are described in very negative terms. The word *mšwš* is sometimes associated in context with other ethnonyms or toponyms, but without any systemic opposition. If the *mšwš* are obviously feared in texts reflecting the actual everyday life in the New Kingdom, the ideological discourse is very different. Indeed, they are described as cowards and submitted to the respect and fear of pharaoh.

Ex. 17. *mšwš ꜥḥi.sn kꜣp.w m tꜣ.sn* 
"as for the *mšwš*, they were uncertain and hidden in their land" (Medinet Habu, First Libyan War, KRI V, 24, 5)[23]
20th Dynasty; royal

Summary of the highlighted semantic features:

---

[20] *Ramsès* text ID 3436.
[21] *Ramsès* text ID 3232.
[22] *Ramsès* text ID 128.
[23] *Ramsès* text ID 1290.

mšwš
- individuality
+ agentivity
+ enemy
+ foreigner

Tab. 4.
Semantic features highlighted for *mšwš*.

***ṯmḥ(.w)/ṯḥn.w* (Libyans, Libya)**

Distribution and classifiers

The lexemes *ṯḥn.w*[24] and *ṯmḥ.w*[25] are respectively attested from the Old Kingdom and the Middle Kingdom. They can still be found in the New Kingdom, in epigraphic texts. The two lexemes *ṯmḥ.w* and *ṯḥn.w* appear to be closely connected and both name Libyan people in the New Kingdom. The term *ṯḥn.w* seems to have appeared first and to originally name the land (Libya), while *ṯmḥ.w* tends more towards an initial ethnonym.

The distribution of the two terms *ṯḥn.w* and *ṯmḥ.w* becomes exactly the same from the New Kingdom: they are both only attested in literary (fictional, wisdom, miscellanea), royal texts and funerary texts. They are also both mainly used as ethnonyms. The only mentions I found of *ṯmḥ.w* and *ṯḥn.w* as toponyms in Late Egyptian hieratic texts are in the Tale of Woe (P. Pushkin 127).

Ex. 18. *ḳd<i> nꜣy.s nhrty <m> ꜥnḫ.t <n> ḫꜣs.t ṯmḥw* 
ꜥḳ<.i> <r> ṯḥnw 
"I followed their sacred wells in the West of the foreign land of *ṯmḥw* and I walked into the (land of) *ṯḥnw*." (P. Pushkin 127, col. 3,1)[26]
Third Intermediate Period(?); lit. fiction

In this passage, the spelling of the foreign lands *ṯmḥw* and *ṯḥnw* includes the classifier 𓊖, in addition to the group . My interpretation is that this adjunction expresses the fact that the traveller learned to know what was previously unknown ("foreign") to him. Indeed, the classifier 𓊖 is used in the context of an urban area, but also a territory marked as Egyptian or under Egyptian influence. By extension, the use of this classifier could mark a place/territory as known (the protagonist became used to it while travelling), by opposition to a place that appears as totally foreign. The complete passage says:

Ex. 19. "I joined the crowd of a ship that was not mine, since mine had been stolen in front of me. I travelled through the land on the river, escaping on its depths. I reached the North at Chemnis, I crossed the highlands and the marshes of the

[24] Wb. 5: 394, 5–9; Hannig 1997: 961; *TLA*: lemma no. 176680; *Ramsès*: ID THnw_1006_37370 and THnw_1014_91129.
[25] Wb. 5: 368, 11–13; Hannig 1997: 953; *TLA*: lemma no. 175490; *Ramsès*: ID TmHw_1004_62798 and TmHw_1014_91126.
[26] *Ramsès* text ID 2469.

Delta in the East of the land of *pḏtiw-šw*. I followed their sacred wells in the West of the foreign land of *ṯmḥw* and I walked into the (land of) *ṯḥnw*." (P. Pushkin 127, Tale of Woe, col. 2, 12–3, 1)

Individuality and foreignness

Both lexemes *ṯmḥ.w* and *ṯḥn.w* are always used as a plural/collective, except for some cases in the Greco-Roman period.[27] There are no corresponding feminine lexemes[28] and no derived personal name. Consistently, they are also not considered as *rmṯ* by the Egyptians.

Agentivity

The terms *ṯmḥ.w* and *ṯḥn.w* are rather low on the agentivity scale, since they mostly fulfil the semantic roles of patients. In the few cases where the lexeme has the function of subject, it generally has the role of experiencer. One notable exception though: the lexemes *ṯmḥ.w* and *ṯḥn.w* fulfil the role of agent with a couple of motion verbs expressing the idea of "flying away", "escaping".

Ex. 20. *Pꜣ tꜣ* <*n*> *ṯmḥw pꜣd*

ir.w nhr

"The land of the *ṯmḥw*  fled, they made a running off" (Medinet Habu, First Libyan War, great inscription year 5, KRI V, 24, 4)[29]
20th Dynasty; royal

Enemy?

Looking at the cotextual elements associated to the *ṯmḥ.w* and the *ṯḥn.w* people, we can observe that they are described as a real stereotype of the enemy to slaughter. Indeed, both lexemes are used as direct object complement of the following verbs: *sksk* (to destroy), *thi* (to transgress, to attack), *gbgb* (to slaughter), *smꜣ* (to kill), *ẖsf* (push aside), *dr* (to expel), *ḥw* (to smite), *dḫ* (to pull down), *sꜣw* (to break), *ṯfi* (to remove), *ḥꜣḳ* (to catch).

Ex. 21. *sꜣw iꜣ.t ṯmḥ.w r km ḏ.t*

"the back of the *ṯmḥ.w* was broken for the whole eternity" (Medinet Habu, First Libyan War, Year 5 inscription, KRI 2 4, 1–2)
20th Dynasty; royal

They are, moreover, qualified as mean (*ẖsi*), and inspiring fear (*snḏ*). But, thanks to the courage of Pharaoh they quickly become sad (*ihm*) and despaired (*bdš*), before being killed (*smꜣ*).

[27] These examples are not taken into account in the frame of this study since the corpus includes only texts up to the Third Intermediate Period.

[28] This is true for the current corpus. A feminine term *ṯmḥ.t* is however attested as divine epithet (LGG VII: 466).

[29] *Ramsès* text ID 1147.

Summary of the highlighted semantic features:

ṯḥn.w/ṯmḥ.w
- individuality
- agentivity
+ enemy
+ foreigner

Tab. 5.
Semantic features highlighted for *ṯḥn.w/ṯmḥ.w*.

The Asiatics

***ḫꜣrw* "Syrian, Levantine"**

Distribution and classifiers

Both the toponym and the ethnonym *ḫꜣrw* are attested from the 18th Dynasty. A regular distinction seems to be made between them since the beginning. However, in some cases, the distinction between the ethnonym and the adjective "Syrian, Levantine" can be difficult to establish. In the 18th Dynasty, *ḫꜣrw* designates specifically the Hurrians. From the 19th Dynasty though, the meaning becomes more general and evolves towards designating the people from the Syro-Palestinian region.[30]

The term *ḫꜣrw* is attested in the following genres: royal texts, literary fictional texts, wisdom texts, miscellanea, letters, amuletic/oracular texts and, later, legal texts.

From the 21st Dynasty, the toponym *ḫꜣrw* (Syria-Palestine) sometimes takes the classifier 𓊖, as it is the case for the toponym *kš* (Kush). This shows a higher level of integration and is also a way of marking the Egyptian influence on these lands. This spelling follows the reorganizational process of the classifiers system that took place in the New Kingdom. Indeed, this addition fits within the dynamics at work during the third phase of this process.[31]

Ex. 22. *ir.i smtr pꜣ ḫꜣrw* *n pr ḏḥwty i.hꜣb.k n.i ḥr.f*
"I questioned the Syrian of the domain of Thoth about whom you wrote to me" (P. Bologna 1086, 9 = KRI 7 9, 12)[32]
Ramesses II; letter

Ex. 23. *my <sḏd.i> n.k pꜣy.f šm.t r ḫꜣrw* *mšꜥ ḥr nꜣ ṯs.wt*
"Come, so that I tell you about his travel in Syria, about his expedition on the mountains" (P. Anastasi 3, 5, 9 = LEM 26, 9)[33]
Merenptah; miscellanies

[30] Cf. Vernus 1977 and M. Kilani (personal communication, November 2018).
[31] Cf. Chantrain 2014.
[32] *Ramsès* text ID 696.
[33] *Ramsès* text ID 194.

Individuality and foreignness

The lexeme *ḫ3rw* can be used in the singular, like *nḥsy*. A personal name "*ḫ3rw*" is attested as well. It does not seem to have a real feminine counterpart but can be found with the feminine classifier . The combination of these three features points towards an acknowledgement of the individuality of the *ḫ3rw*-people by the Egyptians.

Ex. 24. *iw ḫ3[rw(.t)]*  *nḥsy.t*  *iw mr.f sy iw.f (ḥr) di.t n.s ḫ.wt.f*

"(Even if it is not his own wife), but a Syrian woman or a Nubian woman he loves and to whom he bequeaths his goods (…)" (P. Turin 2021 + P. Genève D. 409, r. 3,11 = KRI IV, 741, 9–10)
Ramesses XI; legal

Agentivity

The lexeme *ḫ3rw* is rarely attested with the grammatical function of subject in the corpus. Moreover, in this case, it does not fulfil the semantic role of agent. The most frequent semantic role attested for *ḫ3rw* is the one of patient, followed with the one of experiencer.

Enemy?

Here again, a difference has to be made between the ideological discourse and the elements provided by other textual genres. The *ḫ3rw*, like the *nḥsy*, symbolises a part of the world, different from Egypt, both in an antagonist and complementary ways. However, the *ḫ3rw* are described in more negative terms than the Nubians.

Ex. 25. *sm3 ḫ3rw*  *ptpt kš* 

"The one who kills Syria and tramples on Kush" (Stela Gebel el-Silsila, KRI I, 60, 2)
Seti I; royal

Ex. 26. *w3ḥ k3 n it.i imn ḥ3 [twi] ḥr km.t mi it it.w nty bw ptr.w ḫ3rw.w* 

"By the *ka* of my father Amun, ah, if only I had stayed in Egypt, like the fathers of my father who have never seen aSyrian" (Qadesh [L1], 50, §188–189)
Ramesses II; royal

Specific cotextual features

As we have seen earlier, in some hieratic texts, the association of *ḫ3rw* and *nḥsy* expresses the idea of "any kind of foreigner" in opposition to *rmṯ n km.t* "the people of Egypt". Interestingly enough, both *ḫ3rw* and *nḥsy* are also called *rmṯ*, which shows a certain level of integration within the extended frame of the Egyptian society and an acknowledgement of their individuality.

This complementarity is attested in several genres and cotextual environments. It is above all recurrent though in amuletic texts, where it comes to protect someone from anything and anyone coming from Egypt and abroad.

ḫ3rw
+ individuality
- agentivity
+ enemy
+/- foreigner

Tab. 6.
Semantic features highlighted for *ḫ3rw*.

ᶜ3m: Asiatic

Distribution and classifiers

The lexeme *ᶜ3m* "Asiatic" is attested from the Old Kingdom, in a letter dated from the 6th Dynasty (P. Strasbourg Cb, v. K2).
This term is found in most of the textual genres, except for amuletic, legal and administrative texts.
The sign  is usually part of the spelling, but not in the position of classifier, even though it is also clearly semantically motivated.
The main classifiers used from the 19th Dynasty are , , , ;  (sometimes in association with ,  (epigraphy) or  (hieratic). The group  it attested as well.

Individuality and foreignness

The lexeme *ᶜ3m* is often used in the singular, to refer to an individual as well as to name the Asiatics in general. It is to be noticed that *ᶜ3m* is an exception in this respect, because the other terms rather use the plural to express the collective. A feminine lexeme *ᶜ3m.t* is also attested[34].

Ex. 27. *ᶜ3m.t*  *tn in-iw.ṯ bs.ti*

"O you, Asiatic woman, did you come?" (P. Berlin P 3027, spell E, 5, 3)[35]
18th Dynasty; magical

There is apparently no personal name derived from *ᶜ3m*, but the *ᶜ3m.w* people are often referred to by their own names, which shows both a high level of integration and of individuality.

Ex. 28. *in n šmᶜw ᶜ3m*  *z-n-wsrt-snb*

"Brought by the singer, the Asiatic *z-n-wsrt-snb*" (P. Berlin 10066, v. 4)[36]
12th Dynasty; letter

Despite this fact, the *ᶜ3m.w* do not seem to be designated as *rmṯ*.

---

[34] Wb. 1, 168, 1–2; Hannig 1997: 130; *TLA*: lemma no. 35410. *Ramsès* has one single entry *ᶜ3m*.
[35] Yamazaki 2003: 20.
[36] Luft 1992: Briefe 1. Luft does not translate *ᶜ3m* and considers it as part of the name. I here follow the translation provided by I. Hafemann in the *TLA*. Parallel attestations of *ᶜ3m* + personal name support the latter interpretation (e.g. P. BM 10021, 3: *ᶜ3m iᶜrtw*).

Agentivity

The *ꜥꜣm.w* can fulfil all semantic roles. They are high on the agentivity scale. This depends however on the kind of texts. Indeed, in royal texts belonging to the ideological discourse, the lexeme *ꜥꜣm* works more frequently as an object, with the semantic role of patient. It is eloquently used with the following verbs: *ini* (to bring), *snḏ* (to fear), *sḫr* (to kill), *ptpt* (to crush), *ḫsf* (to punish), *sḫi* (to strike), *ḥwi* (to hit).

In the same texts, the term *ꜥꜣm* can fulfil the semantic role of agent or experiencer. In the first case, the most frequent context is a depiction of the *ꜥꜣm.w* bringing some tribute to the pharaoh, and/or coming to him (centripetal motion, cf. infra). In the second case, the *ꜥꜣm.w* are in a sufferance state, or about to die.

The way the *ꜥꜣm.w* people are qualified in the ideological discourse leaves also little room for doubt: the most recurrent adjective referring to them is by far *ḫsy* (miserable, vile, mean).

In texts from the everyday life, however, the context tends to be much more neutral and the *ꜥꜣm.w* are depicted as being part of the society, even if in rather subordinate roles.

Enemy?

The way the *ꜥꜣm.w* people are qualified in the ideological discourse leaves also little place to doubt: the most recurrent adjective referring to them is by far *ḫsy* (miserable, vile, mean) and the fear of them is a well-known topic for the Egyptian travelling abroad.

The *ꜥꜣm.w* are also openly designated as enemies (*ḫrw.w*).

In texts from the everyday life, however, the context tends to be much more neutral and the *ꜥꜣm.w* are depicted as being part of the society, even if in rather subordinate roles (*šmsw* (servant), *šmꜥw* (singer)).

Ex. 29. *in n šmsw ꜥꜣm*  *sṯi-rꜥ*

"Brought by the servant, the Asiatic *sṯi-rꜥ*" (P. Berlin 10081 C, v. 3)[37]
12th Dynasty; letter

Tab. 7.
Semantic features highlighted for *ꜥꜣm*.

ꜥꜣm
+ individuality
+ agentivity
+ enemy
+ foreigner

[37] Luft 2006: 105ff.

Lexical studies: Onomasiology

Recapitulative and comparative tables of the features highlighted for the different lexemes.

The first following table[38] sums up the distribution of the different lexemes according to the textual genre and the diachrony within the corpus[39].

Tab. 8.
Distribution of the different lexemes according to the textual genre and the diachrony.

Genres	Lexemes						
	nḥsy	*sty*	*mšwš*	*ṯḥn.w*	*ṯmḥ.w*	*ḫꜣrw*	*ꜥꜣm*
Royal	OMN	O (topo) MN	OM (topo) N	N (ethn)	MN	N	MN
Autobiography	OM	M	-	-	-	-	OMN
Funerary / relig.	OMN	MN	-	OM (topo)			
N (ethn)	MN	-	OM				
Magical	MN	MN	-	-	-	N	N
Amuletic / oracul.	N	-	-	-	-	N	-
Lit. fiction	-	M	-	N	MN	-	MN
Wisdom	N	-	-	-	N	N	MN
Poetry / hymns	N	-	-	-	-	-	N
Satirical	N	-	N	-	-	-	N
Miscellanies	N	N	-	-	-	N	N
Letters	OMN	-	N	N	-	N	OMN
Legal texts	N	-	N	-	-	N	-
Administrative	N	-	N	-	-	-	-

The next table shows the distribution of the main classifiers attested for each lexeme, according to the writing system and support and to the diachrony.

Looking at the distribution of the data, several points can be highlighted. First, the classifiers used vary according to the writing system and support. Indeed, there is, in a general way, more variety in the spellings from epigraphic texts. Furthermore, the use of classifiers is far from being systematic in that kind of texts, especially before the Second Intermediate Period. In hieratic texts, we can notice more consistency in the spellings: there are usually one or two fix groups. This is especially true for the New Kingdom, where the use of these groups becomes

[38] O = Old Kingdom and First Intermediate Period; M = Middle Kingdom and Second Intermediate Period; N = New Kingdom and Third Intermediate Period. Topo = toponym; ethno = ethnonym.

[39] Only the results for the corpus made of the texts from the *TLA* and *Ramsès* are displayed here.

systematic (which is the main difference with the Middle Kingdom–Second Intermediate Period for the same writing system and support).

The lexemes appearing at the beginning of the New Kingdom or being of re-actualised use in the Ramesside period[40] show more similar spellings for hieratic and hieroglyphic epigraphic texts. In this case, an influence from hieratic can clearly be seen in the hieroglyphic spellings: the groups 𓌙𓀀𓏥 and 𓌙𓀀𓁐𓏥 are by far the majority.

In hieratic texts, and in texts from the New Kingdom in general, we can see an increasing use of superordinate[41] classifiers, while there is a variety of subordinate classifiers used in Old Kingdom and Middle Kingdom epigraphic texts, with a general, but yet reduced, continuation of this trend in Ramesside texts written in "égyptien de tradition"[42]. Not all of them are listed here since I included only the most frequent ones in the table. We can however mention, among others, the following ones: 𓀏, 𓁐, 𓀐.

The common sign to almost all the groups of classifiers attested is 𓌙, which marks the word as designating a foreign entity.[43]

Tab. 9.

Distribution of the main classifiers attested for each lexeme, according to the writing system and support and to the diachrony.

Lexemes	Mainly attested classifiers[44]			
	OK-FIP / MK-SIP	MK-SIP (hieratic)	NK-TIP (hieratic)	NK-TIP (epigraphic)
nḥsy	𓈉; 𓌙; 𓌙𓈉𓏥; Ø	𓌙;	𓌙𓀏; 𓌙𓀀𓁐𓏥	𓌙; 𓌙𓈉𓏥; 𓌙𓈉
sty	𓈉; 𓌙; Ø	𓌙𓀀𓏥; 𓌙𓀀𓁐𓏥 (rare)	𓌙𓀀𓏥; 𓌙𓀀𓁐𓏥 (rare)	𓌙𓀏; 𓌙𓀀𓁐𓏥; 𓌙𓀀𓁐𓏥
mšwš	-	-	𓌙; 𓌙𓀀𓏥; 𓌙𓀏; 𓌙𓀀𓁐𓏥	𓌙𓀏; 𓌙; 𓌙𓌙; 𓌙𓀀𓏥; 𓌙𓀀𓏥𓈉; 𓌙𓀀𓁐𓏥; 𓌙𓈉; 𓌙𓀏𓈉
ṯḥn.w	𓌙; 𓌙𓈉𓏥; Ø	𓌙𓀀𓏥; 𓌙𓀀𓁐𓏥; (rare)	𓌙𓀀𓏥; 𓌙𓀀𓁐𓏥; 𓌙𓀀𓁐𓏥𓈉 (rare)	𓌙𓀀𓁐𓏥; 𓌙𓀏𓁐𓏥𓈉
ṯḥnw (topo)	𓌙𓈒; 𓌙𓈒𓈒𓈒; 𓌙𓈉; Ø	𓌙𓈉	𓌙𓈉𓊖 (1)	𓌙𓈒𓈒𓈒; 𓌙𓈒𓈉; 𓌙𓈉
ṯmḥ.w	𓀏; 𓌙; Ø	𓌙𓀀𓏥; 𓌙𓀀𓁐𓏥 (rare)	𓌙𓀀𓏥; 𓌙𓀀𓁐𓏥 (rare)	𓌙𓀀𓏥; 𓌙𓀀𓁐𓏥; 𓌙𓀏𓁐𓏥𓈉
ṯmḥ.w (topo)	-[45]	-	𓌙𓈉𓊖 (1)	𓌙𓈉
ḫ3rw	-	-	𓌙𓀏; 𓌙𓀏	𓀏; 𓌙𓀀𓏥; 𓌙𓈉
ḫ3rw (topo)	-	-	𓌙𓈉; 𓌙𓈉𓊖	𓌙𓈉; 𓌙𓈉𓏥
ꜥ3m	𓌙𓀏; 𓀏; 𓌙; Ø		𓌙𓀏; 𓀏; 𓌙𓀀𓁐𓏥; 𓀀𓏥𓈉	𓁐𓏥; 𓀏; 𓌙𓀏; 𓈉

[40] As an example, I will here refer more specifically to a long series of attestations of the *ṯmḥ.w* and *ṯḥn.w* people in the texts from Medinet Habu. All these attestations show similar hieratic-influenced spellings.

[41] On the taxonomic organisation of the classifier system, cf. Goldwasser 2002 and Lincke 2011.

[42] The amount of different signs will know a new increasing phase from the Late Period, prefiguring the extensive variety of the Ptolemaic system. This phase, however, is still under investigation (Chantrain in preparation).

[43] Allon 2010.

[44] This list is not exhaustive but contains the most recurrent classifiers and significant variants attested for the different lexemes.

[45] Middle Kingdom–Second Intermediate Period: *t3 n ṯmḥ.w*: "the land of the Libyans".

Finally, the last table below summarizes the differences that have been highlighted between the lexemes through the distributional analysis, according to four distinctive features: individuality, foreignness, Agentivity and "enemicity".

Interestingly, the only two terms that have exactly the same distribution of features are *ṯḥn.w* and *ṯmḥ.w*, which appear as semantically very close in the New Kingdom, since the initial distinction between toponym and ethnonym seems to have become less systematic than in the previous periods.

Lexemes	Criteria			
	+/- individuality	+/- foreignness	+/- agentivity	+/- enemy
nḥsy	+	+/-	+	+/-
sty	-	+	+	+/-
mšwš	-	+	+	+
ṯḥn.w	-	+	-	+
ṯmḥ.w	-	+	-	+
ḫ3rw	+	+/-	-	+
ꜥ3m	+	+	+	+

Tab. 10.
Summary of the sematic features highlighted for each lexeme.

Narrative frame and ratio of power

In the narrative frame, several elements can work as indicators of "egyptianity" or "non-egyptianity"[46]. Three of them will be investigated here: 1) the agent and environment of the action, 2) the structure of the action and 3) the motion dynamics (centrifugal motion *vs.* centripetal motion as relevant factor).

Environment of the action: protagonist alone vs. "in the middle of"

The first element is the environment of the action. The protagonist marked as [+ Egyptian] rather acts alone/is on his own, while the protagonist marked as [+ foreigner] and/or [+ enemy] is *in the middle of* a group of people (army, tribe, ...). This point may be linked to the criterion of individuality that we have seen before. It also puts the emphasis on the courage of the Egyptian protagonist, in opposition with the cowardice of the enemy. In the fictional texts, the foreign protagonists are usually Asiatics: the Nubians, as we have seen, do not seem to be given a role in the fictional world.

This theme is very recurrent in the ideological discourse of royal texts, where the king fights alone against a multitude of enemies. The following passage of the Battle of Qadesh offers a good example:

[46] On this concept, see Loprieno 1988; Moers 2001.

Ex. 30. (Qadesh, L1, § 65) *ist pꜣ wr ḫsy n ḫtꜣ ꜥḥꜥ m ḥry-ib mšꜥ nty ḥnꜥ.f*

"while the vile prince of Ḫatti was standing in the middle of his army, which was with him"

n pr.n.f r ꜥḥꜥ n snḏ n ḥm.f

"he didn't dare to go out, by fear of his Majesty"

(...)

§ 82 *iw.f wꜥ ḥr-tp.f nn ky ḥnꜥ.f*

"while he (Ramesses) was on his own, without anybody else"

A similar configuration *singular vs. collective* is found in Sinuhe, in the passage narrating the fight between Sinuhe and the strong man of the Retjenu. Sinuhe is alone, facing the strong man of the Retjenu, who has all his allies behind him. He is in this situation marked as [+ Egyptian], while the strong man is marked as [+ foreigner] and [+ enemy]. The parallel is clear between this scene and the ideological discourse[47].

Ex. 31. *ḥḏ.n tꜣ tnw iy.t(j)*

ḏdb.n.s wḥy.t.s

sḥw.n.s ḫꜣs.wt n gs.sy

"At dawn, the Retjenu was there, it had assembled its tribes, it had gathered its neighbouring foreign countries" (Sinuhe B130)

Another example on the other hand rather qualifies Sinuhe as [- Egyptian]/ [+ foreigner]. Indeed, when the Egyptian messenger (who is on his own) in charge of the royal decree reaches him, he is in the middle of his tribe, like an Asiatic ruler.

Ex. 32. *spr.n wḏ pn r.i ꜥḥꜥ.kwi m ḥry-ib wḥy.t.i*

"this decree reached me while I was standing in the middle of my tribe" (Sinuhe B 200)

Structured vs. unstructured action

The second element concerns the structure of the action. There is a clear opposition between the well-ordered, structured action of the Egyptians and the unstructured action of the foreigners/enemies. This topic is well represented in the texts from the ideology:

Ex. 33. *gm.n.i pꜣ 2500 n ꜥ-n-ḥtr.w wn.i m-ḫnw.sn ḫpr.w m gbgby.t r-ḥꜣ.t ssm.t.i*

"I found out that the 2500 chariots in the middle of which I was had turned into a mass in front of my horses" (Qadesh, Poem, §132)

§ 134: *bw gm.n wꜥ ḏr.t.f r ꜥḥꜣ im.sn*

[47] Cf. Parkinson 2002: 158 (with previous bibliography).

"none of them was able to fight anymore (lit.: could find his hand to fight)"
(…)
§ 136: *bw rḫ.sn st.t*
"they were not able to use their bows anymore"
§ 137: *bw gm.n.w ḥ3ty.sn r ṯ3i.t n3y.sn niwy.w*
"they couldn't find the courage to take their javelins anymore"

Here as well, a parallel can be found in the same passage of Sinuhe. Where the action of the strong man is disorganized and ineffective, the one of Sinuhe is quick, precise and deadly.

Ex. 34. *rdi.n.i sw3 ḥr.i ꜥḥ3.w.f zp n ntt wꜥ ḥr ḫn m wꜥ*
"I let his arrows pass me by without effect, one following the other. Then, when he charged me, I shot him, my arrow sticking his neck" (Sinuhe B 136–137)

"šm-oriented" vs. "iy.t-oriented motions"

The back and forth dynamics (repeated back and forth motions of the protagonists in a short section of text) in the narrative has at least two functions: it highlights the key-moments of the story and makes explicit the position of strength or weakness of the main protagonists. Centripetal motion (to come) is associated with the position of relative inferiority of one of the protagonists in respect to the other, while centrifugal motion (to go, to send) is a marker of a position of superiority. In the texts belonging to the ideological discourse, the ratio of power is naturally in favour of the Egyptians.

In some texts though, this situation can be reversed, a particularity that can be highlighted by the use of motion verbs and, in some case, by the use of irony (for example, in Wenamun or in Sinuhe)[48].

During the exchanges between Wenamun and Tjekerbaal, the prince makes Wenamun move to him twice. The accumulation of *iy.t*-oriented motions performed by Wenamun makes obvious the fact that he is in a position of weakness, of inferiority, in comparison with Tjekerbaal.

The prince first makes Wenamun come to his palace:
Ex. 35. (1, 47) *iw.f (ḥr) h3b*
"he sent (to me)"
iw.f (ḥr) iṯ3.i r-ḥry
"and he brought me up"

A long speech follows, where the prince mocks Wenamun by using irony.[49] Furthermore, to put the self-confident attitude of Wenamun into perspective, he adds,

[48] Parkinson 2002: 157.
[49] Cf. the repeated use of *mk*, as stressed in Winand 2004; on the use of irony in Wenamun, see also Eyre 1999: 238–239.

among others, that if Egypt was indeed created first, his own country had no reason to be envious (Wenamun: 2, 21). To sum up, Wenamun praises the omnipotence of Egypt and Amun, but the circumstances remind him of his current condition of inferiority.

The prince makes him come to the shore:
Ex. 36. (2,45) *iw.f (ḥr) hꜣb n.i r-ḏd mi*
"then he sent to me saying: come!"
ẖr-ir twi (ḥr) ms r-ḳr.f
"when I brought myself into his presence..."
(...)
(2,47) *iw.i (ḥr) ms r-ḳr.f*
"I came close to him"
(...)
(2,49) *i.ir n ḥꜣty.i*
mtw.k iy.t r ꜣtp.s
"do as I wish, and come to load it"
ẖr in bn iw.w (r) di.t.s n.k
"for has it not been given to you?"
m iri iy.t r ptr tꜣ ḥry.t n pꜣ ym
"do not come to see the terror of the sea"
(...)
(2,52) *iw.f (ḥr) ḏd n pꜣy.f wdpw: ṯꜣ sw*
"then he said to his attendant: take him!"

The position of weakness of Wenamun, as well as Tjekerbaal's behaviour remind a section of *Sinuhe*, which makes very explicit the role of motion in a ratio of power:

Ex. 37. (B154) *btꜣ z n gꜣw hꜣb.f ink ʿšꜣ.w mri.w*

"a man runs for lack of one to send, I am rich in servants"

This play on fuzzy boundaries between Egyptians and foreigners is also present in this allusion made to the Syrian crew of Wenamun. This is also stressed on the level of the classifiers, with the adjunction of the sign ⊗ to ⊔⊔. This example is well-known, but is part of a broader phenomenon and illustrates the complexity of the relations between Egyptians and foreigners, as well as the fact that integration of people from abroad in the Egyptian mental world is a multi-level synergy.

Ex. 38. (1, 54) *sw ṯnw pꜣ imw n ʿš i.di n.k ny-sw-bꜣ-nb-ḏd.t*
"where is the ship of cedar that Smendes gave to you?"
(1, 55) *sw ṯnw tꜣy.f is.t n ẖꜣrw.w?* 
"where is its crew of Syrians?"
(1,55–56) *in i.ir.f ḥn.k n pꜣy ḥry mnš ḏrḏr r rdi.t ẖdb.f tw*
"if he left you with this foreign captain, is it not to have him kill you?"

(1,57) *in bn mnš n km.t*
"Is it not an Egyptian ship?"
(1, 57–58) *ḫr is.t n km.t nꜣ nty ḥr ḫnw ḥr ny-sw-bꜣ-nb-ḏd.t*
"those who sail under Smendes are Egyptian crews"
in wn m-di.f is.wt ḫꜣrw
"does he not have Syrian crews?" 

Conclusions

The distribution of the different lexemes studied shows differences according to the diachrony and the textual genres. Some of them are almost exclusively part of the ideological discourse, while others are found in texts from the everyday life.

The vision of the foreigner reflected in the texts highly depends on the textual genre they belong to and, consistently, on the influence of the ideological discourse. The cotextual environment of these terms makes explicit the existence of differences in the way the different groups of people were considered, and in the position they hold within the cultural and textual landscape.

Concerning the use of the classifiers, differences can be seen according to two main criteria: the writing system and support (epigraphic hieroglyphic texts *vs.* hieratic texts on papyri and ostraca), the textual genre and the diachrony. In the hieratic texts, the lexemes studied seem to follow the reorganisation taking place during the Ramesside period,[50] with an augmentation and systematisation of superordinate classifiers usage. The most attested group for the ethnonyms is by far  and it tends to become generalised from the end of the 19th Dynasty, and in the 20th Dynasty. More uniformity is consequently visible in the classifiers used for lexemes appearing in the New Kingdom, in all kind of texts and supports. An evolution is still possible though, as it is the case for the toponym *ḫꜣrw*, taking the sign 𓊖 in adjunction to 𓈉 from the 21st Dynasty in certain contexts. This corresponds to the third phase of reorganisation of the classifiers system and reminds the features [+individuality] and [+/- foreigner] of the corresponding ethnonym *ḫꜣrw*. In a general way, plays on the visual dimension (including classifiers, thus) tend to be more exploited in literary texts.

Some of the ethnonyms and toponyms studied in this article work as elements of a systemic opposition exemplifying the Egyptian vision of the world. This is the case of *nḥsy*, *ḫꜣrw* and *rmṯ n km.t*, which are specific case of the general dichotomy between *ḫꜣsti* and *rmṯ*, stressed by Loprieno, among others.[51] Interestingly, and despite this actual opposition, one can note that in the New Kingdom, both *nḥsy* and *ḫꜣrw* can be named *rmṯ*. This feature highlights in my opinion the complementarity of these terms and the relatively high level of integration of these people in the Egyptian mental world and society.

---

50 Chantrain 2014.
51 Loprieno 1988.

The concepts of "foreignness" and "egyptianity" are not always as clearly defined as in the ideological texts. There are indeed many cases of play with the system, as we have seen through the study of some elements of the lexicon and the narrative frame.

The features of individuality vs. plurality/collectiveness associated to the ethnonyms under consideration seem thus to correspond to different degrees of integration of these people within the Egyptian society and mental world.

The relations between the Egyptians and the people they were considering as foreigners can be thus be described in terms of both opposition and of continuum. Indeed, all these terms can find their place in a continuum between two poles [+ foreigner] and [- foreigner], and this distribution evolves with time. The oppositions that have been highlighted are used in a perspective of complementarity. Indeed, the concept of "egyptianity" is also defined by contrast with the way people from the neighbouring countries are perceived.

The ration of power between protagonists marked as [+ Egyptian] *vs.* [-Egyptian]/[+ foreigner] is made explicit by several elements of the narrative.

Two of them, the environment of the action and the motion dynamics, respectively correspond to the features of [individuality] and [Agentivity] highlighted in the lexical studies, in the first part of this article.

The third element, the structure of the action, echoes some cotextual elements highlighted for some of the ethnonyms (*mšwš*, *ṯmḥ.w*, *ṯḥn.w*, *ḫꜣrw*, *ꜥꜣm.w*). The main features are the flight (cowardice) and the disorganisation of the enemy's action.

References

Allon, N., 2010. At the Outskirts of a System. Classifiers and Word Dividers in Foreign Phrases and Texts. *LinAeg* 18, 1–17.

Černý, J., 1939. *Late Ramesside Letters*. BiAeg 9. Brussels: Fondation Égyptologique Reine Elisabeth.

Chantrain, G., 2014. The Use of Classifiers in the New Kingdom. A global Reorganization of the Classifiers System?. *LinAeg* 22, 39–59.

Chantrain, G., in preparation *Classification strategies from the end of the Ramesside Period until the Late Period: a living system.*

Edwards, I.E.S., 1960. *Oracular Amuletic Decrees of the Late New Kingdom*. London: British Museum.

Gardiner, A.H., 1937. *Late-Egyptian Miscellanies*. BiAeg 7. Brussels: Fondation Égyptologique Reine Elisabeth.

Goldwasser, O., 2002. *Prophets, lovers and giraffes. Wor(l)d classification in Ancient Egypt; with an Appendix by Matthias Müller*. GOF 38/3 = Classification and Categorization in Ancient Egypt 3. Wiesbaden: Harrassowitz Verlag.

Hannig, R., 1997. *Die Sprache der Pharaonen. Großes Handwörterbuch Ägyptisch-Deutsch* (2800-950 v. Chr.). Hannig Lexica 3. Mainz: Philipp von Zabern.

Kitchen, K.A., 1975–1990. *Ramesside Inscriptions*. 8 volumes. Oxford: BH Blackwell.

Klug, A., 2002. *Königliche Stelen von der Zeit Ahmose bis Amenophis 3*. MonAeg 8. Turnhout: Brepols.

Koch, R., 1990. *Die Erzählung des Sinuhe*. BiAeg 17. Brussels: Fondation Égyptologique Reine Elisabeth.

Leitz, Chr., 2002. *Lexikon der Ägyptischen Götter und Götterbezeichnungen*. OLA 129. Leuven: Peeters.

Lincke, E.-S., 2011. *Die Prinzipien der Klassifizierung im Altägyptischen*. GOF 38 = Classification and Categorization in Ancient Egypt 6. Wiesbaden: Harrassowitz.

Loprieno, A., 1988. *Topos und Mimesis: zum Ausländer in der Ägyptischen Literatur*. ÄA 48. Wiesbaden: Harrassowitz.

Luft, U., 1992. *Das Archiv von Illahun*. Berlin: Akademie Verlag.

Luft, U., 2006. *Urkunden zur Chronologie der späten 12. Dynastie, Briefe aus Illahun*. Vienna: Verlag der Österreichischen Akademie der Wissenschaften.

Moers, G., 2001. *Fingierte Welten in der ägyptischen Literatur des 2. Jahrtausends v. Chr.: Grenzüberschreitung, Reisemotiv un Fiktionalität*. PdÄ 19. Leiden: Brill.

Parkinson, R.B., 2002 *Poetry and culture in Middle Kingdom Egypt: a dark side to perfection*. London – New York: Bloomsbury.

Quack, J.F., 1994. *Die Lehren des Ani. Ein neuägyptischer Weisheitstext in seinem kulturellen Umfeld*. OBO 141. Göttingen: Vandenhoeck and Ruprecht.

Sethe, K., 1906–1909. *Urkunden der 18. Dynastie*, 1–4. Leipzig: J.C. Hinrichs.

Vernus, P., 1977. Les Hurrites dans les sources égyptiennes, in: Anonymous (ed.), *Problèmes concernant les Hurrites*. Paris: CNRS, 41–49.

Wente, E.F., 1967. *Late Ramesside Letters*. SAOC 33. Chicago: The University of Chicago Press.

Yamazaki, N., 2003. *Zaubersprüche für Mutter und Kind: Papyrus Berlin 3027*. Schriften zur Ägyptologie B, 2. Berlin: Achet-Verlag.

NOT SO VILE? RHETORIC AND REALITY IN EGYPTIAN-LEVANTINE RELATIONSHIPS IN SINAI DURING THE OLD AND MIDDLE KINGDOMS

Susan Cohen (Montana State University)

Introduction

During the history of pharaonic Egypt, Egyptian official text and image described and presented foreign peoples and enemies of Egypt (both real and perceived) using specific rhetoric, hyperbolic language, and canonized visual representation designed to emphasize the concept of foreign subjugation to Egyptian sovereignty. Whether the people and places in question were the "vile Asiatics" or "miserable Kush", image and text combined to create a formal rhetoric and trope of the non-Egyptian as enemy, as "other", and as fully deserving of the violence and disdain they received (see Chantrain in the present volume). Further, Egyptian ideology in which pharaoh was responsible for maintaining order (*maat*) in the kingdom and overcoming chaos (*isfet*) furthered these ideals. Traditional imagery showing the ruler subduing foreign "others" served to bolster the ideology of the office of the king and graphically illustrated the challenges or threats to Egypt and its peoples that the ruler, by definition, overcame. As such, the images of pharaoh "smiting" foreign enemies of Egypt, who lie or cower helplessly before or under him, stand out as some of the most iconic visual representations from ancient Egypt, regardless of era.

However, in addition to the classic "smiting" images, other representations and descriptions present not only less violent interaction with southern Levantine peoples, but suggest other relations, interactions, and views of these foreign "others" that range anywhere from neutral to collaborative to favorable. Further, while the image of the king smiting helpless foreigners at his feet is timeless (despite minor changes in the canon in different historical eras), the individualized representations of interaction with specific groups of foreign individuals are often historical in nature, and as such they may be contextualized within both era and region. This creates a contrast between the formalized representation of the idealized world as presented in the official rhetoric of Egyptian sovereignty over foreign lands and peoples and the subsequent presentation of the actual reality of the world as shown in descriptions and representations of activities that occurred during the course of Egyptian encounters with other peoples.[1] Examination of

[1] The contrast may be described in terms of *topos* and *mimesis* (Loprieno 1996) The former refers to the ideological expectations regarding Egyptian worldview, self-expression, and actions, while the latter is the actual response to real situations, encounters, and circumstances (also see discussion in Hikade 2007).

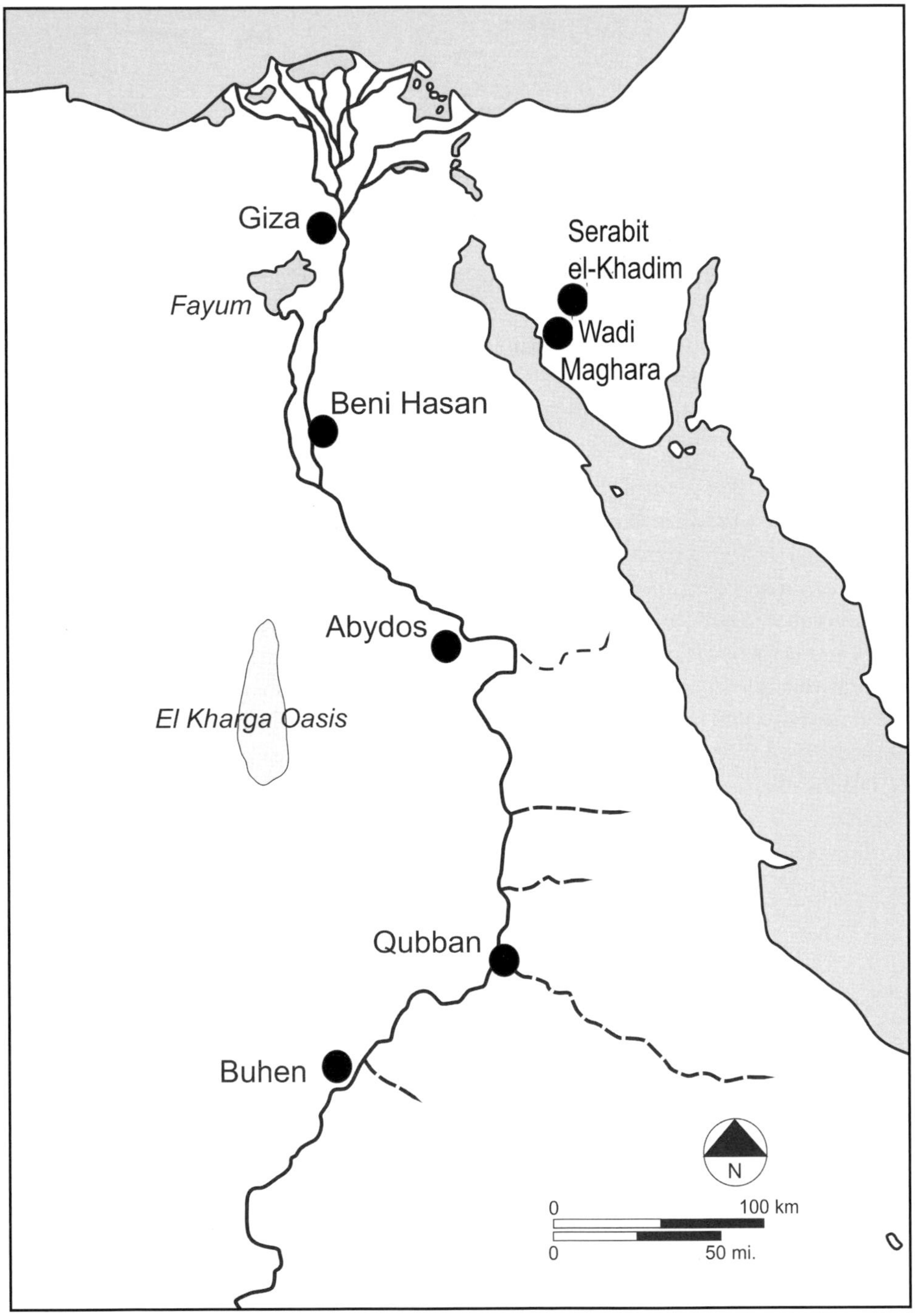

Fig. 1.
Map of Sinai showing location of Wadi Maghara and Serabit el-Khadim (adapted from Shaw 1998: fig. 15.1; drawing by W. Więckowski).

both types of presentation of southern Levantines therefore allows for contrast between views and treatment of this group of foreigners, as well as for discussion of how these differences might be interpreted. This contrast is particularly noticeable in the Egyptian inscriptions dating to both Old and Middle Kingdoms found in Sinai at Wadi Maghara and Serabit el-Khadim (Fig. 1).

Egyptian Inscriptions in Sinai

The Egyptian inscriptions found in Sinai (Gardiner – Peet 1952; Gardiner – Peet – Černý 1955; Tallet 2012) were left by expeditions sent by Old and Middle Kingdom pharaohs that sought valuable resources, most commonly copper, malachite, and other hard and/or semi-precious stones (Shaw 1998; Nicholson – Shaw 2000: 62).[2] During these expeditions, Egyptians encountered "Asiatics", both as the indigenous inhabitants of Sinai, and from other regions in the southern Levant. Many of the inscriptions depicting or citing these peoples date to individual rulers and often to specific regnal years, providing precise knowledge of when these expeditions occurred, which, by extension, allows for correlations with specific periods in the southern Levant.

It has long been noted that the Old Kingdom inscriptions at Sinai uniformly present a hostile view of the foreign "other", depicting the Asiatic in the iconic position of subjugation. By contrast, those dating to the Middle Kingdom instead suggest collaboration between Egyptians and southern Levantines, often listing individuals by name and rank. Further, the accompanying imagery in the Middle Kingdom inscriptions shows independent individuals, while simultaneously the iconic representation of the smiting pharaoh is largely absent (Černý 1935; Gardiner – Peet 1952; Gardiner – Peet – Černý 1955; Tallet 2012).

While the foreigners in the Old Kingdom imagery remain stereotyped and anonymous, more information exists concerning the identity and nature of those "Asiatics" listed in the Middle Kingdom inscriptions (e.g., Goldwasser 2012–2013). However, the primary point of discourse for both groups of data traditionally has been the Egyptian view of southern Levantines, and, accordingly, the actions, views, and policies held by Egypt regarding Sinai and the southern Levant. In these discussions, therefore, southern Levantines exist as objects of Egyptian action and representation, and, by extension, the geographic region they inhabit likewise appears as a passive recipient of Egyptian policy and activities. This approach to analysis of the presentation of the foreigner in Old Kingdom and Middle Kingdom inscriptions found in Sinai, therefore, does not account for developments in the southern Levant itself, or for the actions and activities of those peoples who lived there that may have affected the interactions between the two groups.

In part, of course, this inequality of discussion stems from the fact that the available evidence is, unquestionably, Egyptian, and thus reflects Egyptian activities, views, and representations. The sheer paucity of representational material from Palestine likewise precludes examination of local southern Levantine visual

[2] Resources in Sinai included copper, malachite, turquoise, azurite, chrysocolla, and rock crystal. The Egyptian term *mfꜣkt*, used to describe the items procured in Sinai, has variously been interpreted as turquoise or malachite (Nicholson – Shaw 2000: 44, 62). In their study of Egyptian materials, Nicholson and Shaw (2000: 44, 62) question the amount of turquoise mined and the frequency of its use by Egypt and suggest instead that one of the primary goals of the Sinai expeditions was copper, with turquoise acquired as a byproduct of that procurement.

presentations of interactions with Egyptians or other foreign peoples.[3] However, despite these drawbacks, the differences in representation and presentation of southern Levantine peoples seen in the Old Kingdom and Middle Kingdom inscriptions in Sinai still may be analyzed from a southern Levantine perspective as well as from the Egyptian one. Examination of these differences, together with analysis of contemporary southern Levantine developments, contextualizes both the rhetoric and the reality of the Egyptian presentation of the "other" in both eras and helps to provide further explanation for them.

Old Kingdom

While a small number of inscriptions date to Predynastic rulers (see Tallet 2012) the majority of third millennium inscriptions in Sinai are from the Old Kingdom, predominately found in Wadi Maghara (see Fig. 1). In these inscriptions, the sole visual presentation of southern Levantines depicts them in their role as subjugated enemy in the traditional smiting scene, which stands out as one of the most common visual images found in the Old Kingdom inscriptions in Sinai (Gardiner – Peet – Černý 1955: 25). While some of the individual descriptive details may vary, the overall image of the "Asiatic" on his knees in an attitude of helplessness and submission before the pharaoh does not.

The basic depiction shows the king grasping the kneeling foreigner by the hair with his left hand, with his right hand back and holding a mace in preparation for smiting the Asiatic on the head (Fig. 2). In each case, the Asiatic kneels in an attitude of abject submission, face up toward the king, with the left arm on the knees, and gesturing with the right arm toward pharaoh, perhaps as an indication of submission, perhaps as a request for mercy. In other scenes, the prisoner holds the feather marking him as a foreigner, presumably taken from his own head, as a further symbol of submission (Gardiner – Peet – Černý 1955: 26).

This iconic scene appears on inscriptions throughout the Old Kingdom with little variation, through the reigns of Sahure and Niuserre of the 5th Dynasty (e.g., Gardiner – Peet 1952: pls. V–VI). However, beginning in the late 5th Dynasty with the reign of Djedkare and continuing into the 6th Dynasty, some of the inscriptions, while still including the traditional hostile imagery, also indicate additional, and perhaps alternative, forms of interaction with southern Levantines, often from the reign of the same ruler. For example, Inscription 13 (Gardiner – Peet 1952: pl. VII.13), dating to Djedkare of the 5th Dynasty, mentions both an "overseer of interpreters" and a "second in charge of interpreters" (Gardiner – Peet – Černý 1955: 14, 62–63), while Inscription 14 (Gardiner – Peet 1952: pl. VIII.14), dating to the same pharaoh, shows the king smiting a southern Levantine, with the caption, "Smiting the chief of the foreign country" and a statement about the "subduing of foreign countries" (Gardiner – Peet – Černý 1955: 62–63).

[3] See Beck 2002 for discussion of Bronze Age southern Levantine imagery and representation.

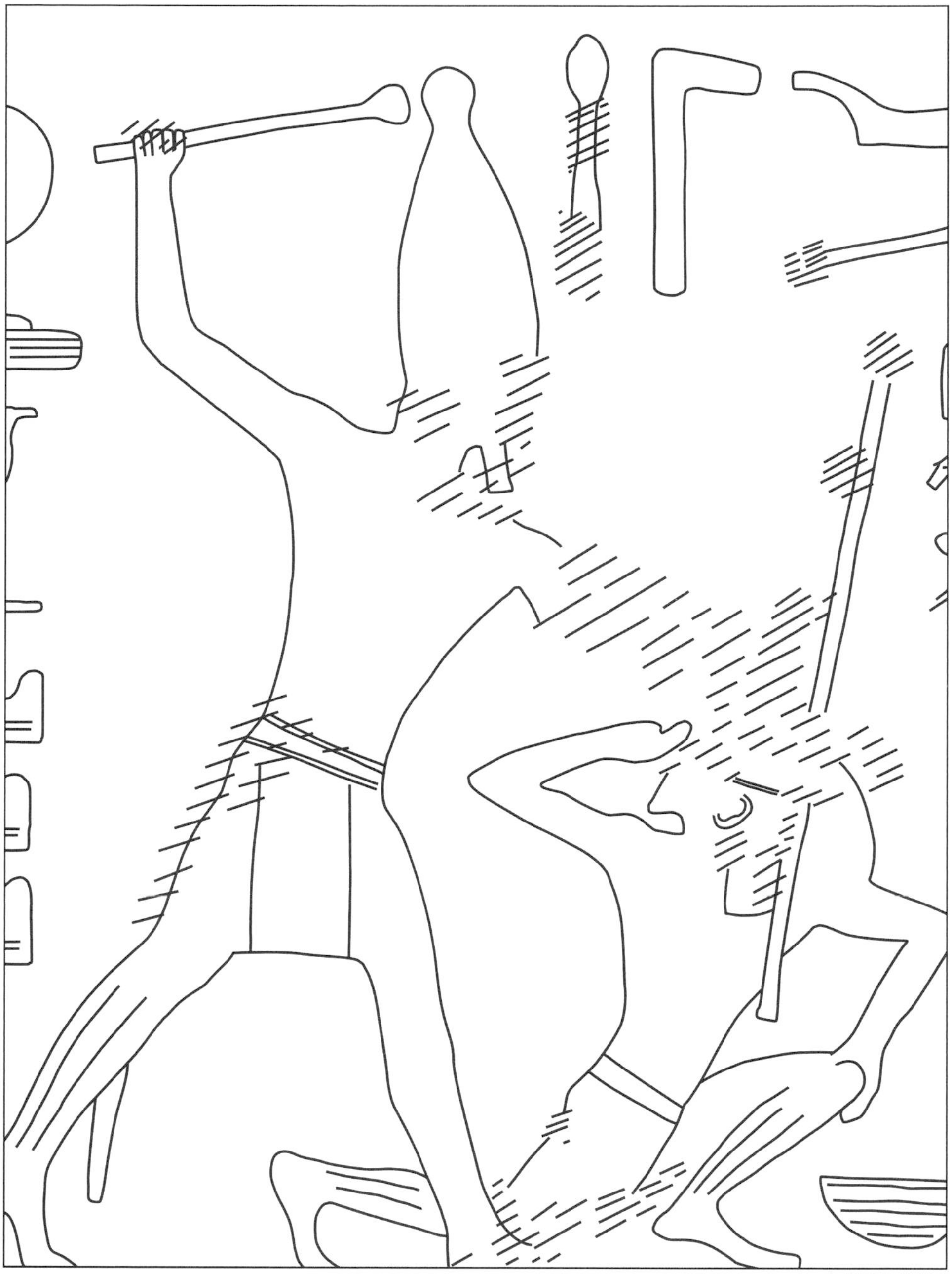

Fig. 2.
Image of Sahure from the 5th Dynasty "smiting" a kneeling foreigner from the Old Kingdom inscriptions at Wadi Maghara (adapted from Gardiner – Peet 1952: pl. V; drawing by W. Więckowski).

In the 6th Dynasty, an inscription of Pepi I (Gardiner – Peet 1952: pl. VIII.16), depicts the king in the traditional stance, smiting a foreign captive, with the caption of "Smiting" and "Subduing the Mentji and all foreign countries" (Gardiner – Peet – Černý 1955: 63). At the same time, the accompanying inscription listing expedition members names three different individuals in the position of "pilot and overseer of interpreters" (Gardiner – Peet – Černý 1955: 63). Another inscription from Pepi II (Gardiner – Peet 1952: pl. IX, 17) lists two individuals as "Pilot, overseer of interpreters" and an additional person as "second-in-charge of interpreters" (Gardiner – Peet – Černý 1955: 64).

The juxtaposition of formulaic images of smiting a foreigner together with clear evidence for the presence of people who interpret foreign speech allows for the possibility that additional interaction beyond the simply bellicose occurred between Egyptians and the indigenous inhabitants of Sinai or of the southern Levant in the later dynasties of the Old Kingdom. Certainly, the canonized imagery maintained official rhetoric and policy, upholding Egyptian formal perspective and view of the "other." Practically speaking, however, the presence of not just a single interpreter, but an entire group of individuals identified as interpreters, and present in enough numbers to occasionally warrant a "second-in-charge", implies alternative modes of interaction beyond the simply hostile (Mumford – Parcak 2003: 87; Parcak 2004: 55).

This is not to imply any significant change in the formal Egyptian perspective of the foreigner as either inferior or unworthy, or that hostile relations did not exist; however, it does suggest a degree of interaction between the two groups whereby Egyptian communication with local inhabitants of Sinai may have become both necessary and desirable. The presence of interpreters suggests a more interactive, if still markedly uneven, relationship. The traditional imagery thus maintained the formal relationship and perspective demanded by Egyptian worldview, while the presence of interpreters in expeditions bowed to the practicality of a more complex reality.

The Old Kingdom inscriptions in Sinai may be contextualized chronologically with contemporary eras in the southern Levant. The traditional basic correlations between Egypt and the southern Levant synchronized the end of the Egyptian Old Kingdom with the decline and end of the Palestinian EB III. However, most recent data instead indicate that the end date of EB III must be raised by as much as 300 hundred years, to ca. 2500 BC (Tab. 1) (Regev et al. 2012; Höflmayer et al. 2014). This places the late 5th Dynasty and the 6th Dynasty contemporary with the Intermediate Bronze Age in the southern Levant, and accordingly, the Old Kingdom inscriptions found in Sinai in Wadi Maghara that juxtapose traditional rhetoric and imagery with citation of individuals identified as "interpreters"—and the appearance of both in the same inscription—must be examined against the social, economic, and political organization of that era.

Egypt	Southern Levant/Sinai
2nd / 3rd Dynasty – 4th / 5th Dynasty	Early Bronze Age III
Late 5th Dynasty – 6th Dynasty	Intermediate Bronze Age
First Intermediate Period	Intermediate Bronze Age
Early Middle Kingdom	Intermediate Bronze / Early Middle Bronze Age
12th Dynasty (Senusret II →)	Early Middle Bronze Age I →
12th Dynasty (Amenemhet III →)	Late Middle Bronze Age I – early Middle Bronze Age II

Tab. 1.
Chart showing chronological synchronisms between the Egyptian historical dynastic sequence and the periodization of the southern Levant.

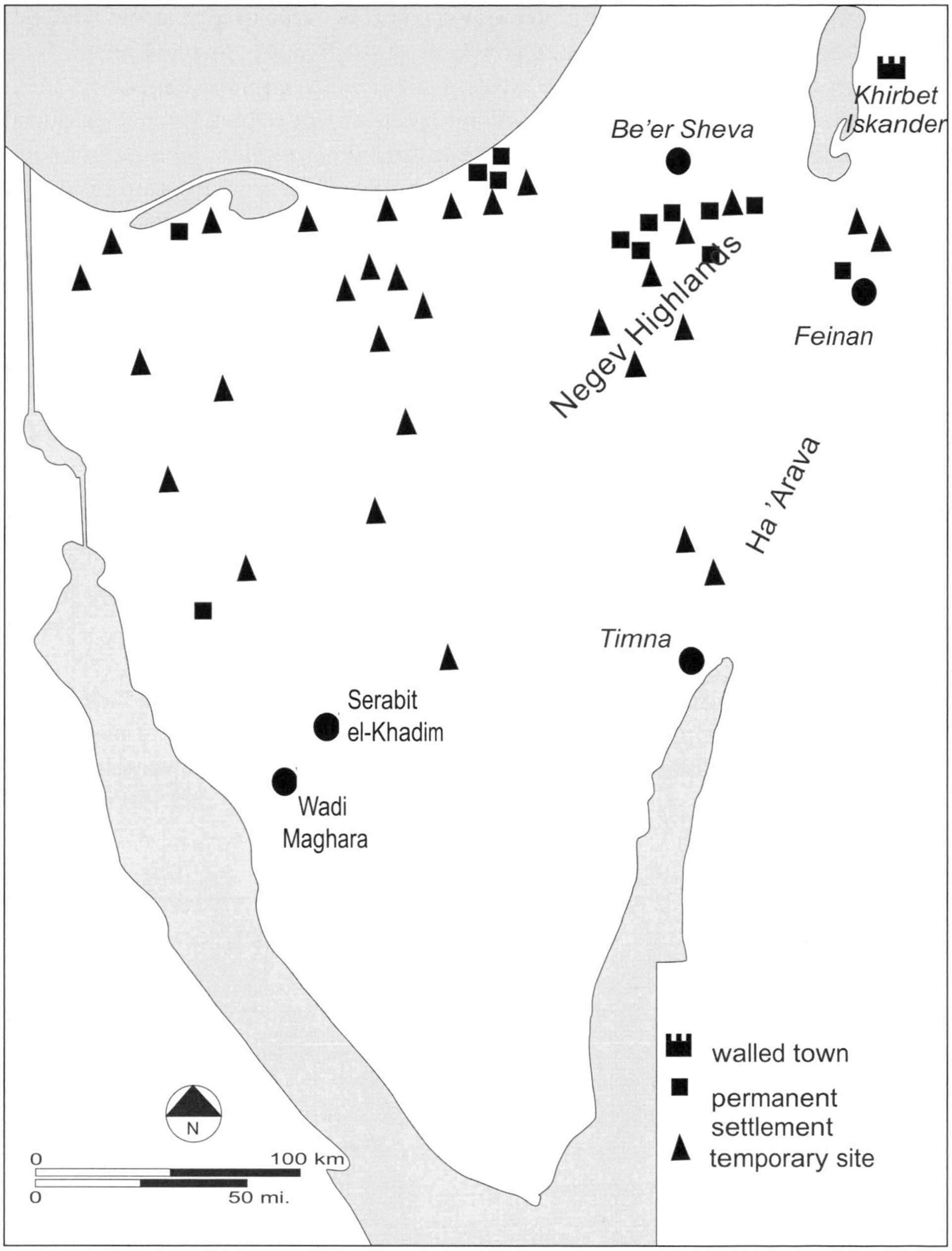

Fig. 3.
Map of Intermediate Bronze Age settlement in Sinai and the southern Negev (adapted from Haiman 1996: fig. 12; drawing by W. Więckowski).

The decline and end of Early Bronze Age III and the beginning of the Intermediate Bronze Age in Palestine are marked by the disappearance of large walled fortified cities in the southern Levant and a concurrent shift to smaller unfortified dispersed sites throughout the region. At the same time, the Intermediate Bronze Age saw the rise of a network of settlements throughout the marginal regions of the Negev and Sinai (Fig. 3) (Haiman 1996; 2009; Cohen 2019). The location of many of these sites in regions unlikely to be conducive to long-term and/or permanent settlement suggests that their growth and development stemmed from broader changes in social and/or economic patterns in the greater southern Levant (Finkelstein 1995). It is possible that these Intermediate Bronze Age settlements in the Negev and Sinai were linked to copper mining, exploitation, and subsequent trade with Egypt (Haiman 1996; 2009).[4] As a result, there is clear evidence for increased human occupation and activity in these regions, which may have resulted in both hostile encounters with Egyptian expeditions, stemming perhaps from competition for scarce subsistence or marketable resources (Mumford – Parcak 2003; Parcak 2004), and in increased interaction between southern Levantines and Egyptians that necessitated some degree of communication.[5]

Overall, the Sinai inscriptions dating to the Old Kingdom reveal a pattern of presentation, interaction, and perspective on the southern Levantine "other" that corresponds to changes in southern Levantine development. While the traditional rhetoric remained constant, upholding as it did the official trope regarding foreigners, and southern Levantines specifically, the inclusion of individuals whose purpose was to communicate with foreigners reflects a more complex reality of interaction. The initial inscriptions from the 3rd Dynasty into the early 5th Dynasty, corresponding to the end of EB III (see Tab. 1), and hence the final stage of large urban fortified occupation in Palestine, show only the formulized and formulaic images of pharaoh smiting the kneeling and subjugated foreigner. The inscriptions of the later Old Kingdom, correlating with the decentralized Intermediate Bronze Age and increased southern Levantine occupation and presence in the Negev and north Sinai, while still maintaining the trope of formal hostility, also cite the inclusion of interpreters among the ranks of individuals, presenting a mixture of both rhetoric and reality in interaction and view of the southern Levantine "other".

Middle Kingdom

There is considerably more evidence dating to the Middle Kingdom regarding Egyptian presentation of Levantine peoples, both visually and in text, outside the traditional and formulaic smiting of the "other". While the image of the conquering pharaoh and foreigners cowering in submission continues throughout the Middle Kingdom, as do the verbal descriptions that reinforce the inferior status of the peoples of the southern Levant,[6] other texts and images provide contrasting perspectives that may be contextualized and historicized as evidence for specific interactions. As noted above, this contrast may be observed in Middle Kingdom inscriptions in Sinai as compared to those from the previous era. In addition, the famous procession of Aamu in the tomb of Khnumhotep II at Beni Hasan must also be considered.

---

[4] This interpretation has been disputed (see discussion in Cohen 2019).

[5] For example, the Egyptian fortress at Tell Ras Budran dating to the 6th Dynasty illustrates the perceived Egyptian need for defenses in the Eastern Desert during this period (Mumford 2006: 57–58), perhaps as much for military purposes as to safeguard Egyptian access to and acquisition of resources.

[6] This may be found, for example, in the language describing southern Levantines in The Prophecy of Neferti, or in the encomium of Senusret I in The Tale of Sinuhe, in which Sinuhe states that Retjenu belongs to the pharaoh as do Senusret's hunting dogs (Wente 1990: 23).

Fig. 4.
Image of a southern Levantine individual—possibly Khebded—on a donkey (adapted from Gardiner – Peet 1952: pl. XXXIX; drawing by W. Więckowski).

Significantly, the inscriptions dating to the Middle Kingdom at Wadi Maghara and Serabit el-Khadim in Sinai (see Fig. 1), notably do not include the traditional "smiting" scene. Instead, these inscriptions, both verbally and visually, indicate collaborative interaction between Egyptians and southern Levantines. Although there are inscriptions from all the 12th Dynasty pharaohs at Sinai, the majority date to the reign of Amenemhet III, with another large group from the reign of his successor Amenemhet IV, which are the focus of examination here.

Three of these inscriptions, Nos. 85, 87, and 92 (Gardiner – Peet 1952: pls. XXIII.85, XXIV.87, XXVII.92), mention the "brother of the prince of Retjenu Khebded" (Gardiner – Peet – Černý 1955: 94–95), while a fourth (No. 112) (Gardiner – Peet 1952: pl. XXXVII), provides the same caption with a slight variation on the proper name, hence "the brother of the prince of Retjenu, Khebdem" (Gardiner – Peet – Černý 1955: 114). Three inscriptions, Nos. 112, 115, and 405 (Gardiner – Peet 1952: pls. XXXVII, XXXIX, LXXXV) include imagery depicting a man riding a donkey, led by another individual—either a boy or a man—and driven by yet a third figure (Fig. 4). In inscriptions 115 and 405, some of the individuals are depicted carrying weapons.[7] In the images that retain color, these figures are painted yellow, the conventional method of indicating Semites (Černý 1935; Goldwasser 2012–2013: 364).[8]

[7] In inscription 112, the driver of the donkey instead carries a large vase in one hand and is identified as "His [Khebdem's] attendant, *Ḳeḳbỉ*" (Gardiner – Peet – Černý 1955: 114).

[8] Saretta (2016: 184–187) suggests that the labels associated with in the donkey riding scene in Inscription 405 also link the individuals with specific regions in the Levant.

The association of these foreign individuals with donkeys is indicative both of perceived ethnicity by the Egyptians, and of the status of the seated individual himself (Parcak 2004: 56; Goldwasser 2012–2013: 358; and see discussion in Stadelmann 2006). It is generally assumed that this individual is Khebded; if not, it is still apparent that the individual is clearly an Asiatic of rank and status.[9] The presentation of this individual, his mode of transportation, the description of his rank, and the weapons carried by both him and his attendants all point to the relationship between Khebded, and the southern Levant more generally, and Egypt as one of cooperation and collaboration, rather than hostility, while still maintaining the distinction of the southern Levantine "other" through visual cues of color, donkey-riding, and other elements in the scene (Goldwasser 2012–2013: 366ff).[10]

This interpretation derives support from other Middle Kingdom inscriptions that list the participants in these expeditions, as these include southern Levantines, some of whom are referred to by their given name. For example, Inscription 24A, found at Wadi Maghara, cites the "Asiatic Esni" in the last line, with a figure of seated bearded man holding a throw stick serving double duty as both image and determinative for the proper name (Gardiner – Peet 1952: pl. XI; Gardiner – Peet – Černý 1955: 68). Another group of inscriptions (Nos. 93, 95, 98) (Gardiner – Peet 1952: pls. XXVIII.93, XXX.95, XXXIII.98) lists an individual who is described as "conceived of Ituneferu, 'the Asiatic'" (Gardiner – Peet – Černý 1955: 101). This individual appears to rise in status over time and is cited in Inscription 98 as having received the accolades "possessing honor" and "true of voice" (Gardiner – Peet – Černý 1955: 105). This clearly indicates that southern Levantine parentage, or part-southern Levantine parentage, did not inhibit his participation or gaining increased status in Egyptian mining expeditions, although the fact that it was necessary to mention it still implies a perceived "difference".

A significant number of inscriptions also list anonymous southern Levantines as members of the expeditions, although without mention of their specific role or function.[11] Inscription 85, for example, cites "men of the *ỉmnw* 60" and "Asiatics, 10" (Gardiner – Peet – Černý 1955: 94); Inscription 110 cites "Asiatics of Ḥami, 20" (Gardiner – Peet – Černý 1955: 113); Inscription 114 mentions "from Retjenu, 10 Asiatics" (Gardiner – Peet – Černý 1955: 118); Inscription 115, written above the scene of the man mounted on a donkey, lists "[Re]tjenu, 6" (Gardiner – Peet – Černý 1955: 119); and Inscription 120 notes "Retjenu 20" (Gardiner – Peet – Černý 1955:

[9] See Goldwasser 2012–2013 for a thorough discussion of Khebded, the linguistic variation of his name, his role and persona, and likely rise in prestige over time.

[10] Classifiers for "Asiatics" differentiate between those viewed as "friendly" and those deemed "unfriendly" (Allen 2008: 33; Goldwasser 2012–2013: 355 n. 14); the imagery used to write Khebded's name further illustrates the spirit of collaboration and non-hostile relations.

[11] Interpretations of the specific role played by the foreign members of the expeditions vary. One interpretation suggests that these relatively small numbers of southern Levantines were employed by the Egyptians as local experts on the terrain and the surrounding region more generally (Černý 1935; Debono 1947; Chesson – Darnell 2005: 89–90). A different view proposes that these individuals were "press-ganged" from the local population for unskilled labor (Shaw 1998: 246). In yet another interpretation, based on her reading of *ỉmnw*, Saretta (2016: 131ff.) has suggested that the Asiatics were included in the expeditions as artisans.

Fig. 5.
Procession of "Asiatics"—Aamu (*ꜥꜣmw*)—from Tomb 3 at Beni Hasan (Newberry 1893: pl. XXXI).

123). Finally, many inscriptions (e.g., Nos. 85, 92, 112, 121, 136, 412) also include interpreters in the lists of participants.

Further evidence indicates that collaborative relationships with southern Levantine peoples during the Middle Kingdom was not limited to interactions in Sinai. An inscription of the "general of the Asiatics, Bebi" (*ỉmy-rꜣ mšꜥ n(y) ꜥꜣm.w Bbỉ*) (Chesson – Darnell 2005: 88), found in Wadi el-Ḥol in the Western Desert further attests to interactions with Asiatics in this period. Likely dating to the reign of Amenemhet III, this text thus provides a contemporary parallel to the Sinai inscriptions. The inscription also mentions Bebi's daughter, and other persona, and implies the existence of a sizeable group of "Asiatics" interacting with Egyptians in the Western Desert.

Finally, although earlier in date, the primary parallel to these scenes of collaboration in Sinai and the Western Desert found in Egypt proper is the famous procession of Aamu in the tomb of Khnumhotep II at Beni Hasan (Fig. 5). Part of the middle register of the northern wall of Tomb 3, the image shows fifteen individuals, including men, women, and children, identified as "Aamu (*ꜥꜣmw*) from Shu (*šw*)" (Newberry 1893: 69, pls. XXX, XXXI). The accompanying text, however, lists the total number of the group as 37 (Newberry 1893: 69, pl. XXXVIII).

The historicity, interpretation, and accuracy of this representation of this group of people has been discussed extensively elsewhere (Cohen 2015; Kamrin 1999; 2009). Here, however, as imagery of foreigners produced by Egyptians, this procession of peoples provides vivid contrast to the traditional trope of hostility to the "other." In this scene, rather than cowering before Khnumhotep II, the Aamu are walking upright, with no gesture or indication of obeisance; they are fully clothed, belying with the stereotypical presentation of the foreigner as naked or nearly naked prisoner; they have possessions, including both material objects and animals; and finally, and significantly, they are armed. In sum, both image and text make it explicitly clear that they are being presented to Khnumhotep II not as captives but as visitors or guests, who likely are there of their own free will.[12]

It is quite clear that the Beni Hasan Aamu are real people, and the scene may very well be representative of a real event or a series of events. In either case, however, rather than focus on their inherent inferiority and suitability for subjugation, the artistic rendering of the Aamu seems instead to have striven for a certain level of accuracy. There is no reason to show the Aamu women with red boots unless indeed this bears some resemblance to the actual footwear worn. Further, although much (likely far too much) has been made of the importance of the "duck-billed" axe carried by one of the men, the fact remains that the weaponry depicted in the scene appears to be credible attempts at faithful renditions of real Levantine types—as does the imagery of the weaponry carried by the individuals shown in the inscriptions from Sinai—adding further realism to the scene.

The Beni Hasan inscription dates to the reign of Senusret II, roughly half a century earlier than the inscriptions at Sinai dating to Amenemhet III and IV. While it is unclear if this image represents a single event, or commemorates an iterative one, it indicates either an ongoing or one-time exchange relationship between the Aamu and Egypt, and a relationship in which the Aamu, while perhaps not equal partners, were viewed with equanimity, or at least not with official disdain.[13] Rather, this representation of foreigners appears to acknowledge both their difference and their value in providing desired commodities to Egypt, further implying interaction based in part on mutual collaboration.

All data, therefore, point to a substantial degree of collaborative interaction and contact between Egypt and southern Levantine peoples in the Middle Kingdom.[14] This appears to have started early in the 12th Dynasty and increased over time, reaching its greatest extent during the reigns of Amenemhet III and IV, both of whom, in addition to their efforts in Sinai, focused on increasing contacts with the Levantine world (Goldwasser 2006: 131). This is clearly borne out by the inscriptions from Sinai and the Western Desert, and importantly, by the rise of Asiatic settlement at Tell el-Dabʿa in the Delta. Notably, the discovery of a statue of an Asiatic man, seated, robed and with a distinctive hairstyle, in cemetery F/I at Tell el-Dabʿa, upholds the image of independent southern Levantine peoples at the site (Schiestl 2006: fig. 3), and their presumed interaction and collaboration with Egyptians.

---

[12] See also Aufrère (2002: 211) for a discussion of interactions between Asiatics from the Eastern Desert and Egypt in the context of this image.

[13] This does not contradict the simultaneous interpretation that the Aamu depicted on the tomb wall help to illustrate the "disorder" of the desert that Khnumhotep, as governor of the Oryx Nome, was responsible for controlling (see discussions in Kamrin 1999; 2009; Cohen 2015). In the Egyptian worldview in which more than one seemingly contradictory "truth" may exist at the same time, the Beni Hasan Aamu might easily have represented and symbolized multiple concepts simultaneously.

[14] The presence of foreigners in a variety of roles in society in Egypt throughout the Middle Kingdom is well-attested (see Schneider 2003 for a more complete discussion).

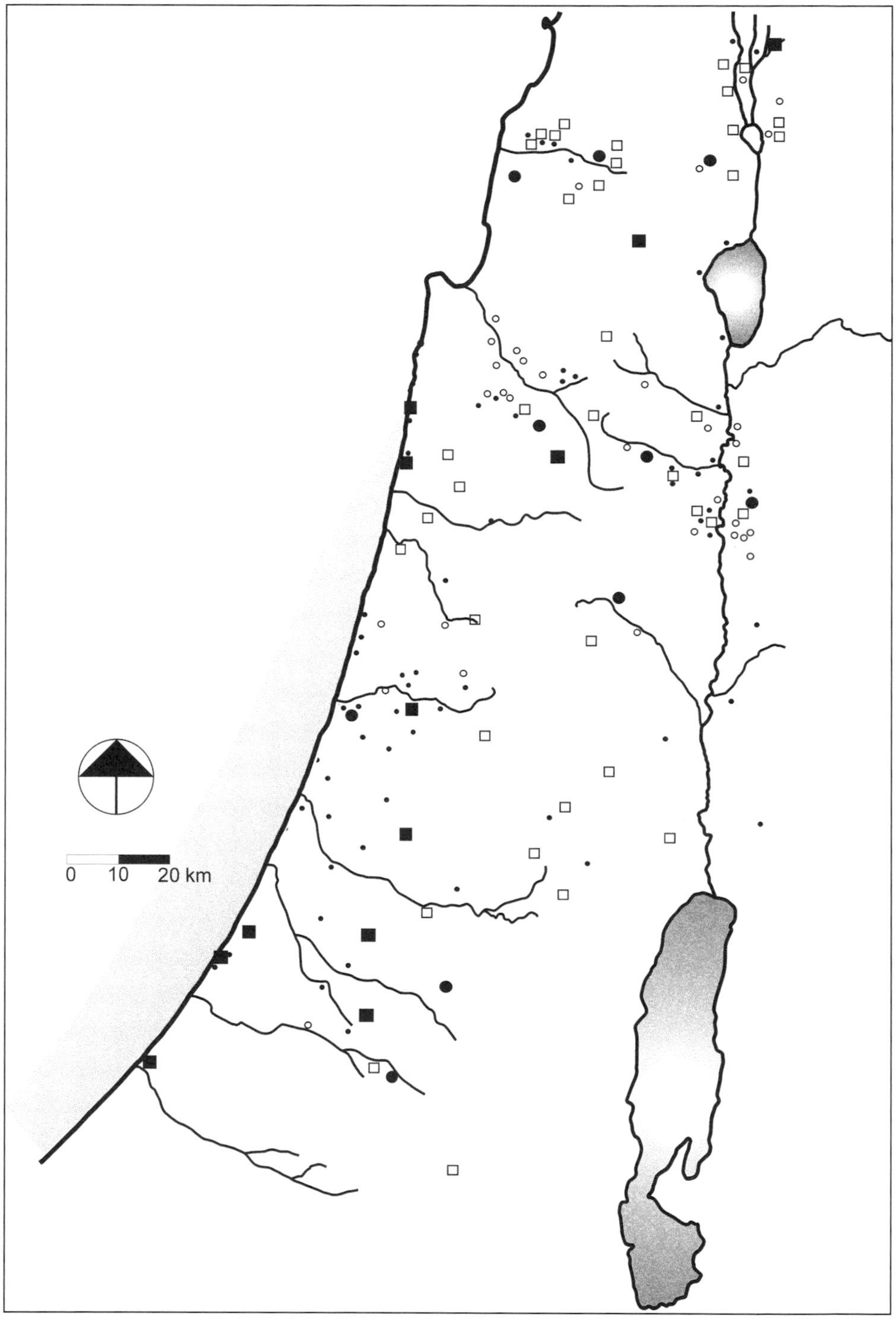

Fig. 6.
Map showing MB I settlement in the southern Levant (from Cohen 2016: fig. 6.7).

Currently there is no solid consensus regarding the chronological synchronisms between Egypt and the southern Levant, and the precise chronological connections between the different reigns of the Middle Kingdom and various subphases of the Palestinian Middle Bronze Age are subject to considerable debate (see, for example, the articles in Höflmayer – Cohen, eds. 2017). However, in broad terms, the correlations are such that the beginning of the Middle Kingdom corresponds to the end of the Intermediate Bronze Age in the southern Levant, with the beginning of the Middle Bronze Age (MB I) likely contemporary with the early rulers of the 12th Dynasty (see Tab. 1) (Cohen 2012; 2017). As such, the Aamu represented in the Beni Hasan tomb painting have a solid early Middle Bronze Age context, and the Middle Kingdom inscriptions in Sinai dating to the reigns of Amenemhet III and IV correlate to the final phases of MB I in the southern Levant and the transition to MB II.

In both cases, the presentation of foreigners in these Middle Kingdom representations and texts reflect the relationships between Egypt and the southern Levant. The early phases of MB I, contemporary with Senusret II, saw increased settlement activity in the southern Levant; by the reigns of Amenemhet III and IV, strongly organized settlement networks focused on regional urban centers existed throughout the region, except for the Negev (Fig. 6). Evidence for trade and exchange found at southern Levantine sites such as Ashkelon and Tel Ifshar, suggest Egyptian-Levantine commercial interaction, albeit on a small scale in MB I (Cohen 2016: 46–47). The lack of settlement in the marginal regions of the Negev and Sinai may have contributed to both lack of overt hostility as well as the development of collaborative efforts in resource acquisition.

However, despite the obvious cooperation and lack of hostility apparent in the evidence for trade and the collaboration visible in the Sinai inscriptions, reflecting the reality of interactions between the southern Levant and Egypt, the official rhetoric of subjugation of the foreign other remained unchanged. While this is easily apparent through even a cursory examination of other contemporary material from the Middle Kingdom, the most obvious example is the Execration Texts, which also date to Amenemhet III and thus are precisely contemporary with the Sinai inscriptions. In the Middle Kingdom, the Execration Texts curse peoples and places in both the southern Levant and in Nubia. However, by the time of Amenemhet III, neither of these two areas presented a threat to Egypt in actual fact. Nubia existed largely as Egyptian territory, controlled by the massive fortresses that lined the Nile down past the Second Cataract (see discussion in Cohen 2016). Likewise, with the one exception of Khu-Sobek's account of Senusret III's expedition to *Skmm*, which itself may be overly exaggerated (Baines 1987: 60), there is no evidence for any overtly hostile encounters between Egypt and the indigenous inhabitants in the southern Levant. The Texts therefore, highly formulaic and ritualized as they are, appear to have functioned primarily as defensive or preventative magic, serving to uphold the ideological trope of Egyptian superiority and control over foreign places and their peoples, but which may not necessarily have reflected a contemporary factual reality. Simultaneously, other evidence from Sinai, Beni Hasan, and the Western Desert, and the incontrovertible fact that "Asiatics" existed peacefully within the traditional borders of Egypt, present a very different reality.

Conclusions

The stereotypical presentation of the "other" is endemic in Egyptian materials, whether text or image or both. The development of the idea of who was Egyptian, by definition, also created an idea of who was not: the foreign "other." Thus, the stereotyped image of foreigner, most commonly presented as the recipient of the king's action of smiting and subduing—itself intrinsically linked to the official ideology of the king—served not only to illustrate the nature and place of the "other" but also functioned as a means of upholding official perspective, order, organization, and Egyptian worldview. By and large created by and on behalf of the elite, the ideology of the elite thus dominated both text and image (Baines 1996: 341), combining to portray official perspectives, presented through formal rhetoric and canonized imagery that conveyed specific meaning essential to maintaining formal ideology.

However, interaction with the "other" also was a contemporary reality throughout much of Egyptian history, which waxed and waned in accordance both with Egyptian internal developments and in response to changes in those foreign regions with which Egypt had contact. The contrasts and differences between the Sinai inscriptions from the Old and Middle Kingdom, as well as the unique image of the Aamu from Beni Hasan in the Middle Kingdom, illustrate that the historical reality of relationships between Egypt and foreign regions influenced the views and presentations of foreigners in Egyptian visual and textual records. Increasing frequency of contact in the Middle Kingdom may also have contributed to depiction outside the stereotypical imagery, as increased familiarity with the "other" may change that "other" from inferior to simply "different" (see Liverani 1990: 36).[15] As the differences between Old Kingdom and Middle Kingdom inscriptions show, the broader familiarity with the peoples of Sinai and the southern Levant led to a greater range of representation of those peoples. While this is not to imply that Egyptians of the Middle Kingdom ever relaxed their official impression of the "otherness" of the "Asiatics", or decreased the ideology that the king was entitled to destroy and conquer them, the increased contacts and interactions between Egypt and southern Levantines in the Middle Kingdom clearly also led to a change in perception of both value and activity of the "Asiatic other" (also see discussion in Baines 1996).

Further, the specificity of these presentations also allows for greater understanding of the relationships between Egypt and the southern Levant. There is a clear correlation between the political/economic development in the southern Levant and the changes in Egyptian presentation of southern Levantine peoples between the Old and Middle Kingdoms. Again, this stands out strongly in the Sinai inscriptions. The Old Kingdom material, contemporary with Intermediate Bronze Age and increased settlement and activity in marginal regions, clearly

---

[15] In his study of Egyptian mining ventures, Shaw (1998: 255) suggested also that these expeditions, outside traditional Egyptian territory, allowed for, if not encouraged, increased Egyptian contact with foreigners.

forms part of the traditional canon of hostility to the "other"; the Middle Kingdom stele and inscriptions, however, contemporary with the late MB I – MB II southern Levant and a contemporary absence of settlement and activity in Negev and Sinai, just as clearly indicate active collaboration and cooperation.

Finally, it may also be important to note that the discussion of "who is a stranger" and the "other" is remarkably one-sided. By virtue of the nature of the available evidence, scholarship looks at foreignness from the point of view of literate societies and the textual and artistic representations they produced, which are, in this specific case, the views presented by ancient Egypt. With almost no exception (e.g., Mumford – Parcak 2003: 116) there is no discussion of the southern Levantine perspective of Egyptians as foreigners.[16] While the Egyptian official trope and rhetoric may have viewed the "vile Asiatic" as representative of chaos, lesser and worthy of subjugation, with a decidedly inferior place in the order of the world, there is no evidence that provides us with the southern Levantine view of the Egyptian. It is tempting to speculate about a formal southern Levantine trope of the foreign Egyptian "other" as overbearing, brutal, barbaric invaders, tempered by individual accounts of a reality that consisted of occasional trade, cooperation and tentative truces. The question of "who was a stranger" surely always had two sides, even if we only ever see the one.

References

Allen, J., 2008. The Historical Inscription of Khnumhotep at Dahshur: Preliminary Report. *BASOR* 352, 29–39.

Aufrère, S., 2002. The Deserts of the Fifteenth and Sixteenth Upper Egyptian Nomes during the Middle Kingdom. In R. Friedman, ed., *Egypt and Nubia: Gifts of the Desert*. London: British Museum Press, 207–214.

Baines, J., 1987. The Stela of Khusobek: private and royal military narrative and values. In J. Osing – G. Dreyer, eds., *Form und Mass. Beiträge zur Literatur, Sprache und Kunst des alten Ägypten. Festschrift für Gerhart Fecht zum 65. Geburtstag am 6. Februar 1987*. ÄAT 12. Wiesbaden: Harrassowitz, 43–61.

Baines, J., 1996. Contextualizing Egyptian Representations of Society and Ethnicity. In J. Cooper – G. Schwartz, eds., *The Study of the Ancient Near East in the 21st Century*. Winona Lake, IN: Eisenbrauns, 339–384.

Beck, P., 2002. *Imagery and Representation. Studies in the Art and Iconography of Ancient Palestine: Collected Articles*. Edited by N. Na'aman, U. Zevulun, and I. Ziffer. Journal of the Institute of Archaeology of Tel Aviv University, Occasional Publications 3. Tel Aviv: Emery and Claire Yass Publications in Archaeology.

Černý, J., 1935. Semites in Egyptian Mining Expeditions to Sinai. *ArOr* 7, 384–389.

Cohen, S., 2012. Synchronisms and Significance: Reevaluating Interconnections between Middle Kingdom Egypt and the Southern Levant. *JAEI* 4, 1–8.

Cohen, S., 2015. Interpretative uses and abuses of the Beni Hasan tomb painting. *JNES* 74, 19–38.

[16] Mumford – Parcak (2003: 116) refer to the Egyptians in Sinai as an "intrusive Nile Valley pharaonic culture".

Cohen, S., 2016. *Peripheral Concerns. Urban Development in the Bronze Age Southern Levant.* Sheffield: Equinox.

Cohen, S., 2017. Reevaluation of Connections between Egypt and the Southern Levant in Light of the New Higher Chronology. *JAEI* 13, 34–42.

Cohen, S., 2019. Continuity, Innovation, and Change. The Intermediate Bronze Age in the Southern Levant. In A. Yasur-Landau – E. Cline – Y. Rowan, eds., *The Social Archaeology of the Levant: From Prehistory to the Present*. Cambridge: Cambridge University, 183–198.

Chesson, M.S. – J.C. Darnell, 2005. *Results of the 2001 Kerak Plateau Early Bronze Age Survey. Two Early Alphabetic Inscriptions from the Wadi el-Ḥôl. New Evidence for the Origin of the Alphabet from the Western Desert of Egypt*. AASOR 59. Boston, MA: American Schools of Oriental Research.

Debono, F., 1947. Pics en pierre de Sérabit el-Khadim (Sinaï) et d'Égypte. *ASAE* 46, 265–285.

Finkelstein, I., 1995. *Living on the Fringe: The Archaeology and History of the Negev, Sinai, and Neighbouring Regions in the Bronze and Iron Ages*. Monographs in Mediterranean Archaeology 6. Sheffield: Sheffield Academic.

Gardiner, A. – T. Peet, 1952. *The Inscriptions of Sinai.* Part I. Egypt Exploration Society Excavation Memoir 36. London: Egypt Exploration Society.

Gardiner, A. – T. Peet – J. Černý, 1955. *The Inscriptions of Sinai.* Part II. Egypt Exploration Society Excavation Memoir 45. London: Egypt Exploration Society.

Goldwasser, O., 2006. Canaanites Reading Hieroglyphs: Horus is Hathor? – The Invention of the Alphabet in Sinai. *ÄuL*16, 121–160.

Goldwasser, O., 2012–2013. Out of the Mists of the Alphabet – redrawing the "Brother of the Ruler of Retenu". *ÄuL* 22/23, 353–374.

Haiman, M., 1996. Early Bronze Age IV Settlement Pattern of the Negev and Sinai Deserts: View from Small Marginal Temporary Sites. *BASOR* 303, 1–32.

Haiman, M., 2009. Copper Trade and Pastoralism in the Negev and Sinai Deserts in the EB IV. In P. Parr, ed., *The Levant in Transition. Proceedings of a Conference Held at the British Museum on 20–21 April 2004*. Palestine Exploration Fund Annual 9. Leeds: Maney, 38–42.

Hikade, T., 2007. Crossing the Frontier into the Desert: Egyptian Expeditions to the Sinai Peninsula. *Ancient East and West* 6, 1–22.

Höflmayer, F. – S. Cohen, eds., 2017. *Chronological Conundrums. JAEI* 13.

Höflmayer, F. – M. Dee – H. Genz – S. Riehl, 2014. Radiocarbon Evidence for the Early Bronze Age Levant: The site of Tell Fadous-Kfarabida (Lebanon) and the End of the Early Bronze III Period. *Radiocarbon* 56, 529–542.

Kamrin, J., 1999. *The Cosmos of Khnumhotep II at Beni Hasan*. London – New York: Kegan Paul International.

Kamrin, J., 2009. The Aamu of Shu in the tomb of Khnumhotep II at Beni Hasan. *JAEI* 1, 22–36.

Liverani, M., 1990. *Prestige and Interest. International Relations in the Near East ca. 1600–1100 B.C.* HANE/S 1. Padova: Sargon srl.

Loprieno, A., 1996. Defining Egyptian Literature: Ancient Texts and Modern Theories. In A. Lopreino, ed., *Ancient Egyptian Literature. History and Forms*. PdÄ 10. Leiden – New York: Brill, 39–58.

Mumford, G., 2006. Tell Ras Budran (Site 345): Defining Egypt's Eastern Frontier and Mining Operations during the Late Old Kingdom (Early EB IV/MB I). *BASOR* 342, 13–67.

Mumford, G. – S. Parcak, 2003. Pharaonic Ventures into South Sinai: el-Markha Plain Site 346. *JEA* 89, 83–116.

Newberry, P.E., 1893. *Beni Hasan*, Part I. Archaeological Survey of Egypt 1. London: Egypt Exploration Fund.

Nicholson, P. – I. Shaw, eds., 2000. *Ancient Egyptian Materials and Technology*. Cambridge: Cambridge University.

Parcak, S., 2004. Egypt's Old Kingdom 'Empire' (?): A case study focusing on South Sinai. In G. Knoppers – A. Hirsch, eds., *Egypt, Israel, and the Ancient Mediterranean World. Studies in Honor of Donald B. Redford*. PdÄ 20. Leiden – Boston: Brill, 41–60.

Regev, J. – P. de Miroschedji – R. Greenberg – E. Braun – Z. Greenhut – E. Boaretto, 2012. Chronology of the Early Bronze Age in the Southern Levant: New Analysis for a High Chronology. *Radiocarbon* 54, 526–566.

Saretta, P., 2016. *Asiatics in Middle Kingdom Egypt. Perceptions and Reality*. Bloomsbury Egyptology. London – New York: Bloomsbury.

Schiestl, R., 2006. The Statue of an Asiatic Man from Tell ed-Dabʿa Egypt. *ÄuL* 16, 173–185.

Schneider, T., 2003. *Ausländer in Ägypten während des Mittleren Reiches und der Hyksoszeit, Teil 2: Die ausländische Bevölkerung*. ÄAT 42. Wiesbaden: Harrasowitz.

Shaw, I., 1998. Exploiting the desert frontier; the logistics and politics of ancient Egyptian mining expeditions. In E. Herbert – A.B. Knapp – V. Pigott, eds., *Social Approaches to an Industrial Past: the archaeology and anthropology of mining*. London – New York: Routledge, 242–258.

Stadelmann, R., 2006. Riding the Donkey: A Means of Transportation for Foreign Rulers. In E. Czerny – I. Hein – H. Hunger – D. Melman – A. Schwab, eds., *Timelines: Studies in the Honor of Manfred Bietak*, Vol. II. OLA 149. Leuven: Peeters, 301–304.

Tallet, P., 2012. *La zone minère pharaonique du Sud-Sinaï – I. Catalogues complémentaire des inscriptions du Sinaï*. MIFAO 130. Le Caire: Institut français d'archéologie orientale.

Wente, E., 1990. *Letters from Ancient Egypt*. WAW 1. Atlanta, GA: Scholars Press.

IT IS YOU, MY LOVE, YOU, WHO ARE THE STRANGER.[1] AKKADIAN AND ELAMITE AT THE CROSSROADS OF LANGUAGE AND WRITING

Katrien De Graef (Ghent University)

Introduction

From old, Mesopotamian civilizations have been in close contact with the neighbouring eastern lands through pillaging and warfare, exchange and trade, and diplomatic relations and collaboration (see, among others, Potts 1994). It goes without saying that these continuous encounters, both negative and positive, profoundly impacted both sides. This was particularly manifest in the large lowland-highland border area alongside the Zagros mountains in modern western Iran, where a duality of cultures developed as a result of the millennia-long interaction and balancing between lowland and highland traditions, values and influences—a duality still existing today (see, among others, Ingham 1994).

Especially interesting in this regard is the Susiana plain, geographically the prolongation of the Mesopotamian alluvial plain and therefore a contact area par excellence.

Although contacts between lowland Mesopotamian and highland Iranian cultures surely predate the written record (see, among others, Algaze 1989), interregional contacts and trade networks intensified during the third millennium BC (see, among others, Selz 1991, and Potts 1994). Later in the same millennium, both the Old-Akkadian and the Ur III kings conquered parts of the Iranian highlands and incorporated them—albeit with varied success—into their respective kingdoms, imposing their respective writing systems and languages for administrative and governmental purposes.[2]

At the beginning of the second millennium BC, the picture changes altogether. After the fall of the Ur III empire, in which the Elamites had a considerable part (see De Graef 2012 and 2015 with references), an Elamite dynasty rose to power, which ruled the Iranian highlands and lowland Susiana, and even shortly conquered parts of the Mesopotamian plain. Generally called "the Sukkalmaḫ dynasty" after the Sukkalmaḫ as assumed highest authority, the political structure and organisation of this empire seems to have been that of a federal state, with a king as highest authority, under whom two Sukkalmaḫs each ruled over a part

[1] The Stranger Song (Leonard Cohen).

[2] Whereas the Old-Akkadian case is rather understudied, the eastern expansion drive and conquests of the Ur III kings and the commercial and diplomatic relations between Sumer and the Iranian highlands have been extensively studied, see most recently Steinkeller 2007; 2013; 2014 and forthcoming.

of the territory, Elam and Šimaški in the north and Susa and Anšan in the south. Further down, smaller and local officials, such as Sukkals and Teppirs, supervised smaller territories or cities (see De Graef 2012 and 2019 with references). Early on in the second millennium BC, the Elamite federation emerged as a major power broker in the web of relations between Babylon, Ešnunna and Mari, amongst others, as is shown in various studies on the Mari letters in which these rulers acknowledge the Elamite superiority (see, among others, Charpin and Durand 1991; Charpin 2013; Durand 2013 and Peyronel 2013). After Hammurabi's conquests put an end to this situation, Elam ceased foreign interventions.

As a result of the continuous interaction and balancing between foreign (Mesopotamian) and local (Elamite) traditions, values and influences in political, legal, economic and administrative matters, a basic duality of cultures developed throughout the second millennium BC, to give way, only at the very end of this millennium, to a more or less unilingual Elamite society. This interaction between Elamite and Mesopotamian cultures and its eventual resolution is a fascinating evolution that can be observed at the level of families, households and individuals, both in a private and an institutional context, as is shown by the documentary texts found in Susa, Haft Tappeh, Tall-i Malyan, Chogha Gavaneh, Tappeh Bormi and other sites. In what follows, I will try to shed some light on this basic duality as it is shown in the legal and administrative formulas used in the documentary texts from Sukkalmaḫ Susa (first half of the second millennium BC).

Documentary Texts from Sukkalmaḫ Susa

The overall majority of the nearly 1000 administrative, economic and legal texts from Sukkalmaḫ Susa (published in MDP 10, 18, 22, 23, 24, 28, 55 and De Graef 2007) are written in Akkadian. The usage of Akkadian as a written language outside of the Mesopotamian heartland in itself is not exceptional or surprising.[3] From the late third millennium BC onwards, Akkadian—and to a lesser degree Sumerian—has been used as a written language in both literary and administrative contexts in Iranian highland cultures (see De Graef 2013a), which was no doubt in part due to the fact that both the Old-Akkadian and Ur III empires conquered parts of the Iranian highlands and imposed their languages and writing systems for administrative and governmental purposes.

What is somewhat surprising, however, is the fact that the newly created Elamite federal state, which covered a very large territory, originating in the Iranian highlands of the Fars and maintaining its capital there, instead of using its own language, kept on using Akkadian as its official written language and continued to do so for half a millennium. This is the more surprising, as there had

[3] Texts written in Akkadian are found in many sites outside Mesopotamia, in modern Syria, Turkey, Iran, Egypt, and the Levant. The language of these texts is generally termed "Peripheral Akkadian" although there is no consensus whether these texts reflect in all cases an actual form of spoken Akkadian, see von Dassow 2010 and the other papers in the section "Peripheral Akkadian" in Kogan et al. 2010.

been previous attempts to develop a local writing system in order to write the Elamite language, such as the Linear-Elamite script of Puzur- or Kutik-Inšušinak (see most recently Desset 2018).

Akkadianized or Not?

The documentary texts of Sukkalmaḫ Susa being written in Akkadian had led the majority of modern scholars to the assumption that the greater part of western Iran was "Akkadianized" and even that Susa was a sort of Babylonian "colony" whose population was for a large part Akkadian.[4]

The question arises, however, whether this hypothesis holds true until today, or whether it should at least be nuanced in the light of the following (new) information.

First, it has been generally assumed that the onomasticon in the documentary texts from Sukkalmaḫ Susa was for the greater part Akkadian, implying a predominantly Akkadian ethnicity—or at least Akkadian speaking character—of its population. Moreover, both Malbran-Labat (1996: 40) and Tavernier (2010: 206–207 and 2018: 309) assume there was barely any interaction between the Akkadian and Elamite ethnic/linguistic groups, referring to a link between personal names and professional categories mentioned by Amiet (1992: 86) who, citing Lambert (1971: 220), distinguishes between the Elamite ethnic population (descended from the highlands) and the native Akkadian speaking population of Susa, based on the fact that only princes and shepherds bear Elamite names, whereas the majority of the urban elites bear Akkadian names.

It is certainly true that most rulers and important functionaries—sukkalmaḫ's, sukkal's, teppir's and the like—bear Elamite names. However, the preliminary results of a study of the onomasticon of the documentary texts from Sukkalmaḫ Susa[5] clearly shows that not all inhabitants of Susa bear Akkadian names. Only ca. 45% of the personal names mentioned in these texts can be identified linguistically and etymologically with certainty as (Sumero-)Akkadian. A small part (ca. 15%) can be identified as Elamite and a fairly large part (ca. 40%) is uncertain, hybrid or foreign. This is no doubt due to our poor understanding of Old-Elamite, the rather large amount of hypocoristica or so-called "banana-names" which are very difficult to allocate linguistically[6] and the use of logographs that can be read in any language.

---

[4] The hypothesis that Susa and Susiana was "Akkadianized" due to a mass arrival of Mesopotamians emigrated from the Lagaš and Umma region because of a famine following Amorite incursions in the beginning of the second millennium BC was originally formulated by Lambert (1991) and since then taken over by many scholars, among which Malbran-Labat 1996: 40; Steve – Vallat – Gasche 2002: 451–452; Tavernier 2010: 206–207 and 2018a: 309; and Potts 2016: 154.

[5] Ghent University BOF funded project "East Side Story. Susa under the Sukkalmaḫ Dynasty (1930–1450 BC): a Prosopographical Study".

[6] Zadok (1983; 1984; 1987 and 1991) allocates a great part of these names to Elamite verbal and nominal roots, but there is no consensus on this, see, among others, Foster 1982; Emberling 1995 and Blažek 1999.

More importantly, though, is the fact that within one and the same family, both Akkadian and Elamite (or hybrid) personal names were given,[7] implying at least a certain degree of biculturality and / or bilingualism within the urban population of Susa. The presupposition that shepherds (i.e. highlanders) bear Elamite names, originally formulated by Lambert (1971: 220) and since then adopted without question by others, is based on three texts mentioning sheep and fields on the one hand and persons bearing Elamite names on the other.[8] Needless to say that this does not make sense, as none of these persons are actually designated as shepherd in these texts, and there are many more texts mentioning sheep and fields in combination with persons bearing Akkadian and other personal names. Moreover, the only person actually designated as shepherd (SIPA) whose name is not broken, bears a Sumero-Akkadian name, viz. Warad-Sîn (ir-^{d}EN.ZU) in MDP 18 159.

The preliminary results of a study of the onomasticon of the Sukkalmaḫ Susa texts shows that there is no link between personal names and professional categories, on the contrary, persons bearing Akkadian, Elamite and other names are represented in most professional categories. Moreover, persons bearing typically Elamite titles, such as šati (a kind of priest, see ElW II *sub* šà-ti) or kipar (a functionary, see ElW I *sub* ki-pa-ru) often bear Akkadian names,[9] and persons bearing typically Sumero-Akkadian titles, such as di.kud (judge) and ugula (overseer) often bear Elamite names.[10] Most characteristic for this biculturality and bilingualism among the urban elites is the fact that there are scribes (dub.sar) with both Akkadian and Elamite (or hybrid or foreign) names.[11]

Second, it has been generally assumed that the usage of Akkadian was limited to the western part of the Sukkalmaḫ kingdom (i.e. Susa and Susiana) whereas Elamite was used in the eastern part—the highland (see, among others, Malbran-Labat 1996: 34). Hence the idea that (the bulk of) royal inscriptions written in Akkadian were intended for the western part and those (few) written in Elamite for the eastern part, as put forward by Tavernier (2018: 309).

However, letters between officials in Susa and the palace in Tall-i Malyan, ancient Anšan, suggest that the use of Akkadian as an official written language was far more wide-spread. Indeed, four unpublished letters, part of a group of 139 tablets found in a dividing wall of the Royal City of Susa by Ghirshman, sent by the penultimate Sukkalmaḫ Temti-halki to Kuk-zuḫzupi, start with the expression

---

[7] E.g. Kuk-luḫurater (El.), son of Iqbi-ul-īni (Akk.) in MDP 23, 174, 175 and 176; Atta-ḫaštuk (El.), son of Šēlebum (Akk.) in MDP 23 315; Kuk-gešṭû (El. / Akk.), son of Šamaš-gāmil (Akk.) in MDP 23 325; Aḫīya (Akk.) and Annu-pī-Simut (Akk. / El.), sons of Sîn-iddinam (Akk.) in MDP 24 340; Kuk-adar (El.) and Abi-ili (Akk.), sons of Atanaḫ-ili (Akk.) in MDP 24 341; Kuppakra (El.), son of Šamaš-gāmil in MDP 28 471; Abi-ili (Akk.), son of Napratep (El.) in MDP 28 472.

[8] *MDP* 28 512, 515 and 540, see Lambert 1971: 220, fn. 10.

[9] E.g. Abīšunu šati in MDP 23 246, Ana-ilīma-atkal šati in MDP 23 279 and 280, Nūr-Šamaš šati in MDP 28 430, Ḫabil-kīnu kipar in MDP 22 136.

[10] E.g. Atta-ḫaštuk judge in MDP 23 320, Uduk-Simut overseer in MDP 28 438.

[11] Although the majority of the scribes bear Akkadian names, there are quite some scribes bearing Elamite (or at least non-Akkadian) names, e.g. Adaruru (MDP 23 185, 188, 256 and 258), Ḫudiliya (MDP 22 18), Yaye (MDP 22 29), Ibibi (MDP 24 331, 334; 28 405), Kuk-Inšušinak (MDP 28 548 seal), Kuk-Inzu (MDP 43 1769).

"The palace is fine, Anšan is fine!" (*ekallum šalim Anšan šalim*), implying that Temti-ḫalki resided in his palace in Anšan when he wrote these letters to Kuk-zuhzupi, who was obviously in Susa where the letters were found.[12] The fact that these letters are written in Akkadian seems to imply that it was also used as an official (written) language in Anšan. Note, moreover, that both sender and addressee bear Elamite names, which might imply they were of Elamite ethnicity and Elamite speaking, or at least identified themselves as Elamite.

Third, it has been generally assumed that the structure, phrasing and content of the Akkadian administrative, economic and legal texts from Sukkalmaḫ Susa are similar to those of Mesopotamia proper (see Tavernier 2010: 208).

It goes without saying that the basic structure of some of the genres—subject, verb, oath, witnesses—are indeed very similar. However, the legal and administrative formulas seem to be for a great part typically local, no doubt reflecting local legal practices, and some even include Elamite expressions or words. It is clear that this is not just a question of a simple transfer of formulas. This usage of Elamite phrases and expressions as well as Akkadian ones only used in texts from Iran—but not in texts from Mesopotamia—again implies that we are dealing with a bilingual and bicultural society.

The Akkadian of the Susa contracts has been studied by De Meyer (1962) and Salonen (1962 and 1967). However valuable a contribution these studies certainly were back then, time has come now to reappraise the language(s) and script of these Susa texts in the light of new insights in multilingual societies (see, most recently, Braarvig and Geller 2018).

It goes without saying that such a reappraisal is a long-term study, requiring a number of book volumes rather than a small conference contribution such as this one. The purpose of this contribution, therefore, is to put forward new research questions, ideas and hypotheses in order to set out some new lines of inquiry for the study of the language(s) and script of the Sukkalmaḫ texts from Susa (and other sites) in general and their legal and administrative formulas in particular.

For, the question must be asked why we naturally assume that these texts were written by Akkadian speaking people, whereas we do not automatically do so with other so-called "peripheral Akkadian" texts. Why do we consider writers of "peripheral Akkadian" texts in Anatolia, Nuzi, Ugarit, Egypt etc. to have been "bilingual" in so far that they wrote Akkadian but spoke (and wrote) their own local mother tongue, but do we believe the writers of the texts from Susa (and other sites in Elam) to be unilingual Akkadian? Why do we consider the possibility (or probability) that the writers of the Mari texts were bilingual Akkadian-Amorite (see, most recently, Charpin 2016), but do we not take this possibility in account for the writers of the Susa texts?

The main reason seems to be Lambert's "Akkadianization" theory from 1991, in which he suggests that a part of the population of the Lagaš area migrated to

---

[12] See my paper read at the 58th *Rencontre Assyriologique Internationale* in Leiden in 2012 "The Writing *In* the Wall. A Study of the Letters of Temti-ḫalki Found in a Cache in Old Babylonian Susa". A revised publication of this paper is forthcoming.

Elam at the beginning of the second millennium BC, a hypothesis in need of revision.[13] It goes without saying that it is not inconceivable that (southern) Babylonians migrated to the east during the Sukkalmaḫ period. Indeed, Gasche (2013) found archaeological evidence in Susa implying that during the period of depopulation in southern Babylonia during Samsuiluna's reign, a part of its population migrated eastwards. It seems thus that there were various waves of migration from Babylonia to Elam during the first half of the second millennium BC, which could explain why the share of Akkadian names in Susa seems fairly stable throughout the whole Sukkalmaḫ period. However, this does not imply that (the majority of) the population of Susa was, and especially remained, Akkadian and therefore Akkadian speaking. On the contrary, though there certainly must have been Babylonians—and other foreigners for that matter—living either temporarily or permanently in the Susa area at the time, the greater part of the population was no doubt Elamite. And whereas the urban elites—whether they be newly migrated Babylonians, Elamites, of mixed origin or foreigners—certainly must have known (at least some) Akkadian, one cannot but assume that the spoken language of the greater part of the population must have been Elamite.

Starting from this much more logical assumption that Elamite was the vernacular within the Elamite federation, the so-called Sukkalmaḫ State—including Susiana—a second question automatically arises: if they spoke Elamite, if the statements and aphorisms accompanying their rites, rituals, ceremonies and dealings as part of (daily) commerce and (customary) law within the existing social structures were uttered in Elamite, what language did they write?

Did they write Akkadian? In other words, did they adopt a complete and ready-made Mesopotamian administrative system, including cuneiform writing and Akkadian, which they interspersed here and there with Elamite expressions to fill the gap not covered by the Mesopotamian ones? The finding of school tablets in Susa from all phases of the Sukkalmaḫ period (see Malayeri 2014), implying local Susian scribes received a regular education in cuneiform, Sumerian and Akkadian, seems indeed to indicate this. However, if they "simply" adopted their administrative system from the Babylonians, we would expect to find much more similarities with the existing documentary corpus from Babylonia proper. We would expect then to be able to discern a particular "school" with its typical language, tablet formats, syllabary and shape of signs, as is the case in Mari where at the beginning of the reign of Yaḫdun-Lim the system of the school of Ešnunna was adopted (Charpin 2012 and 2016: 14–16). This is not the case in the Susa ma-

[13] This hypothesis is to a large extent based on the incorrect impression that the overall majority of personal names in the Susa texts are Akkadian, and in particular on the attestation of five names with the theophoric element Nazi or Nanše and Šara, patron deities of Lagaš and Umma (Lambert 1991: 56). It seems rather hard, in my opinion, to substantiate a claim based on the theophoric elements of five personal names (out of more than 6500). It is obviously not inconceivable that in the politically and socially unstable early second millennium BC southern Babylonia groups of people migrated to the east, but this should be considered in light of a complete and comprehensive study of the onomasticon of the Sukkalmaḫ texts from Elam in combination with new findings on the history of early second millennium BC Babylonia and Elam.

terial. On the contrary, as mentioned earlier, the legal and administrative formulas seem to be for a great part typically local and some even include Elamite expressions or words, which makes it less plausible that we deal here with a straightforward adopted system from Mesopotamia.

Did they write a mixed language? The uniqueness of some of the legal and administrative formulas, including newly created Akkadian words as well as Elamite words—"Akkadianized" or not—indeed seems to imply that we are dealing with the development of a new language—or at least legal, administrative jargon to be used in the context of economic and legal agreements—by persons who were fluent in both source languages, in all probability Elamites educated in cuneiform, Sumerian and Akkadian on a high level. Especially as the legal formulas to a large extent go back to local Elamite customary law, including the accompanying customs, rites, acts, utterances, oaths and spells, which needed to be fitted into an administrative system, the basic structures of which were derived from Mesopotamia, it seems but logical that specific elements of Elamite customary law resonate in these formulas. Was this a newly created officialese, using lexical and structural resources of both source languages, developed by Susa's intelligentsia as a manifestation of their Elamo-Akkadian identity? For it was not, after all, a spoken language, but an artificially created *lingua administrativa*.

As mentioned earlier, the spoken language of the greater part of the population must have been Elamite, and although the majority of these texts were commissioned by members of the urban elites, the propertied class, whom we might expect to have known at least some Akkadian, it seems very unlikely that they were all perfectly bilingual and, moreover, literate. We can assume that, although they may have had some basic knowledge and could roughly identify their contracts and documents, in most cases they needed a professional scribe, not only to draft their contracts and documents but also to be able to read them. It is even anything but unthinkable that this scribe would have translated the content of these in officialese written documents into the spoken language, viz. Elamite, just as the commissioners would have expressed their desiderata and needs in Elamite for the scribe to translate them into the written language necessary for official documents. Taking this one step further, we might even consider the possibility of alloglottography, a term introduced by Gershevitch (1979) to describe the use of Elamite to write Old Persian in the Persepolis tablets. The concept of alloglottography, viz. "using one writable language to write another language", is not only interesting but it appears to have not been so rare (Rubio 2006). Indeed, von Dassow (2004: 642) believes the hybrid of Canaanite and Akkadian used by the Canaanite scribes not to have been an actual language, but an "artefact of these scribes' use of cuneiform". According to her, the language underlying their writing was not Akkadian but Canaanite, or in other words, they used Akkadian words, spelled in cuneiform, to write Canaanite. Could some form of alloglottography have already existed in the Sukkalmaḫ period? Did the Susian scribes use Akkadian words in cuneiform to write Elamite? Fanciful as this may look at first sight, it is not unimaginable that day-to-day documents such as sales, loans or receipts, which were written in Akkadian were read in Elamite. In view of the formulaic nature of such texts this would not even have been difficult to do, and the presence of some untranslatable Elamite titles and expressions would have made this even easier. However interesting as this may sound, it remains difficult if not impossible to prove.

It is, however, certain that there was a certain degree of biculturality and bilingualism within the urban population of Susa (and no doubt also other cities in the Sukkalmaḫ State). This cultural and linguistic duality is apparent not only from the onomasticon, but also from the *lingua administrativa* used in their documentary texts, containing both Akkadian and Elamite elements.

A necessary step in trying to understand this biculturality and bilingualism and its evolution, is the analysis of both the adoption and adaptation or even "creation" of Akkadian formulas and the introduction of (often "Akkadianized") Elamite expressions, so that their precise use and meaning in a new bilingual and bicultural legal and administrative Susian context can be determined. This will shed light on the evolution of Akkadian as a written language in a largely non-Akkadian-speaking context, and on the evolving use of Elamite titles, phrases and expressions in these texts.

One of the key questions in this context is which model formed the basis: the Akkadian or the Elamite one? Were Susian legal and administrative practices to a large extent based on a Mesopotamian and thus foreign model, or was this primarily an Elamite model, adopting some Akkadian norms and values through the use of the Akkadian language and writing system?

Or in other words, who was the stranger in the house: Akkadian or Elamite?

Administrative and Legal Formulas

Two groups of administrative and legal formulas or expressions used in the Susa texts are of interest for us here:

(1) completely Akkadian formulas or expressions without Elamite words or elements that appear uniquely in Susa texts and are not—or only very marginally—used in heartland Mesopotamian texts, and

(2) Akkadian formulas or expressions containing one or more Elamite words or elements.

As stated earlier, it is by far not the intention to give a complete overview of all administrative and legal formulas or expressions used in the Susa texts. The purpose of this paper is above all to put forward new research questions, ideas and preliminary hypotheses in order to set out some new lines of inquiry for study, which I will do by discussing a few examples for each of the two groups.

Akkadian Formulas or Expressions without Elamite Words or Elements

The first group consists of formulas or expressions rendered in correct Akkadian. The only particularity is that they are as yet not—or only very marginally—attested in heartland Mesopotamian texts. This implies they were not simply adopted from Mesopotamian practice but adapted or maybe even created to serve the local Susian practice.

CAD mentions more than 100 words, verbs and expressions which are attested only in Elam, or are used only in a specific sense in Elam. A part of these are actually Elamite words (e.g. *sukkir* "king",[14] *teppir* "a scribe or official"[15]) or words which are probably derived from an Elamite root (e.g. *kiparu* "an official",[16] *sumītu* "part of temple or installation within temple"[17]). Others are undoubtedly Akkadian words, expressions or verbs that are attested up to now only in Elam, or are used only in a specific sense in Elam.

In what follows, I will discuss three compound prepositional phrases (*ina ṭūbātīšu ina nar'amātīšu, ina dūr u pala,* and *ana esip tabal*) and the word *kubussûm* which is used in two legal clauses.

Ina ṭūbātīšu ina nar'amātīšu

Ina ṭūbātīšu(/ša/šunu) ina nar'amātīšu(/ša/šunu) is generally translated "of his/her/their own free will, of his/her/their own consent".[18] It is a perfectly correct and sound Akkadian double prepositional phrase with adverbial sense, the first part of which (*ina ṭūbātīšu*) is moreover attested in heartland Mesopotamia.[19] The double prepositional phrase *ina ṭūbātīšu(/ša/šunu) ina nar'amātīšu(/ša/šunu)*, however, is up to now only attested in Elam, more particularly in the texts from Susa and the so-called "Malamîr texts", which have recently been attributed to Tappeh Bormi by Mofidi-Nasrabadi (2018). It is used to express an act of free will by one or more persons who play an active role in an economic and/or legal agreement, especially in divisions of inheritance,[20] bequests and donations,[21] and to a lesser extent in sales and redemptions,[22] rents,[23] adoptions,[24] litigations, verdicts and declarations on oath.[25]

---

[14] CAD S *sub* sukkir and ElW II *sub* su-un-gìr, su-un-ki-ir, zu-kir.

[15] CAD T *sub* teppir and ElW I *sub* de-bi-ir, te-ip-pi-re, te-ip-pír, te-pír.

[16] CAD K *sub* kiparu and ElW I *sub* ki-pa-ru (vermutlich akkadisiert, ...; die eigentlich elam. Wortform war vielleicht kipar)

[17] CAD S *sub* sumītu (part of a temple or an installation within a temple) and ElW II *sub* su-h-mu-tú (Stèle).

[18] CAD Ṭ *sub* ṭūbātu b) 1', CAD N_1 *sub* narāmu 3. b) 2', De Meyer 1962: 52, and Salonen 1967: 63 and 97. CAD N_1 *sub* narāmu 3. b) 2' transcribes *narāmātišu* whereas De Meyer (1962: 52) and Salonen (1967: 63) transcribe *nar'amātīšu* due to the broken spelling VC-V (*na-ar-a-ma-ti-šu*) in the Susa texts, implying an 'aleph.

[19] CAD Ṭ *sub* ṭūbātu b) 1' gives some OB examples, viz. BAP 107 (division on inheritance, Sippar, Aṣ 16/01/03—a duplicate of this tablet is published in Van Lerberghe and Voet 1994), Szlechter 1953 nr. 19 (division of property, Ṣupur-Šubula, Ae A), to which YOS 13 198 (loan/deposit (?) of bread, Kiš, Ae i) should be added. Note also the double prepositional phrase *ina ṭūbātīšu(/šunu) u mitgurtīšu(/šunu)* "of his/their good will, of his/their agreement"—more or less reminiscent to the Elamite *ina ṭūbātīšu(/ša/šunu) ina nar'amātīšu(/ša/šunu)*—attested in two Old Babylonian Sippar texts, viz. CT 4 11a (division; Si 28/06/10) and MHET 455 (field exchange; Si 30/12/20).

[20] MDP 22 6, 7, 9, 11, 12, 13, 14, 15, 17, 18, 19; 23 166, 168, 177, 24 335, 336, 337 and 340.

[21] MDP 22 10, 16, 133, 135, 136, 137, 138; 24 379, 381 and 382.

[22] MDP 22 76, 154; 23 206, 209 and 234.

[23] MDP 23 241.

[24] MDP 22 1 and 3.

[25] MDP 22 160, 164; 23 242; 24 373 and De Meyer 2001.

Ana dūr u pala

A similar compound—we might even say pleonastic—prepositional phrase is to be found in the sales contracts, viz. *ana dūr u pala* "for continuation and change", almost always in combination with *ana šer šerri* "for (all) future generations"[26]. This formula expresses the irreversibility and perpetual validity of the sale and is mentioned in more than 3/4 of the sales contracts from Susa.[27] The prepositional phrase *ana dūr u pala* consists of two nouns in the absolute state, *dūr* from *dūrum* "continuity" or "permanent status or property" and *pala* from *palûm* "rotation in office", combining as such two basic time concepts, viz. continuity and circularity. Glassner (1996 and 2011) discusses these two time concepts in depth.

The meaning of the concept bala/*palûm* includes an important notion of circularity: the rotation of functions, like the reign of a king or the position of an officer, can indeed be seen as a circular movement. In addition, bala/*palûm* also expresses some sort of duration, a time span with a beginning and an end; it can be short or long, but is always limited: a delineated period of time (Glassner 1996: 175 and 2001: 183). In contrast with this, *dūrum* or *dārum*[28] indicate a time that elapses, in a continuous flow, from an expired (sometimes distant) past, to a more or less distant future. *Dūrum* or *dārum* express an infinite time span and seems to indicate a rather linear time concept. However, Glassner (2001: 183) argues that it includes a sense of circularity as well, refuting the generally accepted idea that *dārum* "continuity" and *dārum* "generation"[29] are not connected, the latter being a West-Semitic loanword.

In other words, *dūr* and *pala* are no mere opposites: they are both representatives of a time concept that unites the idea of linear and cyclic time movement. Their main difference is the contrast between the unlimited and limited time span. By combining two basic time concepts, *ana dūr u pala* intends to embrace all of time, in particular all of the time that is yet to come. Whereas it is generally translated "for continuation and change", trying to catch the meaning of both components, or "for all future time", with the intention of reflecting the sense of the expression as a whole, it seems more adequate to translate "forever and always", an English expression that also expresses an eternity of time by joining two time concepts.

Apart from its twofold character, which seems to have been typical for Elam, *ana dūr u pala* is semantically clearly different from common Akkadian expressions

---

[26] CAD D *sub* dūru B 1. c), Salonen 1962: 111 and 1967: 24, CAD P *sub* palû A 4., Salonen 1967: 66, CAD $Š_2$ *sub* šer šerri, and Salonen 1967: 87.

[27] MDP 22 41–46, 48–51, 53–59, 61–63, 66–69, 77–80, 82; 23 200–210, 212–221, 224, 227–229, 231–232, 234, 236, 238, 239; 24 347, 350, 353–355, 357–358, 364; 28 412, 414–418 and 420. In MDP 22 41 and 24 350 *ana šer šerri* is omitted. In MDP 22 47, the scribe erroneously wrote *ana esip tabal ana šer šerri*, mixing up the clauses for leases with those for sales (cf. *infra* for *ana esip tabal*). MDP 22 41 has a deviant spelling *dú-ár* for *du-úr*. MDP 22 48; 23 215, 224, 227, 229 and 28 414 have the logogram BALA instead of the syllabic spelling *pa-la*.

[28] CAD D *sub* dār.

[29] CAD D *sub* dārum A.

for "forever" such as *ana dārâtu* or *ana dārīti*, which are also used in the Susa texts[30]. The addition of the concept of *pala* might be linked with the other typical Elamite, but unfortunately still obscure, BALA-formulas (De Graef 2018b: 274–284).

Ana esip tabal

A third example of an Akkadian compound prepositional phrase typical for the Susa texts is the *ana esip tabal* or "to 'gather and take away'!" formula. This formula is extensively studied in Oers 2013. The phrase is used in field lease contracts, in which it is stipulated that the rent of the field is to be paid in advance in silver, as a result of which the lessee can take the entire crop of the field at harvest time, contrary to the "normal" field leases, where the rent of the field was paid out of the yield of the field at harvest time (Oers 2013: 155).

There are a few references to individuals who may or will take away and gather (*issim-ma itabbal*) the yield of a field (see Oers 2013: 165), but the exact clause "*ana* + the imperatives of the verbs *esēpum* and *tabālum*" is as yet not attested in leases from heartland Mesopotamia. Interestingly though, the expression *esip tabal* is mentioned in §49 of Hammurabi's Code in which it is stated that "If a man borrows silver from a merchant and gives the merchant a field prepared for planting with either barley or sesame and declares to him: 'cultivate the field and gather and take away as much barley or sesame as will be grown' (*eriš-ma šeʾam ulu šamaššamī ša ibbaššû esip tabal*)—if the cultivator should produce either barley or sesame in the field, at the harvest it is the owner of the field who shall take the barley or sesame that is grown in the field, and he shall give to the merchant only the barley equivalent to his silver which he borrowed from the merchant and the interest on it and also the expenses of the cultivation" (see Roth 1997: 90–91).

Whereas the *esip tabal* leases were widespread in Susa (about 80% of all leases are *esip tabal* leases), the practice of paying an amount of silver in advance in exchange for the right to cultivate the field and to collect the entire yield seems not to have been common in Mesopotamia. What's more: the fact that it is mentioned in Hammurabi's Code clearly indicates that it was considered problematic. The reason is obvious: speculators would give silver to people in acute financial distress in exchange for the right to cultivate their field and collect the entire yield of the field, which was worth much more than the amount initially paid by the speculator. As a righteous shepherd, Hammurabi restricted this highly exploitative lease practice by ordering that the speculator / lessee was not entitled to the entire yield of the field but only to a part of it equivalent to the capital he invested, the interest on that capital since time would elapse between payment and reimbursement and the expenses he made in order to cultivate the field. The rest of the yield belonged to the owner / lessor of the field. As such, Hammurabi turned this lease practice de facto into a loan for which a field serves as an antichretic pledge.

Considering the fact that *esip tabal* leases are as yet not attested in heartland Mesopotamia, one is tempted to imagine that the Elamites, who occupied

---

[30] CAD D *sub* dārâtu b) and dārītu b), and Salonen 1967: 23.

Ešnunna and various cities on the Tigris and thence advanced along the Tigris and the Euphrates at the time (see Charpin 2004: 213–226), introduced the practice. Although they were never able to conquer Babylon, they occupied briefly the northern part of Babylonia including Upi and Ḫirītum. Eventually Hammurabi was able to oust the Elamites and reconquer the territories they held, but it is not far-fetched to imagine that the Elamite presence, however short-lived, led to exchange and / or introduction of Elamite practices. It is however clear that the *esip tabal* lease did not find acceptance in heartland Mesopotamia.

Kubussûm

Another example of a typical Susian expression is *kubussûm*. Although never attested in texts from heartland Mesopotamia, *kubussûm* is a perfectly correct Akkadian afformative form derived from the root K-B-S. It is translated as "regulations governing specific legal procedures" and "regulations concerning the release of private debts" in CAD K *sub* kubussû 1. and 2., and as "Rechtsregel" by Salonen (1967: 45–46).

Kubussûm is used in two kinds of clauses:

(1) *warki kubussê ša* [object] DN_1 (*u* DN_2) / RN_1 (*u* RN_2) *ikbusu* / *iškunu*, and

(2) *kidinnam* (or *ṣullam*) *u kubussâm* (*ul*) *umaḫḫar(u)* / *išu*

The first clause refers to a kind of measure or decree that was issued by either one or two deities or one or two rulers. These decrees concern

(1) the legal status of biological and adopted siblings and children (*aḫḫūtam aḫḫūtam mārūtam mārūtam*)—issued by the gods Inšušinak and Išme-karab,

(2) real estate (E$_2$.DU$_3$.A.MEŠ)—on most occasions issued by Inšušinak, but once by two rulers, and

(3) certain professional or social groups—issued by two rulers

The *kubussûm* concerning the legal status of biological and adopted siblings and children is mentioned in only two texts: a litigation and an adoption.

MDP 23 321–322 is a litigation concerning a part of the inheritance of Damqīya. His sons pressed charges against Belî, claiming a field that Belî had inherited from his father Aḫuḫutu, who himself had been adopted by Damqīya. They appeared together in court where Belî was heard and defended himself by saying: "Damqīya, son of Aniḫ-Šušim, adopted him as a brother. According to the *kubussûm* that the position of a brother (by adoption) is as valid as the position of a (biological) brother (and) the position of a son (by adoption) is as valid as the position of a (biological) son, which Inšušinak and Išme-karāb established, the property of my father Aḫuḫuti [… and] had been returned to me",[31] implying that the field was at first claimed by and assigned to the sons of Damqīya, after which Belî lodged an appeal which he won and the field was returned to him.[32]

---

31 MDP 23 321–322: (14) *um-ma* ^{I}*be-li-i-ma* ^{I}*dam-qí-ia mār*(DUMU) *a-ni-iḫ-*⸢*šu-ši-im*⸣ (15) *a-na aḫ-ḫu-ti il-qé-šu-ú-ma* (16) *i-na ku-bu-us-sé-e šà aḫ-ḫu-tam aḫ-ḫu-tam* (17) *ù ma-ru-tam ma-ru-tam šà* ^{d}*Inšu-šinak*(MUŠ$_3$.EREN) (18) *ù* ^{d}*iš-me-ka-ra-ab* <<*ku-bu-us-sà*>> *iš-ku-nu-ú-ma* (19) ⸢*makkāram*(NÍG.GA)⸣ *šà a-hu-hu-ti a-bi-ia* (20) [...] ⸢x⸣ [...] *it-tu-ra-am-mi*.

32 See De Graef 2018a: 132–134 for an analysis and interpretation of this text.

MDP 22 3 states the adoption by Ilšu-bani of his paternal aunt Atûtu as his sibling. As a result of this, he has no claim on her property (both personal and real estate), but his property (real estate) is donated to her. It is not clear why exactly the clause is added here—especially as it is not inserted in other adoption contracts including an explicit bequest by the adopter to the adoptee (e.g. MDP 22 1) —and unfortunately the tablet is broken at this point.[33] It seems logical that it must have been linked to the adoptee's rights on the property inherited, but, contrary to MDP 23 321–322 where Belî says *ina kubussê ša* ... "according to the *kubussê* ...", MDP 22 3 has egir *kubussê ša* ... "after the *kubbussê* ..." which seems to emphasize the fact that the adoption and donation were concluded *after* the *kubussûm* was issued, as is the case in the other *kubussûm* clauses. This might then explain why it is added to this adoption contract, but not standard to all adoption contracts.

The *kubussûm* concerning real estate is to be found in five sales of (parts of) houses (MDP 22 44, 45, 50, 51 and 55) and one rent of a house (MDP 22 85). In all sales it is stated that the buyer bought the house after the *kubussûm* concerning real estate that Inšušinak issued (*warki*(EGIR) *ku-bu-us-sé-e šà bītātim*(E_2.DU_3.A.MEŠ) ^d^*Inšušina*k(MUŠ$_3$.EREN) *ik-bu-sú-ma bītam*(E_2.DU_3.A) *i-šà-am*). In the rental contract, it is said that the tenant paid the rent of this year, viz. 2 šeqels of silver, after the *kubussûm* that Temti-ḫalki and Kuk-našur issued concerning real estate (*ki-ṣí-ir šà-at-ti-šu* 2 ⸢*šiqil*(GÍN)⸣ *kas*⸢*pam*(KÙ.BABBAR)⸣ *iš-qú-ul wa-ar-ki ku-bu-us-sé-e šà* RN_1 *ù* RN_2 *šà bītātim*(E_2.DU_3.A.MEŠ) *ik-bu-sú*).

The *kubussûm* concerning certain professional or social groups is to be found in three field sales and one wheat loan, each time stating that the contract had been concluded after the *kubussûm*. MDP 23 206: 29–33 states that the field has been bought after the *kubussûm* concerning the replacements (*attārī*),[34] messengers (*lāsimī*)[35] and the *zukkizukki bābil* ⸢x⸣-[...][36] that Tan-uli, sukkal, and Kuk-

---

[33] MDP 22 3: (13) *warki*(EGIR) *ku-bu-us-*⸢*sé*⸣-[*e šà*] (14) *aḫ-ḫu-ti aḫ*-[*hu-ti*] (15) *ma-ru-tam* [*ma-ru-tam*]—broken "After the *kubussê* that the position of a brother (by adoption) is as valid as the position of a (biological) brother (and) the position of a son (by adoption) is as valid as the position of a (biological) son", no doubt followed by "issued by one or more gods or rulers".

[34] CAD A_2 *sub* attaru a) 3′.

[35] CAD L *sub* lāsimu e) and Salonen 1967: 48.

[36] *Zukkizukki* is an Elamite word, the meaning of which is not clear: ElW II *sub* zu-uk-ki.zu-uk-ki translates "Regierung(?)", based on the fact that abstract nouns are formed through reduplication. CAD S *sub* sukkisukki gives "(a class of persons of a certain status)". Considering the context, it seems indeed likely that a particular group of people is meant. Grillot (1987: 85–86) differentiates between *zukkir* and *sunkir*: *sunkir*, "king" in delocutive 3rd person animate singular, derives from the nominal base *sunki*, whereas *zukkir* derives from the nominal base *zukki*, the corresponding verbal base being *zukka*. Since a *zukkir* seems to have been an administrator in Achaemenid Elamite, Grillot (1987: 85) argues to translate *zukkir* in the Middle-Elamite texts as "governor" or "mandatary". In line with this, *zukkizukki* might have been used to designate the "ruling class" or group or class of "government officials" or "civil servants" in the context of the *kubussûm* clause. In MDP 23 206: 31 *zukkizukki* is followed by *ba-bi-*⸢*il* x⸣-[...]. It not clear how to interpret this correctly. According to Scheil (MDP 23: 55) the sign after IL might have been ⸢*ki*⸣-[...]. Unfortunately, collation of the tablet could not give a definitive answer, and it is not clear how many more sings could have followed as the right edge is broken. A possible interpretation is 'bringer/carrier of *ki*-[...]' with *bābil* as a G participle in the construct state from *babālum* (CAD A_1 *sub* abālu), in which case *zukkizukki* is a to be interpreted as a singular collective noun.

našur issued. MDP 23 208: 18′–22′ states that the field has been bought and the silver has been received after the *kubussûm* concerning the [(...)] BALA.MEŠ[37] and the *zukkizukki* that Temti-ḫalki, sukkal, and Kuk-našur issued. MDP 23 209: 4′–9′ states that the field has been bought and the silver has been received after the *kubussûm* concerning the *zukkizukki* that Temti-ḫalki, sukkal, and Kuk-našur issued. MDP 23 208 and 209 refer in all probability to the same *kubbussûm*.

In one wheat loan (MDP 23 181), it is stated that the debtors, seven associates from the city of Madat, received the wheat in the month *šabati* of the BALA URU.DAG,[38] after the *kubussûm* of the inhabitants of Susa (*mārū*(DUMU.MEŠ) *Šušim*) and the *zukkizukki*. The same text adds that they (the debtors) may not appeal to the *kidinnum* and / or *kubuššûm*,[39] a clause known from five other loans.[40] As for MDP 23 181, it is clear that the debtors cannot appeal to the *kidinnum* and / or *kubuššûm* because the contract was concluded after the *kubussûm*. It is not clear whether the same goes for the other loans, as it is not explicitly mentioned they were concluded after a *kubussûm*.

Often the *kubussûm* clause is simply abbreviated as *warki kubussê* or *warki kubussê ša Inšušinak*, which makes it difficult to know which *kubussûm* is meant.

All five texts referring to the *kubbussûm* of Inšušinak are field leases (four of which *esip tabal* leases) in which it is stated that the lessee leased the field, and paid the lease price in case of the *esip tabal* leases, in a particular month from a particular BALA after the *kubussûm* of Inšušinak.[41]

Three of the texts that simply mention *warki kubussê* are also *esip tabal* field leases in which it is stated that the lessee leased the field and paid the lease price in the month *abi* of the BALA GAL after the *kubussûm*.[42] It seems therefore probable that they also refer to the *kubussûm* of Inšušinak. One sale of a field (MDP 23 228) adds at the end after the witnesses and the oath *warki kubbussê*,

---

37 The bala.meš must refer to the three BALA sectors that are known from the BALA formulas (De Graef 2018b: 274–284). As the left margin of the revers is broken, it is not clear if BALA.MEŠ on l. 19′ might have been preceded by one or two signs: [*šà*] BALA.MEŠ *ù zu-uk-ki-zu-uk-ki* or [*šà* x] BALA.MEŠ *ù zu-uk-ki-zu-uk-ki*, especially as we would expect to have a group of people or collective—people responsible for, in charge of or in any other way involved in the BALA sectors?—considering the context.

38 According to Reiner (1973: 100) *šabāti* is the 12th month of the Elamite calendar. Month names are often followed by one of the three BALA-formulas, implying that every BALA had its own calendar, as already suggested by Koschaker (1931: 99 and fn. 4). See also De Graef 2018b: 274–284.

39 MDP 23 181: (21) *ki-di-na ù ku-bu-us-sà-a-am* (22) *ú-ul ú-ma-aḫ-ḫa-ru-šu* "the *kidinnum* and / or the *kubussûm*, they may not appeal (to it)". For *kidinnum* see *infra*.

40 MDP 23 270, 271 and 272, all three business / partnership loans of silver. MDP 24 344, a business loan of silver and barley, has the variant *kidinnam u kubussâm ul išu* 'it has no *kidinnum* and / or *kubussûm*' and MDP 22 28, a *ḫubuttatum* loan of silver, has the variant *ṣulla u kubussâ ul išu* 'it has no *ṣullum* and / or *kubussûm*'.

41 Month *šabāti* of the BALA IGI.URU.KI in MDP 22 103 and 104, month *ḫultuppi* of the BALA IGI.URU.KI in MDP 22 105 and 126, and month *adari* of the BALA IGI.URU.KI in MDP 23 252. According to Reiner (1973: 100) *adari, ḫultuppi* and *šabāti* are respectively the 1st, 11th and 12th months of the Elamite calendar.

42 MDP 23 249, 250 and 251. According to Reiner (1973: 100), *abi* is the 5th month of the Elamite calendar.

which might refer to a *kubussûm* concerning certain professional or social groups issued by two rulers. One rent of a house (MDP 22 84) states that the tenants entered the house in the month *šerʾi-ša-erēši* of BALA URU.DAG[43] after the *kubussûm*, which might refer to a *kubussûm* concerning real estate issued by two rulers.

In sum, there are *kubussûm*'s issued by rulers concerning real estate and particular social groups attested in sales of fields, a rent of a house and a loan of wheat, and *kubussûm*'s issued by gods concerning real estate and the equal status of adopted vs. biological children and siblings, attested in sales of houses, an adoption contract and a litigation. Excepting the litigation MDP 23 321–322 stating Belī's words "according to the *kubussûm* concerning …" (*ina kubbussê ša …*), all other texts have "after the *kubussûm* concerning …" (EGIR or (*w*)*arki kubussê ša …*". It was, in other words, important to add that a sale, rent, lease, loan or adoption / donation was concluded *after* a *kubussûm* was issued. The importance of the posteriority of the conclusion of the contract is even more stressed by adding the month and BALA: the contract was concluded in that particular month of that BALA *after* the issuing of the *kubussûm*. By adding this, the contractors state that the sale, lease rent or loan they participate in, is not subject to the measures demanded by a particular *kubussûm*.

This obviously reminds us to the decrees (*ṣimdatum* or *mīšarum*) issued by the Old Babylonian kings in order to restore the economic balance by cancelling non-commercial debts or returning alienated real estate to their original owners (see in general Renger 2002 and Hudson 2002 with references)—hence the translation of *kubussûm* given in the CAD "regulations concerning the release of private debts" (CAD K *sub* kubussûm 2).

But, can we simply assume that *kubussûm* is the Elamite variant of the Old Babylonian *mīšarum* or *ṣimdat šarrim*? As for the *kubussûm*'s issued by rulers concerning real estate and particular social groups, this might hold true. The *kubussûm*'s issued by gods, however, are problematic. At first, they seem hardly compatible with a temporary economic measure taken by a king only when necessary and consequently at irregular intervals, but on the contrary seem to tend towards a generally valid and timeless custom. This holds especially true for the *kubussûm* stating that equal legal status of adopted vs. biological children and siblings—a custom also known in Mesopotamia—which can hardly have had anything to do with restoring an economic balance. Or can it? The fact that the adoption contract *MDP* 22 3 has "after the *kubussûm* …" (EGIR *kubussê* …) instead of "according to the *kubussûm* …" point at a temporary measure taken by rulers or gods—especially as other adoptions do not mention a *kubussûm*. The fact that temporary measures were taken by gods, such as the *kubussûm* concerning real estate issued by Inšušinak, is, however, very interesting. A possible explanation may lie in the fact that *kubussûm*'s issued by Inšušinak were local Susian decrees—

[43] CAD Š$_2$ sub *šerʾu* d) and Salonen 1967: 87. According to Reiner (1973: 100) *šerʾi-ša-erēši* is the 8th month in the Elamite calendar.

Inšušinak being the patron deity of Susa embodying the Susian authorities[44]—whereas the *kubussûm*'s issued by rulers applied in the entire Sukkalmaḫ state.

However, even if both the Old Babylonian *mīšarum* or *ṣimdat šarrim* and the Elamite *kubussûm* were temporary measures taken by rulers (and in Susa by the patron deity embodying the city authorities), there is no indication whatsoever that the Elamite *kubussûm*'s cancelled debts or returned alienated real estate to their original owners. But then what did the Elamite *kubussûm*'s entail?

Two texts give more information regarding the *kubussûm* and the implications for the contract. MDP 24 355 states the sale of an orchard by Ipquša to Kūbu-rabû, at the end of which is added that should the orchard be smaller or larger, after the *kubussûm*, the buyer will deduct from or add to the silver.[45] This is odd, since it is said that the orchard has been surveyed by the scribe (l. 2: *šiddat ṭupšarrim*(DUB.SAR). The reason for this addition must lie in the fact that the peg of Awīltum had been driven in the property (l. 1b: *sikkatum*(gišGAG) ⸢*šà a-wi-il-tim*⸣) implying that it was pledged. The addition seems to imply that the actual area of the orchard and consequently its price could be subject to change after the *kubussûm*. How should we understand this?

Being a hypothecary pledge, (a part of) the orchard could be claimed by Awīltum in case Ipquša would not be able to redeem, making the field smaller and thus cheaper, but this has nothing to do with the issuing of a *kubussûm*. *MDP* 24 358, another sale of an orchard by Ipquša to Kūbu-rabû, might shed light on the case. At the end of this contract is added that this orchard was assigned (by means of a legal document) in exchange for the orchard of Awīltum after the *kubussûm*.[46] In other words, this orchard is a replacement for another orchard which became the property of Awīltum after the *kubussûm*. Of importance here is that in both sales the orchard is said to have been adjacent to that of Nūratum, implying that both are parts of one and the same larger orchard. One could then hypothesize that Ipquša had a large orchard, a part of which was 'pegged' by Awīltim.[47] He then decided to sell a part of his "pegged" orchard to Kūbu-rabû, adding that after the

[44] Note in this regard the seal belonging to a legal body authorized to deal with claims impressed on MDP 23 242 and 325 in which Inšušinak is called *šarrum*(LUGAL) *ša Šušim* "king of Susa" (see De Graef 2018a: 134–141). The same goes for the *kubussûm* issued by Inšušinak and Išme-kārab mentioned in MDP 23 321–322 on which the seal is impressed of Išme-karāb who is called *šar* (LUGAL) uru*Šušim* "king of Susa" and of whom it is said that he provided the seal with legal power, embodying as such the 'supreme court' (see De Graef 2018a for an analysis of both the seal and the litigation *MDP* 23 321–322).

[45] *MDP* 24 355: (21) *kirûm*(gišKIRI$_6$) *i-ma-ṭì-ma* (22) *kaspam*(KÙ.BABBAR) *i-ḫa-ra-aṣ* (23) *wa-ar-ki ku-bu-ṣe-*[*e*] (24) *i-wa-ti-ir-ma* (25) *kaspam*(KÙ.BABBAR) *ú-ṣa-ab*.

[46] *MDP* 24 358: (20) *wa-ar-ki ku-bu-ṣe-e* (21) *a-na pu-uḫ kirîm*(gišKIRI$_6$) *šà a-we-el-tim* (22) *kirâm*(gišKIRI$_6$) *an-na-am iš-ṭu-ru*.

[47] The reason why the peg of Awīltim has been driven in Ipquša's orchard is not given. As explained by Oers (2010), this was done on three occasions: (1) in case of a loan, the creditor could drive a peg in the property of the debtor until the loan was repaid, (2) in case of sales, the buyer could drive a peg in another property of the seller in case the property sold should be claimed by a third party, and (3) in case of *esip tabal* leases, the lessor could drive a peg in another property of the lessee in case the field he leased should be claimed by a third party. No other documents involving Ipquša and Awīltim are found, so it is impossible to know whether Ipquša lent from Awīltim, sold her a part of his property or leased her a field.

kubussûm the area and price of the orchard could be subject to change. And this was indeed the case, as Kūbu-rabû gets another part of the same orchard later on, in exchange of the earlier part that became property of Awīltim after the *kubussûm*. In other words, *MDP* 23 358 (*pre kubussûm*) replaces *MDP* 23 355 (*post kubussûm*).

It seems thus that a *kubussûm*—in all probability a *kubussûm* concerning real estate, or that part of the *kubussûm* concerning real estate if we assume that the *kubussûm*'s concerning real estate, the *zukkizukki* and the BALA's and *zukkizukki* issued by Temti-ḫalki and Kuk-našur are actually one and the same *kubussûm* covering various issues—settled the situation of pledged property. This is not at all surprising, considering the fact that the act of driving a peg into property, turning it into a hypothecary pledge, was a fairly common practice, not only in case of possible insolvency in loans, but also in case of a hypothetical future claim of real estate by a third party in sales and leases (see Oers 2010). This practice must have resulted in a situation in which the majority of all property was pledged, especially as pledging another property of the seller by the buyer in case of a possible future claim by a third party was not limited in time. Once the majority of all property was pledged, the functioning of the system itself was jeopardized, leading to an economic standstill, and rulers or gods embodying the authorities had to intervene by assigning the pledged property to its legitimate owner, being either the original owner in case there had not been any claim by a third party, or the one who took the property in pledge in case of insolvency of the debtor or a claim by a third party on real estate leased or bought. This might also explain why the actual area of real estate and consequently its price could be subject to change after the *kubussûm*. In a situation where members of the urban elites had each other's property pledged, the decision to assign the pledged property to the legitimate owner at a certain point in time, could either increase or reduce one's estate.

Another hint to the meaning of a *kubussûm* and its implications is given in *MDP* 23 282, a so-called "royal charter" in which Kuk-našur, sukkal of Elam and Šimaški, granted privileges to his servant Sîn-imguranni. The text states that Kuk-našur established the *mašûtum* of his fields and irrigation flows, the fields of the shepherds, soldiers, replacements, nomads and messengers that he has bought for the full price and that, since Temti-agun established a *kubussûm*, and Kuk-našur renewed (it), returned to him.[48] The following important conclusion can be drawn from this text:

---

[48] *MDP* 23 282: (5b) *eqlēt*(A.ŠA$_3$.ḪI.A)-*šu agâ*(A.GE$_5$)-*šu* (6) *eqlēt*(A.ŠA$_3$.ḪI.A) *rēʾî*(SIPA.MEŠ) *rēdî*(AGA.UŠ.MEŠ) *wa-at-ta-ri* (7) *a-mu-ur-ri-i ù la-sí-⸢mi⸣* (8) *šà a-na ší-mi-im ga-am-ri-im i-šà-mu-ma* (9) *iš-tu te-em-ti-a-gu-un ku-bu-⸢us⸣-sà-am* (10) *iš-ku-nu-ú-ma ku-uk-*^{d}*na-šu-úr ú-uš-ší-iš-ma* (11) *ú-ti-ir-šum ma-šu-us-sú iš-ku-un*. I translate *amurrî* here as 'nomads' as it is very improbable that the Amorites (as a people) are meant here. It seems much more likely that the (semi-sedentary) nomads (highlanders? / non-urban population?) are meant here. I choose not to translate *mašûtum* as it is one of those words only attested in texts from Elam the meaning of which is unclear. CAD M$_1$ *sub* mašûtu translates "(freedom from certain legal obligations applicable to landowners)", but unpublished letters from Susa from level A XII (cited in CAD) mention the *mašûtum* of a canal and of fields, contradicting the translation proposed by CAD. The royal charters and the specific terminology used in them are in great need of a thorough study, but awaiting the time to be able to do this and in light of the evidence from the A XII letters, I prefer to interpret *mašussu* in MDP 282: 11 not as "his (i.e. Sîn-imguranni's) *mašûtum*" but as "the *mašûtum* of it (i.e. the land listed)" for now.

1) Kuk-našur renewed a *kubussûm* originally established by Temti-agun.[49] It seems thus very probable that when our texts mention "the *kubussûm* that Temti-ḫalki and Kuk-našur issued", "the *kubussûm* that Temti-ḫalki issued earlier and was now renewed by Kuk-našur" is meant. The same goes for the "the *kubussûm* that Tan-uli and Kuk-našur issued".[50]

2) Kuk-našur, who renewed the *kubussûm* issued earlier by Temti-agun, identifies himself as Sukkal of Elam and Šimaški, which seems to confirm my earlier assumption that *kubussûm*'s issued by rulers applied, or at least could apply, in the entire Sukkalmaḫ state.

3) Because of the renewal of the *kubussûm* by Kuk-našur, fields that Sîn-imguranni bought for the full price, return to him. The fact that they return to him implies that he somehow temporarily lost ownership of them. The fields in question are designated as the fields of particular groups of people (shepherds, soldiers, replacements, nomads and messengers) two of which are known from the *kubussûm* mentioned in MDP 23 206, viz. the one concerning the replacements, messengers and *zukkizukki* issued by Tan-uli and (renewed by) Kuk-našur. One could then hypothesize that private owned land could for some reason be assigned temporarily to particular groups in society but were returned to their original and rightful owner through a *kubussûm*.

In all, it seems that one of the main goals (and results) of a *kubussûm* was the settlement of pledged property (the *kubussûm* concerning houses) and property assigned to (or claimed by the authorities for) particular groups in society (the *kubussûm* concerning particular groups in society) to the legitimate owners. An Elamite *kubussûm* therefore seems to have been something completely different than a Babylonian *mīšarum* or *ṣimdat šarrim*. Indeed, it seems to have met specific needs typical for Elamite economy and society rather than being some kind of clean slate adopted and adapted from Babylonia.

If a *kubussûm* is indeed a typical Elamite custom, the question arises why they "invented" an Akkadian word for it, for it seems indeed to be a perfectly correct Akkadian afformative form derived from the root K-B-S, but it is never attested elsewhere and a translation remains highly problematic. According to GAG §56 o *PuRuSSûm* expresses deliberate activities, giving as an example *rugummûm* "claim" from R-G-M "to claim". However, K-B-S has various meanings in different contexts, but none of them seem to fit the picture, especially as both the noun and

[49] There are two Elamite rulers named Temti-agun: one who ruled at the very beginning of the Sukkalmaḫat (Vallat 2007) and one who ruled probably *ca.* 1700 BC (De Graef 2013c). There are at least three Elamite rulers named Kuk-našur, one of which is a contemporary of king Ammiṣaduqa of Babylon (1646–1626 BC) (Steve – Vallat – Gasche 2002: 383–386). Based on a prosopographal study of the Susa texts, it seems very probable that we are dealing in this text with Temti-agun II and Kuk-našur II or III.

[50] Both Tan-uli and Temti-ḫalki ruled probably between 1675 and 1600 BC (De Graef 2013b and 2013d). The ruler of the name Kuk-našur who renewed the *kubussûm*'s of Tan-uli and Temti-ḫalki is probably one and the same person (Kuk-našur III or IV) who ruled at the very end of the Sukkalmaḫat.

the verb stem from K-B-S: *kubussê ša … ša* DN / RN_1 *u* RN_2 *ikbusu*.[51] On some occasions, *ikbusu* is replaced by *iškunu* "they established, they placed" but this does not make them synonymous. The basic meaning of K-B-S being "to stride, to tread" *kubussâm kabāsum* could be translated as "to surely perform the striding away"[52] (intensified by the *figura etymologica*), but this does not make much sense in the context of our texts.

Maybe the question to be asked here is whether *kubussûm* is an Akkadian word altogether. After all, it is used in an expression together with *kidinnum* (*kidinnam u kubussâm ul umaḫḫar* "they may not appeal to the *kidinnum* or the *kubussûm*") which at first glance appears to be an Akkadian word, but is in reality the "Akkadianized" Elamite word *kitin*, and was later on adopted as loanword in Mesopotamia.[53] Is it possible that also *kubussûm* is an "Akkadianized" Elamite word? Unfortunately, Old-Elamite is hardly known, due to a lack of sources, but could it be possible that the Elamite word *kup* "pledge"[54] is hidden behind the "Akkadian" *kubussûm*—especially as one of the purposes of a *kubussûm* seems to have been the settlement of pledged property? Was it originally a clever wordplay by witty Elamite scribes who created a formal correct Akkadian word in which an Elamite root is hidden by using an existing (but semantically unrelated) Akkadian root, and combined it with the Akkadian verb of the same root to add some extra effect, that got adopted in the legal jargon? For now, these are wild guesses, and it goes without saying that it needs further research, but it is in all not unimaginable. Especially as the aforementioned *kidinnum* is another example of an "Akkadianized" Elamite word, which brings me to the next group of administrative and legal formulas: those containing one or more Elamite words.

Akkadian Formulas with a Typical Elamite Word or Element

In what follows, I will discuss two Elamite words or expressions that are used in legal clauses: *kidinnum*, used in two clauses, and *parputtu* and *parkutu*, used in two variants of one and the same clause.

---

51 CAD K *sub* kabāsu 1. to step into something (unclean) accidentally, 2. to step upon something on purpose, to trample, to crush, defeat an enemy, to bother, to make people do work, to press people, to stamp out a fire, to suppress noise, to make compact, to full cloth, to let time pass, 3. to stride, to walk upon, to pace off, 4. to exert oneself, to put pressure upon a person, to drop a claim, a case, to forgive, pardon a sin. *Sub* 3. CAD also gives "(with *kubussû*) to make regulations to come in" referring to *kubussû* 1. regulations governing legal procedures b) with *kabāsu* and translates the various passages with *kubussâm ikbusu* as "to set up regulations", but this translation of *kabāsum* is clearly based on the assumption that *kubussûm* means "regulations".

52 See in this regard AHw II *sub* kubussûm 1) "Abschreitung (von Grundstücken / Beamten) vornehmen".

53 *AHw* II *sub* kidi / ennu(m) and ElW I *sub* ki-den, kidennu(m), ki-di, ki-di-en, ki-te-en, and ki-tin. See also Leemans 1946.

54 *ElW* I *sub* ku-up mE "Unterpfand (?)" and ku-up-pu-h-ti mE "Ihr habt verpfändet (?)".

Kidinnum

Kidinnum or *kidennum* is used in two legal clauses: the aforementioned
(1) *kidinnam* (or *ṣullam*) *u kubussâm* (*ul*) *umaḫḫar(u)* / *išu*, and
(2) *ša ibbalakkatu rittašu u lišāššu inakkissū kiden Inšušinak ilput imât*

As mentioned above, the first clause is attested in six loan contracts. The loans state that the debtor(s) may not appeal to the *kidinnam* and / or *kubussâm*. One of these loan contracts (MDP 23 181) mentions that the debtors, seven associates from the town of Madat, received the wheat they lent after the *kubussûm* concerning the inhabitants of Susa and the *zukkizukki*. This explains why they cannot appeal to the *kubussûm* but it is not clear how to interpret this. As shown earlier, it seems that one of the main goals (and results) of a *kubussûm* was the settlement of pledged property (the *kubussûm* concerning houses) and property assigned to (or claimed by the authorities for) particular groups in society (the *kubussûm* concerning particular groups in society) to the legitimate owners. It is as yet not clear to me how this could affect the status of a debtor. It thus appears that other measures could be taken by means of a *kubussûm*, about which we are still groping in the dark. In any case, it does not seem to refer to the release of non-commercial debts, similar to the Old Babylonian *mīšarum* decrees as suggested by the translation of the CAD (*sub* kubussûm 2), as five of the six loans in which the clause is mentioned are business loans (and it is not mentioned in the other 25 business loans from Susa). Moreover, it does not explain why they cannot appeal to the *kidinnum* and what that means.

In one of these loans (MDP 22 28), *kidinnam* is replaced by *ṣullam*. Both *kidinnum* and *ṣullum* are being interpreted as some kind of "(divine) protection" (CAD K *sub* kidinnu and CAD Ṣ *sub* ṣullu). Koschaker (1936: 46), followed by Leemans (1946) and Klíma (1963), interpreted the phrase *kidinnum u kubussûm* as expressing both sides of the legal order, viz. the divine order and the profane order, or in other words, divine and profane law. This interpretation does not seem to be fully sustainable though, considering the fact that a *kubussûm* could be issued by one or more gods, as discussed above.

Moreover, the other clause in which the *kidinnum* is mentioned, as well as other attestations of the word in the Susa texts, seem to indicate that a *kidinnum* was (also) a sacred object, and by extension a sacred space, providing divine coverage or protection.

Indeed, the penalty clause stating that "he who breaks the agreement, they will cut off his hand and tongue; because he has touched the *kidinnum* of Inšušinak, he shall die" (*ša ibbalakkatu rittašu u lišāššu inakkissū kiden Inšušinak ilput imât*) is commonly used in economic agreements and legal documents from Susa. The clause is often abbreviated to *kiden Inšušinak ilput* "he has touched the *kidinnum* of Inšušinak" which led to the assumption that the touching of the *kidinnum* being the outcome of the breaking of the agreement, must have implied a violation or desecration and that touching the *kidinnum* was taboo (Hinz 1950 and 1964: 87, but see also ElW I *sub* ki-di-en). As Charpin (2001) has shown, this interpretation is wrong, since touching (violating or desecrating) the *kidinnum* is not the outcome of breaking the agreement, but on the contrary is an act of commitment understood to prevent one from breaking the agreement. By breaking the agreement, one violates or desecrates the *kidinnum* and thus loses divine protection. In one silver loan (MDP 23 273), the *kidinnum* of Inšušinak is replaced by that of Ruḫurater in the (abbreviated) penalty clause.[55] Ruḫurater being the patron deity of Ḫuḫnur (Henkelman 2008) implies that the contract was concluded (and the tablet written) in Ḫuḫnur, which is corroborated by the fact that the silver lent is weighed with the weight stone of the city of Ḫuḫnur.[56]

It is clear from the foregoing that in the context of this clause, the *kidinnum* of Inšušinak should be interpreted as an image or emblem representing this deity which one could touch, especially as MDP 24 337, a division of inheritance between four women (sisters?), adds that "they swore (and) were touching the head of their god"[57] (as already mentioned by Charpin 2001). A similar hypothesis was already suggested by Leemans (1946: 40–41) who saw similarities between the Elamite *kidinnum* and the Babylonian *šurinnum*, a (divine) emblem or standard, used in judicial procedures, among other things.[58]

This is corroborated by the legend of the seal impressed on the litigation MDP 23 321–322, in which the *kidinnum* of Napiriša and Inšušinak is mentioned: "he or his adversary in court, should they contest the agreement again, the *kidinnum* of Napiriša and Inšušinak has been touched upon, and he who shall alter this seal(ed tablet) must go away upon the command of Napiriša and Inšušinak".[59] Since both Napiriša, patron deity of Anšan (de Miroschedji 1980), and Inšušinak, patron deity of Susa, are mentioned, the clause of the seal inscription covers the whole Sukkalmaḫ state, from the capital Anšan to Susa—the fact that Napiriša is mentioned before Inšušinak moreover hints at the supremacy of Anšan over Susa during this period. What is more, the seal has a particular presentation scene featuring a deity represented as worshipper, standing on a platform and facing another much smaller deity, who is holding the rod and ring and sits on a snake throne placed on a platform supported by two snakes whose entwined bodies form a post (see for a drawing and photos De Graef 2018a: 124). The deity sitting on the snake throne—or "god with the snake and spring waters" as he was called by de Miroschedji (1981)—could represent both Napiriša and Inšušinak, even simultaneously. Contrary to "normal" presentation scenes featuring a worshipper and a deity where both are of equal size, the "god with the snake and spring waters" on the seal impressed

[55] MDP 23 273: (8′) *šà ib-ba-la-ak-ka-tu ri-˹ta˺-[šu]* (9′) *ù li-šà-aš-šu i-na-[ki-sú]* (10′) *ki-de-en* ^{d}*ru-ḫu-ra-˹ti˺-[ir il-pu-ut]*.

[56] MDP 23 273: (1) 1/2 ma.na kù.babbar na$_4$ uru^{ki} *ḫu-[uḫ-nu-úr]*. Ḫuḫnur has been identified with Tappeh Bormi by Modifi-Nasrabadi (2005).

[57] MDP 24 337: (12′) *ta-mu-ú qa-aq-qa-ad* (13′) *ì-lí-šu-nu la-ap-tu*.

[58] CAD Š$_3$ *sub* šurinnu 1. For *šurinnum*, see, most recently, Richardson 2012 and Stol 2012, both with references. Note, however, that *šurinnum* (written with the logogram šu.nir) is attested in one Susa text to be dated in the early Sukkalmaḫat, in which it is stated that Atta-ḫušu made a copper *šurinnum*: (1) [*ad*]-˹*da*˺-*ḫu*-[*šu*] (2) *šurinnam*(˹^{urudu}˺ŠU.NIR$^{\text{-a-˹x˺}}$) (3) ˹*i*˺-*pu-uš*-˹*ma*˺.

[59] Seal impressed on MDP 23 321–322: (8b) *šu-ú* (9) *ù be-el di-ni-˹šu˺* (10) *i-tu-ur-ru-ma i-na-ak-ki-ru-šu* (11) ˹*ki*˺-*di-na šà* ^{d}*Napiriša*(GAL) *ù* ˹^{d}*Inšušinak*(MUŠ$_3$.EREN)˺ *la-pi-it* (12) ˹*ù*˺ *šà-a ku-nu-uk-ka an-na-a i-in-˹nu˺* (13) [*i*]-*na a-wa-at* ^{d}˹ *Napiriša*(GAL)˺ *ù* ^{d}˹ *Inšušinak*(MUŠ$_3$.EREN) *li-ṣí*˺, see De Graef 2018a.

on MDP 23 321–322 is small and placed on a platform, implying that he is represented here as an image on a standard, or in other words, that the scene in fact depicts that which is described in the seal inscription, viz. the *kidinnum* of Napiriša and Inšušinak, an image of both deities (depicted as one) on a standard to be touched as an act of commitment (De Graef 2018a: 130–131).

According to Grillot (1973: 139), *kidinnum* is to be understood in the context of legal documents as a place in the sacred domain of a god in which legal acts and ceremonies took place. This is indeed corroborated by some texts in which the *kidinnum* seems to have been a locale. Two sales contracts mention that the contract has been concluded in the *kidinnum* of Inšušinak. MDP 23 211, the sale of a house, states that the buyer bought the house in the *kidinnum* of Inšušinak,[60] without further explanation. However, MDP 23 200, the sale of a field, gives us a glimpse as to why the agreement might have been concluded in the *kidinnum*. The contract describes how the field was inherited within the family during four generations: from Iškur-gugal to his daughter Ubārtu, to her daughter Ramātu to her daughter Waqartu who is the seller. It then states that the field does not belong to Ilum-muttabbil or Ilum-ēriš—who must have been the children of Waqartu—nor their heirs, who will be punished should they claim the field.[61] In other words, Waqartu sells her share of the family estate to an unrelated person, being apparently an exceptional situation, which explains why the sale was concluded in the *kidinnum* of Inšušinak, as special regulations were due in order to safeguard the buyer from possible future claims by the seller's heirs.

Two litigations mention the *kidinnum* of Inšušinak. In MDP 22 160, a litigation concerning the redemption of cattle, it is stated that both parties have come to an agreement before 11 witnesses in Susa, in the *kidinnum* of Inšušinak.[62] MDP 24 391, a litigation concerning Bēlšunu's house, describes a rather peculiar situation: Awīlta, the wife of Iškuppi, is sent up to the *kidinnum* by Inšušinak-umballiṭ and is only allowed to come down after Inšušinak-umballiṭ compensated Bēlšunu's

---

[60] *MDP* 23 211: (9′) ^{I}⸢*mu*⸣*-ti-ia-tu-ù* (10′) *i-na ki-de-en* ^{d}*Inšušinak*(MUŠ$_3$.EREN) (11′) *bītam*(E$_2$.DU$_3$.A) *a-na da-ra-*[*ti*] (12′) ⸢*i*⸣*-šà-am*.

[61] MDP 23 200: (32) *eqlam*(A.ŠA$_3$) *šà* ^{d}IŠKUR-GU.GAL *ma-*⸢*aḫ*⸣*-*[*ru*] (33) ^{d}IŠKUR-GU.GAL *a-na u-bar-ti* (34) *ma-ar*$^{!}$*-ti-šu i-qí-iš-sí* (35) *u-bar-tum a-na ra-ma-at-ti* (36) *ma-ar-ti-šà ta-qí-iš* (37) *ra-ma-a-tum a-na wa-qar-ti* (38) *ma-ar-ti-šà ta-qí-iš* (39) *wa-qar-tum a-na ší-mi ga-*⸢*am*⸣*-*[*ru-ti*] (40) *i-na ki-di-nim šà* ^{d}*Inšuši-nak*(MUŠ$_3$.EREN) (41) *a-na* ^{d}GUL*-a-zi-ir* (42) *ta-di-in* (43) *eqlum*(⸢A⸣.ŠA$_3$) *ù-ul šà ilum*(DINGIR)*-mu-ut-ta-bi-il* (44) ⸢*ú*⸣*-ul šà ilum*(DINGIR)*-e-ri-iš* (45) ⸢*ap*⸣*-lu šà ilum*(DINGIR)*-mu-ut-ta-bi-il* (46) ⸢*ù*⸣ *ilum*(DINGIR)*-e-ri-iš* (47) *eqlum*(A.ŠA$_3$) *nu-ut-tum i-qa-*⸢*bu-ú-ma*⸣ (48) *it-ti re-i it-ti wa-*⸢*at*⸣*-*[*ta-ri*] (49) *i-la-ak i-qa-bu-ú-ma* (50) *i-na a-wa-at ṣi-we-pa-la-*[*ar*]*-/ hu-úh-pa-ak* (51) *ù ku-du-zu-lu-uš* (52) *li-i-ṣí* "The field that Iškur-gugal received, Iškur-gugal bequeathed (it) to Ubārtu, his daughter, Ubārtu bequeathed (it) to Ramātu, her daughter, Ramātu bequeathed (it) to Waqartu, her daughter, Waqartu sold (it) for the full price in the *kidinnu* of Inšušinak to GUL-azir. The field does not belong to Ilum-muttabbil, does not belong to Ilum-ēriš. Should an heir of Ilum-muttabbil or Ilum-ēriš say 'The field is ours', he must go with the shepherds and the replacements. Whomever should say (it), must go away upon the command of Ṣiwepalar-ḫuppak and Kuduzuluš."

[62] MDP 22 160: (35) *maḫar*(⸢IGI⸣) 11 *šībūtim*(AB.MEŠ) *an-nu-ti* (36) ⸢*i-na*⸣ *šu-ší-im i-na ki-de-en* (37) $^{[d]}$*In-šušunak*(⸢MUŠ$_3$.EREN⸣) *im-ta-*⸢*ag*⸣*-ru*.

damage and performed the necessary repair works in his house.[63] The ins and outs of the story are not clear as the interrelation between the three protagonists is not known, but it seems that people could be sent to the *kidinnum* (to perform rituals?) for a longer period. This is corroborated by MDP 24 390 in which a person states in the first person singular that "while he was staying (a first time?) in the *kidinnum* of Šimut, Šimut-ilum cut two of his trees and gave them away, and while he was staying (a second time?) in the *kidinnum* of Šimut, he cut another eight trees and gave them away".[64] The texts does not refer to a specific locality and the cult center of Šimut is as yet unknown (Henkelman 2009).

In sum, we can conclude that there was more than one *kidinnum*. Indeed, it seems that all deities had their own *kidinnum* in their cult center. The penalty clause known from the texts of Susa and Ḫuḫnur shows that a *kidinnum* of a deity was an image or emblem representing the deity which one was supposed to touch as an act of commitment. This is corroborated in text and image by the seal impressed on MDP 23 321-2, in which the *kidinnum* of Napiriša and Inšušinak, an image of both deities (depicted as one) on a standard is to be touched as an act of commitment (De Graef 2018a: 130–131). Some texts show that a *kidinnum* of a deity was also an actual place in which actions could be performed, one could be sent to and one could even stay. This was no doubt the sanctuary in which the standard of the deity was placed, which by extension was given the same name.

Now coming back to the *kidinnam u kubussâm ul umaḫḫar* clause, one could hypothesize it meant that the debtor, should he not be able to repay the creditor, could not settle his case by means of performing a ritual before (or in) the *kidinnum* nor could his pledged property, in case of insolvency, be returned to him by means of a *kubussûm*. In other words, the debtor did not enjoy the protection of the "safety nets" one could normally fall back on in Elamite society.

It is clear that the word *kidinnum* is polysemic: depending on the context in which it is used, it can designate (1) a sacred object, emblem or standard, representing the deity, which was to be touched upon as an act of commitment, providing as such protection for the participants in economic and legal agreements, (2) the sacred space in which the *kidinnum* was located, in which rituals could be performed and people could stay, no doubt also to provide them with divine coverage or protection, and by extension (3) the concept of divine protection provided by a *kidinnum*. Importantly, it was considered necessary to use an Elamite word,

---

[63] MDP 24 391: (2) ⸢I⸣^{d}*Inšušunak*(MUŠ$_3$.EREN)-*um-ba-al-li-iṭ* (3) *a-wi-il-ta aš-ša-at iš-ku-up-pi* (4) *i-na ki-di-ni ú-še-la-am-ma* (…) (9b) ^{Id} *Inšušunak*(MUŠ$_3$.EREN)-*um-ba-li-iṭ* (10) *kaspam*(KÙ.BABBAR) *šà daltim*(^{giš}IG) *i-šà-aq-qa-al* (11) *ù mi-it-ḫa-ra* ^{d}*Inšušunak*(MUŠ$_3$.EREN)-*um-ba-li-*[*iṭ*] (12) *ú-ṣa-al-la-al* (13) *ù pa-pa-ḫa ṭì-da-am i-šà-ka-an* (…) (21) [x] *an-na i-pu-*[*šà*]-⸢*am*⸣-*ma* (22) ⸢*a*⸣-*wi-il-ta iš-tu ki-di-ni* (23) *ú-še-ri-da* "Inšušinak-muballiṭ has sent Awilta, wife of Iškuppu, up to the *kidinnu* (…) Inšušinak-muballiṭ must pay the silver for the door, and Inšušinak-muballiṭ must roof the *mitḫara*-room, and he must place plaster in the *papaḫu*-room (…) when he has done this, he let Awilta come down from the *kidinnu*."

[64] MDP 24 390: (1) [*a*]-*na-ku* [*i*]-*na ki-de-*⸢*en*⸣ [^{d}*ší-mu-ut*] (2) *aš-ba-ku-ma* (3) 2 *i-ṣi-ia ik-ki-is-ma* (4) *a-na ì-lí-šukkalum*(SUKKAL) *id-di-in* (5) *i-na ki-de-en* ^{d}*ší-mu-ut aš-ba-ku-ma* (6) 8 *i-ṣi-ia ik-ki-is* (7) *napḫar*(ŠU.NÍGIN) 10 *iṣī*(GIŠ.ḪI.A) (8) *šà* ^{d}*ší-mu-ut-ilum*(DINGIR) (9) *ik-ki-sú-ma* (10) *a-na a-wi-li-ia id-di-nu*.

kiten, for lack of an Akkadian equivalent, implying it was a not just an image, an emblem or a sanctuary, but an ingrained and inherent Elamite concept. Remarkably, though, instead of simply using the Elamite word, they "Akkadianized" the word to fit the otherwise Akkadian context.

Ina muḫḫi parputtu šebir & ina muḫḫi parkutu šebret

Ina muḫḫi [cattle/flock] *parputtu šebir* and its variant *ina muḫḫi* [cattle/flock] *parkutu šebret* "over [cattle/flock] the *parputtu* / *parkutu* is broken" appear in eight loan contracts from Susa. Until recently, we were groping in the dark about the origin and meaning of the words *parputtu* and *parkutu*.[65] Recently, a new hypothesis has been proposed by Oers (2019). According to her, both words are in fact Elamite words, each composed of two elements: *par* "offspring, seed" (ElW I *sub* pa-ar) in first position, and respectively *putu* "small goat" (ElW I *sub* pu-tú) and *kutu* "cow" (ElW I *sub* ku-tu) in second position. In other words, *parputtu* is the offspring of a goat, or a kid, and *parkutu* the offspring of a cow, or calf. As the clause always follows "until he (i.e. the debtor) returns/pays the silver/barley wheat", Oers (2019) interprets the breaking of a kid or calf over the cattle and flock as a way of marking the cattle and flock of the debtor as a hypothecary pledge, parallel with the driving in of a peg in property in order to pledge it. She tentatively suggests that the back of the pledged animals was marked with the blood of the "broken" young, which would have a temporary visual effect. However, it also might have been a mere symbolic act or rite in the presence of witnesses, as its recording in the written contract was decisive, and it is hard to understand why a (probably valuable) young animal had to be sacrificed to mark the rest of the herd. Oers (2019) gives as an alternate possible explanation that the "breaking" could refer to an interruption of the marking of the young animals, whose status would thus be undetermined, awaiting repayment (and allowing their marking by the debtor) or not (allowing their marking by the creditor) of the debt for which they were pledges.

Conclusions

The examples discussed above clearly show that the administrative and legal formulas attested in documentary texts from Sukkalmaḫ Susa were not simply adopted from Mesopotamia and adapted to local use. The use of Akkadian terms in a different meaning and/or context, the development of new formulas, the formation of new words in Akkadian and the introduction of Elamite expressions seems to imply that we are dealing with a primarily Elamite society that developed its own idiom and register.

Striking is their preference for compound or double and often almost pleonastic expressions: *ina ṭūbātīšu ina narʾamātīšu, ana dūr u pala, ana esip tabal, kidinnum*

---

65 CAD P *sub* parputtu (or *parbuttu, parkuttu*) '(an object representing ownership) OB Elam; foreign word(?) and AHw II *sub parputtum, parkuttum* (elam. Fw.) ein Stab?? aB Susa.

u kubussûm and so forth. Might this be a typical Elamite way of expressing things? It seems that by combining each time two similar but not equal terms, such as *ṭūbum* "goodness, good will" and *narāmum* "love, free will", by combining two aspects of the same concept, such as *dūrum* "continuity, unlimited time" and *palûm* "circularity, limited time", they seek to grasp the ideal of totality. The urge to make complementary yet perfectly parallel pairs seems to have been particularly large, also formally, as they "invent" a feminine plural form of *narāmum* (*nar'amātum*)—otherwise never attested in Akkadian—to match the feminine plural of *ṭūbātum*.

The same might go for the pair *kidinnum u kubussûm*, each representing different yet complementary aspects of the concept of protection. Remarkably, when they introduce an Elamite word, such as *kitin*, they often "Akkadianize" the word by adding a case ending, in order to fit the otherwise Akkadian context. The question is whether this kind of "Akkadianization" was only expressed in writing or also in the spoken language. Most likely, this was limited to the writing, as it would have been rather odd for a speaker of Elamite to use the artificially "Akkadianized" *kidinnum* instead of the correct *kitin*. In other words, it seems that one wrote *ki-di-nam* but read *kitin* (or however the Old-Elamite pronunciation of this word might have been). One could thus argue that *ki-di-nam* was an Akkadograph for *kitin.* Thinking along the same line, this might have been the case for more words and phrases. Indeed, as suggested above, *kubussûm* might also be an "Akkadianized" Elamite word or an artificially created word based on an existing (but semantically unrelated) Akkadian root resonating the Elamite word *kup*, in which case *ku-bu-us-sà-am* could have been an Akkadograph for the Elamite word in question (*kup*-something).

The traces, echoes and resonances of Elamite terms in the formally Akkadian-looking texts appear to have been much more widely spread than previously thought: not only the inexplicable terms, such as until recently *parputtu* and *parkutu*, are in fact Elamite words, but also the formally correct Akkadian words can hide Elamite roots. It is all the more unfortunate that the Old-Elamite language is so little known, as it would certainly give a much greater insight into the mixed language of this legal and administrative jargon developed in the Sukkalmaḫ State.

Especially Elamite terms and concepts from the religion or religious sphere, possibly linked to the rites and spells used in customary law, find their way in this mixed language. Klíma (1963: 300–301) already noticed this, but he assumed that they were remnants of an older (i.e. non-Akkadian but Elamite) legal tradition that resisted within an "Akkadianized" society. Once one abandons the myth of the "Akkadianization", the reality is much simpler: these texts reflect Elamite society and Elamite traditions but cast in a written Akkadian mould.

Most striking, however, is the fact that some of those "Akkadianized" Elamite words, concepts and expressions seem to have found their way to Babylonia, such as the word *kidinnum,* which was originally "Akkadianized" by the Elamites to fit the written Akkadian context, and later adopted as such in Mesopotamia. The same might hold true for the concept of the *esip tabal* lease practice. Who was the stranger in that case? It is you, my love, you, who are the stranger.

References

Algaze, H., 1989. The Uruk Expansion: Cross-cultural Exchange in Early Mesopotamian Civilization. *CA* 30, 571–608.

Amiet, P., 1992. Sur l'histoire élamite. *IrAnt* 27, 76–94.

Blažek, V., 1999. Elam: a bridge between Ancient Near East and Dravidian India? In R. Blench – M. Spriggs, eds., *Archaeology and Language IV. Language Change and Cultural Transformation*. London – New York: Routledge, 48–78.

Braarvig, J. – M.J. Geller, eds., 2018. *Multilingualism, Lingua Franca and Lingua Sacra*. Max Planck Research Library for the History and Development of Knowledge Studies 10. Berlin: Max Planck Institute for the History of Science.

Charpin, D., 2001. Manger l'*asakkum* en Babylonie et toucher le *kidinnum* à Suse. *N.A.B.U.* 2001/54.

Charpin, D., 2004. Histoire politique du Proche-Orient Amorrite (2002–1595). In D. Charpin – D.O. Edzard – M. Stol, *Mesopotamien. Die altbabylonische Zeit*. OBO 160/4. Fribourg – Göttingen: Academic Press – Vandenhoeck & Ruprecht, 25–480.

Charpin, D., 2012 Mari à l'école d'Ešnunna: écriture, langue, formulaires. In C. Mittermayer – S. Ecklin, eds., mu-ni u$_4$ ul-li$_2$-a-aš ĝa$_2$-ĝa$_2$-de$_3$. *Altorientalische Studien zu Ehren von Pascal Attinger*. OBO 256. Fribourg – Göttingen: Academic Press – Vandenhoeck & Ruprecht, 119–138.

Charpin, D., 2013. «Ainsi parle l'empereur»: à propos de la correspondance des *sukkalmah*. In K. De Graef – J. Tavernier, eds., *Susa and Elam. Archaeological, Phililogical, Historical and Geographical Perspectives.* MDP 58. Leiden – Boston: Brill, 341–353.

Charpin, D., 2016. Quelques aspects du multilinguisme dans la Mésopotamie antique. In J.-L. Fournet – J.-M. Mouton – J. Paviot, eds., *Civilisations en transition (II): sociétés multilingues à travers l'histoire du Proche-Orient. Actes du Colloque Scientifique Internationale 3-4-5 septembre 2015.* Byblos: UNESCO/CISH, 11–36.

Charpin, D. – J.-M. Durand, 1991. La suzeraineté de l'empereur (*sukkalmaḫ*) d'Élam sur la Mésopotamie et le 'nationalisme' amorrite. In L. De Meyer – H. Gasche, eds., *Mésopotamie et Élam: actes de la XXXVIème rencontre assyriologique internationale, Gand, 10–14 juillet 1989.* Mesopotamian History and Environment Occasional Publications 1. Ghent: University of Ghent, 59–66.

De Graef, K., 2007. Les textes de V récent du chantier B à Suse (fin Sukkalmaḫat – ca. 1575-1530 av. notre ère). *IrAnt* 52, 41–59.

De Graef, K., 2012. Dual Power in Susa: Chronicle of a Transitional Period from Ur III via Šimaški to the Sukkalmaḫs. *BSOAS* 75, 525–546.

De Graef, K., 2013a. The Use of Akkadian in Iran. In D.T. Potts, ed., *The Oxford Handbook of Ancient Iran*. Oxford: Oxford University Press, 263–282.

De Graef, K., 2013b. Tan-Uli. *RlA* 13, 445.

De Graef, K., 2013c. Tem(p)ti-Agun. *RlA* 13, 584–585.

De Graef, K., 2013d. Tempti-ḫalki, *RlA* 13, 585–586.

De Graef, K., 2015. Susa in the Late 3rd Millennium: From a Mesopotamian Colony to an Independent State (MC 2110-1980). In W. Sallaberger – I. Schrakamp, eds., *ARCANE 3: History and Philology*. Turnhout: Brepols, 289–296.

De Graef, K., 2018a. The Seal of an Official or an Official Seal? The Use of Court Seals in Old Babylonian Susa and Haft Tepe. *JAOS* 138, 121–142.

De Graef, K., 2018b. In Susa's Fields. On the Topography of Fields in Old Babylonian Administrative Documents from Susa. In J. Tavernier – E. Gorris – K. Abraham – V. Boschloos, eds., *Topography and Toponymy in the Ancient Near East. Perspectives and Prospects*. PIOL 71. Leuven: Peeters, 267–311.

De Graef, K., 2019. The Powers That Be. On the Institutionalization and Political Structure of the Early Sukkalmaḫ Regime. In K. Maekawa, ed., *Ancient Iran: New Perspectives in Archaeology and Cuneiform Studies. Proceedings of the International Colloquium Held at the Center for Eurasian Cultural Studies, Kyoto University, December 6-7, 2014*. Ancient Text Sources of the National Museum of Iran 2. Teheran: National Museum of Iran (*in press*).

De Miroschedji, P., 1980. Le dieu élamite Napirisha. *RA* 74, 129–143.

De Miroschedji, P., 1981. Le dieu élamite au serpent et aux eaux jaillissantes. *IrAnt* 16, 1–25.

De Meyer, L., 1962. *L'Accadien des contrats de Suse*. Suppléments à Iranica Antiqua 1. Leiden: Brill.

De Meyer, P., 2001. Un meurtre à Suse. In W.H. van Soldt – J.G. Dercksen – N.J.C. Kouwenberg – Th.J.H. Krispijn, eds., *Veenhof Anniversary Volume. Studies Presented to Klaas R. Veenhof on the Occasion of his Sixty-fifth Birtday*. PIHANS 89. Leiden: NINO, 31–38.

Desset, F., 2018. Linear Elamite writing. In J. Alvarez-Mon – G.-P. Basello – Y. Wicks, eds., *The Elamite World*. Abington: Taylor and Francis, 397–415.

Durand, J.-M., 2013. La «suprématie Élamite» sur les Amorrites. Réexamen, vingt ans après la XXXVIe *RAI*. In K. De Graef – J. Tavernier, eds., *Susa and Elam. Archaeological, Phililogical, Historical and Geographical Perspectives.* MDP 58. Leiden – Boston: Brill, 329–339.

Emberling, G., 1995. *Ethnicity and the State in Early Third Millennium Mesopotamia*. PhD dissertation University of Michigan.

Foster, B.R., 1982. Ethnicity and Onomastics in Sargonic Mesopotamia. *Or NS* 51, 297–354.

Gasche, H., 2013. Transferts culturels de la Babylonie vers Suse au milieu du 2e millénaire av. n. ère. In K. De Graef – J. Tavernier, eds., *Susa and Elam. Archaeological, Philological, Historical and Geographical Perspectives.* MDP 58. Leiden – Boston: Brill, 71–82.

Gershevitch, I., 1979. The Alloglottography of Old Persian. *Transactions of the Philological Society* 77/1, 114–190.

Glassner, J.-J., 1996. Les temps de l'histoire en Mésopotamie. In A. de Pury – T. Römer – J.-D. Macchi, eds., *Israël construit son histoire*. Genève: Labor et fides, 167–189.

Glassner, J.-J., 2001. Le devin historien en Mésopotamie. In T. Abusch – P.-A. Beaulieu – J. Huehnergard – P. Machinist – P. Steinkeller, eds., *Historiography in the Cuneiform World. Proceedings of the XLVe Rencontre Assyriologisue Internationale*. Bethesda: CDL Press, 181–193.

Grillot, F., 1973. La postposition génitive -na en élamite. *CahDAFI* 3, 115–169.

Grillot, F., 1987. Notes à propos des bases élamites zukki – zukka. *CahDAFI* 8, 85–88.

Grillot, F. – F. Vallat, 1984. Dédicace de Šilhak-Inšušinak à Kiririša. *IrAnt* 19, 21–29.

Henkelman, W., 2008. Ruḫurater. *RlA* 11, 449.

Henkelman, W., 2009. Šimut. *RlA* 12, 511–512.

Hinz, W., 1950. Elamisch. *Or NS* 18, 282–306.

Hinz, W., 1964. *Das Reich Elam*. Stuttgart: Kohlhammer.

Hudson, M., 2002. Reconstructing the Origins of Interest-Bearing Debt and the Logic of Clean Slates. In M. Hudson – M. Van De Mieroop, eds., *Debt and Economic Renewal in the Ancient Near East*. International Scholars Conference on Ancient Near Eastern, Economies 3. Bethesda, MA: CDL Press, 7–58.

Ingham, B., 1994. Ethno-linguistic links between southern Iraq and Khuzistan. In K. McLachlan, ed., *The Boundaries of Modern Iran*. London – New York: Routledge, 93–100.

Klíma, J., 1963. Le droit élamite au IIme millénaire av. n. è. et sa position envers le droit babylonien. *ArOr* 31, 287–309.

Koschaker, P., 1935. Göttliches und weltliches Recht nach den Urkunden aus Susa. *Or NS* 4, 38–80.

Kogan, L.E. – N. Koslova – S. Loesov – S. Tischenko, eds., 2010. *Proceedings of the 53e Rencontre Assyriologique Internationale, Vol. 1. Part 2. Language in the Ancient Near East.* Babel und Bibel 4/2. Winona Lake, IN: Eisenbrauns.

Lambert, M., 1971. Investiture de fonctionaires en Élam. *JA* 259, 217–221.

Lambert, W.G., 1991. The Akkadianization of Susiana under the Sukkalmaḫs. In L. De Meyer – H. Gasche, eds., *Mésopotamie et Élam. Actes de la XXXVIe Rencontre Assyriologique Internationale, 10-14 juillet 1989*. Mesopotamian History and Environment. Occasional Publications 1. Ghent: Ghent University, 53–57.

Leemans, W.F., 1946. Kidinnu: Un symbole de droit divin babylonien. In M. David – B.A. Van Groningen, eds., *Symbolae ad jus et historiam antiquitatis pertinentes Julio Christiano Van Oven dedicatae*. Leiden: Brill, 36–61.

Malayeri, M., 2014. *Schülertexte aus Susa*. PhD dissertation, Eberhard Karls Universität Tübingen.

Malbran-Labat, F., 1996. Akkadien, bilingues et bilinguisme en Élam et à Ougarit. In F. Briquel-Chatonnet, ed., *Mosaïque de langues, mosaïque culturelle. Le bilinguisme dans le Proche-Orient ancien. Actes de la Table-Ronde du 18 novembre 1995, organisée par l'URA 1062 «Etudes Sémitiques»*. Antiquités Sémitiques 1. Paris: Maisonneuve, 33–61.

Mofidi-Nasrabadi, B., 2005. Eine Steininschrift des Amar-Suena aus Tappeh Bormi (Iran). *ZA* 95, 161–171.

Mofidi-Nasrabadi, B. 2018. Who was "^{d}MÙŠ.EREN.EŠŠANA.DINGIR.MEŠ"? In B. Mofidi-Nasrabadi – D. Prechel – A. Pruß, eds., *Elam and its Neighbors. Recent Research and New Perspectives. Proceedings of the International Congress Held at Johannes Gutenberg University Mainz, September 21-23, 2016*. Elamica 8. Hildesheim: Verlag Franzbecker, 113–126.

Oers, L., 2010. A Round Peg in a Square Hole? The *Sikkatu* in Old Babylonian Susa. *Akkadica* 131, 121–143.

Oers, L., 2013. To Invest in Harvest. Field Leases in Old Babylonian Susa. *ZAR* 19, 155–169.

Oers, L., 2019 Broken Young. *Parputtu* and *parkutu* in Old Babylonian Susa. *RA* 113 (*in press*).

Peyronel, L., 2013. Elam and Eshnunna: Historical and Archaeological Interrelations during the Old Babylonian Period. In K. De Graef – J. Tavernier, eds., *Susa and Elam. Archaeological, Philological, Historical and Geographical Perspectives.* MDP 58. Leiden – Boston: Brill, 51–70.

Potts, T.F., 1994. *Mesopotamia and the East: An Archaeological and Historical Study of Foreign Relations ca. 3400-2000 B.C.* Oxford: University of Oxford Press.

Potts, D.T., 2016. *The Archaeology of Elam. Formation and Transformation of an Ancient Iranian State (second edition)*. Cambridge: Cambridge University Press.

Reiner, E., 1973. Inscription from a Royal Elamite Tomb. *AfO* 24, 87–102.

Renger, J., 2002. Royal Edicts of the Old Babylonian Period. Structural Background. In M. Hudson – M. Van De Mieroop, eds., *Debt and Economic Renewal in the Ancient Near East*. International Scholars Conference on Ancient Near Eastern, Economies 3. Bethesda, MA: CDL Press, 139–162.

Richardson, S., 2012. "The Crowns of Their bābtum": On Wives, Wards, and Witnesses. *JAOS* 132, 623–639.

Roth, M., 1997. *Law Collections from Mesopotamia and Asia Minor (second edition)*. WAW 6. Atlanta, GA: Scholars Press.

Rubio, G., 2006. Writing in Another Tongue: Alloglottography in the Ancient Near East. In S.L. Sanders, ed., *Margins of Writing, Origins of Cultures.* OIS 2. Chicago: Oriental Institute of the University of Chicago, 33–70.

Salonen, E., 1962. *Untersuchungen zur Schrift und Sprache des Altbabylonisch von Susa*. StOr 27. Helsinki: Societas Orientalis Fennica.

Salonen, E., 1967. *Glossar zu den altbabylonischen Urkunden aus Susa*. StOr 36. Helsinki: Societas Orientalis Fennica.

Selz, G., 1991. "Elam" und "Sumer" — Skizze einer Nachbarschaft nach inschriftlichen Quellen der vorsargonischen Zeit. In L. De Meyer – H. Gasche, eds., *Mésopotamie et Élam: actes de la XXXVIème rencontre assyriologique internationale, Gand, 10-14 juillet 1989*. Mesopotamian History and Environment Occasional Publications 1. Ghent: University of Ghent, 27–43.

Steinkeller, P., 2007. New Light on Šimaški and Its Rulers. *ZA* 97, 215–232.

Steinkeller, P., 2013. Puzur-Inšušinak at Susa: A Pivotal Episode of Early Elamite History Reconsidered. In K. De Graef – J. Tavernier, eds., *Susa and Elam. Archaeological, Phililogical, Historical and Geographical Perspectives.* MDP 58. Leiden – Boston: Brill, 293–317.

Steinkeller, P., 2014. On the Dynasty of Šimaški: Twenty Years (or so) After. In M. Kozuh – W.F.M. Henkelman – C.E. Jones – C. Woods, eds., *Extraction and Control. Studies in Honor of Matthew W. Stolper*. SAOC 68. Chicago: The Oriental Institute of the University of Chicago, 287–296.

Steinkeller, P., forthcoming. *The Grand Strategy of the Ur III Empire: Babylonia's Foreign Policy and Territorial Expansion at the End of the Third Millennium BC.*

Steve, M.-J. – F. Vallat – H. Gasche, 2002. Suse. *DB Suppl.* 73, 359–512.

Stol, M., 2012. Renting the Divine Weapon as Prebend. In T. Boiy – J. Bretschneider – A. Goddeeris – H. Hameeuw – G. Jans – J. Tavenier, eds., *The Ancient Near East, A Life! Festschrift Karel Van Lerberghe*. OLA 220. Leuven: Peeters, 561–583.

Szlechter, E., 1953. Les tablettes juridiques datées du règne d'Abî-ešuḫ conservées au Musée d'art et d'histoire de Genève. *JCS* 7, 81–99.

Tavernier, J., 2010. Migration des savoirs entre l'Élam et la Mésopotamie. *RANT* 7, 199–222.

Tavernier, J., 2018. Multilingualism in the Elamite Kingdoms and the Achaemenid Empire. In J. Braarvig – M.J. Geller, eds., *Multilingualism, Lingua Franca and Lingua Sacra.*

Max Planck Research Library for the History and Development of Knowledge Studies 10. Berlin: Max Planck Institute for the History of Science, 307–320.

Vallat, F., 2007. Temti-Agun I. Un nouveau Sukkalmaḫ. *Akkadica* 128, 73–84.

Van Lerberghe, K. – G. Voet, 1994. An Old Babylonian Clone. In H. Gasche – M. Tanret – C. Janssen – A. Degraeve, eds., *Cinquante-deux reflexions sur le Proche-Orient ancien offertes en homage à Léon De Meyer*. MHEO II. Leuven: Peeters, 159–168.

Von Dassow, E., 2004. Canaanite in Cuneiform. *JAOS* 124, 641–674.

Von Dassow, E., 2010. Peripheral Akkadian Dialects, or Akkadography of Local Languages? In L.E. Kogan – N. Koslova – S. Loesov – S. Tischenko, eds., *Proceedings of the 53e Rencontre Assyriologique Internationale, Vol. 1. Part 2. Language in the Ancient Near East*. Babel und Bibel 4/2. Winona Lake: Eisenbrauns, IN, 895–924.

Zadok, R., 1983. A Tentative Structural Analysis of Elamite Hypocoristica. *BzN* 18, 93–120.

Zadok, R., 1984. *The Elamite Onomasticon*. Annali Suppl. 40/3. Napoli: Instituto Universitario Orientale.

Zadok, R., 1987. Peoples from the Iranian Plateau in Babylonia during the Second Millennium B.C. *Iran* 25, 1–26.

Zadok, R., 1991. Elamite Onomastics. *SEL* 8, 225–237.

A RELUCTANT SERVANT: UGARIT UNDER FOREIGN RULE DURING THE LATE BRONZE AGE

Elena Devecchi (University of Turin)*

Since their first discoveries, the epigraphic finds from Ugarit (modern Ras Shamra) provided a unique insight into the relationship between the Hittite kingdom and one of its most important Syrian vassals. These texts constitute an exceptional corpus, because Ugarit is the only Hittite vassal whose archives cover its political history in such great detail and for the whole period of Hittite domination. The texts found at Ḫattuša, the Hittite capital, contribute very little to our knowledge of Ugarit, and the few references to Ugarit that do appear in the Hittite texts are of little use in reconstructing the relationship between that city and Ḫatti;[1] conversely, other Hittite vassals (in Syria as well as in Anatolia) are amply represented in the documents from Ḫattuša, but often we have no sources from the vassals themselves. Indeed, if Ugarit's archives had not been discovered, we would barely know that it was part of the Hittite kingdom, not only because of the paucity of references to the city in Hittite textual sources, but also because Hittite dominion over Ugarit is not reflected in the material culture of the site, where objects of possible Anatolian origin are extremely rare (Genz 2006; Glatz 2013: 36–43).

The recent publication of Akkadian texts discovered in the so-called "House of Urtenu" (Lackenbacher – Malbran-Labat 2016) adds valuable information on the interaction between Ugarit and Ḫatti in the final phase of the Late Bronze Age. The new evidence reinforces the impression that the last kings of Ugarit regularly tried to shirk their obligations towards their Hittite suzerains and at the same time provides a different historical framework for some events known from earlier textual finds, altogether allowing a better understanding of the occasions on which the kings of Ugarit showed insubordinate behaviour and of the Hittite response.

Even though this contribution focuses on the last decades of Ugarit's history in the second half of the 13th century BC, it will be useful to quickly recall its earlier history as a Hittite vassal in order to appreciate how the interaction between subordinate and overlord changed over time.

---

* This paper was written within the framework of the PRIN-project (2015) "L'Anatolia antica: politiche imperiali e culture locali tra XV e VII secolo a.C. Problemi di etnicità, assetti urbani e territoriali, tradizione e innovazione".

[1] Ugarit is attested only in the following handful of Hittite texts: KBo 1.10+: letter of Ḫattusili III to Kadašman-Enlil II (CTH 172); KBo 16.39+: fragment of a historical text (CTH 215); KUB 26.66: inventory of metals, tools, and weapons (CTH 242); KUB 42.84: acknowledgment of receipt (CTH 247); KUB 15.35+ and KBo 35.170: ritual for Ištar of Nineveh (CTH 716); KUB 15.34: evocation ritual (CTH 483).

Ugarit became part of the Hittite empire around 1330 BC, in the wake of Suppiluliuma I's military campaigns that led the Hittites to overpower the kingdom of Mittani, previously the leading power in the area, and then conquer northern Syria. At that time, Niqmaddu II (ca. 1350–1315 BC) was on the throne of Ugarit. We do not know the details of the Hittite conquest of his kingdom, since the documents recovered in the "international archive" of Ugarit's royal palace inform us only of the events that followed Ugarit's subjugation, not of those that led to it.[2] It seems, however, that Ugarit did not resist the Hittites and remained loyal to its new overlord even when a group of neighbouring Syrian kings (the kings of Mukiš, Nuḫašše, and Niya)[3] revolted against Suppiluliuma and, by invading Ugarit, tried to involve Niqmaddu in the rebellion. However, Niqmaddu refused to participate and his loyalty was rewarded by Suppiluliuma, who issued edicts granting Niqmaddu territories on the border with Mukiš as well as the right to retain fugitives who might have entered his country from Mukiš and Nuḫašše (Devecchi 2012: 640–643; 2013: 85–87).

Little is known about the rule of Ar-Ḫalba (ca. 1315–1313 BC), Niqmaddu II's successor. To explain his presumably very short reign, it has been suggested that he had been plotting against Ḫatti at the time of the Egyptian-supported rebellion of the Syrian vassals during the reign of Muršili II and therefore was deposed relatively soon after his accession (Singer 1999: 637–638). A travertine vase bearing the name of Horemheb discovered at Ugarit (RS 17.420+17.421) has been traditionally interpreted as evidence supporting Ugarit's alliance with Egypt and its involvement in the rebellion (Lagarce 2008: 268–269, 274–275). However, it is possible that Ḫatti and Egypt were at peace during at least part of Horemheb's reign, thus one should at least consider the possibility that Horemheb's vase reached Ugarit during such a period (Devecchi – Miller 2011: 145–146). In that case, its presence at Ugarit would be an indication that the coastal kingdom was naturally exploiting this favourable situation and entertaining friendly relations with a Hittite ally (Devecchi 2015: 120). Lastly, there is no conclusive evidence supporting Ugarit's involvement in the rebellion and, as Itamar Singer suggested, "Ar-ḫalba's prompt disappearance could simply have been caused by non-political circumstances, such as sudden illness and death" (Singer 1999: 638).

As far as we know, Niqmepa, the next king of Ugarit (ca. 1313–1260 BC), remained loyal to the Hittites throughout his entire reign. He was a contemporary of no less than four Hittite kings (Mursili II, Muwatalli II, Mursili III, and Ḫattusili III), none of whom seems to have had reason to complain about his behaviour. Most importantly, Niqmepa was ready to fight alongside the Hittites on the occasion of the crucial battle of Qadeš against Egypt (see Singer 1999: 644 with n. 122).

---

[2] For this dating of the documents issued by Suppiluliuma I for Niqmaddu II, see Devecchi 2013 with references to previous literature.

[3] Referred to either as "the kings of Nuḫašše and the king of Mukiš" (CTH 45 and 47) or by their personal names: Itūr-Addu, king of Mukiš, Addu-Nīrārī, king of Nuḫašše, and Aki(t)-Teššup, king of Niya (CTH 46).

While the interaction between Ugarit and Ḫatti seems to have been relatively easy and smooth during the first decades of Hittite dominance, towards the mid of the 13th century BC the relationship between vassal and overlord starts to fray.

A certain disregard for Hittite authority is first shown by Ammistamru II (ca. 1260–1235 BC), who had a relatively long reign towards the mid-13th century BC and was a contemporary of Ḫattusili III and Tutḫaliya IV. This is witnessed by an episode recorded in two Akkadian letters sent by Takuḫli, a representative of Ugarit at the court of Karkemiš, to his master, who is simply addressed as the king of Ugarit but with all likelihood should be identified with Ammistamru II.[4] In the first letter (RS 17.383),[5] Takuḫli complains to his lord about the dispatch of a load of inferior stone instead of genuine lapis lazuli to the king of Karkemiš, who is infuriated:

> (10–11)What is this matter you repeatedly wrote about to the king (of Karkemiš), saying: (12)"Herewith I sent you some lapis lazuli"? (13)The king became very angry (14)and took it out on me, saying: (15–17)"Is this (man) not making fun of me? He picked up some *kammu*-stone from the ground (18–20)and sent it to me saying 'Herewith I sent you some lapis lazuli'!" (…) (28–29)Now, find from somewhere lapis lazuli and send it to the king: (30–31)may the king not become (even more) angry towards my lord![6]

Takuḫli subsequently sends a second message urging his lord to look for some lapis lazuli (RS 17.422),[7] noting that the king of Karkemiš is very upset but a shipment of lapis lazuli would restore Ammistamru to his good graces. Interestingly, Takuḫli stresses that "until now, they have not been unfriendly to me in the Land of Ḫatti" and implores his lord to save him from the embarrassment this situation is causing him.

This episode is representative of a rather contemptuous attitude on the part of the king of Ugarit towards the king of Karkemiš, who was the highest Hittite authority in Syria. This is quite surprising, considering that Ammistamru II was the protagonist of a serious diplomatic incident that must have put him in a rather awkward position within the Hittite empire. I refer to Ammistamru's well-known decision to divorce the so-called "fille de la Grande Dame", who was a daughter of Bentešina, the king of Amurru, and of the Hittite princess Gassuliyawiya, therefore a direct descendant of the Hittite royal family. This issue is the subject of a number of documents exchanged between Ugarit, Amurru, Karkemiš, and Ḫatti, which testify to the great trouble that it must have caused for all involved parties (Kühne 1973; Arnaud – Salvini 1991–1992; Singer 1999: 680–681). At last, the conflict was resolved in favour of Ammistamru with the endorsement of the Hittite authorities, who probably were mainly concerned about the mutual relations of

---

[4] On the career of Takuḫli(nu) and the synchronism with Ammistamru II, see Singer 2011b: 152ff.

[5] *Editio princeps*: PRU 4, 221–223; see Lackenbacher 2002: 91–92.

[6] If not otherwise indicated, all translations of Akkadian texts are of the present author.

[7] *Editio princeps*: PRU 4, 223–225; see Lackenbacher 2002: 92.

their vassals and wanted to make sure "that possible damage to the stability of Syria caused by this affair was kept to minimum" (van Soldt 2010: 202).

We do not know whether the "lapis lazuli issue" reported in Takuḫli's letters should be dated to before or after Ammistamru's divorce from the "fille de la Grande Dame". If it took place while he was still married to her, one could argue that it was precisely this prestigious marriage that emboldened him to cheat the king of Karkemiš; but if it took place after Ammistamru repudiated the "fille de la Grande Dame", i.e. after the Hittite king Tutḫaliya IV and the king of Karkemiš Ini-Teššub spent so much energy to resolve the complicated diplomatic crisis caused by his divorce, such deceitful behaviour would have been perceived as a real outrage by the Hittites.

Ammistamru was succeeded by his son Ibiranu (ca. 1235–1225/20 BC), who quickly got into trouble with the Hittites. In a letter by the Hittite prince Piḫawalwi (RS 17.247; PRU 4, 191), Ibiranu is scolded because he did not pay a visit to the Great King upon his ascent to the throne of Ugarit and is urged to quickly send messengers with presents for His Majesty and for Piḫawalwi:

> (6–7)Since you have assumed kingship in Ugarit, (8–9)why have you not come to the presence of His Majesty? (10–11)And why didn't you send regularly your messengers? (12–15)Now, His Majesty is very angry about this matter. (16–18)Now, send your messengers quickly to the presence of His Majesty (18–20)and send presents for His Majesty, together with presents for me.

This, as we shall see, is a recurrent issue: paying regular visits and sending presents to the Hittite court were among the duties of Hittite vassals, explicitly ratified in the treaties imposed upon them, and the last kings of Ugarit constantly tried to evade these obligations.

Another document, however, is often cited in the secondary literature as evidence of Ibiranu's treacherous behaviour towards the Hittites. I refer to the famous letter of an Assyrian king, probably Tukultī-Ninurta I, discovered at Ugarit in the so-called "House of Urtenu" (RS 34.165).[8] The letter reports on an Assyrian victory against the Hittites and is usually thought to have been written in the wake of the battle of Niḫriya, which probably took place during the reigns of Tutḫaliya IV and Tukultī-Ninurta I (Singer 1999: 689 with previous literature; Bányai 2011). The text is usually interpreted as the Assyrian king's overture for the cooperation of Ibiranu, whose name is traditionally restored in the position of the addressee in Obv. 2 (Klengel 1999: 281; Singer 1999: 689; Dietrich 2003: 118–119; Schwemer 2006:

[8] See the editions in Lackenbacher 1991: 90–100 and Dietrich 2003, and the translation by Schwemer 2006: 254–256. The poor state of preservation of this text's opening lines makes it difficult to identify sender and addressee. The content suggests that the sender was an Assyrian king, either Salmanassar I or Tukultī-Ninurta I (see most recently Llop 2015: 249 n. 25 for a review of the different opinions). Even though the Assyrian origin of the letter was called into question because of its palaeographical and linguistic features (Mora – Giorgieri 2004: 17 n. 86 with references to previous literature; d'Alfonso 2006: 307), I will maintain the identification of the sender as the Assyrian king Tukultī-Ninurta I as a working hypothesis.

254; Glatz 2013: 32). However, a different solution was put forward by Lorenzo d'Alfonso, who proposed to restore in Obv. 2 the name of the pharaoh Ramesses II ([*a-na* ^{m}*Ri-a-ma-še-ša ma-a-i* ^{d}*a-ma*]-*na*) instead of Ibiranu's name ([*a-na* ^{m}*I-bi-ra*]-*na*) and suggested that the letter might have been intercepted in Hittite-controlled territory while on its way to Egypt (d'Alfonso 2006: 304 n. 3). This possibility fits very well with the fact that the Assyrian king addresses his counterpart as "my brother" (Obv. 6), a title which would be very unusual if the addressee was a "small king", such as the king of Ugarit. Furthermore, as already noted by the text's editor, not even the name of the addressee's country is certain: instead of LUGAL KUR ⌜*Ú*⌝-[*ga-ri-it*], the traces at the end of Obv. 2 permit a reading LUGAL KUR ^{u}[^{ru}...] (Lackenbacher 1982: 149), which can be restored LUGAL KUR ^{u}[^{ru}*Mi-iṣ-ri*]. Another element that renders the identification of Ibiranu as the letter's addressee less certain is the find spot of the tablet it was discovered in the so-called "House of Urtenu", which yielded almost exclusively documents from the reigns of Niqmaddu III and Ammurapi. In any case, there is no evidence suggesting that Ibiranu actually defected to Assyria, unless one assumes that he was the king of Ugarit whom the Hittites exempted from contributing a military contingent in the war against Assyria (RS 17.059), and that this decision was motivated by the Hittites' mistrust of his loyalty.[9] Thus, the above-mentioned letter of Piḫawalwi remains the only source witnessing tensions between Ibiranu and the Hittites, which resulted in the usual tug-of-war between the king of Ugarit and his overlord, the former trying to elude his vassal duties and the latter trying to bring him into line by talking tough.

With the reign of Niqmaddu III (ca. 1225/20–1215 BC) we enter the phase of Ugarit's history that is now amply documented by the texts of the so-called "House of Urtenu". As we shall see, Niqmaddu challenged the patience of the Great King and of his representatives in Syria on several occasions and on different matters. Even though it is difficult to reconstruct the chronology of these episodes, one gets the impression that they might have recurred throughout Niqmaddu's whole reign.

Following the (bad) example of his father Ibiranu, Niqmaddu too irritates the Hittites with his reluctance to comply with his most basic duties: paying a visit to the Hittite court and sending presents. He is reprimanded for this by Puduḫepa, the famous Hittite queen who played a major political role during the reigns of her husband Ḫattusili III and of her son Tutḫaliya IV. The Ugaritic version of a letter sent by her to Niqmaddu (RS 17.434+)[10] contains the following complaint:

[9] See d'Alfonso 2005: 174–176 for this reconstruction of the political background behind the issuing of the edict RS 17.059. The name of the king of Ugarit who received the edict is not preserved: it could have been either Ammistamru II or Ibiranu.

[10] See Singer 2011a: 656ff. for the identification of Puduḫepa as the wife of Ḫattušili III, here acting as Queen Mother during the reign of Tutḫaliya IV.

> (1–2)[Messa]ge of Puduḫepa, [Great] Quee[n, que]en [of Ḫatti: To] Niqmaddu say: (…) (5–13)Concerning the fact that you have sent to the royal palace your message (as follows): "Now, [I?] hereby remit [the g]old of my tribute [to] the Sun [and] as for you, the M[R]T that you stipulated in the tre[aty, certainly] you will receive it," (…) But to me you have not come [… and] your messenger-party you have not sent to me. (translation adapted after Pardee 2002: 96).

In this context, one should mention also a letter of the king of Karkemiš to Ammurapi, Niqmaddu's successor, which recalls an episode that happened during Niqmaddu's reign (RS 34.136 = RSO 7 7). The king of Karkemiš complains to the king of Ugarit about an unsatisfactory shipment of presents to Ḫatti and reminds him of what transpired during the reign of his father:

> (25–29)When your father, the son-in-law of His Majesty, was in Ḫakapišša and in Kizzuwatna because of the presents, (30)how did they treat him? (31–32)Didn't they put his servants into fetters?

The letter refers to the father of the current king of Ugarit as "the son-in-law of His Majesty"; this points to Ammurapi as the addressee of the letter, since it was his father Niqmaddu III who married the Hittite princess Eḫli-Nikkal, probably a daughter of Tutḫaliya IV, and was therefore a son-in-law of the Hittite king.[11] Singer (1999: 695–696) contextualized this letter by assuming that "Eventually, Niqmaddu must have managed to appease the angry Hittite king, for a Hittite princess was given to him in marriage. Marital connections with the imperial family were usually considered as a great privilege for a vassal king, but surely they were no less in the interest of his suzerain. The Hittite king and his resourceful mother may have thought that a suitable match would provide a good possibility of keeping an eye on this assertive vassal". If this was the goal the Hittites hoped to achieve through the presence of Eḫli-Nikkal at the court of Ugarit, they must have been deeply disappointed. In fact, one of the recently published Akkadian letters from the "House of Urtenu" shows that Niqmaddu's behaviour did not improve much after his prestigious marriage. RSO 23 38 (RS 94.2562) is a letter whose sender and addressee are unknown, but its content allows one to assign it to the correspondence between Ḫatti and Ugarit and, more precisely, to the messages sent to Niqmaddu III, since it refers to his position as son-in-law of the Hit-

[11] The events related to this marriage have been the subject of different reconstructions. Most scholars identified the king of Ugarit who married Eḫli-Nikkal with Ammurapi (see e.g. Dijkstra 1990; Klengel 1992: 148; Klengel 1999: 301, 303; Beckman 1999: 183–185; Lackenbacher 2002: 126–130; Glatz 2013: 34), but it was also convincingly argued that she was married to Niqmaddu III (Singer 1999: 701–704). The second hypothesis has now been conclusively demonstrated by the letter RSO 23 23, addressed by a Hittite prince to Eḫli-Nikkal after the death of her husband (Lackenbacher – Malbran-Labat 2016: 51–52). This letter also shows that the documents recording the division of Eḫli-Nikkal's patrimony between her and the kingdom of Ugarit (see Nougayrol 1956: 208–210; Beckman 1999: 183–185; Lackenbacher 2002: 126–130) were not issued because the couple divorced, but because Eḫli-Nikkal left Ugarit after she became a widow.

tite king. The message deals with an individual whom the king of Ugarit should deliver to the Hittites:

> (17')(If) you will not give (him) to him, (18')do not rely on your being a son-in–law: (19')considering how you treat the Hittites, (20')if you do not deliver that servant of mine, (21'–22')on the day you will come to me, you will see how I will treat you!

The reference to a future visit might suggest that the letter's author was the Hittite king, who was expecting Niqmaddu to travel to Ḫatti to fulfil his vassal duties. This passage clearly demonstrates that the presence of a Hittite princess at Niqmaddu's side was not enough to spare him the reprimands of the Great King, nor did it render him more submissive.

In fact, other Akkadian letters from the "House of Urtenu" supply ample new evidence about Niqmaddu's insubordination. In RSO 23 4 (RS 94.2352) Niqmaddu is scolded by the Hittite king, who must have been Tutḫaliya IV, for his behaviour towards Zuzulli, a courtier (LÚ *ša* SAG) of the king[12]. The Great King regards this behaviour as so outrageous that he can hardly believe what he heard:

> (1–2)Thus speaks His Majesty, the Great King: say to Niqmaddu. (3)Now, I, His Majesty, have heard this: (…) (5–9)you have hampered? Zuzulli, the courtier of the king, who came to you, and did not allow [him] to enter your country. (10–12)Now, I, His Majesty, cannot believe this statement (13–14)but if (this) statement is true and you have inter[fered? with] the courtier of the king, (…) (15–16)be [aware] of how much you did wrong towards His Majesty. (…) (22–25)And if Zuzulli will send a (negative) report to His Majesty, be aware that a punishment will be imposed upon you.

As a courtier of the king, Zuzulli belonged to the innermost circle of high officials who were closely involved in the state administration, which explains why the latter was so upset about the fact that Niqmaddu did not show the respect due to him.

Another troubling issue produced a whole dossier of letters dealing with the pressing request for troops and chariots in order to carry out some "works" (KIN^{meš}) at Alalaḫ.

First of all, one should consider a letter of the king of Karkemiš to Niqmaddu III (RSO 23 31 = RS 94.2079+2367), which gives a clear and vivid image of what was going on:

---

12 I prefer Miller's (2013: 294–295) cautious approach in rendering this title as "courtier", rather than "eunuch" (favoured by Peled 2013), since it is still open to debate whether or not the Hittite *ša rēšis* were castrated; both studies refer to previous literature It is possible that Zuzzulli was at the service of the king of Karkemiš: see most recently Bilgin 2018, 331-332.

> (1–4)Thus speaks the king [of Karkemiš]: to Niqm[addu], king of Ugarit, say: (5)may you be well! (6–7)Didn't His Majesty entrusted to you the (re)construction of Alalaḫ? (8–10)(Then), why are your troops not carrying out the works at Alalaḫ? (10–13)And (even) if you send your troops to Alalaḫ, they stay for 5, 6 days, then get up and disappear. (14–16)Now, herewith I am sending you the scribe Madī-Dagān: (16–18)give him 200 men (lit. troops)! (18–19)If you do not give (them) to him, be aware: (20–22)I will write to His Majesty and (his) punishment will be inflicted on you.

Thus, the Hittites were upset because Niqmaddu was failing to complete some works at Alalaḫ with which he had been entrusted. The nature of these "works" is not very clear: this letter speaks of "(re)construction" (*raṣāpa*), while other texts in the dossier suggest that his duties included also the plantation of orchards and the digging of canals. In any case, the issue seems to be required urgent attention, and the king of Karkemiš threatens to inform the Hittite king about Niqmaddu's noncompliance and promises that he will be duly punished by the overlord.

Not only the king of Karkemiš, but also the *uriyanni*, one of the highest officials of the Hittite kingdom,[13] repeatedly writes to Niqmaddu about the same matter. Among the three letters of the *uriyanni* dealing with this problem, one in particular (RSO 23 28 = RS 94.2578) echoes very explicitly the content of RSO 23 31:

> (32–35)Herewith: in Alalaḫ, there are neither chariots nor troops of yours in Alalaḫ. (35–37)Did they not entrust to you the works in Alalaḫ? (37–38)Then give orders (about it) accordingly! Now, herewith (39–41)I am sending you the scribe[?] Madī-Dagān: give him 200 men (42–43)who will carry out the works in Alalaḫ!

The connection between this letter and the message of the king of Karkemiš is quite obvious, as the two texts are phrased almost identically. Another fragmentary letter of the *uriyanni* to Niqmaddu mentions Alalaḫ and warns the king of Ugarit that "the punishment of His Majesty will be inflicted on you!" (RSO 23 30:44–46).

Niqmaddu III, however, did not seem to be terribly bothered by these threats. In fact, further texts testify to his tenacious reluctance to comply with his orders and the consequent frustration of the Hittites in this matter. RSO 23 32 (= RS 94.2389), for instance, is a letter whose upper half is missing, leaving the identity of sender and addressee unknown. However, what remains of the message is enough to assign it beyond doubt to the dossier about the "Alalaḫ issue" and to hypothesize that it was another letter sent to Niqmaddu either by the king of Karkemiš or by the *uriyanni*,[14] as demonstrated by the following lines:

---

[13] I follow Lackenbacher – Malbran-Labat 2016: 63 in understanding [m]*ú-ri-ia-an-ni* as a title, rather than as a personal name, despite the presence of the personal determinative; on the office of *uriyanni*, see most recently Pecchioli Daddi 2010 and Bilgin 2018: 176–190.

[14] The text's editors favor the second possibility (Lackenbacher – Malbran-Labat 2016: 69).

> (13′–15′)Once, twice I gave you instructions about the troops that have to carry out works in Alalaḫ, (16′–17′)but you would not listen to my words!

Similarly, another fragmentary letter whose sender and addressee are unknown can be assigned to this dossier because it deals again with Alalaḫ (RSO 23 33 = RS 94.2506) and says:

> (3′–5′)Does His Majesty not treat you as a son of him? Then why don't you listen to [his] wor[ds]?

The new evidence provided by these texts allows a different interpretation of another Akkadian letter from the king of Karkemiš to an unnamed king of Ugarit discovered in the "House of Urtenu" and published in 1991 (RSO 7 6 = RS 34.143). Here, the king of Karkemiš accuses the king of Ugarit of having mislead him by claiming that his troops were camped in Mukiš,[15] while according to the king's informers Ugarit's troops were located in the northern part of the kingdom of Ugarit; the king of Karkemiš also accuses Ugarit's king of having refused to send chariots and horses, adducing the excuse that they were in poor shape, and of having kept for himself the best *mariyannu*-troops while sending to the king of Karkemiš only worthless soldiers.

Singer (1999: 723–725) suggested that the historical background for this letter was an attack of the Sea Peoples during the reign of Ammurapi, at the end of the 13th – beginning of the 12th century BC, and proposed to link it with a rather fragmentary message in Ugaritic sent by a certain Iriri-Šarruma to the queen of Ugarit, which mentions the presence of enemies in Mukiš (RS 16.402 = KTU 2.33; see translation in Pardee 2002: 105–106).

While this possibility cannot be ruled out conclusively, RSO 7 6 has so many points in contact with the newly published Akkadian texts from the "House of Urtenu" that it seems quite likely that they deal with the same issue. Therefore, I believe that RSO 7 6 dates to the reign of Niqmaddu III and should not necessarily be regarded as evidence for some impending danger in Mukiš, given that it can be connected to the construction works that needed to be carried out by Niqmaddu's troops at Alalaḫ.

There is no explicit evidence about the conclusion of this arm-wrestling between Niqmaddu and the Hittites on the "Alalaḫ issue", and we must rely on archaeological and textual *argumenta ex silentio*. While the nature of the "works" entrusted to Niqmaddu is not entirely clear, the recent archaeological excavations carried out at Alalaḫ did not reveal traces of major construction works that could be associated with this undertaking. The results of the archaeological excavations rather suggest that "Atchana's final phase of widespread Bronze Age habitation ended by around 1300 BC with the exception of the temple area, and that most of

---

[15] Zeeb 1992 gives a different interpretation of RSO 7 6: 7–8, but I retain the translation of Malbran-Labat 1991: 28, which was followed also by Singer 1999: 723; this interpretation is now supported also by the phrasing of RSO 23 28:34–35.

the site lay deserted throughout the 13th century with only a resettlement sometime in the mid-12th century, the Iron Age" (Yener 2013: 12), thus long after Niqmaddu III and the Hittites were exchanging messages about this matter.

Furthermore, with the exception of the imprisonment of Niqmaddu's emissaries in return for the delivery of insufficient presents (cf. RSO 7 7 above), we do not know of any other form of punishment inflicted upon Ugarit during his reign. Thus, we can imagine that the Great King reluctantly accepted Niqmaddu's refusal to comply with his duties and eventually refrained from trying to impose his will on this unruly vassal.

Certainly, one would expect the Hittites to have been terribly annoyed by Niqmaddu's behaviour. It is therefore surprising to find a positive description of Niqmaddu's reign in the Ugaritic version of a later letter sent by the Hittite king to Ammurapi, Niqmaddu's successor (RS 18.038). Here, His Majesty (probably Suppiluliuma II) complains about Ammurapi's behaviour by contrasting it with that of his father in a sort of "historical prologue" (Fink 2006) to the letter:

> (1–4)Message of the Sun: to Ammurapi say: With the Sun everything is well. (5–8)Before the Sun's [fa]ther, [your] fath[er], his servant, did indeed dwell submissively; for a se[rvant] indeed (and) his possession was he, and [his] l[ord] he did indeed guard. My father never lacked g[rain], (but) you, for your part, have not recognized (that this was how things were). (translation by Pardee 2002: 94–95)

Amazingly enough, despite Niqmaddu's troubled relations with the Hittites, one generation later he was regarded – or at least presented – as a paragon of virtue, the submissive and faithful vassal *par excellence.*

With Ammurapi (ca. 1215–1190/85 BC), the Hittites face again the same old problems: the last king of Ugarit is reprimanded for not paying a visit to the Great King and not sending enough presents. The "presents issue" is recorded by the above-mentioned letter of the king of Karkemiš, which recalls the imprisonment of Niqmaddu's emissaries as a warning (RSO 7 7 = RS 34.136):

> (5–7)Your messenger you sent to Ḫatti and the presents you sent to the Greats (8–9)are very scarce. Was it me who told you: "May the presents (10–11)you send to the Greats be scarce"? (11–15)Didn't I write to you as follows: "Send to the Chief Scribe an extraordinary present, don't send him one less than extraordinary"? (16–18)So, precisely with regard to him didn't you send such presents? (19–20)Why do you act like this?

The "visit issue" is dealt with in the above mentioned letter sent by a Hittite king, most likely Suppiluliuma II (RS 18.038), where Niqmaddu is surprisingly presented as a compliant vassal, while Ammurapi must be reminded that:

> (11–16)Now you also belong to the Sun your master; a serv[ant] indeed, his possession are you. But [yo]u, for your part, you have not at all recognized

> (your responsibility toward) the Sun, your master. To me, the Sun, your master, from year to year, why do you not come? (translation after Pardee 2002: 95)

The same letter addresses also another matter that Ammurapi is apparently trying to evade: the dispatch of grain to Ḫatti.

> (17–21)Now, concerning the fact that you have sent a tablet to the Sun, your master, regarding food, to the effect that there is no food in your land: the Sun himself is perishing.

While Ḫatti's need of grain is a recurring topic in several cuneiform texts from the final phase of the Late Bronze Age and has been interpreted as evidence for an actual food shortage in Anatolia,[16] it has been suggested that the claim that grain was lacking in Ugarit was simply an excuse for not complying with the Great King's request (Singer 1999: 717). However, also in this case the new evidence from the "House of Urtenu" offers new data which allow to review this reconstruction: in fact, a letter from Egypt records a request for grain by the king of Ugarit because his country is indeed "very hungry" (RSO 23 40 = RS 94.2002+2003).

This and a few other letters exchanged with Egypt at the time of Ammurapi[17] have been interpreted as evidence that Ammurapi's relations with Egypt were too intense and friendly. Two of them, in particular, record repeated declarations of loyalty by the king of Ugarit towards Pharaoh Merneptah, who is addressed as Ammurapi's "lord". This raised understandable doubts about the propriety of Ammurapi's behaviour towards Ḫatti: the Syrian kingdom was seeking help and protection from a still powerful Great King who could guarantee him much needed grain supplies, while his Hittite overlord was losing his grip on his territories and was himself struggling with a food shortage (Singer 1999: 708–715). This does not imply that Egypt and Ugarit had concluded a formal alliance at this time, as suggested by Morris (2015), because one should remember that a Hittite vassal was allowed to entertain diplomatic contacts with other Great Kings, as long as they were Hittite allies (Devecchi 2015). Since at this time the Pharaoh was at peace with Ḫatti, Ugarit's correspondence with Egypt does not necessarily con-

[16] See de Martino 2018 for a recent review of the relevant sources; as the author stresses, the evidence supports the possibility that Ḫatti suffered from temporary shortages of food, but should not necessarily be linked to a long-lasting situation of emergency; see also Miller in press.

[17] The relevant Akkadian texts are two letters of Merneptah? to Ammurapi? (RSO 14 1 = RS 88.2158, RSO 23 40 = RS 94.2002+2003), a letter of Sethi II to Ammurapi (RSO 23 41 = RS 94.2176), and a letter of Beya "Chief of the troops of the Great King, King of the Land of Egypt" to Ammurapi (RSO 14 18 = RS 86.2230); for the Ugaritic texts, see Pardee 2002: 99ff. I agree with Arnaud's (2001: 278) cautious approach in regarding Beya's letter simply as evidence for contacts between Egypt and Ugarit with no major political implications, because only the letter's heading and greeting formula are preserved, while the content is completely lost; Morris (2015: 343) sees it instead as evidence that a pact between Egypt and Ugarit had indeed been forged, because "were the two countries not militarily allied at that time, the reason for this correspondence would be difficult to discern".

stitute treacherous behaviour *tout court*, but could rather represent an attempt to exploit all available diplomatic channels in a context of general uncertainty and insecurity. As for Ammurapi's addressing the Pharaoh as his "lord", that is what diplomatic etiquette required of a small king writing to a Great King.

There are no further sources reporting on Ammurapi's insubordination, and indeed other texts witness his rather obliging attitude towards the Hittites. Two parallel letters of the Great King and of Pendi-Šarruma, a very high-ranking official at the Hittite court (RSO 23 8–9), to Ammurapi report that the Great King is "very happy" (*ḫadi danniš*) about a dispatch of excellent lapis lazuli and the fact that Ammurapi "showed respect" (*tuktabitanni*) to His Majesty, who finally saw his authority acknowledged.

The interaction between Ḫatti and Ugarit in the final phase of the Late Bronze Age is characterized by some recurring patterns. The last three kings of Ugarit (Ibiranu, Niqmaddu III, and Ammurapi) are regularly scolded because they do not comply with two basic obligations of a good vassal: paying visits and sending presents to the Hittite court. Niqmaddu III seems to have been the most problematic offender: he is also accused of hindering Hittite officials from fulfilling their duties, of ignoring the orders that are given to him and refusing to carry out some works at Alalaḫ, and in general of not treating the Hittites with respect. Perhaps precisely because of his assertive attitude, the Great King gave a Hittite princess in marriage to Niqmaddu, whom he perhaps hoped would have a positive influence on his recalcitrant vassal. As we saw, though, even this was not enough to bring him into line.

Such behaviours prompted the reaction and intervention of individuals at all levels of the imperial hierarchy: the kings of Ugarit are reprimanded directly by the Hittite king and queen, by the king of Karkemiš, by princes, and by high officials such as the *uriyanni*. All of these figures complain repeatedly and even promise harsh punishments, but we know of only one occasion when a punishment was actually carried out and Niqmaddu III's emissaries were imprisoned because of some issue related to the delivery of presents.

How shall we explain the accommodating reaction of the Hittites? It certainly depended to some degree on the growing weakening of royal authority that characterized the reigns of the last Hittite kings. The origin of this crisis[18] might be sought in the *coup d'état* through which Ḫattusili III seized power from Urḫi-Teššub / Mursili III and the consequent rift within the Hittite royal family and court, but other factors played a role as well: the conflict with Assyria on the eastern border of the empire, security problems in western Anatolia, perhaps an attempt of the king of Tarhuntašša to seize power in southern Anatolia, the general instability caused in the whole region by the migrations of the "Sea Peoples", and maybe even a shortage of grain.

[18] For a recent overview of the factors that might have contributed to the fall of the Hittite kingdom, see de Martino 2018; cf. Miller in press, who is sceptical about the possibility of identifying any evidence for a collapse in the textual documentation from Ḫattuša.

In this situation, the Hittite kings must have been reluctant to invest any energy in an exemplary punishment against Ugarit, even though they probably had the military strength to do so; in fact, despite the difficulties they were facing, the last Hittite kings were still able to conduct successful military campaigns, which led them, for instance, to annex Alašiya / Cyprus during the reign of Suppiluliuma II. However, campaigning to conquer new territories was worth the effort, while in the larger scheme of things, the troubles caused by Ugarit might have been regarded as minor inconveniences that could be tolerated, as long as they remained confined to forms of "disobedience and delay" (Glatz 2013: 35) and did not precipitate an overtly aggressive rebellion that threatened the entirety of the kingdom.

As we saw, the kings of Ugarit did not lack occasions for betraying their overlords and siding with different enemies: with other Syrian vassals, who rebelled against the Hittite authorities during the reigns of Suppiluliuma I and Mursili II; with Egypt, again during the reign of Mursili II and also afterward, until the peace treaty between Ḫattusili III and Ramesses II inaugurated the age of the so-called *Pax Hethitica;* and finally with Assyria, mainly during the reign of Tutḫaliya IV. However, as far as we can tell, they never graduated to open revolt. It rather seems that they simply tried to exploit Ḫatti's growing weakness to their own advantage, perhaps in order to bargain for better economic treatment or more freedom, without necessarily planning to subvert the established order. This might be the reason why even Niqmaddu III could be presented in the end as a good subject, who "dwelt submissively and guarded his lord": he could be accused of being a reluctant servant, but not a disloyal one.

References

Arnaud, D., 2001. Lettres. In M. Yon – D. Arnaud, eds., *Études ougaritiques*. RSO 14. Paris: Éditions Recherche sur les Civilisations, 257–322.

Arnaud, D. – M. Salvini, 1991–1992. Le divorce du roi Ammistamru d'Ougarit: un document redécouvert. *Semitica* 41–42, 1–22.

Beckman, G., 1999². *Hittite Diplomatic Texts*. WAW 7. Atlanta, GA: Scholars Press.

d'Alfonso, L., 2005. *Le procedure giudiziarie ittite in Siria (XIII sec. a.C.)*. StMed 17. Pavia: Italian University Press.

d'Alfonso, L., 2006. Die hethitische Vertragstradition in Syrien (14.–12. Jh. v.Chr.). In M. Witte – K. Schmidt – D. Prechel – J.C. Gertz, eds., *Die deuteronomistischen Geschichtswerke. Redaktions- und religionsgeschichtliche Perspektiven zur „Deuteronomismus" – Diskussion in Tora und Vorderen Propheten*. BZAW 365. Berlin – New York: De Gruyter, 303–329.

Bilgin, T. *Officials and Administration in the Hittite World.* SANER 21. Boston – Berlin: De Gruyter.

Devecchi, E., 2012. Treaties and edicts in the Hittite world. In G. Wilhelm, ed., *Organization, Representation, and Symbols of Power in the Ancient Near East. Proceedings of the 54th Rencontre Assyriologique Internationale, Würzburg, 21–25 July 2008*. Winona Lake, IN: Eisenbrauns, 637–645.

Devecchi, E., 2013. Suppiluliuma's Syrian campaigns in light of the documents from Ugarit. In S. de Martino – J.L. Miller, eds., *New Results and New Questions on the Reign of Suppiluliuma I.* Eothen 19. Firenze: LoGisma, 81–97.

Devecchi, E., 2015. The international relations of Ḫatti's Syrian vassals, or how to make the best of things. In B. Eder – R. Pruzsinszky, eds., *Policies of Exchange. Political systems and modes of interaction in the Aegean and the Near East in the 2nd millennium B.C.E.* OREA 2. Wien: Austrian Academy of Science Press, 117–126.

Devecchi, E. – J.L. Miller, 2011. Hittite-Egyptian synchronisms and their consequences for ancient Near Eastern chronology. In Mynářová, J., ed., *Egypt and the Near East – The Crossroads*. Prague: Charles University in Prague, 139–176.

Dietrich, M., 2003. Salmanassar I. von Assyrien, Ibirānu (VI.) von Ugarit und Tudḫaliya IV. von Ḫatti. RS 34.165 und die Schlacht von Niḫriya zwischen den Hethitern und Assyrern. *UF* 35, 103–139.

Dijkstra, M., 1990. On the identity of the Hittite princess mentioned in label KTU 6.24 (RS 17.72). *UF* 22, 97–101.

Fink, A.S., 2006. The historical prologue in a letter from Šuppiluliuma II to 'Ammurapi' king of Ugarit (RS 18.038). In A.M. Maeir – P. de Miroschedji, eds., *"I Will Speak the Riddles of Ancient Times." Archaeological and Historical Studies in Honor of Amihai Mazar*. Winona Lake, IN: Eisenbrauns, 673–688.

Genz, H., 2006. Hethitische Präsenz im spätbronzezeitlichen Syrien: die archäologische Evidenz. *BaM* 37, 499–509.

Glatz, C., 2013. Negotiating empire. A comparative investigation into the responses to Hittite imperialism by the vassal state of Ugarit and the Kaska peoples of the Anatolian Black Sea region. In G. Areshian, ed., *Empires and Complexity. On the crossroads of archaeology, history and anthropology*. Los Angeles: The Cotsen Institute of Archaeology Press, 21–56.

Klengel, H., 1992. *Syria, 3000 to 300 B.C.: A Handbook of Political History* Berlin: Akademie Verlag.

Klengel, H., 1999. *Geschichte des hethitischen Reiches*. HdO I/34. Leiden – Boston – Köln: Brill.

Kühne, C., 1973. Ammištamru und die Tochter der „Großen Dame". *UF* 5, 175–184.

Lackenbacher, S., 1982. Nouveaux documents d'Ugarit I. Une lettre royale. *RA* 76, 141–156.

Lackenbacher, S., 1991. Lettres et fragments. In P. Bordreuil – D. Arnaud – B. André-Salvini – S. Lackenbacher – F. Malbran-Labat – D. Pardee, eds., *Une bibliothèque au sud de la ville. Les textes de la 34e campagne*. RSO 7. Paris: Éditions Recherche sur les Civilisations, 83–104.

Lackenbacher, S., 2002. *Textes akkadiens d'Ugarit*. LAPO 20. Paris: Les éditions du Cerf.

Lackenbacher, S. – F. Malbran-Labat, 2016. *Lettres en akkadien de la «Maison d'Urtēnu». Fouilles de 1994*. RSO 23. Leuven – Paris – Bristol: Peeters.

Llop, J., 2015. Foreign kings in the Middle Assyrian archival documentation. In B. Düring, ed., *Understanding Hegemonic Practices of the Early Assyrian Empire. Essays dedicated to Frans Wiggermann* (Consolidating Empires Project I). PIHANS 125. Leiden: Nederlands Instituut voor het Nabije Oosten, 244–273.

Malbran-Labat, F., 1991. Lettres. In P. Bordreuil – D. Arnaud – B. André-Salvini – S. Lackenbacher – F. Malbran-Labat – D. Pardee, eds., *Une bibliothèque a sud de la Ville*. RSO 7. Paris: Éditions Recherche sur les Civilisations, 26–64.

de Martino, S., 2018. *The Fall of the Hittite Kingdom*. Mesopotamia 53, 23–48.

Miller, J.L., 2013. *Royal Hittite Instructions and Related Administrative Texts*. WAW 31. Atlanta, GA: Society of Biblical Literature.

Miller, J.L., in press. Are there Signs of the Decline of the Late Hittite State in the Textual Documentation from Ḫattusa? In S. de Martino – E. Devecchi, eds., *Anatolia between the 13th and the 12th Century B.C.E.*, Firenze: LoGisma editore.

Mora, C. – M. Giorgieri, 2004. *Le lettere tra i re ittiti e i re assiri ritrovate a Ḫattuša.* HANE/M 7. Padova: S.a.r.g.o.n Editrice e Libreria.

Morris, E.F., 2015. Egypt, Ugarit, the god Baʿal, and the puzzle of a royal rebuff. In J. Mynářová – P. Onderka – P. Pavúk, eds., *There and Back Again – the Crossroads II. Proceedings of an international conference held in Prague, September 15–18, 2014*. Prague: Charles University in Prague, 315–351.

Nougayrol, J., 1956. *Le palais royal d'Ugarit IV. Textes accadiens des archives sud (Archives internationales)*. MRS 9. Paris: Imprimerie Nationale.

Pardee, D., 2002. Ugaritic letters. In W.W. Hallo, ed., *The Context of Scripture. Volume III: Archival Documents from the Biblical World*. Leiden: Brill, 88–114.

Pecchioli Daddi, F., 2010. lúuri(y)anni: una nuova ipotesi di identificazione. *Or NS* 79, 232–241.

Peled, I., 2013. Eunuchs in Hatti and Assyria. A reassessment. In L. Feliu – J. Llop – A. Millet Albà –J. Sanmartín, eds., *Time and History in the Ancient Near East. Proceedings of the 56th Rencontre Assyriologique Internationale at Barcelona*. Winona Lake, IN: Eisenbrauns, 785–797.

Schwemer, D., 2006. Briefe aus den Archiven von Ugarit. 1. Briefe in akkadischer Sprache. In B. Janowski – G. Wilhelm, eds., *Briefe*. TUAT N.F. 3. Gütersloh: Gütersloher Verlagshaus.

Singer, I., 1999. A political history of Ugarit. In W.G.E. Watson – N. Wyatt, eds., *Handbook of Ugaritic Studies*. HdO I/39. Leiden – Boston – Köln: Brill, 603–733.

Singer, I., 2011a. Dating the end of the Hittite empire. In I. Singer, ed., *The Calm before the Storm. Selected writings of Itamar Singer on the Late Bronze Age in Anatolia and the Levant*. WAW Supplement Series 1. Atlanta, GA: Society of Biblical Literature, 655–660.

Singer, I., 2011b. Takuḫlinu and Ḫaya: Two Governors in the Ugarit Letter from Tel Aphek. In I. Singer, ed., *The Calm before the Storm. Selected writings of Itamar Singer on the Late Bronze Age in Anatolia and the Levant*. WAW Supplement Series 1. Atlanta, GA: Society of Biblical Literature, 147–172.

van Soldt, W.H., 2010. Ugarit as a Hittite vassal state. *AoF* 37, 198–207.

Yener, K.A., 2013. New excavations at Alalakh. The 14th–12th centuries BC. In K.A. Yener, ed., *Across the Border. Late Bronze-Iron Age relations between Syria and Anatolia. Proceedings of a symposium held at the Research Center of Anatolian Studies, Koç University, Istanbul, May 31–June 1, 2010*. ANESS 42. Leuven – Walpole, MA: Peeters, 11–35.

Zeeb, F., 1992. "Die Truppen sind unfähig": Überlegungen zu RS 34.143. *UF* 24, 481–498.

A SUMERIAN STRONGHOLD. STRANGERS IN THE HOUSE OF ENLIL?

Anne Goddeeris (Ghent University)[1]

Strangers come in all shapes and forms. They may come as invading barbarians from the mountains, as guests invited to a party, as refugees seeking safety or escaping poverty or as tourists appreciating the assets of the region. Moreover, strangers must not necessarily come from another region. Just as often intentionally as not, countrysiders stand out in a city, as do Muslims and Jews in a church, or a couple in their fifties on a rave party. Who is the stranger, and who is the "local", is always dependent on the context. Any feature in common—whether it relates to geographical, social, ethno-racial, religious, gender, age or professional identity—may suffice to create small or large groups, and as soon as we have insiders, by definition we have outsiders. These group identities and group compositions are constantly evolving and even depend on the context of the moment. Oppositions can just as well dilute as gain importance, and additional distinguishing attributes are constantly created and implemented. Strangers and outsiders, therefore, may switch position with insiders overtime. After all, as soon as one gets to know him, a stranger is not a stranger anymore.

All this makes it very difficult to investigate historical as well as other questions regarding the concept foreigner in an unambiguous manner. Before addressing the insiders and outsiders in the religious circles of Old Babylonian Nippur, I will establish an operational definition of the term, making use of the concepts developed the frame of the *social identity approach*. Social identity approach is a theoretical framework in social psychology, which offers a combination of psychological and social explanations for dynamics of group behaviour such as in-group favouritism and out-group bias. The approach also offers a framework for interpreting social change. As such it has extended its reach well outside the confines of psychology, and has shown its relevance for all human sciences, from political science via history to economics (Hornsey 2008). Since it acknowledges the ambiguous and dissipating aspects of outsiders and insiders, the theory will allow me to situate foreigners and locals in the Babylonian religious institutions.

With this framework in mind, I will investigate who can be identified as insiders and outsiders in the religious circles of Old Babylonian Nippur, and I will discuss who these categories developed in the course of the 18th century BC.

---

[1] Research for this article was funded by FWO Flanders project 3G006317 "Priests en Profits 2.0. The Role of the Temple in the Old Babylonian Economy (1911-1499 BC)".

An operational definition—The social identity approach.

The social identity approach consists of two complementary branches of research: the social identity theory, developed by Tajfel and his students, and the self-categorization theory elaborated on by Turner and colleagues after Tajfel's death.

Social identity theory is an "integrative theory that attends to both the cognitive and motivational basis of intergroup differentiation" (Haslam 2004: 21). Why do people—sometimes irrationally—discriminate or favour others without direct benefit for themselves?

The principle that lies at the basis of social identity theory is the minimal group paradigm, a process brought to light by Henri Tajfel when he was investigating the minimal conditions that lead members of one group to discriminate in favor of the other (Tajfel – Billig – Bundy – Flament 1971). Much to his surprise, it appeared that even if the groups were formed on a random basis (such as "dot-overestimators" vs. "dot-underestimators") in his laboratory experiments, the participants in the experiment sought a maximization of the difference between in-group and out-group when they had to appoint points to others. The mere act of categorizing themselves suffices for members of one group to discriminate in favour of their fellow group members. No objective conflict is needed. More specific features come only in a second phase, when actions are undertaken to establish distinctiveness to an otherwise empty situation (Haslam 2004: 20–21).

As a probable motive for these irrational decisions, social identity theorists propose achieving, maintaining and protecting a *positive self-concept* (Hornsey 2008: 214–215). In other words, after being categorized in terms of a group membership and having internalized this categorization, individuals seek to achieve positive self-esteem by positively differentiating their ingroup from a comparison outgroup on some valued dimension, seeking positive distinctiveness (Haslam 2004: 21). In case the outgroup has a higher status, this may be achieved by comparing to a different outgroup, or by measuring other aspects, e.g. social or emotional well-fare rather than status or wealth (social creativity). Also, one may attempt to challenge the social order (social competition) or to become a member of the other group (social mobility). The choice of strategy for self-enhancement depends on the permeability of the group boundaries, and on the security of the group's status. For Tajfel, social identity theory was at its heart a theory of social change (Hornsey 2008: 207).

On top of all this, social identity is defined by the (non-)membership of an *unlimited number* of groups. Groups defining one's identity may intersect or overlap, may contain one another, and complement each other. Combined with the constant change of the group identity, this shows that social identity is a highly fluid concept. The salience of any of these memberships depends on context of the moment, and on the extent to which the group membership is internalized.

After Tajfel's death in 1982, Turner further investigated the categorization process that lies at the basis of SIT (Turner – Hogg – Oakes – Reicher – Wetherell 1987). How do particular social identities become internalized and salient?

An individual can "switch" his various social identities on and off, by a process of self-stereotyping through which he sees himself as categorically interchangeable with other ingroup members. This process is labeled "depersonalization" (Haslam 2004: 30). The extent to which the social categories are perceived to reflect social reality is referred to with the term *fit*, once more a very dynamic concept, which is studied in a normative way (normative fit, in line with stereotypical expectations) and in a comparative way (comparative fit, referring to intra-category differences and inter-category similarities) (Hornsey 2008: 208). A group-member is compared to a prototype, but the prototype remains a fleeting concept that fluctuates according to context, reflecting a subjective sense of the defining attributes of a social category. Even the boundaries of apparently fixed categories such as race and ethnicity change and are permeable. In the highly regulated U.S. Census, Huddy has identified examples both of permeable ethnic boundaries, where an ethnic identity such as "American Indian" can be and increasingly is adopted (2001: 138) and of constantly changing attributes for ethnic categories such as "Mexican American" (2001: 142). It goes without saying that group boundaries are much more vague in less regulated daily discourse.

Focusing on the dynamics within a group or category, self-categorization theory addresses the constant shifts of priorities and changing prototypes. Changes in the intergroup relations, but also a natural disaster or a major incident such as 9/11, immediately change the discourse of groups and may cause polarization, so that conflictual members become more prototypical within groups and will gain influence and authority (Turner 2005: 15), and so that certain groups will gain or lose salience (Huddy 2001: 149). Nowadays, we hear this everyday in political rhetorics.

These lines of research have led to an alternative analysis of power. Traditionally, power is supposed to be acquired through control over resources. From the perspective of the self-categorization theory, power results from intragroup dynamics, and may take the form of persuasion, control or coercion (Turner 2005). The advantage of this approach is that it contexualizes the constant changes in power relations that we observe in history and in our surrounding world. Control over resources does not shift fast enough to account for the constant power shifts constituting reality.

For obvious reasons, the exact social and psychological processes that lay at the basis of changes within and between groups cannot be identified in historical sources, but the social identity approach and the processes described in it have shown their universal validity in explaining social change. The approach does justice to the constant changes of group boundaries and power relations that can be observed in historical case studies.

Having established the theoretical framework, we can now return to an operational definition of a foreigner or a stranger. In the following paragraphs, individuals who are not members of an ingroup—in this case the clergy in Old Babylonian Nippur—are taken to be foreigners or strangers. We will investigate the attributes of the clergy in Old Babylonian Nippur as a social category, try to determine (the development of both) its boundaries and its salience in the course of the Old Babylonian period. By the salience of the clergy of Nippur, we refer to its (political, but also social and cultural) influence.

The attributes of a member of the clergy of Old Babylonian Nippur

Having taken the hurdle of the operational definition, we immediately stumble over another one: how can we identify these "strangers" in the legal and administrative documents?

Membership of social groups is expressed in various visible and invisible characteristics, which, for their part, are constantly evolving as well. These characteristics range from fixed attributes such as age, gender, family background and place of origin, over language, accent and professions to features that can easily be adopted and discarded, such as dress code (including haircut and accessories) and behaviour (from posture over table manners to religious practices).

Most of these features cannot be identified in historical case-studies. Babylonian individuals cannot be questioned about their identity or about the meaning of their attributes. However, the legal and administrative documents may contain indications concerning the "foreignness" of the individuals mentioned:

Traditionally, foreigners are identified in cuneiform documents on the basis of three factors:

1) by their city or region of origin

2) by linguistic nature of their personal name or of their patronymic

3) by circumstantial aspects.

If a cuneiform record identifies an individual by his city or region of origin, this leaves no room for doubt. Such a qualification is rarely given, but if it is, it stresses the foreignness of the individual. Thus, even if we cannot locate the toponym mentioned, we know by the simple fact that a toponym is given, that the individual is an outsider.

Personal names are systematically given in legal and administrative documents, but much more questionable as a tool for attributing individuals to an ethnic or even a linguistic category. Gender is marked but cannot always be identified with certainty. Likewise, we cannot always identify the linguistic origin of a name. In Fig. 1, Ekur-andul is marked as Sumerian, but might just as well be read as an Akkadian name Ēkur-ṣullulī, both meaning "the Ekur (= the temple of Enlil in Nippur) is my shade". Only if the name belongs to a more remote language, such as Kassite or Elamite, and if we have other indications (contextual or a foreign patronymic), can we conclude on the foreignness of the individual.

Names may also give an indication regarding the professional category of the owner (Stol 1991: 209–210). In the lower social stratum, we find the slave names (Harris 1977). Higher up the social ladder, members of the clergy (Edzard 1998b: 110) and of the royal administration may adopt distinctive names as well (the so-called "Beamtennamen": Stol 1991: 209; Michalowski 1991: 55; Edzard 1998a: 98–99; Edzard 1998b: 109–110). These professionals probably have adopted their professional name at a certain point in their career, but only a few of these name changes can be identified with certainty. When he became chief dirge singer, Bēlānum changed his name to Ur-Utu (Tanret 2015: 501). Around Šū-Suen's third regnal year Lā-māḫar changes his name to Šū-Suen-lā-māḫar (Sallaberger 1993: part I 222, n. 1057 and part II 128–132, tab. 75). However, a name change must lie behind all the cases where an adult official carries the name of a ruler who is in power only 10 years in his name (Edzard 1998b: 109).

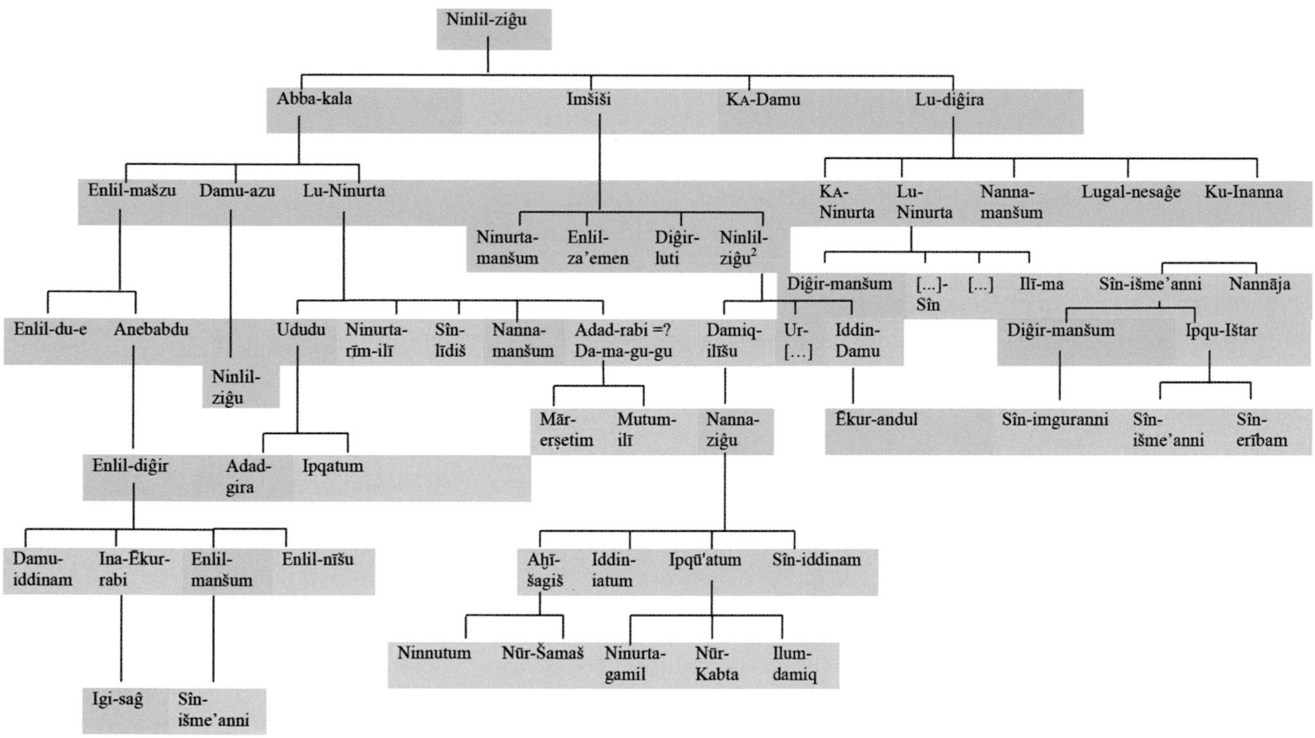

Fig. 1.
Family tree of the descendants of Ninlil-ziĝu, with the Sumerian names marked grey (Goddeeris 2016: 348).

Again, an appropriate name is by no means a *conditio sine qua non* for a cultic or administrative profession. This is illustrated by Fig. 1, which shows the family tree of the descendants of Ninlil-ziĝu, who kept the office of *pašīšum* priest (gudu₄) of Ninlil in Nippur during the Old Babylonian period (Goddeeris 2016: 348). The tree could be reconstructed on the basis of a large number divisions of inheritance pertaining to this family, in which all the male siblings are enumerated. We see that Sumerian names are popular among the *pašīšum* priests (cf. Stol 1991: 197–198): thirty of the sixty names in the family tree are Sumerian, whereas Sumerian names make up 30% of the onomasticon of Old Babylonian Nippur as a whole. Sumerian names are more common in the earlier generations of the family—they seemed to be in fashion in clergical circles around the third generation, but at the same time, it is clear that a parent is free to choose any name. A parent may use this freedom to express his personal taste, to thank a god or also as a means to offer his child a social identity.

These tendencies to display one's cultic affiliation in personal names is observed in the names of the clergy of Nuska. We meet a Nuskatum and two different Nuska-nīšu's amongst it (Goddeeris 2016: 372–374).

Other criteria, besides provenance or linguistic affiliation of the name must help us to determine the "foreignness" of individuals. Below, we will discuss examples of specific professions linking the individual to the king, and thus to Larsa (e.g. dub-sar lugal-la, aga-ús lugal). Again, this factor must be used with caution, since the lú KAxŠU-NE lugal-la, discussed below as well, will appear to be a local Nippurite.

Finally, different language use and diplomatic practices may indicate that we are dealing with tablets drafted at another site, or with families originating from elsewhere (Stone 1987: 62; Charpin 1989: 110; Goddeeris 2016: 110).

To summarize: How can we identify foreigners and outsiders in cuneiform documents?

Most often we are only able to do this when the scribe wants us to. The scribe decides to include the country or city of origin; if he does so, it generates meaning. It shows that he considers the individual as a member of the outgroup, not belonging the social category in which the scribe functions.

Circumstantial evidence can be gained from the personal name of the individual, from his profession, from his function in the transaction recorded, and from the way the transaction is recorded (diplomatic practices and language).

The more details that are given to describe an individual, the further away he stands from the core of the social category in which the transaction takes place. In administrative archives, the main agents are described by their personal name only. Dependents and outsiders will be qualified by their profession or patronymic, by their city of origin, by their relation to third party, or by a combination of these elements—more or less in order of increasing distance.

In bilateral contracts, this scheme functions slightly different, since the identity of the participants must be indisputable. Therefore, a patronymic will be given systematically, and a profession may be added to indicate agency (such as the agency of the scribe in the list of witnesses, or the agency of the temple officials in contracts involving the clergy, cf. Tanret – Suurmeyer 2011). Only the place of origin is unambiguous, and outsiders must be identified on the basis of a combination of elements.

The salience of the clergy in Nippur

As the seat of Enlil, the head of the Sumerian pantheon, Nippur was the religious capital of Sumer, at the latest from the Early Dynastic period II onwards. All monarchs exercising hegemony in southern Mesopotamia during the third and early second millennium showed Nippur the highest esteem, bestowed it with votive gifts and renovated its temples (Klein 1998–2001: 534–535). The kings of Isin regularly proclaim tax exemptions for the citizens of Nippur (Kraus 1984: 17-30). Though still the religious and cultural capital of Babylonia after Hammurabi's conquest of Larsa, it becomes one of the many cities of the Babylonian empire on an administrative level.

In the Ur III and Isin-Larsa periods, Nippur also became the center of scribal education. The curriculum developed in its schools, which flourished between ca. 1820–1720 BC, became normative for all OB scribal schools (Klein 1998–2001: 537–538).

Impersonating this religious and cultural eminence, the priests of Enlil, his wife Ninlil, his son Ninurta, who was the city patron, and of Nuska, the vizier of the family, considered themselves the keepers of the Sumerian identity during this period.

Thanks to their wealth and their relatively high level of literacy, the members of the Nippur clergy produced the majority of the archival sources from the city during the Old Babylonian period. Excavations of Old Babylonian layers have yielded Sumerian literary texts, all kinds of school exercises, files of title deeds keeping track of the family estate of established families, and administrative records keeping track of the management of temples and their personnel (Stol 1998–2001).

Both because of the availability of relevant sources and because of the high salience and the exclusive status of the category, the priestly circles of Nippur form an excellent case-study for an investigation into the dynamics of social categories in Babylonia during the early second millennium BC. Who was allowed as a member of the Nippur clergy? What does a prototypical priest look like? Do we see changes in the course of time? To what outgroups does the Nippur clergy compare itself, and what is the result of this comparison? Where are the strangers, and to what extent can these outsiders participate in the cultic activities?

I will attempt to answer these questions through an exploration of three snapshots of Old Babylonian Nippur, each showing the clergy and the cult from a different perspective. First, I will look for foreigners in the administration of the so-called "central redistributive household" of the city, which managed aspects of the cult and of the urban infrastructure during the second half of the reign of Rīm-Sîn of Larsa. Next, we will investigate the consequences of an adoption that took place in the 28th year of Samsuiluna. A last group of texts dates from Samsuiluna 30, a couple of months before the city is taken over by Ilī-ma-ilum of the Sealand dynasty.

Snapshot 1: Strangers in the central redistributive household of Nippur

Unfortunately, the picture we are able to draw of the Old Babylonian temple management in Nippur remains fragmentary. The administrative files that have been recovered shed light on fascinating details such as the amount of barley spent every day as fodder for donkeys and for animals to be fattened for offerings (Robertson 1984: 153), and on the redistribution the regular bread and beer offerings (*satukku*) given to the members of the temple personnel (Sigrist 1984; Brisch 2017), but we keep groping in the dark about the various responsibilities of these priests and about the sources of income of the temples. One of the main uncertainties is: What falls under the responsibilities of the individual temples of Nippur (which owned fields that are distributed as sustenance fields to temple office holders), and what is managed by an apparently overarching institution (most recently Brisch 2017: 45; see also Goddeeris 2016: 340–341)? Because of this uncertainty, the institution behind the largest administrative file is labeled "central redistributive authority". This file dates from the second half of the reign of Rīm-Sîn (who ruled the kingdom of Larsa from 1822 to 1763 BC[2]; cf. Robertson 1981; 1984; 1989 and 1992; Goddeeris 2016: 335–341). The texts from the file are characterized by an unusual dating system (Robertson 1983; Goddeeris 2016: 336–340) and concern diverse aspects of the management of the cult, the infrastructure and the diplomatic affairs in the city of Nippur.

One group of texts in particular illustrates the variety of destinations associated with these expenditures: the lists of miscellaneous barley expenditures (Goddeeris 2016: 250–265 with the newly published documents TMH 10 161-176, earlier

[2] According to the middle chronology.

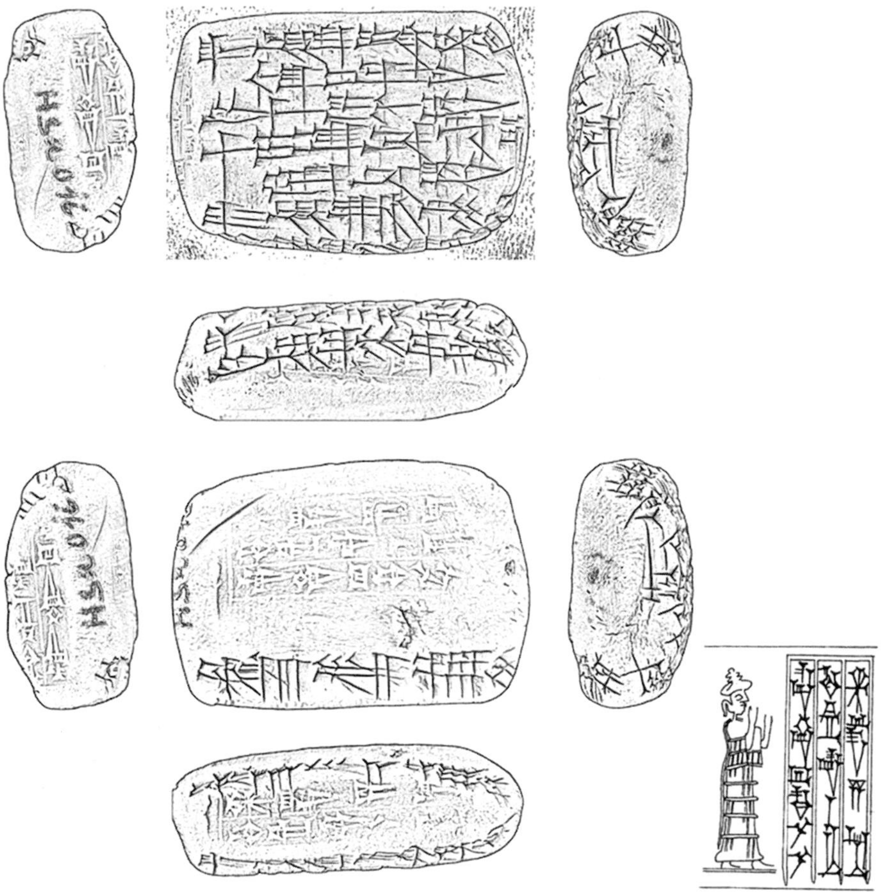

Fig. 2.
PLD recording of TMH 10 174, showing the landscape format and the seal impression, accompanied by a line drawing of the seal, by Ursula Seidl and Anne Goddeeris.

discussions: Robertson 1984). In these lists, disbursements for cultic purposes are listed next to infrastructural expenditures (among other things repairing the city wall) and diplomatic expenses (for delegates of the king and his entourage). Here, we encounter an interesting group of foreigners.

One sub-group of these lists of miscellaneous barley expenditures has a very specific lay-out and seems to contain exclusively diplomatic expenditures. It consists of three documents now located in the Hilprecht Sammlung (Jena), now published as TMH 10 173-175, and 7 documents kept in the University Museum of the University of Pennsylvania (Philadelphia). The tablets in the University Museum have not been discussed by Robertson in his dissertation (1981) because the documents do not mention a year-name. They are published below as an appendix to this article. The tablets have a landscape format and the same seal is enrolled on the reverse and the edges of every one of them (Fig. 2.). The seal bears a religious legend, which provides no information about the authority who seals (Seidl 2016: 313, no. 17).

The tablets all list expenditures of barley or *tappinnu* flour (or of a combination of both), disbursed to an individual who always seems to be acting in an official capacity. The table below gives an overview of the texts from this sub-file in chronological order (first column) and the entries in each text (second column).

Date (text)	Entries
1. iti ki-2 gu_4-si-su u_4-5-kam (TMH 10 173)	a. 60 l. of barley: Enlil-mudammiq, diviner of the house of Enlil-nādā
	b. 80 l.: Kudur-santab, man of Rīm-Sîn-rappašunu
	c. 60 l.: Ubarīja, man of Ilī-ma
	d. 20 l.: refugees
	e. 20 l.: the man of Enlil-magir, brother of Rabut-Sîn, he has brought the share of the yield (to me?) - the house of Ur-Lugalaba.
2. iti sig_4-a u_4-20-kam (CBS 7635)	a. 60 l. of barley: purchase price of various reed; KA-Utu, overseer of the diviners
3. iti sig_4-a u_4-26-kam (CBS 7502)	a. 160 l. of barley: rent of a boat: Sîn-rēmēni, of Iamutbalum
4. iti ki-3 sig_4-a u_4-9-kam (TMH 10 174)	a. 40 l.: Sîn-iqīšam and his colleague, men of the daughter of the king
	b. 10 l. *I-ṣi-da-re-e*, soldier of the king
	c. 30 l. Enlil-ḫāzir, man of Sîn-muballiṭ
5. iti NE-NE-ĝar u_4-20-kam (CBS 7681)	a. 180 l. of *tappinnu* flour, 120 l. of barley: a ram of Ḫaja-mušallim
	b. 180 l. of *tappinnu* flour, 120 l. of barley: a ram, a sheep of Abi-nārim
6. iti NE-NE-ĝar u_4-⌈26⌉-[kam] (CBS 7519)	a. 20 l. of barley: Salilum, man of Talimum
7. iti ki-6 kin di-nanna u_4-7-kam (TMH 10 175)	a. 60 l. of barley: Sâsum, man of the *entum* priestess of Iškur, daughter of the king
	b. 60 l. of *tappinnu* flour, aširtum offering of Sîn-dajjān, man of the town of Ḫubabum
8. no date (CBS 7507)	a. 600 l. of barley: the diviner [ ]
	b. 60 l.: Ḫāziru, ma[n of], man of Sîn-muballiṭ
	c. 20 l.: men of Utu-igiĝu
	d. 10 l.: man of Egigi
9. no date (CBS 7427)	a. 60 l.: Ištaran-emuqi, man of Sîn-muballiṭ: the 27th day
	b. 60 l.: Ištaran-emuqi, man of Sîn-muballiṭ: the 1st day
10. no date (UM 29-16-567)	a. 60? l.: man of Gimil-[ ], sheikh; he brought fish rations (?).

The destinations of the entries can be grouped into different types of foreigners. Several of these sets turn up in other lists of miscellaneous barley expenditures, such as CBS 7110. There, they occur alongside disbursements for local destinations, on unsealed tablets, dated with a year-name.

Disbursement to foreigners from outside Nippur

Three entries describe the recipients as foreigners from elsewhere. This never happens in the unsealed lists of expenditures. The origin of the refugees is not specified, however.

1.d.	20 l.	Refugees
3.a.	160 l.	A man from Iamutbalum[3] for the rent of a boat.
7.b.	60 l. of flour	*aširtum* offering of Sîn-dajjān, man of the town of Ḫubabum

Delegates of the king and his entourage

- of the king himself

4.b.	10 l.	*I-ṣi-da-re-e*, soldier of the king

In CBS 7110, *I-ṣi-da-re-e*, soldier of the king, receives 50 l. of barley when he brought a letter. In CBS 7449 barley (amount broken) is given to an unnamed soldier of the king, who brought a letter as well.

- of the *entum* priestess of Iškur, daughter of the king

4.a.	40 l.	Sîn-iqīšam and his colleague, men of the daughter of the king
7.a.	60 l.	Sâsum, man of the *entum* priestess of Iškur, daughter of the king

Lines 11–13 of CBS 7110, contain an entry of 60 l. issued to Iamaḫḫum, man of the *entum* priestess of Iškur of Karkar. In lines 1–5 of CBS 7435, 60 l. is disbursed to another man of the *entum* priestess of Iškur, daughter of the king, named Iškur-e-x.

These four entries illustrate how the Kudur-mabuk dynasty of Larsa has adopted the practice of appointing their daughters as high priestesses in major shrines, instated by the kings of Akkad and of Ur III. The priestess of Iškur may be a daughter of Rīm-Sîn himself, or of his father Kudur-mabuk.

3 The region of Maškan-šapir, Stol 1976: 63–72.

4.c.	30 l.	Enlil-ḫāzir, man of Sîn-muballiṭ
8.b.	60 l.	Ḫāziru, ma[n of], man of Sîn-muballiṭ
9.a.	60 l.	Ištaran-emuqi, man of Sîn-muballiṭ: the 27th day
9.b.	60 l.	Ištaran-emuqi, man of Sîn-muballiṭ: the 1st day

- of Sîn-muballiṭ, brother of the king

Although Sîn-muballiṭ is a very common name, we can identify this individual with the brother of the king of that name (Charpin 2004: 127), because this Sîn-muballiṭ is clo sely involved with high functionnaries of the king (Veldhuis 2007), some of whom, such as Rīm-Sîn-rappašunu and I/Egigi, send delegates to Nippur as well.

Delegates of Sîn-muballiṭ appear in the other lists of miscellaneous barley expenditures: in UM 29-15-859, Apil-Iškur, son of the man of Sin-muballiṭ, receives 60 l. In CBS 7451, the same individual also receives 60 l. of barley, this time not qualified as the son of a representative, but as a representative himself. In UM 29-15-937, finally, the name of the representative, who receives 10 l. this time, is not given.

- of royal functionaries known from administrative documents from Larsa.

Rīm-Sîn-rappašunu is a striking name, which occurs several times in administrative accounts from Larsa (Riftin SVJAD no. 114, no. 115—where it is written Rīm-Sîn-rapšunu—and no. 116, and Clevenstine 2015)[4], alongside other men with *Beamtennamen*.

A number of tabular accounts from the same group (Seri 2007: no. 43, and BM 85260, BM 85269, BM 16391 and BM 85232, listed in Robson 2004: 131, and to be published in Robson forthcoming) list other functionaries of Rīm-Sîn. On line 1 of Seri 2007: no. 43, we encounter I/Egigi, and on line 9, Seri reconstructs dumu-meš zi-da-re. However, the parallel she refers to (BM 85232, of which a copy by Robson can be found on CDLI) reads *i-ṣi-da-re-e*. I/Egigi also sends a representative to Nippur, and we have encountered *I-ṣi-da-re-e* already as a soldier of the king.

1.b.	80 l.	Kudur-santab, man of Rīm-Sîn-rappašunu

In CBS 7110, Ataḫaštum is the representative of Rīm-Sîn-rappašunu. He receives 60 l. of barley there.

[4] As also noted by Charpin 2018.

8.d.	10 l.	man of Egigi

In CBS 7535 (l. 3–4), two representatives of Igigi, Aḫī-wedum and his unnamed colleague, get 20 l. of barley.

- of other delegates

The other individuals who send delegates to Nippur cannot be identified any further.

1.c.	60 l.	Ubarīja, man of Ilī-ma
1.d.	20 l.	the man of Enlil-magir, brother of Rabut-Sîn, he has brought the share of the yield (to me?)—the house of Ur-Lugalaba

Rabut-Sîn must be a well-known individual. In CBS 7510, he sends his own delegate to Nippur: Nūr-Amurrum, man of Rabut-Sîn, who brought the boats, receives 60 l. of barley.

6.a.	20 l.	Salilum, man of Talimum
8.c.	20 l.	men of Utu-igiĝu

Representatives of Utu-igiĝu occur in two other entries, always unnamed: in CBS 7440, a delegate receives 10 l. of barley, and in UM 937, the amount is not preserved.

10.a.	60? l.	man of Gimil-[ ], sheikh; he brought fish rations (?)

Diviners

A last group of individuals receiving barley in these sealed administrative notes are the haruspices (máš-šu-gíd-gíd). Sallaberger and Huber Vulliet (2003–2005: 633) have noted that their sphere of influence is the palace rather than the temple.

1.a.	60 l.	Enlil-mudammiq, diviner of the house of Enlil-nādā
2.a.	60 l.	purchase price of various reeds; KA-Utu, overseer of the diviners
8.a.	600 l.	the diviner [ ]

The first entry of CBS 7110 records a disbursement involving a diviner as well: Šu-Amurrum, diviner, receives 300 l. of barley, wages for builders, a caravan to Adab. The exact meaning of this entry remains hidden for me. Just as in the damaged entry of CBS 7507 (reference 8.a.), the amount disbursed is much larger than the amounts given to individuals.

In this overview, the entries of text no. 5 have not been included, since they do not refer to individuals, but apparently to disbursements (of *tappinnu* flour and barley) for rams to be offered.

Some concluding remarks on the strangers in the "central redistributive household" of Nippur

Some unsealed texts on tablets with portrait orientation contain references to these outsiders as well. CBS 7110 (Robertson 1984: 176–178), for one, contains a lot of entries related to foreigners. However, it also lists several large disbursements for wages for builders, and several smaller for the purchase of reed and fish, certainly products to be acquired and used locally. CBS 7535 is another unsealed and non-landscape tablet recording nearly exclusively expenditures to representatives. However, the last entry records the disbursement of 120 l. of barley to a textile worker for embellishing the dress of Damiqtum (?).[5]

Thus, there is a clear distinction between the lists of the miscellaneous expenditures and the lists with expenditures to foreigners, formally as well as in substance. The foreigners, who are often affiliated to the palace in Larsa in some way, move at the outer fringes of the institution: a seal has to be enrolled in order to account for the expenditures on their behalf.

Although we cannot identify these foreigners on the basis of their personal names, there are some clear Elamite names (Egigi, Ataḫaštum, Iamaḫḫum and Kudur-santab) among the foreigners. Two officials whose representatives receive barley in the lists carry *Beamtennamen* referring to Rīm-Sîn. We have discussed Rīm-Sîn-rappašunu above, and a certain Rīm-Sîn-nādā appears in CBS 7535 and in UM 29-15-877.

The king appears in the affairs of the "central redistributional household" on two other occasions. Huber Vuillet (2010) discusses extensively two multi-column tablets with expenditures of meat to the urban authorities of Nippur, cultic personnel of different temples in Nippur, and members of a delegation from Larsa, including the cup-bearer of the king, who came by boat to the city. On the basis of the order of the disbursements, she reconstructs the course of events of the festival of Ninurta. The tablets are dated to the second month of Rīm-Sîn's 21st regnal year, and may record the celebration of Rīm-Sîn's ultimate recognition as supreme ruler of Babylonia in Nippur.[6]

Most recently, Charpin (2019) has drawn attention to the implications of TMH 10 26, a document recording two a-ru-a dedications by the king and by Simat-

[5] CBS 7535, l. 11–12: túg *da-mi-iq-tum* ku$_7$-ku$_7$-na-šè.

[6] This idea was proposed to me by Dominique Charpin in an personal communication.

Ištar, one of his wives, to the sancturies of Nippur. He situates these deeds in the aftermath of the conquest of Isin by Rīm-Sîn. Persons dedicated as a-ru-a often are prisoners of war.

Both these texts have a markedly earlier date than the other texts of the file. Could we conclude that they have been kept in the archives because of their exceptional nature?

Foreigners occur frequently in the file of the "central redistributional household", because hosting representatives from the entourage of the king and the palace in Larsa forms part of its responsibilities. Rīm-Sîn clearly attaches a lot of importance to his relations with the authorities of Nippur. These foreigners receive amounts of barley, but they do not participate in the household. Unfortunately, the unusual dating system of the file prevents us to situate the visits in the Babylonian calendar.

Snapshot 2: Adopting a stranger.

We may assume that the priests of the major sanctuaries are members of the established families of Nippur. In all the branches that could be identified in the reconstructed family tree of the descendants of Ninlil-ziĝu (Fig. 1), we meet holders of this temple office.

Although an exception to the rule, TMH 10 10 seems to confirm this assumption (Goddeeris 2016: 51–54). TMH 10 10 is an adoption contract dated to the 28th year of Samsuiluna: Tabni-Ištar, daughter of Ki-a'aĝaniše, the *nešakkum* priest, has adopted Lipit-Enlil, scribe of the king, son of Tarībum, as her heir. Through this transaction, Lipit-Enlil receives Ki-a'aĝaniše's term of the *nešakkum* office of Enlil. The document has several remarkable features:

1. lines 1–2: The adoptive mother is designated as "heiress of her father's estate". The scribe seems to be confused about the correct Sumerian term for "heiress": on the tablet he writes "dumu-munus ibila <é> ad-da-na-kam", whereas the case reads "munus-ibila é ⌈ad⌉-da-[...]". The—also atypical— division of inheritance TMH 10 15 uses still another combination of signs to discribe the concept: dumu-munus munus-UŠ (l. 27). Clearly, a sign combination for the concept of a female heir is not taught in the well-established schools of Nippur, which otherwise cover all the possible legal situations.

2. line 3: The profession of the adoptive son is "scribe of the king". This profession is otherwise not attested in Nippur either. The personal name of the adoptee, Lipit-Enlil, points to local roots, but Lipit-Enlil's profession places him outside the category of the Nippur clergy.

3. lines 5–15: The property transferred both ways: as said above, Lipit-Enlil receives Ki-a'aĝaniše's term of the *nešakkum* office of Enlil, together with its sustenance fields. However, he enters his adoptive house with 1 mina of silver, and he will provide his adoptive family with yearly rations of barley (1800 l.), oil (12 l.) and wool (5 kg.), which amount to triple the standard sustenance amount. Moreover, the deed stipulates that Lipit-Enlil, who is adopted as "eldest brother", compensates Ninurta-muballiṭ and Lu-Ninurta, sons of Tabni-Ištar, for the *nešakkum* office of Enlil with a term of 6 months of the offices of *pašīšum*, brewer, doorkeeper,

courtyard sweeper and buršuma of the temple of Baba. This compensation raises more questions than it answers. Why did Tabni-Ištar have to alienate this temple office, when she had two sons as heirs? Apparently, this transaction did not arise from poverty, or from the lack of successor. What would be the value of (this term of) the *nešakkum* office of Enlil and its sustenance fields? Who did the temple offices of Baba belong to prior to this transaction, to Tabni-Ištar or to Lipit-Enlil?

4. lines 16–23: The penalty clauses are nearly equal: if they do not adhere to the agreement, both parties have to pay 3 mina of silver. Tabni-Ištar loses any claim on the *nešakkum* office of Enlil, whereas Lipit-Enlil forfeits his income[7] (?).

5. lines 22–24: The oath, on the other hand, is sworn by Tabni-Ištar only. This is a clear-cut indication of her dependent position in this transaction.

In Old Babylonian Nippur, the large number of temple office sales give the impression that temple offices can be freely sold. However, the eminent priest offices of Nippur, such as the *pašīšum* and *nešakkum* offices of Enlil, Ninlil, Ninurta and Nuska, never occur in these purchase deeds. The deeds always concern minor offices such as the *pašīšum* office of Ningirgilu, Nindu and Pabilsaĝ (PBS 8/1 15) or *pašīšum* office, the office of overseer and the buršuma office of the temple of Amurrum (TMH 10 57). And in many cases, seller and buyer must have been related to each other. This becomes visible when large genealogies could be reconstructed, such as the family of Mannum-mēšu-liṣṣur (most recently described by Meinhold 2015) and in the family of Ninlil-ziĝu (cf. Goddeeris 2016).

In this adoption agreement, the heiress of the *nešakkum* priest of Enlil clearly does not willingly dispose of the temple office. Why she does so, while she has two sons, remains an enigma. Being described as a scribe of the king, the new *nešakkum* priest of Enlil, does not belong to the established clergical families. Only through an adoption, and at a large expense, he can enter this exclusive category. This transaction takes place during the last years of Samsuiluna's rule over Nippur, and agrees well with the developments observed in the file described below.

Snapshot 3: Who is in charge? Strangers in the house.

On two texts, both dating from the second day of 3rd month of Samsuiluna's 30th year, the last year of his rule over Nippur[8], TMH 10 no. 185 and no. 186, a seal that links the documents to the palace is enrolled. The legend of the seal (Fig. 3.) reads:

⌈lú⌉-^{d}nin-[urta]
⌈ugula⌉ é ^{d}nin-[urta]
lú KAxŠU-NE lugal-la
dumu ^{d}nin-urta-me-š[a$_4$]
ìr *sa-am-su-i-*[*lu-na*]

---

[7] TMH 10 10, l. 20: Á-ka-a-ni-ta.
[8] To be corrected in the edition (Goddeeris 2016: 273–274).

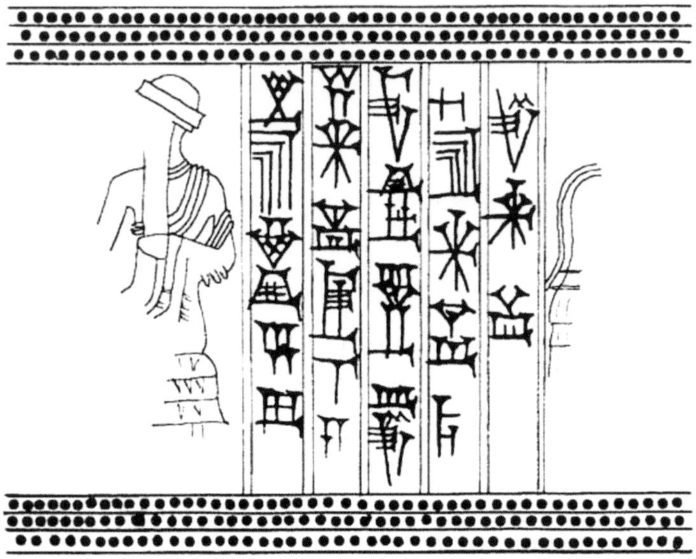

Fig. 3.
Line drawing of the seal enrolled on TMH 10 185 and 186 by Ursula Seidl and Anne Goddeeris (Seidl 2016: 306, seal no. 5).

Because Lu-Ninurta's father, Ninurta-meša, was an overseer of the temple of Ninurta as well, we can be sure that Lu-Ninurta is a member of the established clergical families in Nippur. On this seal, he has acquired a new title, lú KA-kešda lugal-la. This is the earliest mention of this title, which occurs only on seals. We know one example from Nippur (only these two texts with Lu-Ninurta), and several later ones from Sippar and Dūr-Abiešuḫ (De Graef – Goddeeris, forthcoming).

The two documents fit in a small administrative file of bullae and short accounts of expenditures dating to these last months of Samsuiluna's rule over Nippur.[9] These documents refer to several institutional buildings that do not appear in the earlier archival documents from Nippur such as the storehouse (araḫ$_x$), the storehouse of the palace (ésaĝ é-gal). Entries both refer to the palace in Babylon (the animal fattener of the palace, a journey to Babylon and the tax collector) and the temples in Nippur (*satukkum* offerings for Nin-Nibru, oil for Nin-Nibru, *tappinnu* flour for Ninšubur).

At this stage, the palace has gained access to the management of the temples in Nippur. It is not possible to reconstruct how exactly this was achieved. The economic crisis in the middle of the reign of Samsuiluna has certainly changed the situation.

Epilogue

After Nippur was lost to the first dynasty of Babylon, in the 30th year of Samsuiluna, its cult was reinstated in Dūr-Abi-ešuḫ (Charpin 2015: 153). The kings of Babylon did this for other cults as well, in order to establish themselves as the

[9] Goddeeris, in preparation.

rightful heirs of Babylonian kingship (Richardson 2018). The documents published by Van Lerberghe and Voet (2009) show how offering material and other resources are acquired through the agency of the well-known palace agents Utul-Ištar and his son Marduk-mušallim. Thanks to the funds of the palace in Babylon, the clergy of Nippur continues to exist in another location and is able to continue its activities in a "virtual Nippur" (Charpin 2015: 153)—be it on a smaller scale.

Conclusions

For kings in late third and early second millennium Babylonia, controlling Nippur was paramount to be recognized as the supreme ruler of Babylonia. In order to control the eminent city Nippur, the palace—whether it was located in Isin, Larsa or in Babylon—must get a foot in the door of its clergy. The clergy of Nippur was a powerful category, stable and undisputed. Especially in the context of the competing city-states Isin and Larsa, the category of the Nippur clergy was extremely salient.

Rīm-Sîn, king of Larsa, who acquired control over southern Babylonia in the course of the first half of his 60-year long reign, treated the clergy with the respect it was due. On a regular basis, all the members of his family and entourage sent representatives, who were in turn received with high regards (see *snapshot 1*).

The Babylonian kings are of a different category. Hammurabi conquered the kingdom of Larsa as a whole, and as one of the many kingdoms to be conquered, albeit a very prestigious one. The clergy of Nippur remained a stable and undisputed category. The small administrative file from the end of the reign of Samsuiluna (see *snapshot 3*) shows that the palace has managed to play a more active role in the management of the cult in Nippur. The question remains open whether the transaction discussed in *snapshot 2* could have taken place during the reign of Rīm-Sîn, when the king sought recognition by the clergy.

The case of the Nippur clergy shows how, in the course of a few generations, individuals who must remain at the fringes of a category—in this case the representatives of the palace—gradually take up a central place in the category, and a reference to palace connections (the inclusion of the phrase lú KAxŠU-NE lugal-la on the seal) becomes a prototypical characteristic of the category. These developments are indicative of transitions, in this case from a political system of city states to one of territorial states.

Appendix: The diplomatic accounts of the "central redistributive household" in the University Museum

These tablets have been studied during two research stays in the University Museum. I wish to thank Stephen Tinney, Professor of Assyriology and Associate Curator of the Babylonian Section of the Penn Museum, for allowing me to study these documents and Grant Frame, Professor of Assyriology, for allowing me the use of his office. Photos of the tablets can be found on the CDLI website.

The seal shown above and published by Goddeeris and Seidl (Goddeeris 2016: 263; Seidl 2016: 313) is enrolled on all the tablets published below.

CBS 7502

Obverse

2(bariga) 4(bán) še

á ^{giš}má

^{d}EN.ZU-*re-me-ni*

dumu *ià-mu-ut-ba-lum*

Reverse

iti sig$_4$-a u$_4$-26-kam

Translation

160 l. lease of a boat: Sîn-remēni, inhabitant of Iamutbalum.

Date.

CBS 7507

Obverse

2(gur) še gur máš$^{!}$-šu-gíd-gí[d] eš

1(bariga) *ḫa-zi-ru* l[ú$^{?}$] ^{d}en-líl$^{?}$

lú ^{d}en.zu-*mu-ba-*[*lí-i*]*ṭ*

2(bán) lú-me ^{d}utu-igi-[ĝu$_{10}$]

1(bán) lú e-gi$_4$-gi$_4$

2(gur) 1(bariga) 3(bán) še-gur

Reverse

uninscribed

Translation

600 l. of barley the diviner [ ]

60 l. *Ḫasīru* [ ] of Enlil, man of Sîn-muballiṭ

20 l. the men of ^{d}utu-ši-[ ] x

10 l. the man of Egigi

690 l.

Remarks

line 1: Tablet reads lú šu-gíd-gí[d-]

line 4: Reconstructed on the basis of CBS 7440: l. 5.

line 6: total

CBS 7519
Obverse
2(bán) še *sà-li-lum*
lú *ta-li-mu-um*

Reverse
iti ne-ne-ĝar u$_4$-⌈26⌉-[kam]

Translation
20 l. Salilum, man of Talimum
Date.

CBS 7527
Obverse
1(bariga) ^{d}ištaran-*e-mu-qí*
lú ^{d}en.zu-*mu-ba-lí-iṭ*
u$_4$-27-kam
1(bariga) ^{d}ištaran-*e-mu-qí*
u$_4$-1-kam

Reverse
uninscribed

Translation
60 l. Ištaran-emuqi, man of Sîn-muballiṭ; day 27
60 l. Ištaran-emuqi; day 1

CBS 7635
Obverse
1(bariga) še
šám gi-ḫi-a
KA-^{d}utu ugula máš-šu-gíd-gíd

Reverse
iti sig$_4$-a u$_4$-20-kam

60 l. barley, to buy reed; KA-Utu, overseer of the diviners
Date.

UM 29-16-567

Obverse

1$^{?}$(bariga) lú *gi*$_4$*-mi-i*[*l*]

ad-da MA[R.TU]

šuku ka-mar[^{ku6}]

ma an d[u$^{?}$]

Reverse

uninscribed

Translation

60(?) l. the man of Gimil-[ ], adda MAR.TU, who brought fish rations.

CBS 7681

Obverse

3(bariga) dabin 2(bariga) še

1 udu-nita

^{d}ḫa-ià-*mu-ša-lim*

3(bariga) dabin 2(bariga) še

1 udu-nita

im-me-er ^{d}*a-bi-na-ri-im*

Reverse

iti ne-ne-ĝar u$_4$-20-kam

Translation

180 l. flour, 120 l. barley: 1 sheep of Ḫaja-mušallim

180 l. flour, 120 l. barley: 1 sheep of Abi-nārim

Date.

References

Brisch, N., 2017. To Eat Like a God: Religion and Economy in Old Babylonian Nippur. In Y. Heffron – A. Stone – M. Worthington, eds., *At the Dawn of History: Ancient Near Eastern Studies in Honour of J. N. Postgate*. Winona Lake, IN: Eisenbrauns, 43–53.

Charpin, D., 1989. Un quartier de Nippur et le problème des écoles à l'époque paléo-babylonienne. *RA* 83, 97–112.

Charpin, D., 2015. Chroniques bibliographiques 17. Six nouveaux recueils de documents paléo-babyloniens. *RA* 109, 143–196.

Charpin, D., 2018. En marge d'ARCHIBAB, 29: à propos de TMH 10. *N.A.B.U.* 2018/97.

Charpin, D., 2019 En marge d'Archibab, 32 : du nouveau sur la famille royale de Larsa du temps de Rim-Sin I. *N.A.B.U.* 2019/18.

Çig, M., 1992. Eski Babil Çağına ait iki Tüketim Listesi. In H. Otten – E. Akurgal – A. Ertem – A. Süel, eds., *Hittite and other Anatolian and Near Eastern studies in honour of Sedat Alp*. Ankara: Türk Tarih Kurumu Basimevi, 91–96.

Clevenstine, E., 2015. MAH 15886 + 16295, a Rim-Sin Tabular Account in Geneva. *CDLN* 2015:9.

De Graef, K. – A. Goddeeris, forthcoming. Dangerous Liaisons? Temple Personnel with Royal Seals in the Old Babylonian Period.

Edzard, D.O., 1998a. Namen, Namengebung (Onomastik). A. Sumerisch. *RlA* 9, 94–103.

Edzard, D.O., 1998b. Namen, Namengebung (Onomastik). B. Akkadisch. *RlA* 9, 103–116.

Goddeeris, A., 2016. *The Old Babylonian Legal and Administrative Texts in the Hilprecht Collection Jena. With a contribution by Ursula Seidl. Texte und Materialien der Frau Hilprecht Sammlung* 10. Wiesbaden: Harrassowitz.

Goddeeris, A., in preparation. Samsuiluna's last efforts in Nippur.

Harris, R., 1977. Notes on the Slave Names of Old Babylonian Sippar. *JCS* 19, 46–51.

Haslam, A., 2004. *Psychology in Organizations: The Social Identity Approach*. London: Sage Publications (3rd edition).

Hornsey, M., 2008. Social Identity Theory and Self-categorization Theory: A Historical Review. *Social and Personality Psychology Compass* 2, 204–222.

Huber-Vuillet, F., 2010. Un festival nippurite à l'époque paléobabylonienne. In H.D. Baker – E. Robson – G. Zólyomi, eds., *Your Praise is Sweet. A Memorial Volume for Jeremy Black from Students, Colleagues and Friends.* London: British Institute for the Study of Iraq, 125–150.

Huddy, L., 2001. From Social to Political Identity: A Critical Examination of Social Identity Theory. *Political Psychology* 22, 127–156.

Klein, J., 1998–2001. Nippur. A. I. *RlA* 9, 532–539.

Michalowski, P., 1991. Charisma and control: on continuity and change in early Mesopotamian bureaucratic systems. In R.D. Biggs – McG. Gibson, eds., *The Organization of Power. Aspects of Bureaucracy in the Ancient Near East.* SAOC 46. Chicago: Oriental Institute of the University of Chicago, 45–58.

Meinhold, W., 2015 Das Vermögen der Familie des Mannum-mēšu-liṣṣur. *ZA* 105, 7–29.

Robertson, J.F., 1981. *Redistributive Economies in Ancient Mesopotamian Society: A Case Study from Isin-Larsa Period Nippur*. Ph.D. Dissertation. Philadelphia: University of Pennsylvania.

Robertson, J.F., 1983. An Unusual Dating System from Isin-Larsa Period Nippur: New Evidence. *ASJ* 5, 147–161.

Robertson, J.F., 1984. The Internal Political and Economic Structure of Old Babylonian Nippur: The Guennakkum and His "House". *JCS* 36, 145–190.

Robertson, J.F., 1989. Agriculture and the Temple Estate Economies of Old Babylonian Nippur. In H. Behrens – D. Loding – M.T. Roth, eds., *Dumu-e2-dub- ba-a. Studies in Honor of Åke W. Sjöberg*. Philadelphia: University of Pennsylvania Press, 457–464.

Robertson, J.F., 1992. The Temple Economy of Old Babylonian Nippur: The Evidence for Centralized Management. In M. deJ. Ellis, ed., *Nippur at the Centennial, Papers Read at the 35e Rencontre Assyriologique Internationale, Philadelphia, 1988*. Philadelphia: University of Pennsylvania Press, 177–188.

Robson, E., 2004. Accounting for change: the development of tabular book-keeping in early Mesopotamia. In M. Hudson – C. Wunsch, eds., *Creating economic order: record-keeping, standardization and the development of accounting in the Ancient Near East.* Bethesda, MD: CDL Press, 107–144.

Sallaberger, W., 1993. *Der kultische Kalender der Ur III-Zeit.* UAVA 7. Berlin: De Gruyter.

Sallaberger, W. – F. Huber Vulliet, 2003–2005. Priester. A.I. Mesopotamien. *RlA* 10, 617–640.

Seidl, U., 2016. Seal impressions (in German). In A. Goddeeris, *The Old Babylonian Legal and Administrative Texts in the Hilprecht Collection Jena. With a contribution by Ursula Seidl. Texte und Materialien der Frau Hilprecht Sammlung* 10. Wiesbaden: Harrassowitz, 303–326.

Sigrist, M., 1984. *Les satukku dans l'Ešumeša durant la periode d'Isin et Larsa.* BiMes 11. Malibu: Undena Publications.

Stol, M., 1976. *Studies in Old Babylonian History.* PIHANS 40. Leiden: Nederlands Instituut voor het Nabije Oosten.

Stol, M., 1991. Old Babylonian Personal names. *SEL* 8, 191–212.

Stol, M., 1998–2001. Nippur. A. II. Altbabylonisch. *RlA* 9, 539–544.

Stone, E., 1987. *Nippur Neighborhoods.* SAOC 44. Chicago: The Oriental Institute of the University of Chicago.

Tajfel, H. – M.G. Billig– R.P. Bundy– C. Flament, 1971. Social Categorization and Intergroup Behaviour. *European Journal of Social Psychology* 1, 149–178.

Tanret, M., 2015. Ur-Utu. C. Chief dirge-singer of Sippar. *RlA* 14, 501.

Tanret, M. – G. Suurmeyer, 2011. Officials of the Šamaš temple of Sippar as contract witnesses in the Old Babylonian Period. *ZA* 101, 78–112.

Turner, J.C., 2005. Explaining the nature of power: A three-process theory. *European Journal of Social Psychology* 35, 1–22.

Turner, J.C. – M.A. Hogg – P.J. Oakes – S.D. Reicher – M.S. Wetherell, 1987. *Rediscovering the Social Group: A self-categorization Theory.* New York: Blackwell.

Van Lerberghe, K. – G. Voet, 2009. *A late old Babylonian temple archive from Dūr-Abiešuḫ.* CUSAS 8. Bethesda, MD: CDL Press.

Veldhuis, N., 2008. Old Babylonian Documents in the Hearst Museum of Anthropology. *RA* 102, 49–70.

EGYPTIANS AS FOREIGNERS IN THE WESTERN DESERT DURING THE EARLY DYNASTIC PERIOD

Caleb R. Hamilton (Monash University)

Introduction

From the outset, I note that evidence for Egyptian interests in the Western Desert during the Early Dynastic Period is sporadic. The nature of this evidence is scattered across a wide region (Fig. 1), and can be difficult to interpret; however, in outlining the evidence, we are presented with a distinct opportunity to comment on this material and how it reflects a different type of interaction at this time. This is because of the nature of the evidence for Egyptian interactions, into what was then a non-Egyptian area. The types of Egyptian interactions with the indigenous culture in the Western Desert are unique for this time, and may be interpreted as a reflection of the Egyptians as foreign peoples entering a part of the Egyptian desert that had not yet been incorporated into the nascent Egyptian state.

It is also important to note that while the occurrence of evidence is not numerous, its existence is significant, and when explored it helps to provide a better holistic understanding of the capabilities, interests, and motivations of the expanding Egyptian state during the Early Dynastic Period. Here I present evidence to convey that, during the Early Dynastic Period, the Egyptians were foreigners in the Egyptian Western Desert.

I begin this discussion here by briefly setting out evidence closer to the Nile Valley from the Early Dynastic Period, which seems to indicate movement by the Egyptians out of the valley towards the Western Desert. I then turn to material further afield in Kharga and Dakhleh Oases, and how evidence here can present the Egyptians as non-native to the Western Desert based on the type and amount of archaeological evidence available. I then present concluding remarks on the nature of this evidence and how it can present the Egyptians as a foreign entity entering and encroaching towards the Western Desert during this time. Throughout this discussion the evidence is not exhaustive, though as much has been incorporated as possible, providing a geographical focus within a chronological framework, to allow coverage of a large region and across multiple dynasties.

A Prelude to Egyptian Activity in the Western Desert

Prior to the main discussion below, a brief comment on the nature of the evidence from the beginning of the dynastic era is useful, as it presents a particular attitude towards a group of people often linked to the Western Desert (though doubtfully the Western Desert region and Dakhleh area). Two artefacts from the reign of Narmer show representations of the king smiting the Ṯḥnw (Hamilton 2019),

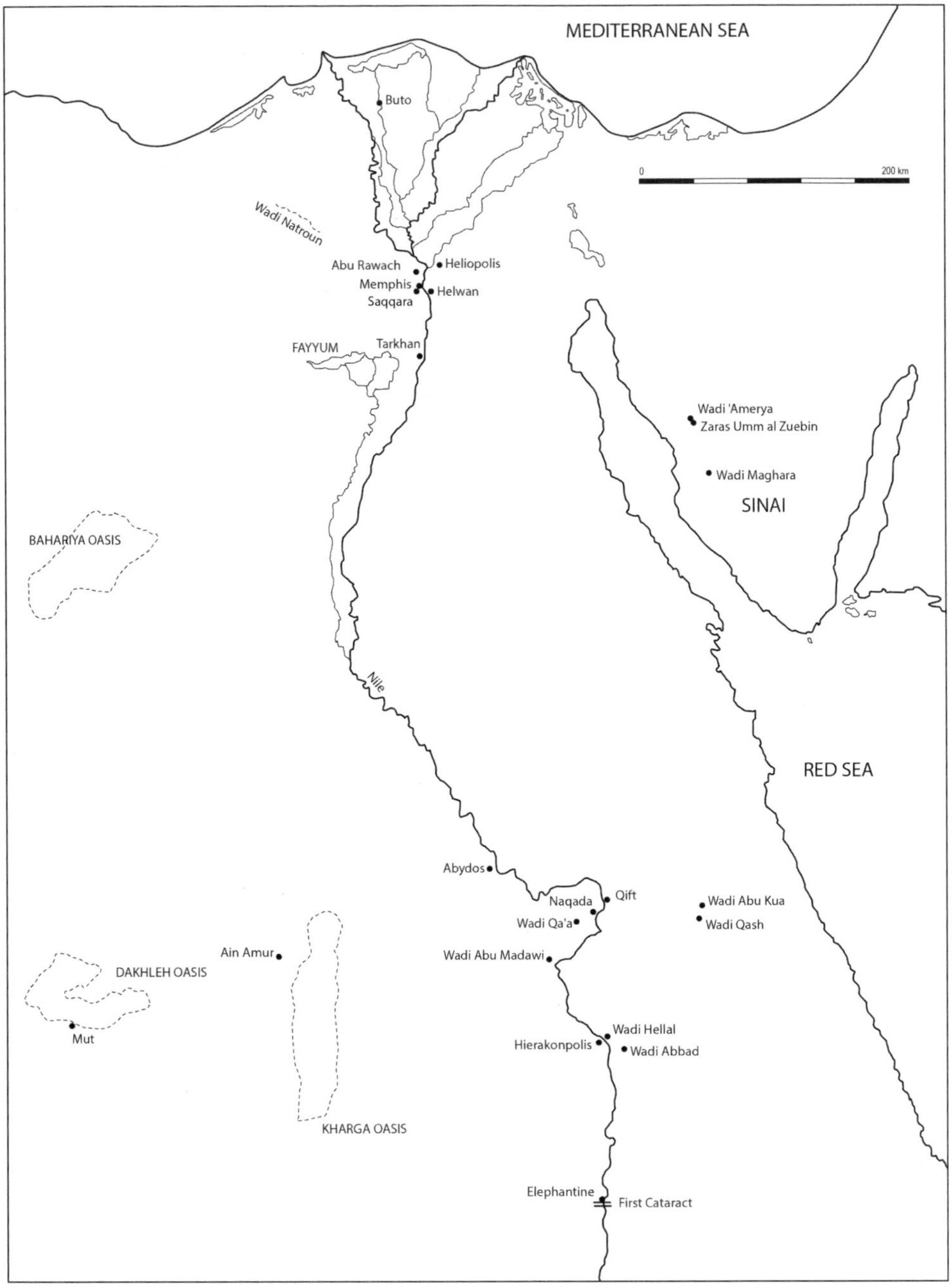

Fig. 1.
Map of Early Dynastic Sites.

though the location of these peoples and the meaning of this representation are contentious (Quibell 1900: pl. 15.7; Whitehouse 2002: 439; Dreyer et al. 1998: 33, 139, Abb. 29; 2005; Wilkinson 1999: 162). Other evidence alluding to interactions with the Ṯḥnw was unearthed at Umm al-Qaʿab (Dreyer at al. 1998: 162–163, pl. 12.a; 2003: 93, pl. 18.f). A label, divided into three registers, was found with the *serekh* of Djet on the uppermost register in front of arms raised towards the *tꜣ-stj* bow-sign. On the far right of the middle register is a figure with arms raised above

Fig. 2–3.
Serekh-signs of an unnamed ruler at Wadi Abu Madawi.

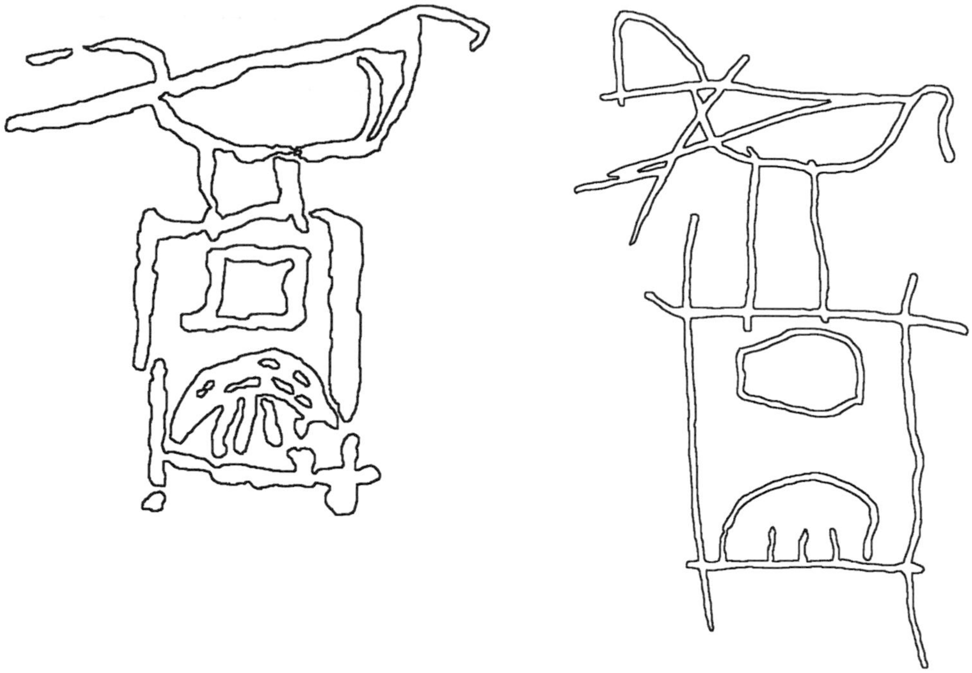

the throw-stick sign for Ṯḥnw (Gardiner 1957: 513, sign-list T14 and T15). The exact location of Ṯḥnw, either as a geographical region or a place where the Ṯḥnw-people came from, is unknown. It has been suggested that it could be an area to the west or north-west of Egypt, or west of the Delta (Hope 2007: 402). The same register from the label also details the foundation of a fortress, which Dreyer (1998: 163) suggests was a measure for controlling the western Delta. On the bottom register a delivery for Ṯḥnw-oil is alluded to, which has similarities with labels dating to the reign of Netjerykhet (Hamilton 2016a: 200). This label may indicate an economic relationship with the Ṯḥnw, though at the same time the two references to conflict with the Ṯḥnw and Nubia (in the form of *T3-Sty*), may suggest a dominant attitude towards them.

Care should be exercised with the analysis of such images, as not all records are comparable in nature. The Egyptian records are written or engraved from their own perspective and reflect their own cultural ideology, with a self-serving purpose. This would present the Egyptians as *the* dominant culture, aligning with aspects of their ideological system developing at this time. I return to this aggressive imagery below, within the context of Egyptian foreign interactions.

Two potential *serekh*-signs (Figs. 2–3) found in Wadi Abu Madawi allude to an unidentified ruler from the Protodynastic Period that seems to have had an interest in the desert margins near Armant (Winkler 1938: 10, pl. 10.2–3; Wilkinson 1995: 210; 1999: 56, fig.2.3(4)). While this evidence is presented elsewhere (see Hamilton forthcoming a, for a new interpretation), it is suggested that the rock-carved signs at this site, when linked with a later *serekh* (below) may allude to the importance of this desert margin region as a conduit from the Nile Valley out towards the desert and oases beyond.

More evidence into the desert margin of the Western Desert for a potential *serekh*-sign of Narmer has been found at Gebel Tjauti (Friedman – Darnell 2002: 19–22; see also Jiménez-Serrano 2001: 84; 2003: 111; Regulski 2010: 45). This *serekh*, attributed to Narmer, is not deep into the region of focus here, but does at least reflect the Egyptians interest beyond the Nile Valley, and links well with more evidence from this time, in this area, that is considered below and helps to show the movement towards the western oases.

The Desert Margins

I turn to evidence from the early 2nd Dynasty, which shows a continuation of interest in the desert margins. This evidence dates to the reign of Raneb (Fig. 4), where his *serekh* was found by Winkler (1938: 10, pl. 11.4) in the Wadi Abu Madawi, near Armant during his 1936–37 season. The reading of Raneb's name, while contentious at times (see Wilkinson 1999: 84, 293; Kahl 2007: 7–12, tab. 1; Regulski 2010: 50), can now be confirmed, and the *serekh* at this site attributed to the 2nd Dynasty king (Hamilton 2016b: 189–192).

This inscription may be indicative of expeditions into the Western Desert during Raneb's reign, taking trade routes from the Armant region towards the western oases' (Wilkinson 1995: 208; 1999: 84, 173).[1] An interesting thought regarding the nature of inscriptions has been raised by David and Wilson (2002: 6). They note that because inscriptions are often long-lasting or intended to be permanent marks on the landscape in which they are inscribed, they may trigger a memory with anyone viewing the inscription. This is noteworthy because Raneb's inscription at Wadi Abu Madawi can be viewed in the wider scope of the landscape there, where other earlier inscriptions have been left by a late Protodynastic ruler, mentioned above (Wilkinson 1995; Wilkinson 1999: 173; Hamilton forthcoming a).[2]

The two Protodynastic *serekh*-signs and Raneb's *serekh* may have been left in this general area as a mark for an entry or exit point from the Armant region into the Western Desert, perhaps onto Kharga Oasis. Raneb may have had his *serekh* left here in an attempt to evoke his ability to send expeditions to the Armant region and perhaps further afield. The combination of all three inscriptions would indicate that this area near Armant could have been an important departure point for the Western Desert during the Protodynastic and into the Early Dynastic Period.

This movement of the Egyptians out beyond the peripheral, towards the oases is reflected in the ceramic record found in the Yabsa Pass, which includes Nile Valley forms that date to the late Predynastic and Early Dynastic Periods. This could indicate that either Nile Valley Egyptians were passing between this region, towards Kharga Oasis during the Early Dynastic Period, or that items were traded

[1] The later Persian rock inscriptions at the same site appear to refer to Kharga Oasis, see Di Cerbo – Jasnow 1996: 32–38.

[2] Tallet (2015: 10–11, pls. 7–8, 10) has raised the possibility that there may be a parallel between the name in these *serekh*-signs and a *serekh* in the Wadi ʿAmeyra.

Fig. 4.
Serekh of Raneb at Wadi Abu Madawi.

with other people using this route (D. Darnell 2002: 166; Hope 2007: 405). D. Darnell (2002: 166) suggests that due to the volume of ceramic evidence from Yabsa, this interaction was intensive and repetitive. This seems to be similar for the route from Gebel Qarn al-Gir, in the Hour region, westwards from the Nile Valley towards the Western Desert, probably towards north-eastern Kharga (D. Darnell 2002: 166).

Towards Kharga Oasis

That the Egyptians undertook expeditions to the oases' during the Early Dynastic Period is supported by the presence of another *serekh* in the Kharga Oasis region. During the 2003–2004 season of the North Kharga Oasis Survey, Ikram and Rossi (2004) identified a *serekh* that was not clearly discernible (Fig. 5). The *serekh* is surrounded by other images of a possible hunting scene (Ikram – Rossi 2004: 212, fig. 1).

When interpreting the *serekh*, Ikram and Rossi (2004: 213, fig. 3) note that the falcon adorns the palace-façade with the arm-sign inside (Gardiner's sign-list D36) (Regulski 2010: 46). The falcon tilts forward slightly, with a straight top along the palace-façade, above the name compartment, which generally dates the *serekh* no earlier than the reign of Aha. Ikram and Rossi (2004: 213) initially suggested that

Fig. 5.
Serekh of Qaʾa at Ayn Amur.

the name of the owner of this *serekh* may be "Aa", an otherwise unattested king of the Protodynastic. This conclusion has been challenged by Hendrickx et al. (2009: 230), who suggest that the *serekh* belongs to Qaʾa. This is based on the crouching position of the falcon, which indicates an early date; however, the wing as a single line which continues above the body of the bird, and the upright position of the head, may contradict an early date. The identification of a known king is more appropriate than speculation of a hitherto unattested ruler. Thus, it is better to interpret the name as a defective writing of the name of Qaʾa. This *serekh* therefore indicates an Early Dynastic expedition to the Kharga Oasis region, strengthening the notion that the Egyptians ventured away from the Nile Valley during the 1st Dynasty. To inscribe a *serekh*-sign in this manner may reflect a notion that Darnell (2002; 2007: 34; 2009: 85) suggests could reflect a physical marking, and incorporation of an area into the Egyptian world, as well as their world-view related to their need to promote an ideological dominance of the world around them (see Hamilton 2016a: 23–25). This could be seen as their engagement with a foreign area, noting that they saw themselves as not of this region, and as such, desired to incorporate this into the new state, both ideologically and physically.

This evidently shows an early Egyptian interest in the Kharga region, though the scope and range of this Egyptian interest in Kharga or beyond into the Dakhleh region is difficult to gauge due to the limited archaeological evidence for this period this far into the Western Desert (see Hope – Pettman 2012: 157–158; Hamilton 2019: 171–172). The *serekh* of Qa᾿a in the Kharga region may link with an expansion of activity in the Western Desert, through the desert margins, during his reign, and was possibly continued into the 2nd Dynasty, suggested by the engraving of Raneb's name along an entry and exit route to the region (see Hamilton 2016b: 194–196).

Dakhleh Oasis: the Egyptian Material

Evidence from the Dakhleh region is not specifically dated, with some material generally dated to the Early Dynastic Period (Fig. 6). Early during the survey of the oasis, vessels with parallels to the 1st Dynasty forms were found in Grave 1 at 32/390-L2-1 in Dakhleh Oasis (Hope 1980: 288–289, pl.17.b–c; Mills 1980: 258; Hope – Pettman 2012: 161). This site is around 1.5 km south-east of Amhida, with graves cut into the red clay which were re-used during the Roman period. The grave contained a semi-contracted burial of an elderly male (Mills 1980: 258), with three vessels and a large body sherd. These were originally ascribed generally to the Early Dynastic Period (Hope 1980), though reservations about this date were raised by Giddy (1987: 166). More recently Hope and Pettman (2012: 161) paralleled the slender necked jar and deep bowls found with others which date to the reign of Aha (see Bestock 2008). This again seems to suggest that the 1st Dynasty Egyptians may have been interested in the Western Desert (Hamilton 2019: 176–77), with Mills (1999: 174) suggesting that these pieces were the result of trade. Whether this is down-the-line trade or direct trade ventures by the Egyptians into Dakhleh is hard to establish so far.

Other evidence in this region has recently been dated to the 2nd Dynasty. Such evidence comes from Locality 229 (30/450-G8-2), a watch-post in Dakhleh Oasis. Activity at Locality 229 (30/450-G8-2), has been dated as early as the 2nd Dynasty based on an analysis of the ceramic corpus for this site (Pettman forthcoming). This first phase of activity was followed by a second, which has been dated to the late Old Kingdom (McDonald 1990: 49; Pettman forthcoming). This is indicative of an Egyptian presence here during the Early Dynastic Period within the southern part of the oasis, perhaps in hunting huts, or to form a position which could better survey the surrounding area, and to help with expeditions and exploration. If the dating of these ceramic forms is correct, then they are not suggestive of a permanent settlement, rather it alludes to the Egyptians moving through this area from the Nile Valley. This notion may link with evidence from beyond Dakhleh outlined below.

These vessels indicate that the first phase of use for Locality 229 was sometime during the Early Dynastic Period, most likely during the 2nd Dynasty. A significant proportion of vessels from Locality 229 are of imported Nile Valley fabric which is a good indication of early interaction with this part of the region, though the nature of this interaction is at best speculative, especially considering that there is no intervening ceramic evidence at the site between these two phases of use. This may be the result of limited excavations carried out at the site. Again, the

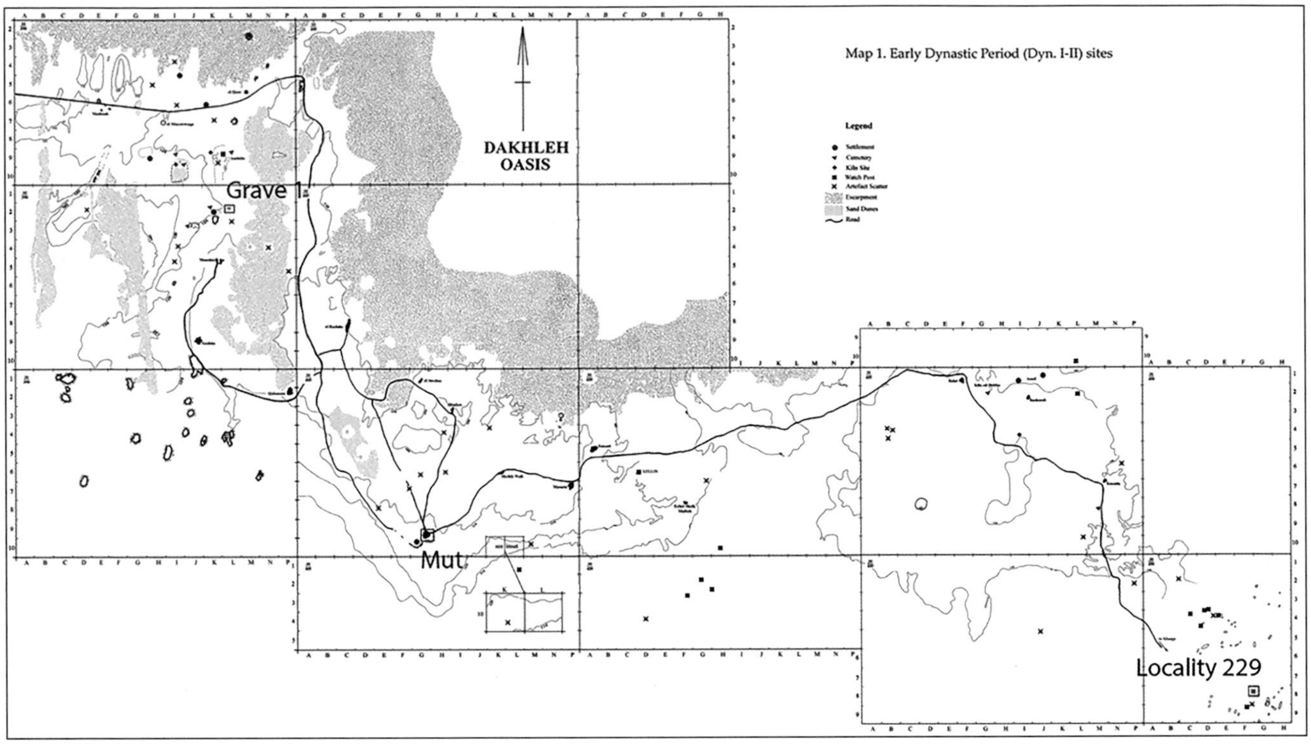

Fig. 6.
Map of Early Dynastic sites in Dakhleh Oasis.

finds here could indicate direct or indirect trade, but at least the vessels were definitively brought from the Egyptian Nile Valley.

The site of Mut al-Kharab has provided a unique example of Sheikh Muftah-Egyptian interactions. The ceramic evidence from the site seems to indicate a permanent Egyptian settlement some time during the 3rd or 4th Dynasty, with Sheikh Muftah inhabitants also present (Hope et al. 2018: 203). The ceramic finds at Mut al-Kharab have led to a reinterpretation of the Egyptians arrival in Dakhleh (see Hope – Pettman 2012; Hamilton 2016a: 202; Pettman 2016). The ceramic assemblage from the central part of the site is a mixture of Nile Valley ware, locally-made copies of the Nile Valley types, and Sheikh Muftah pottery. This was found in differing proportions within different archaeological contexts, with the lowest contexts assigned to the Sheikh Muftah and the upper most dated to the early Old Kingdom (Hope – Pettman 2012: 156–158). Mut may have originally been occupied by the Sheikh Muftah, with initial Egyptian contact taking place during the 1st–2nd Dynasty, though this was not a permanent occupation at this time (Hope – Pettman 2012: 159). Hope and Pettman (2012: 160) have interpreted this evidence as indicting a symbiotic relationship between the Sheikh Muftah and Egyptians at a site that was strategically located within the oasis. From this site, the exploitation of surrounding resources could be achieved, and could be aided by monitoring the activity within this part of the oasis. The Egyptian interests became more intense within the Western Desert into the 3rd and 4th Dynasty, when Egyptian settlement of Mut al-Kharab probably took place (Hope – Pettman 2012: 162; Hope et al. 2018: 193, 203). It is noteworthy that the redisposition of material during Egyptian building activity could have occurred, and may explain some of the mixed nature of the ceramic corpus.

Preliminary evidence from ʿAyn al-Gazzarin suggests that there may have been Egyptian-Sheikh Muftah interaction at this site (see Pettman 2016; Pettman et al. forthcoming). Below an Old Kingdom wall, ceramics were excavated that have been linked to a possible Sheikh Muftah campsite. The evidence of co-habitation is not as clear when compared with Mut al-Kharab. It is possible that there may have been episodic Sheikh Muftah occupation at ʿAyn al-Gazzarin, contemporary with the Egyptians. This builds in the notion that peaceful interactions took place between the Sheikh Muftah and Egyptians (Mills 1999: 220; Hope 2007: 407).

Dakhleh Oasis: the Sheikh Muftah Cultural Unit and the Egyptians

I turn now to discuss the indigenous culture of the Western Desert at the time the Early Dynastic Egyptians began to venture into this area. The Sheikh Muftah Cultural Unit occupied Dakhleh Oasis prior to the Egyptian encroachment, settlement and eventual annexation of this area of the Western Desert, and later, seemingly co-existed with them into the Old Kingdom. Their archaeological identification was originally proposed by Mary McDonald (1999: 117, 122–130). The growing body of material culture, especially ceramic and lithic material for the Sheikh Muftah allows for a re-interpretation of the interactions between these two cultures (see Hope 2007; Warfe 2003; 2017; Hope – Pettman 2012; Hamilton 2016a; Hamilton 2019; Pettman 2016; Ricketts 2015; 2017; forthcoming; Hope et al. 2018).

By detailing some of the evidence of the Sheikh Muftah, it will become apparent that they occupied parts of the Western Desert, primarily in the Dakhleh Oasis area, prior to the Egyptians, and that during the Early Dynastic Period, they probably had an influence on the Egyptians exploring this region.

Dates for the Sheikh Muftah Cultural Unit correlate with the Pre- and Early Dynastic Periods, as well as the Old Kingdom. This is based on radiocarbon dates, and the relative dating via imported Egyptian ceramic evidence in the Western Desert, and also locally produced wares (Hope 2002: 51, 56–58). Unfortunately, dates for Sheikh Muftah sites are not secure, with only a handful of radiocarbon dates published (McDonald 2002: 113). These range from 3800 to 2900 BC cal, though notably evidence for the Sheikh Muftah continues into the 5th Dynasty (Kaper – Willems 2002: 81; McDonald 2002: 113; Hope – Pettman 2012; Hope et al. 2018: 193; Pettman et al. forthcoming).

A significant Sheikh Muftah site for our discussion here is El Kharafish 02/5. Located on the southern plateau of the escarpment, north of the Dakhleh depression, this site has been radiocarbon dated with dates aligning to the Early Dynastic Period. However, the dates could fall between the 2nd and 4th Dynasty, leaving an overly large timeframe to date the occupation, though a later date seems more likely (Riemer at al. 2008: 602–603; Riemer 2011: 705). Excavations yielded a small amount of Egyptian pottery (1.5%) amongst the Sheikh Muftah assemblage, which was consistent with Old Kingdom forms, similar to pottery found at Khufu 01/01 which is dated to the 4th Dynasty (Riemer at al. 2008: 591–592). This pottery could be indicative of exchange between the Sheikh Muftah and Egyptians, rather than an Egyptian presence at El Kharafish 02/5. This seems to indicate a lack of permanence of the Egyptians here during the Early Dynastic Period, and from a non-Egyptian perspective indicates a more dominant culture in this area.

Another important site is the Sheikh Muftah encampment of Balat North/1. This site is situated approximately 90 m north of the enclosures at ʿAyn Asil. A Sheikh Muftah occupation has been identified by a cluster of fireplaces, concentrations of bone, ceramic, and flint items (Jeuthe 2014: 105; 2017: 166–170). The preliminary analysis of this site dates it to the late 3rd Dynasty, or the early 4th Dynasty (Jeuthe 2017: 167). This seems to be similar to the co-existence at Mut al-Kharab (Hope 2007: 405; Hope – Pettman 2012: 156; Pettman et al. forthcoming), when during the Old Kingdom that the Egyptian settlement seems to take place.

Balat North/1 provides evidence of both imported and locally produced Egyptian pottery, which was excavated from the dwelling pit at Camp 1 (Jeuthe 2017: 173). This can be coupled with the use of Egyptian-like techonology (Hope – Pettman 2012: 159), such as mudbricks, which were used to construct short-term features sucgh as storage pits in the campsite (Jeuthe 2017: 170–173). It is also notable that six fragments of clay sealings were excavayed, possibly originating from ʿAyn Asil (Jeuthe 2014: 110), though the original date of these is not exact and re-depositing can be preposed. It seems from this evidence that interactions between the Sheikh Muftah and Egyptians resulted in some entanglement, though the exact nature of this is debatable (Ricketts forthcoming). Siginificantly, it seems that the Egyptians movement in to the region did benefit the local indigenous culture, suggesting a somewhat symbiotic relationship at times.

It is possible that groups of Sheikh Muftah and Egyptians may have co-existed peacefully within Dakhleh Oasis, which is inferred from the mixed ceramic assemblages at some other sites in the oasis, such as Locality 136, Locality 404, and Mut al-Kharab (McDonald et al. 2001: 6, 8; Hope and Pettman 2012: 149). Based on ceramic evidence from Mut, some Sheikh Muftah interacted with the Egyptians at this site, perhaps in a symbiotic manner.

Beyond Dakhleh Oasis: the Jaqub Stela

A notable piece of evidence for an early Egyptian presence in the Western Desert was found at Jaqub 02/50 (Riemer 2006: 3; Förster 2015: 263–269). A stela was found associated with charcoal and dung from a shelter at this site, which has been dated between ca. 2900 and 2700 cal BC (Riemer 2011: 188–193; Hope – Pettman 2012: 161; Förster 2015: 515). An incised falcon on the stela has been dated based on stylistic features (Fig. 7), to the end of the 1st Dynasty or the beginning of the 2nd Dynasty (Hendrickx et al. 2009: 203, figs. 13–14, 17; Hendrickx et al. 2011: 142–143; Förster 2015: 265; Hamilton 2016a: 192–193). This seems to correlate well with these radiocarbon dates. Also present on the stela are two Barbary sheep, as well as a *wꜥs*-sceptre. This iconography was often used as an expression of elite Egyptian activity (Hendrickx et al. 2009: 228–231). Barbary sheep are also depicted

Fig. 7.
Stela from Jaqub 02/50.

at Meri 02/12, which is close to Jaqub 02/50 and the Abu Ballas Trail. These sites have yielded Sheikh Muftah pottery (Riemer 2006: 3), which when combined with the iconographic evidence may indicate Egyptian interactions with local Sheikh Muftah people at these sites, or may have been directed to them with the Sheikh Muftah acting as guides (Förster 2015: 263, 515). This evidence may be suggestive of cooperation between these two cultures in the Western Desert. While evidence of Egyptian interaction with the inhabitants of this region is limited before the 3rd or 4th Dynasty, it is possible to suggest that the stela from Jacub 02/50 may have been carved by a member of an Egyptian expedition, far away from the Nile Valley. It is probable that the Sheikh Muftah people may have accompanied Egyptian expeditions into the Western Desert, as attested by Sheikh Muftah ceramics at such sites (Hendrickx et al. 2009; Förster 2015: 263–269; Hamilton 2016a: 193).

The hieroglyphic inscriptions from Khufu 01/01 details an expedition during the reign of Khufu and Djedefre (Förster 2007). Based on these inscriptions, it has been suggested that the aim of the expedition was the procurement of a powder (*mfꜣt*) and pigment (*sš*) (Kuhlmann 2002: 134–136; Kuper – Förster 2003: 26; Kuper et al. 2004: 6–7; Kuhlmann 2005: 247–251). This shows the Egyptians interest ranged beyond Dakhleh Oasis, from at least the beginning of the 4th Dynasty, though knowledge of this powder and its sources may date to a time before Khufu's reign, prior to the beginning of the Old Kingdom. The pottery excavated at Khufu 01/01 is an oasis fabric, possibly from Dakhleh, though some Nile Valley imports were also present. The latter was characteristic of early Old Kingdom forms, matching the inscriptions (Kuper – Förster 2003: 27–28; Kuper et al. 2003: 10). A small quantity of Sheikh Muftah ceramics may suggest that they acted as guides for the Egyptian expeditions (Hope 2007: 407; Hope – Pettman 2012: 160; Hope et al. 2018: 206). This is similar to the evidence from sites on the Abu Ballas trail.

A Foreign Egyptian Entity into the Western Desert

The evidence for interactions between the Egyptians and Sheikh Muftah is limited during the Early Dynastic Period (Hendrickx et al. 2009: 193; Förster 2015: 146–154; Hope et al. forthcoming: 5). Evidence for Egyptian interactions in the Western Desert began slowly, with a small amount of evidence for the 1st and 2nd Dynasty (see Hamilton 2019). This evidence seems to indicate seasonal ventures beyond Dakhleh Oasis. These ventures may have involved an element of trade and exchange with the Sheikh Muftah. Notably, the evidence of interactions with the Sheikh Muftah does not indicate violence, or the Egyptianisation of this group (Mills 1999: 177; Hamilton 2016a: 244). Indeed, co-habitation may have occurred at Mut al-Kharab (Hope at al. 2006: 38). Hope et al. (2018: 203–206) note that the interactions between the Egyptians and Sheikh Muftah should not be considered static, highlighting that different groups of the Sheikh Muftah people may have reacted to the arrival of the Egyptians in differing ways. Some may have been hostile, resisting the Egyptians, while others may have left the oasis (Hope et al. 2018: 204). It is hard to gauge the quantification of non-homogenous objects found at a site and what they represent in regards to cultural interaction. The higher quantity of foreign objects found at a site can indicate a permanent presence of those that made or brought such objects to that place; though it could also reflect a large quantity of these objects traded or moved via exchange networks, which would not necessarily require a permanent presence at the site. Both possibilities indicate interactions between different groups of peoples; therefore, this evidence is reliable as an indication of cultural contact (Caple 2006: 138). The nature of this contact at Mut seems to have been co-habitation, though an extant Sheikh Muftah presence still needs to be ascertained with future excavations under the Egyptian occupation. This would seem to indicate the earliest example of permanent settlement in the Western Desert by the Egyptians; thus, setting-up a new period of the incorporation of this area into an expanding Egyptian state, with the associated Egyptian ideology and world-view. This leads to a time when the Egyptians are no longer foreigners in this peripheral region to their well-established presence in the Nile Valley during the Early Dynastic Period.

The Abu Ballas trail, as mentioned earlier, dates to the late Old Kingdom (see Förster 2015: 146–154). Sheikh Muftah ceramics were found on this road with Egyptian ceramics, though association and dating of these requires caution as they were collected as surface material. However, other evidence from the Western Desert, beyond Dakhleh Oasis, could be indicative of reconnaissance or hunting expeditions, perhaps originating from Dakhleh or even from the Nile Valley or perhaps even resources at this early stage of Egyptian history (Hendrickx et al. 2009: 229; Hamilton 2016a: 226). It is notable that there was no Egyptian pottery found at Jaqub 02/50 or Meri 02/12, which may indicate that the Egyptians were cooperating with the Sheikh Muftah, who may have acted as guides for the Egyptians during the Early Dynastic Period (Hendrickx et al. 2009: 230–231; Förster 2015: 263; Hamilton 2016a: 192). It is also possible that the Egyptians did not drop any ceramics at these sites, or they may have only been infrequently visited by them, and could have been predominantly used by the Sheikh Muftah. Ultimately, this evidence can be interpreted as a foreignness exhibited by the Egyptians, with a reliance on others in the Western Desert for the Sheikh Muftah's expertise.

Concluding Remarks

Apart from belligerent representations of the Egyptians over the Ṯḥnw, during the Protodynastic Period and the early 1st Dynasty, there is a lack of conflict or an aggressive attitude apparent in the Western Desert from extant evidence during the Early Dynastic Period or early Old Kingdom (see Hamilton 2016a: 241, 244; Hamilton 2016c: 107; Hamilton 2019: 176–177). It is not clear whether these representations of the Ṯḥnw relate to a specific group of people, or alternatively an area of the Western Desert. Therefore, the aggressive policy towards the Ṯḥnw during the reign of Narmer and Djet may reflect episodic conflict, or simply a reflection of ideological fervour.

Egyptian interactions with the Western Desert began in an explorative nature, with evidence of a specific policy towards the region evident during the reign of Qaʾa at the end of the 1st Dynasty. During the early 2nd Dynasty, Raneb is the only king who shows specific interest towards this region, though this is only in the desert margin. The extent of these kings' policies towards the Western Desert is not overly clear, with resource exploitation a possibility, or access to trade networks from sub-Saharan Africa. By the 3rd Dynasty it seems that the Egyptians had developed a specific interest and eventually established a more permanent presence in Dakhleh Oasis, evident from the ceramics excavated at Mut al-Kharab. This may have been the beginning of the incorporation of this part of the region into the developing Egyptian state (Hope – Pettman 2012; Hamilton 2016a: 238; Hope et al. 2018). When contextualising the activities of the Egyptians in the Western Desert, it is apparent that these interactions contrasted those from other areas of Egyptian interest (see Hamilton 2016a). This could be attributed to the reliance they had on the indigenous peoples from the region, and is perhaps an acknowledgment of the notion that they were not the first to occupy the area. This is not the usual attitude that the Egyptian evidence conveys towards other cultures during this time; as they usually present themselves in alignment with their traditional ideological manner, as aggressive and dominant over the "other", often smiting, or exploiting other cultures and regions for resource procurement, of defence of Egyptian interests (see Hamilton 2016a: 239–244; Hamilton 2016c).

Notably, the evidence discussed extends the timeframe of cohabitation of Dakhleh Oasis beyond previous estimates (Mills 1999: 177). This aligns better with the intermittent contact between the Egyptians and the Western Desert during the 1st and 2nd Dynasty. The Egyptians may have been venturing to this part of the Western Desert in order to gain more direct access to commodities from the sub-Saharan trade that could filter through Dakhleh Oasis (Hamilton 2016a: 197). Until further evidence of the Egyptians expeditions further into Abu Ballas area, as noted by the carving at Jaqub 02/50, then it can be postulated that economic control within the region was a motivation for the Egyptians to move into the region as a non-indigenous culture. In doing so, they would bring their established administration and organisation, as well as their religion and ideology. A pre-existing knowledge of tradeable resources could be implied by the established expeditions to Khufu 01/01 during the first reign of the 4th Dynasty, with the possibility that such raw materials were already known during the 3rd Dynasty. Such ventures may have been conducted in conjunction with Sheikh Muftah assistance. This assistance is notable with earlier expeditions to Jaqub 02/50 and Meri 02/12, highlighting the Egyptians reliance on these people in the Western Desert prior to their occupation of the area. This strengthens the notion of the Egyptians as foreigners, initially into the Western Desert.

Increasing interest was paid to the Western Desert from the 1st Dynasty to the 3rd Dynasty. Beginning with a cursory amount of evidence, this region may have been explored by a small number of Egyptians, perhaps for hunting trips (Hendrickx et al. 2009: 229; Förster 2015: 263–269). It is not until the reign of Qaʾa at the end of the 1st Dynasty that definitive evidence exists for an Egyptian expedition beyond the desert margins of the region. While Qaʾa was seemingly more interested than other kings in the margins of the Western Desert and the oases, some expeditions may have taken place with the *serekh*-signs of two early kings and Raneb marking possible routes to and from the Western Desert near Armant. Ceramic forms from the archaeological evidence at Mut al-Kharab may suggest that there was an increasing Egyptian presence in Dakhleh Oasis, perhaps late in the 3rd Dynasty. This evidence suggests that there was an eventual expansion of Egyptian culture into the Western Desert, which would be solidified during the 4th Dynasty (Hope – Pettman 2012; Hope et al. 2018).

In tracing Egyptian foreign interactions during the Early Dynastic period, I have tried to show that different forms of evidence are available to illuminate how the Egyptians can be interpreted as encroaching on the Western Desert, initially during the Early Dynastic Period, then increasingly towards the Old Kingdom, as a non-Western Desert culture. The increasing need and reliance on the commodities from this region shaped the nature and character of the expeditions to retrieve them. While the ideological system directed towards non-Egyptians dictated a specific way in which interactions were represented, the archaeological evidence indicates a more symbiotic and cooperative nature of exchange. Indeed, the establishment of a permanent settlement in foreign regions may have been related to the protection or definition of Egyptian borders from external threats, which aligns with the ideological system of how the Egyptians viewed foreigners as a source of chaos (Köhler 2002: 501; Hamilton 2016a: 23–25).

References

Bestock, L., 2008. An Undisturbed Subsidiary Burial from the Reign of Aha. In E.M. Engel – V. Müller – U. Hartung, eds., *Zeichen aus dem Sand: Streiflichter aus Ägyptens Geschichte zu Ehren von Günter Dreyer*. Menes 5. Wiesbaden: Harrassowitz, 41–57.

Caple, C., 2006. *Objects: Reluctant Witnesses to the Past*. London: Routledge.

Cerbo, Di C. – R. Jasnow, 1996. Five Persian Period Demotic and Hieroglyphic Graffiti from the site of Apa Tyrannos at Armant. *Enchoria* 23, 32–38.

Darnell, D., 2002. Gravel of the Desert and Broken Pots in the Road: Ceramic Evidene from the Routes between the Nile and Kharga Oasis. In R.F. Friedman, ed., *Egypt and Nubia: Gift of the Desert*. London: British Museum Press, 156–177.

Darnell, J.C., 2002. The Narrow Doors of the Desert: Ancient Egyptian Roads in the Theban Western Desert. In B. David – M. Wilson, eds., *Inscribed Landscapes: Marking and Making Place.* Honolulu: University of Hawai'i Press, 104–121.

Darnell, J.C., 2007. The Deserts. In T.A.H. Wilkinson, ed., *The Egyptian World*. London – New York: Routledge, 29–48.

Darnell, J.C., 2009. Iconographic Attraction, Iconographic Syntax, and Tableaux of Royal Ritual Power in the Pre and Proto-Dynastic Rock Inscriptions of the Theban Western Desert. *Archéo-Nil* 19, 83–108.

Darnell, J.C. – D. Darnell – R.F. Friedman – S. Hendrickx, 2002. *Theban Desert Road Survey in the Egyptian Western Desert 1: Gebel Tjauti Rock Inscriptions 1-45 and Wadi al-Hôl Rock Inscriptions 1-45*. OIP 119. Chicago: Oriental Institute of the University of Chicago.

Dreyer, G. – U. Hartung – T. Hikade – E.C. Köhler – V. Müller – F. Pumpenmeier, 1998. Umm al-Qaab. Nachuntersuchungen im frühzeitlichen Königsfriedhof, 9./10. Vorbericht. *MDAIK* 54, 77–167.

Dreyer, G. – R. Hartmann – U. Hartung – T. Hikade – H. Köpp – C. Lacher – V. Müller –A. Nerlich – A. Zink, 2003. Umm al-Qaab: Nachuntersuchungen im frühzeitlichen Königsfriedhof. 13./14./15. Vorbericht. *MDAIK* 59, 67–138.

Dreyer, G., 1998. *Umm el-Qaab I. Das prädynastische Königsgrab U-j und seine frühen Schriftzugnisse.* AV 86. Mainz: Verlag Philipp von Zabern.

Dreyer, G., 2005. Narmerpalette und Stadtepalette. Die Unterwerfung des Deltas. In K. Daoud – S. Bedier – S.A. al-Fatah, eds., *Studies in Honor of Ali Radwan*. Supplément aux ASAE 34. Cairo: The Supreme Council of Antiquities, 253–261.

Friedman, R.F. – J.C. Darnell, 2002. Gebel Tjauti Rock Inscription 2. In J.C. Darnell – D. Darnell – R.F. Friedman – S. Hendrickx, eds., *Theban Desert Road Survey in the Egyptian Western Desert 1: Gebel Tjauti Rock Inscriptions 1-45 and Wadi al-Hôl Rock Inscriptions 1-45*. OIP 119. Chicago: Oriental Institute of the University of Chicago, 19–24.

Förster, F., 2007. With Donkeys, Jars and Water-Bags into the Libyan Desert: The Abu Ballas Trail in the late Old Kingdom/First Intermediate Period. *BMSAES* 7, 1–36.

Förster, F., 2015. *Der Abu Ballas-Weg: Eine Pharaonische Karawanenroute durch die Libysche Wüste*. Africa praehistorica 28. Köln: Heinrich Barth Institut.

Gardiner, A.H., 1957. *Egyptian Grammar: Being an Introduction to the Study of Hieroglyphs.* Oxford: Griffith Institute.

Giddy, L., 1987. *Egyptian Oases: Bahariya, Dakhla, Farafa and Kharga during Pharaonic Times*. Warminster: Wiltshire – Aris and Philips.

Hamilton, C.R. 2016a. *Egyptian Foreign Interactions during the Early Dynastic period.* Ph.D. Dissertation, Monash University, Melbourne.

Hamilton, C.R., 2016b. Enlightening the Enduring Engravings: The Expeditions of Raneb. *Archéo-Nil* 26, 185–204.

Hamilton, C.R., 2016c Conflict in the Iconography of the Protodynastic and Early Dynastic Periods. In R. Landgráfová – J. Mynářová, eds., *Rich and Great: Studies in Honour of Anthony J. Spalinger on the Occasion of his 70th Feast of Thoth*. Prague: Charles University in Prague, 99–114.

Hamilton, C.R., 2019. Mapping Early Dynastic evidence in the Dakhleh Region. In G.E. Bowen – C.A. Hope – B. Parr, eds., *Oasis Papers IX: Proceedings of the Ninth International Dakhleh Oasis Project Conference. Papers Presented in Honour of Anthony J. Mills.* Dakhleh Oasis Project Monographs. Oxford: Oxbow, 171–179.

Hamilton, C.R., forthcoming a. An Early Egyptian king in the Western Desert Margin. In J.C.R. Gill – C.R. Hamilton – A.J. Pettman – D.A. Stewart – A.R. Warfe, eds., *Dust, Demons and Pots: Studies in Honour of Colin A. Hope.* Leuven: Peeters.

Hendrickx, S. – H. Riemer – F. Förster – J.C. Darnell, 2009. Late Predynastic / Early Dynastic Rock Art Scenes of Barbary sheep hunting in Egypt's Western Desert: From Capturing Wild Animals to the Women of the 'Acacia House'. In H. Riemer, ed., *Desert Animals in the Eastern Sahara: Status, Economic Significance, and Cultural Reflection in Antiquity: Proceedings of an Interdisciplinary ACACIA Workshop held at the University of Cologne December 14–15, 2007.* Colloquium Africanum 4. Köln: Heinrich Barth Institut, 189–244.

Hendrickx, S. – R.F. Friedman – M. Eyckerman, 2011. Early Falcons. In L.D. Morenz – R. Kuhn, eds., *Vorspann oder formative Phase? Ägypten und der Vordere Orient 3500-2700 v. Chr.* Phillipika 48. Wiesbaden: Harrassowitz, 129–162.

Hope, C.A., 1980. Dakhleh Oasis Project – Report on the Study of the Pottery and Kilns. *JSSEA* 10, 283–313.

Hope, C.A., 2002. Early and mid-Holocene ceramics from the Dakhleh Oasis: Traditions and Influences. In R.F. Friedman, ed., *Egypt and Nubia: Gift of the Desert*. London: British Museum Press, 39–61.

Hope, C.A., 2007. Egypt and 'Libya' to the End of the Old Kingdom: A View from Dakhleh Oasis. In Z. Hawass – J. Richards, eds., *The Archaeology and Art of Ancient Egypt: Essays in Honour of David B. O'Connor*. Vol. 1. Supplément aux ASAE 36. Cairo: American University in Cairo Press, 399–415.

Hope, C.A. – A.J. Pettman, 2012. Egyptian Connections with Dakhleh Oasis in the Early Dynastic Perod to Dynasty IV: New Data from Mut el-Kharab. In C.A. Hope – R.S. Bagnall – P. Davoli, eds., *Oasis Papers 6: Proceedings of the Sixth International Conference of the Dakhleh Oasis Project.* Oxford: Oxbow, 147–166.

Hope, C.A. – A.J. Pettman – A.R. Warfe, 2018. The Egyptian annexation of Dakhleh Oasis: New Evidence from Mut al-Kharab. In K. Kuraszkiewicz - E. Kopp - D. Takács, eds., *The Perfection that Endures...: Studies in Old Kingdom Art and Archaeology.* Warsaw: University of Warsaw Press, 191–208.

Ikram, S. – C. Rossi, 2004. An Early Dynastic Serekh from the Kharga Oasis. *JEA* 90, 211–215.

Jeuthe, C., 2014. Initial results: the Sheikh Muftah occupation at Balat North/1 (Dakhla Oasis). *Archéo-Nil* 24, 103–114.

Jeuthe, C., 2017. Balat/Dakhla Oasis: the Sheikh Muftah camps during the Old Kingdom. In B. Midant-Reynes – Y. Tristant – E.M. Ryan, eds., *Egypt at its Origins 5. Proceedings of the Fifth International Conference "Origin of the State, Predynastic and Early Dynastic Egypt," Cairo, 13th–18th April 2014*. OLA 260. Leuven: Peeters, 165–174.

Jiménez-Serrano, A., 2001. Horus Ka and the cemetery of Helwan. *GM* 180, 81–87.

Jiménez-Serrano, A., 2003. Chronology and Local Traditions: The Representations of Power and the Royal Name in the Late Predynastic Period. *Archéo-Nil* 13, 93–142.

Kahl, J., 2007. *"Ra is my Lord". Searching for the Rise of the Sun God at the Dawn of Egyptian History*. Menes 1. Wiesbaden: Harrassowitz.

Kaper, O. – H. Willems, 2002. Policing the Desert: Old Kingdom Activity around the Dakhleh Oasis. In R.F. Friedman, ed., *Egypt and Nubia: Gift of the Desert*. London: British Museum Press, 79–94.

Köhler, E.C., 2002. History or Ideology? New Reflections on the Narmer Palette and the Nature of Foreign Relations in Pre and Early Dynastic Egypt. In T.E. Levy – E.C.M. van den Brink, eds., *Egypt and the Levant: Interrelations from the 4th through the early 3rd millennium BCE*. London – New York: Leicester University Press, 499–513.

Kuhlmann, K.P., 2002. The "Oasis Bypath" or the Issue of Desert trade in Pharaonic Times. In T. Lenssen-Erz – U. Tegtmeier – S. Kröpelin, eds., *Tides of the Desert – Gezeiten der Wüste. Beiträge zu Archäologie und Umweltgeschichte Afrikas zu Ehren von Rudolph Kuper*. Africa praehistorica 14. Köln: Heinrich Barth Institut, 125–170.

Kuhlmann, K.P., 2005. Der "Wasserberg des Djedefre" (Chufu 01/1). Ein Lagerplatz mit Expeditionsinschriften der 4. Dynastie im Raum der Oase Dachla, *MDAIK* 61, 244–289.

Kuper, R. – F. Förster, 2003. Khufu's 'mefat' expeditions into the Libyan Desert. *EA* 23, 25–28.

Kuper, R. – H. Riemer – S. Hendrickx – F. Förster, 2003. Preliminary Report on the Field Season 2002 of the ACACIA Project in the Western Desert. Köln: University of Cologne, Cooperative Research Centre 389, 1–12.

Kuper, R. – H. Riemer – S. Hendrickx – F. Förster, 2004. Preliminary Report on the Field Season 2003 of the ACACIA Project in the Western Desert. Köln: University of Cologne, Cooperative Research Centre 389, 1–22.

McDonald, M.M.A., 1990. The Dakhleh Oasis Project: Holocene Prehistory: interim report on the 1988 and 1989 seasons. *JSSEA* 20, 24–53.

McDonald, M.M.A., 1991. Origins of the Neolithic in the Nile Valley as seen from Dakhleh Oasis in the Egyptian Western Desert. *Sahara* 4, 41–52.

McDonald, M.M.A., 1999. Neolithic cultural units and adaptations in Dakhleh Oasis. In A.J. Mills – G.S. Churcher, eds., *Reports from the Survey of Dakhleh Oasis, Western Desert of Egypt, 1977–1987*. Oxford: Oxbow, 117–32.

McDonald, M.M.A., 2002. Dakhleh Oasis in predynastic and Early Dynastic times: Bashendi B and the Sheikh Muftah cultural units. *Archéo-Nil* 12, 109–120.

McDonald, M.M.A. – C.S. Churcher – U. Thanheiser – J. Thompson – I. Teubner – A.R. Warfe, 2001. The mid-Holocene Sheikh Muftah Cultural Unit of Dakhleh Oasis, South Central Egypt: A Preliminary Report on Recent Fieldwork. *Nyame Akuma* 56, 4–10.

Mills, A.J., 1980. Dakhleh Oasis Project: Report on the Second Season of Survey, September-December. 1979. *JSSEA* 10(4), 251–282.

Mills, A.J., 1999. Pharaonic Egyptians in the Dakhleh Oasis. In A.J. Mills – C.S. Churcher, eds., *Reports from the Survey of Dakhleh Oasis, Western Desert of Egypt, 1977–1987*. Oxford: Oxbow, 171–178.

Pettman, A.J., 2016. *Tracks Through the Sand: Understanding the Date and Nature of Old Kingdom Egyptian Activity in the Western Desert*. Ph.D. Dissertation, Monash University, Melbourne.

Pettman, A.J., forthcoming. Dakhleh's Old Kingdom Watch Posts: An Examination of the Ceramic Evidence for their Date. *CCÉ* 10.

Pettman, A.J. – C. Beauchamp – A.R. Warfe, forthcoming. Examining the Old Kingdom-Sheikh Muftah Connection at Ain al-Gazzareen through the Ceramic Evidence.

Quibell, J.E., 1900. *Hierakonpolis*. London: Quaritch.

Regulski, I., 2010. *A Palaeographic Study of Early Writing in Egypt*. OLA 195. Leuven: Peeters.

Ricketts, S.M., 2015. Approaches to lithic analysis: the assemblage from Mut al-Kharab. In J. Cox – C.R. Hamilton – K.R.L. McLardy – A.J. Pettman – D.A. Stewart, eds., *Ancient Cultures at Monash University: Proceedings of a Conference Held Between 18–20 October 2013 on Approaches to Studying the Ancient Past*. BAR international series 2764. Oxford: Archaeopress, 57–67.

Ricketts, S.M., 2017. *Sheikh Muftah and Old Kingdom Connections at Mut al-Kharab: A Lithic Study*. M.A. Thesis. Monash University, Melbourne.

Ricketts, S.M., forthcoming. The Sheikh Muftah Cultural Unit: insights into Social Relations with Old Kingdom Egyptians, Dakhleh Oasis and Desert Surrounds. In J.C.R. Gill – C.R. Hamilton – A.J. Pettman – D.A. Stewart – A.R. Warfe, eds., *Dust, Demons and Pots: Studies in Honour of Colin A. Hope*. Leuven: Peeters.

Riemer, H., 2006. Control Posts and Navigation System of the Pharaonic Abu Ballas Trail. Köln: University of Cologne, Cooperative Research Centre 389, 1–8.

Riemer, H., 2011. The lithic material from the Sheikh Muftah desert camp site El Kharafish 02/5, western desert of Egypt. In R.F. Friedman – P. Fiske, eds., *Egypt at its Origins 3: Proceedings of the Third International Conference "Origin of the State: Predynastic and Early Dynastic Egypt," London, 27th July–1st August 2008*. OLA 205. Leuven: Peeters, 705–725.

Riemer, H. – N. Pöllath – S. Nussbaum – I. Teubner – H. Berke, 2008. El Kharafish: a Sheikh Muftah desert camp site between the Oasis and the Nile. In B. Midant-Reynes – Y. Tristant, eds., *Egypt at its Origins 2: Proceedings of the International Conference "Origin of the State: Predynastic and Early Dynastic Egypt," Toulouse, 5th-8th September 2005*. OLA 138. Leuven – Dudley, MA: Peeters, 585–608.

Tallet, P., 2015. *La zone minière pharaonique du Sud-Sinaï. II: Les inscriptions pré- et proto-dynastiques du Ouadi 'Ameyra (CCIS no 273-335)*. MIFAO 132. Cairo: Institut françis d'archéologie orientale.

Warfe, A.R., 2003. Cultural origins of the Egyptian Neolithic and Predynastic: an evaluation of the evidence from the Dakhleh Oasis (South Central Egypt). *AAR* 20(4), 175–202.

Warfe, A.R., 2017. *Prehistoric Pottery from Dakhleh Oasis, Egypt*. Dakhleh Oasis Project Monograph 18. Oxford: Oxbow.

Whitehouse, H., 2002. A Decorated Knife Handle from the 'Main Deposit' at Hierakonpolis. *MDAIK* 58, 425–445.

Wilkinson, T.A.H., 1995. A New King in the Western Desert. *JEA* 81, 205–210.

Wilkinson, T.A.H., 1999 *Early Dynastic Egypt.* London: Routledge.

Winkler, H., 1938. *Rock-Drawings of Southern Upper Egypt: Sir Robert Mond Desert Expedition: Preliminary Report.* London: Egypt Exploration Society.

Wilson, M. – B. David, 2002. Introduction. In B. David – M. Wilson, eds., *Inscribed Landscapes: Marking and Making Place.* Honolulu: University of Hawai'i Press, 1–12.

AN EGYPTIAN'S FOOTPRINT: MEMBERS OF THE EGYPTIAN ADMINISTRATION AND MILITARY IN LB I SOUTHERN LEVANT

Ann-Kathrin Jeske (University of Vienna)

"Then Sharuhen was besieged for three years. Then his majesty despoiled it. Thereupon I carried off spoil from there: two women and a hand" (Wilson 1955: 233). With these words, Ahmose, son of Ibana, recorded what is presumably the first Egyptian encounter with the southern Levant in the 18th Dynasty. This was followed by a gradual increase in the number of written documents referring to Egyptian activities in the "northern foreign lands" Canaan, *ḏ3hj* or *rṯnw*. The study of such documents was quite popular during the last century and many scholars trained in Egyptology and Near Eastern studies or archaeology contributed their research and opinions concerning Egypt's involvement in the Levant. Many tended to put the emphasis of their research on the textual record and demoted the archaeological remains to an auxiliary source to support arguments. Although one cannot neglect the significance of the preserved texts, Egyptian material culture uncovered in the southern Levant should be entitled to its own "voice" and be regarded as a valuable independent source to test and potentially challenge results gained by text analysis. Furthermore, in the light of the sometimes quite positivist and uncritical reading of the preserved textual record, our approach ought to change. *We should not ask: Why does the archaeological evidence not provide the needed information to verify statements in texts?*[1] Instead, we should thoroughly discuss any discrepancies between the archaeological and textual evidence. We need to find arguments to explain what might be causing inconsistencies, without favouring textual evidence as the "better" type in order to accordingly adjust our interpretations.

This paper presents and discusses a method to filter Egyptian archaeological material discovered in the southern Levant in order to generate a suitable data set that facilitates studying the activities of members of the Egyptian administration and military in the region. The backbone of this selection process are hypotheses derived from the two theoretical approaches *object itinerary* and *cultural appropriation*, while the concept of *affordance* offers a way to identify objects with which tasks could have feasibly been executed. This filtering method has been applied to Egyptian material culture excavated in the southern Levant with a LB I context to demonstrate the work process, on the one hand, and, on the other hand, to discuss how much knowledge can be gained by solely examining archaeological material.

---

[1] Höflmayer already pointed out the tendency of some, often referred to as "maximalists", to acknowledge missing archaeological evidence but to still not alter their interpretation(s); see Höflmayer 2015: 202. E.g. Morris 2005: 141: "Assuming that the textual references to forts and other buildings on foreign soil have a basis in fact, some explanation for their invisibility in the archaeological record must be discovered".

Theoretical background—*object itinerary, cultural appropriation and affordance*

Object itinerary

The *object itinerary* concept is a derivate of the more popular *object biography*[2] theory and was recently introduced by Hans Peter Hahn (2015) after criticising the application of a biography metaphor to objects. For the current study, the application of *object itinerary* was preferred, because it places more emphasis on the spatial mobility of objects, which better meets the requirements of this research. Within the chosen concept, the utilisation period of items is described as a succession of waystations that may represent spatial and chronological movements, physical alterations as well as changes in the perception of objects (Hahn et al. 2013: 8–9; Gosden et al. 1999: 169; Hahn 2015: 27). Generally speaking, waystations represent the production, utilisation and deposition of an item (Fig.1). Rephrased, each waystation stands for one or more interaction(s) between people and the objects with which they surround themselves. Thus, developing object itineraries of items that can be grouped, may allow for information about their users (as well as possibly their lives and cultures) to be deduced.

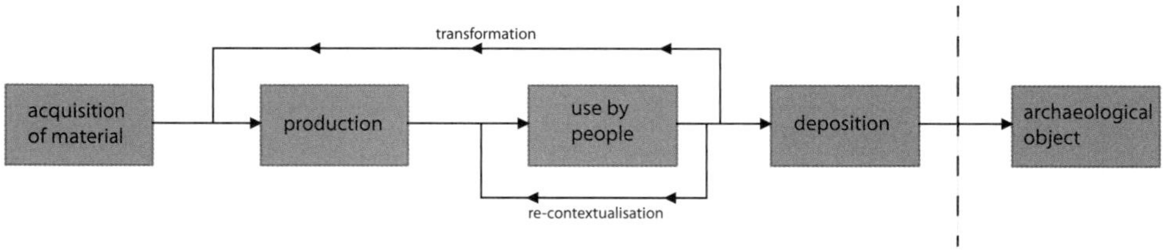

Fig. 1.
Succession of general waystations of any object within the framework of object itinerary.

Cultural appropriation

How does a society deal with objects alien to them, and how does it incorporate such objects into its own material culture? Silverstone et al. proposed a formalised description of such phenomena that they developed in the context of their consumption research (Silverstone et al. 1992: 15–28). Several anthropologists (e.g., Hahn 2014: 99–109) and archaeologists (e.g., Schreiber 2013[3]; Stockhammer 2012) adopted this theoretical approach—*cultural appropriation*—and altered it slightly in order to suit the needs of their research areas. To meet the requirements of my research, I too slightly altered the description of the appropriation processes: I renamed some of the processes in order to describe appropriation phenomena, because I did not consider some of the terminology decisive enough. Further, I bundled together some processes since they partially overlap, and because separating every single aspect does not necessarily enrich this study.

[2] Sergej Tretjakow and Igor Kopytoff developed independently from each other their object biography concepts. The core idea was to describe the environment and culture of people through objects with which they surround themselves; see Tretjakow 2007; Kopytoff 1986.

[3] Schreiber discussed very neatly the potential, but also the limitations, of this theoretical approach.

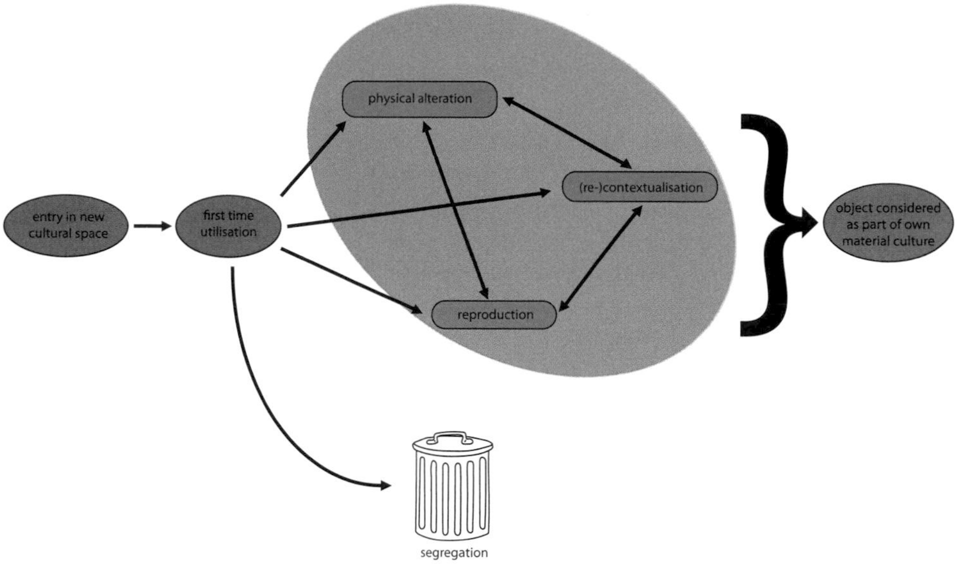

Fig. 2.
Cultural appropriation processes.

Therefore, processes of cultural appropriation are described as follows (Fig. 2): People are confronted for the first time with an object alien to them. With the first handling, people decide if the object might be useful or interesting to them, or if they will set it aside. Objects, which were considered as worthy of dealing with, can be subject to up to three different processes: physical alteration, (re-)contextualisation and reproduction. Physical alteration can be either visible or invisible, e.g., the cleaning of an item. All types of alterations were intended to meet the requirements of the new setting of utilisation. The process of (re-)contextualisation involves cultural negotiation[4] about the new "Sitz im Leben". The third process is the reproduction of items in the new cultural setting.[5] The three processes do not follow any set sequence, and not all of them must occur for a shift in the perception of an object—from that of being foreign to that of being part of the indigenous repertoire of material culture.

Affordance

With every new object, people are confronted with the question of how to use it. James Gibson examined how people handle objects within perception studies and coined the theoretical concept *affordance* (Gibson 1982). He postulated that items afford possibilities in their use via their physical properties. Therefore, a person is able to decode the full repertoire of an object's functions by interpreting their

---

[4] The use of the expression does not imply a verbal negotiation. Negotiation is rather a metaphor and denotes a process which is unconscious and may spread from small units of a culture to superordinate units, whereby the "correct" use is constantly negotiated; compare Wimmer 2005: 25–49.

[5] Egyptian scarabs which were reproduced in Levantine workshops, sometime after their first introduction in the region, are an excellent example of this process.

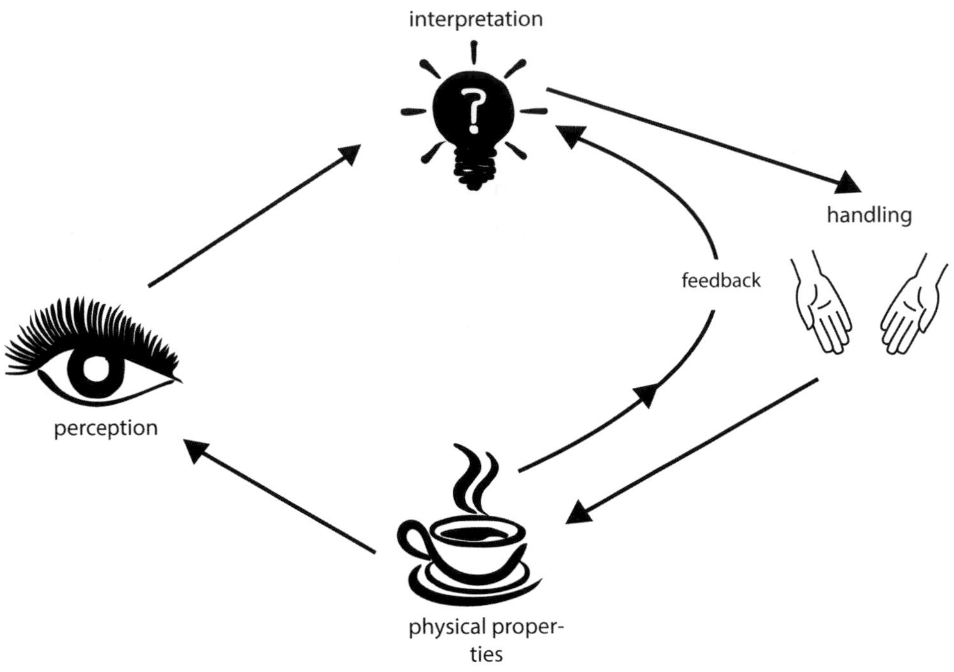

Fig. 3.
The affordance concept.

perception of its physical properties. But the proper interpretation needs to be learned, and it is open to misinterpretation (Fig. 3).[6] Archaeologists criticised Gibson in his approach for failing to include the cultural background of an object's user (Knappett 2004: 44–45). This criticism is expedient because archaeologists are confronted every day with the challenge of perceiving and interpreting the affordances of items which are not situated in their local material culture. Yet, while dealing with objects that were present in several cultural settings, the affordance concept offers a valuable perspective because it weakens the link between the function intended during the production process and the later function. The initially intended function is only one option, from a set of several theoretically possible functions. Therefore, functions actually applied in certain contexts might not necessarily equal the "proper" (negotiated) function, because a user's cultural influence may alter his or her perception of potential functions (Knappett 2004: 48–49; Keßeler 2015: 349).

[6] Using the example of a water glass: Firstly, it is a transparent vessel that can contain liquids and solids: beverages, yoghurt, pens/pencils, etc. Yet the use as container suitable for pens and pencils is only possible from a certain vessel height onwards; otherwise the pens could either fall out of the glass or due to high center of gravity, the glass could fall over with its content. Further, its shape and weight qualify it to be used as a projectile, yet, a user risks its destruction in this function due to its material. Both, that some physical properties afford the use as a projectile and that others do not, is something a person needs to learn.

Ideal object itinerary of Egyptian objects uncovered in the southern Levant

Who could transport Egyptian items to the southern Levant? To answer this question, which is crucial to the present study, an ideal object itinerary (Fig. 4) was created that is valid for all imported Egyptian objects excavated in the southern Levant.

To begin with, an item was manufactured in Egypt after the acquisition of its raw materials, which may have been imported into the Nile Valley. The item was used in Egypt for an undefined length of time before it was transported to the Levant by either regular Egyptians, non-Egyptians, or soldiers and officials in the service

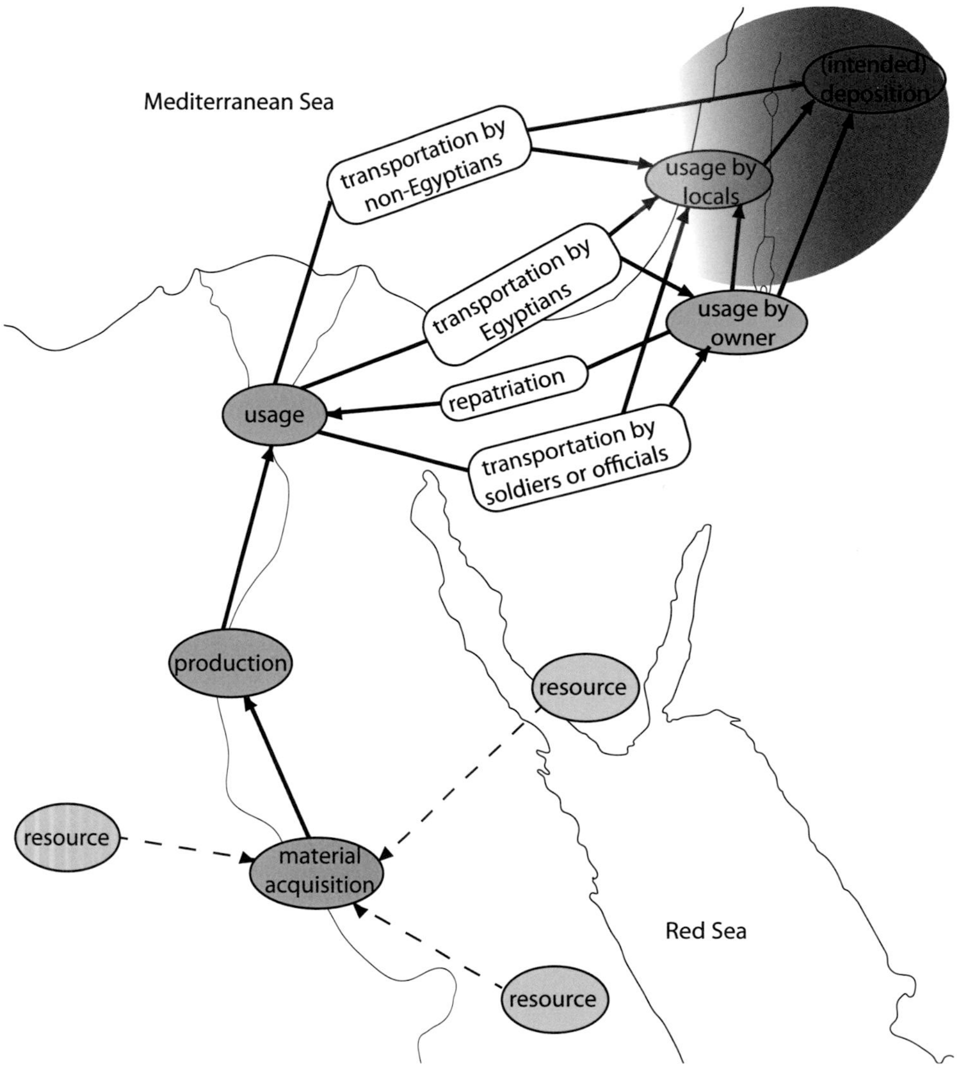

Fig. 4.
Ideal itinerary of Egyptian objects excavated in the southern Levant.

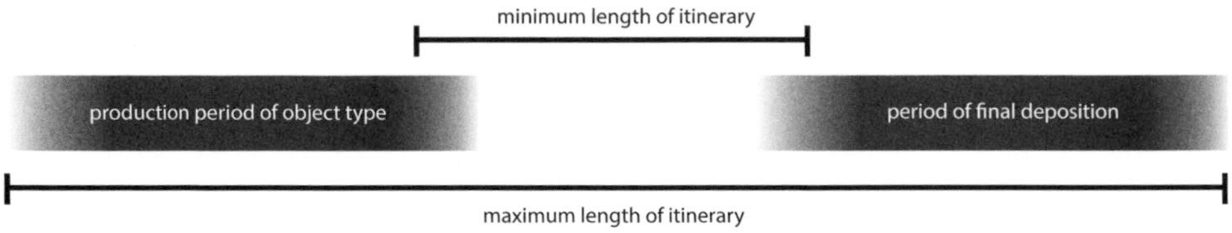

Fig. 5.
Definition of minimum and maximum length of itinerary.

of Egypt.[7] Two different groups of objects were transported: One, items intended for local use, like gifts and trade goods. Two, those intended for the personal use of the importer, i.e., equipment and personal objects. Objects of the latter group were supposed to return to Egypt but could have remained in the region for various reasons. They may have been deposited directly by their Egyptian owners or may have been used, secondarily, by locals prior to their deposition and were therefore exposed to the processes of cultural appropriation. The most common indicator of cultural appropriation are Egyptian objects that functioned as grave goods in a southern Levantine cultural setting. Yet, this phenomenon also demonstrates that it is not possible to conclude on the basis of the find context, who initially brought an Egyptian object from Egypt to the Levant.

The so-called length of an object itinerary, which is the chronological distance stretching between the production and the final deposition of an object (Fig. 5), can only be approximated because the when of production and deposition cannot be narrowed down to less than a generation. It is however possible to determine an itinerary's minimum and maximum length. An object's maximum itinerary length is the time passed between when objects of that type first began to be produced in Egypt and the end of the period in which the respective object was deposited. The minimum length of an object's itinerary is defined by the time passed between the end of its production period and the starting phase of its last deposition period.

Compilation of data set and discussion of discarded material

The aforementioned theoretical approaches—*object itinerary* and *cultural appropriation*—represent the mesh used to filter objects of Egyptian material culture excavated in the southern Levant. This filtering is done in order to compile a data set that allows for conclusions about the activities of Egyptian soldiers and officials at the objects' find locations. For this study's data set, all Egyptian objects must meet three criteria:

First, the find context in which the item was uncovered needs to be associated with a contemporary, notable settlement. Activities of Egyptian functionaries in the southern Levant required human-to-human contact[8] which is rather unlikely in a cemetery. I claim that the deposition of objects in burials not closely linked to

[7] The ethnic origin of these functionaries does not matter within the study. They are considered as Egyptian members of the administration and of the military if they acted on behalf of Egypt.

[8] See below concerning potential responsibilities of such.

a settlement is due to processes of cultural appropriation. Thus, such objects do not reliably indicate activities of Egyptians at the find location. Since there haven't been any notable occupation sites as of yet discovered in Gezer, Jerusalem[9] or Jericho, material discovered in contexts that date to LB I from these sites were ruled out.

The second criterion concerns the length of the object itinerary. The minimum length ought not exceed 50 years (~ 2 generations), whereas the maximum length must be less than 150 years (~ 6 generations). These boundaries were chosen due to the following considerations: Neither the date of the find context nor the production date typically provides a tighter time resolution than a quarter-to-a-half a century; rarely is a provided time resolution shorter than a decade. We also need to take into account a tolerance margin in the synchronisation between the Egyptian historical and Levantine relative chronologies[10] as both have a different conceptual foundation which can hamper proper synchronisation. Due to these considerations, the length of the object itinerary needs to be granted a certain minimum duration in order to meet the given demands of the objects. At the same time, the length must be as short as possible to minimize interferences such as cultural appropriation, which might for example, affect the spatial distribution of items. Every assemblage from sites yielding objects of Egyptian material culture includes some material that does not meet these boundaries.

The composition of a site's assemblage is the third and last criterion. The local and contemporary assemblage must contain additional objects of Egyptian material culture. One single object may have reached a site for any one of several reasons, but several Egyptian items, which also meet all of the criteria, hint more strongly at Egyptian activities. At Tel Dan, Yoqneam, Jericho, Jerusalem, and Tel Mor, the uncovered Egyptian objects are rather singular finds and therefore do not qualify for inclusion in the study's data set.

Summing up those sites that yielded Egyptian material in LB I but did not contribute to the data set: Tel Dan, Yoqneam, Jericho, Jerusalem, Gezer, and Tel Mor; because the objects uncovered at these sites failed to meet all three of the criteria. It should be noted that all of these sites (with the exception of Tel Mor) are located in the north or in the Judean and Samarian highlands.

I considered all Egyptian-styled pottery (locally produced pottery using Egyptian forms and production techniques) uncovered at LB I sites for the data set. This was done as this kind of pottery can be considered as an indicator of an Egyptian presence at the site; as already suggested by Martin (2004: 279). The non-prestige nature of Egyptian pottery justifies this assumption (Martin 2004: 279). Thus, it is rather unlikely that processes of cultural appropriation were triggered by

[9] Of course, Jerusalem stands out due to its long and continuous occupation that severely hampered research of older occupational levels. But if we do not have proper proof of a notable settlement at this site, from an archaeological point of view, we need to assume that there has not been one.

[10] For this study, the traditional synchronisation between Egypt and the southern Levant is applied: While the reigns from Ahmose to the end of the co-regency of Hatshepsut and Tuthmose III is contemporary to LB IA, the period from the beginning of the sole-reign of Tuthmose III up to the end of Tuthmose IV's reign covers LB IB.

such ware. Adding to this, certain Egyptian vessel shapes strongly resemble those in the Canaanite repertoire (Martin 2011: 23, 30), such that a Canaanite reproduction might appear redundant.[11]

Returning to the length of object itinerary, it is necessary to discuss the disadvantage of a tight chronological framework limiting the length of itinerary to less than 150 years. Several object types do not change their appearance over a period of time that easily exceeds the set 150 years, which means that all of those objects are ruled out from the study's data set. To mitigate this downside, all objects that meet all other requirements (including a minimum length of itinerary of less than 50 years) were assigned to an auxiliary data set. This auxiliary data set has only been used for an extended argument and to underline certain discussed aspects, because the estimated arrival of objects assigned to this set cannot be narrowed down to less than 150 years.

Responsibilities Egyptian functionaries might have had

In order to identify those objects that were transported by members of the Egyptian military and members of the administration, it is necessary to ask: *What could these individuals have done in LB I southern Levant?* While creating a potential repertoire of tasks Egyptian soldiers and officials might have engaged in, it is appropriate to consult the textual record. The consideration of texts does not undermine the study's aim to analyse and interpret the archaeological remains independently, if we do not exclusively focus on documents referring to LB I southern Levant. Potential responsibilities of Egyptian functionaries can be grouped into four categories: administrative,[12] diplomatic,[13] military,[14] and economic.[15] The assumption is that by identifying those Egyptian items that might have served in the execution of one of these potential tasks, it is possible to draw conclusions on the particular activities conducted by Egyptian soldiers and officials at the find site. With the appliance of the theoretical approach *affordance,* all objects that qualified for the data set were examined in order to check if they afford the use complying with the execution of one or several of the potential tasks.

Footprints of Egyptian functionaries in LB IA

The composed data set lists only Egyptian objects from Tell el-ʿAjjul (Fig. 6) that were uncovered in contexts dating between the accession of Ahmose and the end

[11] I would like to again emphasise at this point that compiling the data set is only intended as a means to rule out material that is unlikely to help understand the activities of Egyptian soldiers and officials in the southern Levant. During the analysis of the assembled data set, further explanations, within the sites' context and their general assemblage of material culture, are considered for the occurrence of this kind of pottery.

[12] E.g., documenting the arrival of goods, (re-)destribution of products and human resources.

[13] E.g., keeping contact with local elites.

[14] E.g., military campaigns, protection of Egyptians.

[15] E.g., trading, collecting tribute.

Fig. 6.
Distribution of Egyptian (-styled) material selected for the study's data set in the southern Levant during LB IA.

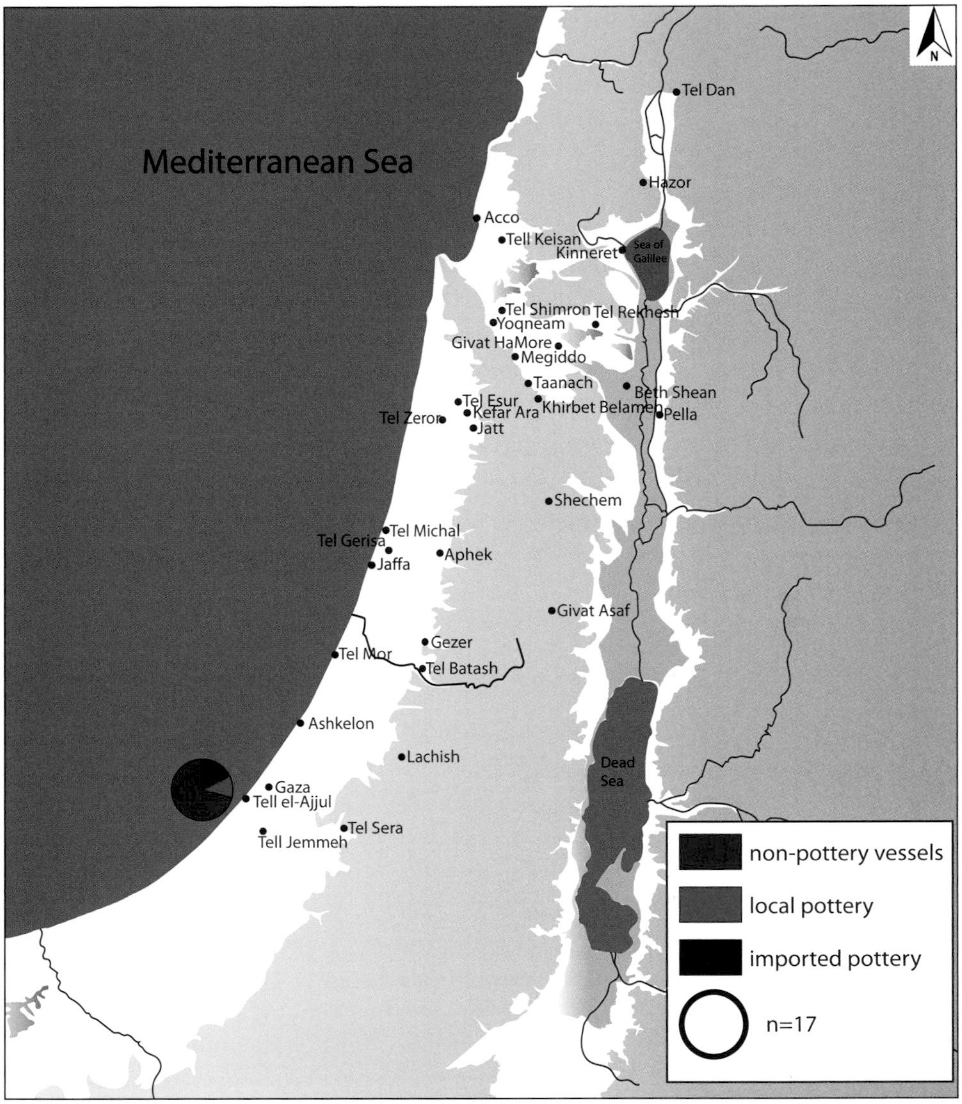

of the co-regency of Hatshepsut and Tuthmose III (LB IA). The site yielded a large amount of Egyptian material culture, among it, imported and Egyptian-styled pottery as well as stone vessels. Yet, only a small portion of preserved remains of Egyptian material culture could be considered for study due to major stratigraphical issues with the site. These issues were partially caused by Petrie's documentation; already a few years later, his stratigraphical interpretation was adjusted by Albright (1938), who was the first, but not the last to do so.

Petrie uncovered a large number of Egyptian and Egyptian-styled pottery, but the precise quantity and their find contexts can rarely be properly determined. Moreover, most of the pottery was not examined visually by specialists. Therefore the distiction the distinction between an imported or locally-produced pottery vessel is lacking. Fischer's two-campaign excavation conducted in a rather limited area yielded three imported jars that could have been used to transport goods (Fischer et al. 2002: 122–123; 2000: 224). Further, one bowl and one so-called flowerpot that were both locally produced were excavated (Fischer 2003: 281–82). Adding to the pottery, ten stone vessels of differing shapes were also discovered in five different burials (Sparks 2007: 282–283, 299, 303, 305, 309, 318–319, 321) and two stone vessels came from a settlement context (Sparks 2007: 318, 321) during Petrie's excavation.

The three imported ceramic jars afford the function as containers for trade goods or supplies, but due to their outer appearance, they were not trade items themselves. In contrast, a few small closed vessels made from stone could have been used in both functions: as containers (e.g., for cosmetic products) and as trade goods. Further, such a vessel could also have been presented as a gift. All stone vessels generally afford the use as trade goods and gifts.

Judging from the evidence provided by the objects in the data set, there is a slight indication of an Egyptian population living together with locals at Tell el-ʿAjjul. But since none of the objects' affordances is limited to a specific use associated with a potential task of Egyptian functionaries, it is unlikely that such were present at the site.

Footprints of Egyptian functionaries in LB IB

There is an increase in the remains of Egyptian material in LB IB; both in general and in the study's data set (Fig. 7). Again, Tell el-ʿAjjul yielded the largest number of objects.[16] Eight seals (Keel 1997: 146, 148, 184, 190, 192, 268, 270 and 270) and one seal impression (Keel 1997: 210) were considered for the data set. Among other symbols, the seal impression on a bulla bears the name of Tuthmose III from which one might conclude that this kind of seal—with royal names—were used particularly in Tell el-ʿAjjul to conduct administrative activities. Four of the eight seals that are shaped as scarabs or oval plaques bear royal names. The bulla and the four seals which could evidently have been used for sealing practices suggest administrative activities were conducted at the site. Further, the four seals afford the function as objects of legitimacy to identify oneself as a representative of an Egyptian institution. In addition to these objects, four stone vessels, 16 seals and another seal impression were uncovered in Tell el-ʿAjjul, but since their maximum itinerary length is too long, we cannot determine whether they arrived in the southern Levant within the LB IB period.

In Beth Shean, only Egyptian-styled pottery qualified for the study. Besides this, no other object type was uncovered in clean LB IB contexts at the site. The pottery assemblage consists of three so-called flowerpots (Martin 2011: 135), 14 bowls (Martin 2011: 135), and six jars (Martin 2011: 135–136). Although we do not have a complete repertoire of Egyptian pottery shapes, we do have a good indication for Egyptians inhabiting the site. Martin already reached a similar conclusion,

[16] Concerning pottery uncovered at this site, I would like to refer to the remarks mentioned in association with LB IA Tell el-ʿAjjul.

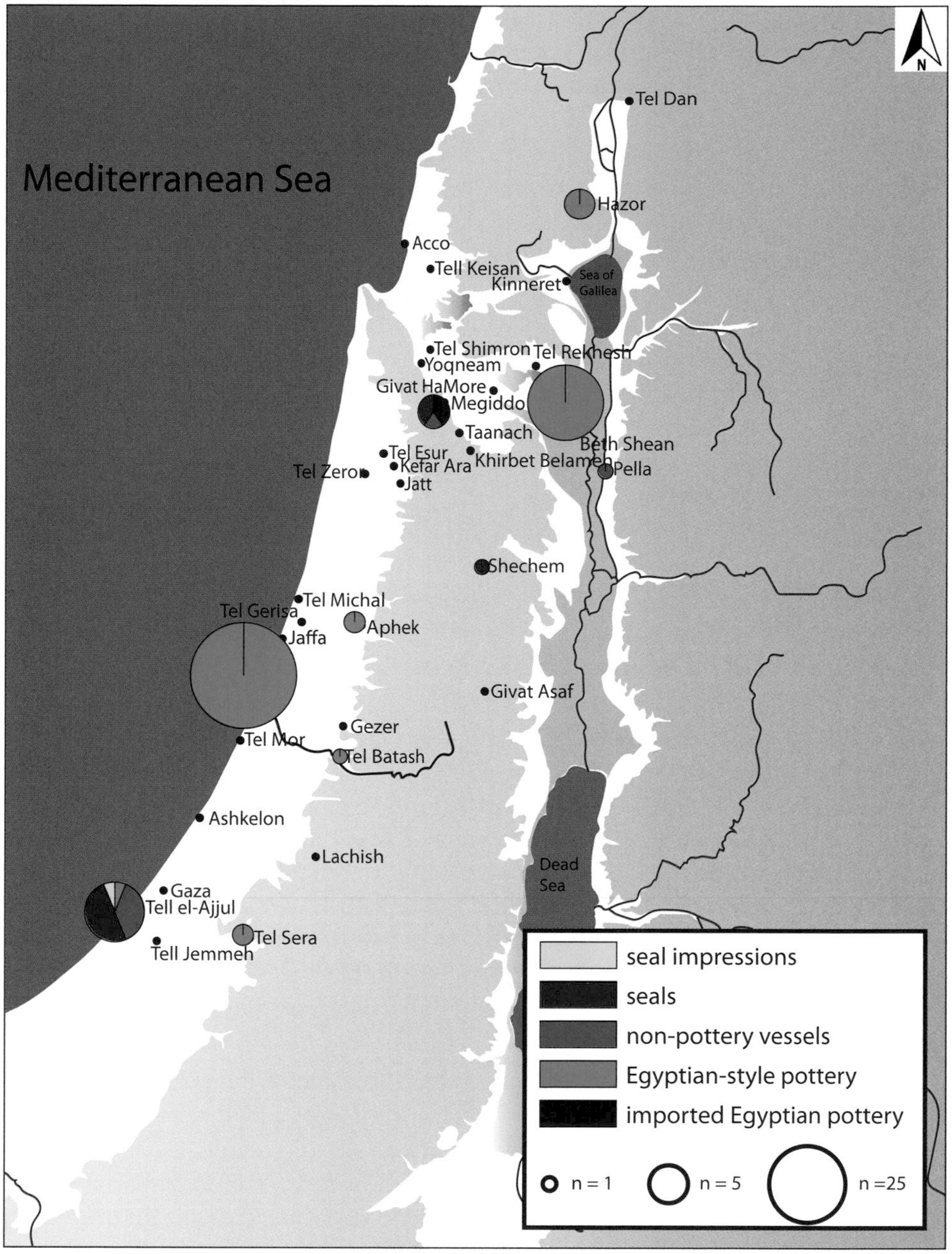

Fig. 7.
Distribution of Egyptian (-styled) material selected for the study's data set in the southern Levant during LB IB.

due to the considerable output of pottery produced locally in an Egyptian style (Martin 2004: 279). Martin's analysis of pottery assemblages in the southern Levant of the Late Bronze Age revealed that there is not any evidence for "pure" Egyptian pottery assemblages in the region. Egyptian and Levantine ware were used side-by-side, and especially Canaanite cooking pots were present in overwhelming amounts (Martin 2011: 256, 2004: 280). Although we have rather conclusive evidence that Egyptians resided in Beth Shean, there is not any support for the assumption that Egyptian soldiers and officials conducted activities at the site.

A comparable situation to that in Beth Shean can be observed in Jaffa. Almost double the amount of Egyptian-styled pottery—consisting of at least 20 flowerpots, 19 bowls, 6 jars, 3 *zir*-storage jars, and 2 stands – was uncovered in one building at the site (Burke et al. 2011: 261–270; Burke et al. 2017: 97). The find context of the pottery itself adds further evidence that favours Egyptians living at the site. The find spot indicates that food and pottery production took place within in the same enclosed area, which is often considered an Egyptian phenomenon (Burke et al. 2017: 94). Jaffa also did not yield evidence of any activity by Egyptian functionaries at the site. Three imported jars included in the auxiliary data set afford a use as containers for supplies or trade objects but do not necessarily suggest activities on the part of members of the Egyptian military and administration at the site.

At Jaffa's nearby site Aphek, a few scattered pieces of Egyptian-styled pottery were excavated in layer X-14a (Gadot 2009: 255, 260; Martin 2011: 182). One explanation for their occurrence could have been intrusion, if not for the fact that the layer above yielded no Egyptian pottery (Martin 2011: 182). The discoveries of Egyptian-styled vessels in Tel Seraʿ (Martin 2011: 223-224), Lachish, (Martin 2011: 219; Tufnell et al. 1940, Pl. LI), Tel Batash (Martin 2011: 240) and Ḫazor (Martin 2011: 237; Yadin et al. 1989: 223, 233) are also rather challenging to interpret. Petrographical examinations of these sherds may help to produce more information to understand the occurrence of Egyptian-styled pottery at these sites.

Two seals (Lalkin 2010: 431–432), one diorite alabastron (Sparks 2007: 299) and two imported jars (Martin 2011: 158) were excavated in occupational layer F-10a in Megiddo. The co-occurrence of one scarab seal and one jar in the same locus—debris above a floor—may offer a small indication of activities of Egyptian functionaries. Although the scarab does not bear a royal name or depiction, it could have also been used to conduct administrative activities. A short-term presence of members of Egyptian institutions is at least feasible at the site due to its location at a junction of major routes leading to the north and east. That the three other Egyptian objects were uncovered each in a separate tomb is the result of cultural appropriation, but nevertheless the possibility exists that these objects arrived at the site with representatives of Egypt.

Pella and Shechem each yielded one object that meets the necessary criteria. Other Egyptian objects found with these items had to be excluded because their maximum itinerary length is too long. Therefore, two seals (Eggler et al. 2006: 202, 208) and parts of an ivory box or boxes in Pella (Smith et al. 1992: 59–63) as well as two seals in Shechem[17] were included in the auxiliary data set. A tube jar—the one which meets all requirements—from Pella is made of gypsum (Sparks 2007: 310) and affords the use as an item of trade rather than as a diplomatic gift. Thus, there is no conclusive indication that Egyptian officials and soldiers were active at the site.

The seal bearing the name of Queen Tiye from Shechem[18] could have been used for legitimation, as a seal or as a diplomatic gift—executing administrative and diplomatic activities. Yet, seals also afford the general function of being trade

[17] Keel, Stempelsiegelkartei Sichem No. 24 and 44; kept in Fribourg/Switzerland.
[18] Keel, Stempelsiegelkartei Sichem No. 43; kept in Fribourg/Switzerland.

items. This said, such a seal tentatively suggests activity by Egyptian soldiers and officials at Shechem. But due to Shechem's remote location in the Samarian highlands, other explanations are more likely.

Discussion of Egyptian activities in LB I according to archaeological remains

During LB IA, one site shows evidence of Egyptian activities: Tell el-ʿAjjul. Analysing the archaeological evidence alone supports a minimalist reading of the textual record, as argued for example by Redford (2010: 193–194) and Höflmayer (2015). Redford phrased his critique—which I wholeheartedly support—rather strikingly concerning a maximalist interpretation that often includes assumptions not even backed up by textual evidence:

> "Those who assume that, prior to the first campaign, some sort of supervenient status of legal force had been already imposed by Egypt on the Canaanite headman, have adopted the mindset which ancient Egyptian public relation assumes is universally valid: viz. that all peoples on earth are bound by ties of loyalty to the Son of the sun and the Heir of Geb. Apart from this claim, arising solely out of Pharaonic ideology, there is no evidence for a legal status of subservience before Thutmose's Megiddo campaign" (Redford 2010: 194).

One of the maximalists Redford criticises is Hoffmeier. Although Hoffmeier remarks that the kings of the early 18th Dynasty focused their activities and therefore their resources on Nubia rather than the Levant (Hoffmeier 2004: 121, 123), he concludes that Egypt deployed military troops stationed in the southern Levant prior to LB IB. Further, he proposes Megiddo, Taanach, Gaza, and Sharuhen as possible locations where the troops could have been stationed. He admits however that the archaeological evidence does not support his assumptions (Hoffmeier 2004: 124–125). Taking into account the analysis of the archaeological record presented in this study, I consider not only this kind of reconstruction as an unjustified stretch of evidence, I would even propose a more minimalistic interpretation than those of Redford and Höflmayer: Tell el-ʿAjjul yielded evidence for Egyptians residing at the site, but there is not any indication of activity by Egyptian soldiers or officials, and therefore, one ought to doubt whether a garrison was stationed at all within the entirety of the Levant prior to the Tuthmosid period.

In the subsequent period, four sites display Egyptian activity (in differing intensity): Tell el-ʿAjjul, Jaffa, Beth Shean, and Megiddo. The archaeological remains in Tell el-ʿAjjul suggest not only a continuity from the previous period, one might even conclude the site served as an Egyptian centre. Since the affordance of some Egyptian objects includes the necessary functions, it seems reasonable to infer an administrative centre was maintained.

The evidence in Beth Shean and Jaffa appears to be sufficient to support the presence of small groups of Egyptians living at both sites—similar to Tell el-ʿAjjul during LB IA. We do not have any indication that administrative and military activities were conducted at either site. This interpretation of evidence is partially aligned with Redford's who raised the suggestion that the Egyptians did not deploy people to the area during the reign of Tuthmose III (Redford 2010: 257).

At some point in Jaffa, an Egyptian fortress was erected of which only the gate could be excavated as of yet. Unfortunately, neither datable finds nor an associated floor could be identified, and therefore, the necessary information to suggest a date for the gate's construction is lacking. The most recent excavators proposed that the gate may have been erected at the transition of LB IB to LB IIA based on stratigraphical considerations (Burke et al. 2017: 107). At first glance, this proposition seems to be probable. But by analysing the evidence presented in this study, I would oppose their suggestion that "Thutmose III may have designated Jaffa an *ḫtm*-base along with such sites as ʿAkko, Yarimuta, Byblos, and Ullaza" (Burke et al. 2017: 90).[19] Nonetheless, the evidence in Jaffa and Beth Shean leads to an interesting suggestion: since both sites became Egyptian centres in the following LB IIA period, it seems reasonable to suggest that the establishment of Egyptian administrative and military centres stemmed from an already present Egyptian group at those sites. Further indication for this assumption is provided by Tell el-ʿAjjul, where the suggested "evolution" from a settlement with Egyptian inhabitants to an Egyptian centre happened presumably a few generations earlier. One may even raise the hypothesis that small enclaves at the three sites in their respective periods provided Egypt with sufficiently secured waystations such that a permanent deployment at these sites was not needed. Pushing the evidence even a bit further, one might suggest that Egyptian inhabitants at each site were recruited for campaigns along with people living in the Nile Valley. Recruiting people already present in the region would have also an economic advantage: one did not need to invest the resources to move recruits to the southern Levant.

The evidence in Megiddo may tentatively suggest activities conducted by Egyptian officials, but it certainly does not indicate a permanent presence.

Although the archaeological record indicates an Egyptian presence in LB IB southern Levant, administrative activities are limited to Tell el-ʿAjjul. It should be noted that Ben-Tor argues the opposite based on her study of royal name scarabs found in the region—a group of objects that affords functions suitable to the execution of administrative activities. She interprets the evidence provided by this one object group as marking the Egyptian Empire's expansion into the southern Levant as already occurring during the reign of Tuthmose III (Ben Tor 2011: 203). In my opinion, she does not give the dates of the find context enough weight. There are indeed a large number of scarabs bearing the name Tuthmose III, but most of them were discovered in LB IIA or later contexts. Hoffmeier similarly argues, on the basis of an increase in Egyptian activities visible along the northern Sinai during LB IB, for the establishment of the Egyptian empire in the

[19] Although Burke stretches the general interpretation, while proposing the establishment of a *ḫtm*-base, he is basically aligned with the common interpretation (e.g., Höflmayer 2015: 202 and Weinstein 1981: 14 although without naming sites).

southern Levant already during the reign of Tuthmose III (Hoffmeier 2004: 124). Although his argument has valid points, the establishment of appropriate infrastructure and secured waystations along the Way of Horus to supply passing groups of Egyptians does not imply Egyptian centres in the Levant. From a strategic point of view, it would be reasonable to first establish a direct link between Egypt and the Levant, before advancing further with more permanent installations in the southern Levant.

Out of the four major responsibilities—administrative, military, diplomatic and economic—members of the Egyptian military and administration might have had in the southern Levant, only administrative activities are traceable within the archaeological record. Such can be deduced from the presence (scarab) seals that afford the use as an object to seal or to legitimise oneself as representative of Egypt.

None of the objects excavated in the LB I indicates Egyptian military activities in the southern Levant. In fact, there is not any evidence for Egyptian military activity in the archaeological evidence during the entire 18th Dynasty.[20]

Only one site during LB I, namely, Megiddo, has evidence tentatively indicating diplomatic and economic activity. However, the evidence only offers the possibility of such activities. It does not confirm them. In order to generate viable hypotheses about whether diplomatic activities occurred or whether products were traded or acquired at certain locations, the written documents that refer to those sites—at which the material was excavated—need to be consulted.

Conclusion

The archaeological evidence presented above favours a model with more limited involvement than is typically proposed for Egyptian institutions in the southern Levant during the 18th Dynasty until the rise of the "International Age" in the Amarna Period. Although we may conclude that parts of Tell el-ʿAjjul's population were Egyptian, there is not sufficient indication to reconstruct the deployment of a garrison before the Tuthmosid period. Similar to Tell el-ʿAjjul during the early 18th Dynasty/LB IA, the evidence from Jaffa and Beth Shean suggests some Egyptian inhabitants, but yields little evidence of any military or administrative elements during LB IB.

In addition, no contemporary text characterises Tell el-ʿAjjul during LB IA as an Egyptian stronghold, neither does a contemporaneous source concerning Jaffa and Beth Shean in LB IB. In cases where documents do not reveal much information, the necessity of an independent approach to analyse archaeological remains and interpreting Egypt's involvement in the region becomes obvious. As demonstrated in this paper, the presented approach to select and analyse Egyptian material culture excavated in the southern Levant is appropriate to detect administrative activity at sites with a long-term presence. But,

[20] This observation also emphasis one of the many obstacles one encounters while linking destruction horizons to events described in written record; see Höflmayer 2015 for the most recent overview of the discussion.

of course, the approach also has its shortcomings: As the discussion about the remains in Megiddo, Shechem and Pella has shown, it is rather difficult to detect and analyse the short-term presence of Egyptian functionaries; thus, these interpretations may be challenged. In such cases, it is necessary to consult the preserved textual record to evaluate and interpret the hints visible in the archaeological record.

References

Albright, W.F., 1938. The Chronology of a South Palestinian City, Tell el-Ajjul. *AJSL* 55, 337–359.

Ben-Tor, D., 2011. Political Implications of New Kingdom Scarabs in Palestine During the Reigns of Tuthmosis III and Ramesses II. In D. Aston, ed., *Under the Potter's Tree: Studies on Ancient Egypt Presented to Janine Bourriau on the Occasion of Her 70th Birthday*. OLA 204. Leuven: Peeters, 201–214.

Burke, A.A. – A. Mandell, 2011. Egyptian "Flowerpots" from Kaplan's Area A Excavations. Cultural and Historical Implications. In A.A. Burke – M. Peilstöcker, eds., *The History and Archaeology of Jaffa*. The Jaffa Cultural Heritage Project Series 1. Los Angeles, CA: Cotsen Institute of Archaeology Press University of California, 261–270.

Burke, A.A. – M. Peilstöcker – A. Karoll – G.A. Pierce – K. Kowalski – N. Ben-Marzouk – J.C. Damm – A.J. Danielson – H.D. Fessler – B. Kaufman – K.V.L. Pierce – F. Höflmayer – B.N. Damiata – M. Dee, 2017. Excavations of the New Kingdom Fortress in Jaffa, 2011–2014. Traces of Resistance to Egyptian Rule in Canaan. *AJA* 121, 85–133.

Eggler, J. – O. Keel, 2006. *Corpus der Siegel-Amulette aus Jordanien. Vom Neolithikum bis zur Perserzeit.* OBO 25. Fribourg – Göttingen: Academie Press – Vandenhoeck & Ruprecht.

Fischer, P.M., 2003. The Preliminary Chronology of Tell el-Ajjul. Results of the Renewed Excavations in 1999 and 2000. In M. Bietak, ed., *The Synchronisation of Civilisations in the Eastern Mediterranean in the Second Millennium B.C. II. Proceedings of the SCIEM 2000 – EuroConference, Haindorf, 2nd of May – 7th of May 2001.* Wien: Verlag der Österreichischen Akademie der Wissenschaften, 263–294.

Fischer, P.M. – M. Sadeq, 2000. Tell el-Ajjul 1999. A Joint Palestinian-Swedish Field Project. *ÄuL* 10, 211–226.

Fischer, P.M. – M. Sadeq, 2002. Tell el-Ajjul 2000. Second Season Preliminary Report. *ÄuL* 12, 109–154.

Gadot, Y., 2009. *Aphek-Antipatris II. The Remains on the Acropolis. The Moshe Kochavi and Pirhiya Beck Excavations.* Tel Aviv: Emery and Claire Yass Publications in Archaeology Institute of Archaeology Tel Aviv University.

Gibson, J.J., 1982. *Wahrnehmung und Umwelt. Der Ökologische Ansatz in der Visuellen Wahrnehmung.* München – Wien: Urban & Schwarzenberg.

Gosden, C. – Y. Marshall, 1999. The Cultural Biography of Objects. *WA* 31, 169–178.

Hahn, H.P., 2014. *Materielle Kultur. Eine Einführung.* Berlin: Reimer.

Hahn, H.P., 2015. Dinge sind Fragmente und Assemblagen. Kritische Anmerkungen zur Methapher der 'Objektbiographie'. In D. Boschung, ed., *Biography of Objects. Aspekte eines Kulturhistorischen Konzepts*. Paderborn: Fink, 11–33.

Hahn, H. P. – H. Weiss, 2013. Introduction. Biographies, Travels and Itineraries of Things. In H.P. Hahn – H. Weiss, ed., *Mobility, Meaning and the Transformations of Things. Shifting Contexts of Material Culture through Time and Space*. Oxford: Oxbow, 1–14.

Hoffmeier, J.K., 2004. Aspects of Egyptian Foreign Policy in the 18th Dynasty in Western Asia and Nubia. In G.N. Knoppers – A. Hirsch, eds., *Egypt, Israel, and the Ancient Mediterranean World. Studies in Honor of Donald B. Redford*. PdÄ 20. Leiden: Brill, 121–142.

Höflmayer, F., 2015. Egypt's "Empire" in the Southern Levant During the Early 18th Dynasty. In B. Eder – R. Pruzsinszky, eds., *Policies of Exchange. Political Systems and Modes of Interaction in the Aegean and the Near East in the 2nd Millennium B.C.E. Proceedings of the International Symposium at the University of Freiburg. Institute for Archaeological Studies, 30th May – 2nd June 2012*. Vienna: Austrian Academie of Sciences Press, 191–206.

Keel, O., 1997. *Corpus der Stempelsiegel-Amulette aus Palästina/Israel. Von den Anfängen bis zur Perserzeit. Katalog Band I: Von Tell Abu-Farag bis ʿAtlit.* OBO SA 13. Freiburg – Göttingen: Universitätsverlag – Vandenhoeck & Rupprecht.

Keßeler, A., 2015. Affordanz, oder Was Dinge Können!. In K.P. Hofman, ed., *Massendinghaltung in der Archäologie. Der Material Turn und die Ur- und Frühgeschichte*. Havertown: Sidestone Press, 343–364.

Knappett, C., 2004. The Affordances of Things. A Post-Gibsonian Perspective on the Relationality of Mind and Matter. In E. DeMarrais – C. Godsen – C. Renfrew, eds., *Rethinking Materiality. The Engagement of Mind with the Material World*. Cambridge: McDonald Institute for Archaeological Research, 43–51.

Kopytoff, I., 1986. The Cultural Biography of Things. Commoditization as Process. In A. Appadurai, ed., *The Social Life of Things: Commodities in Cultural Perspective*. Cambridge: Cambridge University Press, 64–91.

Lalkin, N., 2010. Chapter 20. The Scarabs. In I. Finkelstein – D. Ussishkin – B. Halpern, eds., *Megiddo IV. The 1998-2002 Seasons*. Tel Aviv, Israel: Emery and Claire Yass Publications in Archaeology, 430–436.

Martin, M.A.S., 2004. Egyptian and Egyptianized Pottery in Late Bronze Age Canaan. Typology, Chronology, Ware Fabrics, and Manufacture Techniques. Pots and People? *ÄuL* 14, 265–284.

Martin, M.A.S., 2011 *Egyptian-Type Pottery in the Late Bronze Age Southern Levant.* CChEM 29. Wien: Verlag der Österreichischen Akademie der Wissenschaften.

Morris, E.F., 2005. *The Architecture of Imperialism. Military Bases and the Evolution of Foreign Policy in Egypt's New Kingdom.* PdÄ 22. Leiden: Brill.

Redford, D.B., 2010. *The Wars in Syria and Palestine of Thutmose III.* CHANE 16. Leiden, Boston: Brill.

Schreiber, S., 2013. Archäologie der Aneignung. *Forum Kritische Archäologie* 2, 48–123.

Silverstone, R. – E. Hirsch, 1992. *Consuming Technologies. Media and Information in Domestic Spaces.* London – New York: Routledge.

Smith, R.H. – T. Potts, 1992. The Middle and Late Bronze Age. In A.W. McNicoll – P.C. Edwards – J. Hanbury-Tenison – J.B. Hennessy – T.F. Potts – R.H. Smith – A. Walmsley – P. Watson, eds., *Pella in Jordan 2. The Second Interim Report of the Joint University of Sydney and College of Wooster Excavations at Pella 1982-1985*. Sydney: Meditarch, 35–68.

Sparks, R.T., 2007. *Stone Vessels in the Levant.* Leeds: Taylor and Francis.

Stockhammer, P., 2012. Identität durch Aneignung. Zur Funktion Fremder Keramik im Spätbronzezeitlichen Ostmittelmeerraum. In I. Heske – B. Horejs, eds., *Bronzezeitliche Identitäten und Objekte. Beiträge aus den Sitzungen der AG Bronzezeit auf der 80. Tagung des WSVA in Nürnberg 2010 und dem 7. Deutschen Archäologenkongress in Bremen 2011*. Bonn: Habelt, 107–114.

Tretjakow, S., 2007. Biographie des Dings. In Forschungsprojekt "Das populäre deutschsprachige Sachbuch im 20. Jahrhundert", ed. *Sergej Tretjakow – Biographie des Dings*. Arbeitsblätter für die Sachbuchforschung 12. Berlin – Hildesheim, 4–8 (https://edoc.hu-berlin.de/bitstream/handle/18452/6147/12.pdf?sequence=1&isAllowed=y, accessed on 15 May 2019).

Tufnell, O. – C.H. Inge – G.L. Harding, 1940. *Lachish (Tell Ed Duweir) 2. The Fosse Temple.* London: Oxford University Press.

Weinstein, J.M., 1981. The Egyptian Empire in Palestine. A Reassessment. *BASOR* 241, 1–28.

Wilson, J.A., 1955. Egyptian Historical Texts. In J.B. Pritchard, J. B., ed. *Ancient Near Eastern Texts Relating to the Old Testament with Supplement*. Princeton, NJ: Princeton University Press, 227–264.

Wimmer, A., 2005. *Kultur als Prozess. Zur Dynamik des Aushandelns von Bedeutungen.* Wiesbaden: VS Verlag für Sozialwissenschaften.

Yadin, Y. – A. Ben-Tor – S. Geva, 1989. *Hazor III-IV. An Account of the Third and Fourth Seasons of Excavation, 1957-1958.* Jerusalem: Israel Exploration Society – Hebrew University of Jerusalem.

"THE MEN OF URA ARE A HEAVY BURDEN UPON YOUR SUBJECT!": THE ADMINISTRATION AND MANAGEMENT OF STRANGERS AND FOREIGNERS IN UGARIT

Kevin McGeough (University of Lethbridge)*

Preface

King Niqmepa of Ugarit complained to the Hittite king Ḫattusili III about the growing economic power of foreign merchants within Ugarit, stating that, in Beckman's translation, "The men of Ura are a heavy burden upon your subject".[1] These merchants were, at least in King Niqmepa's conception, foreigners at Ugarit (Ura was in Cilicia) and it would seem that their economic power within Ugarit, leveraged through debt relationships, had become too great. The juridical ruling of the Hittite king was that these merchants were not allowed to own real estate in Ugarit and that real estate could not be used to fulfill debt obligations owed towards them. However, individual Ugaritians could enter into service with them as a means of fulfilling debt obligations. Furthermore, the merchants of Ura were only allowed to be physically present at Ugarit during favorable seasons, seemingly based on the concern that they might be stranded their permanently (more on that shortly).[2]

The particular case of the merchants of Ura points to a number of interesting issues related to the subject of foreigners at Ugarit. Minimally it attests to the presence of foreigners with what could be described as a liminal residency status. That is to say they are not permanent residents but their presence at the site (both physically but perhaps economically and politically) was sufficient enough to make Ugaritians nervous about that presence. That the merchants of Ura were not necessarily welcome at Ugarit is hinted at through some of the actions that were known to have been taken against them. RS 17.319 records an instance when they were robbed (their property was ordered restored) and so one must presume that the presence of foreigners was contested in different ways, such as by criminal acts or violence being enacted against them. The Hittite king's role in the dispute resolution shows that the internal administration of Ugarit lacked final authority over the presence and activities of these merchants within the kingdom and that the resolution of disputes had both formal and informal qualities. The formal qual-

* I would like to thank Jana Mynářová, the other organizers, the Charles University, and the Czech Science foundation for their hospitality and commitment to scholarly dialogue that is so explicitly international in its scope.

[1] For a translation of this text, see text 32 in Beckman 1999: 177. It is preserved in three copies: RS 17.130, RS 17. 461, and RS 18.03. See the original publications in PRU 4, 103–104.

[2] For more on this historical situation, see Klengel 1992: 137 and Singer 1990: 660–664.

ities are reflected by the juridical role of the king of the Hittites and the legal mechanisms and processes that inform the resolution of the dispute. Yet there is an *ad hoc* element to this situation that is resolved through international correspondence. The decision of the Hittite king further informs about Hittite views of what constitutes fair obligations in respect to foreign merchants. It is fine for these foreign merchants to press Ugaritians into service in fulfillment of debt obligations. The holding of real estate, however, lies beyond the scope of what foreigners should be allowed. The people are alienable but the land is not. Debt was clearly recognized as a fundamental means through which relations were structured, through which foreigners could become entangled with locals, and so was subject to juridical oversight.

The Construction of Difference in the City

The site of Ugarit (modern Ras Shamra), located on the Mediterranean coast of Syria has been identified as a locus of Late Bronze Age cosmopolitanism since the first excavations in 1929 under the direction of Claude Schaeffer. The varieties of material culture and languages attested at the site, seemingly Hittite, Hurrian, Egyptian, Mesopotamian, Aegean, and Canaanite led scholars to presume that the city was a lynchpin of eastern Mediterranean trade. As the political history of the site has become clearer over the past almost one hundred years of research and scholars have gained a greater understanding of the hybridity of LBA North Syrian material culture it is now possible to complicate our understanding of the issue of foreigners and strangers as manifest at Ugarit.

It may be useful to shift the focus of this issue: rather than considering how difference was found at the site and at the city, it may be interesting to think about how difference was made at the city. This shift of focus references two levels of thinking about Ugarit. The first level shifts our thinking from the kind of simplistic approach to ethnicity and difference that was typical of culture-history approaches in archaeology, where material correlates directly to some fixed, stable, and unchanging category that presumes that Late Bronze Age people shared nineteenth-century AD conceptualizations of identity. This is not necessarily new; post-processualists have been critiquing these kinds of "pots equal people" readings since the 1980s. Yet this older logic of otherness is charismatic and often lurks beneath otherwise sophisticated understandings of the geo-political realities of the Late Bronze Age. Thus, this paper shall examine difference as something that was continuously negotiated, was dynamic, and possibly, but not necessarily, corresponded with contemporary methods for defining and negotiating difference.

The second level of thinking is at more of a metahistorical level for it involves shifting the discussion of otherness from something that archaeologists "find" in the archaeological record to something that archaeologists, philologists, and art historians "make" from their interactions with the archaeological record. This does not mean that scholars cannot find evidence for difference that is meaningful or perhaps corresponds to some kind of historical truth. What is emphasized here is that a greater degree of complexity of consideration of otherness should be allowed for than merely postulating national, ethnic, or perhaps religious difference as primary and fixed categories predicated on rigid ontologies. Otherness should be taken as a process not a fact.

Over the course of this paper, rather than providing an overarching view of how otherness was manifest at Ugarit and what life was like for strangers, and rather than explaining a series of set conditions in which strangeness functioned at Ugarit, different moments within the operation of otherness shall be examined as exemplars of these processes. Here the approach is explicitly bottom-up rather than top-down. The paper takes specific situations that are explicitly apparent from an evidentiary perspective and uses those as examples of potential other past moments and situations. Thus, for this paper, I have selected different evidence that relates to the questions upon which this conference volume has been predicated and have selected different bodies of critical theory that can be invoked to make sense of these situations.

Who were "others" at Ugarit then? While Ugarit is often associated with Canaanite culture in contemporary scholarship with qualifications, it is clear from the Ugaritic texts that Ugarit was not perceived to be part of Canaan in antiquity. The textual record from Ugarit also clearly distinguishes Egyptians, presumably Cypriotes, and others in a manner that seems consistent with Ugaritians deeming people from these regions as foreign (as one would expect). Issues are less clear when dealing with Hittite and Hurrian culture and in terms of identifying boundaries within Syria. Similarly, the administration of locations within the kingdom of Ugarit but outside of the city points to more complex forms of identification beyond simple self and other. The territorial boundaries of Ugarit's kingdom are clear from the Hittite treaties and so there is a sense in which the conceptions of who is part of and who is not part of the kingdom is established by an external polity. Van Soldt (1999: 769–773) has studied this issue in great detail and has noted that there is a consistent ordering of site names listed in the administrative documents related to the periphery and concludes that there was some kind of administrative division of the periphery. This issue shall be returned to later but the use of toponyms in these lists presupposes some element of difference from Ugarit but formally, the borders of who is Ugaritian and who is not are established by the Hittite king. For everyday life, however, this probably meant the simple of binary of foreign or not foreign was blurrier than usually presumed. Can an administrative act of the Hittites make an urban Ugaritian feel a sense of connectedness with someone from a rural location more than a day's walk from the city? Operating from a patrimonial model, a scholar would assume "yes" and from a two-sector perspective, a scholar would assume "no". Perhaps both are correct and the feelings of connectedness were inconsistent not only with different people and places but constantly shifting.

Thinking about the City

Since this particular paper is predicated upon the construction of otherness at the level of the city, it is useful to start out at that scale of consideration. Thinking about what a city actually "is" or "was" has become more complicated as scholars have come to realize that an urban environment was not a monolithic space and that becoming urban was not simplistic as a binary urban or non-urban. "The Urban Mind" project, under the IHOPE umbrella, presumes from the outset that urbanism needs to be understood in relation to, not distinct from, human cognition (Sinclair 2010: 12–13). Take for example Ben Jervis's recent work on Medieval British towns. By employing a form of assemblage theory (Jervis 2018: 141–142), he is able to illustrate that the city is not just physical, bounded space but a form of social performance. The performance of urbanism by the actors within the city space actually shapes different aspects of life and thus the city is not just a reflection of social roles but an agent of their creation. Fluidity, rather than stability is to be expected, even if the archaeological record is suggestive of one particular moment in the process of being urban.

As already mentioned, the city is understood here as a location where difference is made not where it is found. This conceptualization is borrowed from the field of human geography and specifically from the work of Engin Isin and others who have built on that work. Julie Young (2011: 544) characterizes Isin's readings of the city as: "a 'difference machine' because it is a space in which differences are labelled and perpetuated through spatial practices and technologies of governance". The city is not a monolith but a spatial location in which numerous individuals who varying align themselves with others in the city in different ways negotiate and live their lives while consciously and unconsciously making sense of otherness. Perhaps residency may seem like a fundamental constraint on the sense of self or other manifest at Ugarit. Certainly, it was a potentially contested status as evidenced by the merchants of Ura incident. Yet as shall be explored, residency is not the sole defining trait of non-foreign-ness and different factors play a role in who is welcomed in the city as part of the power of the city was as a meeting place for different individuals. Perhaps the observation of Patricia Wood (2006) that people outside of the city must go to the city to engage in politics is relevant for consideration of Late Bronze Age life, and that even though she is discussing a situation that emerged out of industrial capitalism, perhaps we can see situations where this is true before the emergence of that structuring of economic relationships. In a Late Bronze Age context, can we think of a dominant modality that imposes a normative model of who belongs where and legitimizes certain locations for encounters with the other? Or, is this anachronistic and is the process of legitimization and access one that emerges *ad hoc* from lived practice? Furthermore, the evidence at Ugarit suggests that power relations were also manifest more complexly than merely foreigner versus self and that economic wealth and status of both categories further complicated issues. While we often think of the foreigner as "precarious" in a Late Bronze Age context and travel literature of the ancient Near East seems to support this, other evidence suggests that the city may have been a more precarious location for poor individuals within Ugarit who would not have been considered foreigners. Wealthy foreigners seemed to have experienced the city with a level of privilege that was alien to non-elite resident Ugaritians.

Rather than thinking of the city as an almost primordial, bounded and coherent entity in which the stranger is a similarly bounded and coherent entity that is in full juxtaposition to the city, this paper shall attempt to make this dichotomy messier. David Seitz's (2016) use of queer theory in the context of contemporary human geography is helpful for he uses it to invoke unstable identities that are formed more out of power relations than any particular connection. Thus, people with little to do with one another end up with shared identity; in the case of this volume, did those constituted as "foreigners" at Ugarit bear a shared identity? Or is this a latter scholarly imposition? Using Amin's notion of micropublics (2002: 976), this paper shall explore some of the locations of everyday life in which identities like "foreigner" or "stranger" may emerge or be elided. It shall explore specific instances, constituted as spatial locations of interactions or as administrative moments in which identity is imposed, negotiated, or asserted and presumes that there is a situational flexibility in these constitutions of identity.

For Julie Young (2011: 535–536), who studies contemporary issues of refugee status, the city is a place of contestation where, as she explains in regards to young refugees in Toronto (2011: 566), "their ascribed identities as non-citizens are negotiated in everyday spaces and relations of the city". For her, it is the intersection of everyday life and bureaucratic imposition that lead to the ascription and negotiation of different statuses and these statuses do not remain stable in all spaces of the city. For Young (2011: 536), "notions of hospitality and sovereignty exclude people from membership in the state" but, simultaneously, what she refers to as the practice of the city by its inhabitants, the lived experiences of navigating the city, provide alternative means of belonging that lie outside identities defined by the state. Despite the temporal difference between Young's Toronto refugees and the Late Bronze Age, her approach offers opportunities for thinking about the ancient world because she concentrates on urban refugees' interaction with the city since it is through municipal affairs that these individuals engage with the state materially, not merely in an abstract ideological form.

Urban legibility

That urban design plays a role in people's engagement with a city environment is a presupposition of much work in human geography. One of the classic books in this field, Kevin Lynch's *The Image of the City* (1960) established a now seemingly self-evident concept in urban design of "legibility" (Lynch 1960: 2–6). It is a concept that moves urban design out of simple considerations of physicality by demonstrating how cognitive issues such as memory, sensation, emotion, and symbol all interact as the individual passes through the urban environment. It presumes that cities have both temporal and spatial elements, with components created by many different people with diverse motivations, and are experienced differently by individuals in embodied fashions that are framed by a variety of factors that are not consistent. For strangers or foreigners, the embodied experience of the city is a fundamental, potentially troubling, but perhaps unconscious means through which a sense of "out-of-placeness" is established. How legible the city is has implications for those experiences. For Lynch (1960: 49–83) there are five components of urban legibility, all of which there is evidence for at Ugarit: paths (how one moves through the city); edges (essentially borders although not necessarily explicitly marked as such); districts (spaces of common function or status); nodes (locations like squares); and landmarks (visually distinct physical features that act, perhaps unintentionally, as important spatial markers).

The question that this poses for the discussion here is how "legible" was Ugarit to foreigners? In relation to urban legibility, Pamela Robinson (2018: 30) uses the design competition for the Yucca Mountain nuclear waste facility in Nevada as an interesting point of entry. This was not a competition to make a real set of signage but rather an artistic exhibition intended to expose the problems associated with the long-term storage of nuclear waste. The fundamental question is how to make a warning sign that will be effective for 10,000 years; presuming language changes and other changes to the cognitive elements of legibility, how can a sign explain the dangers of nuclear waste in a way that will remain legible for the 10,000 years over which such waste will still be dangerous? Invoking the Yucca Mountain exhibition in the context of a discussion of the Late Bronze Age brings up two interesting issues: what elements of urban legibility are still intelligible to us three thousand years after their use; and, what elements of urban legibility would have made the city comprehensible to non-residents at the time? Perhaps the first question will be answered indirectly here; the second should be addressed explicitly and so here the discussion will be oriented along Lynch's components of urban legibility.

Paths

Thinking about paths, the roads in the city of Ugarit were, as is expected, the main means of orienting movement throughout the city. Yon's analysis of the road infrastructure of the site suggests a generally *ad hoc* approach to the planning, construction, and maintenance of these paths (Yon 1992b: 25–27; Callot – Yon 1995: 161). Terrain was not leveled before the construction of the roads and the width of the streets is highly variable throughout the site, although most would readily facilitate the movement of wagons and animals. In particular, the roads around the palace seem to have been more labyrinthine than elsewhere and while perhaps not purposefully intended to limit access, provided invisible social messages that others were not welcome. However, the excavators have identified a major thoroughfare in the middle of the city that they have designated "main street" (Yon 2006: 85). In the location excavated, this north-south thoroughfare is intersected by a large east-west road, suggesting that this would have been the main road for traffic in the city. To the north, this road likely leads to a major plaza in the "south city" and southwards seems to lead directly to a bridge over the Nahr ed-Delbeh. This main street also seems to be surrounded by very high quality buildings, of the construction type typical of the elite areas. Of course, it is not just the physical movement facilitated by paths that conveys meaning. The paths are framed by various kinds of material culture that offer their own messages. For example, the roads leading into ancient Rome communicated directly to visitors who the most powerful families in the city where. This emerged out of Roman prohibitions against burial within the city; mausoleums were not forbidden directly outside of the city so monuments to the dead, through their varying degrees of lavishness, communicated important information about whose descendants were the most important people within the city. Monumental and public architecture within Rome and other Roman cities that flanked different paths functioned similarly. Visitors to Ugarit, walking along the main street would have seen imposing monumental architecture on either side, have been somewhat limited in being able to actually gain access to those regions, and would have seen the acropolis and acropolis temples from these vantage points.

Nodes

A number of nodes where roads meet and space widens into plazas are discernible. The "main street" likely led up to a plaza in the south city and between the fortifications and palace another plaza has also been discerned. The royal plaza was demarcated by walls and benches surrounding the walls suggest that this was a location that allowed the possibility of lingering (Yon 2006: 35). Staircases led up to the acropolis and the temples themselves have walls that delimit large enclosures. Thus, the ritual space would have acted as nodal space but likely access to these nodes was limited based on liturgical and other criteria.

Edges

While the large buildings and narrow side roads (in comparison to the wide main road) would have presented potentially permeable borders, more significant edges to the urban space where the walls and gates. As with other Levantine cities, Middle Bronze Age Ugarit likely featured a substantial fortification system, which, in the Late Bronze Age, was reused and heavily modified (Yon 2006: 31). The best understood wall and gate complex is that on the western edge of the tell that gave access to the palace. Its exact appearance at the last phase of Ugarit's habitation is not clear but at least at some point in the city's history, it was an impressive, monumental structure flanked by a tall tower. The complex certainly signaled the control of access to this part of the tell and to the royal complex.

Districts

Distinct districts of the city have been identified by the excavators and these could be generally categorized as the royal zone, the elite area, the domestic quarters, and the acropolis. The physical construction and layout of these different zones signals the distinctiveness of these sectors. The acropolis was set apart by its height in relation to the rest of the tell. The elite and palatial zones feature fine ashlar construction in comparison to the cramped spacing and less high quality building materials used in the residential areas. The different zones would likely have been readily apparent to strangers to the city.

Landmarks

A number of different landmarks would have also been legible to strangers. The palace would have been very obvious. Almost 7000 square meters, the palace was constructed in numerous stages through the Late Bronze Age. Made of finely hewn ashlars, and cut timbers, the palace was by far the largest structure on the Late Bronze Age mound, and an imposing symbol of authority. Yon has suggested that access to the palace was limited and that entrance was gained through the western side (Yon 1997: 48). This was in keeping with other major Levantine cities of the Late Bronze Age where palaces were located not on the acropolis but on the western edge of the site near a gate system. Thus, strangers to the city who were at least familiar with Levantine cities would have found the palace where it was expected. The palace and activities related to foreigners will be returned to later but it should be noted that the physical structure of the palace offered easily legible arguments about royal authority.

The temples on the acropolis were likely the most readily apparent landmarks and likely would have been legible as such to strangers to the city. Both the Temple of Baʿl and the Temple of Dagān would have been visible from outside of the city and from most exterior locations within the city (Yon 2006: 106). That seventeen stone anchors were found within the courtyard of the Baʿl temple suggests that sailors offered their thanks or requested favour from Baʿl in this location (Yon 2006: 110). If at least some of these anchors can be presumed to have been offered by non-residents, than here is evidence for the kinds of activities that foreigners engaged in at the site. However, this cannot be known for certain so a softer claim is that at the very least the visitor to the city would have had visual cues of the importance of this cultic activity and the prominence of these temples within the community.

Urban Legibility Conclusion

Based on this brief survey of the materiality of urban Ugarit, some key elements of legibility in Lynch's sense are readily apparent. Parts of the city were extremely legible for the foreigner. The palace location was consistent with Late Bronze Age norms and the acropolis temples were likely apparent as such from far outside of the city's confines. A southern entrance and large main street channeled the flow of people and goods axially into the city and the few plazas that have been identified suggest that spatial nodes for lingering were available. The distinct architecture of different locations told visitors where they were to some extent and nodal control points, like near the palace, allowed for the management of access. Despite what may look like a complex urban environment depending on the scale of map viewed, specific sections of the city would have been highly legible to foreigners and the areas that were less legible, like the domestic areas, were where less legibility would have been expected (and would have been less appropriate space for visitors to enter, so that lack of legibility fulfilled a function as well). Much of Ugarit could be described as an "open city", one that enables and encourages unpredictable encounters between people who did not necessarily know one another (Sennett n.d.).

Regulations and International Law

Moving away from embodied experiences of the city, considering the more abstract issues of law and regulation, did the city constitute a level of ancient emic thinking about difference? It would seem so from the ample textual evidence in which that is presupposed by the authors. This issue shall be returned to again in a discussion of administrative categories used in specific administrative moments. From the Hittite juridical and administrative perspective, certainly Ugarit, as a city with a hinterland, was a meaningful designation of otherness and was understood as a distinct polity.

There is multiple evidence that illustrates that there were administrative means of regulating foreignness at the site. For example, there is some contestable evidence that trade concessions at Ugarit could be purchased. This is indicated by administrative tablets in which the term *ntbt* is employed. The word, which may have cognates in Aramaic and Eblaite, seems to have a base meaning of "path". Sasson (1966: 136) and Astour (1970: 120) equate it with Akkadian *ḫarrānu* and Sumerian KASKAL, which both mean not only road but trade venture. In KTU 2.36, Egypt is said to have a *ntbt* through Ugarit and in 4.366, an individual purchases one for 220 units of gold. While the mechanisms of this are not clear from the evidence, it seems that foreigners could purchase rights to economic activities within the kingdom.

As already discussed in terms of the well-known merchants of Ura case, extra-municipal legal obligations seemed to have facilitated and regulated the movement of foreigners into and out of the city. Sauvage (2011: 435–436) has argued that the activities of merchants were highly regulated through a complex series of diplomatic policies and laws. Basing her analysis on the Hittite legal corpus, Ugaritic correspondence, and stories like Wenamun, she has shown that the safety of traders was one of the key issues addressed in this fashion. When traders were robbed, even if this was by the actions of individuals and not the state, as Sauvage argues (2011: 429), punishment or restitution was made at the international level. She argues that this indicates that the traders were "controlled by the throne in their own country" (Sauvage 2011: 431) but this does not need to have been the case. These traders may have been acting independently, and as Routledge and I have argued elsewhere, the distinction between public and private is not so clear cut in the Late Bronze Age (Routledge – McGeough 2009). Rather, the state-based level of compensation reflects how the larger international system of the Late Bronze Age facilitated the movement of peoples by providing protection for both foreigners and people who welcomed foreigners through recourse to a judicial authority beyond the scale of the individual. These travelers need not have been directed by their home thrones; rather they need merely have been seen to have been under their jurisdiction in order to make sense of this evidence.

How strictly enacted these laws and regulations where is debatable; it is the same problem for dealing with any Near Eastern code of laws. Take for example the issue of when traders were allowed to enter Ugarit. There is some discussion about how safe the Mediterranean Sea was for shipping during all seasons and that laws existed that prevented ships from sailing during the more difficult times (see, for example, Tammuz 2005). One of the key sources of evidence for this is the Hittite king's edict about the merchants of Ura where the king makes it explicit, as part of his larger forbidding of them owning real estate, that these men were not allowed to remain at Ugarit during the winter. Often this is taken to mean that trade was conducted mainly in non-winter months and that arriving in Ugarit in winter meant that one was stuck there for an extended period due to the conditions. Whether or not this was the case is not as important for what this instance does show is that the actual residency of these men, regardless of weather, was predicated on the *ad hoc* decree of the Hittite king. For real purposes, that was the limiting factor. Thus, however regulated one perceives Late Bronze Age trade to have been, the actual movement of foreigners was conditional upon the negotiations of elite and especially royal agents.

That being said, international elite contacts were numerous and there is significant evidence in the Ugaritic epistolary record to indicate that elites, both royal and non-royal from Ugarit engaged in relations of various sorts with other elites outside of the city. Dynastic alliances with Amurru indicate that a queen potentially viewed as foreign would not have been unusual at Ugarit. Close commercial connections with Emar, Carchemish, and other Syrian locales are well attested. How much these people would have been viewed as "foreign" is not clear, but as shall be discussed further, gentilic categories are one of the primary identifiable administrative categories related to identity.

Foreign-ness in Internal Administration

Returning to the scale of otherness within the city, textual records offers some evidence of how "selfhood" and "otherness" were dealt with in local administration. The most significant micropublic in which administration occurred at Ugarit was the Royal Palace. Here, invoking David Seitz's use of queer theory, the palace administration renders all of those who come into its orbit as "queer" and then labels them with an administrative identity, an identity that is constituted in relation to the palace and its invocation of power. These identities are normalized through a variety of different processes but most powerfully through their repeated invocation in administration.

In his early reports (see especially Schaeffer 1952; 1957; 1962), Schaeffer noted that there are five major groups of rooms with tablet depositions, as well as numerous individual rooms. The five major sections of the palace are in the west, the east, the south, the southwest, and the centre and are often called "archives". Many individual rooms also contained large amounts of tablets. The designation of sections of the palace as "archives" is based on early suppositions that the tablets were purposefully placed by officials who acted in an administrative or custodial function. There are some common characteristics of each of these five "archives". Each of the archives is in close proximity to, or has fallen into, a courtyard. This is a functional attribute, since it is much easier to read tablets in direct light. It seems that each "archive" was kept in rooms on both the ground and upper floor of the palace. Van Soldt has shown that what was once considered separate strata by the excavators were actually collapsed upper stories that had fallen onto the ground floor (van Soldt 1991: 57, 107). By making joins through separate layers of deposition, van Soldt has shown that texts cannot be associated with a trustworthy stratigraphic context. Scholars at the University of Chicago continue to work on this issue and so perhaps in the future more substantive conclusions will be drawn. The collapse of the upper story of the palace on to the ground floor prevents an exact reconstruction of the palace's layout.

Despite efforts of many to identify a rigid bureaucratic system within the palace archive, most scholars have described the filing system as haphazard and disorganized. From this, some have concluded that the palace's role in governance was indirect and decentralized (see, for example, Whitt 1993). However, when one considers the administrative activities that include organizing people, activities that do not necessarily involve rigid, definable structures and offices, then we can see that many aspects of ancient lives were affected by administration. Given the uneven amounts of data preserved in the archaeological record, this day-to-day influence must have been striking.

Here perhaps David Seitz's (2016: 6) metaphor of the waiting room is helpful. In the context of his work, the waiting room is both literal and metaphorical, the physical space in which refugee claimants are made into a formal category of "asylum seeker" in relation to the state government and the metaphorical location of liminality where their old identities are transformed into new ones. The Ugaritic palatial administration categorized and organized people into specific groups and perhaps this was one of the most meaningful elements of administrative power—to render individuals into categories that were meaningful to the state and inscribe upon people identities in relation to this power. Perhaps the palace administration can be seen as a body that renders the stranger into the non-strange?

To identify what the Ugaritic palace found to be "strange" and "not strange", some effort must be made to identify ancient emic categories and not presume that these categories line up with contemporary identity categories. Lynn Meskell has recognized that archaeology has tended to not be successful in reconstructing emic categories, given that archaeologists themselves have tended to focus on particular topics of identity of interest in Western political discourse (i. e., gender, age) without acknowledging the complexity and mutability of how other variables may have been at play in the individual's own understanding of identity (Meskell 2001: 187–188). Indeed, Meskell has suggested that Western notions of identity tend to be rigid and she states, "that rigidity necessitates that all individuals be neatly pigeonholed and categorized according to a set of predetermined labels" (Meskell 2001: 187). The concern here is that the scholar attempting to understand how the palace pigeonholed people ends up simply coming up with her or his own types of pigeonholes.

Administrative categories that are employed offer one particular avenue for exploring emic categories, at least as seen by the palace. The very act of inscribing a tablet is symbolic of the agency held by an institution or person engaging in record keeping. Tablets record instances of administrative relation—moments when social roles are circumscribed and reified. These documents, the remnants of a particular administrative moment, are witness to a specific instance when social identities are designated by the administrator and the message of the administrator is passed on in a subtle but very powerful way to those being administrated. Documentation and the ability to document gives administration the power to label and create identity at a very fundamental level. Here is where, in Seitz's waiting room metaphor, the stranger is made recognizable and determined to be foreign or not.

Administration, when enacted, becomes a part of everyday, lived experience. At Ugarit, people encountered the palace administration in many situations, including when land was transferred; debts were incurred or repaid; inventories of ships, agricultural estates or available military equipment were taken; requests for raw materials were made; trading concessions were given; and various goods were distributed to or received from specific individuals and places—to name a few. In these kind of day-to-day activities, administration became a fundamental, and often unquestioned component of everyday life. This lack of questioning is the truly powerful force behind successful, administrative practice. When those on both sides of the administrative schema, the administrators and the administered accept the system (or series of values) as a "proper" way of relating to one another, then this means of interaction becomes a dominant, though nearly unconscious means of orientation.

Bourdieu labels this kind of "naturalization of arbitrariness" as "doxa" (Bourdieu 1977: 164). "Doxa" describes the understanding of the world or environment that the individual takes for granted or sees as self-evident. These are the unquestioned classificatory categories of everyday life (such as age, gender, race, class, ethnicity) that are considered as given for the purposes of day to day functioning, and are not recognized as arbitrary criteria for organization. These classificatory categories are much more powerful than ideology. Whereas ideology involves a conscious argument (although to varying degrees), doxa becomes an unquestioned aspect of everyday life. Even more powerful is that each time a participant in a society acts according to one of these underlying organizing principles, that participant is reinforcing, and reeifying that value—entrenching it even more.

The work of Anthony Giddens provides similar insight. Giddens states (Giddens 1984: 19) "that the rules and resources drawn upon in the production and reproduction of social action are at the same time the means of system reproduction." Human social activity is recursive. It is through actions that the conditions for the enacting of these same actions is made possible (Giddens 1984: 2). This creates agency, which is the ability to engage in action (as opposed to the intent to engage in action) (Giddens 1984: 9). It is this agency (gained by day-to-day activities, based on unquestioned but not unquestionable assumptions) that creates the power of the administrative apparatus.

In the process of the constitution of the self, Peirce's conceptions can merge well with Bourdieu's and Giddens' observations on the perpetuation of knowledge. As will be shown at Ugarit, but presumably the process is similar elsewhere, administrative identity creation involves the creation of sign categories that become an accepted component of the ontological framework of the object. The evidence from Ugarit is such that it is possible to identify emic categories (emic from the perspective of the palace) that were used in the day-to-day administration of economic and juridical life at the site. The identification of the usage of specific types of referents for the identification of the individual in the ancient context, through a Peircean perspective helps understand the role that ancient authority played in the articulation of ancient identity and rendering the stranger into a known quantity, perhaps a foreigner, perhaps not.

Peirce's notion of "Thirdness" is instructive for analysis of administration and the articulation of categories of identity through administration. Working from the philosophies of Hegel and Kant, Peirce articulated three interdependent categories of phenomena (Peirce 1931: 148). Lele well summarizes these three categories (Lele 2006: 53–54): "Firstness corresponds with undifferentiated possibility, pure quality ... Secondness corresponds with the existent or predominance of a dyadic relationship ... Thirdness corresponds with habit,...law-governed phenonomena ... representation...and mediation..." Administrating, and the act of governing cannot be untangled from all three of these categories, and certainly, it is no use to attempt to rigidly attempt to categorize a phenomenon solely into one of these three groups. However, the manner in which administration and government create and reify identity can well be understood through the concept of Thirdness. As shall be shown at Ugarit, a significant component of royal administration involved the organization of people through categories of identity. While most of these administrative categories (as shall be shown) have a "real" or First or Second component (such as an indication of the city where the person lives or the type of work that they engage in), the use of certain categories of identity as administrative markers indicates, from a semeiotic perspective, the creation or reification of a sign of identity (based on Secondness) through a relationship of Thirdness.

Peirce was the first to demonstrate that "Thirdness" has a direct bearing on an individual's own sense of identity. As Lele demonstrates, Peirce is explicit in demonstrating that habits (regulative and practical) help formulate a notion of the self that extends beyond isolated moments or encounters (Lele 2006: 55). The bombardment of messages, manifest as signs, especially the interpretant component of a sign that reflects only some aspects of the object, condition the object's sense of self, and especially informs the object about which aspects of the self differentiate the object from other "selfs".

Internal Administrative Categories at Ugarit

In the Ugaritic administrative system, different referents are used in different contexts—though never uniformly. That is to say, there are a wide variety of possible ways of referring to a specific individual—there are a number of possibilities for the scribe to choose from. The palace used a limited set of categories by which to identify people and in reifying these as natural categories the palace claimed them in its role as designator and arbiter. These choices are further conditioned by the particular circumstances of the administrative moment. Some referents are just not appropriate in all contexts.

bêtu âbi *terminology*

Referents using familial terminology are commonly employed in the Late Bronze Age throughout the Near East. The use of these kinds of referents has been well-discussed by many scholars including Mario Liverani (2001) and David Schloen (2001). Schloen has illustrated that this terminology rooted in the household is a dominant metaphor for the structuring of social relations at Ugarit. Following Stager's Weberian study of ancient Israel, Schloen has illustrated how authority was nested in various levels of patrimonial authority (Schloen 2001).

Thus, it is not surprising that one of the most frequent means of recording individuals is by patronym. Individuals at Ugarit are frequently referred to (in the administrative record) as "x son of y" or simply as "son of y." This identifies the individual in patrimonial terms and is by the far the most common means of identifying the individual in records kept by the palace. Schloen has shown that the individual's name, patronym, or name and patronym together can be used interchangeably (Schloen 2001: 211). That is to say, all three of these methods of identification are used within the same contexts. For example, KTU 4.371 is a list of individuals living in a particular village. Individuals are listed in all three ways. The fact that all three are used interchangeably indicates that all three types of identification, revolving around the use of names and patronyms were used to provide essentially the same information—the identity of the individual in question.[3] Here then is one referent through which someone's identity is constituted as non-foreign—as someone with a recognizable or administratively "categorizable" genealogy.

Another kind of referent is used (often in reference with a name or patronym) that indicates a specific social relationship between two individuals, not necessarily of the same household. These attached referents express this specific, social relationship to a particular individual by the addition of a possessive suffix. This possessive suffix specifies a particular person to whom the reference is made. The most common four terms of this nature (besides familial terms such as wife, brother, and daughter) are *nḥl*[4], *lmd*[5], *s/ś*ǵ*r*, and *n*ʿ*r*, meaning "heir", "apprentice", "servant/child"[6], and "assistant" or "youth", respectively. The use of each of these terms (though the exact meanings are arguable) indicates that person could be identified to the palace solely by their social relationship to an individual identi-

[3] The name and/or patronym is used extremely frequently in the Ugaritic administrative corpus. Examples of alphabetic texts where this is the sole referent used include (note that incomplete tablets are marked with an * to indicate that other referents may have been employed in the tablet, but simply have not survived: include KTU 4.334, KTU 4.114, KTU 4.115*, KTU 4.84, KTU 4.97, KTU 4.130*, KTU 4.147*, KTU 4.148*, KTU 4.159*, KTU 4.289, KTU 4.662, KTU 4.672, KTU 4.678, KTU 4.679, KTU 4.321, KTU 4.445, KTU 4.448, KTU 4.449, KTU 4.452, KTU 4.453, KTU 4.455, KTU 4.458, KTU 4.520, KTU 4.524, KTU 4.537, KTU 4.539, KTU 4.543, KTU 4.354, KTU 4.364 *, KTU 4.372, KTU 4.406, KTU 4.229, KTU 4.233 *, KTU 4.112, KTU 4.543. This type of text is also well attested in the syllabic corpus. Examples include: PRU 3 196 (RS 15.42 + 110), PRU 6 82 (RS 17.242), PRU 6 83 (RS 17.430), PRU 6 84 (RS 19.30), PRU 6 85 (RS 19.79), PRU 6 86 (RS 19.82), PRU 6 88 (RS 19.94), PRU 6 89 (RS 19.110), PRU 6 90 (RS 19.114), PRU 6 91 (RS 19.132), PRU 6 92 (RS 19.173A), Ug. 5 97 (RS 20.20), and Ug. 5 98 (RS 20.07).

[4] This referent can be found in: KTU 4.311, KTU 4.315, KTU 4.413, KTU 4.571, KTU 4.581, and KTU 4.605.

[5] See tablets KTU 4.194 and KTU 4.227 for examples of this.

[6] This word is somewhat problematic in that it appears mostly in the context of shepherding activities, and Watson understands this term to reflect some sort of lower-ranked shepherd (Watson 2002: 204–205). Del Olmo Lete and Sanmartín (2004: 755) suggest that this is cognate to the Akkadian *suḫāru* and suggest a related translation of "child" or "servant".

fied by name or patronym. KTU 4.69 is a text that lists individuals by occupation. A common expression within this list is "son of PN and his heir." Whether these terms originate in household terminology is not clear, but what is clear is that they are not derived from terminology used to designate biological family members.

Geographic terminology

Related to patronymic references but separate from them are descriptions of individual by location of residence or origin. Here is, arguably, the most clear evidence for conceptions of foreign-ness within the Ugaritic administration. This kind of referent manifests itself in two basic forms: the description of individuals who are at a specific location and the description of individuals with a geographic name modified by a gentilic ending.

The first type of individual referent is employed when the important aspect of the administrative relationship is the determination of residence. In KTU 4.122 individuals (possibly plowmen, although the first line of the tablet is somewhat broken) are listed who are at a specific geographic location. These people are further listed by patronym, but their administrative *connection* is where they are located at that administrative moment.

More related to issues of identity and identity creation at Ugarit are instances of the use of gentilic descriptions. The gentilic at Ugarit is rendered by a geographic name with a *-y* suffixed to the end of the word. Individuals can be designated with a gentilic for a specific village within the kingdom of Ugarit (see for example KTU 4.45; 4.50; 4.51; and 4.85), or neighboring Northern Levantine villages (for example see KTU 4.96:3). Or individuals are referred to in less local terms, possibly national terms, like Egyptian (see for example KTU 4.96:7; KTU 4.352:4) or Cypriote (KTU 4.352:2).

The location of origin, and possibly ethnic identity, was an important criterion for establishing boundaries of *otherness* within the city of Ugarit—both in terms of other villages and other states. The need to list and account for these groups is very closely tied to the creation of identity through opposition. Certainly, every time an individual was recorded as a non-Ugaritian in a list, this difference was reified. Sorting out which localities were thought to be "foreign" is difficult and likely this conception was not consistent, shifting depending on circumstances and individuals.

Occupational terminology

Scholars have argued that some of these gentilic titles (especially "Egyptian") actually refer to professions (Pardee – Bordreuil 1992: 715).[7] Whether this was the case or not, occupational groups were another important category of identification

[7] Certainly, this is the case with the Sherdana at Ugarit. While this is the name of one of the groups of Sea People, at Ugarit it appears listed along with other military professionals (see for example KTU 4.137). See Astour 1972 for more on his suggestion that the use of "Egyptian" (*mṣr*) similarly refers to an occupational group (Astour 1972: 23).

in the administrative record. Occupational designation is an important organizing principle in many of the economic texts at Ugarit. That this was the case is clear from the consistent order of occupational categories within administrative records at Ugarit. Gray had noticed as early as 1952 that occupation names appeared in a consistent order, with *mryn* always appearing at the top (Gray 1952: 51). His conclusion based on this, which was followed by Rainey (1962: 166) was that these occupational groups reflected "guilds". The evidence that these groups reflected "guilds" in the Medieval sense of the term is minimal, and this kind of structured, internally organized corporation in opposition to royal authority was not likely present at Ugarit (*contra* Craigie 1982; Gray 1952: 50–51; and Rainey 1962: 166–167).

However, there does seem to be evidence that people of the same occupational category took some collective economic action in terms of resource acquisition. KTU 4.626 records the request for various items by "potters". Wool distributions are made to shepherds and recorded in KTU 4.378. And the account of some sort of smith (*sbrdn*) is preserved in KTU 4.337. Whether these were groups organized by the palace or independently organized, or even organized at all, is not clear.

Other evidence that the palace thought of people in terms of occupational category can be found in those texts explicitly recording and listing people according to occupational category. There are numerous examples of texts at Ugarit with the heading "Tablet of x occupational group". This heading is then typically followed by a list of personal names.[8] Other times, lists of personal names beneath various different occupational headings can be found in the same texts.[9] In these cases, the occupational groups are listed in the standard order. Sometimes this type of list also records distributions to individuals. Distributions include fields[10]; equipment and weapons[11]; silver[12]; and other precious metals[13].

In other situations, the occupational category when used as a referent seems to be simply secondary information recorded by the scribe. KTU 4.332 and KTU 4.224 both list personal names with an occupational category in apposition. The purpose of these texts seems to be to record the geographic location of certain individuals; it is telling of the role of occupational category as identity referent that this information would be included.

The occupational category was clearly a meaningful referent for individuals from the palace's perspective. People were grouped and identified by specialized skills; at some level this was an important component of individual identity. Here then is perhaps a way that individuals were made known from the palace's perspective. How much being categorized as a member of a specific occupational group made one more or less "foreign" is again unclear but the confluence of oc-

---

8 See for example, KTU 4.134; KTU 4.155; KTU 4.320; and KTU 4.542.
9 See for example, KTU 4.412 and possible KTU 4.183.
10 For example, KTU 4.416.
11 For example, KTU 4.624 (RS 19.049 [A] + [C]).
12 For example, KTU 4.69; KTU 4.71; and PRU 6 136 (RS 17.240).
13 For example, KTU 4.396.

cupational and geographic referents within the same list suggest that this kind of identity complicated the conception of who was foreign.

A Designation of Possession and/or Obligation

A particularly controversial subject in the study of Ugaritic economics and social structure is the designation *bnš*. This term used to identify individuals in the Ugaritic administrative record is often modified by its appearance in construct with another noun (most often *mlk* = king). For example, KTU 4.370 is a list of *men of the king* who had been requested by a certain individual. Differing models of Ugaritic society have been proposed based on understandings of this word. We are certain that *bnš* is equated with the Akkadian term *amīlum* (=*awīlum*) in the Ugaritic polyglots. Roth (1997: 268) suggests that it can have two uses in Akkadian literature. It can refer to a member of a privileged class, in distinction to the *muškēnu* class and the slave class, a use most notably found in the Laws of Hammurabi. In this same text, it can also refer to, according to Roth (1997: 268): "a general, non-specific person." The latter of these uses seems the most likely in the Ugaritic administrative material. The word *bnš* is often used to simply refer to a "person" (without reference to that person's name, patronym, geographic origin, or profession). The kinds of contexts in which it is used are the same as the contexts for other kinds of chattel, such as animals and mobilia. When *bnš* is used in construct with another noun, there is an implication of possession, control, origin and/or obligation.[14] For example, Márquez Rowe (2002) takes the more specific *bnš mlk* as indicating that a person owes some kind of debt service to the palace; Prosser (2010) takes it as referencing an almost patron-client relationship. Here then, either a debt relationship or a patronage relationship makes an individual "belong" in the sense of identity referents, to another and thus may be another meaningful category that intersects with and complicates the foreign-self binary.

Census Texts

Particularly direct evidence about the presence of foreigners at Ugarit may be what have been referred to as census texts that were recovered from the palace archives. The lists identify the occupants (human and sometimes oxen) in the houses of various individuals who, it is stated on the tablets, are Cypriotes. A typical tablet is KTU 4.102 (II:4–7), which reads:

> A pre-eminent wife in the house of PN (*arttb*).
> A wife and her two sons in the house of PN (*iwrpzn*).
> A wife and an unmarried woman in the house of PN (*ydrm*).
> Two pre-eminent wives and an unmarried woman in the [house of PN?]

---

[14] For more on the nature of the grammatical relationship of words in construct at Ugarit, see Sivan 1997: 82–86, 209.

Van Soldt (2002: 816–817) notes that these names seem Semitic but the tablet does indicate that these people are Cypriote, so there is some confusion about the situation as presented here. Given the case that there is some Cypriote connection to these tablets, there are interesting implications for the consideration of foreigners at the site. Since these types of tablets are not attested for Ugaritians themselves, it suggests that there was some degree of administrative oversight of the presence of foreigners at Ugarit, to the extent that their household members are listed. Presumably these are the family members of the men listed in the tablets although, given that we know that Ugaritians could enter into debt service to foreigners, perhaps the reason for the palace's recording of this information was to keep track of just such service. If these are family members and not Ugaritians in service, then it suggests that resident foreigners were not just the individuals engaged directly in economic activity but family as well. Since oxen are also indicated, these foreigners seem to have been involved in some degree of agricultural activity and the palace seems to have been interested in this kind of record keeping. Many uses for these texts have been postulated; Astour (1970: 121–122) suggested that these were foreigners with a trade concession at the site and Rainey (1965: 11–12) argued that this was some kind of fiscal record in which the debtor's family members were kept track of in case the foreigner defaulted on a loan (and thus the palace would seize a family member in response). No firm conclusions can be reached about these texts other than that they illustrate the palace's concern to keep records of foreigner's household composition within Ugarit.

Foreign-ness, Strange-ness, and Known-ness as Constructed Through Internal Administration

These administrative tablets represent moments of contact between individuals and a larger administrative body. Each time this kind of contact is made, the social roles of the players are identified and the classificatory categories are strengthened. The act of circumscribing an individual or group by a specific designation upholds the social norm in a very conservative fashion. These distinctions become a kind of "common-sense"—unquestioned assumptions about the natural ordering of the everyday world. It may seem obvious that the palace would record people by the criteria mentioned above, but this is exactly the point. There is no *natural* imperative that these are the ways people should be identified, but each time the individual is identified and recorded as such, the right of the palace to do so (its agency) is strengthened.

While Ugarit is an unusual Late Bronze age site for its volume and variety of preserved texts in many different languages, evidence from other sites (such as Alalaḫ) suggest that administration at Ugarit seems to broadly reflect administrative *mentalités* throughout Late Bronze Age Syria. Administration is understood as a means of organizing from the top down, and one of the ways it does this is through *naturalizing* arbitrary categories and using them to label individuals and create identities, a process recoverable in the archaeological record through tablets. This evidence should not *just* be viewed as the remnant of information storage. These documents were intended to communicate a message to the parties privy to the administrative moment - and in fact acted as a symbol of that administration. The actual practice of administration, as well the symbolic (in the Peirceian sense) messages conveyed through administrative practice both reflect phenomena of Thirdness.

Cosmopolitanism

So, these are identifications of self and other that are made explicit by the palace administration. Does this mean that the state had the authority to define self and other? To what degree does this palatial administration mirror the 21st-century state's ability to define citizenship? Let us now turn to other signs of foreign-ness at the site; the site's seemingly explicit cosmopolitanism. When thinking about cosmopolitanism in the Late Bronze Age, we are most likely to look to signs of internationalism as evidence of positive views of foreign-ness, that the other is welcome in the context in which such evidence is discovered. Yet we should consider the contrary as well, that cosmopolitanism is often a language through which otherness is made explicit and defined. Here I return to Julie Young's work on Toronto refugees and her observations derived from reading Derrida. Derrida (2001: 19) toys with Kant's law of cosmopolitanism in respect to its dictum that foreigners be treated with specific rights as visitors. These rights of hospitality are explicitly invoked to encourage safe travel to other places. Yet they are just as important in preserving the boundaries of self and otherness when the other enters one's space. Hospitality serves to preserve the "other" as "other" even if done in gentle and appealing ways. There is, in Derrida's view, an underlying hostility that Young has categorized as "hostipitality" (2011: 540). The city, or whichever political body is viewed as the "host" comes to be defined as a concrete entity in relation to the hosted who, must by definition, be an "other" to the host. Thus, signs of cosmopolitanism at Ugarit signify both an acceptance of otherness (or perhaps a fetishization of otherness) but also the creation of boundaries that define otherness.

Hints of Foreign Forms of Administration

A curious class of object found at Ugarit hints at potential methods of regulating or administering those who may have been thought of as foreigners. Two clay balls inscribed with what Ferrara believes are names seem to be analogous to the types of Cypro-Minoan clay balls found especially in Cyprus (Ferrara – Valério 2017: 72). While these types of objects are well attested in the Aegean there is some disagreement in regards to their function and significance. Most scholars seem to believe that these are some kinds of identity bearing device. Some suggest that the inscriptions bear the names of labourers; others suggest that they bear the names of elites (Ferrara – Valério 2017: 73). Ferrara and Valério (2017: 85), basing their argument on the round shape of the balls and the fact that they were baked, suggest that these were lots. If this is the case, the casting of lots may have been a means of choosing labourers for a work assignment, settling disputes, or for other religious, ceremonial, juridical, or economic activities.

Perhaps this should be considered in tandem with the Ugaritic inscription found at Tiryns. The inscription appears on a broken ivory rod (of which 3.7 cm survives). While it is too fragmentary to know for sure, the original publishers of the rod suggest that it was either a label or some sort of measuring device (Cohen – Maran – Vetters 2010: 11–12). Identifying its exact use is not necessary here; what is important for this discussion is it suggests that just as administrative activities in Cypro-Minoan are apparent at Ugarit, so too are activities in Ugaritic (or at least some sort of cuneiform) in the Peloponnese.

The use of different languages and writing systems at Ugarit is often cited as further evidence of the city's cosmopolitanism and returning to the questions posed for thought during this conference, perhaps sheds light on the role of the scribe in facilitating the presence of foreigners in the city. Both van Soldt (van Soldt 2001) and Cohen (Cohen 2017: 281) have identified Assyrian scribes who operated in the city, with Cohen arguing for one whose traces have been identified in the *Maison aux tablettes*, a location in which many works of the Mesopotamian scribal tradition have been recovered. Within that building school texts have been identified and, while this is not surprising, provides evidence of individuals who may have been understood as foreigners participating in delivering a scribal curriculum. Mesopotamian lexical, literary, and omen texts found at the site show that Mesopotamian education was available at the site and perhaps an Assyrian teacher resided in the city.

More broadly speaking, the material culture of Ugarit defies easy description of foreign or local. Varieties of cylinder seals, stamp seals, art, and other material culture reflect connections from around the Mediterranean and Near East. Feldman's (1998) argument that some of the artistic themes constitute an international koine is well known and need not be explained in any detail here yet it is an important point to reiterate within the context of this discussion. That symbols of foreignness are invoked at Ugarit in a way that communicates elite status points to the role of foreignness in articulating and mediating local identity. One's relationship to the foreign provides a means for articulating one's identity within the city.

Conclusions: Foreigners at Ugarit

This discussion has wound between different examples of engagements with otherness at Ugarit and different kinds of critical theory that can help make these engagements more apparent. As a form of conclusion, I want to return to some of the critical questions that were posed as a means of orienting Crossroads III. First, how do we recognize a foreigner in an ancient society? The short answer here is that this is more difficult than is typically thought. The usual stance has been that gentilics and personal names offer an easy diagnostic but when one looks at this evidence at Ugarit, there seems to be a greater fluidity here than a simple "self-other" binary could accommodate. There is much evidence for people with non-Ugaritian names or gentilics operating within the city with as much or even more fluidity and/or power than those who might be deemed Ugaritic by such standards. Where the situation is most clear in regards to significant "foreign" status, from an administrative perspective, seems to be when another polity has authority over the legal or juridical status of the individuals in question. Thus, the merchants of Ura were, at least emically, foreigners.

Despite the murkiness of clearly identifying foreigners, it is perhaps easier to offer answers to the question of what were the roles of foreigners at Ugarit. From the administrative perspective addressed here, the obvious answer is that they operated as mediators of exchange relationships, facilitating the movement of goods in different ways. A mere economic reading is insufficient, even though that is mostly what has been discussed so far. Feldman's identification of an international koine shows one way in which foreign-ness operated as a means for the articulation of power and identity within the city. This is not the place to address this further but Egypt seems to have offered much exotic or auratic appeal that has long been identified, and this perhaps goes beyond mere displays of power but hints at the religious and ideological value that the foreign can play. And, as well discussed by Devecchi (2015), Hittite suzerainty played a complex role as a foreign power holding political and juridical authority over Ugarit.

Debt may have been one of the most meaningful economic relationships that connected foreigners with Ugaritians. The case of the merchants of Ura shows that this was not only a significant means for which foreigners could gain economic power in the city, it was also a contested means of doing so. The palace census texts, the category of *bnš mlk*, and perhaps other types of administrative tablets demonstrate that in this non-monetary economy, debt and credit were important instruments that foreigners could access.

Thinking about the experiences of foreigners at Ugarit, this paper has attempted to understand what that embodied experience would have been like, trying to evaluate the legibility of the city to a newcomer. It was possible to identify locations that were legible and those that were less so and these seem consistent with where one would imagine a stranger would want to participate in civic life. The roads and urban planning not only facilitated movement towards these areas and away from non-legible space, the physical layout of the city communicated messages of power that seem consistent throughout the Late Bronze Age eastern Mediterranean.

Another guiding question has been what were the roles of scribes and interpreters in the interactions between foreigners and Ugaritians? The answer is not monolithic. Typical Mesopotamian scribal curricula have been identified at Ugarit and the multilingualism of the site is clear. How multi-lingual individuals were, is less clear but this is an academic problem that is typical of the Late Bronze Age. What Ugarit perhaps offers that is different are the hints of foreign administrative practices that have been identified at the site and the fact that an Ugaritic inscription was found at Tiryns. While the foreign administrative elements do not constitute a large proportion of the administrative tools in evidence, their presence suggests a level of *ad hoc* flexibility in these experiences. More systematic roles of scribes are perhaps less evocative but more meaningful. The actual textual recording of individuals, by the palace, in relation to specific categories of identity naturalized categories in a way that made these identities perhaps unquestionable. If this logic can be pushed further, and maybe exaggerated, one could argue that the scribes actually generated these identities to some extent, or at least were the arbiters of who was foreign and who was not.

If we consider Henri Lefebvre's (1996) more activist argument that citizenship should not be a binary status constituted by a relationship to the city-state but rather, as Julie Young (2011: 537) paraphrases him, reframed as the "substantive practice engaged in by all residents of the city", then perhaps our thinking of foreignness in antiquity needs to be reconsidered. Is our work in defining ancient foreigners just continuing the larger enterprise of 18th and 19th-century nationalism, where the mechanisms of the state are naturalized as entangled and inseparable with a kind of racialized ethnicity? Or perhaps a softer reading, are we perpetuating early 20th-century archaeological "culture-history" approaches that no longer need be adopted given the more advanced state of our discipline? Here the conclusion is not that the concept of "foreign" was foreign to the Late Bronze Age Near East. Rather, it is suggested that scholars also approach the issue from avenues distinct from the state, the nation, or the ethnos, or at least allow that these may not have been the constitutive elements of what it means to be foreign. Administratively, the city of Ugarit was not as coherent of an entity as academic approaches tend to presume. Lived experience at Ugarit was one of different scales of power, with nested hierarchical and heterarchical spheres that were fluid and situational. It was not the place where Ugaritian and foreigner met but was one of the locations where the idea of Ugaritian and non-Ugaritian was created and enacted.

References

Amin, A., 2002. Ethnicity and the Multicultural City: Living with Diversity. *Environment and Planning A* 34, 959–980.

Astour, M., 1970. Ma'ḫadu, the Harbor of Ugarit. *JESHO* 13, 113–127.

Astour, M., 1972. The Merchant Class of Ugarit. In D.O. Edzard, ed., *Gesellschaftsklassen im Alten Zweistromland und in den angrenzenden Gebeiten*. Munich: Beck, 11–26.

Beckman, G., 1999². *Hittite Diplomatic Texts*. WAW 7. Atlanta, GA: Scholars Press.

Bourdieu, P., 1977. *Outline of a Theory of Practice*. Translated by R. Nice. Cambridge: Cambridge University Press.

Callot, O. – M. Yon, 1995. Urbanisme et Architecture. In M. Yon – D. Arnaud, eds., *Le pays d'Ougarit autour de 1200 av. J.-C. Actes du colloque international Paris, 28 Juin-1er juillet 1993*. RSO 11. Paris: Éditions Recherche sur les Civilisations, 155–168.

Cohen, C. – J. Maran – M. Vetters, 2010. An Ivory Rod with a Cuneiform Inscription, Most Probably Ugaritic, from a Final Palatial Workshop in the Lower Citadel of Tiryns. *Archäologischer Anzeiger* 2, 1–22.

Cohen, Y., 2017. An Assyrian Teacher at Ugarit? A New Reading of the Colophon of *ŠIMÂ MILKA* ("Hear the Advice") from the *Maison Aux Tablettes*. *BiOr* 74/3–4, 274–283.

Craigie, P., 1982. Amos the nōqed in the Light of Ugaritic. *Sciences Religieueses/Studies in Religion* 11, 29–33.

Del Olmo Lete, G. – J. Sanmartín, 2004². *A Dictionary of the Ugaritic Language in the Alphabetic Tradition*. Second revised edition. Edited and translated by W.G.E. Watson. HdO I/67 (2 volumes). Leiden – Boston: Brill.

Derrida, J., 2001. *On Cosmopolitanism and Forgiveness (Thinking in Action)*. London: Routledge.

Devecchi, E., 2015. The International Relations of Hatti's Syrian Vassals, or How to Make the Best of Things. In B. Eder – R. Pruzsinszky, eds., *Policies of Exchange: Political Systems and Modes of Interaction in the Aegean and the Near East in the 2nd Millennium B.C.E.* OREA 2. Wien: Austrian Academy of Sciences Press, 117–126.

Feldman, M., 1998. *Luxury Goods from Ras Shamra – Ugarit and their Role in the International Relations of the Eastern Mediterranean and Near East during the Late Bronze Age.* Ph.D. Dissertation, Harvard University.

Ferrara, S. – M. Valério, 2017. Contexts and repetitions of Cypro-Minoan Inscriptions: Function and Subject Matter of Clay Balls. *BASOR* 378, 71–94.

Giddens, A., 1984. *The Constitution of Society*. Berkeley: University of California Press.

Gray, J., 1952. Feudalism in Ugarit and Early Israel. *ZAW* 64, 49–55.

Jervis, B., 2018. Assemblage Urbanism. Becoming Urban in Late Medieval Southampton. *Archaeological Dialogues* 25 / 2, 135–160.

Klengel, H., 1992. *Syria 3000 to 300 B.C.: A Handbook of Political History.* Berlin: Akademie Verlag.

Lefebvre, H., 1996. *Writing on Cities.* Translated by E. Kofman and D. Nicholson-Smith. Cambridge: Blackwell.

Lele, V., 2006. Material Habits, Identity Semeiotic. *Journal of Social Archaeology* 6 / 1, 48–70.

Liverani, M., 2001. *International Relations in the Ancient Near East, 1600-1100 BC*. New York: Palgrave.

Lynch, K., 1960. *The Image of the City.* Boston: MIT Press.

Márquez Rowe, I., 2002. The King's Men in Ugarit and Society in Late Bronze Age Syria. *JESHO* 45 / 1, 1–19.

Meskell, L., 2001. Archaeologies of Identity. In I. Hodder, ed., *Archaeological Theory Today*. Cambridge: Polity Press, 187–213.

Pardee, D. – P. Bordreuil, 1992. Ugarit: Texts and Literature. In D.N. Freedman, ed., *The Anchor Bible Dictionary*. Vol. VI. New York: Doubleday, 706–721.

Peirce, C., 1931. *The Collected Papers of Charles Sanders Peirce, Vol. I: The Principles of Philosophy.* Cambridge: Harvard University Press.

Prosser, M., 2010. *Bunušu in Ugaritic Society*. Ph.D. Dissertation, University of Chicago.

Rainey, A.F., 1962. *The Social Stratification of Ugarit.* Ph.D. Dissertation, Brandeis University.

Rainey, A.F., 1965. Family relationships at Ugarit. *Or NS* 34, 10–22.

Robinson, P., 2018. Design Interventions for a Digital Future. *Spacing* Spring 2018, 30–31.

Roth, M., 1997[2]. *Law Collections from Mesopotamia and Asia Minor*. WAW 6. Atlanta, GA: Scholars Press.

Routledge, B. – K. McGeough, 2009. Just What Collapsed? A Network Perspective on Trade, Exchange, and the Palace at Ugarit. In C. Bachhuber – G. Roberts, eds., *Forces of Transformation: The End of the Bronze Age in the Mediterranean*. London: Oxbow, 22–29.

Sasson, J., 1966. Canaanite Maritime Involvement in the Second Millennium B.C. *JAOS* 86, 126–138.

Sauvage, C., 2011. Evidence from Old Texts: Aspects of Late Bronze Age International Maritime Travel and Trade Regulations in the Eastern Mediterranean? In K. Duistermaat – I. Regulski, eds., *International Contacts in the Ancient Mediterranean: Proceedings of the International Conference at the Netherlands-Flemish Institute in Cairo, 25th to 29th October 2008*. OLA 202. Leuven: Peeters, 427–437.

Schaeffer, C., 1952. Nouvelles fouilles et découvertes de la mission archéologique de Ras Shamra dans le Palais d'Ugarit (campagne 1951). *AAS* 2, 3–22.

Schaeffer, C., 1957. Résumé de résultats de la XIXe campagne de fouilles à Ras Shamra-Ugarit, 1955. *AAS* 7, 35–66.

Schaeffer, C., 1962. Fouilles et découvertes des XVIIIe et XIXe campagnes, 1954–1955. In C. Schaeffer, ed., *Ugaritica IV*. MRS 15. Paris: Imprimerie Nationale.

Schloen, J.D., 2001. *The House of the Father as Fact and Symbol Patrimonialism in Ugarit and the Ancient Near East*. SAHL 2. Winona Lake, IN: Eisenbrauns.

Seitz, D., 2016. Limbo Life in Canada's Waiting Room: Asylum-seeker as Queer Subject. *Environment and Planning D: Society and Space* 35/3, 438–456.

Sennett, R., n.d. The Open City. Available at https://www.richardsennett.com/site/senn/UploadedResources/The%20Open%20City.pdf (accessed on January 14, 2019).

Sinclar, P., 2010. The Urban Mind: A Thematic Introduction. In P. Sinclair – G. Nordquist – F. Herschend – C. Isendahl, eds., *The Urban Mind: Cultural and Environmental Dynamics.* Uppsala: Uppsala University Press.

Singer, I., 1999. A Political History of Ugarit. In W.G.E. Watson – N. Wyatt, eds., *Handbook of Ugaritic Studies*. HdO I/39. Leiden – Boston – Köln: Brill, 603–733.

Sivan, D., 1997. *A Grammar of the Ugaritic Language*. HdO I/28. Leiden – New York – Köln: Brill.

Tammuz, O., 2005. *Mare clausum?* Sailing Seasons in the Mediterranean in Early Antiquity. *Mediterranean Historical Review* 20/2, 145–162.

van Soldt, W., 1991. *Studies in the Akkadian of Ugarit: Dating and Grammar.* AOAT 40. Kevelaer – Neukirchen-Vluyn: Butzon & Bercker – Neukirchener Verlag.

van Soldt, W., 1999. Studies in the Topography of Ugarit (4): Town Size and Districts. *UF* 31, 749–796.

van Soldt, W., 2001. Nahiš-šalmu, an Assyrian Scribe Working in the "Southern Palace" at Ugarit. In *Veenhof Anniversary Volume: Studies Presented to Klaas R. Veenhof on the Occasion of his Sixty-Fifth Birthday*. PIHANS 89. Leiden: Nederlands Instituut voor het Nabije Oosten, 429–444.

van Soldt, W., 2002. Studies on the *sākinu*-Official (2): The functions of the *sākinu* of Ugarit. *UF* 34, 805–828.

Watson, W.G.E., 2002. The Meaning of Ugaritic *s/śġr*. *JSS* 47/2, 203–207.

Whitt, W., 1993. *Archives and Administration in the Royal Palace of Ugarit.* Ph.D. Dissertation, Duke University.

Wood, P., 2006. The 'Sarcee War': Fragmented Citizenship and the City. *Space and Polity* 10/3, 229–242.

Yon, M., 1992. Ugarit: The Urban Habitat, The Present State of the Archaeological Picture. *BASOR* 286, 19–34.

Yon, M., 2006. *The City of Ugarit at Tell Ras Shamra.* Winona Lake, IN: Eisenbrauns.

Young, J., 2011. "A New Politics of the City": Locating the Limits of Hospitality and Practicing the City-as-Refuge. *ACME: An International E-Journal for Critical Geographies* 10/3, 534–563.

ETHNIC ENCLAVES: A MODERN UNDERSTANDING OF HOW MIGRATORY GROUPS PRESERVE ETHNIC IDENTITY AS A POTENTIAL EXPLANATION FOR THE LIBYANS' RETENTION OF A NON-EGYPTIAN IDENTITY IN THE LATE NEW KINGDOM AND THIRD INTERMEDIATE PERIOD.

Edward Mushett Cole (University of Birmingham)

Introduction

The Libyan Period, dating roughly from the 21st to 24th Dynasties, saw the rise to power of a group within the Egyptian elite who not only altered or ignored some of the key conventions of Egyptian society but who also appear to have maintained elements of a non-Egyptian identity, one considered to be "Libyan".[1] Representations of members of the elite with non-Egyptian markers, from names, to titles, and even dress, alongside wider changes to aspects of Egyptian culture has led to the identification of this group as one of non-Egyptian background (Yoyotte 1961: 4–30). This identification of the Libyan nature of the elite during the Libyan Period has grown over the last few decades through the research of Leahy (1985), Jansen-Winkeln (1994; 1999; 2005), Ritner (2009a), and Broekman (2010), amongst others, establishing that the assumption of the Libyans' "egyptianisation" has been exaggerated in past scholarship. This is despite some contemporary Egyptian texts claiming that the Libyans were settled in groups and "converted" to Egyptian culture and language and the strong Egyptian conventions surrounding textual and imagery representations for the elite which emphasised the need to be represented as "Egyptian" irrespective of background.

Despite this increasing recognition that the Libyans retained at least some aspects of their non-Egyptian identity long after their arrival within Egypt, there have been no formal attempts to explain how such a group might have retained this non-Egyptian identity, particularly given this group's likely long residence in Egypt prior to their rise to power. Nor has there been any explanation of the motivation for the Libyans to mark out their non-Egyptian identity given the Egyptian decorum regarding elite representation which had endured across the New Kingdom, and arguably much longer (Baines 1995: 26, 33–35). It is this gap that this article will address.

[1] Note that for the purposes of this paper the term "Libyan" is used as convenient shorthand for all of the groups that appear to have originated from the Western Desert, such as the Meshwesh/Ma, Libu, Seped, Tehenu, and Temeh, to avoid confusion as to whether I am referring to specific groups or more generally to individuals from all of those groups.

Urban social studies have examined this problem within modern societies, where new migrants often do not integrate or assimilate into the majority culture and through such studies the concept of "ethnic enclaves" has been developed. Ethnic enclaves are based on a noticeable preponderance for modern migrants who arrive in regions where there is an existing dominant culture to gather and settle together for a number of reasons, but as a consequence often preserves and even enhances their minority identity. This paper will present the concept of ethnic enclaves as a possible explanation for how the Libyans were able to retain such a distinctly non-Egyptian identity even as they rose through Egyptian society.

Arrival and settlement of the Libyans into Egypt

Before outlining what ethnic enclaves are and why they might provide a useful explanation for the preservation of the Libyans' non-Egyptian identity it is important to clarify the methods by which the Libyans arrived into Egypt, where known from the surviving Egyptian sources. These sources suggest that this entry into Egypt was as part of two main groups; via captives being resettled following the major invasions of the late New Kingdom and through low-level Libyan migration that probably took place throughout the late New Kingdom and Third Intermediate Period. It is important to note though that as the evidence for this entirely comes from Egyptian sources there is likely a high level of ambiguity and lack of details regarding Libyans and their origins and culture (Ritner 2009b: 43–56), as is the case with all the foreign cultures with which they were in contact (Liszka 2011: 154).

Non-Egyptian evidence for the Libyans is largely non-existent, except for some possible rock art in the Western Desert of unknown date or origin (Ritner 2009b: 48–49). From the Egyptian record the most extensive evidence is for the Libyan "invasions" of the late New Kingdom and the subsequent settlement of captives following the Egyptians' victories. During the late 19th and 20th Dynasties there were a number of Libyan invasions where large Libyan groups who were moving into the Nile Valley were defeated militarily by the Egyptians. The first of these incursions was in Merneptah's Year 5 (ca. 1210 BC) and further such large-scale movements took place in Ramesses III's Year 5 (ca. 1178 BC) and Year 11 (ca. 1172 BC).

Merneptah recorded his victory on both the walls of Karnak and on stelae set up across Egypt, including the now well-known "Israel Stela", whilst those from Ramesses III's reign were recorded on the walls of his mortuary temple at Medinet Habu, as well as in the "Rhetorical Stela" from Chapel C at Deir el-Medina, and in the "historical section" of the Great Harris Papyrus. For the perspective of the Libyans' arrival into Egypt the most important part of these texts are the sections detailing what happened to the Egyptians' captives after their victory. These texts outline the New Kingdom practice of settling captives within Egypt, often away from the areas closest to where the invading group was from or through which they had entered Egypt, and incorporating them into the state workforce either in the military or through the other major state institutions such as the temples (Davies 1943: 47–48; 1943b: pl. LVI–LVII; Eyre 1987: 189; Haring 2009: 5; Grandet

2013: 731). The practice itself is attested in inscriptions throughout the New Kingdom including Tuthmose III's and Rameses II's campaign inscriptions and those of officials in Tuthmose III's reign:

> "Number of Asiatic men and women and Southern men and women my majesty gave to my father Amun, beginning in year 23 until the recording of this tablet upon this temple (*ḥwt-nṯr*); Syrians (*ḫ3rw*) 1,578" (Annals of Tuthmose III, Urk. IV 742.10–743.8; translation by author).

> "The captives which his majesty [Tuthmose III] brought away for the works of the temple [of Amun]" (Davies 1943a: 55; 1943b: pl. LIX).

> "Now then, his Majesty had made ready his army and his chariotry, and the Sherden of his Majesty's [Ramesses II's] plunder, whom he had brought back by the victory of is strong arm" (Battle of Kadesh inscriptions at Karnak; KRI II 11:6–10).

The Merneptah and Ramesses III inscriptions are no different from this, recording the settlement of Libyan captives within Egypt and their being branded with the king's name for service:

> "The plains and hill countries were cut off, and carried to Egypt as slaves presented together to its conclave of the gods" (Great Inscription of Year 5 at Medinet Habu; KRI V 22:2).

> "Their leaders were rounded up and made into groups, in fortresses, and branded with the name of his majesty" (Great Inscription of Year 5 at Medinet Habu; KRI V 24:1–2).

> "I settled their leaders in forts bearing my name. I appointed troop-commanders for them and tribal chiefs (*ˁ3 n mhwt*), branded and reduced (to the status of) slaves with cartouches in my name, their wives and children being similarly treated." (P. Harris I 77:5–6; Grandet 1994: 337).[2]

The use of these settled foreign groups in the military is best demonstrated by the group known as the Sherden. There are references to units of the Sherden in Merneptah's army in P. Anastasi II (Caminos 1954: 45) and in Ramesses III's Medinet Habu reliefs where Sherden are depicted as being an element of the Egyptian army as it fought the "Sea Peoples" in his Year 8 (Edgerton – Wilson 1936: 36). This group is even recognisable in imagery due to the distinctive armour and weaponry with which they were depicted (with horns on their helmets and distinctive swords), marking them as different from the Egyptian soldiers they served alongside (see the "Sea Peoples" Medinet Habu reliefs in OIP 8:

[2] Translation from the original French by the author.

pl. 29, 30–43). As with other captive groups we have textual references to them being settled in "fortresses", apparently primarily in the Fayyum region, although they appear in records all the way through Middle Egypt such as P. Amiens and P. Ashmolean Museum 1945.96 (Cavillier 2010: 342–343; Adams – Cohen 2013: 648–650). For the Sherden there appears to have been a recognition that they were a distinct group who retained some differentiation from other Egyptians across the New Kingdom. For example, there are references to an individual called the "Sherden Hori" despite his Egyptian name in the Late Ramesside Letters P. BM 10326, P. Turin 2026, and P. BM 10375 from the reign of Ramesses XI (Wente 1990: 190–194). They are also referenced in land records such as P. Wilbour with the title of "Sherden" (*Srdn*) (e.g. Text B 9.1–9.9, Gardiner 1948: 115), as well as in P. Amiens (Gardiner 1941: 38–41), along with references to a possible donation to a god of the Sherden in Text B of P. Wilbour (*nṯr šrdn*; B 9.13.20; Gardiner 1941: 120). This is despite many of the individuals identified as "Sherden" holding Egyptian names along with their descendants and no distinctive archaeological evidence has been located to reveal the cultural practices of this group. Suggestive of a similar military role for the captive Libyans is that many of the Libyan elite held military titles during the Libyan Period (Moje 2014: 87), with the kings Shoshenq I and Osorkon I both first attested as military commanders (Ritner 2009c: 169; Payraudeau 2014b: 28–29). Most of the Libyan elite continued to hold military titles into the later Libyan Period, often combined with the high priesthood of the local temple (Jansen-Winkeln 1999: 16–17; Moje 2014: 87–88), all of which is probably indicative of their origins as prisoners-of-war conscripted into the Egyptian military (Leahy 1985: 56).

Importantly, it is unclear whether these large-scale Libyan "invasions" were indeed purely military. The Egyptian records detail the presence of both women and children as part of the Libyan groups as well as large quantities of livestock in the items recorded as being captured by the Egyptians in the text accompanying the scenes of the second Libyan invasion in Year 11 (KRI V 53:1–54:8):

> "His warrior-runners were carried off [...] their wives and their children [bound by?] their arms and their heads, as prisoners, with their property and their children weighing down upon their backs, their cattle, and their horses brought to Egypt" (Great Inscription of Year 11 at Medinet Habu; KRI V 61:14–62:1).

The Egyptians even seem to have understood this to be the motivation of the Meshwesh during that "invasion" in Year 11: "'We will settle in Egypt', so they had said" (Great Inscription of Year 11; KRI V 60:0). This has led to suggestions that these Libyan "invasions" were much closer to migrations or simply nomadic groups moving to new pasture areas than a pure military invasion (Peden 1994: 43, 61). This is significant as it might have meant that the captives would have included significant numbers of families who might have been expected to be settled together – immediately forming a Libyan community within Egypt.

However, given that this implies that there might have been a settled "Libyan" community within Egypt as a product of the settling of Libyan prisoners-of-war, the description of what happened to those captives in Ramesses III's "Rhetorical Stela" from Chapel C at Deir el-Medina is particularly important:

> "They are settled ("made") into strongholds for the victorious king, they hear the language of (Egypt's) people, in serving the king. He abolished their language, he changed their tongue" (KRI V 91:5–10).

This text implies that, on at least some level, the Libyans who were settled in Egypt by the Egyptian state and co-opted into the state system may have been forced to adopt Egyptian culture. A significant proportion, therefore, of the first Libyans to arrive in Egypt were probably prisoners-of-war who were subsequently settled in forts together, possibly as part of the Egyptian army, and who may well have been indoctrinated in Egyptian culture and language (Leahy 1985: 56).

This was, however, not the only way in which Libyan groups entered into and settled in Egypt. It is clear from some of the textual sources that low-level migration into Egypt by groups from the Western Desert, and particularly into the western Delta region, was a common event across the New Kingdom. References in Merneptah's records of his defeat of the Libyans implies that the Libyans had been in the region for some time and it was only as they moved further into Egypt into the eastern Delta and towards Heliopolis and Memphis that the Egyptians stopped them, probably somewhere in the southwestern region of the western Delta (Manassa 2003: 27):

> "tents before Perbaset which reached the Shakana Canal at the artificial lake of the Ati Canal" (Great Karnak Inscription of Merneptah line 7; Manassa 2003: 13).[3]

Similarly, in some of Ramesses III's inscriptions he explains his need to act because the Libyans had been crossing and then settling in Egyptian territory, again presumably the western Delta, and there is an implication that they had been there for some time, especially in the description of the first "invasion" in the Harris Papyrus which even has the Libyans in control of towns in the western Delta:

> "He has carried off the land of Libya (Temehu), Sepedu, and Meshwesh, who were ruining Egypt daily" (Text accompanying scenes of First Libyan war at Medinet Habu; KRI V 15:1–3).

> "and they kept penetrating Egypt's frontiers" (Great Inscription of Year 11 at Medinet Habu; KRI V 60:10).

---

[3] For the identification of these places as locations in the eastern Delta see Manassa 2003: 13–16 notes a–f.

> "The Libu and the Meshwesh were settled in Egypt, having seized the cites of the western border (of the Delta), from Houtkaptah (Memphis) to Qerben, (then) having held the Great-River on all (the length of) its bank. And it was they who robbed the cities of the nome of Xois[4] for very many years while they were in Kemet." (P. Harris 1, 76–77; Grandet 1994: 337).[5]

Following the invasions of Ramesses III's reign we have a number of records that indicate that this low-level migration was continuing into the western Delta, but also now further down in the Nile Valley at the points where the desert roads reach the floodplain. These records are primarily from the day-journal of the workmen's village at Deir el-Medina on the west bank of the Nile at Thebes. These detail repeated disruption to the workmen's work on the royal tombs in the Valley of the Kings due to the presence of Libyans (*Libu* and *Meshwesh*) or unnamed "enemies", "foreigners", throughout the 20th Dynasty. Specifically there are references to their presence from the reigns of Ramesses III (O. Deir el-Medina (ODM) 35; KRI V 521:1–2), Ramesses V (P. Turin 2044; McDowell 1999: 228), Ramesses VI, where it appears that their presence may have delayed the burial of Ramesses V (O. Cairo CGC 25.254; KRI VI 343:14–15), Ramesses IX (P. Turin 2074; KRI VI 608:10–609:6; P. Turin 2071/224; KRI VI 637:7–638:14), and Ramesses X (P. Turin 1898, 1937, 2094/244, P. Chabas-Lieblein 1; KRI VI 687:14–689:2). This gives us a sense that during this period, at least, there was considerable movement into the Nile Valley from the Western Desert and there has been some suggestion that these movements continued into the Libyan Period (Yoyotte 1961: 43–44; Leahy 1985: 55).

This continued migration may even have led Ramesses III to renew or newly fortify temple enclosures in Middle and Upper Egypt, at Siut, Abydos, Hermopolis, Asyut, and This (P. Harris I, 57:11–59:4; Grandet 1994: 304–306; Kitchen 2012: 11; Snape 2012: 421). Such arrivals of groups through the desert roads from the Western Desert is further suggested by a letter from Ramesses XI's reign, P. Louvre 3169, requesting a local official to gather some men in order to track a group of Meshwesh and determine their intentions:

> "and with all the men of the Chiefs of the Medjay who are in Per-hebyt, the town which is under you. So, do not hold back (even) one man of them! By their names which are with me in writing, I shall summon them; and you shall come, once you know thoroughly the state of mind of the Meshwesh." (KRI VI 523:1–523:10).

There is no mention in any of these texts, however, of whether these later arrivals were (re-)settled by the Egyptian state in specific locations, as is known from the textual sources regarding the Libyan captives. This perhaps suggests that they may have been able to settle wherever they chose, but certainly appears to indicate

---

[4] Literally *ḫ3sww* – the 6th Lower Egyptian nome.
[5] Translated from the original French by the author.

that they were not part of a formal indoctrination programme by the Egyptian state to which the captives had supposedly been subjected. This last factor, that there would have been no formal mechanism for them to gain Egyptian language and culture, is significant as it makes them more akin to modern migrants arriving in a region or state with a very dominant culture—the very group of people that create ethnic enclaves in the modern era—something that will be explored later.

The Libyan nature of the Libyan Period

The "Libyan" nature of the Libyan Period (approximately the 21st to 24th Dynasties) has been much debated in the last few decades, ever since Leahy's 1985 article "The Libyan Period in Egypt: An Essay in Interpretation". Influenced by the Egyptian texts recording the indoctrination of the Libyan captives, scholars have created a tradition of identifying the Libyans settled this way as largely if not entirely "egyptianised" (O'Connor 1983: 238–241; 1990: 106–107; Kemp 1997: 128; Hüneberg 2003: 71–74; Moreno García 2013: 97). Establishing the actual extent of the Libyans' "egyptianisation" is complicated by the fact that it is difficult to distinguish ethnicity in the past, especially within the archaeological record (McGuire 1982: 163; Jones 1997: 119–127; Liszka 2011: 161), and particularly for ancient Egypt where text and imagery conventions concealed such ethnic backgrounds (Leahy 1985: 54; Booth 2005: 6), as is clear from attempts to locate the ethnicity of the various "Sea Peoples" (Drews 1993: 62–72). Differences from those conventions within the Libyan Period, however, make it clear that the Libyans' level of egyptianisation continues to be overstated in scholarship (Leahy 1985: 57).[6] That a group wanted to distinguish themselves from other members of a society reflects a clear preservation of an ethnic identity and its boundaries (McGuire 1982: 166; Jones 1997: 84; Dever 2007: 51).

Forced conversion to a new identity and culture often leads to the development of a distinctive "counter identity" to resist such changes (Assmann 2011: 134–135; Liszka 2011: 161). Ethnic identities are often produced in societal contexts that are delineated by relations of power, where a dominant culture "decides" how a group should be represented and constructs an ethnic identity for a group based on their preconceptions of that identity (Jones 1997: 143). Indeed, the Libyans may even have deliberately constructed an identity based on the stereotype the Egyptians had created for people from the Western Desert once it provided them with a benefit, perhaps by providing group cohesion in the face of the presence of Egyptian culture. This would be what other, earlier groups in Nubia appear to have done with the "Nehesy" and "Medjay" identities but again only when those identities had become a benefit to individuals who identified as them (Liszka 2011: 164–167). Additionally, settling the Libyans in groups away from others by placing them in specific settlements would have made it easier for them to maintain their ethnic identity (Leahy 1985: 56; Jansen-Winkeln 1994: 88; Ritner

[6] For examples of such overstatement see Kitchen (1990: 21) and Hüneberg (2003: 68–70).

2009a: 332).[7] Indeed, it is increasingly argued that the Libyans retained some level of non-Egyptian identity and were not, therefore, as thoroughly "egyptianised" as other captured peoples had been (Leahy 1985; Jansen-Winkeln 1994; Ritner 2009a; Broekman 2010; Mushett Cole 2015: 113; 2017: 248–256).

The evidence for this identity is largely iconographic and onomastic in nature, with some support from wider cultural changes that took place during the Third Intermediate Period which are perceived as being the product of the Libyans' differences (Leahy 1985: 61; Jansen-Winkeln 1994: 92–93; 1999: 19; Broekman 2010: 89). The political divisions visible under the later 22nd and 23rd Dynasties are argued to be a product of the Libyans' lack of assimilation, not just because they divided the country, but also because the Egyptian concept of a sole king was unimportant for rulers of this period (Leahy 1985: 59; Jansen-Winkeln 1994: 95; 1999: 19–20; Broekman 2010: 91).

From the middle of the 22nd Dynasty onwards there is increasing evidence for a number of kings, great chiefs and chiefs of the Ma. Unlike previous Egyptian periods of political division (Moreno García 2015: 83–84), however, there is very limited evidence for conflict between the various regions, with no apparent restrictions on local leaders becoming king. This change to the understanding of kingship is visible on the statue of Nakhtefmut which dates to the middle of the 8th century BC. The statue is inscribed with the titles of Horsiese (A), who granted him the statue, and those of Horsiese (A)'s northern contemporary Osorkon II, with no indication that this was unusual (Broekman 2010: 91). On Piye's "Victory stela" four kings are recorded, at Hermopolis, Herakleopolis, Leontopolis and Tanis respectively, along with a number of great chiefs and chiefs of the Ma and Libu (Grimal 1981: 2–3), reflecting the direct opposite of the traditions of Egyptian kingship. Even local leaders who did not assume a form of Egyptian kingship appear to have appropriated a number of royal attributes. Donation stelae from the later Libyan Period provide some of the best examples of this, with the local Libyan ruler depicted in the traditional place of the king (Yoyotte 1961: 30–31; Leahy 1985: 59; Jansen-Winkeln 1999: 17; Moje 2014: 5; 107), even though the stelae were still dated to a specific king's reign. In some instances the king's cartouches were even left blank (Yoyotte 1961: 32–33, 58–59; Moje 2014: 144–145). This loss of significance for the role of the king(s) is also shown by the importance of genealogies which demonstrated an individual's inheritance of their titles from their ancestors (Lange 2008: 140; Moje 2014: 125–126), reflecting the king's lack of control over the appointments to most positions.

Most significantly, there was large-scale retention of Libyan culture in names, titles and in depictions of individuals, many of which continued into the Kushite Period and on into the Late Period (Leahy 1985: 57; Ritner 2009a: 332; Moje 2014: 125). The names of the kings and much of the elite during the Libyan Period did not conform to Egyptian styles, instead being distinctly Libyan in origin, such as

[7] This is particularly true if Ritner's (2009a: 332) retranslation of the relevant section of P. Harris (I, 75: 5) is correct, "I settled their leaders in strongholds in my name. I gave to them captains of archers and elders of the tribes".

Shoshenq, Takeloth, Nimlot, and Osorkon (Leahy 1985: 54–55; Jansen-Winkeln 1994: 93). Unlike previous groups of foreigners who adopted Egyptian names, or gave them to their children (Shaw 2000: 326), and thus assimilated into the wider population, the Libyans continued using distinctively Libyan names, with some popular throughout the entire Third Intermediate Period (Leahy 1985: 55). These names were even incorporated into classic Egyptian compound names such as "Ankh – King's name", e.g. Ankhshoshenq (Leahy 1992: 146–163). This lack of assimilation is also apparent in the continuation of Libyan titles, such as great chief and chief of the Ma / Libu (Leahy 1985: 57). During the Libyan Period these titles were often deemed more important by an individual than their Egyptian titles (Ritner 2009a: 336; Broekman 2010: 90). This is best demonstrated by Padiese A's Serapeum stelae where, despite having an Egyptian name, he not only replaced the king before the gods, but was depicted with only his Libyan titles and attributes, with his title of high priest of Ptah instead attached to his son Peftjauawybast (Louvre IM 3749; Ritner 2009c: 388–390). This trend is apparent even at the top of the Egyptian hierarchy; Osorkon II desired that his sons would become "great chiefs" (Lange 2008: 138–139), an unusual request for an Egyptian king whose sons were much higher in the Egyptian social hierarchy than a foreign chief could ever be (Lange 2008: 139; Ritner 2009a: 336).

There are other "Libyan" elements which appear to confirm the Libyan elite's retention of an ethnically Libyan identity. Despite individuals being depicted with traditionally Egyptian features, several items were added, in particular the ostrich feather on the head, that do not conform to the conventions of Egyptian depiction (Leahy 1985: 57; Moje 2014: 125). Such items appear in Egyptian depictions of the inhabitants of the Western Desert, as in the reliefs accompanying Ramesses III's Libyan invasions inscriptions at Medinet Habu (OIP 9: pl. 73–78). That these elements could be considered "native" Libyan markers of identity, however, is supported by their appearance on rock art across the Western Desert of Egypt, particularly representations of people wearing the ostrich feathers on their head in the styles attributed to both the Meshwesh and Libu (Ritner 2009b: 48–49). Even if not a specifically "Libyan" tradition, its use by these individuals demonstrates its importance in marking an individual's membership of a group with a distinctive non-Egyptian identity. Such signposting of ethnic boundaries is an important element of ethnic identity, whether that marking is done by those who are members of the group or by those outside it who perceive an individual to be a member of it (Jones 1997: 128–129). There was also the appearance of genealogical inscriptions, often recording the inheritance of a specific set of titles by an extended family line. The most notable of these are those of Basa (Ritner 2009c: 25–31), the Memphite priests (Ritner 2009c: 21–25), and most importantly that of Pasenhor (Ritner 2009c: 17–20). Their importance is argued to be an indication of the need for the previously nomadic Libyan elite to record and display their lineages, something common to many tribal societies (Leahy 1985: 55; Jansen-Winkeln 2005: 139; Ritner 2009a: 335; Broekman 2010: 86).

Other changes show the Libyans not only maintained elements of their ethnic identity, but also did not adopt Egyptian cultural norms, with dramatic changes in burials from large necropolises to "family" burials, argued to be a product of the importance of "family" to the Libyans (Leahy 1985: 61–62; Jansen-Winkeln 1994: 93), in the use of the hieratic script on monuments (Leahy 1985: 60), and in the increased importance of women (Jansen-Winkeln 1994: 92–93). These changes are apparent from early in the 21st Dynasty, even before the first Libyan king Osorkon "the elder", in the family names of HPA Herihor, and in changes in the burial practices of the kings (Leahy 1985: 61; Jansen-Winkeln 1994: 92–93; 1999: 19; Broekman 2010: 89).

This retention of a non-dominant identity often happens when a smaller, possibly newer, ethnic group clusters, or is clustered, together within a different society forming an "ethnic enclave", a possibility that will be explored in the rest of this paper.

Ethnic Enclaves—a modern urban social pattern

Ethnic enclaves are, in reality, not so much a theoretical concept as a term used by social scientists to explain a pattern noticeable in modern urban areas (Abrahamson 2006: 1–4; Laguerre 2010: 255), even though it was first used as a concept in the 1920's (Abrahamson 2006: 1) and such enclaves have been identified in urban settlements as far back as the pre-medieval period (Laguerre 2010: 255). Ethnic enclaves and its associated theories attempt to explore why newly arrived migrants often seek out areas where existing migrants from the same group have settled, what benefits this provides to both the newly arrived migrants and those already in place, and how this grouping informs how the migrants interact with both the dominant local culture and their own (Laguerre 2010: 255–256).

Ethnic enclaves were first identified in the 1920's and 1930's through the discovery and confirmation of the existence of such enclaves within American cities following the major migrations of the late 19th and early 20th centuries (Park 1925: 40). Subsequently there has been research to identify distinctions between ghettos and enclaves (choice being an important part of the latter—see Gans 2008: 353–357). The concept has been further refined and updated for the 21st century with the "enclave" concept now understood to apply not only to groups who share an ethnic identity but to those who have a group identity where gathering together provides additional benefits, protection, and support (Abrahamson 2006: 1–4; Laguerre 2010: 255–256). Although the concept of enclaves originated in modern urban studies (particularly the emphasis on their distinction from ghettos) and there are case studies from across history including those closer in time to ancient Egypt, such as medieval Italian and Middle Eastern cities (Raymond 1985: 131), in order to suggest their presence in ancient Egypt it is important to understand the underlying original concept. This is particularly the case as the enclaves within Egypt may have been formed in similar circumstances to those in the modern era, through gradual but persistent migration into a region with a dominant local culture. It has also been noted that there is probably a common set of drivers that create the social clustering in urban areas across history (York et al. 2010: 2401–2406) and thus it is possible to compare modern circumstances and urban centres with ancient ones (York et al. 2010: 2408–2409).

Ethnic enclaves are where each distinct group, along with its stores and institutions, occupies a geographic area that becomes intimately associated with that group, e.g. "little Italy" or Chinatowns in American cities (Abrahamson 2006: 1). Through this linkage, areas acquire symbolic qualities that include their place names and social histories. Enclaves are created when a group moves into a new location where there is a dominant culture that is different from their own (Massey 1990: 69; Abrahamson 2006: 1–4; Duncan and Waldorf 2009: 11; Laguerre 2010: 255–256; *The Economist* UK Special Report 2013: 11). Typically there is only a specific area where they are able to settle, often in poorer areas within an urban settlement (irrespective of the location of that area within the city), and the newly arrived group often keeps together for protection and mutual support, or because they are unable to go anywhere else.[8] As later migrants from the same group move into the same location, however, they then actively choose to settle in the same areas as those original migrants, starting to form "clusters" of members of that particular group (Wilson – Portes 1980: 302–303; Abrahamson 2006: 4–11). This is because new "migrants" often settle in areas where there are others from their own ethnic and cultural background, forming an enclave which provides them with support networks and access to institutions associated with their group (Massey 1990: 68–70; Abrahamson 2006: 4–5).

The actual numbers of a specific group present in an area do not need to be very significant for it to be identified as an ethnic enclave, with some modern enclaves identified as such despite the local population containing less than 25% of the group with whom the enclave is identified (Logan – Alba – Zhang 2002: 303–305; Abrahamson 2006: 4). Indeed, some modern enclaves can have as low as 3% of the local population identified as belonging to the relevant enclave group (Logan – Alba – Zhang 2002: 308–311). Thus, it is not simply the presence of members of the distinct group who bring about the identification of an enclave, it is also the presence of institutions designed to cater solely for that group that also supports that identification, such as specific places of worship, food shops and restaurants, and the presence of non-dominant languages on signs (Logan – Alba – Zhang 2002: 307; Abrahamson 2006: 196–198; Laguerre 2010: 255–256). They are also perceived as marked "territories" where members of that group live, both by their residents and by those who live outside the enclave, irrespective of an individual's membership of the relevant ethnic group (Abrahamson 2006: 6–9). As the group becomes more established the ethnic enclave can even act as a destination for incoming migrants as they are aware that on their arrival they will find support and protection from members of their own group and will gain the benefit of localised institutions (Wilson – Porte 1980: 314–315; Wilson – Allen Martin 1982: 155–157; Massey 1990: 68–70).

---

[8] The location of these areas is somewhat culturally or historically specific, with some groups specifically settled by the state in more privileged areas, whilst those with no connection to the existing elite (as with modern migrants and arguably the Libyans) move into the poorer areas, wherever those areas are, sometimes on the outskirts but often (especially in the modern era) in deprived areas in the centre of settlements.

Being able to settle in an ethnic enclave has been demonstrated to allow a new group to preserve their non-dominant cultural identity (ethnic or otherwise) despite being surrounded by that dominant culture and needing to interact with it on a daily basis (Logan – Alba – Zhang 2002: 299–301; Donzer – Yaman 2013: 315–319, 323). From the earliest identification of ethnic enclaves it has been identified that their members have their most meaningful relationships with those inhabit their enclaves (Park 1925: 40; Wilson – Portes 1980: 296; Abrahamson 2006: 1). Indeed, ethnic enclaves have been seen in some instances as actively inhibiting the residents' integration into the dominant society in which they live (Chiswick – Miller 1996: 19–35; Donzer – Yaman 2013: 312–313), by offering fewer incentives and opportunities for integration, especially a lack of inter-ethnic contact, leading to a general lack of self-assessed identification with the host country (Donzer – Yaman 2013: 322–323).

If the captive Libyans were settled together in specific locations by the Egyptian state then these could have formed the nuclei of ethnic enclaves within Egypt, in the same way that such enclaves have been formed in the modern era. By settling the Libyans together as groups the Egyptians would have enabled them to be able to maintain some of their cohesion as a group, helping them to establish themselves within Egypt as a settlement of Libyans with a distinct, non-Egyptian identity. Even if the Egyptians did attempt to indoctrinate the captives in Egyptian culture this may have simply created a "counter-identity" that helped bind the Libyans even more tightly to their group identity. Such enclaves may also have developed, or even have been perpetuated, as a result of the low-level migration into the western Delta and Nile Valley via the oases that occurred during the 20th Dynasty, as recorded in the Deir el-Medina journal (Vernus 2003: 6; KRI VI 609:5–10, 687:10, 688:15), and the Libyan Period (Yoyotte 1961: 43–44; Leahy 1985: 55). As further Libyan groups entered the Nile Valley they would have aimed for areas where they might feel they would be safe and able to find assistance in dealing with the Egyptian administration—such as the locations where existing Libyans were already settled. With increasing numbers settled together there would have been ever less requirement to adopt full Egyptian customs. In order to secure power, however, there would have been a requirement to adopt Egyptian traditions as had been required in the past (Kemp 1997: 128; Panagiotopoulos 2006: 403–404).

When an individual from a minority group needs to participate in the social system created by the dominant group they are often required to adopt or assimilate the culture of that group. It has been noted within studies of ethnic enclaves, however, that often members who are engaging with the dominant culture retain very specific markers of their alternative ethnic identity as a way of demonstrating to members of their own group their ethnic "authenticity" in a practice called "strategic assimilation" (Meghi 2017: 1008–1009). Thus, Meghi argues that in modern UK society black individuals often feel the need to adopt aspects of white culture in order to be accepted as members of a social class, but still mark their black identity in certain ways in order to maintain their "authenticity" with the black community and prevent accusations of betraying their own community (Meghi 2017: 1015–1021). Thus, individuals in a minority group living in a region with a majority culture move "back and forth the class divides within different social spheres populated by audiences and actors of varying race and class backgrounds" (Rollock et al. 2011: 1088). The Libyans, therefore, may well have practised a form of "strategic assimilation" to secure power in Egypt. This in indicated through their adherence to Egyptian norms, for example representing themselves on monuments with Egyptian physiognomy, using Egyptian language, and offering to Egyptian gods, whilst simultaneously employing specific markers of a "Libyan" identity (Libyan names, titles, and occasionally dress) to emphasise their authenticity as a Libyan individual to members of that group, emphasising that they had not given up their Libyan identity.

Summary

Thus, a plausible reconstruction might see that following an initial forced relocation of Libyan captives into locations across Egypt by the Egyptian state in the late New Kingdom, subsequent low-level migration may have helped turn these early Libyan settlements into enclaves where Libyans were not only able to retain their non-Egyptian identity but also some of their social structure—explaining why non-Egyptian titles continued to retain their significance for the Libyan elite even after they had risen to power within the Egyptian social hierarchy. With the Libyans' increasing political power and wealth there would have been ever less incentive to assimilate into Egyptian culture in order to achieve high office (Leahy 1985: 56). Its allied concept of "strategic assimilation" provides further explanation for why the Libyans chose not only to have themselves represented as Egyptians and participate in Egyptian society as a method for securing power and prestige, but also their retention and public display of markers of a non-Egyptian identity. The next step would be to try to tie this explanation to the available existing evidence through identifying where possible Libyan ethnic enclaves might be located. This, however, is significantly complicated by the complete absence of any distinctive material culture that might be attributed to them. The lack of any of the records or institutions that modern urban studies rely on for identifying such enclaves in modern cities, such as census records, food shops, or religious institutions, would make this process of locating potential Libyan enclaves highly challenging, as does our total lack of knowledge about what the Libyans were like prior to their arrival into Egypt. Nonetheless, the presence of identified ethnic enclaves in societies across history where greater evidence is available (such as specific quarters of medieval cities for foreign groups) does suggest that the concept of ethnic enclaves might provide an explanation for how a group were able to retain their non-Egyptian identity long after their arrival into Egypt, thus it is reasonable to conclude that such Libyan enclaves did exist and it is perhaps the Delta where we should look to identify them. This is especially so given the evidence for the existence of other such enclaves in Egyptian history, as with the presence of Canaanites in the eastern Delta at Tell el-Dabʿa (Bietak 2018: 78–81) or the "Carian Quarter" in Memphis (Adiego Lajara 2007: 2). There is a long-standing awareness that there appear to have been greater concentrations of the Libyans in the Delta, especially in the western Delta and at points where the desert roads reached the Nile Valley, such as Herakleopolis (Pérez-Die 2009: 304; Payraudeau 2009: 401–403), (as might be expected given its proximity to the Western Desert origins of the Libyans), although there are no definitive known "settlements" of Libyans or Libyan "quarters" of Egyptian settlements. Moreover, the preponderance of Libyan rulers were marked by Piye as being located in the Delta.

Probably the only way to identify potential enclaves within Egypt using the current evidence base is to compile all the archaeological and iconographic evidence for Libyans from key locations, such as Bubastis, Tanis, Herakleopolis and others, to create a chart of the numbers of Libyan individuals, or families, present at the sites. This, therefore, might give us a sense of the proportion of known Libyans at these sites and suggest potential locations for Libyan enclaves. Although these records are compromised by the fact that they appear once the Libyans have joined the elite and are thus not necessarily located where the original enclaves might have been, and might instead be expected to be located in centres of political power, they are currently probably our only option for attempting to locate any such ethnic enclaves. Ultimately, it may be impossible to definitively demonstrate the location of such an enclave as is possible with the presence of Canaanites in the eastern Delta at Tell el-Dab^ca, but even if this is case, the concept of ethnic enclaves provides us with a potential method of understanding how ethnicity can be retained within a region dominated by another culture that has been extensively demonstrated elsewhere and thus cannot be dismissed even without this definitive proof.

References

Abrahamson, M., 2006. *Urban Enclaves. Identity and Place in the World*. Contemporary Social Issues. New York, NY: Worth Publishers.

Adams, M. – M. Cohen, 2013. The "Sea Peoples" in Primary Sources. In A. Killebrew – G. Lehmann, eds., *The Philistines and other "Sea Peoples" in Text and Archaeology*. Society of Biblical Literature – Archaeology and Biblical Studies 15. Atlanta, GA: Society of Biblical Literature, 645–664.

Adiego Lajara, I.-J., 2007. *The Carian Language*. HdO I/86. Leiden – Boston: Brill.

Assmann, J., 2011. *Cultural Memory and Early Civilisation: Writing, Remembrance and Political Imagination*. Cambridge – New York: Cambridge University Press.

Bietak, M., 2018. The Many Ethnicities of Avaris: Evidence from the northern borderland of Egypt. In J. Budka – J. Auenmüller, eds., *From Microcosm to Macrocosm: Individual Households and Cities in Ancient Egypt and Nubia*. Leiden: Sidestone Press, 73–92.

Booth, C., 2005. *The Role of Foreigners in Ancient Egypt: A study of non-stereotypical artistic representations*. BAR International Series 1426. Oxford: BAR Publishing.

Broekman, G., 2010. Libyan Rule Over Egypt: The Influence of the Tribal Background of the Ruling Class on Political Structures and Developments during the Libyan Period in Egypt. *SAK* 39, 85–99.

Caminos, R., 1954. *Late Egyptian Miscellanies*. London: Oxford University Press.

Cavillier, G., 2010. "Shardana project" – Perspectives and Researches on the Sherden in Egypt and Mediterranean. *Syria* 87, 339–345.

Chiswick, B. – Miller, P., 1996. Ethnic Networks and Language Proficiency among Immigrants. *J. Popul. Econ.* 9, 19–35.

Davies, N., 1943a. *The Tomb of Rekh-mi-Rē at Thebes. Volume 1.* Publications of the Metropolitan Museum of Art Egyptian Expedition 11. New York, NY: Metropolitan Museum of Art.

Davies, N., 1943b. *The Tomb of Rekh-mi-Rē at Thebes. Volume 2.* Publications of the Metropolitan Museum of Art Egyptian Expedition 11. New York, NY: Metropolitan Museum of Art.

Dever, W., 2007. Ethnicity and the Archaeological Record: The Case of Early Israel. In D. Edwards – C. McCollough, eds., *The Archaeology of Difference: Gender, Ethnicity, Class, and the 'other' in Antiquity. Studies in Honor of Eric M. Meyers.* AASOR 60/61. Boston, MA: American Schools of Oriental Research, 49–67.

Donzer, A. – F. Yaman, 2013. Do Ethnic Enclaves Impede Immigrants' Integration? Evidence from a Quasi-experimental Social-interaction Approach. *Review of International Economics* 21.2, 311–325.

Drews, R., 1993. *The End of the Bronze Age: Changes in Warfare and the catastrophe ca. 1200 B.C.* Princeton, NJ: Princeton University Press.

The Economist, 9th November 2013 (Print Edition). Special Report: 'Britain: Looking for a future', 1–22.

Edgerton, W. – J. Wilson, 1936. *Historical Records of Ramesses III: The Texts in Medinet Habu Volumes 1 and 2 translated with explanatory notes.* SAOC 12. Chicago: University of Chicago Press.

Eyre, C., 1987. Work and the organisation of work in the New Kingdom. In M. Powell, ed., *Labor in the Ancient Near East.* American Oriental Series 68. New Haven, CT: American Oriental Society, 167–221.

Gans, H., 2008. Symposium on the *Ghetto*. Involuntary Segregation and the *Ghetto*: Disconnecting Process and Place. *City and Community* 7.4, 353–357.

Gardiner, A., 1941. Ramesside Texts Relating to the Taxation and Transportation of Corn. *JEA* 27, 19–73.

Haring, B., 2009. Economy. In E. Frood – W. Wendrich, eds., *UCLA Encyclopedia of Egyptology*, Los Angeles.
http://digital2.library.ucla.edu/viewItem.do?ark=21198/zz001nf64c (accessed on November 22, 2018).

Hüneberg, M., 2003. Essay: Soziologische Überlegungen zum Partikularisierungsprozeß Ägyptens nach dem Ende des Neuen Reiches und während der Dritten Zwischenzeit. In R. Gundlach – U. Rößler-Köhler, eds., *Das Königtum der Ramessidenzeit. Voraussetzungen – Verwirklichung – Vermächtnis. Akten des 3. Symposions zur ägyptischen Königsideologie in Bonn 7.–9. 6. 2001.* ÄAT 36/3. Wiesbaden: Harrassowitz, 57–75.

Jansen-Winkeln, K., 1994. Der Beginn der Libyer Herrschaft in Ägypten. *BN* 71, 78–97.

Jansen-Winkeln, K., 1999. Gab es in der altägyptischen Geschichte eine feudalistische Epoche? *WdO* 30, 7–20.

Jansen-Winkeln, K., 2005. Die Entwicklung der genealogischen Informationen nach dem Neuen Reich. In M. Fitzenreiter, ed., *Genealogie-Realität und Fiktion von Identität.* Internet-Beiträge zur Ägyptologie und Sudanarchäologie 5. London: Golden House Publications, 137–146.

Jones, S., 1997. *The Archaeology of Ethnicity. Constructing Identities in the Past and Present.* London: Routledge.

Kemp, B., 1997. Why Empires Rise. *CAJ* 7.1, 125–131.

Kitchen, K., 1969–1990. *Ramesside Inscriptions: Historical and Bibliographical,* Volumes 2–6. Oxford: Wiley-Blackwell.

Kitchen, K., 2012. Ramesses III and the Ramesside Period. In E. Cline – D.O'Connor, eds., *Ramesses III: The Life and Times of Egypt's Last Hero.* Ann Arbor: University of Michigan Press, 1–26.

Laguerre, M., 2010. Ethnic Enclaves. In R. Hutchinson, ed., *Encyclopedia of Urban Studies.* Thousand Oaks, CA: SAGE Publications, 255–257.

Lange, E., 2008. Legitimation und Herrschaft in der Libyerzeit. *ZÄS* 135, 131–141.

Leahy, A., 1985. The Libyan Period in Egypt: An Essay in Interpretation. *LibStud* 16, 51–65.

Leahy, A., 1992. "May the King live". The Libyan rulers in the onomastic record. In A. Lloyd, ed., *Studies in Pharaonic Religion and Society in Honour of J. Gwyn Griffiths.* London: Egypt Exploration Society, 146–163.

Liszka, K., 2011. "We have come from the well of Ibhet". Ethnogenesis of the Medjay. *JEH* 4, 149–171.

Logan, J. – R. Alba – W. Zhang, 2002. Immigrant Enclaves and Ethnic Communities in New York and Los Angeles. *Am. Sociol. Rev.* 67.2, 299–322.

Manassa, C., 2003. *The Great Karnak Inscription of Merneptah: Grand Strategy in the 13th Century BC.* YES 5. New Haven, CT: Yale University Press.

Massey, D., 1990. The Social and Economic Origins of Immigration. *AAPSS* 510, 60–72.

McDowell, A.G., 1999. *Village Life in Ancient Egypt: Laundry lists and love songs.* Oxford: Oxford University Press.

McGuire, R., 1982. The Study of Ethnicity in Historical Archaeology. *J. Anthropol. Archaeol.* 1, 159–178.

Meghi, A., 2017. Positionings of the black middle-classes: understanding identity construction beyond strategic assimilation. *Ethn. Racial Stud.* 40.6, 1007–1025.

Moje, J., 2014. *Herrschaftsräume und Herrschaftswissen ägyptischer Lokalregenten: Soziokulturelle Interaktionen zur Machtkonsolidierung vom 8. bis zum 4. Jahrhundert v.Chr.* Topoi 21. Berlin: De Gruyter.

Moreno García, J.-C., 2013. Limits of Pharaonic administration: patronage, informal authorities, 'invisible elites' and mobile populations. In M. Bárta – H. Küllmer, eds., *Diachronic trends in ancient Egyptian history: studies dedicated to the memory of Eva Pardey.* Prague: Charles University in Prague, 88–101.

Mushett Cole, E., 2015. Foreign Influence in the Late New Kingdom and Third Intermediate Period. In M. Pinarello – J. Yoo – J. Lundock – C. Walsh, eds., *Current Research in Egyptology 2014.* Oxford: Oxbow Books, 113–122.

O'Connor, D., 1983. New Kingdom and the Third Intermediate Period. In B. Trigger – B. Kemp – D.O'Connor – A. Lloyd, eds., *Ancient Egypt: A Social History.* Cambridge: Cambridge University Press, 183–278.

O'Connor, D., 1990. The Nature of Tjemhu (Libyan) Society in the Later New Kingdom. In A. Leahy, ed., *Libya and Egypt.* London: Centre of Near and Middle Eastern Studies, SOAS and the Society for Libyan Studies, 29–112.

Panagiotopoulos, D., 2006. Foreigners in Egypt in the Time of Hatshepsut and Thutmose III. In E. Cline – D.O'Connor, eds., *Thutmose III: A New Biography*. Ann Arbor: University of Michigan Press, 370–412.

Park, R., 1925. The City: Suggestions for the Investigation of Human Behavior in the Urban Environment. In R. Park – E. Burgess – R. McKenzie, eds., *The City*. Chicago: The University of Chicago Press, 1–46.

Payraudeau, F., 2009. Un linteau de Shéshonq III à Bubastis et les origines de la XXIIe Dynastie. *BIFAO* 109, 397–406.

Payraudeau, F., 2014. *Administration, société et pouvoir à Thèbes sous le XXIIe dynastie bubastite*. Volume 1. BdÉ 160. Paris: Institut français d'archéologie orientale.

Peden, A., 1994. *Egyptian Historical Inscriptions of the Twentieth Dynasty*. Documenta Mundi 3. Jonsered: Paul Åstroms förlag.

Pérez Die, M.-C., 2009. The Third Intermediate Period cemetery at Herakleopolis Magna. In G. Broekman – R. Demarée – O. Kaper, eds., *The Libyan Period in Egypt: Historical and Cultural Studies into the 21st–24th Dynasties. Proceedings of a conference at Leiden University*. EU 23. Leuven: Nederlands Instituut voor her Nabije Oosten – Peeters, 303–326.

Raymond, A., 1985. *Grandes villes arabes à l'époque ottomane*. Paris: Sinbad.

Ritner, R., 2009a. Fragmentation and Re-Integration in the Third Intermediate Period. In G. Broekman – R. Demarée – O. Kaper, eds., *The Libyan Period in Egypt: Historical and Cultural Studies into the 21st–24th Dynasties. Proceedings of a conference at Leiden University*. EU 23. Leuven: Nederlands Instituut voor her Nabije Oosten – Peeters, 327–340.

Ritner, R., 2009b. Egypt and the Vanishing Libyan: Institutional Responses to a Nomadic People. In J. Szuchman, ed., *Nomads, Tribes, and the State in the Ancient Near East: Cross-disciplinary Perspectives*. OIS 5. Chicago: The University of Chicago Press, 43–56.

Ritner, R., 2009c. *The Libyan Anarchy: Inscriptions from Egypt's Third Intermediate Period*. WAW 21. Atlanta, GA: Society of Biblical Literature.

Rollock, N. – D. Gilborn – C. Vincent – S. Ball, 2011. The Public Identities of the Black Middle Classes: Managing Race in Public Spaces. *Sociology* 45.6, 1078–1093.

Shaw, I., 2000. *Oxford History of Ancient Egypt*. Oxford: Oxford University Press.

Snape, S., 2012. The Legacy of Ramesses III and the Libyan Ascendancy. In E. Cline – D.O'Connor, eds., *Ramesses III: The Life and Times of Egypt's Last Hero*. Ann Arbor: University of Michigan Press, 404–441.

The Epigraphic Survey, 1932. *Later Historical Records of Ramesses III. Medinet Habu Volume 2*. OIP 9. Chicago: The University of Chicago Press.

Vernus, P., 2003. *Affairs and Scandals in Ancient Egypt*, translated by D. Lorton. Ithaca, NY: Cornell University Press.

Wente, E., 1990. *Letters from Ancient Egypt*. WAW 1. Atlanta, GA: Scholars Press.

Wilson, K. – A. Portes, 1980. Immigrant Enclaves: An Analysis of the Labor Market Experiences of Cubans in Miami. *Am. J. Sociol.* 86.2, 295–319.

Wilson, K. – W. Allen Martin, 1982. Ethnic Enclaves: A comparison of the Cuban and Black Economies. *Am. J. Sociol.* 88.1, 135–160.

York, A. – M. Smith – B. Stanley – B. Stark – J. Novic – S. Harlan – G. Cowgill – G. Boone, 2010. Ethnic and Class clustering through the ages: A transdisciplinary approach to urban neighbourhood social patterns. *Urban Studies* 48.11, 2399–2415.

Yoyotte, J., 1961. *Les principautés du Delta au temps de l'anarchie libyenne: études d'histoire politique*. Recherches d'archéologie, de philologie et d'histoire 34. Le Caire: Institut français d'archéologie orientale.

ARE YOU AN EGYPTIAN? ARE YOU A STRANGER? EGYPTIANS IN THE LEVANT IN THE BRONZE AGE.

Jana Mynářová*

"But tell me this, and tell me the truth: Who are you, and where do you come from?".[1]

Contrary to ancient evidence, modern concepts of "foreigners" or "strangers", as well as "ethnicity", "nationality", or "citizenship" are nowadays known and recognized by individual states as well as international organizations, anchored in modern international law and its procedures. For the purpose of uniformity of interpretations, multinational organizations such as UNESCO provide extensive sets of information and definitions of these terms[2]—terms, that are generally understood by a majority of the population, without being extensively introduced and examined on a daily basis. For example, the concept of "nationality"—very closely associated with the topic of the present paper—is bound to the concept of a national state with its sovereignty and mechanisms, a concept known and experienced in modern "Western" societies since the 19th century, but unknown in the ancient states of the Bronze Age Near East.

In her contribution on foreigners in the contact zone stretching along the Middle Euphrates, Regine Pruzsinszky (Pruzsinszky 2019, in this volume)—and following the methodology of van Driel (2005)—lists the indicators for constructing an ethnic group as *language, tradition, religion, way of life, structure of society*, and *material culture*. She also mentions the limitations of the respective categories, and importantly, emphasizes the existence of transitional forms. In this respect the key question is, how can we identify these indicators in sources from the Bronze Age Near East? And how can we evaluate those in order to achieve a more representative picture on the various ethnic groups living in contact with one another? It is the aim of this paper to address these questions, as well as to touch upon the problems of Egyptians as foreigners in "other"—or in other words "non-Egyptian"—societies.

Contacts and interactions between the inhabitants of the Nile Valley with neighboring regions of the ancient Near East have been treated extensively both

---

* This study is a result of a research funded by the Czech Science Foundation as project GA ČR P401/12/G168 "History and Interpretation of the Bible".

[1] Homer, *The Odyssey*, Bk. I, 183–184; transl. by Lombardo 2000: 6.

[2] See the UNESCO's *Glossary of Migration Related Terms*, http://www.unesco.org/new/en/social-and-human-sciences/themes/international-migration/glossary/ (last accessed on 6 September 2018).

in the past as well as in the most recent literature,[3] from a chronological perspective covering the long range starting with the earliest periods, when the first centers of power started to develop in the Nile Valley, to the moment when Egypt became an integral part of the vast empires of the Hellenistic and Roman worlds. Ever since the Neolithic period, the key area of interaction between the land on the Nile and the regions situated further to the north-east was represented by the eastern Nile Delta and the Sinai Peninsula.[4] By crossing both, the Egyptians first gained access to regions located in close vicinity in the southern, as well as more distant northern Levant, and later to the even more remote regions of Anatolia and Mesopotamia. For the Prehistoric period, the information on Egyptians living outside the Nile Valley is very limited. The evidence presently available is not sufficient to reconstruct a complete picture of the mechanisms of these contacts, especially with regards to the daily life of a single individual. The understanding and interpretation of the policy of Egyptian rulers towards the Levantine polities and their peoples is hence largely dependent upon a study of the nature of Egyptian—and sometimes even Egyptianizing—objects discovered at Near Eastern sites. But the same holds true for the Levantine perspective on Egypt as well. The study of imports—both Egyptian imports in the Levant and Levantine imports in Egypt—is a prevalent method for studying cultural contacts between the two regions especially for the Chalcolithic and Early Bronze Age, when the number of imported objects, as well as locally made imitations increases. Such a steep increase is being interpreted as a sign of intensification of trade relations.[5] But the individual imports are not the only topic in the discussion. Considerable attention is also given to the dissemination of ideas, reflected—for example—in domestic architecture.

A significant role in the formalization of the contacts played the formation of the Egyptian state, and as P. de Miroschedji clearly showed,[6] in the latter part of the 4th millennium BC, the Egyptian state and its administration was firmly set in the southern Levant, where it formed a type of state-organized settlement structure whose main goal was to make economic use of the local environment and wealth, making it easier to access and exploit (including the mining activities in the region of Wadi Feinan). It is the material culture that provides evidence on the

---

3 See especially Helck 1962 (with references to earlier literature); Lorton 1974; Redford 1986; Liverani 1990; Redford 1992; Davies – Schofield, eds. 1995; Teissier 1996; Schneider 1998; Cohen – Westbrook, eds. 2000; Higginbotham 2000; Liverani 2001; van den Brink – Levy, eds. 2002; van den Brink – Braun 2003; Vittmann 2003; Knoppers – Girsch, eds. 2004; Sparks 2004; Morris 2005; Ben-Tor 2007; Sowada 2009; Breyer 2010; Schneider 2010; Bar – Kahn – Shirley, eds. 2011; Mumford 2014; Ahrens 2015; Creasman – Wilkinson, eds. 2017; Morris 2018.

4 Hassan 1998; Braun – van den Brink 2008; Braun 2014; Tassie 2014; Mączyńska 2018.

5 For an overview of Egyptian and Egyptianizing objects in the Chalcolithic and EBA I–III, see Sparks 2007 (stone vessels); Sowada 2009. For Egyptian-Transjordanian contacts see Fischer 2002; and recently Sala 2014.

6 Miroschedji 2002; for an over see also Gophna 2000; Braun 2002; Braun 2003; and Miroschedji 2014. For the individual sites see especially Gophna – Gazit 1985 (ʿEn Besor); Brandl 1989 (Tel Erani); Gophna 1995 (ʿEn Besor); Beit-Arieh – Gophna 1999 (Tel Maʾaḥaz); Miroschedji – Sadeq – Faltings – Boulez – Naggiar-Moliner – Sykes – Tengberg 2001 (for Tell es-Sakan); Czarnowicz – Pasternak – Ochał-Czarnowicz – Skłucki 2014 (Tel Erani).

Fig. 1.
Imitations of Syro-Palestinian vessels with two handles and flat bottoms found together with common Egyptian pottery in the burial chamber of Qar Junior, Abusir South, 5th Dynasty (©Archive of the Czech Institute of Egyptology).

rise and the very existence of a system of Egyptian *emporia* that formed a part of the state-controlled economy in the southern Levant, as evidenced by the finds of clay seals or fragments of pottery vessels bearing royal *serekhs*.[7] But with the arrival of the Early Bronze Age II the system underwent a significant change leading to a completely different organization with autochthonous political centers replacing the original system organized by the Egyptian administration. In this stage, the local elites residing in fortified cities formed new power entities controlling the resources and their distribution. The changes in the pattern of contacts is once again visible in the material culture, especially when the *repertoire* of pottery vessels imported from the Levant to Egypt is taken into consideration. Not only does one observe a sudden drop in imported pottery to Egypt, but the southern Levantine production is largely replaced by that of the Lebanese coast (Porat 1989: 70–75); it is the time when Byblos becomes Egypt's main trading partner, as suggest the presence of Egyptian objects discovered at the site.[8] The contacts between Egypt and the southern Levant did not disappear but changed their very character in the EBA II–III.[9] In the new system, the role of the Egyptian *emporia* was taken over by royal emissaries acting as mediators between the Egyptian administration and the Levantine rulers (Miroschedji 2002: 46–47). It is at this time, when a significant change in the composition of sources is clearly visible: the until then dominant evidence of material culture becomes more regularly supple-

[7] For the glyptics see Schulman 1976; 1980; 1983; 1992; Kaplony 2002; Hill 2016.
[8] Diego Espinel 2002; Sparks 2003: 47–48; Sowada 2009: 128–141 with a review by Diego Espinel 2012; Collona 2018.
[9] For the overview and evaluation of *Aegyptiaca* east of the Jordan see recently Sala 2014.

mented by Egyptian iconographic and written data of a very formalized character. This combination of material, iconographic, and written sources—though their relative ratio might differ—has been preserved practically until the mid-second millennium BC. It is noteworthy that even from the stages when more formalized relations of the Egyptian administration towards the Levantine city states prevailed, no records of the legal aspects of these relations were preserved (or ever existed). Our knowledge of the actual procedures and individual activities are therefore very limited. Such absence of one type of evidence can be explained on an ideological level with the role of the Egyptian king—the earthly incarnation of Horus—as a ruler and a universal guarantor of the security and the very existence of the Egyptian state. The earliest written and iconographic sources thus only reflect this role, serving as powerful tools of royal propaganda, intended exclusively for the domestic audience. On the other hand, the only role of the opposite side in these contacts, i.e. the rulers and peoples of the Levant, is to emphasize and confirm the role of the Egyptian king. The Egyptian royal ideology thus strongly affects our perception of the functioning of the state and the role of its sovereign until the mid-second millennium BC, when other types of records start to appear. It is the figure of the king who represents the focal point of these texts. The image of the king, his government and the relationship with the neighboring regions thus seem—and practically is—quite flat on the ideological level, reflecting the character and purpose of the preserved sources. These types of written sources can by no means provide reliable evidence on the reality of everyday life of an anonymous Egyptian individual living in another society. And the same image is provided by the Near Eastern written sources. There are practically no ancient Near Eastern records mentioning the men of Egypt living outside the Nile Valley.

Until the mid-second millennium BC our perspective on the presence or absence of the Egyptians in the Levant is largely formed by the lack or manifestation, decrease or increase of objects of Egyptian origin or produced locally using Egyptian forms or technology, set against the evidence of Egyptian written sources, attesting to the existence of military and trading expeditions to the Levant. Presently, the synchronization of the individual events with material sources is under discussion having the potential to fundamentally change our understanding of the Egyptian-Levantine interactions during the Middle Bronze Age. A proposed High Chronology, based on a series of radiocarbon dates from the southern Levant, creates a new framework for the re-evaluation of these relations.[10] Regardless of the absolute dates, a glimpse of both the presence and the character of Egyptian(s) living in the Levant is provided by the literary evidence of The Story of Sinuhe. The Egyptian text provides both a picture of a successful man, a chief of a tribe, and a perspective on his actual life:

[10] "Changing the chronology of the Middle Bronze Age would have significant impact on current views on history and development of Near Eastern societies during the first half of the second millennium BC." Höflmayer – Cohen 2017: 1. For a summary of the current discussion see Höflmayer 2017.

> He set me at the head of his children; he let me marry his daughter; [he let me choose for myself from his] land, of his belongings, to the borders of another land. [It was indeed a beautiful land,] [I]aa was its name and there was no other (land) like this one on earth. There were figs and grapes, wine was more plentiful than water, [with plenty of honey and moringa]-trees, there was every (kind of) fruit on its trees; there was barley and wheat, and infinity of cattle. … Provisions were made for me daily in fare and wine, cooked meat, roast fowl, as well as desert game. It was hunted for me and fished for me, in addition to the catch of my dogs. Sweets were made for me and a lot of milk was in every cup. … The messenger (*wpw.tj*), who travelled north or south (lit. sailed downstream or upstream) from the residence stayed with me. … I [gave water to the thirsty,] I showed the way to the one, who went astray, I rescued the one, who was robbed. When the Asiatics conspired to attack the rulers of foreign lands, I opposed their movement. For this ruler of Retjenu, he let me lead many of his missions, I was the commander of his troops. Every foreign land in which I marched I attacked and destroyed (its) plants and wells, I plundered its cattle, I carried off its serfs, I seized its food, and I killed its people by my strong arm (and) by <my bow>, by my movements and by my (skillful) plans. (P Berlin 3022, ll. 77–106).[11]

The picture provided by the Egyptian text shows a man with a successful career, giving details of his everyday life. But in fact, the story narrated in this passage is two-sided. On the one hand, there is a righteous and mighty hero, killing his opponents and ensuring justice, but he is also the one who is elevated to his position, who is inferior to the one who elevated him. After defeating his opponent in a fight, and after he "passed many years" with his children becoming strong men, each at the head his own tribe, it is still the Egyptian god Montu who is praised by Sinuhe after his victorious fight. His reference to envoys travelling through the Levant is once again echoed in the Satire of the Trades (or The Teaching of Dua Khety).[12] During this period there are two types of Egyptians in the Levant—those living there permanently (or semi-permanently), like Sinuhe—and those, passing by carrying communication (and business) from and to the residence or participating in military or trading expeditions. Combining the information provided by the Story of Sinuhe with data retrieved from other textual sources[13] and the material culture might actually provide us with a more complex picture of an Egyptian living in the Levant. Leaving the written sources aside, the resulting image of the life of the Egyptians in the Levant would not be much different from that provided by the Old Kingdom sources. But the importance of the written sources for the understanding of the role of the Egyptians in the Levant

---

[11] All translations in the contribution are of the present author unless stated otherwise. For the most recent translation and analysis of the text see Koch 1990; Parkinson 1997: 21–53; Parkinson 2002: 149–168; Simpson, ed. 2003: 54–66; Quirke 2004: 58–70; Feder – Hays – Morenz, eds. 2014.

[12] See among others Parkinson 1997: 273–283; Simpson, ed. 2003: 431–437; Quirke 2004: 121–126.

[13] For Annals of Amenemhet II see Altenmüller – Moussa 1991; Lupo 2004; Altenmüller 2015.

is especially valid when we take into consideration the evidence provided by the Execration Texts of the 12th and 13th Dynasties.[14] Although the composition of the sources is somewhat different, the fact that all these written sources provide an Egyptian view of this region is the same as in the Old Kingdom.

It is only during the Second Intermediate Period (ca. 1700–1550 BC), when the situation changed, especially with regards to the typology of sources and patterns of communication between Egypt and the Near East. Similar to other periods of Egyptian history, the earliest witness of this change is related to trade and the royal sphere. It is once again the Eastern Nile Delta, representing the bridge between Egypt and the other parts of the Eastern Mediterranean, that yielded so far the earliest evidence of cuneiform writing in Egypt.[15] Therefore, it is only in the second part of the second millennium BC, when the written evidence—both Egyptian and non-Egyptian—becomes slightly more balanced and even sufficient to provide a more detailed account on the Egyptians in the Levant.

At the beginning of the New Kingdom, there was a new consolidation of the power of the Egyptian kings. Royal edicts show that it was the king and his government who made a number of legal decisions and that some disputes could result in a hearing in his presence. Despite the complexity of the administrative apparatus, it was ultimately the king and his decision that had the highest validity. A similar role of the Egyptian ruler is also identifiable in the documents of Levantine origin, or more precisely, in areas that gradually reached the economic and political sphere of influence of the Egyptian state.

Following the early campaigns of rulers of the 18th Dynasty, that are only briefly mentioned in the Egyptian records, the material culture of the Levant once again reveals an increasing number of Egyptian or Egyptianizing objects,[16] reaching its peak in the mid-18th Dynasty (LBA IB)[17]— during the period of the most intense military activity of the Egyptian forces in the Levant. It is the period when some parts of the Levant were incorporated into the Egyptian administrative apparatus with annual taxes or tribute. For the very first time the information provided by the material culture and written sources of both Egyptian and Levantine origin can be put together and critically evaluated. But similar to previous periods, it is the king and his image that is constantly rising to the fore when dealing with the Near Eastern polities. The written sources—mostly in the form of correspondence written in Akkadian—reveal that the relations between the various political units were personified by their rulers: in this particular case the Egyptian king on the one hand and one of the Levantine rulers on the other. Such a personified form of relationships allows us to better understand both the character and procedures related to the communication between the individual kings but do not reveal any details pertaining to the daily life of "Egyptians" in the Levantine societies. The

---

[14] For a recent re-evalution of the evidence see Streit 2017 with references to earlier literature; for standard editions see Sethe 1926; Posener – van de Walle 1940; Vercouter 1963; Koenig 1990.

[15] Radner – Van Koppen 2009; Van Koppen – Lehmann 2012–2013.

[16] See the contribution of Ann-Kathrin Jeske in the present volume (2019).

[17] Mumford 2014: 75; for the topic consult especially the thorough study of Mumford 1998.

structure of sources once again represents the most serious problem when trying to understand and describe the role of an Egyptian individual. Their repertoire is in fact very limited. For the Levantine polities holds that we mostly deal with the correspondence of their rulers, addressed to the king of Egypt and representing a superior power, which is especially true for the southern Levant. On the other hand, for more remote regions like Anatolia or Mesopotamia not even the Egyptian king himself was important enough to be the subject of communication of the others (Mynářová 2015) and therefore it is of no surprise that hardly any references to "ordinary" Egyptians can be identified in the set of the "international" letters (Egypt, Babylonia, Assyria, Mittani, Ḫatti, Alašiya, and Arzawa). There are two cases only revealing a more eloquent view on Egyptians "abroad", from Ḫatti and Ugarit.

The contributions of Elena Devecchi and Kevin McGeough in the present volume clearly show[18] that the textual records discovered at the site of ancient Ugarit (modern Ras Shamra) offer a unique insight both into the inner structures of the Ugaritic society and the extensive relations with the Hittite kingdom. During the Late Bronze Age, and especially from the middle of the 14th century BC until the end of the 13th century BC, one of the neuralgic points for the political history of the Levantine region is represented by the relations between Egypt and Ḫatti, with a changing character and intensity. From a chronological perspective, the textual evidence for these relations is imbalanced—on the one hand there is a long-lasting flow of communication attested by means of both the Amarna letters and the Ramesside correspondence, and the legal aspects are extensively articulated by means of a series of treaties.[19] Other written sources from Ḫatti and mentioning the Egyptians are extremely limited (Mynářová 2015: 10–18). The Egyptians are mentioned as the "men of (the land of) Egypt" (LÚ^{meš} KUR ^{uru}*Mizra*) in the Hittite treaties. In these cases, however, they are identified as subjects of the Egyptian king; they are the "men of Egypt". But the term clearly refers to the geographical concept and their position as "Egyptians" is of no difference from the "men of Kizzuwatna" etc., or even the "men of Ḫatti"—their "ethnicity" is thus seen through a geographical concept. Similarly, in the Amarna letters it is the local rulers of Levantine polities that are identified as "men of GN", referring once again to the same, i.e. geographical concept. The identification of the "Egyptians" in the Hittite treaties is therefore two-fold; they are defined by both a geographical concept (as the men of Egypt) and their social status (subjects of the Egyptian king).

Looking at the Hittite material from a wider perspective, it is obvious that the Hittite texts mention foreigners only rarely (Klinger 1992). We find them mostly as prisoners of wars. One of the reasons for this, however, might be related to the repertoire of preserved texts; especially administrative texts are not sufficient to provide a more representative picture on the social dynamics inside the Hittite society in relation to foreigners. The material culture from the Hittite *milieu* also

[18] Devecchi 2019; McGeough 2019.
[19] Devecchi – Miller 2011.

provides only a limited evidence on the Egyptian-Hittite relations with only a low number of Egyptian artefacts discovered in Ḫattuša.[20] Most of these objects, however, do not reveal anything about the possible presence of Egyptians in the city. And their evidential value for understanding the Egyptian-Hittite relations is also very limited. The individual artefactsdo not disclose much about when, how, or even from where the objects made it to Ḫattuša. Their interpretation is also often biased by the archaeological context. This is for instance the case of a fragment of a 19th Dynasty stela discovered in a layer of debris on Büyükale, where in level III an Egyptian alabaster vessel was found, dated to the 13th century BC. A New Kingdom axe was discovered in Temple 26 in the Upper City and an Egyptian scarab in the northern Lower City, but once again, the actual find context is insecure (Genz 2006: 189). Thus, the situation that we encounter in the Hittite environment is not fundamentally different from that in the Levant, i.e. only a mutual evaluation of written sources and material culture can give us a more complete picture of the nature of the Egyptian-Hittite relations, but it tells us virtually nothing about the presence or life of individual Egyptians in Ḫattuša.

Similar to other regions and historical periods, onomastics has been widely used in the discussion on ethnicity and "foreignness". Egyptian personal names appear in the Late Bronze Age written sources from the Levant, as it is already attested in the Amarna letters (Hess 1993), but many of the bearers of "Egyptian" names can hardly be identified as "Egyptians". Given the chronological extents of the Late Bronze Age, it is quite plausible that after a number of generations, some of the originally Egyptian names became domesticated. The name-giving practice is a complex issue combining both elements of tradition with innovations, often motivated by current political or social reality or realities. From the evidence provided by the Levantine written sources, there is nothing to suggest that the Egyptian or Egyptianizing names were considered unusual, strange or foreign. As mentioned earlier, changing preferences in the name-giving are yet another element reflecting changes in the politics and historical realities. An example well-illustrating the changing character of the Egyptian-Hittite relations represents the distribution of the personal name Mizramuwa "(Having) the strength of (the gods of) Egypt",[21] attested in the Hittite sources.[22] There are at least two or even three individuals with the name, both male and female.[23]

The most important of these individuals is prince Mizramuwa, a brother of Upparamuwa, who participated in the Hittite embassy to Egypt after the peace treaty was concluded (KUB 3.43+; Edel 1994: 26).[24] In his letter to Ibiranu, the king

---

[20] For a thorough overview see Genz 2006; for the political overview of the relations consult esp. Devecchi – Miller 2011; Genz 2011.

[21] For the interpretation of the personal name with a theophoric element consult Yakubovich 2013: 106 with further literature.

[22] For the attestations see Imparati 1994 and Bilgin 2018: esp. 284–287.

[23] KUB 6.18 obv. 8; Bilgin 2018: 287.

[24] For the overview and evaluation of sources see recently Bilgin 2018: 212–213; for his role in Amurru see an Akkadian letter TK 02.1; Roche 2003.

of Ugarit, it is probably the king of Carchemish who writes: "And may you know that he is the brother of Upparmuwa, who is the son of the king" (RS 17. 423 rev. 16–21; PRU 4, 193). Indirect evidence on the contacts between the royal courts at Carchemish and Egypt, and more specifically Ini-Teššub offers Ostracon Cairo CGC 25807, considered to be probably a model letter:[25] "The ruler of Carchemish, Ini-Teš(š)ub greets [...]". As the passage does not correspond to standard forms of an address and greeting formulae employed in contemporary documents[26] issued by either the Egyptian royal office or the royal office of Carchemish, the identification of the document as a model letter is highly probable. As Kitchen correctly pointed out,[27] by its content the text very likely ranks among other hieratic documents such as parts of Papyrus Anastasi II (BM EA 10243,1)[28] and its parallel in Papyrus Anastasi IV (BM EA 10249,3)[29] and this suggestion is further supported by the dating of the respective documents to the latter part of the 19th Dynasty.

In general, personal names[30] containing the geographical element "Egypt", or "The Egyptian"[31] are attested only rarely in the Late Bronze Age sources, either from the Levant[32] or from Anatolia[33]. In his paper on "Anatolian Names in *-wiya* and the Structure of Empire Luwian Onomastics" I. Yakubovich correlates the chronological distribution of the individuals bearing the name of Mizramuwa in the second part of the 13th century BC with the events following "the inconclusive war between the Hittite Empire and Egypt" and the possible acculturation of the foreign—in this case Egyptian—gods by the Hittites (2013: 194–195). It can be also added that the presence of the divine witnesses in the respective state treaties might have played its role in the process.[34] Nevertheless, only during the period of peaceful relations between the two Great Powers, we can find an "Egyptian" element set deeply in the Hittite *milieu*.

As Elena Devechi clearly demonstrated in her contribution to the present volume, the changing nature of the Hittite-Ugaritic relations were crucial for the political and cultural history of the Eastern Mediterranean at the end of the Late

---

[25] Černý 1935: I 94, 115*; II pl. CXI; *KRI* II, 233: 4 (No. 65); Barnett – Černý 1947: 94; *KRITAT* II, 86; *KRITANC* II, 145–146.

[26] Edel 1994 (Ḫatti), Lackenbacher 2001 and Lackenbacher – Malbran-Labat 2016 (both Ugarit); for the correspondence of Carchemish see Yamada 1992.

[27] *KRI* II, 233: 2–3 and especially *KRITANC* II, 146.

[28] Praise of the Delta Residence; Gardiner 1937: 12–13; Caminos 1954: 37–40.

[29] Praise of the Delta Residence; Gardiner 1937: 40–41; Caminos 1954: 153–155.

[30] The opinion of M. Astour (1972) that a gentilic term *mṣry* "an Egyptian", attested widely in Ugaritic texts, is related to certain occupational roles cannot be confirmed based on the re-evaluation of the Ugaritic sources; see especially McGeough 2011; Van Soldt 2015; Vita 2018.

[31] Known, for example, from the Neo-Assyrian sources, Jursa 2001: 772 (*sub* Akk. Muṣurāiu, WS Muṣurī). Nevertheless, other PNs containing a geographical element "Egypt" are not known from the Neo-Assyrian Period.

[32] Cf. Hess 1993 (Amarna); Mayer 2001: 39–69 (Ekalte); Pruzsinszky 2003 (Emar); Richter – Lange 2012: 173–180 (Qaṭna); Horowitz – Oshima – Sanders 2018: 191–195 (southern Levant). For the attestations in Ugaritic sources consult Gröndahl 1967.

[33] Laroche 1966; Laroche 1981; De Martino 2011; Trémouille 2014.

[34] The fact that the lists of divine witnesses represent an important source on political and cultural events as well as a good dating argument has been recently emphasized by I. Singer for the Egyptian-Hittite treaty (2013).

Bronze Age and have also directly influenced the policy of Egypt towards Ugarit. Leaving aside standardized mentions of Ugarit in Egyptian lists of toponyms—by its character revealing no information on the presence of Egyptians in the kingdom—it is the written evidence from Ugarit that brings the most extensive evidence on Egyptians in the LBA Levant.

Conclusions

The overview of the image of the Egyptians as reflected in non-Egyptian records shows that there is nothing like a universal image of "an Egyptian" in the LBA Near Eastern sources and clear evidence of a historically conditioned changing view on the Egyptians in the Levant is difficult to postulate. Regardless of the politics of Egyptian kings, when mentioned, the "Egyptians" are considered integral components of local society or societies, the respective individuals. There is no evidence that the "men of the land of Egypt" would gain any special status or an occupational role because they were "from the land of Egypt". The records do not bear witness to any special qualities of the "Egyptians", either good or bad; there are no "vile" Egyptians in the written sources. In none of the autochthonous documents an "Egyptian" is identified as "a foreigner" or "a stranger". In reaction to S. Richardson's introduction to the topic of "foreignness" in the present volume, this essay cannot present "a coherent single picture of" Egyptians as strangers, because there is none. Being an "Egyptian" is not "a single cultural phenomenon" (Richardson 2019: 316).

It is not only the different character and imbalance of preserved sources that does not allow us to shape a clear perspective on the problem. The evidence shows that at the same time, an individual could be both, an "Egyptian" and also a member of a local community and society with his or her rights and responsibilities on all levels, including those of an economic character. Such fluidity, although difficult to be recognized in the preserved evidence, is an omnipresent phenomenon in the LBA Levant, but its nature is already reflected in earlier sources, such as the Story of Sinuhe.

References

Ahrens, A., 2015. Objects from Afar – The Distribution of Egyptian Imports in the Northern Levant. In: B. Eder – R. Pruzsinszky, eds. *Policies of Exchange: Political Systems and Modes of Interaction in the Aegean and the Near East in the 2nd Millennium BCE*. OREA 2. Vienna: Österreichische Akademie der Wissenschaften, 141–156.

Altenmüller, H., 2015. *Zwei Annalenfragment aus dem frühen Mittleren Reich*. SAK Beihefte 16. Hamburg: Helmut Buske Verlag.

Altenmüller, H. – A.M. Moussa, 1991. Die Inscrift Amemenhets II. aus dem Ptah-Tempel von Memphis. Ein Vorbericht. *SAK* 18, 1–48.

Bar, S. – D. Kahn – J.J. Shirley, eds., 2011. *Egypt, Canaan and Israel: History, Imperialism, Ideology and Literature. Proceedings of Conference at the University of Haifa, 3–7 May 2009*. CHANE 52. Leiden: Brill.

Beit-Arieh, I. – R. Gophna, 1999. The Egyptian Protodynastic (late EB I) site at Tel Ma'aḥaz: A Reassessment. *Tel Aviv* 26/2, 191–207.

Ben-Tor, D., 2007. *Scarabs, Chronology and Interconnections: Egypt and Palestine in the Second Intermediate Period.* OBO Series Archaeologica 27. Fribourg – Göttingen: Academic Press – Vandenhoeck & Ruprecht.

Bilgin, T., 2018. *Officials and Administration in the Hittite World.* SANER 21. Berlin – Boston: De Gruyter.

Brandl, B., 1989. Observations on the Early Bronze Age Strata of Tel Erani. In: P. de Miroschedji, ed., *L'urbanisation de la Palestine à l'âge du bronze ancien: Bilan et perspectives des recherches actuelles. Actes du colloque d'Emmaüs (20–24 octobre 1986).* Vol. 2. BAR International Series 527. Oxford: B.A.R., 357–387.

Braun, E., 2002. Egypt's first sojourn in Canaan. In: E.C.M. van den Brink – T.E. Levy, eds., *Egypt and the Levant: Interrelations from the 4th through the Early 3rd Millennium B.C.E.* London – New York: Leicester University Press, 173–189.

Braun, E., 2003. South Levantine encounters with ancient Egypt at the beginning of the Third Millennium. In: R. Matthews – C. Roemer, eds., *Ancient Perspectives on Egypt.* London: UCL Press, 21–38.

Braun, E., 2014. Observations on Contacts between the Nile Valley and the Southern Levant in Late Prehistory Prior to Dynasty 0. In: M.A. Jucha – J. Dębowska-Ludwin – P. Kołodziejczyk, eds., *Aegyptus est imago caeli. Studies Presented to Krzysztof M. Ciałowicz on His 60th Birthday.* Kraków: Institute of Archaeology, Jagellonian University in Kraków, 223–234.

Braun, E. – E.C.M. van den Brink, 2008. Appraising south Levantine-Egyptian interaction: recent discoveries from Israel and Egypt. In: B. Midant-Reynes – Y. Tristant, eds., *Egypt and Its Origins 2: Proceedings of the International Conference "Origin of the State, Predynastic and Early Dynastic Egypt", Toulouse (France), 5th–8th September 2005.* OLA 172. Leuven: Peeters, 643–675.

Breyer, F.A., 2010. *Ägypten und Anatolien. Politische, kulturelle und sprachliche Kontakte zwischen dem Niltal und Kleinasien im 2. Jahrtausend v. Chr.* CChEM 43. Wien: Österreichische Akademie der Wissenschaften.

Caminos, R.A., 1954. *Late-Egyptian Miscellanies.* BES 1. London: Oxford University Press.

Cohen, R. – R. Westbrook, eds., 2000. *Amarna Diplomacy: The Beginnings of International Relations.* Baltimore: The Johns Hopkins University Press.

Collona, A., 2018. Gods in translation: dynamics of transculturality between Egypt and Byblos in the III millennium BC. *Studi e materiali di storia delle religioni* 84/1, 65–90.

Creasman, P.P. – R.H. Wilkinson, eds., 2017. *Pharaoh's Land and Beyond. Ancient Egypt and its Neighbors.* New York: Oxford University Press.

Czarnowicz, M. – M. Pasternak – A. Ochał-Czarnowicz – J. Skłucki, 2014. The Egyptian Presence at Tel Erani. In: M.A. Jucha – J. Dębowska-Ludwin – P. Kołodziejczyk, eds., *Aegyptus est imago caeli. Studies Presented to Krzysztof M. Ciałowicz on His 60th Birthday.* Kraków: Institute of Archaeology, Jagellonian University in Kraków, 235–243.

Černý, J., 1935. *Catalogue général des antiquités égyptiennes du Musée du Caire, Nos 25501-25832. Ostraca hiératiques.* I–II. Le Caire: Imprimerie de l'Institut français d'archéologie orientale.

Černý, J. – R.D. Barnett, 1947. King Ini-tešub of Carchemish in an Egyptian document. *JEA* 33, 94.

Davies, W.V. – L. Schofield, eds., 1995. *Egypt, the Aegean and the Levant: Interconnections in the Second Millennium BC*. London: The British Museum Press.

De Martino, S., 2011. *Hurrian Personal Names in the Kingdom of Ḫatti.* Eothen 18. Firenze: LoGisma.

Devecchi, E., 2019. A Reluctant Servant: Ugarit under Foreign Rule during the Late Bronze Age. In: Mynářová, J. – Kilani, M. – Alivernini, S., eds. *A Stranger in the House – the Crossroads III. Proceedings of an International Conference on Foreigners in Ancient Egyptian and Near Eastern Socities of the Bronze Age Held in Prague, 10–13 September 2018.* Prague: Charles University, 121–135.

Devecchi, E. – J.L. Miller, 2011. Hittite-Egyptian Synchronisms and their Consequences for Ancient Near Eastern Chronology. In: J. Mynářová, ed., *Egypt and the Near East – the Crossroads. Proceedings of and International Conference on the Relations of Egypt and the Near East in the Bronze Age, Prague, September 1–3, 2010.* Prague: Charles University in Prague, 139–176.

Diego Espinel, A., 2002. The Role of the Temple of Baʿalat Gebal as Intermediary between Egypt and Byblos during the Old Kingdom. *SAK* 30, 103–119.

Diego Espinel, A., 2012. Egypt and the Levant during the Old Kingdom. *AuOr* 30, 359–367.

Edel, E., 1994. *Die ägyptisch-hethitische Korrespondenz aus Boghazköy in babylonischer und hethitischer Sprache*. ARWAW 77. Opladen: Westdeutscher Verlag.

Hays, H.M. – F. Feder – L.D. Morenz, eds., 2014. *Interpretations of Sinuhe: inspired by two passages (proceedings of a workshop held at Leiden University, 27–29 November 2009.* EU 27. Leiden – Leuven: Nederlands Instituut voor her Nabije Oosten – Peeters.

Fischer, P., 2002. Egyptian-Transjordanian Interaction during Predynastic and Protodynastic Times: The Evidence from Tell Abu al-Kharaz, Jordan Valley. In: E.C.M. van den Brink – T.E. Levy, eds., *Egypt and the Levant: Interrelations from the 4th through the Early 3rd Millennium B.C.E.* London – New York: Leicester University Press, 323–333.

Gardiner, A.H., 1937. *Late-Egyptian Miscellanies.* BiAeg 7. Bruxelles: Fondation Égyptologique Reine Élisabeth.

Genz, H., 2006. Imports and their Methodological Implications for Dating Hittite Material Culture. In: D.P. Mielke – U.-D. Schoop – J. Seeher, eds. *Strukturierung und Datierung in der hethitischen Archäologie. Voraussetzungen – Probleme – Neue Ansätze. Internationaler Workshop, Istanbul, 26.–27. November 2004.* Byzas 4. Istanbul: Ege Yayınları, 185–196.

Genz, H., 2011. Foreign Contacts of the Hittites. In: H. Genz – D.P. Mielke, eds., *Insights into Hittite History and Archaeology.* Colloquia Antiqua 2. Leuven – Paris – Walpole, MA: Peeters, 301–331.

Gophna, R., 1995. *Excavations at ʿEn Besor*. Tel Aviv: Tel Aviv University.

Gophna, R., 2000. Egyptian settlement and trade in Canaan at the waning of the Early Bronze Age I: New discoveries and old questions. In: K.M. Ciałowicz – J.A. Ostrowski, eds., *Les civilisations du basin Méditerranéen: Hommages à Joachim Śliwa*. Cracovie: Université Jagellonne, Institut d'Archéologie, 99–104.

Gophna, R. – D. Gazit, 1985. First Dynasty Egyptian Residency at En Besor. *Tel Aviv* 12, 9–16.

Gröndahl, F., 1967. *Die Personennamen der Texte aus Ugarit*. Studia Pohl 1. Rom: Päpstliches Bibelinstitut.

Hassan, F.A., 1998. Relations culturelles entre l'Égypte et ses orientaux durant la Préhistorie récente. In: D. Valbelle – Ch. Bonnet, eds., *Le Sinaï durant l'antiquité et le Moyen-Age: 4000 ans d'histoire pour un désert. Actes du colloque «Sinaï» qui s'est tenu à l'UNESCO du 19 au 21 septembre 1997*. Paris: Errance, 12–19.

Helck, W., 1962. *Die Beziehungen Ägyptens zu Vorderasien im 3. und 2. Jahrtausend v. Chr.* ÄA 5. Wiesbaden: Harrassowitz.

Hess, R.S., 1993. *Amarna Personal Names*. American Schools of Oriental Research Dissertation Series 9. Winona Lake, IN: Eisenbrauns.

Higginbotham, C.R., 2000. *Egyptianization and Elite Emulation in Ramesside Palestine: Governance and Accommodation on the Imperial Periphery*. CHANE 2. Leiden: Brill.

Hill, J.A., 2016. *Cylinder seal glyptic in Predynastic Egypt and neighboring regions.* BAR International Series 1223. Oxford: Archaeopress.

Höflmayer, F., 2017. A Radiocarbon Chronology for the Middle Bronze Age Southern Levant. *JAEI* 13/1, 20–33.

Höflmayer, F. – S.L. Cohen, 2017. Chronological Conundrums: Egypt and the Middle Bronze Age Southern Levant. *JAEI* 13/1, 1–6.

Horowitz, W. – Oshima, T. – Sanders, S.L., 2018. *Cuneiform in Canaan. The Next Generation. Second Edition.* Eisenbrauns: University Park, PA.

Imparati, F., 1994. Mizramuwa. In: *RlA* 8-3/4, 316–317.

Jeske, A.-K., 2019. An Egyptian's Footprint: Members of the Egyptian Administration and Military in LB I Southern Levant. In: Mynářová, J. – Kilani, M. – Alivernini, S., eds. *A Stranger in the House – the Crossroads III. Proceedings of an International Conference on Foreigners in Ancient Egyptian and Near Eastern Socities of the Bronze Age Held in Prague, 10–13 September 2018*. Prague: Charles University, 179–196.

Jursa, M., 2001. Muṣurāiu, Muṣurī. In: H.D. Baker, ed., *The Prosopography of the Neo-Assyrian Empire*. Vol. 2, Part II: L-N. Helsinki: The Neo-Assyrian Text Corpus Project, 772.

Kaplony, P., 2002. The ʿEn Besor seal impressions revisited. In: E.C.M. van den Brink – T.E. Levy, eds., *Egypt and the Levant: Interrelations from the 4th through the Early 3rd Millennium B.C.E.* London – New York: Leicester University Press, 487–498.

Klinger, J., 1992. Fremde und Aussenseiter in Ḫatti. In: V. Haas (ed.), *Aussenseiter und Randgruppen: Beiträge zur einer Sozialgeschichte des Alten Orients*. Xenia 32. Konstanz: Universitätsverlag, 187–212.

Knoppers, G.N. – Girsch, A., eds., 2004. *Egypt, Israel and the Ancient Mediterranean World: Studies in Honor of Donald B. Redford*. PdÄ 20. Leiden: Brill.

Koch, R., 1990. *Die Erzählung des Sinuhe.* BiAeg 17. Bruxelles: Fondation Égyptologique Reine Élisabeth.

Koenig, Y., 1990. Les textes d'envoûtement de Mirgissa. *RdÉ* 41, 101–117.

Lackenbacher, S., 2001. Une lettre d'Égypte. In: M. Yon – D. Arnaud, eds., *Étuder ougaritiques. I. Travaux 1985-1995.* RSO 14. Paris: Éditions Recherche sur les Civilisations, 239–248.

Lackenbacher, S. – F. Malbran-Labat, 2016. Lettres d'Égypte. In: S. Lackenbacher – F. Malbran-Labat, *Lettres en akkadien de la "Maison d'Urtēnu". Fouilles de 1994.* RSO 23. Leuven: Peeters, 81–88.

Laroche, E., 1966. *Les noms des Hittites*. Études linguistiques IV. Paris: Libraire C. Klincksieck.

Laroche, E., 1981. Les Noms des Hittites: Supplément. *Hethitica* IV, 3–58.

Liverani, M. 1990. *Prestige and Interest: International Relations in the Near East ca. 1600–1100 BC*. HANES 1. Padova: Sargon.

Liverani, M. 2001. *International Relations in the Ancient Near East, 1600–1100 B.C.* Studies in Diplomacy and International Relations. Hampshire: Palgrave Macmillan UK

Lombardo, S., 2000. *Homer. Odyssey*. Indianapolis: Hackett Publishing Company Inc.

Lorton, D. 1974. *Juridical Terminology of International Relations in Egyptian Texts through Dynasty XVIII*. Baltimore: The Johns Hopkins University Press.

Lupo, S., 2004. The Inscription of Amenemhet II in the Temple of Ptah in Memphis. Was there a real control of the Egyptian state over Kush during the Middle Kingdom? *GM* 198, 43–54.

Mączyńska, A., 2018. Is there a place for prehistoric Egypt in Near Eastern archaeology? Some remarks on early relations between Egypt and its neighbours. In: B. Horejs – Ch. Schwall – V. Müller – M. Luciani – M. Ritter – M. Guidetti – R.B. Salisbury – F. Höflmayer – T. Bürge, eds., *Proceedings of the 10th International Congress on the Archaeology of the Ancient Near East (10 ICAANE)*. Vol. 1. Wiesbaden: Harrassowitz, 45–56.

Mayer, W., 2001. *Tall Munbāqa – Ekalte – II. Die Texte.* Saarbrücken: SDV.

McGeough, K., 2011. *Ugaritic Economic Tablets. Text, Translations and Notes*. ANES Supplement Series 32. Leuven: Peeters.

McGeough, K., 2019. "The Men of Ura are a Heavy Burden Upon Your Subject!": The Administration and Management of Strangers and Foreigners in Ugarit. In: Mynářová, J. – Kilani, M. – Alivernini, S., eds. *A Stranger in the House – the Crossroads III. Proceedings of an International Conference on Foreigners in Ancient Egyptian and Near Eastern Socities of the Bronze Age Held in Prague, 10–13 September 2018*. Prague: Charles University, 197–220.

Miroschedji, P. de, 2002. The socio-political dynamics of Egyptian-Canaanite interaction in the Early Bronze Age. In: E.C.M. van den Brink – T.E. Levy, eds., *Egypt and the Levant: Interrelations from the 4th through the Early 3rd Millennium B.C.E.* London – New York: Leicester University Press, 39–57.

Miroschedji, P. de, 2014. The southern Levant (Cisjordan) during the Early Bronze Age. In: M.L. Steiner – A.E. Killebrew, eds., *The Oxford Handbook of the Archaeology of the Levant, c. 8000-332 BCE.* Oxford: Oxford University Press, 307–329.

Miroschedji, P. de – M. Sadeq – D. Faltings – V. Boulez – I. Naggiar-Moliner – N. Sykes – M. Tengberg, 2001. Les fouilles de Tell es-Sakan (Gaza): nouvelles données sur les contacts égypto-cananéen au IVe–IIIe millénaires. *Paléorient* 27, 75–104.

Morris, E.F., 2005. *The Architecture of Imperialism: Military Bases and the Evolution of Foreign Policy in Egypt's New Kingdom*. PdÄ 22. Leiden: Brill.

Morris, E.F., 2018. *Ancient Egyptian Imperialism*. Hoboken, NJ: Wiley.

Mumford, G.D., 1998. *International Relations between Egypt, Sinai, and Syria-Palestine during the Late Bronze Age to Early Persian Period (Dynasties 18-26: c. 1550-525 B.C.): A spatial and temporal analysis of the distribution and proportions of Egyptian(izing) artefacts and pottery in Sinai and selected sites in Syria-Palestine*. An unpublished PhD dissertation. Toronto: University of Toronto.

Mumford, G.D., 2014. Egypt and the Levant. In: Steiner, M.L. – Killebrew, A.E., eds.

The Oxford Handbook of the Archaeology of the Levant c. 8000–332 BCE. Oxford: Oxford University Press, 69–89.

Mynářová, J., 2015. Who's the King? An Image of the Egyptian King According to Non-Egyptian Evidence. In: F. Coppens – J. Janák – H. Vymazalová, eds., *Royal versus Divine Authority. Acquisition, Legitimization and Renewal of Power, Prague, June 26–28, 2013. 7. Symposium zur ägyptischen Königsideologie*. KSGH 4,4. Wiesbaden: Harrassowitz, 9–30.

Parkinson, R.B., 1997. *The Tale of Sinuhe and other Ancient Egyptian Poems 1940–1640 BC*. Oxford: Clarendon Press.

Parkinson, R.B., 2002. *Poetry and Culture in Middle Kingdom Egypt. A Dark Side to Perfection.* Athlone Publications in Egyptology and Ancient Near Eastern Studies. London – New York: Continuum.

Porat, N., 1989. *Composition of Pottery – Application to the Study of the Interrelations between Canaan and Egypt during the 3rd millennium B.C.* Unpublished Ph.D. Dissertation. Jerusalem: Hebrew University of Jerusalem.

Posener, G. – B. van de Walle, 1940. *Princes et pays d'Asie et de Nubie. Textes hiératiques sur des figurines d'envoutement du Moyen Empire.* Bruxelles: Fondation Égyptologique Reine Élisabeth.

Pruzsinszky, R., 2003. *Die Personennamen der Texte aus Emar.* SCCNH 13. Bethesda, MD: CDL Press.

Pruzsinszky, R., 2019. The Contact Zone along the Middle Euphrates: Interaction, Transaction and Movement. In: Mynářová, J. – Kilani, M. – Alivernini, S., eds. *A Stranger in the House – the Crossroads III. Proceedings of an International Conference on Foreigners in Ancient Egyptian and Near Eastern Socities of the Bronze Age Held in Prague, 10–13 September 2018*. Prague: Charles University, 269–284.

Quirke, S., 2004. *Egyptian Literature 1800 BC questions and readings.* GHP Egyptology 2. London: Golden House Publications.

Radner, K. – F. Van Koppen, 2009. Ein Tontafelfragment aus der diplomatischen Korrespondenz der Hyksosherrscher mit Babylonien. In: M. Bietak – I. Forstner-Müller, Der Hyksos-Palast bei Tell el-Dabʿa. Zweite und dritte Grabungskampagne (Frühling 2008 und Frühling 2009). *ÄuL* 19, 91–120.

Redford, D.B., 1986. Egypt and Western Asia in the Old Kingdom. *JARCE* 23, 125–43.

Redford, D.B., 1992. *Egypt, Canaan, and Israel in Ancient Times*. Princeton: Princeton University Press.

Richardson, S., 2019. Aliens and Alienation, Strangers and Estrangement: Difference-Making as Historically-Particular Concept. In: Mynářová, J. – Kilani, M. – Alivernini, S., eds. *A Stranger in the House – the Crossroads III. Proceedings of an International Conference on Foreigners in Ancient Egyptian and Near Eastern Socities of the Bronze Age Held in Prague, 10–13 September 2018*. Prague: Charles University, 307–340.

Roche, C., 2003. La tablette TK 02.1. *Berytus* 47, 123–128.

Sala, M., 2014. EB II-III *Aegyptiaca* East of the Jordan: A Reevaluation of Trade and Cultural Interactions between Egypt and the Transjordanian Urban Centres. *VO* 18, 65–81.

Schneider, T., 1998. *Ausländer in Ägypten während des Mittleren Reiches und der Hyksoszeit*. ÄAT 42. Wiesbaden: Harrassowitz.

Schneider, T., 2010. Foreigners in Egypt: Archaeological Evidence and Cultural Context. In: W. Wendrich, ed., *Egyptian Archaeology*. Blackwell Studies in Global Archaeology. Oxford: Blackwell, 143–63.

Schulman, A.R., 1976. The Egyptian seal impressions from ʿEn Besor. *ʿAtiqot* 11, 16–26.

Schulman, A.R., 1980. More Egyptian seal impressions from ʿEn Besor. *ʿAtiqot* 14, 17–33.

Schulman, A.R., 1983. In the dating of the Egyptian seal impressions from ʿEn Besor. *JSSEA* 13/4, 249–251.

Schulman, A.R., 1992. Still more Egyptian seal impression from ʿEn Besor. In: E.C.M. van den Brink, ed., *The Nile Delta in Transition: 4th–3rd millennium BC. Proceedings of the seminar held in Cairo, 21–24 October 1990 at the Netherlands Institute of Archaeology and Arabic Studies*. Tel Aviv: E.C.M. van den Brink, 395–417.

Sethe, K., 1926. *Die Ächtung feindlicher Fürsten, Völker und Dinge auf altägyptischen Tongefäßscherben des Mittleren Reiches*. Abhandlungen der preussischen Akademie der Wissenschaften, Phil.-hist. Klasse 5. Berlin: Verlag der Akademie der Wissenschaften.

Simpson, W.K., ed., 2003. *The Literature of Ancient Egypt: An Anthology of Stories, Instructions, Stelae, Autobiographies, and Poetry*. New Haven – London: Yale University Press (3rd edition).

Singer, I., 2013. Hittite Gods in Egyptian Attire: A Case Study in Cultural Transmission. In: D.S. Vanderhooft – A. Winitzer, eds., *Literature as Politics, Politics as Literature. Essays on the Ancient Near East in Honor of Peter Machinist*. Winonna Lake, IN: Eisenbrauns, 433–457.

Sowada, K., 2009. *Egypt in the Eastern Mediterranean during the Old Kingdom: An Archaeological Perspective*. OBO 237. Fribourg – Göttingen: Academic Press.

Sparks, R.T., 2003. Egyptian Stone Vessels and the Politics of Exchange (2617–1070 BC). In: R. Matthews – C. Roemer, eds., *Ancient Perspectives on Egypt*. London: UCL Press, 39–56.

Sparks, R.T., 2004. Canaan in Egypt: Archaeological Evidence for a Social Phenomenon. In: J. Bourriau – J. Phillips, eds., *Invention and Innovation. The Social Context of Technological Change 2. Egypt, the Aegean and the Near East, 1650–1150 BC*. Oxford: Oxbow, 25–54.

Sparks, R.T., 2007. *Stone Vessels in the Levant*. Palestine Exploration Fund Annual 8. Leeds: Maney.

Streit, K., 2017. A Maximalist Interpretation of the Execration Texts – Archaeological and Historical Implications of a High Chronology. *JAEI* 13, 59–69.

Tassie, G.J., 2014. *Prehistoric Egypt. Socioeconomic Transformations in North-east Africa from the Last Glacial Maximum to the Neolithic, 24,000 to 6,000 cal BP*. London: Golden House Publications.

Teissier, B. 1996. *Egyptian Iconography on Syro-Palestinian Cylinder Seals of the Middle Bronze Age*. OBO Series Archaeologica 11. Fribourg – Göttingen: University Press – Vandenhoeck & Ruprecht.

Trémouille, M.-C., 2014. *Répertoire onomastique*, http://www.hethport.uni-wuerzburg.de/hetonom/reponomast.php (last accessed on July 30, 2019).

van den Brink, E.C.M. – Braun, E., 2003. Egyptian Elements and Influence on the Early Bronze Age I of the Southern Levant: Recent Excavations, Research and Publications. *Archéo-Nil* 13, 77–91.

van den Brink, E.C.M. – Levy, T.E., eds., 2002. *Egypt and the Levant: Interrelations from the 4th through the Early 3rd Millennium B.C.E.* London – New York: Leicester University Press.

van Driel, G., 2005. Ethnicity, How to Cope with the Subject. In: van Soldt, W. – Kalvelagen, R. – Katz, D., eds. *Ethnicity in Ancient Mesopotamia. Papers Read at the 48th Ren-*

contre Assyriologique Internationale, Leiden, 1–4 July 2002. PIHANS 102. Leiden: Nederlands Instituut voor het Nabije Oosten, 1–10.

Van Koppen, F. – M. Lehmann, 2012–2013. A Cuneiform Sealing from Tell el-Dabʿa and its Historical Context. *ÄuL* 22–23, 91–94.

Van Soldt, W., 2015. Crafts and Craftsmen at Ugarit. In: A. Archi, ed., *Tradition and Innovation in the Ancient Near East. Proceedings of the 57th Rencontre Assyriologique Internationale at Rome, 4–8 July 2011*. Winona Lake, IN: Eisenbrauns, 567–575.

Vercoutter, J., 1963. Textes exécratoires de Mirgissa. *CRAIBL* 107 / 1, 97–102.

Vita, J. P., 2018. Terminology related to Work Force and Job Categories in Ugarit. In: Garcia-Ventura, A., ed., *What's in a Name? Terminology related to the Work Force and Job Categories in the Ancient Near East*. AOAT 440. Münster: Ugarit-Verlag.

Vittmann, G., 2003. *Ägypten und die Fremden im ersten vorchristlichen Jahrtausend*. Mainz: Philipp von Zabern.

Yakubovich, I., 2013. Anatoliyan Names in *–wiya* and the Structure of Empire Luwian Onomastics. In: A. Mouton – I. Rutherford – I. Yakubovich, eds., *Luwian Identities. Culture, Language and Religion Between Anatolia and the Aegean*. Culture and History of the Ancient Near East 64. Leiden – Boston: Brill, 87–123.

Yamada, M., 1992. Reconsidering the letters from the 'King' in the Ugaritic Texts: Royal Correspondence of Carchemish?. *UF* 24, 431–446.

Wastlhuber, Ch., 2010. *Die Beziehungen zwischen Ägypten und der Levante während der 12. Dynastie. Ökonomie und Prestige in Außenpolitik und Handel*. Unpublished Ph.D. dissertation. München: Ludwig-Maximilians-Universität, Fakultät für Kulturwissenschaften.

ASSESSING FOREIGNNESS AND POLITICS IN THE LATE BRONZE AGE

Emanuel Pfoh
(National Research Council [CONICET] / National University of La Plata)

Introduction

Foreigners are particularly relevant to any local community because, with their presence, the local community is forced, willingly or not, to acknowledge otherness and to reflect on its own collective identity and constitutive features. This assertion, most valid nowadays, should also be considered for thinking about ancient Near Eastern realities, especially for the Late Bronze Age (ca. 1550–1200 BC). I would like to offer in the following pages some considerations on the incidence of foreignness in Late Bronze politics and exchange practices, in particular regarding the presence of foreign specialists.

Foreigners, Hospitality, Politics: Some Ethnographic Insights

Let me begin with some general socio-political considerations to then proceed with a few ethnographic insights relevant for the present discussion. We may affirm that political communities in the second millennium BC Near East were structured by clear hierarchic networks, merging basic kinship ties at the bottom of the societal pyramid with more complex yet often changing relationships like patron-client ties, or in the case of some city-states like Ugarit, Alalaḫ or Emar, with state agents, like officers or the military exerting royal authority. In any case, I think we can make a case for understanding these political communities as integrated into patrimonial structures and spheres of socio-political practices. These patrimonial structures were built upon extended kinship and family relationships, as noted, having political or economic reciprocity integrated at the core of the fabric of society (cf. Gouldner 1960; Sahlins 1972: 185–220). This patrimonial reciprocity—expressed more accurately as proper redistribution from the centre of the political community—emulates in ideological terms the reciprocity and the language of the family, although it does not keep the parity of exchange. Indeed, what characterises also patrimonial or household polities is the inherently asymmetrical nature of the social bond through redistribution, even though it might appear as royal reciprocity (the king takes care of his subjects and they in return remain loyal to him—and pay him taxes!). It is against this patrimonial society that foreigners during the Late Bronze Age were confronted and at the same time related—even if at a negative degree (they are "non-kinsmen", "non-members of the community"; cf. Sahlins 1972: 195–196). Yet, coming the foreigners themselves—most probably—from other patrimonial societies, we might assume that they already knew the rules of engagement[1].

Making a general statement from the Mediterranean ethnographic record, one could say with Julian Pitt-Rivers that the foreigner's condition was often addressed by means of the protocols and the practice of hospitality, which was probably a manner of dealing with such alien agents without resorting to violence. According then to Pitt-Rivers (2012 [1977]: 513):

> "The law of hospitality is founded upon ambivalence. It imposes order through an appeal to the sacred, makes the unknown knowable, and replaces conflict by reciprocal honour. It does not eliminate the conflict altogether but places it in abeyance and prohibits its expression. [...] the custom of hospitality invokes the sacred and involves the exchange of honour. Host and guest must pay each other honour. The host requests the honour of the guest's company—(and this is not merely a self-effacing formula: he gains honour through the number and quality of his guests). The guest is honoured by the invitation. Their mutual obligations are in essence unspecific, like those between spiritual kinsmen or blood-brothers; each must accede to the desires of the other. To this extent the relationship is reciprocal. But this reciprocity does not obscure the distinction between the roles."

Even more, explains Pitt-Rivers (2012 [1977]: 507–508) that

> "[...] by dispensing hospitality honour was acquired within the community and allies outside it and considerations of personal advantage are thereby added to the general utility of the association between the stranger and the sacred. [...] The stranger belongs to the 'extra-ordinary' world, and the mystery surrounding him allies him to the sacred and makes him a suitable vehicle for the apparition of the God, the revelation of a mystery."[2]

Another relevant aspect of the presence of foreigners is that their interaction with the local community needs to be carried out through some sort of accorded alliance or subordination for it to be possible at all. Of this, we possess some ethnographic evidence. As Meyer Fortes (1975: 231) observed regarding the Tallensi of

---

1 See the interpretation and discussions in Schloen 2001; Pfoh 2016. Mario Liverani (2014: 240–242) has also noted the family treatment in the Amarna diplomatic greetings between kings, comparing it to modern practice in the Middle East (although without linking it to a patrimonial understanding of society). For an ethnographic account of this sort of "house politics", although at a micro-scale, and its importance in modern Jordan—assessing also instances of hospitality—see Shryock – Howell 2001.

2 Auffarth (1992) relates the moral obligation of providing asylum and protecting strangers in ancient Israel and Greece, rather than with personal honour, with instances akin at honouring the gods. See further also the critical ethnographic remarks on honour and hospitality in Herzfeld 1987; Shryock 2004; 2012.

Tongo during the 1930s and 1960s:

> "To be safe, a person from outside must have either a kinsman or affine or at least a friend to vouch for him, initially at any rate, in the community he entered. There was one exception to this rule. Strangers who could enter a Tallensi community without such protection were the non-Tallensi clients of the external Boghar cult of the Hill Talis."

The acceptance of some sort of *personal* connection of the foreigner with a member of the community ("fictive" kinship, friendship, clientship; Pitt-Rivers 1968: 29) seems to be paramount for any social interaction to be established. In this sense, most foreigners are welcome initially as guests to the community, since "[t]he status of the guest [...] stands midway between that of hostile stranger and that of a community member" (Pitt-Rivers 1968: 16). Furthermore, as Fortes (1975: 233) indicated for the Tallensi:

> "[...] the status of the stranger who comes in from outside their society varies with time and circumstance. He may be regarded as a virtual enemy at the outset; but may at once or later be accepted as welcome or at least as tolerated guest. To be able to stay permanently, he must be given status in the host's domestic group and be thus brought into the community's kinship sphere or into the quasi-kinship sphere of adherence to a common ancestor cult."

By all means, these rules of hospitality and the sociability implied by it must be taken as general instances present in some way or the other in most agrarian or pre-capitalist societies. By evoking situations in which envoys, messengers or officers arrived to a foreign court, we should understand that the overall instances of reciprocity between the host (a king) and the guest (the messenger, the ambassador) was without a doubt less "equilibrated" or symmetrical than those alluded by Pitt-Rivers and Fortes and attested in the ethnographic record referring to more "primitive"[3] or traditional societies. Nonetheless, the key issue is to be aware of such ethnographic possibilities in order to shed more light when interpreting the textual-epigraphic record, especially of the Amarna period.

Some Clues from the Late Bronze Age

Let us focus on the Late Bronze Age specialist, as he (at times, she) plays a particular role as a *situational foreigner*, in the sense that the specialist would go through a process whereby he appears initially as a stranger, to become then a guest that should be welcome and cared for, although during a liminal period, and then remains subordinated to a host who is politically superior to him and a mediator

3 On the "primitive" misnomer for ethnographically attested hunter-gatherer communities, later extended to generic "tribal" societies, cf. the critical assessment in Kuper 2005: 1–36.

between the specialist-stranger and the local community (i.e., the royal court).[4] The Late Bronze specialist belongs essentially to a palatine realm of production. However, we know that during this period there was an important level of interregional contact among the great powers, contacts aiming at exchanging goods, women—as future wives of kings or princes—and, precisely, specialists (Zaccagnini 1987; Liverani 2001; Bryce 2003; Pfoh 2016: 63–88). According to Carlo Zaccagnini, the spatial mobility of craftsmen may well be understood through patterns following at least two of the modes of economic activity originally proposed by Karl Polanyi for pre-modern societies, namely redistribution and reciprocity—with the commercial mode discarded for pre-Hellenistic Near Eastern societies.[5] In this sense, the movement of specialists goes from one palace, where he is already an integrated member, to another palace, where he must go through the different stages of integration, as suggested in the beginning of this section.

The redistributive pattern in the mobility of craftsmen can already be evidenced at a previous period, in the correspondence of the kingdom of Mari, although it might be extended as well to the rest of analogous situations in other palatine economies of the Middle and Late Bronze Ages (Sasson 1968; Zaccagnini 1983a: 247–249; 1983b; Durand 1992; and for Mari epistolary references to artisans and specialists [Akk. *mârû ummênî*], cf. Durand 1997: 221–317). The textual evidence allows to witness then a mobility of varied specialists—healers and seers, physicians, masons, scribes, builders, architects, musicians, metalworkers, furriers—from the palace to the periphery of the kingdom, where they were required (Zaccagnini 1983a: 247–248). This could certainly be understood as patrimonial redistribution, as observed above.

The reciprocal pattern is particularly represented in the Amarna epistolary evidence. Comparing the mobility of specialists to the rhythm of the exchange of gifts and women: the specialists themselves would represent a kind of "symbolic capital" (Bourdieu 1992: 112–121) offered as a gift exchanged between the royal courts,[6] as possessors of key techniques but also embodying a prestige that arrived to the court from a distant location, they were imbued with a certain sacredness. Indeed, as Kristian Kristiansen and Thomas B. Larsson (2005: 39) note, space and

---

[4] On the different attitudes towards different kinds of foreigners in the ancient Near East, and especially their absorption into the host communities, see Beckman 2013.

[5] Polanyi 2001 [1944]: 45–58. Zaccagnini 1983a: 247, also 257: "The singling out of a 'commercial' pattern of mobility raises extremely complex problems, mainly because the operation of such a scheme must be evaluated in relation to a specific socio-economic background, for which ancient Near Eastern sources offer only partial and still problematic evidence. In short, the crucial point to be examined is the following: to what extent are we entitled to recognize the presence of a free-labor market in the pre-Hellenistic Orient (and the Levant) or at least some embryonic stage of such a socio-economic situation?".

[6] Cf. Zaccagnini 1983a: 250: "The sending of specialized workers is well attested in the framework of the diplomatic relations between the 'great' kings and, to a certain extent, between the 'great' and 'small' kings of the Late Bronze Age. The skilled workers who were sent from one court to another were viewed as prestige goods, and their transfers are inserted into de dynamics and formal apparatus of the practice of gift-exchange".

distance possess political and especially also ideological and symbolical connotations, as these are constructed by each society. Therefore, "knowledge acquired from travels to such distant places may form part of a corpus of esoteric knowledge controlled by 'specialists' (chiefs, artisans, priests) as an attribute and legitimisation of their status, power and authority". Also, the welcoming and especially the permanent presence of foreign specialists at the court helped to gain prestige, to be duly displayed to the inside of the community—in this case, the royal court, but also the general public—reinforcing in that manner the royal authority.

Some examples can be presented to illustrate this. In EA 35:26, the king of Alašiya asks for a specialist in vulture omens to the king of Egypt; and in EA 49:22–26, the king of Ugarit requests of the Pharaoh the sending of a physician and two black servants (slaves). According to Zaccagnini (1983a: 251–252), the two black servants (slaves) represent in fact a prestige good, "exotic curiosities to be shown at court among the king's entourage"; furthermore, says Zaccagnini, "both physicians and diviners were considered luxury goods, whose appreciation was not exclusively based on their 'value of use' but primary on their 'exchange value': in a way, they were on a level which is not very different from that of the foreign princesses who were part of marriage exchanges". In the same fashion, in the epistolography between the kings of Ḫatti and the kings of Egypt, we find a petition by Ḫattusili III to Ramesses II of a physician (an obstetrician) so her sister may conceive a child (the Pharaoh shows reluctance concerning the petition and answers back, not without mockery, that only a miracle from the gods would allow for a woman so advance in age as the Hittite princess to conceive [Beckman 1999[2]: 135–137]). Likewise, in a letter from Ḫattusili III to Kadašman-Enlil II of Babylon, the Hittite king declares to have taken care of the physician sent to Ḫatti by the Kassite king, and denies having prevented his return to Babylon (Beckman 1999[2]: 142–143; on the physicians at the Hittite court, cf. Edel 1976; also Caramello 2018). This assertion should be contextualised within the common practice in this period of withholding foreign specialists in the courts, as a particular means of ostentation of individuals bearing a singular symbolic capital, which—as noted above—bestows prestige upon their host. Such a withholding of foreign specialist depends intrinsically on the normal rules of hospitality found in other contexts, yet they are now subsumed under a display of royal authority considering the internal public, a situation which is nonetheless in agreement with the ethnographic attestation of the guest as politically and symbolically subordinated to the host.

Another particular episode in EA 23:13–25, which is not exactly an exchange of specialists, informs about the sending of objects carrying an important symbolic capital: Tušratta, king of Mittani, sends the king of Egypt, his son-in-law, the statue of a goddess: "Thus [speaks] Šauška of Niniveh, mistress of all lands: "I wish to go to Egypt, a country that I love, and then return". Now I herewith send her, and she is on her way" (after Moran 1992: 61; slightly variant renditions in Liverani 1999: 374; Rainey 2015: 185). The exchange of these objects are indeed part of the cosmopolitics of diplomacy, by which not only earthly agents interact politically and economically but divine agents also take part in the procedures of interconnection between political communities of the Late Bronze (cf. Liverani 1989–1990; 2001: 160–182).

Perhaps the main figure of the specialist travelling through the kingdoms' capitals in this period is the messenger (Akk. *mār šipri*, Eg. *wpwty*). In fact, as is well known, the semantic field of the term *mār šipri* is broad and in the Amarna texts it is used to refer both to messengers and couriers properly but also to ambassadors and ministers.[7] The messenger orally delivering a letter is the formal and normal manner of communication between the kings of the Late Bronze Age, as shown in the very form of the written message. The function of the messenger transcended the sole delivery of the message, as he also had to answer questions and explain the intentions of the sender (cf. EA 299:12–14; EA 302:11–18; EA 329:13–20). Of course, the messenger had as well a key role in marriage negotiations, which were at the same time commercial negotiations,[8] acting in that manner as ambassador and as exchange agent too.[9]

Two aspects of the mobility of the messengers are worth noting in relation to the present discussion. The first one is the danger that was implied in travelling to foreign courts. Messengers, with the exception of a courier, would travel in convoys of some twenty people or more, which made the trip a long and slow journey—the longer it took, the more the possible danger of an attack by bandits or semi-nomads, or even desert animals: as the Egyptian text "The Satire on the Trades" (ANET^3: 433) notes, "[t]he courier goes out to a foreign country, after he has made over his property to his children, being afraid of lions and Asiatics". Often, messengers would carry passports with them in order to avoid detention or attacks in the territory they were passing through, as it appears in a letter to the king of Mittani: "To the kings of Canaan, servants of my brother: Thus [says] the king. I herewith send Akiya, my Messenger, to speed posthaste to the king of Egypt, my brother. No one is to hold him up. Provide him with safe entry into Egypt and hand (him) over to the fortress commander of Egypt. Let (him) go on immediately, and as far as his pre<sents> are concerned, he is to owe nothing" (EA 30; after Moran 1992: 100; cf. also Knudtzon 1907: 268–271; Liverani 1999: 405).

---

7 Cf. Bryce 2003: 63; Pfoh 2016: 34–42. Note also Holmes 1975: 376: "Although the letters mention that a foot soldier filled the [messenger] position in one instance [EA 149:83], generally someone closely associated with the palace was used. One passage states that a Mittani princess acted as a courier [EA 24: III,22–23], while another passage indicates that a Mittani family was used in the messenger service [EA 29:156–162]". In general, see the studies by Meier 1988, for the messengers in the Semitic-speaking world, and Vallogia 1976, for the Egyptian messengers. On the procedures and logistics of long-distance communication in the ancient Near East, see Crown 1974; Knapp – Demesticha 2017: 30–35.

8 Cf. EA 5:16–17; EA 11:7–9; EA 19:17–23. Holmes 1975: 379–381: "The messenger functioned as a trade representative for the king. […] The foreign powers were interested in a messenger exchange with Egypt, not so much for diplomatic reasons, but because of the exchange of gifts. […] The messenger exchange was the main source of trade between Egypt and the other important powers, whereas it did not serve this function between Egypt and her vassals".

9 So Oller (1995: 1466): "The distinction between messenger and diplomat is sometimes blurred. Since along with their messages they often carried goods as 'gifts', which in international diplomatic practice was a major means by which foreign trade of the king was carried on, they can also be seen as merchants". For the case of Ugarit, as observed by McGeough (2015: 91): "These economic agents acted with a high degree of autonomy and still seemed to have a close relationship to the palace and to have, at least at times, acted as agents of the palace. Thus, in these cases, it is difficult to argue for a significant public/private distinction in ancient Ugaritic society".

Rainey (2015: 325) translates this last sentence as "And let there be no bri‹bes› demanded from him". This might possibly be referring to instances where "protection money" (Arabic *huwa*, as it is called in the nomadic Middle East) is expected, as noticed among tribal political communities in more recent times in the region (cf. Kark – Oren-Nordheim 2001: 278). One could indeed wonder if this letter is providing us evidence of an attempt by the Egyptian state to overrule the tribal Levantine custom of dealing thusly with travelling foreigners.

The second aspect is related to instances of hospitality when a messenger arrived, as they were not only socio-politically, but also—and equally relevant—symbolically foreign to the host court or community. Messengers were expected to be received according to the already mentioned rules of hospitality, which implied care and protection of the foreigner during a period of time. Interestingly, as we have already observed, in the Amarna letters there is evidence that this principle of hospitality was overturned in the practice, for reasons of local royal prestige, but also in order to execute political pressure, as messengers and ambassadors, as well as other specialists, were withheld in the court in order to gain some advantage from their presence (cf. EA 3:13–14; EA 7:49–50; EA 28:16–22; EA 29:40–42, 110, 113–116, 148–152, 155–161, 167–169; EA 59:13–14). This situation expresses well the notion that, after a liminal period of welcoming, the foreigner *qua* guest becomes a subordinated stranger to the host community (or actually to one of its members), and remains never fully integrated while his political relevance for inter-court negotiation lasts.

A final example related to the importance of feasts for creating bonds between foreigners could be noticed. In the context of a marriage negotiation, the king of Babylon Kadašman-Enlil, complaints to the Pharaoh for not having observed the expected actions of hospitality and reciprocity between two kings who are bonded by means of "brotherhood" (*aḫḫūtu*):

> "Previously, my father would send a Messenger to you, and you would not detain him for long. You qui[ck]ly sent him off, and you would also send here to my father a beautiful greeting-gift [*šulmānu*]. But now when I sent a messenger to you, you have detained him for six years, and you have sent me as a greeting-gift, the only thing in six years, 30 minas of gold that looked like silver. [...] When you celebrated a great festival, you did not send your Messenger to me, saying 'Come t[o eat an[d drink'. No[r did you send me] my greeting-gift in connection with the festival. It was just 30 minas of gold that you [sent me]. My g[if]t [does not amount] to what [I have given you] every yea[r]."[10]

Food and beverage are essential elements for ritually overcoming foreignness, but also for the maintenance of friendship through hospitality. There is a special relation created between host and guest by consuming together a certain sub-

[10] EA 3:9–22, after Moran 1992: 7; cf. also Knudtzon 1907: 70–71; Liverani 1999: 348. On the political (and ontological) asymmetry between the Egyptian king and Southwest Asia's kings, cf. Pfoh 2018.

stance: "Food and drink always have ritual value, for the ingestion together of a common substance creates a bond. Commensality is the basis of community in a whole number of contexts" (Pitt-Rivers 1968: 28; cf. also Appadurai 1981: 502–505; Candea – da Col 2012: 9–10).[11] These expectations and codes of behaviour were shared and understood in the ancient Near East both by the royal courts and the lower echelons of society—not only urban society, but also tribal society, if such a distinction have some merits—as they in fact belong to the normal patrimonial set of rules for interacting with foreigners.[12]

Final Remarks

The function of specialists in Late Bronze Age societies was at least twofold. In the first place, there was the specific task they would perform within the production sphere of the temple or the palace. Without scribes, especially, the relations between the powers would have been much different than what we can reconstruct from the letters and treaties. Second, they would play a key role towards the exterior of their polity, creating contacts between the kingdoms as messengers-ambassadors-exchange agents. Their performance as travelling specialists could of course be understood under the proper rules of diplomacy and inter-polity relations, as this matter is usually treated from a more institutional perspective. However, I hope to have made the case for showing the relevance of a more socio-anthropological interpretation—something pioneered by Liverani and Zaccagnini (Liverani 1972; 1979; Zaccagnini 1973; 1983a; 1983b)—in particular, attending not so much to offices and titles as they appear in the sources of the period but rather to *situations* and *practices* of hospitality expressed in them, after which we may attempt to decode a cultural world which is partially accessible to us and only through the extant textual data manifesting particular social and political logics of behaviour and expectation. Ethnographic insights on the workings of hospitality and politics—although not the exclusive interpretative path to follow—may indeed provide us with clues and perspectives to assess foreignness in the ancient Near East beyond the limitations of the textual corpora.

---

[11] Furthermore, as Lev-Tov – McGeough (2007: 87) indicate: "Religious feasts in the ancient Near East [...] were intimately intertwined with social status, and proper conduct at feasts was determined according to participants' usual group memberships within society". See also further a variety of ancient Near Eastern examples in Milano 2012, and a relevant discussion for early Greek society in Rundin 1996.

[12] See in this context also the story of Sinuhe, especially his reception at the local tribal society: "The sheikh among them, who had been in Egypt, recognized me. Then he gave me water while he boiled milk for me. I went with him to his tribe. What they did (for me) was good" (*ANET*[3], 19, vv. 26–29).

References

Appadurai, A., 1981. Gastro-Politics in Hindu South Asia. *AE* 8, 494–511.

Auffarth, C., 1992. Protecting Strangers: Establishing a Fundamental Value in the Religions of the Ancient Near East and Ancient Greece. *Numen* 39, 193–216.

Beckman, G., 1999². *Hittite Diplomatic Texts*. WAW 7. Atlanta, GA: Scholars Press.

Beckman, G., 2013. Foreigners in the Ancient Near East. *JAOS* 133, 203–215.

Bourdieu, P., 1992. *The Logic of Practice*. Stanford: Stanford University Press.

Bryce, T., 2003. *Letters of the Great Kings of the Ancient Near East: The Royal Correspondence of the Late Bronze Age*. London – New York: Routledge – Taylor & Francis.

Candea, M. – G. da Col, 2012. The Return to Hospitality. *JRAI (N.S.)* 18, 1–19.

Caramello, S., 2018. Physicians on the Move! The Role of Medicine in the Late Bronze Age International Gift Exchange. In B. Horejs *et al.*, eds., *Proceedings of the 10th International Congress on the Archaeology of the Ancient Near East, 25–29 April 2016, Vienna*. Wiesbaden: Harrassowitz, 275–285.

Crown, A.D., 1974. Tidings and Instructions: How News Travelled in the Ancient Near East. *JESHO* 17, 244–271.

Durand, J.-M., 1992. Unité et diversité au Proche-Orient à l'époque amorrite. In D. Charpin – F. Joannès, eds., *La circulation des biens, de personnes et des idées dans le Proche-Orient ancien. Actes de la XXXVIIIe Rencontré Assyriologique Internationale (Paris, 8–10 juillet 1991)*. Paris: Éditions Recherche sur les Civilisations, 97–128.

Durand, J.-M., 1997. *Documents épistolaires du palais de Mari, I*. LAPO 17. Paris: Éditions du Cerf.

Edel, E., 1976. *Ägyptische Artze und ägyptische Medizin am hethitischen Königshof: neue Funde von Keilschriftbriefen Ramses' II. aus Boğazköy*. Opladen: Westdeutscher Verlag.

Fortes, M., 1975. Strangers. In M. Fortes – S. Patterson, eds., *Studies in African Social Anthropology*. London: Academic Press, 229–253.

Gouldner, A.W., 1960. The Norm of Reciprocity: A Preliminary Statement. *ASR* 25, 161–178.

Herzfeld, M., 1987. "As in your own house": Hospitality, Ethnography, and the Stereotype of Mediterranean Society. In D.D. Gilmore, ed., *Honor and Shame and the Unity of the Mediterranean*. A Special Publication of the American Anthropological Association 22. Washington, DC: American Anthropological Association, 75–89.

Holmes, Y.L., 1975. The Messengers of the Amarna Letters. *JAOS* 95, 376–381.

Kark, R. – M. Oren-Nordheim, 2001. *Jerusalem and Its Environs: Quarters, Neighborhoods, Villages, 1800-1948*. Jerusalem – Detroit: The Hebrew University – Magness Press – Wayne State University Press.

Knapp, A.B. – S. Demesticha, 2017. *Mediterranean Connections: Maritime Transport Containers and Seaborne Trade in the Bronze and Early Iron Ages*. London: Routledge.

Knudtzon, J.A., 1907. *Die El-Amarna-Tafeln mit Einleitung und Erlauterungen*. Anmerkungen und Register bearbeitet von O. Weber und E. Ebeling. VB 2. Leipzig: J. Hinrichs.

Kristiansen, K. – T.B. Larsson, 2005. *The Rise of Bronze Age Society: Travels, Transmissions and Transformations*. Cambridge – New York: Cambridge University Press.

Kuper, A., 2005. *The Reinvention of Primitive Society: Transformations of a Myth*. London: Routledge.

Lev-Tov, J. – K.M. McGeough, 2007. Examing Feasting in Late Bronze Age Syro-Palestine through Ancient Texts and Bones. In K.C. Twiss, ed., *The Archaeology of Food and Identity*. Center for Archaeological Investigations Occasional Paper 34. Carbondale, IL: Southern Illinois University Carbondale, 85–111.

Liverani, M., 1972. Elementi «irrazionali» nel commercio amarniano. *OA* 11, 297–317.

Liverani, M., 1979. Dono, tributo, commercio: ideologia dello scambio nella tarda età del bronzo. *AIIN* 26, 9–28.

Liverani, M., 1989–1990. Scambi umani e scambi divini. *Scienze dell'Antichità* 3–4, 99–101.

Liverani, M., 1999 *Le lettere di el-Amarna, 2. Le lettere dei «Grande re»*. TVOA 3/2. Brescia: Paideia.

Liverani, M., 2001. *International Relations in the Ancient Near East, 1600-1100 BC*. Studies in Diplomacy. New York: Palgrave Macmillan.

Liverani, M., 2014. *Dal testo alla storia nell'Antico Oriente*. Atti della Accademia Nazionale dei Lincei. Memorie, Serie IX, Vol. XXXIV, Fasc. 2. Roma: Science e Lettere.

McGeough, K.M., 2015. "What Is Not in My House You Must Give Me": Agents of Exchange According to the Textual Evidence from Ugarit. In B. Eder – R. Pruzsinszky, eds., *Policies of Exchange: Political Systems and Modes of Interaction in the Aegean and the Near East in the 2nd Millennium B.C.E. Proceedings of the International Symposium at the University of Freiburg, Institute for Archaeological Studies, 30th May – 2nd June 2012*. Wien: Austrian Academy of Science Press, 85–96.

Meier, S.A., 1988. *The Messenger in the Ancient Semitic World*. HSM 45. Atlanta, GA: Scholars Press.

Milano, L., ed., 2012. *Mangiare divinamente. Pratiche e simbologie alimentari nell'antico Oriente*. Eothen 20. Vicchio: LoGisma.

Moran, W.L., 1992. *The Amarna Letters*. Baltimore – London: The Johns Hopkins University Press.

Oller, G.H., 1995. Messengers and Ambassadors in Ancient Western Asia. In J.M. Sasson, ed., *Civilizations of the Ancient Near East*. Vol. III. New York: Scribner's Sons, 1465–1473.

Pfoh, E., 2016. *Syria-Palestine in the Late Bronze Age: An Anthropology of Politics and Power*. CIS. London: Routledge.

Pfoh, E., 2018. Reconsidering International Relations in Southwest Asia during the Late Bronze Age. In P. Attinger – A. Cavigneaux – C. Mittermayer – M. Novák, eds., *Text and Image. Proceedings of the 61e Rencontre Assyriologique Internationale, Geneva and Bern, 22-26 June 2015*. OBO Series Archaeologica 40. Leuven: Peeters, 489–496.

Pitt-Rivers, J., 1968. The Stranger, the Guest and the Hostile Host: Introduction to the Study of the Laws of Hospitality. In J. Peristiany, ed., *Contributions to Mediterranean Sociology: Mediterranean Rural Communities and Social Change. Acts of the Mediterranean Sociological Conference, Athens, July 1963*. Paris: Mouton, 13–30.

Pitt-Rivers, J., 2012 [1977]. The Laws of Hospitality. *Hau: Journal of Ethnographic Theory* 2, 501–517.

Polanyi, K., 2001 [1944]. *The Great Transformation: The Political and Economic Origins of Our Time*. Boston: Beacon Press.

Rainey, A.F., 2015. *The El-Amarna Correspondence: A New Edition of the Cuneiform Letters from the Site of El-Amarna based on Collations of all Extant Tablets*, 2 vols. Edited by W. Schniedewind and Z. Cochavi-Rainey. HdO I/110. Leiden – Boston: Brill.

Rundin, J., 1996. A Politics of Eating: Feasting in Early Greek Society. *AJP* 117, 179–215.

Sahlins, M.D., 1972. *Stone Age Economics*. Chicago, IL: Aldine.

Sasson, J.M., 1968. Instances of Mobility among Mari Artisans. *BASOR* 190, 46–54.

Shryock, A., 2004. The New Jordanian Hospitality: House, Host, and Guest in the Culture of Public Display. *CSSH* 46, 35–62.

Shryock, A., 2012. Breaking Hospitality Apart: Bad Hosts, Bad Guests, and the Problem of Sovereignty. *JRAI (N.S.)* 18, S20–S33.

Shryock, A. – S. Howell, 2001. "Ever a guest in our house": The Emir Abdullah, Shaykh Majid al-ʿAdwan, and the Practice of Jordanian House Politics, as Remembered by Umm Sultan, the Widow of Majid. *IJMES* 33, 247–269.

Vallogia, M., 1976. *Recherche sur les "messagers" (wpwtjw) dans les sources égyptiennes profanes*. Centre de Recherches d'Histoire et de Philologie de la IVème section de l'École pratique des Hautes Études, II / Hautes Études Orientales 6. Genève: Droz.

Zaccagnini, C., 1973. *Lo scambio dei doni nel Vicino Oriente durante i secoli XV-XIII*. OAC 11. Roma: Centro per le Antichità e la Storia dell'Arte del Vicino Oriente.

Zaccagnini, C., 1983a. Patterns of Mobility among Ancient Near Eastern Craftsmen. *JNES* 42, 245–264.

Zaccagnini, C., 1983b. On Gift Exchange in the Old Babylonian Period. In O. Carruba – M. Liverani – C. Zaccagnini, eds., *Studi orientalistici in ricordo di Franco Pintore*. Pavia: GJES, 189–253.

Zaccagnini, C., 1987. Aspects of Ceremonial Exchange in the Near East during the Late Second Millennium B.C. In M. Rowlands – M.T. Larsen – K. Kristiansen, eds., *Centre and Periphery in the Ancient World*. Cambridge: Cambridge University Press, 57–65.

THE CONTACT ZONE ALONG THE MIDDLE EUPHRATES: INTERACTION, TRANSACTION AND MOVEMENT

Regine Pruzsinszky (Albert-Ludwigs-University Freiburg)

Prolegomena

Who and what is a foreigner? How can we distinguish them from locals in a multilingual and multicultural society, when only seldomly native terms for "foreigner", such as *aḫûm* or the less neutral *nakrum* occurred? These two Akkadian words referred to different categories of outsiders, such as invaders, merchants, diplomats, experts, brides, refugees, captives, or deportees, etc. (Beckman 2013). This wide range of foreigners covered societies from a lower level up to highly specialized groups of people and members of the elite who entered their new world either voluntarily or were forced to move. Some moved to new places permanently, others might have established semi-autonomous residential quarters or second homes in their host city. As such, they are likely to appear in clusters or groups of foreigners in our records. Depending on their status, some foreigners, with their connections to the host society, their professional function, or their specific form of foreignness were warmly received and respected, while others were made fun of, as we have seen with the Gutians who were compared with monkeys in the most unflattering way (see Reichel in this volume).

Seldomly was a person defined as a foreigner, or known to be a foreigner, as a historical fact in our cuneiform sources. In our search for foreigners, we usually apply objective criteria such as onomastics, gentilics, and language use. However, for the latter there is no general consensus as to which language (Akkadian, West Semitic, Hurrian) was actually spoken in the politically heterogeneous area of Late Bronze Age Syria (de Martino 2017: 151–162; Vita 2015: 375–404). Also, the linguistic evaluation of names has its weaknesses and limitations. Take, for example, naming practices over generations and mixed marriages and the consequences for the naming of children, or ambiguous cases, such as "Mischnamen" (multilingual names) or instances in which someone with a good Akkadian or, even Sumerian, name is labelled as an Amorite (de Boer 2014: 94). Being foreign does not necessarily mean that one has a foreign name or a name including elements known to be foreign. Furthermore, the use of different orthographies, such as the logographic writing of a name, often makes it difficult to determine the correct reading and linguistic analysis of a name.

In the Rencontre volume on the challenging subject "Ethnicity in Mesopotamia" van Driel (2005: 1–10) pointed out that group identity is largely a construct and that ethnic groups are self-defining systems, as the negative stereotypes vividly show. He stressed that the study of "ethnic process", the sequence of events by which one ethnic group removes, absorbs, or merges with another by force, by gradually taking over or by some form of acculturation, is the most promising way to explore the possibilities and limitations of this subject based on our evidence. Three principal stages were defined in this process:

1) Contact (the normal relation between groups)
2) "Landnahme", indicating the likely phase of a conflict involving vital economic interest
3) Acculturation, indicating all forms of (mutual) adaption between ethnic groups

Indicators for constructing an ethnic group are primarily language (which is often problematic, since the spoken language does not necessarily correspond to the written language), tradition, religion, way of life, structure of society, and material culture—each one is subject to contact phases resulting in ethnic change that is almost always connected to considerable social changes.

The Middle Euphrates during the Late Bronze Age

Our main focus first lies on identifying foreigners and determining which strategies the host society had towards foreigners and how they interacted with one another. Understanding their legal and social contexts and the form of contacts foreigners had within their host society may provide a better understanding of various aspects of foreignness. In this paper, I will focus on the texts from the Middle Euphrates area, specifically from Emar, the capital of Aštata, which provides interesting evidence on the social, legal, and economic systems in the Late Bronze Age (Faist – Finkbeiner – Kreuzer 2011). Together with the information provided by texts from other findspots along the Euphrates bend and at the crossroads of East and West in the border region between various political entities, a new picture of a diversified Late Bronze Age culture in inner Syria emerged.

In the 1970s, hundreds of cuneiform tablets were unearthed in the Tabqa Dam area along the Middle Euphrates after several seasons of rescue excavations took place at Tell Meskene (ancient Emar). Along with Emar, additional, closely situated, sites were discovered, all of which shed light on the historical developments and cultural contacts of this region, which had only been referenced in external records until then. Among the sites with text finds along the Middle Euphrates were Ekalte (Tell Munbāqa), Azû (Tell Hadidi)[1] and Baṣīru (Tell Bazi) —all of them dating slightly earlier than, or partly overlapping with, the Emar tablets into the late 15th / early-mid 14th centuries, a period when this region was under the influence and control of Mittani (Otto 2014: 33–60; von Dassow 2014: 11–32; de Martino 2018: 37–50). It appears that the western border of the core of Mittani ran along the Euphrates. Despite a strong Hurrianization

[1] Only recently, a reevaluation of the chronological setting of the texts from Azû has been presented by Torrecilla – Cohen 2018: 149–158 and Torrecilla 2019: 40–43.

of the local population further west, according to the Qaṭna tablets, there is no evidence of Mittanian imperial presence.[2]

The Mittanian sovereignty came to an end when Suppiluliuma I conquered the land of Aštata ca. 1340/30 (on the chronology see Cohen – d'Alfonso 2008: 1–25). Texts report of a Hurrian siege of the city in the time of Pilsu-Dagān, the Emarite king at the beginning of the 13th century. Since no Hittite intervention is documented, this obviously happened at a time when the Hurrian protectorate still existed on the Eastern bank of the Euphrates and tried to regain lost territories. After the Hittite submission of Mittani by the time of Muršili II, more attacks by *tar*-PI troops, perhaps semi-nomadic hostile bands, caused "years of hardship", famine, and inflation of prices by the end of the 13th century (Vita 2002: 113–127; Cohen – d'Alfonso 2008: 22–23). From the reign of Muršili II onwards, Emar was under Hittite control, which monitored its power over Syrian states from Carchemish via the viceroys Šaḫurunuwa and his successors. The *pax hethitica* established in Syria lasted for ca. 150 years until the fall of the Empire.

The Emarite cuneiform archives spanned about 200 years covering seven generations of two local dynasties (Pruzsinszky – Solans 2015: 319). Almost all our evaluation is based on ephemeral documents in which private individuals were attested next to members of a dynastic family, the city administration, and Hittite representatives. 90% of the texts derive from the building M_1, a "private dwelling" which housed over 1700 cuneiform tablets in Akkadian, Sumerian, Hittite, and Hurrian, including schooling texts, a library with various compositions, and an archive of a mixed nature that was closely associated with the legal activities of the city and the diviner's family of Emar (on a detailed study of the findspots of the Emar archives, especially from the M_1 building, see Rutz 2013).

In area A, in the north-west, the so-called "palace" with a *bīt ḫilāni* structure was uncovered. Relatively few texts were found there and, according to Cohen (2009: 11), they shed no light "on any particular royal prerogatives" and thus the structure is to be interpreted as a domestic unit (Otto 2014: 37[21]). A private archive of foreigners derived from House 5 in area A. Further private archives were detected in areas V and T, the latter being under water today.

Two different scribal traditions

From the beginning, the different shape and format of the texts was striking (for a summary see Cohen 2012: 33–45). Subsequent observations on scribal practices, including the palaeography, orthography, language, grammar, and legal phrasing, as well as prosopography, soon revealed that two phases are reflected in the corpus: the first, when the city was still under Mittanian control, and the second, when the city was under Hittite control. Mittanian control is also reflected in the tablets from Ekalte, Azû and Baṣīru, characterized by the Syrian (S) format texts. These represent the so-called "local order" of the earlier Late Bronze Age texts

2 See Map 1 in Eder – Pruzsinszky 2015: 7.

and resemble the Old Babylonian style. The better attested phase under Hittite sovereignty, with the introduction of the Syro-Hittite (SH) tablets, clearly reflects "the Hittite presence and administrative shadow of Carchemish", which "colored everyday scribal practices" (Fleming – Démare-Lafont 2009: 24–25) and resemble the contemporary Middle Babylonian style.[3] In terms of chronology, which is linked to the local dynasties and the diviner's family, the S format texts spanned from the early 14th century to the mid 13th century (ca. 175 years), while the SH tradition started ca. 1275 and ceases with the fall of the city ca. 1175 BC.

On S format tablets the writing runs parallel to the shorter side (vertical shaped tablets), while the SH format texts have a horizontal orientation. The S tablets show signs that are close to the Post-Old Babylonian ones found in Syria, while the SH tablets reveal palaeographic features comparable to the younger Carchemish and Mittanian script. SH texts were sealed with newly-introduced SH type of seals in the middle of the reverse, some of which show Hieroglyphic Luwian or even bi-graphic inscriptions. These seals certainly contributed to the diffusion of the hieroglyphic communicative code in Syria (Balza 2012: 27–28; Hawkins 2017: 247–265). Many local inhabitants adopted the new glyptic style and local craftsmen probably produced SH seals in their workshops (a regional emulation of an Anatolian style). This production provides valuable information on the re-thinking and adaptation of Anatolian hieroglyphs and iconographical motifs in Syria. On S format tablets, traditionally styled anepigraphic cylinder seals of the Syro-Mittanian type were rolled across the upper edge and the left margins.

Both formats were linked with specific cultural groups (Endesfelder 2017: 64[187]). The Syro-Hittite format was employed by scribes who were trained in Carchemish, or other parts of the Hittite Empire, and adapted their tablets according to the local requirements, while the Syrian scribal tradition was closely linked to the local authorities. As a newly developed tradition, the SH scribal tradition was not as consolidated as the Syrian one and is to be regarded as a result of a very productive form of cultural contact between Syria and the Hittite Empire, which overlapped with, and eventually overlaid, the local Syrian scribal tradition (Cohen 2009: 231–240 and Cohen 2012: 33–45).

Written versus spoken language

The majority of the tablets were written in Akkadian, the predominant language of writing throughout the Near East in the Late Bronze Age. Some have termed the language as "Western Peripheral Akkadian", which usually is understood as a "byproduct of a *longue durée* core-periphery relationship" (Rutz 2013: 327). However, Rutz (2013: 8, 327–328) argued that this binary opposition does not suffice the dynamics of integration, adaptation and assimilation of scribal practices, which eventually "become naturalized and perceived as local." Even if Emar was

[3] Instead of the widely used terminology of "Syrian" and "Syro-Hittite" styled tablets, Fleming – Démare-Lafont 2009 introduced the labels "Conventional" and "Free Format" tablets.

located in a peripheral political zone in Northern Syria, it remains unclear where its actual centre was because all, Babylonia, Mittani, Assyria, as well as Ḫatti, influenced the Late Bronze Age script communities in Syria. Different types of materials arrived by different transmission routes, and despite thorough studies on the scholarly texts we still lack the knowledge to pinpoint the time and way(s) of transmission other than through the two waves represented by the two basic scribal traditions mentioned above. Accepting the idea of a script community, the whole centre-periphery idea and questions of foreignness in script become obsolete, since within only 200 years, with few innovations in the script, it is hard to tell "after how many generations writing was perceived to be a local phenomenon" (Rutz 2013: 328). Similarly, Cohen (2009: 243) characterized Emar as a "relatively minor city", with many scribes leaving behind large amounts of ephemeral documents and scholarly material that had absorbed various traditions arriving from different sources throughout a long period of time (e.g. omen texts with Old Babylonian traits and an incantation with Assyro-Mittanian tradition). The local spoken language, Emarite, a North West Semitic tongue related to Ugaritic, was never committed to writing apart from isolated cultic words and topographic terms interspersed in Akkadian religious and legal documents (Cohen 2009: 13–14; Vita 2015: 376–382). Interestingly, lexical lists were not supplied with a column of the local language, as it is known from Ugarit or Ḫattuša, and no religious writing nor literature is documented in Emarite. The large West Semitic component in the city's population is mainly evident from the onomastics (Pruzsinszky 2003; Zadok 1989–1990: 45–61). Gelb (1962) observed that in the ancient Near East, personal names tend to be given in the then-living language. Akkadian may have only been spoken by highly specialized professionals who used the prestigious language, for which they naturally adopted the Mesopotamian cuneiform script that had also been used for Hittite and Hurrian, but not for their mother-tongue of Emarite. This situation is reflected in other scribal centres along the Middle Euphrates in the second millennium, where the local languages were never put into writing. Thus, some effective form of barrier blocking the diffusion of linguistic elements from the local language into written Akkadian must have existed (Cohen 2009: 242–243; Vita 2015: 381–382). It has been argued that the geographical position in the Middle Euphrates region may have contributed to a low language barrier between the local spoken language and written Akkadian, whereas in the coastal Levant or in Anatolia the language barrier was much higher. Another reason, according to Cohen (2009: 243), who points out the absence of Emarite in literature, might have been a certain degree of conservatism. In addition, the scribal centres were monitored by Babylonian and Assyrian scribes, who successfully promoted the prestige of Akkadian. Also, the use of Old Babylonian calligraphic script demonstrates the awareness and interest of scribes in Mesopotamian scribal traditions (Cohen 2012: 38–40).

Personal names as an indicator for foreigners

"A personal name is inextricably linked to the individual's identity" (Negri-Scafa 2005: 245). Every group has its own tradition in naming conventions, reflecting religious beliefs and/or social structures of the group. Thus, a systematic study of the percentages of name types and the linguistic affiliation in a particular area may provide evidence for the presence of a group speaking that language there. However, the use of personal names as an indicator of ethnicity must be applied cautiously, as can be shown, for example, with the Akkadian names of scribes in a clearly Hittite, Hurrian, or West Semitic environment, which were used for professional and cultural purposes along with prestige. However, for some ethnicities' early history, such as the Hurrians and Amorites, we depend entirely on the presence of personal and geographical names.

Torrecilla (2014: 188–189) presented an analysis of the linguistic distribution of personal names in Ekalte, in which West Semitic names comprised 60%, Akkadian names 15%, and Hurrian (and uncertain Hurrian/Semitic) names 9% (next to a number of uncertain West Semitic substrate, hybrid, or unknown substrate names). We observe a clear predominance of the West Semitic substrate names and very little foreign influx. Remarkably, the foreign influx in Ekalte consisted almost exclusively of Hurrian personal names, which represented less than 10% of the onomasticon and reflects the distribution of this ethnic group throughout Aštata (de Martino 2018: 46).

The evidence from Emar compiled by Zadok (1989–1990) and myself (2013) also shows that almost 80% of the PNs were of Semitic origin. The majority of personal names at Emar were West Semitic, and to a lesser degree Akkadian, with their distinction being controversial at times (see Fleming 2004a: 595–599). Most of the West Semitic names borne by locals contained theophoric elements representing a god common in the Euphrates area, such as Baʿl or Dagān. Akkadian substrate names are considerably less evident in Emar. Clearly, Mesopotamian deity names are Marduk, Ea, and Sîn, as they appear, for instance, in the scribes' names Ea-damiq, Marduk-muballiṭ and Sîn-aḫa-iddinam. However, these were probably all locals adopting Akkadian names for professional purposes (Cohen 2009: 65–66, 70, 81–82).[4] Conversely, Mār-Šerūʾa and Kidin-Gula were clearly scribes of foreign origin who stayed at Emar for business purposes (Cohen 2009: 116, 183–188). Mār-Šerūʾa, "the scribe and the merchant of the king", was an Assyrian who appeared together with a group of fellow Assyrians in a debt note (E 127) involving an Assyrian creditor from Šadikanni (Faist 2001: 168–171). Kidin-Gula either originated from Northern Babylonia or the Land of Suḫu, south of Emar. He was a teacher of family members of the diviner Zū-Baʿla and involved in scholarly life of Emar, as colophons show. In documents found in House 5 of the foreigners' quarter he appeared as a slave owner and creditor and acted as a scribe for his own and others' businesses. Based on this individual, we see that Babylonians were not only interested in directly controlling scribal centres, but also in the mechanisms of trade by means of their scribal and accounting expertise.

[4] Negri-Scafa 2005: 250–251 points out to scribes in the kingdom of Arrapḫa and provincial Hittite areas bearing Akkadian names for the same reason (cultural model). Additionally, prestige and family tradition played an important role. Again, this shows that scribal names are surely not a reliable indicator of ethnic background.

Further individuals with Akkadian names were Marduk and Erība-Marduk, who are attested in ephemeral documents from Ugarit and Emar (Cohen – Singer 2006). They were foreign merchants from the Middle Euphrates region or Babylonia residing in Emar. Marduk's loan of silver (E 75, area T) was weighed using the Emar weight standard – a clear indication that the loan involved an individual who was a foreigner in Emar. Since the creditor Dagān-kabar, son of Ḫima, was a well known Emarite businessman, Marduk must have been the foreigner. This text documents an operation between foreigner and local: when two local parties were involved, there was usually no mention of the weight system. Also, Marduk's Kassite-style seal is another clue for his foreign origin. Erība-Marduk, mentioned in a short memorandum regarding his donkey caravan (E 27), was associated with House 5. Interestingly, the letter RS 34.152 from the Urtenu archive in Ugarit referred to both Marduk and Erība-Marduk. This letter belonged to a dossier, according to which the perhaps-Ugaritic merchant Dagān-bēlu, residing in Emar, demanded from Ugarit metals, dyed textiles, alum, and oil (van Soldt 2011: 193–199; Pruzsinszky – Solans 2015: 326–328). The distinctive Babylonian palaeography of this letter suggests that it was most probably sent from the "foreign trading post" in Emar (= House 5 in area A). Based on the Middle Babylonian script with a strong slanting to the right and the typical Babylonian grammatical, features of this letter and the documents from House 5, Cohen and Singer (2006: 127, tab. 1) have suggested that they may have all been written by the Babylonian Kidin-Gula.

Singular in Emar is the case of the business woman with the Hurrian name Tataše ("Beloved") who is once attested with the Akkadian equivalent of her name, Ra'īndu. Her documents were discovered in the foreigner's House 5 and the text, in which she appeared with her Babylonian name receiving a loan of silver according to the weight of the city (of Emar) from the Emarite Kāpī-Dagān, was dated with a Babylonian month name (E 24: operation between local and foreigner). In a private gentlemen's agreement (E 23), in which she is referred to by her Hurrian name, she reimbursed silver according to the big "Subarean" (= Mesopotamian[5]) weight for the foreign merchant Ali-Nanu from the land Salḫu in northern Syria, situated east of Alalaḫ (operation between two foreigners in Emar). In a letter by her husband Alazaya (E 25), she was again addressed by her Hurrian name. Based on this personal instance one may carefully suppose that she was a Hurrian who adopted a Babylonian name in certain instances for convenience or professional reasons. Assuming a Hurrian etymology for the husband's name (Cohen – Singer 2006: 130[24]), we might be dealing with a Hurrian couple doing business in the foreign merchant's quarter of Emar.[6]

Anatolian personal names in the Emar corpus correspond to the population who arrived in Aštata after the Hittite conquest. As expected, no Anatolian names were found in the Ekalte texts and the few attested Hurrian names indicate that

[5] Zaccagnini 2018a: 56 and Zaccagnini 2018b: 6–10.

[6] Note however the individual with a Hurrian name, Ari-Teššup, who is labeled as an "Assyrian" in the text MFA 1977.114 edited by Owen 1995: 573–584.

the texts were probably written after a period of Mittanian florescence, or that "Ekalte was unaffected by Mittani" during the period of its textual documentation, according to Rutz (2013: 51). Torrecilla (2014: 190) reasoned that the limited quantity of foreign names might have been due to the strong local and agricultural character of Ekalte, which was much less "cosmopolitan" than Emar and in which foreign influences may have found it difficult to leave a permanent mark.[7] There certainly was a difference between the forms of dominance exerted by the Hurrians and the Hittites over their conquered territories in this region: As far as we can tell on the basis of the *arana*-documents, the Hurrian control was mainly based on receiving tribute (von Dassow 2014: 17–18). At the beginning of the Hittite rule, its strategy can be characterized as an annexation with relatively few physical contacts between the main power and its subject territories, who were allowed a high degree of local autonomy as, for instance, the scarce use of foreign administrative terminology demonstrates.

The Hittite forms of control and social change[8]

The Hittites' form of control of Aštata was reinforced by military presence and control of the area through the viceroyalty of Carchemish. Its growing influence can be gleaned from the installation of a new provincial administration, a process that d'Alfonso (2011: 163) described as a "dynamic between centre and periphery and that between indigenous administrations and new Hittite officials in charge in Syria" that had to coexist with local institutions, such as the elders of Emar and the local family clan. The local administration was mainly assigned to local dynasties and Hittite officials in each land, who were directly subordinate to the Great King. Some Hittite governors developed their own vision and guidelines for the many lands in Syria, which led Muršili II to correct the relationship between central command and local administrations by direct intervention and give away part of his command to the local administration in Carchemish. D'Alfonso (2011: 163–176) outlined the efforts to create a "political space" in Syria for a new administration as a "three-step process" centring on negotiating a "political space for the administration", with Carchemish, as the centre of Hittite administration during the latter part of Šaḫurunuwa's reign, having direct control over the lands of Aštata. Although Carchemish maintained a formal internal autonomy, the Great King of Ḫatti remained the supreme authority, appearing as the issuer of political treaties and in important matters such as war, interregional struggles, and the payment of tribute. While the king of Ḫatti ultimately ruled over Emar, the king of Carchemish was, in practice, responsible for its control, acting as the highest political and military authority and directly participating in judicial and economic affairs involving other Syrian kingdoms, such as Ugarit and Amurru.

[7] Beckman 1997: 107 characterized the Middle Euphrates region as "the home of a relatively egalitarian society of traders and small producers."

[8] van Exel 2010: 65–86; d'Alfonso 2010: 81–92; d'Alfonso 2011: 163–176.

Preceding the Hittites as a political force in Syria, the texts from Emar, Ekalte and Baṣīru attest to a purely local tradition of the cultural and socio-political *koiné* of the Middle Euphrates guided by a peer authority (van Exel 2010: 11–12; Faist 2012: 111–128; Solans 2014). Politically, this cultural unit was shaped by the prominence of collective powers, for which a number of terms, including "the city", its "men" or "sons", its "elders" or "great ones", or the "brothers" were employed. Texts also allude to the authority of a main deity of the city (ᵈNIN-URTA, Baᶜlaka or Dagān). Furthermore, there existed a very limited form of kingship. Even though the terms lugal, "king", and e_2-gal, "palace", both occur in the texts from Emar and Ekalte (Fleming 2012: 101–109, Otto 2012: 87–99), no palace-like building has been discovered. Instead, as shown for Tell Bazi, the monumental public building, in which the sealed donation tablets were found, served as the assembly place of the elders or the sons of the city who were perceived as the decisive power in these societies in the 15th century. The two tablets from Tell Bazi record transactions in which the king of Mittani dealt with the people of the town who practiced some form of collective self-governance that was exercised through an assembly or other representative body (von Dassow 2014: 19–20). This reminds us of the *taḫtamum*-assembly of the cities Tuttul and Imar during the Middle Bronze Age and of Idrimi fleeing from Ḫalab to the "men of Emar" (Sallaberger – Einwag – Otto 2006: 93; Fleming 2004b: 207–214; Pruzsinszky – Solans 2012: 321–322). Sources from Emar display a kind of synergy between non-royal and dynastic institutions. The tribute for the Hurrian king was to be satisfied "from the palace", but at the same time the tribute was defined as an "obligation of the city and the king" while the collecting was carried out by a group of entities: ᵈNIN-URTA, the city, the elders, and the king. Sale documents demonstrate that the tribute was so heavy that city property had to be sold to pay it. Whether tribute payments were exceptional or regular cannot be inferred from our limited sources (von Dassow 2014: 17–18). What they do show is that the authority of the "city" had its ideological reference in the figure of the city god ᵈNIN-URTA and that the elders embodied this institution (van Exel 2010: 70) while the members of the dynastic family appear to have acted primarily as representatives of the collective (Solans 2014).

The Hittite sovereignty had a significant impact on local societies and certainly motivated a change in the Emarite leading, or "royal", family. At first, the Hittite control was rather indirect, and we observe that up to the middle of the 13th century the 2nd local dynasty aimed at reinforcing its dynastic identity by distancing itself from ᵈNIN-URTA / the city and the elders. Things changed during Šaḫurunuwa, when the Hittite direct administration over Emar became visible and collaborated with the local authorities involving the family of the diviner Zū-Baᶜla and the "elders of the city." Later, during the reign of Ini-Teššup, in the course of a general reorganization of the relationships between Carchemish and Emar, the local scribal tradition, the royal family of Emar, and ᵈNIN-URTA disappeared. The collaboration between new Syro-Hittite officials and the "elders" or "great ones of the city" intensified and the traditional authority began to serve the Syro-Hittite administrators. The Hittite presence in the city was ensured by the Hittite highest officials (usually carrying Anatolian or Hurrian names) responsible directly to the viceroy (dumu lugal) and the overseer of the land (ugula kalam-ma). In addition, members of the royal family of Carchemish appear in legal texts and letters.

Yamada (2006: 222–234) highlighted the principle of indirect control, by which Emar maintained its own political institutions without Hittites forcing their will on Emar one-sidedly. The Hittite administration was regulated by a *mamītu ša Emar* oath/treaty between the Hittites and Emarites (E 18) and the Hittites gave careful consideration to the customary law of Emar, as shown by the phrase *kīma āli*, "according to the custom of the city" (customary law; see Faist 2012: 120–122). Direct control was exercised via the Emarite diviner Zū-Baʿla, who collaborated closely with and whose property was under control of the kings of Carchemish. The M_1 archive shows that the diviner's family played an eminent role in the cult administration, enjoyed special privileges, obtained its office with the help of the Hittites, and acted as intermediaries between Carchemish and the local power. Furthermore, the diviners were participants in, and preservers of, ritual practices, and possessors of specialized bodies of knowledge as the multi-lingual tablet collection demonstrates. Partial direct control can be gleaned from the fact that the Hittite authority employed a number of Emarite citizens, the Emaro-Hittites, as their local staff through a system by which Emarites were given property in exchange for their services, including military obligations (*šaḫḫan, luzzi,* giš-tukul and *ilku*). Here, one fundamental difference in the understanding of the social concept of "servants of the King [of Carchemish]" carrying out the giš-tukul obligation was highlighted by d'Alfonso (2005: 21–22, 33–34 and 2010: 81–82), as the individuals were considered as "free" (*arawannu*) by Hittites, but slaves by the local community.

Hittite influence on religious life

Hittite influence on the religious life can be gleaned from a unique subset of Akkadian-language rituals referred to as "Anatolian rituals", which describe offerings to gods of Anatolian origin, use Hurrian ritual terms such as *keldi* and *ambašši*, and include ritual acts such as the breaking of bread and libation belonging to central Anatolian festival traditions and the burning of offerings that can be found in Kizzuwatnean rituals. Based on the order of the deities in the "Tablet of the rites of the gods of Ḫatti..." (E 471), many of which are Luwian or Hurrian, Prechel (2008: 243–252) related the ritual texts to the cultic reform of Tutḫaliya IV in the 13th century, whose desire it was to standardize the religious practices throughout the Empire by renewing old traditions and including Hurro-Hittite rites in all the cults.[9] Such rites are also found in the important city cult of Emar, the *zukrum* (such as the blood-rite on the *sikkanum* stones and the procession of Dagān), which was considerably modified over the course of the Hittite takeover (Michel 2013: 187–196). However, since only minor gods are mentioned in the tablet of rites, they are not seen as a vehicle of religious imperialism (Archi 2014: 159), but rather served the organized cultic supply of the gods of the Hittite Empire. The diviner Zū-Baʿla, who was responsible for the local celebrations of the city (installation

[9] On preliminary observations on Hurrian divinatory practices attested in Emar and two paleographical groups within this Hurrian text corpus see Fischer 2017: 31–53.

of *ēntu* and *zukrum*), had to perform his obligations to provide for the cult of the Hittites in the first place. At the order of the Hittite officials, he was also responsible for the appointment of new cult officials as replacements of the clergy of the city, previously in the domain of the royal house of Emar. The control of the local cult and the introduction of a cult for the gods of Ḫatti offered an opportunity "to channel wealth from the province to the imperial overlords" (Cohen 2011: 154).

Emar, the transhipment centre

Emar was located along the main trading routes that lead from Ugarit via Aleppo and Carchemish, or inland via Palmyra to the Euphrates and further on to Mari and central Mesopotamia. Its archives hint at multiple external contacts within the economic network of the Great Empires. Within this vibrant (commercial) network, Emar and Carchemish functioned as transhipment centres in Northern Syria where foreign merchants were known to be stationed from the third millennium onwards (Pruzsinszky – Solans 2015: 315–337).

During the Late Bronze Age, the route along the Euphrates was protected by fortified bases, among which Tell Faqous was the last Hittite post bordering Assyria to protect Emar. Although Emar was situated right within the sometimes tense political sphere of Ḫatti and Assyria, trading activities continued. In the territory dominated by the Hittites, Assyrian merchants acquired gold, copper, and tin, as well as wood, especially cedar and boxwood, olive oil, flavoured essences, honey, and linen. Assyrians mentioned raw materials, such as copper blocks coming from Cyprus or Anatolia via Emar to Assyria, which were transported by Assyrian merchants. Finished Assyrian products, such as bronze knives and various wooden products and textiles are named in Emar texts. Only recently, Zaccagnini (2018a: 44–46) reconstructed a trade venture based on the simple payment record E 21 that mirrors the interacting multi-ethnic merchants in the international trade. It started in Emar with a cargo of Assyrian textiles, which were transported down the Euphrates to Anat, south-east of Mari. From there the Emarite businessman Imlik-Dagān took the caravan road to Palmyra, continuing further west until they reached Qaṭna. Whether the caravan continued further on to Ugarit remains unknown, but it is conceivable that it returned back from there. Interestingly, the Emarite merchant was financed by Atteu, perhaps an Assyrian living somewhere in the Jazirah, who had a servant named Kalbiu ("dog"), whose stamp seal is widely attested at Cyprus and in the Levant. Since the document names two men from Palmyra among the witnesses (and possibly merchants), it has been suggested that Kalbiu might have been from there as well, acting as Atteu's Palymrene representative. Back in Emar, he obviously settled some business with the Emarite Imlik-Dagān for Atteu.

As this payment record E 21 and other documents show, silver was traded by different weight systems which also reveal the international character of the businesses done in Emar. As to be almost expected by now, the documents mentioning Western, Mesopotamian, and local weight measurements derive from the private archives of House 5 in the foreign merchants' quarter and from area T. In the receipt E 87 from area T, a rather high quantity of alum, a typical Levantine export, was measured according to the weight of the *kāru*. This *kāru,* the "harbour" or "trading post", may very well refer to the house or market office of the Emarite family of Ḫima, whose archive was found in area T. Their supra-regional links can be gleaned from loan document (E 75), in which 272 silver shekels, according to the Emarite weight, another weight set, were lent by the Emarite Ḫima family to the Babylonian Marduk, who entertained contacts with Ugarit (see above). Chambon – Faist (2014: 17–26) pointed out that the Emar documents attest to three different weight measurements: one based on the sexagesimal system borrowed from Southern Mesopotamia, the second the Syrian decimal system, and a third one blending both aforementioned systems. This hybrid notation is an important indicator for the region's intense cultural contacts revealing, "the active role of the recipients in the process of cultural transmission." (Chambon – Faist 2014: 17) Also, the great amount of weights discovered in a house close to the Central square of Tell Bazi, perhaps the office of merchants similar to the *kāru* of Emar, shows that at least five different systems had been in use, indicating the presence of foreigners in Bazi with interregional connections (Otto 2006: 260; Fink 2012: 141–160). In addition to the Babylonian, Anatolian, Phoenician, Hittite, and Syrian systems, another set of weights represented a local version. Furthermore, among the small finds discovered in this house were a spindle bottle and a scarab. Based on these objects, the building was interpreted as a residence of merchants from the West who shared contacts with the coastal Levant. Different to the trading centres Emar and Carchemish (Marchetti 2014) at the crossroads of commercial routes, Bazi was only of secondary importance at one of the crossings of the Euphrates trading the local raw material hematite and finished products manufactured from this material.[10]

Also, in Emar foreign merchants found their second home, as I have shown for Dagān-bēlu interacting with Urtenu and the Hurrian couple Tatašše and Alazaya, who were engaged in overland trade and credit activities between Babylonia and Emar. Their tablets were discovered in House 5, home of foreign merchants, among them Babylonians such as Marduk, who traded with the well-known Emarite businessman Dagān-kabar, son of Ḫima. Almost all tablets of House 5 with typically Babylonian characteristics attest to a Babylonian-oriented trading business dating to the very end of Emar. They were probably all written by the Babylonian Kidin-Gula, teacher of the diviners in Emar, who interacted with the local urban authority as well (e.g. financial disputes were settled before the "great ones of Emar"), but apparently acted without any direct Hittite intervention. Even though the Hittite domination caused a number of developments and changes in every-day life, such as a new scribal tradition including the adaption of new glyptic styles, changes within social groups and administrative bodies, and the introduction of Hittite and Hurrian cult practices, its influence on commercial activities of Emar's local and foreign merchants in the contact zone

[10] The rich archaeological material from Emar has not been fully published yet: preliminary reports edited by Beyer 1982 provide a first glimpse on the multifaceted material culture discovered at Tell Meskene with its inter- and transregional relationships.

between the East and West seems to have been very limited, as the *mamītu ša Emar* shows that guaranteed the Emarites the respect for the local norms in regard to the legal and economic life, and might have also served the protection of Syrian equilibrium.

References

Archi, A., 2014. Aštata: A Case of Hittite Imperial Religious Policy. *JANER* 14, 161–143.

Balza, M.E., 2012. Between Anatolia and Syria: High Officials at Emar and Syro-Anatolian Cultural Contacts. The Case of Marianni, Scribe of Ini-Teššup. In P. Coticelli Kurras – M. Giorgieri – C. Mora – A. Rizza, eds., *Interferenze linguistiche e contatti culturali in Anatolia tra II e I millennio a.C. Studi in onore di Onofrio Carruba in occasione del suo 80° compleanno*, StMed 24. Pavia, 27–42.

Beckman, G., 1997. Real Property Sales at Emar. In G.D. Young – M.W. Chavalas – R.E. Averbeck, eds., *Crossing Boundaries and Linking Horizons. Studies in Honor of Michael C. Astour on His 80th Birthday*. Bethesda, MD: CDL Press, 95–120.

Beckman, G., 2013. Foreigners in the Ancient Near East. *JAOS* 133, 203–216.

Beyer, D., ed., 1982. *Meskéné – Emar. Dix ans de travaux 1972-1982*. Paris: Éditions Recherche sur les Civilisations.

Boer, de R., 2014. *Amorrites in the Early Old Babylonian Period*. Ph.D. Dissertation, Universiteit Leiden (available at http://hdl.handle.net/1887/25842, accessed on January 3, 2019).

Chambon, G. – B. Faist, 2014. Metrologische Notierung und Kulturkontakt im altorientalischen Emar (13. Jh. v. Chr.). In R. Rollinger – K. Schnegg, eds., *Kulturkontakte in antiken Welten: Vom Denkmodell zum Fallbeispiel. Proceedings des internationalen Kolloquiums aus Anlass des 60. Geburtstages von Christoph Ulf, Innsbruck, 26. bis 30. Januar 2009*. Colloquia Antiqua 10. Leuven: Peeters, 17–26.

Cohen, Y., 2009. *The Scribes and Scholars of the City of Emar in the Late Bronze Age*. HSS 59. Winona Lake, IN: Eisenbrauns.

Cohen, Y., 2011. The Administration of Cult in Hittite Emar. *AoF* 38, 145–157.

Cohen, Y., 2012. An Overview on the Scripts of Late Bronze Age Emar. In E. Devecchi, ed., *Palaeography and Scribal Practices in Syro-Palestine and Anatolia in the Late Bronze Age. Papers Read at the Symposium in Leiden, 17-18 December 2009*. PIHANS 119. Leiden: Nederlands Instituut voor het Nabije Oosten, 33–45.

Cohen, Y. – L. d'Alfonso, 2008. The Duration of the Emar Archives and the Relative and Absolute Chronology of the City. In L. d'Alfonso – Y. Cohen – D. Sürenhagen, eds., *The City of Emar among Late Bronze Age Empires. History, Landscape, and Society. Proceedings of the Konstanz Conference, 25.-26.04.2006*. AOAT 349. Münster: Ugarit-Verlag, 1–25.

Cohen, Y. – I. Singer, 2006. A Late Synchronism between Ugarit and Emar. In Y. Amit – E. Ben Zvi – I. Finkelstein – O. Lipschits, eds., *Essays on Ancient Israel in Its Near Eastern Context. A Tribute to Nadav Na'aman*. Winona Lake, IN: Eisenbrauns, 123–139.

d'Alfonso, L., 2000. Syro-Hittite Administration at Emar: New Considerations on the Basis of a Prosopographic Study. *AoF* 27, 269–295.

d'Alfonso, L., 2005. Free, Servant and Servant of the King: Conflict and Change in the Social Organisation at Emar after the Hittite Conquest. In D. Prechel, ed., *Motivation und Mechanismen des Kulturkontaktes in der späten Bronzezeit*. Eothen 13. Firenze: LoGisma, 19–38.

d'Alfonso, L., 2010. "Servant of the King, Son of Ugarit, and Servant of the King": RS 17.238 and the Hittites. In Y. Cohen – A. Gilan – J. Miller, eds., *Pax Hethitica. Studies on the Hittites and Their Neighbours in Honour of Itamar Singer*. StBoT 51. Wiesbaden: Harrassowitz Verlag, 67–86.

d'Alfonso, L., 2011. Seeking Political Space: Thoughts on the Formative Stage of Hittite Administration in Syria. *AoF* 38, 163–176.

De Martino, S., 2017. The Hurrian Language in the Late Bronze Age. In A. Mouton, ed., *Hittitology Today: Studies on Hittite and Neo-Hittite Anatolia in Honor of Emmanuel Laroche's 100th Birthday*. Istanbul: Institut français d'études anatoliennes Georges – Dumézil, 151–162.

De Martino, S., 2018. Political and Cultural Relations between the Kingdom of Mittani and Its Subordinated Polities in Syria and Southeast Anatolia. In A. Gianto – P. Dubovský, eds., *Changing Faces of Kingship in Syria-Palestine 1500-500 BCE*. AOAT 459. Münster: Ugarit-Verlag, 37–50.

Eder, B. – R. Pruzsinszky, eds., 2015. *Policies of Exchange. Political Systems and Modes of Interaction in the Aegean and the Near East in the 2nd Millennium B.C.E. Proceedings of the International Symposium at the University of Freiburg Institute for Archaeological Studies, 30th May 2nd June 2012*. OREA 2. Wien: Austrian Academy of Science Press.

Endesfelder, M., 2017. Die Institutionen in den syrischen Immobiliartransaktionen aus Emar. *ZA* 107 / 1, 35–88.

Faist, B., 2001. *Der Fernhandel des assyrischen Reiches zwischen dem 14. und 11. Jh. v. Chr.* AOAT 265. Münster: Ugarit-Verlag.

Faist, B., 2012. Die Rolle der Stadt im spätbronzezeitlichen Emar. In G. Wilhelm, ed., *Organization, Representation, and Symbols of Power in the Ancient Near East. Proceedings of the 54th Rencontre Assyriologique Internationale at Würzburg 20–25 July 2018*. Winona Lake, IN: Eisenbrauns, 111–128.

Faist, B. – U. Finkbeiner – S. Kreuzer, 2011. Emar. Das wissenschaftliche Bibellexikon im Internet (available at http: / / www.bibelwissenschaft.de / stichwort / 17472 /, accessed on October 2, 2018).

Fink, C., 2012. Gewichte oder bloße Kiesel? Untersuchungen zu Eisenoxidgesteinen aus Tall Bazi, Syrien. In H. Baker – K. Kaniuth – A. Otto, eds., *Stories of long ago. Festschrift für Michael D. Roaf*. AOAT 397. Münster: Ugarit-Verlag, 141–160.

Fischer, S., 2017. Erste Ergebnisse einer Untersuchung der hurritischen Emar-Texte. *Mesopotamia* 52, 31–53.

Fleming, D., 2004a. Review: Die Personennamen der Texte aus Emar by Regine Pruzsinszky. *JAOS* 124, 595–599.

Fleming, D., 2004b. *Democracy's Ancient Ancestors. Mari and Early Collective Governance*. Cambridge University Press: Cambridge.

Fleming, D., 2012. Textual Evidence for a Palace at Late Bronze Emar. In G. Wilhelm, ed., *Organization, Representation, and Symbols of Power in the Ancient Near East. Proceedings of the 54th Rencontre Assyriologique Internationale at Würzburg 20-25 July 2018*. Winona Lake, IN: Eisenbrauns, 101–109.

Fleming, D. – S. Démare-Lafont, 2009. Tablet Terminology at Emar: 'Conventional' and 'Free Format'. *AuOr* 27, 19–26.

Gelb, I.J., 1962. Ethnic Reconstruction and Onomastic Evidence. *Names. A Journal of Onomastics* 10, 45–52.

Hawkins, D.J., 2017. Laroche and the Seals of Meskene-Emar. In A. Mouton, ed., *Hittitology Today: Studies on Hittite and Neo-Hittite Anatolia in Honor of Emmanuel Laroche's 100th Birthday. Istanbul 21-22 novembre, 2014. 5èmes Rencontres d'archéologie de l'IFÉA.* Istanbul: Institut français d'études anatoliennes Georges – Dumézil, 247–265.

Marchetti, N., ed., 2014. *Karkemish. An Ancient Capital on the Euphrates.* Bologna: Alma Mater Studiorum – Università di Bologna, Dipartimento di Storia Culture Civiltà.

Michel, P.M., 2013. Ritual in Emar. In C. Ambos – L. Verderame, eds., *Approaching Rituals in Ancient Cultures. Proceedings of the Conference, November 28-30, 2011, Roma.* Pisa – Roma: Fabrizio Serra Editore, 187–196.

Negri-Scafa, P., 2005. Ethical and Cultural Aspects Related to Personal Names. The Names of the Scribes in the Kingdom of Arrapḫa. In W.H. van Soldt – R. Kalvelagen – D. Katz, eds., *Ethnicity in Ancient Mesopotamia. Papers read at the 48th Rencontre Assyriologique Internationale, Leiden, 1–4 July 2002.* PIHANS 102. Leiden: Nederlands Instituut voor het Nabije Oosten, 245–251.

Otto, A., 2006. *Alltag und Gesellschaft zur Spätbronzezeit: Eine Fallstudie aus Tall Bazi (Syrien).* Subartu 19. Turnhout: Brepols.

Otto, A., 2012. Archaeological Evidence for Collective Governance along the Upper Syrian Euphrates during the Late and Middle Bronze Age. In G. Wilhelm, ed., *Organization, Representation, and Symbols of Power in the Ancient Near East. Proceedings of the 54th Rencontre Assyriologique Internationale at Würzburg 20-25 July 2018.* Winona Lake, IN: Eisenbrauns, 87–99.

Otto, A., 2014. The Organisation of Residential Space in the Mittani Kingdom as a Mirror of Different Models of Governance. In E. Cancik-Kirschbaum – N. Brisch – J. Eidem, eds., *Constituent, Confederate, and Conquered Space. The Emergence of the Mittani State.* Topoi – Berlin Studies of the Ancient World 17. Berlin: De Gruyter, 33–60.

Owen, D.I., 1995. Pasūri-Dagan and Ini-Teššup's Mother. In Z. Zevit – S. Gitin – M. Sokoloff, eds., *Solving Riddles and Untying Knots. Biblical, Epigraphic, and Semitic Studies in Honor of Jonas C. Greenfield.* Winona Lake, IN: Eisenbrauns, 573–584.

Prechel, D., 2008. Hethitische Rituale in Emar? In L. d'Alfonso – Y. Cohen – D. Sürenhagen, eds., *The City of Emar among Late Bronze Age Empires. History, Landscape, and Society. Proceedings of the Konstanz Conference, 25.–26.04.2006.* AOAT 349. Münster: Ugarit-Verlag, 243–252.

Pruzsinszky, R., 2003. *Die Personennamen der Texte aus Emar.* SCCNH 13. Bethesda, MD: CDL Press.

Pruzsinszky, R. – B. Solans, 2015. Emar's Role in Transregional Trade at the Crossroads along the Middle Euphrates. In B. Eder – R. Pruzsinszky, eds., *Policies of Exchange. Political Systems and Modes of Interaction in the Aegean and the Near East in the 2nd Millennium B.C.E. Proceedings of the International Symposium at the University of Freiburg Institute for Archaeological Studies, 30th May 2nd June 2012.* OREA 2. Wien: Austrian Academy of Science Press, 315–337.

Rutz, M., 2013. *Bodies of Knowledge in Ancient Mesopotamia. The Diviners of Late Bronze Age Emar and Their Tablet Collection.* AMD 9. Leiden – Boston: Brill.

Sallaberger, W. – B. Einwag – A. Otto, 2005. Schenkungen von Mittani-Königen an die Einwohner von Baṣīru. Die zwei Urkunden aus Tall Bazi am Mittleren Euphrat. *ZA* 96, 69–104.

Solans, B., 2014. *Poderes colectivos en la Siria del Bronce Final*. Barcino Monographica Orientalia 2. Barcelona: Universitat de Barcelona Publicacions i edicions.

Torrecilla, E., 2014. *Late Bronze Age Ekalte. Chronology, Society, and Religion of a Middle Euphrates Town.* Saarbrücken: Scholar's Press.

Torrecilla, E. 2019. The Dwellers of Azû. A Study on the Tall Ḥadīdī Society and Chronology. *AfO* 46, 33–50.

Torrecilla, E. – Y. Cohen, 2018. A Mittani Letter Order from Azu (Had 8) and its Implications for the Chronology and History of the Middle Euphrates Region in the Late Bronze Age. *RA* 112, 149–158.

van Driel, G., 2005. Ethnicity, how to cope with the subject. In W.H. van Soldt – R. Kalvelagen – D. Katz, eds., *Ethnicity in Ancient Mesopotamia. Papers read at the 48th Rencontre Assyriologique Internationale, Leiden, 1–4 July 2002.* PIHANS 102. Leiden: Nederlands Instituut voor het Nabije Oosten, 1–10.

van Exel, V.J., 2010. Social Change at Emar: The Influence of the Hittite Occupation on Local Traditions. *RA* 104, 65–86.

van Soldt, W., 2011. Some Remarks on RS 34.141: A Letter from the Urtēnu-Archive. In P.M.M.G. Akkermans – B.S. Düring – A. Wossing, eds., *Correlates of Complexity. Essays in Archaeology and Assyriology Dedicated to Diederik J.W. Meijer in Honour of His 65th Birthday*. PIHANS 116. Leiden: Nederlands Instituut voor het Nabije Oosten, 193–199.

Vita, J.-P., 2002. Warfare at Emar. *AoF* 29, 113–127.

Vita, J.-P., 2015. Language Contact between Akkadian and Northwest Semitic in Syria-Palestine in the Late Bronze Age. In A.M. Butts, ed., *Semitic Languages in Contact*. Studies in Semitic Languages and Linguistics 82. Leiden – Boston: Brill, 375–404.

von Dassow, E., 2014. Levantine Polities under Mittanian Hegemony. In E. Cancik-Kirschbaum – N. Brisch – J. Eidem, eds., *Constituent, Confederate, and Conquered Space. The Emergence of the Mittani State.* Topoi – Berlin Studies of the Ancient World 17. Berlin: De Gruyter, 11–32.

Yamada, M., 2006. The Hittite Administration in Emar: The Aspect of Direct Control. *ZA* 96, 222–234.

Zaccagnini, C., 2018a. Capital Investment, Weight Standards and Overland Trade at Emar. *ZA* 108, 43–62.

Zaccagnini, C., 2018b. "Heavy Shekels" in Late Bronze Age Syria. *Annali, Sezione Orientale* 78, 3–18.

Zadok, R., 1989–1990. On the Onomastic Material from Emar. *WdO* 20–21, 45–61.

"HUMAN INSTINCTS, CANINE INTELLIGENCE, AND MONKEY FEATURES": THE GUTIANS AND OTHER "MOUNTAIN PEOPLE" IN MESOPOTAMIAN AND 20TH CENTURY SCHOLARLY PERSPECTIVES

Clemens Reichel (University of Toronto – Royal Ontario Museum)

The impact of foreigners on state societies—their manifestation, recognition, interactions and reception—remains of continued interest for the study of ancient and modern societies. In present times we are seeing unprecedented numbers of people migrating from their homes to often distant lands, whether for economic reasons for fear for their lives due to warfare, famine or genocide. At their final destinations, mostly "western" countries in Europe, the Americas, and Oceania new immigrants and refugees from very different, often disparate cultures find themselves united under the label of "foreigner" with their "otherness", compared to local populations of countries that they are trying to make their homes, representing the often sole unifying factor among them. Numerous examples from recent and not-so-recent times have shown how the formalization of this very "otherness" through what may be called "local" populations can itself become a unifying force through negative integration, i.e. by shaping identity not through finding commonalities *within* the group but by defining the group through those elements that do *not* make it.[1] Numerous examples of the past few years from across the world have shown all too well how xenophobia can be used as a powerful tool to unify disenfranchised groups, evoking a (false?) sense of identity. Highlighting what does NOT make us through negative prefixes (e.g., "un-American", "undeutsch" etc.) can unite disparate groups into a perceived unified entity under the concept of nationalism.[2] The concept of negative integration by stereotyping "others" is by no means a recent one. Countless examples, from the persecution of Christians in the Roman Empire to anti-Semitic actions all across Europe from the Medieval Ages onwards. It comes as no surprise to find forerunners of such tendencies in much earlier time.

Over the past millennia the Middle East has seen its share of population movements through invasions, migrations, and deportations. While those were by no means free of tension and conflict one needs to recognize that in most cases the absorption and integration of newcomers was not only possible but, in fact, mostly successful—whether one thinks of the Amorite and Kassite migrations to Babylonia during the third and second millennium B.C. or the Aramaean in the Neo-Assyrian

---

1 My concept of "negative integration" loosely follows the model described by Hans-Ulrich Wehler for Bismarck's post-1871 attempts to forge a German national identity by ostracizing various minority groups, such as Roman Catholics, Alsatians, Poles, and Social Democrats, through discriminatory laws (Wehler 1969; 1975).

2 "Rassismus braucht keine Fremden, um zu existieren, er produziert sie [racism does not require strangers to exist, it produces them" (el-Tayeb 2016: 14).

statelater on. Some members of these groups—Amorites, Kassites, Mittani, and later on the Arameans—came to represent political leadership, establishing ruling dynasties that lasted for centuries. Trade and manufacturing hubs such as the cities of Ur, Uruk, Babylon, Aššur and later on the Assyrian capital cities of Nimrud and Nineveh boasted foreign merchants, traders and craftsmen while Mesopotamian merchants themselves expanded into distant lands, from the colonies of the Uruk period in the fourth millennium BC to the Old Assyrian *kārum*'s of Central Anatolia.

It would be naïve, of course, to brand the Mesopotamian world as inherently "global" or "cosmopolitan". Throughout times, its leaders' motivation to interact with surrounding regions was generally driven more by economic than intellectual interest, notably by the need to import vital raw materials such as timber, stone and metal that could not be found, or were hard to come by, in the Mesopotamian lowlands. Gilgamesh and Enkidu's journey to the Cedar Forest to slay Humbaba or Sargon's expedition to the Silver Mountain in Anatolia can barely mask an economic reality behind these heroic stories, the necessity to gain and maintain access to the sources of vital raw materials. The equation of foreign lands with mountainous regions is epitomized by the Sumerian logogram for "foreign land" (KUR), showing a group of three mountains. Such pictorial abstractions highlight a clear understanding of the geographic dichotomy between the linearity of the Mesopotamian lowlands on the one hand and the reliefed topography of the surrounding lands, with hilly flanks or mountain ranges traversed by deeply incised river valleys that represented vital, but often treacherous, avenues of access and communication. These areas, geographically and environmentally so different from lowland Mesopotamia, evoked both fear and fascination that are well reflected anywhere from Sumero-Akkadian myth such as the Gilgamesh Epic or Enmerkar and the Lord of Aratta to Neo-Assyrian accounts of military endeavors such as Sargon's eighth campaign. The multi-faceted reception of foreign lands as places that both fascinate but also instill fear is also reflected in the way in which foreigners were depicted in Mesopotamian artwork, mostly as fearful, "loathsome" or "despicable" creatures but not infrequently as displaying virtue or a certain allure.[3] An almost idealized depiction of

---

[3] The modes and conventions in which foreigners were depicted in Mesopotamian artwork would be the topic of a very different paper (see discussions of this topic by Bahrani 2006 and Ciffareli 1998). Whereas foreigners often are shown as meek and cowardly some adversaries can also be shown as strong, honorable, and brave. In the reliefs from the Southwest Palace showing the battle of Til-Tuba between Assyria and Elam, for example, Tammaritu, son of Teʾumman, king of Elam, is shown as bravely defending his father—who in clear contrast is shown as running away, trying to save his life while asking his son to defend him (Patterson 1912–1913: pls. 63–64; captions: Novotny – Jeffers 2018: 314–317 [nos. 25–27]). In a different scene Urtaku, Teʾumman's in-law (*ḫatānu*), is shown on the ground and injured by an arrow, requesting from an Assyrian soldier to cut off his head—both indicated visually through a gesture of his hand at the neck, and also spelled out in a caption (Patterson 1912–1913: pl. 63; captions: Novotny – Jeffers 2018: 318–319 [no. 28]). Clearly the heroic nobility of this gesture was meant to be in stark contrast to the nearby depiction of Teʾumman's own unceremonious end, in which the king is shown face down on the ground while an Assyrian solder cuts off his head (Patterson 1912–1913: pls. 62–64; captions: Novotny – Jeffers 2018: 316). In some ways these scenes remind of earlier depictions from the Akkadian period, in which the strength and masculinity of captured or slain enemies was highlighted in reliefs on stelae (e.g. Strommenger 1962: figs. 114, 117, 118), as base decorations of statues (e.g., Amiet 1972: 105, fig. 7; 1976: 127, figs. 15 a–e) or in smaller scale sculpture (e.g., Amiet 1976: 130, figs. 44 a, b), perhaps in an effort to highlight the achievement of overcoming such strong enemies.

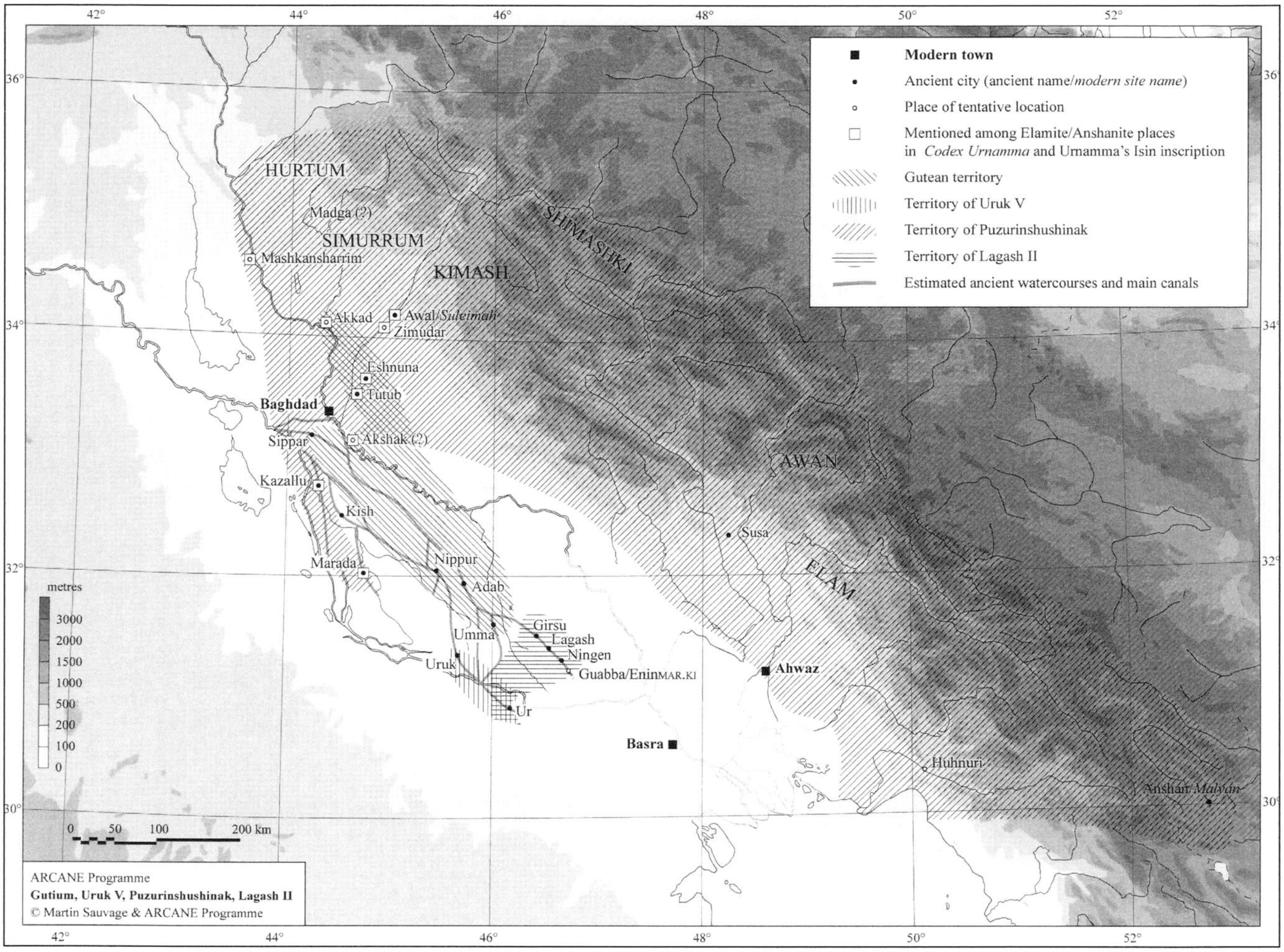

Fig. 1.
Map of the Akkadian State and the extent of the Gutian area of control (adapted from Sallaberger – Schrakamp 2015: 126 [Map 13]).

enemies or adversaries in certain visual narratives highlights the complexity and perhaps futility of making global statements about a Mesopotamian portrayal of foreigners.

There is no doubt, however, that in Mesopotamia's historical and social memory some groups fared worse than others, and few fared as badly as the Gutians (Fig. 1). In this discussion I will not in any way attempt a comprehensive review of the "Gutian period" in terms of historical events and chronological correlations.[4] Instead, I will show how the negative portrayal of the Gutians in Mesopotamia's historical and social memory impacted 20th century attempts to define a cultural setting for a group that was clearly seen as "inferior" or "barbarian".

[4] For a recent comprehensive historical overview see Sallaberger – Schrakamp 2015; also Steinkeller 2015, advocating for a longer Gutian period.

Undoubtedly the best-known Mesopotamian reference to the Gutians is of literary nature, the so-called "Curse of Agade".[5] With earliest copies dating to the Ur III period it represents a poetic, and times clearly non-historical propagandistic retrospective of how, and why, the Akkadian state came to an end. Once stripped of literary embellishments, however, the text reflects certain historical realities that both shed light on the rise of the Akkadian state but also on some of the internal problems that may have let to its ultimate demise.

The story of the "Curse", its historical context and ideological implications, have been while discussed by numerous scholars, so only some of the more seminal points of the story line will be summarized here.[6] The narrative opens with the rise of Agade under Sargon who, at the command of Enlil, established it as his capital city. The text relates its splendor, wealth and the lavish life that its citizens enjoyed. At the center of this successful rise is Inanna, Sargon's divine protagonist, who had set up her residence in É-Ulmaš, her temple at Agade. The text describes what appears to be a perfect symbiosis city and goddess, with Inanna working tirelessly to ensure that Agade's storehouses are filled with provisions, that its people are fed, enjoying celebrations and exotic animals. The presence of emissaries from distant areas such as Elam, Marḫaši, Meluḫḫa and Subartu, bringing precious goods to the city, reflect the extent of campaigns and military expeditions that were undertaken by Akkadian rulers.

By line 55 of the composition, however, the tone had changed. Flooded by lavish offerings that seemingly no longer could be accommodated, there was an urgent need to rebuild or enlarge Inanna's temple—but apparently no permission to do so could be obtained from É-kur in Nippur, whose word in this matter was "like silence" / "disquieting" (l. 57).[7] This latter tidbit of information is notable since it not only indicates that authorization for such temple construction was needed from the highest entity of Mesopotamia's pantheon , but it also seems to reflect misgivings about the fact that this lavish flow of goods that now went to Agade seemingly bypassed other temples, including É-kur.[8] The lack of a building

---

[5] Unless references to terms in the Sumerian text are relevant I will refer to the text translation as provided by the Electronic Text Corpus of Sumerian Literature (ETCSL; http://etcsl.orinst.ox.ac.uk/cgi-bin/etcsl.cgi?text=c.2.1*#; "The cursing of Agade", accessed on August 8, 2019), with occasional borrowings from Cooper's earlier edition where his translation seems to be more appropriate (Cooper 1983). For ease of quotation I have avoided any reference to variant versions of the text.

[6] More prominently, see Falkenstein 1965; Cooper 1983; Glassner 1986; Westenholz 1999.

[7] inim é-kur-ra me-gin$_7$ ba-an-ĝar "The word from Ekur was as silence (Cooper 1983)"; "But the statement coming from the É-kur was disquieting (ETCSL)". Another reference to unsuccessful attempts to seek approval for the temple construction is made later on in the text, making it clear that this word was sought through extispicy: ".... Then he [Narām-Sîn] went to perform extispicy on a kid regarding the temple, but the omen had nothing to say about the building of the temple. For a second time he went to perform extispicy on a kid regarding the temple, but the omen again had nothing to say about the building of the temple. In order to change what had been inflicted (?) upon him, he tried to alter Enlil's pronouncement" (ll. 94–99).

[8] The apparent economic tensions reflected here remind of the "Great Rebellion" against Narām-Sîn towards the beginning of his reign, which is referenced in numerous inscriptions of Narām-Sîn and described in a stela inscription preserved on an Old Babylonian *Sammeltafel* (Kutscher 1989: 13–34, 118 and pl. 1; Frayne 1993: 103–108 [E2.1.4.6]), as well as in "The Great Insurrection against Naram-sin", an Old Babylonian literary composition that reprises the theme of this rebellion (Grayson and Sollberger 1976; see discussions in Frayne 1993: 84–85; Westenholz 1999: 51–54; Tinney 1995).

permission not only caused Inanna to abandon the city (ll. 57–65) but also the other gods to withdraw their divine gifts and decrees (ll. 66–76). Before long, Agade's economic, social and cultic life was brought to a standstill prompting Narām-Sîn, who saw the impending doom that was to overcome Agade in a dream, to fall into a deep seven year-long depression.[9] After repeated further attempts to seek permission for the temple construction Narām-Sîn finally resorted to ultimate measures by mustering his troops and marching towards É-kur. The text describes the attack in graphic detail (ll. 100–148), leaving no doubt that this was planned as a willful, intentional destruction for which tools were specifically cast, followed by extensive looting.[10] Beyond that, Narām-Sîn's actions clearly seemed to be set on intentionally committing any sacrilege that is thinkable, highlighting what can only be seen as an act of revenge for the pain and humiliation that he had received through É-kur's non-compliance with his wish to rebuilt É-Ulmaš.[11] The pyrrhic nature of this campaign and the implied loss of moral and ethical standing following this act of violence is hinted at in ll. 146–148: "With the possessions being taken away from the city, good sense left Agade. As the ships moved away from the docks, Agade's intelligence was removed".

Enlil's ire and desire for revenge following the devastation of his religious homestead is graphically described in the subsequent lines.[12] It is at this point that for the first time we are being introduced to the avengers of Enlil's wrath:

> "He lifted his gaze towards the Gubin mountains, and made all the inhabitants of the broad mountain ranges descend (?). Enlil brought out of the mountains those who do not resemble other people, who are not reckoned as part of the Land, the Gutians, an unbridled people, with human intelligence but canine instincts and monkeys' features. Like small birds they swooped on the ground in great flocks. Because of Enlil, they stretched their arms out across the plain like a net for animals. Nothing escaped their clutches, no one left their grasp." (ll. 152–160).

[9] "Because of the É-kur, he put on mourning clothes, covered his chariot with a reed mat, tore the reed canopy off his ceremonial barge and gave away his royal paraphernalia. Naram-Suen persisted for seven years! Who has ever seen a king burying his head in his hands for seven years?" (ll. 88–93).

[10] "....although the temple was not the Mountains of Cedar-felling, he had large axes cast, he had double-edged *agasilig* axes sharpened to be used against it." (ll. 112–114).

[11] "From its Gate from which Grain is never Diverted, he diverted grain, and the Land was deprived of grain. He struck the Gate of Well-Being with the pickaxe, and well-being was subverted in all the foreign lands. As if they were for great tracts of land with wide carp-filled waters, he cast large spades to be used against the É-kur. The people could see the bedchamber, its room which knows no daylight. The Akkadians could look into the holy treasure chest of the gods. Though they had committed no sacrilege, its *laḫama* deities of the great pilasters standing at the temple were thrown into the fire by Naram-Suen." (ll. 123–133).

[12] "Enlil, the roaring storm that subjugates the entire land, the rising deluge that cannot be confronted, was considering what should be destroyed in return for the wrecking of his beloved É-kur." (ll. 149–151).

The narrative goes on to describe the ravage and devastation across the land[13] caused by these invaders, resulting in everything from lack of public safety, a breakdown of the agricultural system and of urban life, inflation (ll. 162–192), and the establishment of a temporary reed sanctuary at Agade where Enlil entered his bedchamber and laid down fasting. (ll. 193–203). Feeling the pressure from the devastations caused by the Gutian invasions in and around their own cities, the Great Gods (Sîn, Enki, Inanna, Ninurta, Iškur, Utu, Nuska, and Nisaba are named) came around to curse Agade the implied perpetrator that caused their misery (ll. 222–281). Many of the hardships and devastations implied in this curse mirror what the rest of the land has already suffered from the hands of the Gutians. With the phrase "Agade is destroyed—Inanna be praised" the composition closes, suggesting that "justice", on a moral level, had been served, Enlil's anger had been appeased so that an orderly life (in a post-Akkadian world) could go on.

The graphic description of the Gutians in this composition goes beyond any implications of "barbarism" or lack of civilization. To a modern reader the use of animal attributes, notably "canine intelligence" and "monkey-like features",[14] has to evoke notions of extreme racism. It should not surprise, therefore, that during the earlier part of the 20th century, when racial theories still abounded in scholarly worlds on both the ancient and modern the Gutians did not fare well in anthological write-ups of the Ancient Near East. Ironically, those write-ups themselves often were innovative for their time by recognizing the fact that many of modern civilization's greatest achievements did not originate in Greece or Rome, but in fact were invented in the ancient Near East—notably Gordon Childe's "New Light of the Most Ancient Near East" (Childe 1969), which examines the pivotal role of Mesopotamian societies on their way towards urbanism. Alluvial Mesopotamia, with its irrigation agriculture, was seen as a threshold towards urban civilization, whereas "foreign" influences—notably from nearby mountainous regions—were often seen more as disruptors than as a potentially positive impetus. The summary of the Gutian period by Anton Moortgat, published in 1950 in "Ägypten und

---

13 The fact that the text makes references to cities in the land, and in two instances specifically mentions Nippur ("The Gutians drove the trusty (?) goats of Enlil out of their folds .... [ll. 164–165]. "By the Ki᾿ur, Enlil's great place, dogs were packed together ... ." [ll. 184]), is certainly no coincidence. The implication is that "the land" (kalam) is being ravaged by the Gutians whereas Agade itself remains unscathed. While this might indeed reflect a historic reality—the Gutians bypassing the Akkadian homeland and focusing on Sumer instead—the implication here is an intentional divinely ordained "third party punishment": by having the rest of the country suffering the consequences of Enlil's anger over the looting of his sanctuary, the other cities of Sumer and their deities were supposed to develop the same kind of animosity against the capital city. The notion that this supposed "plan" worked is expressed by the fact that the great gods of the land caved in to pressure and cursed Agade.

14 Although not native to the area monkeys were known in ancient early Mesopotamia, imported either from India or East Africa. A figurine from Ishchali, made of amber and dating to the Old Babylonian period, represents a monkey, most likely a baboon (Hill – Jacobsen – Delougaz 1988: pls. 40 e, f). Monkeys are frequently shown on terracotta reliefs, occasionally sitting on a person's back (e.g., Parrot 1961: 292, fig. 359c; Mendelson 1983: pl. 24a; Collon 2003: 99) and cylinder seals (Collon 1987: 187–190). For the Sumerian term for monkey see Klein 1979.

Vorderasien im Altertum", reflects a typical example of elevating achievements of Mesopotamian civilization by contrasting it with the "barbarism" of surrounding populations:

> "None of the many invasions from the north, west and east that Mesopotamia had to endure were quite as associated with the terror of barbarism as the Gutian invasion, one of the semi-wild tribes that—just like the Lullubi had their home in the Zagros mountains, in the area of today's Luristan. 'The Dragons of the Mountains,' as they were referred to in a later text written by those who ousted them, 'who robbed the husband his wife, the children from their parents, and who abducted the kingdom of Sumer off to the mountains." Later generations remembered them as pillagers and defilers of temples (Tempelschänder). ...... For about one century they were able to seize control of the land. Their kings wrote Akkadian and called themselves 'king of Guti,' or 'king of Guti and the Four World Quarters,' indicting their desire to follow in the footsteps of the Akkadian rulers. [.....] We know virtually nothing about the language, ethnic origin or other cultural achievements of these people. [......] Archaeological sources for the Gutian period are even more scant than written sources. Several stylistically completely rotten cylinder seals which reverted from the plasticity of the Akkadian glyptic back to linearity and which, in terms of their narrative, are completely unrewarding, were declared to be Gutian seals."[15]

It would be easy to dismiss Moortgat's work, which by using of terms like "Volkgemeinschaft" inevitably recalls political and social concepts propagated by Nazi ideologists, as ideologically tainted. But Moortgat was by no means alone and in fact, reflected comments and assessments that predated his own scholarly career and the political developments of Germany in the 1930s and 1940s. In his book "The Sumerians", originally published in 1928, Leonard Woolley, for example, likened the Gutian invasion into Mesopotamia to natural disasters and cataclysmic events:

---

[15] "Keiner unter den vielen Invasionen, die das Zweistromland zu erdulden gehabt hat von Nord, West und Ost, haftet so der Schrecken des Barbarentums an wie dem Einfall der Guti, eines der halbwilden Stämme, die wie die Lullubi ihre Heimat im Zagrosgebirge hatten, etwa im heutigen Luristan. 'Die Drachen des Gebirges,' so heißt es über sie etwas später in einem Texte ihrer Besieger, 'die dem Gatten die Gattin, den Eltern die Kinder geraubt, das Königtum von Sumer in die Berge geschleppt haben.' Als Plünderer und Tempelschänder stehen sie im Gedächtnis der Nachkommen. [....] Auf ein Jahrhundert etwa konnten die Fremdlinge die Herrschaft im Lande an sich reißen. Ihre Könige schreiben akkadisch und nennen sich 'König der Guti,' aber auch 'König der Guti und der vier Weltteile,' womit sie die Nachfolge der akkadischen Weltherrscher beanspruchen. [....] Über Sprache, Volksverwandtschaft, politische Organisation und sonstigen kulturellen Stand dieses Volkes wissen wir so gut wie nichts. [....] Die archäologischen Quellen fließen für die Guti-Zeit noch dürftiger als die schriftlichen. Einige im Stil völlig verrottete Rollsiegel, bei denen die starke Plastik der Formen, die die akkadische Glyptik auszeichnete, wieder in Lineares umgesetzt wird und die inhaltlich völlig unergiebig sind, hat man für Guti-Siegel erklärt" (Moorgat 1950: 270).

> "In the reign of Shargalisharri, Naram-Sin's successor, fresh troubles broke out in the north and east and twice there are references to wars with Gutium wherein no victory was claimed. After his time the storm burst in earnest, the Guti invaded the river-land, and the empire built up by Sargon's house crumbled ignominiously: a feeble line of kings maintained a purely local rule at Agade, Erech for a time boasted an independence confined to narrow limits, but the country as a whole was overrun by the northern barbarians 'who knew not kingship'. And the Sumerian scribes wrote in their dynastic lists after the name of Shargalisharri the despairing note 'Who was king, and who was not king?' A period of complete anarchy seems to have followed the invasion, and there are no records to fill the historical gap; but in time the Guti set up kings of their own whose control, however exercised, did certainly extend over the whole delta." (Woolley 1965: 83).

Similar to Moortgat, Woolley went on to contrast the perceived ephemeral nature of the Gutian culture with the resilience of Sumer, highlighting the conquerors' need to assimilate in order to survive:

> "It is to the credit of the Sumerian civilization that it survived the disaster which put an end to the political organization of the country. Doubtless Akkad, which bore the first brunt of the Guti invasion, suffered most material damage, but Sumer also must have been completely devastated by 'the pest.' The temple hymns bewail the violation wrought by the Guti in the shrines of Nippur, Adab, Erech and Kesh and if the accident of time has preserved no records dealing with the destruction of other Sumerian cities the silence if none the less eloquent; during the Guti period of 125 years business documents and works of art are alike lacking. Yet of Sumer too it might be said that capta ferum victorem cepit, and before long the Guti kings were dedicating their offerings in the temples of the Sumerian gods which the first invaders had despoiled, Sumerians were installed as patesis or governors in the cities—the Guti, one must suppose, were ill equipped for such complicated administrative posts, and the foreign trade on which the country so absolutely depended recovered its old important and extension. As the conquerors assimilated, or were assimilated by, Sumerian civilization, the city-states were allowed to regain no small measure of autonomy; the excavations at Lagash have shown what prosperity might be enjoyed by one of them under a line of active native rulers toward the close of the Guti period." (Woolley 1965: 84–85).

A very similar disdain can be discerned in Henri Frankfort's writing, who in his book "The Art and Architecture of the Ancient Near East" (originally published in 1954) stated that:

> ".... the Akkadian dynasty was overthrown by the Guti, wild mountaineers from the north-east who contributed nothing to the civilization of the plain which they ransacked" (Frankfort 1996: 95).

As mentioned earlier, these assessments need to be seen in the context of scholarly views of the early 20th century that themselves were evolving. The rediscovery of ancient Mesopotamia during the 19th century, the fascination that the monuments and documents of Babylon, Assyria and Sumer created in the scholarly and public audiences, fundamentally challenged notions that most of civilization's greater achievements originated in Greece and Rome. "Ex orient lux" was clearly manifested in V. Gordon Childe's work. With new excavations in Iraq throughout the 1920s, at sites like Ur, Uruk, Ubaid, Kish, and Girsu Mesopotamia firmly established its position as a "Cradle of Civilization". It is easily imaginable that an invasion from outside into this "apex of civilization" could only have been seen as disruptive, with its protagonists viewed as "inferior" or "barbarian".

Other textual sources from the Akkadian and post-Akkadian period, whether historical or historiographic, by contrast, do not necessarily portray the Gutian period as a time of chaos.[16] In the Sumerian King List, the transfer of the kingship to Gutium following the defeat of the preceding Second Dynasty of Uruk indicates that the fundamental legitimacy of this process was not questioned. The characterization of the beginning of the Gutian dynasty: "at first no king was famous; they were their own kings and ruled thus for 3 years" (ugnim gu-tu-um^{ki} lugal mu nu-tuku ni$_2$-ta-a lugal-am$_3$ mu 3 i$_3$-ak; ll. 308–309), does seem to indicate a less rigid political structure, with the term "king" being attributed here to what could be more adequately called a tribal leader. The narrative does not reflect the same level of confusion expressed earlier (ll. 284–285) concerning the legitimacy of succession for the time after Šarkališarri in the late Late Akkadian period: "Then who was the king? Who was not the king? Irgigi was king, Imi was king, Nanûm was king, Ilulu was king, and the four of them ruled for only three years". The listing of 21 king for the Gutian dynasty, often with very short reigns over a period of 125 years, however, seems to indicate either political instability with very rapid non-dynastic successions or at least co-regencies of several of these "kings". The numerous differences in names and numbers of regnal years between variants of the King List make it clear that it cannot be seen as a reliable historical source.[17]

---

[16] "In the army (var. land) of Gutium, at first no king was famous; they were their own kings and ruled thus for 3 years. Then Inkišuš ruled for 6 years. Zarlagab ruled for 6 years. Šulme ruled for 6 years. Silulumeš ruled for 6 years. Inimabakeš ruled for 5 years. Igešauš ruled for 6 years. Yarlagab ruled for 15 years. Ibate ruled for 3 years. Yarla ruled for 3 years. Kurum ruled for 1 years. Apilkin ruled for 3 years. Lā-erabum (?) ruled for 2 years. Irarum ruled for 2 years. Ibranum ruled for 1 year. Ḫablum ruled for 2 years. Puzur-Suen, the son of Ḫablum, ruled for 7 years. Yarlaganda ruled for 7 years. ...... ruled for 7 years. Tirigan (?) ruled for 40 days. 21 kings; they ruled for 124 years and 40 days. Then the army of Gutium was defeated and the kingship was taken to Uruk" (ETCSL ll. 308–334; http://etcsl.orinst.ox.ac.uk/cgi-bin/etcsl.cgi?text=t.2.1.1#).

[17] In the words of P. Michalowski, " ... one thing is clear; there is absolutely no reason to trust the data contained in the Kinglist. The unreliable nature of the early sections of the text may be most dramatically demonstrated in the case of the Dynasty of Gutium. It is well-known that almost everything we know of that 'dynasty' comes from the King List. (...) Suffice it to say that of the four known manuscripts which preserve this section, no two agree on the names, order, regnal years, or number of the Gutian Kings." (Michalowski 1983: 239–240).

I will refrain from a comprehensive review of the available historical data, which has been undertaken recently and comprehensively by Sallaberger and Schrakamp, and simply highlight a few points that are seminal for the remainder of this study (Sallaberger – Schrakamp 2015). The feasibility of a stand-alone 125 year-long Gutian period between the end of the Akkadian period and the beginning of the Ur III period has long been questioned by scholars based on the absence of historical sources as well as royal inscriptions to fill such a time frame. Only seven Gutian kings / rulers are attested in contemporary sources—either through their own inscriptions or through external references—but only five of them can be somewhat convincingly matched up with names in the Sumerian King List (Sallaberger – Schrakamp 2015: 127–129). Hallo's fundamental article on "Gutium" in the *Reallexikon der Assyriologie und vorderasiatischen Archäologie* shortened the length of the time between the last year of Šarkališarri of Agade and the first year of Ur-Namma of Ur Ill to 40 years (Hallo 1957–1971), a conclusion that—in spite of cautionary remarks that remain necessary in light of Steinkeller's reconstruction of a 100-year-long Gutian period (Steinkeller 2015)—remains reasonably well corroborated by Sallaberger and Schrakamp's study.[18]

As the latter two authors point out, a shorter independent Gutian period with its beginning and end embedded in the later Akkadian and the Lagash II periods respectively tends to be well received by the archaeological community.[19] No site in the south so far, unfortunately, has so far seen the level of detailed excavations of late third millennium BC remains that would allow us to conclusively draw convincing borderlines between late Akkadian, post-Akkadian and early Ur III assemblages. The levels of devastation mentioned in the Curse of Agade cannot be identified on major Mesopotamian sites, whether at Ur, Uruk, or Nippur,[20] sometimes due to the fact that Ur III reconstructions of major sanctuaries have obliterated many of the remains from the preceding Akkadian period, but quite often simply due to limited resolution in stratigraphic observations during late 19th and early 20th century excavations.

---

18 "Although no convincing arguments can be found to sustain the extreme chronologies of 40 years (Hallo) and 100 years (Steinkeller) respectively, these extreme values cannot be excluded. Our own deliberations came up with an estimate of ca. 80 years for the Gutean period. So long as only provisional solutions for a historical chronology can be proposed, we suggest accepting a mean value of 70 years (+/- 10 years according to our most plausible estimate or +/- 30 years regarding the extreme values) for the Gutean period; this should allow future adjustments of the chronology without major difficulties" (Sallaberger – Schrakamp 2015: 130).

19 Note that the summary on "Mesopotamia" in *Chronologies of Old World Archaeologies* has no section on the Gutian period at all, only a passing reference that links late third millennium BC destructions at Tell Asmar in the Diyala region and at Tell Taya in Northern Iraq, without citing supporting evidence, to activities by "Guti tribes" (Porada – Hansen – Dunham 1992: 116–117).

20 Unfortunately, the relevant excavations of the É-kur at Nippur were largely undertaken in the late 19th century and simply were too unsystematic to be useful to address questions of relative chronology in material culture. The uncritical use of textual sources (notably brick and votive inscriptions) when dating archaeological features was further complicated by a mix-up of Sargon (Šarru-kīn) with Šarkališarri, whose name was misinterpreted at (*šar-ga-ni-šar-ali*(URU) "Sargon, king of the town", making many chronological observations obsolete (e.g, Hilprecht 1903: 517).

In spite of this dearth of archaeological data, occasional references to Gutian material culture can be found throughout 20th century scholarly literature (see, for example, the passage from Moortgat 1950 quoted above). Such associations largely seem to originate in stratigraphic and cultural attributions made by Henri Frankfort, based on his excavation work in the Diyala region on behalf of the University of Chicago's Oriental Institute. Undertaken between 1931 and 1939, these excavations were groundbreaking in establishing a chronology of material culture for Mesopotamia's early history from the late Uruk Period to the Late Old Babylonian period. Unlike many other archeological expeditions to major sites, the Diyala excavations were conceived to be systematic and stratigraphic with a complete recovery of associated archaeological materials, ranging from prestige items to items of daily life, including sculpture, seals, stone vessels, pottery, jewelry, stone tools, and any kinds of implements. Five publications on architecture (Frankfort – Lloyd – Jacobsen 1940; Delougaz 1940; Delougaz – Lloyd 1942; Delougaz – Hill – Lloyd 1967; Hill – Jacobsen – Delougaz 1988) and four on principal artifact classes (Frankfort 1939; 1943; 1955; Delougaz 1952), which remain the backbone of most chronological schemata for early Mesopotamia, give testimony to the fact that this objective was achieved to a large degree. Nonetheless, one has to recognize that on numerous occasions Frankfort to avoid the pitfalls of preemptive interpretations. The uncritical use of textual sources in dating archaeological levels often makes objective chronological reinterpretations difficult.[21] At the site of Tell Asmar (Fig. 2), Frankfort not only identified a post-Akkadian occupation level but also several artifacts from it as "Gutian":

> "We are fortunate in being able for the first time to designate certain seals as products of the barbaric Guti, who overran Mesopotamia during the concluding reigns of the Sargonid dynasty and terrorized and dominated the country for nearly a century. Certain seals executed in a vigorous linear style were found in Houses III at Tell Asmar. This layer lies between an Akkadian stratum and one dated to the Third Dynasty of Ur by the tablets found therein. Since the Akkadian layer contained seal impressions bearing the name of Shudurul, the last king of Agade, our Houses III must be assigned to the Guti period. Most of the seals found there are of Sargonid manufacture or, at least, maintain the Akkadian tradition without modification ... . Three seals, however (Nos. 689-91), though clearly rendering subjects known in Akkadian times, do so in a manner for which there is no parallel in certified Akkadian seals. Normally we would consider them peripheral seals- seals made somewhere on the periphery of Mesopotamia during Akkadian times. Since they were found at Tell Asmar, however, among the remains of a period in which people from the periphery occupied the plain of the Two Rivers, it is the foreign origin of their makers rather than a foreign center of manufacture which accounts for their pe-

[21] This problem is particularly pertinent in the publication of the Palace of the Rulers (Frankfort – Lloyd – Jacobsen 1940) where ruler names and labels such as "Ur III" and "post Ur III" were adopted already during excavation and often turned out to have been assigned prematurely; see my forthcoming republication of this building complex (Reichel, n.d).

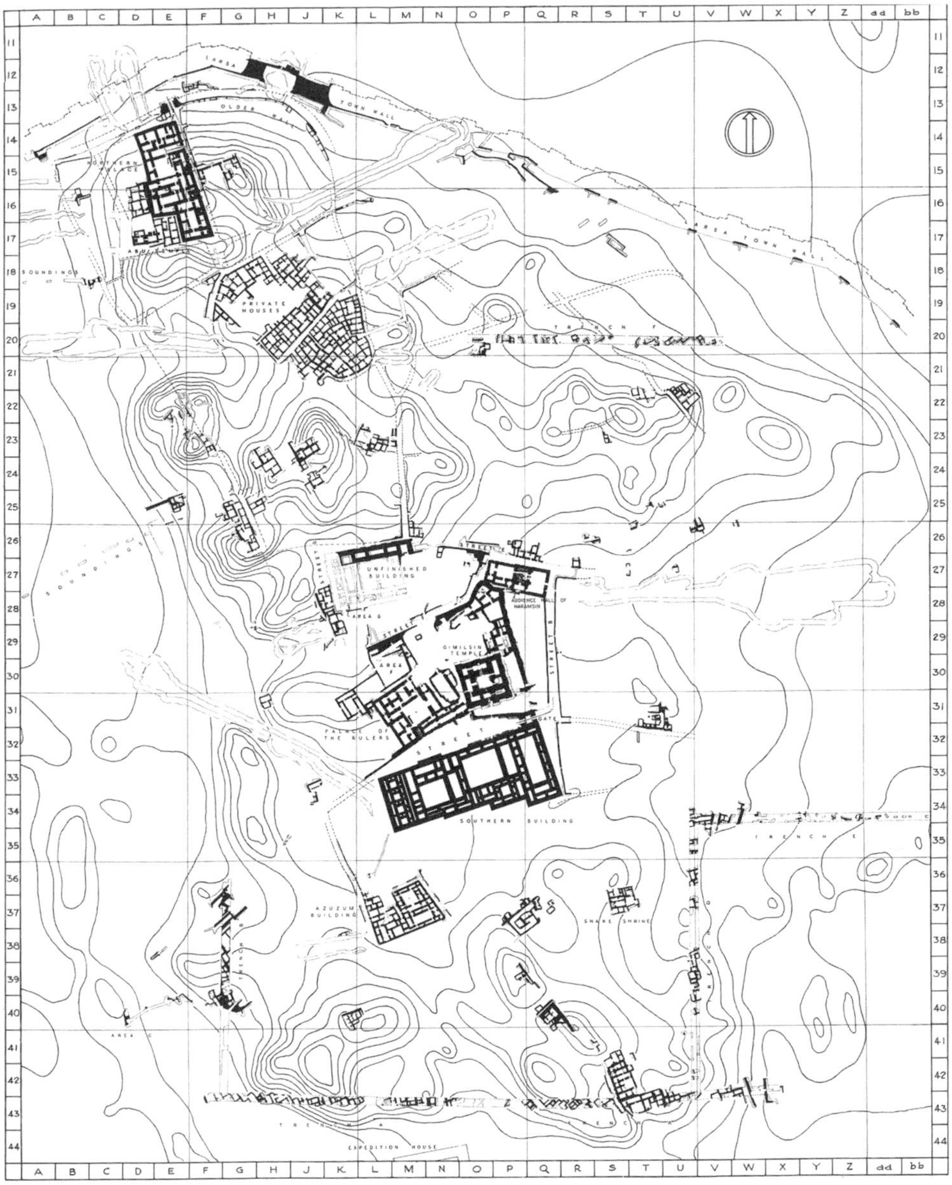

Fig. 2.
Map of Tell Asmar (Delougaz – Hill – Lloyd 1967: pl. 23).

culiarities. Other seals, like Nos. 676-77, may be Guti seals or merely Akkadian seals simplified in a manner which became popular in Guti times" (Frankfort 1955: 33).

It is impossible to address Frankfort's conclusions without first reviewing the archaeological sequence from which these seals were recovered. The so-called "Houses" Area (Figs. 3, 4), where these seals were found, is located in the central / eastern part of the third millennium city of Tell Asmar. The stratigraphic overview published in the volume on private houses and graves indeed assigns "Houses III" to the end of the Gutian period:

Tab. 1.

Houses at Tell Asmar: stratigraphic sequence and suggested dates (after Delougaz – Hill – Lloyd 1967: Table III).

Houses:	Dates:
I	Isin-Larsa
II	Ur III
III	End of Gutium
IVa	Late Akkadian
IVb	Early Akkadian
Va	"Proto-Imperial"
Vb	Early Dynastic IIIb
Vc	

Fig. 3.

Tell Asmar: plan of Houses IVa ("Late Akkadian"); findspot of sealing with seal of Šu-Turul's servant is marked (adapted from Delougaz – Hill – Lloyd 1967: fig. 28).

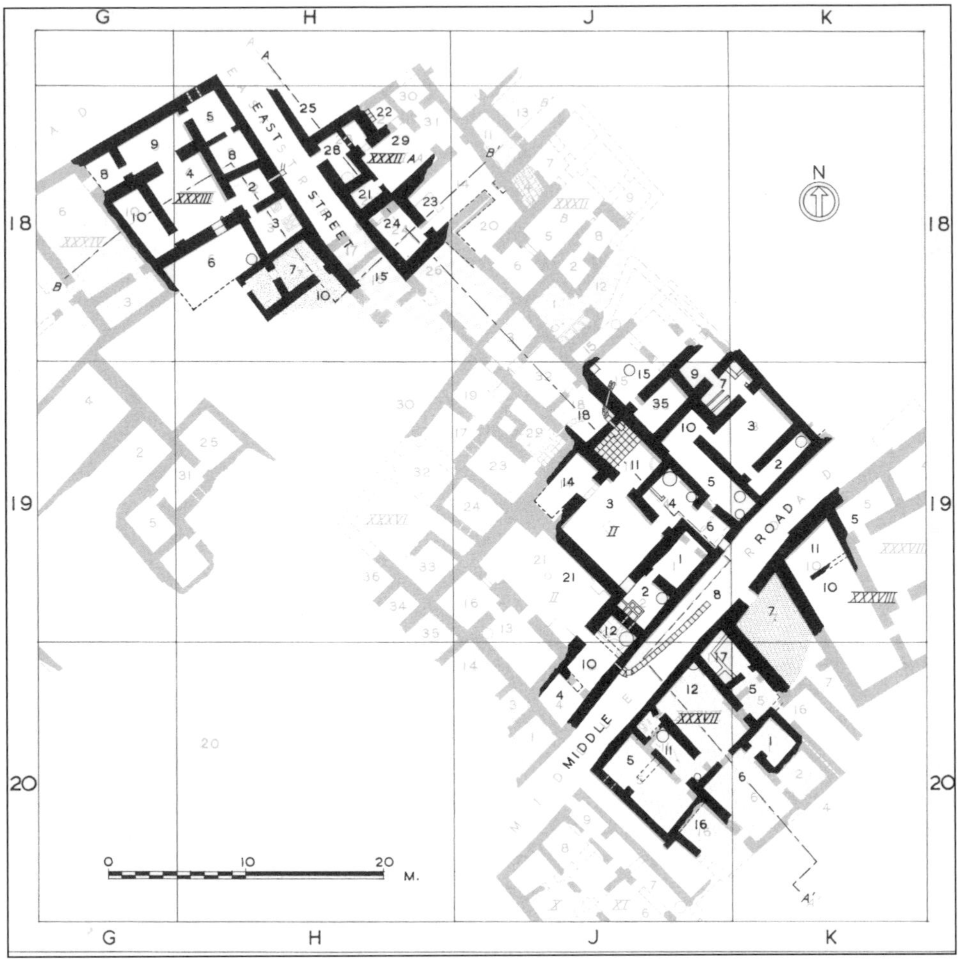

Fig. 4.
Tell Asmar: plan of Houses III ("end of Gutium") with plan of underlying Houses IVa added to sow architectural continuity (adapted from Delougaz – Hill – Lloyd 1967: fig. 29).

As Frankfort had pointed out, a sealing[22] bearing the name of an official of Šu-Turul, the last king of the Akkadian Dynasty (Fig. 5), was found in association with Houses IVa, the level below Houses III, which supports a post-Akkadian date for Houses III—but does it support an association with the "end of Gutium"?

22 Frankfort 1955: no 701 (labelled "As. 31:627"). The published drawing actually is based on three sealing fragments (now catalogued as As. 31:T.671a-c). The largest fragment upon which the drawing was based (As. 31:T.671a) was actually found on a debris dump but can be traced back with some certainty locus H18:7 to Houses IVa, where a smaller sealing fragment bearing the same impression was found a few days later (see Hill – Lloyd – Delougaz 1967: 144, n. 3). The inscription reads:

1. *šu-túr-ùl*	Šu-Turul
2. *da-núm*	the mighty one,
3. lugal	king
4. *a-ga-dè*^{ki}	of Agade
5. [ ]-maḫ	[ ]-maḫ
6. [? ?]	[son of ...?]
7. [ir$_{11}$-*sú*]	[is his servant]

Frayne 1993: 215–216 (E2.1.11 [2002])

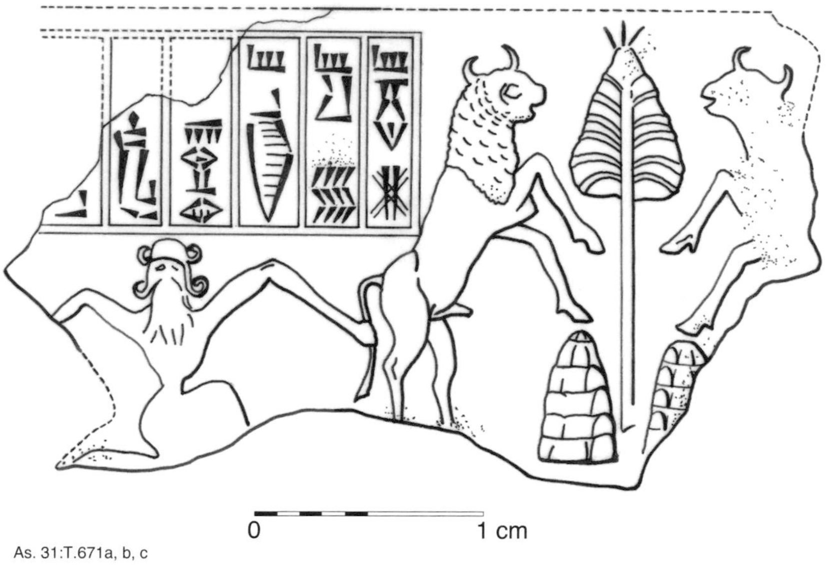

Fig. 5.
Seal of Šu-Turul (unpublished drawing; Diyala Project, Oriental Institute, University of Chicago).

The fact that the name of the last Akkadian king is attested on a sealing from Houses IVa, in fact, strongly suggests that the Diyala region, or at least Tell Asmar, did *not* fall in Gutian control. While it is certainly possible that it fell under Gutian control after the Šu-Turul's reign there is no compelling argument in favor of such an assumption. There is strong architectural continuity between Houses IVa and III, and no evidence of any destruction or other evidence of conquest (Figs. 3, 4). More to the point, the ceramic assemblage associated with Houses III bears several shapes that are already clearly associated with the Ur III period (Fig. 6).[23]

Let us now turn towards the so-called "Gutian seals" from Tell Asmar. Three seals were from Houses III were identified by Frankfort as "Gutian" (Fig. 7) while three more from Houses IVa were tentatively labeled "Gutian?" (Fig. 8). Since only eight seals could be firmly assigned to Houses III (eliminating surface finds and clear heirlooms) it is possible to review their overall assemblage to put Frankfort's cultural assignments into better context. Four of these seals can be dated as Akkadian on stylistic grounds: a beer-drinking scene (As. 31:602 = Frankfort 1955: no. 687 = Boehmer 1965: no. 1617 [fig. 681]),[24] two combat scenes (As. 32:55 = Frankfort 1955: no. 685 = Boehmer 1965: no. 867; As. 31:639 = Frankfort 1955: no. 686 = Boehmer 1965: no. 777 [fig. 267]), and a heraldic scene with two bulls and alternating trees (As. 32:521). The three seals identified as "Gutian" (As. 32:250, As. 32:226, As. 33: 317 = Frankfort 1955: nos. 689–691), on the

[23] The typology numbers given here follow Delougaz 1952. For parallels from Nippur (and other sites) for B.151.210 see McCown – Haines 1967: pl. 82.18–21 (examples from TB IX-II = Ur III – early Isin-Larsa); for B.061.210 see *ibid.* pl. 83.2–3 (examples from TB VIII – VI = Ur III).

[24] Boehmer dates one of these seals to "Akkadisch I b, c" (As. 32:55) and two others to "Akkadisch III (As. 31:602; As. 31:639), which would make all of them heirlooms in Houses III. It is, however, possible that Akkadian stylistic tradition in the lower Diyala region lasted longer than in Sumero-Akkadian realm of Southern Mesopotamia.

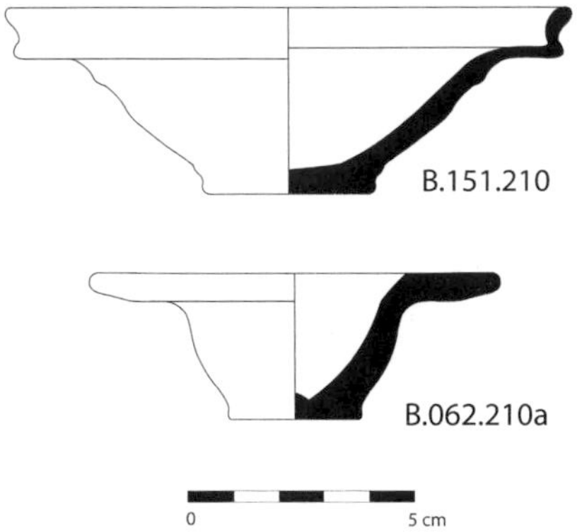

Fig. 6.
Key Ur III ceramic types from Houses III (redrawn from Delougaz 1952: pls. 148, 150).

other hand, show presentations scenes before deities. While originating in the Akkadian period, the theme of the presentation scene becomes dominant in the Ur III period. Two of them (As 32:250 and As. 33:317), in fact seem to show the introduction of a petitioner by a female suppliant ("Lamma") goddess, which becomes a standard scene from the early Ur III period onwards.[25] Iconographically speaking, there is no compelling reason to see them as anything but early Ur III seals. What Frankfort considers ".... a vigorous linear style" may be indicative of ".... peripheral seals" but there is no compelling reason to associate them culturally with the Gutians.

The three seals from Houses IVa that Frankfort had labeled as "Gutian?" are difficult to classify as one group (Fig. 8). Two of them (As. 32:249, As. 32:201 = Frankfort 1955: nos. 676, 677) are indeed executed in a more linear fashion, but so are other seals from the Diyala excavations that Frankfort had classified as "Akkadian" (e.g., Kh. II 45 and As. 32:1230 = Frankfort 1955: nos. 438, 640); Ur III seals that were executed in a very linear fashion also show up on southern Mesopotamian sites.[26] As. 32:201 shows a presentation scene before a god with a saw (the Mesopotamian sun god), for which there are numerous parallels in the Akkadian period and thereafter.[27] The scene on As. 32:201 showing two walking men driving a goat, remind of similar depictions on seals dating the Isin-Larsa and Old Babylonian period from Tell Asmar and elsewhere.[28] As. 32:1370, a fragmentary seal showing two seated figures back to back (albeit at different scales) and a divine attendant with a bucket, seems unusual in terms of the

[25] For typologies and chronological prevalence of presentation scenes see Franke 1977; Winter 1986; Haussperger 1991.

[26] An example for a provenanced Ur III seal executed in a linear fashion would be VA5969, a marble seal from Uruk, which shows a presentation scene with a seated deity holding a cup, to whom a petitioner is introduced by a suppliant goddess (Moortgat 1940: no. 318). Similarly also Buchanan 1981: no. 701 (unprovenanced, late Ur III) with comment regarding "linear" style.

[27] See Boehmer 1965: figs. 426, 437, 438, 464, 465 for comparable simpler renderings of the sun god facing a petitioner, dating to Akkadian III.

[28] E.g., seal As. 31:42 (Frankfort 1955: no. 741) from the Palace of the Rulers; see also my forthcoming discussion on the seals of Ašubliel in Reichel n.d. Also, Porada 1948: nos. 552, 553.

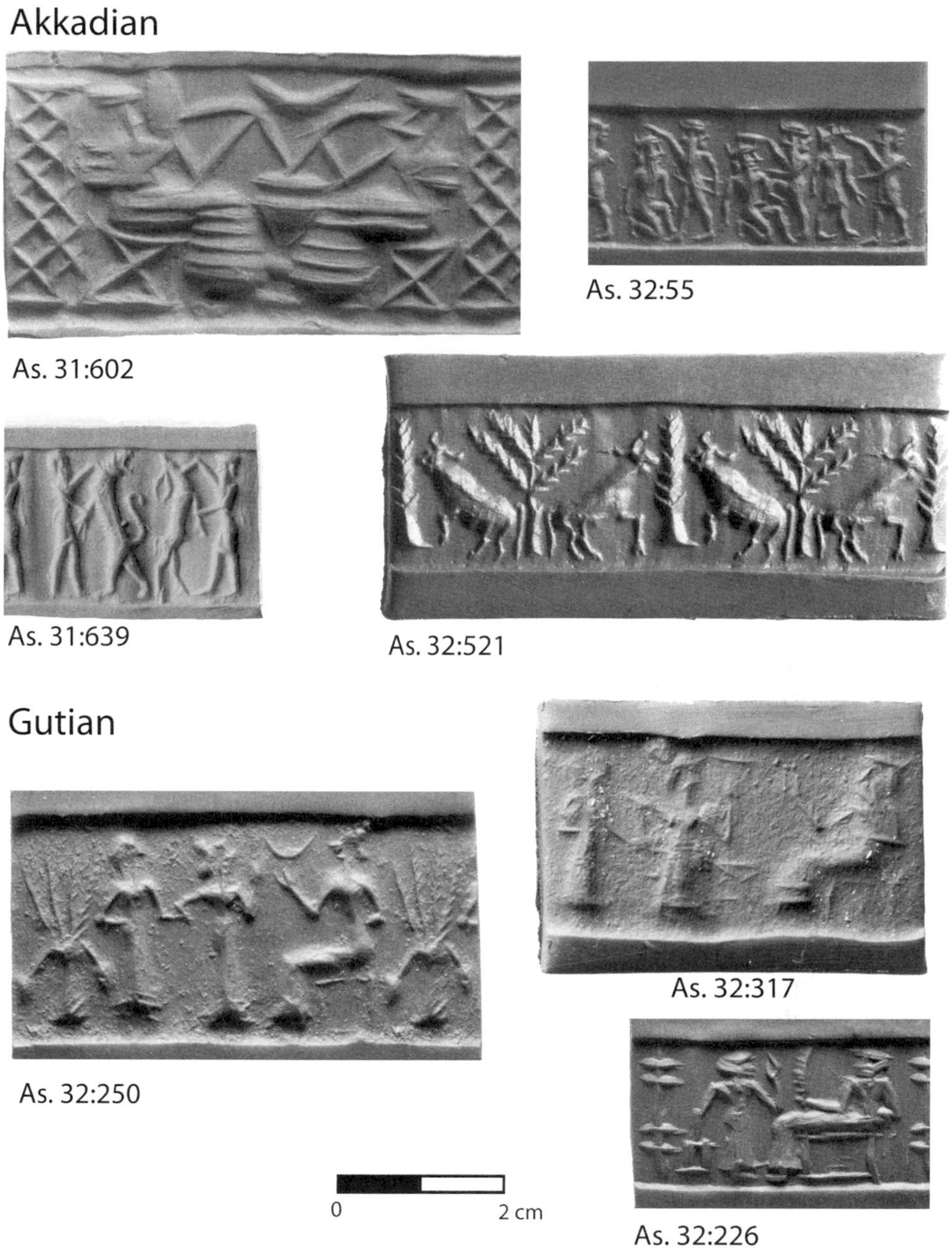

Fig. 7.
Seal assemblage from Houses III ("end of Gutium"). Upper part: seals labeled "Akkadian" by Frankfort (1955). Lower Part: seals labeled "Gutian" by Frankfort (1955).

renderings of garments and facial features. In his discussion of seals of "coarse workmanship" Frankfort includes this seal among his list of later examples of ".... seals (that) stand out for what they are—amateurish or popular products outside glyptic traditions altogether" (Frankfort 1955: 8). While the derogatory tone of this description can be rightfully criticized it also reflects a more widely accepted explanation for varying artistic qualities in seal design (or any prestige artifact, for that matter), i.e., a direct relationship between the quality of artwork

As. 32:201

As. 32:249

As. 32:1370

0 2 cm

Fig. 8.
Seals from Houses IVa (Late Akkadian) labeled "Gutian?" by Frankfort (1955).

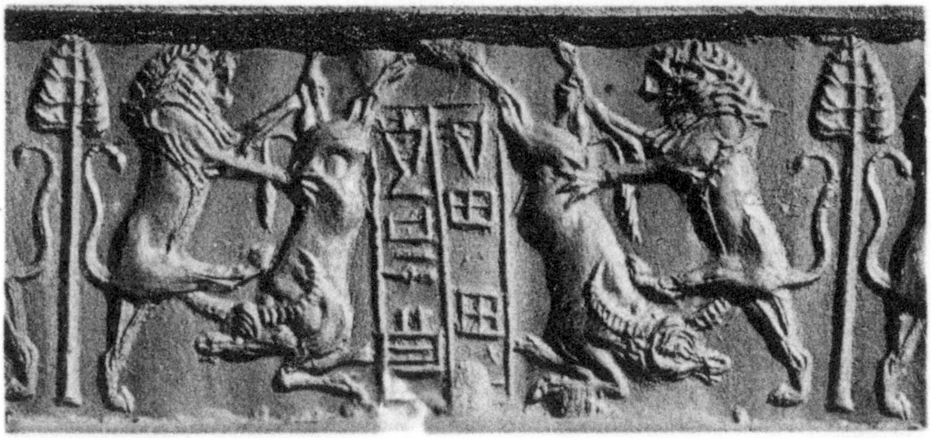

Fig. 9.
Seal of Ilulu, servant of Siʾum (Moortgat 1940: no. 186).

and the social status of its owner. Whether the lower quality of these seals simply reflect the lower social status of their owners can be disputed, but it is clear that their identification by Frankfort as "Gutian," based on nothing more than the presumption that "primitive" and "barbaric" mountain people would not be capable of any expressions of higher quality visual design, cannot be maintained. The architectural, chronological, ceramic, and glyptic evidence from Tell Asmar, therefore, makes it clear that the concept of a Gutian material culture that can be identified through elements of inferiority can be rejected.

The fallacy of finding Gutian traits by looking for stylistic attributes in artifacts can be further demonstrated by looking at cylinder seals that identify their owners as Gutian. An example of that can be seen in VA2929 (Fig. 9), a cylinder seal belonging to Ilulu,[29] servant of Si᾿um, a king of Gutium that seems to not be mentioned in the King List but who is attested in a votive inscription of a subordinate from Umma.[30] While Ilulu is most likely a Gutian name (according to the King List, the same name is born by one of the rulers of Agade during the period of confusion right after Šarkališarri), the seal design itself displays a bull-and-lion fight, and hence a typically Akkadian motive. Stylistically this seal falls into what Boehmer calls "Akkadisch III", dating between Narām-Sîn and Šu-Turul, in his own words a time span that reflects a time span that reflects a highpoint of Akkadian seal cutting skills (Boehmer 1965: 136). Any attempt to trace ethnicity though style or visual narrative falls completely apart here—the seal cutter himself might very well have been of Akkadian origin and, in fact, have been employed by the Akkadian state earlier on.

The major points of my paper, in conclusion, are probably quite obvious: literary sources such as the "Curse of Agade" need to be consulted with great caution when being mined for historical facts. Attempts to connect artifacts or styles with certain groups ethnicities, however, are to be treated with even more caution (here, to be fair, one would have to initiate a much wider discussion about what archaeologists often grandly term "cultures"—itself a highly problematic term). Lastly, when dealing with the topic of foreigners and otherness we need to be careful with established scholarship of the 20th century, which itself has not always been able to avoid the stereotyping that the Curse of Agade has bestowed so effectively onto the Gutians.

---

[29] Moortgat 1940: no. 186; Boehmer 1965: no. 753 [fig. 252]; The seal's inscription reads:

1. *ì - lu - lu*	"Ilulu,
2. ÌR *si - a - um*	Servant of Si'a'um"

[30] This inscription is found on a marble tablet, said to have from Umma (present whereabout of item unknown):

1. lugal-an-na-tuma	
2. ensí	
3. umma^{KI}-ke$_4$	"Lugal-ana-tuma governor of Umma— 35 years having passed since (the province) of Umma had been divided up—
4. umma^{KI}	
5. ba-ba-a	
6. 35 mu	
7. zal-la-ba	
8. e-gidru umma^{KI}	
9. ì-dù	built the E-gidru at Umma.
10. temen-bi	He drove into the earth its foundation pegs and saw after everything that was necessar therein.
11. ki-a ì-si-si	
12. me-bi šà-ba	
13. si ba-ni-sá	
14. u$_4$-ba *si-u-um*	At that point Si᾿um was king of Gutium."
15. lugal-*gu-ti-um*-kam	
Frayne 1993: 268 [E2.11.13.1])	

For the political position of Umma and its independence from Akkad, see Sallaberger – Schrakamp 2015: 120 (8.4.2). In his edition of the Sumerian King List Jacobsen (1939: 120, n. 306) restored the name of the penultimate king of Gutian Dynasty as [*si*]-*u*$_4$ (see cautionary comments regarding this reconstruction in Sallaberger – Schrakamp 2015: 120).

References

Amiet, P., 1972. Les statues de Manishtusu, roi d'Agadé. *RA* 66/2, 97–109.

Amiet, P., 1976. *L'Art d'Agadé au Musée du Louvre.* Paris: Éditions des Musées Nationaux.

Bahrani, Z., 2006. Race and Ethnicity in Mesopotamian Antiquity. *WA* 38/1, 48–59.

Boehmer, R.M., 1965. *Die Entwicklung der Glyptik während der Akkad-Zeit.* UAVA 4. Berlin: De Gruyter.

Buchanan, B., 1981. *Early Near Eastern Seals in the Yale Babylonian Collection.* New Haven – London: Yale University Press.

Childe, V.G., 1969. *New Light on the Ancient Near East.* New York: Norton Library.

Cifarelli, M., 1998. Gesture and Alterity in the Art of Ashurnasirpal II of Assyria. *The Art Bulletin* 80(2), 210–228.

Collon, D., 1987. *First Impressions. Cylinder Seals in the Ancient Near East.* London: British Museum Press.

Collon, D., 2003. Dance in Ancient Mesopotamia. *NEA* 66(3), 96–102.

Delougaz, P., 1940. *The Temple Oval at Khafajah.* OIP 53. Chicago: University of Chicago Press.

Delougaz, P., 1952. *Pottery from the Diyala Region.* OIP 63. Chicago: University of Chicago Press.

Delougaz, P. – H. Hill – S. Lloyd, 1967. *Private Houses and Graves in the Diyala Region.* OIP 88. Chicago: University of Chicago Press.

Delougaz, P. – S. Lloyd, 1942. *Pre-Sargonid Temples in the Diyala Region* (with chapters by Henri Frankfort and Thorkild Jacobsen). OIP 58. Chicago: University of Chicago Press.

El-Tayeb, F., 2016. *Undeutsch. Die Konstruktion des Anderen in der postmigrantischen Gesellschaft.* Bielefeld: transcript.

Falkenstein, A., 1965. Fluch über Akkade. *ZA* 57, 43–124.

Frangipane, M., 2015. Different Types of Multiethnic Societies and Different Patterns of Development and Change in the Prehistoric Near East. *Proceedings of the National Academy of Sciences of the United States of America* 112.30, 9182–9189.

Franke, J., 1977. Presentation seals of the Ur III / Isin-Larsa Period. In McG. Gibson – R. Biggs, eds., *Seals and Sealing in the Ancient Near East.* BiMes 6. Malibu: Undena Publications, 63–66.

Frankfort, H., 1939b. *Sculpture of the Third Millennium B.C. from Tell Asmar and Khafajah.* OIP 44. Chicago: University of Chicago Press.

Frankfort, H., 1943. *More Sculpture from the Diyala Region.* OIP 60. Chicago: University of Chicago Press.

Frankfort, H., 1955. *Stratified Cylinder Seals from the Diyala Region.* OIP 72. Chicago: University of Chicago Press.

Frankfort, H., 1996. *The Art and Architecture of the Ancient Orient.* New Haven – London: Yale University Press (reprint of 1954 edition, with comments).

Frankfort, H. – S. Lloyd – Th. Jacobsen, 1940. *The Gimilsin Temple and the Palace of the Rulers at Tell Asmar.* OIP 43. Chicago: University of Chicago Press.

Frayne, D., 1993. *Sargonic and Gutian Periods (2334-2113 BC).* RIME 2. Toronto: University of Toronto Press.

Glassner, J.J., 1986. *La Chute d'Akkadé. L'événement et sa mémoire.* BBVO 5. Berlin: Dietrich Reimer Verlag.

Grayson, A.K. – E. Sollberger, 1976. L'insurrection générale contre Narām-suen. *RA* 70/2, 103-128.

Hallo, W.W., 1957–1971. Gutium (Qutium). *RlA* 3, 708–720.

Haussperger, M., 1991. *Die Einführungsszene. Entwicklung eines mesopotamischen Motivs von der altakkadischen bis zum Ende der altbabylonischen Zeit.* MVS 11. München: Profil Verlag GMBH.

Hill, H. – T. Jacobsen – P. Delougaz, 1988. *Old Babylonian Public Buildings in the Diyala Region* (with contributions by T.A. Holland – A. McMahon). OIP 98. Chicago: Oriental Institute.

Hilprecht, H.V., 1903. *Explorations in Bible lands during the 19th century.* Philadelphia: A.J. Holman.

Klein, J., 1979. The Reading and Pronunciation of the Sumerian Word for "Monkey". *JCS* 31, 149–160.

Kutscher, R., 1989. *The Brockmon Tablets of the University of Haifa: Royal Inscriptions.* Haifa – Wiesbaden: Haifa University Press – Otto Harrassowitz.

McCown, D. – R.C. Haines, 1967. *Nippur I: Temple of Enlil, scribal quarter and soundings.* OIP 78. Chicago: University of Chicago Press.

Mendelson, C., 1983. More Monkey Business. *AnSt* 33, 81–83.

Michalowski, P., 1983. History as charter: some observations on the Sumerian King List. *JAOS* 103, 237–248.

Moortgat, A., 1940. *Vorderasiatische Rollsiegel.* Berlin: Verlag Gebrüder Mann.

Moortgat, A., 1950. Geschichte Vorderasiens bis zum Hellenismus. In A. Scharff – A. Moortgat, eds., *Ägypten und Vorderasien im Altertum.* München: F. Bruckmann, 191–503.

Parrot, A., 1961. *Sumer: The Dawn of Art.* New York: Golden Press.

Paterson, A., 1912–1913. *Assyrian sculptures; Palace of Sinacherib: plates and ground plan of the palace.* The Hague: Martinus Nijhoff.

Porada, E., 1948. *Corpus of Ancient Near Eastern Seals in the Pierpont Morgan Library Collection.* Vols. I–II. The Bollingen Series. Washington, DC: Pantheon Books.

Porada, E. – D. Hansen – S. Dunham, 1992. The Chronology of Mesopotamia, ca. 7000-1600 B.C. In R. Ehrich, ed., *Chronologies in Old World Archaeology I + II.* Chicago: University of Chicago Press, 77–121 (Vol. I), 90–124 (Vol. II).

Reichel, C., n.d. *Center AND Periphery: The Archaeology of Politics at Ešnunna from the Ur III to the Old Babylonian Period* (submitted to the OIP series, Chicago).

Sallaberger, W. – I. Schrakamp, 2015. The Gutean Period: A problem of 3rd Millennium chronology. In W. Sallaberger – I. Schrakamp, eds., *History and Philology.* ARCANE III. Turnhout: Brepols, 113–130.

Strommenger, E., 1962. *Fünf Jahrtausende Mesopotamien: die Kunst von den Anfängen um 5000 v. Chr. bis zu Alexander dem Grossen.* München: Hirmer Verlag.

Steinkeller, P., 2015. The Gutian period in chronological perspective. In W. Sallaberger – I. Schrakamp, eds., *History and Philology.* ARCANE III. Turnhout: Brepols, 281–288.

Tinney, S., 1995. A New Look at Naram-Sin and the "Great Rebellion". *JCS* 47, 1–14.

Wehler, H.-U., 1969. *Bismarck und der Imperialismus.* Köln: Kiepenheuer & Witsch.

Wehler, H.-U., 1973. *Das deutsche Kaiserreich, 1871-1918.* Göttingen: Vandenhoeck & Ruprecht.

Westenholz, A., 1999. The Old Akkadian Period: History and Culture. In W. Sallaberger – A. Westernholz, A., eds., *Mesopotamien: Akkade-Zeit und Ur III-Zeit.* OBO160/3. Freiburg Schweiz – Göttingen: Universitätsverlag – Vandenhoeck und Ruprecht, 17–117.

Winter, I., 1986. The King and the Cup: Iconography of the Royal Presentation Scene on Ur III Seals. In M. Kelly-Buccellati – P. Matthiae – M. van Loon, eds., *Insight through Images: Studies in honor of Edith Porada.* BiMes 21. Malibu: Undena Publications, 253–268.

Winter, I., 1987. Legitimization of authority through image and legend: seals belonging to officials in the administrative bureaucracy of the Ur III state. In McG. Gibson – R. Biggs, eds., *The Organization of Power. Aspects of Bureaucracy in the Ancient Near East.* SAOC 46. Chicago: Oriental Institute, 69–116.

Woolley, C.L., 1965. *The Sumerians*. New York: W.W. Norton and Company (originally published in 1928).

ALIENS AND ALIENATION, STRANGERS AND ESTRANGEMENT: DIFFERENCE-MAKING AS HISTORICALLY-PARTICULAR CONCEPT

Seth Richardson (University of Chicago)*

Introduction: Reception and Perception in Historical Context

This essay gathers together several disparate narratives about "insiders" and "outsiders" in one specific period. The point of doing so is not to define or distill a single conclusion about what these concepts meant at one time—or, by analogy, in any one time—but rather to draw attention to the constant complication of dyadic concepts of hosts / guests, citizens / strangers, etc., because of their asymmetry. The gentle reader can expect that the essay means not to present a coherent single picture of "concepts of strangers", because it should not. This telling will outline not only the range of unequal grounds on which foreignness was assessed across the Late Old Babylonian period (ca. 1720–1595 BC; hereafter often "Late OB"), but even the shifting semantic and social terms on which ideas of belonging and familiarity were defined. Diachrony plays a role in making this point, in the sense that important changes happened *within* periods, and not only between them. But the even larger point is that attempts to understand the reception of "foreignness" in specific historical contexts without parallel consideration of the fault lines of difference and distinction *within* host societies, and the dynamic between the two arenas, are unsatisfactory acts of comparison when they presume that host cultures are socially stable and unitary entities. Thus, what follows reproduces the complex, confusing, and changing ideas of what was staked in making such distinctions in the Late OB.

What I do hope to give a clear picture of is the contingency of distinction-making practices: not just between insiders and outsiders, but within those categories, for purposes which were often not directly comparable, and which required that acts of self-definition recursively redefined other comparative categories, in a seemingly endless syntagmatic chain. For this, historical contexts which account for change are indispensable.

But I will begin with a basic point: concepts of "strangers" and "foreigners" are social constructions just as identities are—not natural categories, but distinctions and choices made with reference to each other. These concepts are not only

* Abbrevations and translations follow the CAD unless otherwise noted, plus: BTM = Foster 1996; CUSAS 8 = Abraham and Van Lerberghe 2009; CUSAS 29 = Abraham – Van Lerberghe 2017; Haradum II = Joannès 2006; MHET I = Van Lerberghe – Voet 1991; MHET II = Dekiere 1994–1997; TLOB 1 = Richardson 2010b; TLOB 2 = Richardson (in preparation A). Citations of Mesopotamian laws follow Roth 1995. Abbreviations for Late OB year-names follow Pientka 1998: Ae = Abi-ešuḫ, Ad = Ammiditana, Aṣ = Ammiṣaduqa, Sd = Samsuditana.

a matter of relative perspective—of particular peoples coming to seem more or less familiar over time, "progressing" from acculturation to assimilation to integration. The concepts are also categorically protean: for instance, the ethno-linguistic and national terms in which modern Western concepts of foreignness are framed clearly did not carry the same weight in ancient cultures; the entire idea of what "foreignness" *meant* (as opposed to how it was constituted) was differently constructed. Comparisons have always been in dialogue with, for instance, local settlements about what it meant to belong as an insider; social versus spiritual conceptions of alienation vis-à-vis "aliens"; and the relation of "foreignness" to other forms of contemporary social judgement necessary for not only the dipole of inclusion and exclusion, but the larger and more complicated middle ground of recognition.

In the Late Old Babylonian setting I will discuss here, ethnonyms, place of origin, and onomastics for non-Babylonian people were deployed in contexts which were, despite substantial diversity and difference (*per* De Graef 1999), in themselves unmarked as to economic preference or social comparison (which can only be inferred). Our sources (e.g., lists of workers, slave sales, dispersed personal names) give virtually no inflection (positive or negative) as to the ethnic, social, or political identities of foreign people. After a short review of these kinds of data, I will devote my attention to the Babylonian conceptual construction of "strangers" and "strangeness"—what it meant to talk about "enemies", "aliens", and "others" in the contexts where the relevant groups and terms (e.g., *aḫû*, *nak*(*ā*)*ru*, *ubāru*, etc.) appeared. Through a series of historical examples, I will illustrate that Babylonian ideas about foreignness were protean even within a single historical period. The receptions and expressions of what the culture held to be alien, strange, or foreign were mutable, historical particulars. In the context of Late OB state society, these particulars are important clues about not only outsiders and aliens, but ideas of membership and belonging as well. I will argue that a collapse of external ethnic and political markers of foreignness after 1750 BC gave way to a more diffuse and culturally internal sense of what it meant to be an "alien" social being, prefiguring the themes of isolation and alienation arising in Akkadian literature of the later second millennium.

This question of alterity is especially important for ancient Near Eastern history. The cultures we study give so few abstract and introspective statements about *themselves* that one of our few insights is to look at how they defined the terms of Self and Other. But one of the obstacles to evaluating ethnic identity and otherness in antiquity, as Katharina Streit so ably demonstrates in her essay in this volume, is that making visible the kinds of multiple and situational identities that make social comparison possible and powerful requires living informants to make explicit otherwise subtle cultural differences. As Streit acknowledges (2019, this volume), this can be as difficult to locate in the archaeological record as in the textual one when it is not possible to distinguish conscious representation from "cultural automatism", as she puts it. To adopt Streit's terms, the "acquired", "segmentary", and "situational" identities descriptive of ethnic fluidity are almost invisible to us, unless the record makes plain (as it rarely does) the deployment of alternate forms of self-presentation, or perceptions contingent on the kinds of circumstance we would require to be able to say: "Ah, yes: here is a Sutean playing at being a Babylonian in order to be counted as a mercenary / farmworker / trader; and here is a Babylonian viewing a Kassite in this context as a principal in his contract, but here as a hostile tribesman camped out in the border marches. Now which of these is to be considered a 'foreigner,' and how much so?" What we can do instead is to try to excavate and make plain the kinds of structures and situations in which fluidity and alterity might have become operational social and political strategies, with reference to the kinds of difference-making discourses going on within the host culture at the same time.

Focus and Perspective

This marks the twentieth anniversary of a seminal article on "foreigners" in the Late OB, Katrien De Graef's 1999 two-part "Les étrangers dans les textes paléob-abyloniens tardifs de Sippar". One might reasonably wonder what really could or should be added to that excellent work; the short answer would be: "not much." What De Graef did so cleanly and clearly was to distinguish the attested roles for different ethnic people in the cuneiform record of this period: Gutians appeared as slaves and servants, Suheans were workers and owners of slaves, and Elamites, although sometimes slaves, could also be mercenaries, landowners, and bearers of cylinder seals. The several major different ethnicities present in Babylonia, she wrote, were "at different stages of integration", and so "it would be a mistake to take this kaleidoscope in order to create an artificial and general image of 'The Stranger'."[1] Additional relevant evidence which has emerged over the past two decades could be added to her data set (e.g., new onomastic forms, ethnonyms, etc.), but it would little change De Graef's underlying warning, which remains firm and fixed: we must avoid the creation of some kind of Frankenstein image of "The Foreigner" from a composite of very separate particulars.

My goal here is, therefore, rather different: not to make a description of the socio-economic position of foreign people in Babylonia which has already been done, but to analyze the conditions under which the *reception* of that foreignness took place; not of difference, but of difference-*making*. How did Babylonians *think* about foreignness? What did it mean to *perceive* someone as an outsider or as a stranger; what do changes in that thinking reflect about Babylonia itself? (My subject in this sense is closest, among the several goals of this conference, to exploring "the communication patterns between individuals and societies.") If we have a fair understanding of the contexts in which outsiders fit into Babylonian institutions and economies (at least to the extent to which documents make them conform*able*)—that is, the conditions under which they lived—we have less of a sense of how their presence, especially over time, affected the society in which they were hosted. This is not, for better or worse, a theoretical problem so different from the one faced by analysts of host-immigrant dynamics in modern societies.

[1] De Graef 1999b: 13.

Our basic theories in the social sciences do not deal with how immigrants might influence host societies, but rather with how immigrants adapt *to* them. Furthermore, even if one searches in other scholarship, such as the vast literature on social movements, one will not find a model that can be easily crafted to fit the question of how immigrants and/or ethnic groups might work their magic on host institutions. In short, if we want to explain how immigrants or ethnic groups influence the institutions of host societies, we must invent a model to explain these events and to guide our empirical research into their details.[2]

The questions are all the more important *because* the meaning of foreignness was not qualitatively marked within the same record that paradoxically took the trouble to specify it in the first place—ethnically, linguistically, geographically. Indeed, as Gary Beckman (the most recent cuneiformist to address the subject of foreigners at the general level) has noted, even the surface-level onomastic, linguistic, and epithetical criteria we are forced to use are highly inexact.[3] Even setting that issue aside, we could say that the socio-economic positions of Gutians, Subareans, Suheans, Elamites, and Kassites differed in objective and descriptive terms; but they all shared the underlying context that, to the extent that ethnicity was marked at all, there were none of the judgments or opinions that social recognition requires; where the quality of separateness was called out.

De Graef's work was a kind of archaeology that uncovered invisible socio-economic distinctions and hierarchies. Calling out these distinctions was important, because it corrected an instinct to totalize or make legible an otherwise bewildering range of statuses and interactions between proper Babylonians and the many ethnic and political[4] identities given to slaves, workers, mercenaries, traders, servants, itinerants, etc. Still, it remains remarkable that the cuneiform evidence of the Late OB gives us almost nothing in the way of opinions about various ethnicities as desirable/undesirable, hard-working/lazy, clean/dirty, or in any conceivable way substantially different either from Babylonians or between each other.

One might suppose that ethnic foreigners were, in the aggregate, an underclass in some general way relative to Babylonians; but no sooner is this voiced than one must admit that even this is hardly clear. I take it as significant that these kinds of differences almost nowhere rise to the level of comment in the ancient sources—not in letters nor literature nor law. We do not find any discourses of assimilation, acculturation, or accommodation in which it was imperative was voiced for outsiders to become, or become integrated with, Babylonians, or for anyone to resist such forces.[5] On top of that, we have to question whether or to

---

[2] Orum 2005: 922. Beckman (2013: 211) at most concludes of the ancient Near Eastern reception of foreigners: "Although the host civilizations generally absorbed the newcomers without themselves undergoing significant change, when large bodies of invaders belonging to cultures confident of their own superiority … arrived in the region in later centuries, the age-old ways of life in Mesopotamia and Anatolia would be radically transformed."

[3] Beckman 2013: 205.

[4] I use the adjective "political" throughout to mean "polity-of-origin" rather than to refer to politics in its processual or negotiatory aspect.

[5] Waldinger 2003: 29.

what degree the "groupness" of ethnically-designated individuals reflected their own subscription to those names.[6] Did a Subarian perceive anything meaningful in being called a Subarian by a Babylonian? A man of Idamaraṣ probably agreed the he came from that region—but was it important? Did a Bimatî Kassite think of himself as Kassite, Bimatî, or only as a member of some specific kinship unit, a clan or household, Bīt-something-or-other. Did someone from the Middle Euphrates respond to being called a Hanean? Numhaean? Suhean? *Ḫapīru*? Some? All? None? If so: when, and why?

Separateness in the Sources? Limited Returns.

To what degree do our texts reflect different or separate practices where ethnicity is concerned? This is a relatively traditional approach to framing questions about "insiders" and "outsiders" such as De Graef critiqued. But I will use this section not to promise results, but rather to illustrate the insufficiency of this kind of structured analysis, in favor of the narrative vectors explored in the following section. The most common context in which non-Babylonians were identified was administrative, especially in lists of pay or rations for workers and mercenaries, who were individually marked for ethnicity. We can look, for example, to a long paylist like BM 96955 (Aṣ —) and find that it includes two Sutaeans (I:23′, IV:11) and a Ḫanigalbatean (III:9). But not only do they receive no notably different pay than people named Sîn-iddinam or Ina-Esagil-zēri, but there are many other non-Babylonian names on the list not marked with an ethnonym,[7] and conversely at least one detail illustrates that even "good Babylonian names" may hide ethnic identity, since the text lists an Elamite (lú.nim.ma.ki) bearing the name Sippar-liwwir (III:12). Another text (BM 79970 [Late OB]) includes three Suhaeans (two with Babylonian names) and two Kassites, alongside many other names unmarked for ethnicity. In another case, a list of grain delivered by Elamites in BM 97196 (Sd 13) includes only people with Babylonian names, patronyms, and titles, with no Elamite onomastic elements; if they were not labelled as "Elamites", one would never know the difference.[8] Several texts document service-fields distributed to Elamites among others by the Babylonian administration (e.g., AbB IV 107, XI 173, XIV 6, etc.). And so forth. Simply put, even where we find the acknowledgement of separateness by ethnonym, it seems to have had no bearing on any aspect of the administrative transaction documented; nor is there is ever an indication that the *kind* of work being done was in any respect *particular* to that ethnicity, and in fact foreigners are most often listed side-by-side with Babylonians doing the same work.

---

[6] Waldinger 2003: 36–37.

[7] Unmarked non-Babylonian names in BM 96955 include Iamsû s. Ḫunabu (I:16′), Iakburum (II:18″), Kurraḫu (e.g., II:23″, but the name recurs), Iaʾumaṣ (II:24″), Ušgaya (III:10), and more. See Richardson 2005: 278 for more examples with Kassites. Note the remarkable MHET I 43 and 55, with similar transactions between Subareans and Babylonians.

[8] See similarly BM 78658 (n.d.), with four men providing unnamed erén mar.tu.

In private legal contracts, we find the same unconcern for what ethnicity might mean: individual principals could be labelled Suheans, Elamites, etc. But beyond these designations, there is nothing to distinguish them functionally or hierarchically from other principals, either within the contracts where we find them, or in comparison to other contracts. An archive of 27 texts, for instance, illustrates the loan and rental activities of one Galdanu the Sutaean, whose customers included a herald, a *nāditu*, and well-known persons such as Utul-Ištar *abi ṣābim*[9] and Iddin-Ea the judge; in virtually no respect was any transaction of Galdanu's modified by or contingent on his ethnic marking, though it is presented consistently.[10] Other scattered examples seem to support this sense: a Kassite man rents a field in VS 7 64 (Ad 37); a Sutean man held a debt over a man named Enlil-muballiṭ (CUSAS 8 81 [n.d.]); another Sutean receives a loan of chick-peas to pay for seeding work (YOS 13 395 [Sd 14]); yet a third Sutean loans silver to a sanga of Gula (BM 79868 [Aṣ 16]). The number of such instances is small, but then all the more remarkable for their being unremarked-upon. Two important distinctions, however, may be made: the first is that ethnonyms rarely appear in contracts for the sale or lease of real estate, though a scant few exceptions are known;[11] the second is that I am unaware of any instance in which an ethnonym follows the name of a witness to a contract. Without further context, it cannot be clear whether these restrictions existed because they were not legally or socially permitted;[12] and further, in the case of real estate, whether, if the ownership of land was a determining factor of citizen status, the moment of land acquisition was also the moment at which one became a Babylonian and no longer something else, without a need to be identified as anything "other."

None of the above is to ignore instances in which whole contingents of persons were ethnically marked—entire troops called Elamite, Amorite, Kassite, etc.—as clearly separate and discrete units. It is rather only to say that when we encounter such individual workers or soldiers, outside of group references, ethnicity was sometimes marked, but never with any further meaningful distinction from other unmarked persons. One is left to imagine that ethnic marking was an accounting device, ultimately traceable to the function of recording income merely and expense streams. One commonly-recurring feature which does stand out is that ethnonyms marking individuals among heterogeneous groups often (but not exclusively) seem to stand in for the absence of patronyms, the single most common marker of identity in Babylonian texts; that is, that ethnicity was possibly a parallel mechanism of individuation. Moreover, it is rare for a person with a non-Babylonian name to be identified as the son of someone with a Babylonian name,

---

[9] Note another instance in which Utul-Ištar acts together in an official capacity with an Iddin-Sîn *su-ḫu-um*[ki] in YOS 13 69.

[10] TLOB 1 74–84 (pp. 50–58); see also BM 79868 (Aṣ 16).

[11] E.g. VS 7 64 (Ad 37), in which a Kassite man rents a field for new cultivation; MHET II 5 633 (post-Si) lists the house of an Elamite; MHET II 6 913 (Aṣ 16), in which a man of Tukriš rents a field to an ugula máš.šu.gíd.gíd. Cf. e.g. the a.šà *aḫîm*, the "field of strangers," in AbB III 81.

[12] Note the apparent exclusion of "strangers" in e.g. AbB VII 35, but without any further specification.

or vice-versa[13] ... though both are attested![14] And even if patronymic vs. ethnonymic naming practices had the purpose of identifying household membership, this in turn would have to be weighed against the fact that the great majority of non-Babylonian names in administrative texts appear without either patronym *or* ethnonym, which unsettles the idea of even *that* as a regular practice. And so we must step back from assuming that either naming practices were practiced in any consistent way, as tools of either assimilation or ethnic distinction.

Slave sale contracts present something of a different problem. On the one hand, it is commonly observed that many sold slaves were identified as foreigners—ethnically, geographically, and / or onomastically.[15] But, in the first place, the identification of foreign origin in these texts primarily had a legal purpose, namely to document the jurisdiction of sale, for the purpose of adjudicating future claims.[16] And in the second place, it seems significant to me that the foreign names of slaves—as for foreign workers and mercenaries, for whom original onomastic forms were often preserved—were just as often preserved as they were replaced by Babylonian names; no preference can be evinced for one over the other.[17] More to the point, observing only that many slaves were foreign comes without a hint of social paradox that many *other* sold slaves were house-born Babylonians, citizens of native cities; or that fathers could sell their wives, daughters, or even themselves into slavery. It also remains an open question as to whether transfers of native Babylonians into slavery were consistently marked by sale documents, since these transfers were often collections for debt or (what is much the same) the resolution of distraints without redemption, rather than sales per se.[18] The consequence of this is that the sale of native Babylonians into slavery often may simply not have been recorded in contracts, leaving the corpus of slave sale texts to appear as focused on "foreigners" as it does. But slavery itself, as either personal / legal status or institution, was not ethnically marked or for non-Babylonians alone.[19]

Thus we face a conundrum. On the one hand, it was important for some reason(s) for scribes and administrators to identify, in writing, the ethnic or political

---

13 Simply to begin with personal names starting with Ia- (a marker of West Semitic onomastics), we typically find Iabsû s. Išgamu, Iadi'u s. Takti ([lú]Sutû), Iaḫala s. Mudadu, Iapazu s. Aḫḫunanu, and so forth.

14 E.g., Iaditum s. Iddin-Bunene (BM 81255 [Sd 3]), Iammu-Ištar s. Ilšu-ibni and br. Qīš-Marduk (VS 18 19 [Ad / Aṣ]), and Iakraḫ s. Ekur-rabi (BM 81591 [Ad 37]). Conversely, Ibbi-Ilabrat s. Kunnija (VS 7 56 [Ad 24]), Ibni-Marduk s. Abdu-maliki (YOS 13 54 [Aṣ 10]), Ilī-iqišam s. Pejaia (YOS 13 528 [Sd 1], *pe-ia-a*).

15 See esp. van Koppen 2005, and Richardson 2002: 303–305 and 2019a.

16 See below, ad loc. nn. 19 and 28, on Babylonian recognition of foreign slave-holders' property rights.

17 Unlike the case discussed by Pruzsinszky 2019, this volume, there is a very low incidence of so-called "Mischnamen," i.e., names with both Babylonian and non-Babylonian elements, in the Late OB onomasticon.

18 See Richardson 2019a.

19 Indeed, the only point at which the Laws of Hammurabi (§§280–281) take notice of foreign slaves as such has to do with the equal recognition of other jurisdictions and property rights; and that contracts recognized the extended legal indentity of "house-born" (*wilid bītim* GN) to polities other than Babylonian ones, including Numḫia (Kraus Edict v 36) and Suḫûm (see Richardson in preparation A, esp. Text 3); see also AbB VI 80.

identity (never both) of people who were non-Babylonian. On the other hand, and with equal consistency, they never recorded the reason for doing this. What is more (as a corollary), given how often people designated with ethnonyms also bore "good" Babylonian names, we have little idea of how often or when "good" Babylonian names, when and where they appear *without* an ethnonym or any other comment, actually belonged to non-Babylonians without being so disclosed. Did it then in fact matter at all that people came from somewhere else, or belonged to some other ethnic stock? What *were* the criteria and terms by which people perceived, formed, or acted on perceptions of "insideness" and "outsideness"?

We may begin by discarding the explanation that the ancient cultures we are looking at simply didn't care about these distinctions, especially on the understanding that a tolerance of others was something built into ancient societies—a tolerance maybe we lack. This would require that we believe in cultures that just didn't make distinctions and discriminations, which runs against the tone of our otherwise highly opinionated sources, e.g., the cranky discourse of private letters or the highly-charged terms of royal inscriptions.[20]

What seems more likely is that the apparent disinterest of the texts in making ethnic distinctions was produced by generic conditions of the texts—by the fact that contracts, administrative documents, and even letters were focused on the resolution of highly specific and quantifiable issues of property and moveable goods. Given this, ethnicity or foreignness takes on no more interest for a text about, say, the sale of a field than the hygiene of the seller, the weight of the buyer, or the view from the field. It is more likely, then, that where markings of difference do appear, they were consequences of accounting or administrative requirements, or as designations for commercial purposes, real-property ownership, or legal jurisdiction. As McGeough (2019, this volume) puts it, these markers were added as "administratively cognizable forms of genealogy;" or even as a kind of cognatic notion of descent in which the marking of difference, establishing social location, domesticated and *diminished* difference rather than highlighted it, as we might expect. We might construct ethnic marking even more positively still, as an adjunct or extra level of social identity rather than separateness, as the *basis* for collectives or enclaves within the host society—of workers, mercenaries, traders. That is, we cannot exclude the possibility that ethnic terms marked not dependency or subordination in Babylonian society, but elective or *subscriptive* membership, affiliations with the social benefits of a group one might *want* to belong to, by which resident aliens were institutionally recognized in relation to Babylonian state and society; that ethnonyms were related to privileges rather than, or as well as, limitations and rules. This possibility would require us to think about foreign people as less of an underclass and more as a metic community with its own unique relations to the political center, one with perhaps not necessarily equal relations to

20 But compare to the point made by Fales 2018: 484, that letters deliver a "more nuanced" range of meanings about ethnicity and its reception than royal inscriptions, for the "fixed and traditional ideological tenets" of the former, as well as the institutional and class differences in the genres' different productions.

it, but at least bilateral ones. Unfortunately, there is no more evidence to build out such a theory than there is to prove or debunk one which presumes an underclass or subaltern status for all foreigners.

The "standard approach" which follows these threads really leads us primarily to an empty space, if we hope to make of them an account of identities as the basis of alterity. So how *can* we talk about a cultural norm of social distinctions without the evidence to describe it? If this is an empty space, what we can try to do is to account for the norms adjacent to it; to make a silhouette. The remainder of this paper will work to locate a historically-particular idea of "the foreign" within the range of *other* types of social exclusion. We can look at other entities which are labeled or correspond to the status of "enemy", "outsider", "emigrant" in order to develop not just some etic and objectifying concept of *aliens*, but of what *alienation* is; not just *strangers*, but *estrangement*. Just as there is no stable category of "foreigner", as De Graef shows, neither was there a historically uniform perception of what foreignness meant, nor single bases on which outsiders were identified. If one removes foreign origin and ethnic identity as the limiting criteria for alterity, Babylonians had a lot to say about what makes people strange or different. Strangeness was something about which they cared quite a lot.

To think about foreignness as just one kind of social exclusion among others opens up a general theoretical problem for the topic: *perceptions* of foreignness are themselves historically particular—what Mynářová (2019, this volume) calls out as the discourse-based "fluidity" of exclusability, identity, and meaning-making; and what Streit (2019, this volume) particularizes as acquired, situational, and segmentary ideas of ethnicity; all of which the process and practice of labeling only *obscures*. A society's receptivity to outside people and the criteria by which their strangeness is evaluated and acted upon can change even within the supposedly unitary cultures of a single historical period, as I will show. The identity of all kinds of outsiders was conditioned by how Babylonians framed their political, legal, social, labor, cultural, and residential conditions; the personhood of foreigners was thus a malleable and changeable variation of the partial or imperfect personhood relative to normative membership (and imperfect forms thereof) in the host society.[21] I argue against suggestions that the Old Babylonian period, or any other period, had clear and simple conceptual dyads of insiders and outsiders.[22] These categories are always complicated, and our first job is to document and analyze those complexities.

---

[21] Reitz 2002: 1006 on "four dimensions" of social interaction between hosts and immigrants: ethnic relations; labor markets; government policies; changing international situation; cf. the schemae proposed and questions raised by Safran 1991 and Van Oudenhoven et al. 2006, reaching into not only social, political, and economic interactions, but even changes in individual psychology, "cognitive styles," self-stereotyping, stereotype appropriation, etc.

[22] As Pongratz-Leisten (2000: 195) argues, different genres of OB texts "distinguish between concepts" of city vs. countryside, sedentarism vs. nomadism, and homeland vs. enemy, but "intermingle in order to formulate the concept of the inner and the outer world." The same could be said of some idea of "native" vs. "foreign" ethnicity (note [ibid.: 205–206] her discussion of the ambivalent "conflict and contact" and "contempt and need" illustrated even within literary works such as the *Marriage of Martu* text).

Late Old Babylonian stories

Seeking out dyadic structures presupposes their existence and analytically privileges their importance; we must find alternative strategies of explanation to round out the picture. In what follows, I propose to draw several "vectors" about specific contexts of interaction, stories which complicate insider/outsider dyads by tracking them diachronically. From seven descriptions of rather different problematic situations, I hope to draw out the complexity of these relations, to not only comment on specific differences, but on social processes of *differentiation* altogether and their fundamental instability. In effect, differentiation is discourse-based; defining the changing terms of discourses across particular historical contexts tells us about the basis on which political relations are established.

What I propose for the Late OB is that we see an almost complete turning inside-out of perceptions about who were insiders and who were outsiders *within the OB period.* In its middle phase (ca. 1840–1720 BC), Old Babylonian society was indeed characterized by a perception of foreignness primarily centered on (often hostile) foreign nationality, and secondarily on ethno-linguistic identity. But by the Late OB, two processes had begun to fold the outside to the inside: people who were formerly considered to be "outsiders" had, through several transformations, come to be closely associated with the state; while a variety of social and political "insiders" drifted away to become more marginal. The consequences of this were two-fold: politically, it prepared the ground for the great cataclysm of 1595—for state collapse; culturally, it set the stage for a cultural concern with alienation in Akkadian literature.

I will illustrate this through seven stories about "outsiders" and "strangers" in the Late OB, with some comparison between the time of Hammurabi around 1760 to the later 17th century setting—the symbolic landscape of what "foreign" meant to a north Babylonian person in this time that made it different from 2000 or 1300 or 700 BC. By starting at 1760, we already begin two-thirds of the way into the 400-year Old Babylonian period (just to emphasize, once again, that the changes discussed all came within a single period, to illustrate how reductive depictions of culture by period really can be). The stories do not make up a single historical narrative; they don't "go together", or demonstrate a single cultural phenomenon. But they reflect a society in which the perception of who was a "stranger" was undergoing substantial change. I begin with four stories about people we might think of as "foreigners", in ethnic and/or geographic terms; and then three more stories about people we wouldn't.

Classic "Outsiders"?

Story 1: The International situation

The first story to tell has to do with the fact that Babylon in the 1720s was suddenly isolated from the regional world in which it had, until very recently, acted on a vast and complex international stage. In 1760, Babylon was in touch with everywhere from Dilmun and Ur in the south to Assyria and Aleppo in the north; Qaṭna and Ḫazor to the west and Susa to the east. This was patch of ground on the face of the earth not smaller than world of the Amarna letters, with day-by-day knowledge of the doings of foreign cities, courts, and people, with an everyday mingling of messengers, ambassadors, and courtiers.

Yet this communicative episteme disappeared entirely by 1720—within a single lifetime. By 1720, barely a whiff of contact with other lands remained:[23] far-flung places like Šeḫna, Amurru, and Subartu disappeared even from the dynasty's year names and royal inscriptions, as even notional or imagined foreign enemies; private letters mentioned contact only with nearby Ešnunna and Jablija.

Meanwhile, even the southern Babylonian cities that had revolted against Babylon's rule in the 1730s were by 1720 no longer occupied or at least operative as political powers, with the possible exception of Nippur. So even contact with this most nearby old Sumerian south virtually disappears from the record.[24] Across the Near East, the archaeological profile and textual record of many once-great kingdoms suggests that abandonment or at least isolation between cities had set in by the end of the Middle Bronze. Mari, Šubat-Enlil, Ekallatum, Larsa, Uruk—they were all effectively gone. Emar, Ḫazor, Qaṭna,[25] Tigunanum—there is no hint that these places had any contact with Babylon for a century. And even if the old palaces of Aleppo, Aššur, and Susa still kept their hearth fires burning, we have no hint that Babylon knew much of it. Even for the new power of the emerging Sealand Dynasty, we have little to suggest that contact with Babylon was sustained in any meaningful way.[26] Altogether, this was a severe reduction in the footprint of states *as a category of organization*. Whatever the individual health and welfare of the individual kingdoms, a widespread and complex international system had effectively disappeared within the space of four decades.

What is the significance of this disappearance for "perceptions of foreigners"? States are meaningful bases of identity only within systems of *other* states. For cooperation or competition in security, warfare, and commerce, states only have definition as entities organized to interact within a system of peers. One long-term effect of removing an international system is on the local perception of the state itself: if the state in which you live becomes only an organization to collect taxes, administer canal-digging, and provide for local security, it has moved a significant way along the spectrum from statehood towards warlordism. In such a situation,

[23] It is true that, lacking the royal archives of Babylon, we depend to a great degree on the Mari archives for our knowledge of what states Babylon was in contact with. So a great deal of our impression that Babylon becomes isolated depends on our lack of access to a chancery archive which might have contained such letters. We may note a few passing references to foreign agent / missions in other texts, e.g. VS 22 34 (Sd 11), mentioning an "Elamite messenger," PN ^{lú}kin.gi$_4$.a Elam^{ki}; VS 7 67, mentioning Kuk-našer, sukkal of Elam (Aṣ 1); a mention of "envoys of the Sealand" (CUSAS 29 3:9-10, dumu.meš *šiprī ša* a.ab.ba [Ae 14?]); and (probably commercial) journeys from Ḫaradum to Emar and Aššur (Joannès 2006 no. 65 and 70). Notwithstanding these exceptions, the letters from Babylonia simply do not discuss the wider Syro-Elamite-Mesopotamian region with any focused attention.

[24] See Richardson 2018, with literature, and "Story 3," below.

[25] But note the lonely (possible) single mention of erén Qatana^{ki} in CUSAS 29 30:4.

[26] With the exception of the "envoys" mentioned above in n. 23.

it would become relatively meaningless to be a "Babylonian" in distinction to some other political identity, as all identities—native, foreign, and in-between—would be emptied of some degree of political value.

This may not have an immediate effect on how Babylonians thought of the individual "foreign" people who still lived among them or passed through as traders. But their personhood was less clearly defined by the diplomatic protections and sense of peerage that states had previously observed. Further, there was a significant population of foreigners living in Babylonia, not entirely as migrants or visitors on an *elective* basis, but as refugees from the disastrous wars of the previous century—people who maybe could not go home again because there was no home to go *to*. There is a difference between outsiders aspiring to become insiders, and outsiders seeking safety *from* the outside—in one of the few remaining state centers, fearing the insecurity of a larger stateless world. People who had previously been foreign nationals were often now, without the international system, just "foreigners."

What was the meaning of the foreignness of a mercenary from Aleppo, if there were no diplomatic relations with, or news from, or even fighting against Aleppo? How much could it matter whether a worker was "Elamite" if he was a third-generation resident with his own farmed plot and family in Babylonia? International situations always inform the local social and cultural relations of foreigners in host cultures; but what we may wonder as much is how relevant "insiderness" seemed in a kingdom with no structured "outside", and how much of the state's claims to defend those distinctions mattered.

Story 2: The protected and the unprotected

This leads me to a story about foreigners who were legally protected and privileged in Babylonia—and those who weren't. As a starting point, let us take the fact that some foreigners had a degree of legal standing, insofar as the law collections of Babylon and Ešnunna recognized the property rights of foreign slave-owners.[27] It is not clear that these laws limited their protections to slave property only, or if they protected other types of properties by analogy. The few law cases that acknowledge foreign jurisdiction[28] mostly have to do with the return of slaves or other persons over whom there were claims (deserters, runaways, distrainees, etc.), so the limited rights were focused mostly on personal status. Slaves were, of course, highly mobile forms of capital, and often, like their owners, of foreign origin. The recognition of legal rights in other jurisdictions therefore only openly addresses the extended legal personhood of foreign citizens, and not a commitment to protect other crimes against their persons or properties.

In no other respect, however, does OB statute law makes any claim to protect or define legal subjects on an ethnic or political basis.[29] We may contrast this to

[27] LH §§280–281, as *māt nukurtim* and *māt šanītim*; LE §52, a slave "in the safekeeping of a foreign envoy" (*ša itti mār šiprim naṣruma*).
[28] See Westbrook 2009² and Richardson 2017: 34–35.
[29] Note, however, LE §36 and 41, legal requirements for the *ubārum* and *napṭarum*.

Ur-Namma's law, which claimed to protect in its entirety both "Akkadians and foreigners (lú-gir$_5$-ra) in the lands of Sumer and Akkad", an expansive claim one does not find echoed in OB laws. Thus, other than the slave statutes, there is no clear legal pronouncement as to whether foreign persons enjoyed equal, separate, or partial legal rights in Old Babylonian times.

The Edicts of the Late Old Babylonian kings (which were also legal documents) give us a rather different picture. These edicts were published by at least three kings across the century after Hammurabi (namely Samsuiluna, Ammiditana, and Ammiṣaduqa), in largely identical language.[30] The Edicts mostly remitted certain obligations for specific constituencies; few provisions related to large classes of people. The laws may have enumerated a few specific legal rights for all foreigners equally, but they otherwise also ignored this status equally. But the Edicts made implied distinctions between *specific* groups of non-Babylonian origin: people of Suḫûm, but not Sutû; men of Šitullum, but not Širamaḫ; etc. The Edicts did not remit all debts for all people, and they were not concerned with legal rights; in their particularism, they gave *occasional* tax- and debt-relief privileges for *specified* groups. In this, their specificity about some groups and not others tells us that the exemptions were not about foreignness per se, but other, more specific kinds of relationships—most likely political ones, related to the terms on which certain groups had originally accepted the sovereignty of Babylon.

If we break down the Edict of Ammiṣaduqa by types of affected subjects, we find a distribution of people receiving relief distinguished by group in 22 separate measures: most if not all measures affected only *particular* sets of citizens, officers, and corporate bodies. Among these acts, the Edict enumerated exemptions for five non-Babylonian places: Idamaraṣ, Mankisum, Šitullum, Suḫûm, and Numḫia (§§10, 14, 20–21). Of these, Idamaraṣ alone had protections for both "citizens" (dumu GN) and "markets" (kar GN), whereas Mankisum and Šitullum had only its markets exempted; Numḫia had only its citizens exempted; and Suḫûm more obliquely had its "arrears" (lál.ḫi.a) exempted. These places were not in lower Babylonia, and they also were not included in the list of cities in the Code of Hammurabi that defined what the kingdom of Babylon considered itself to rule.[31]

Alongside the exemptions particularized to foreign places, we find exemptions for citizens and markets of six cities which were geographically all Babylonian (§§10, 20–21): Isin, Larsa, and Malgium had both markets and citizens exempted; Borsippa had only its markets exempted; Uruk and Kisurra had only their citizens exempted. All but Kisurra are listed among the kingdom's cities by the Code of Hammurabi.[32] Meanwhile, other political identities we might expect to appear in the Edicts are absent: citizens and merchants of Sippar, Dilbat, or Kiš, the principal

[30] See esp. Charpin 1987 and Veenhof 1997–2000.
[31] Cf. Charpin 2010: 39.
[32] It may be that Kisurra's proximity to Isin accounts for its absence from the Code of Hammurabi's prologue. Two more geographic classes may be notes: a legal domain called "the land" (§§2, 21; cf. §12), with both a market and citizens, and Babylon (§§2 and 10), for which, intriguingly, "citizens" are not mentioned. Whatever the implications of these differences, both were their own special legal and administrative identities.

other cities of the kingdom. Neither did the Edicts which listed Uruk, Isin, Larsa, etc., list any other southern cities which Babylon had otherwise claimed to represent, such as Ur or Nippur. Nor did the Edicts exempt debts for citizens or merchants from places like Aleppo, Elam, Aššur, Jablija, Emar, Arrapḫa, or Ešnunna, places from which Babylon continued to host resident aliens and do some trading business. In no case did the Edicts' exemptions claim powers to levy or remit rents over foreign *places*, but only reliefs for certain people *from* those places, as foreigners of one degree or another resident in the kingdom of Babylon. No ethnic group is mentioned by either the Edicts or the Code of Hammurabi: the legal authority of the state was over citizens and institutions of polities, not ethnoi.

The provisions of the Edicts distinguish between the relief of commercial loans, specified for "Akkadians or Amorites" in §§3–9, likely a merism something like the whole Babylonian population (of citizens?);[33] and in all other passages (§§1–2, 10–22) along two axes: according to political origin, and for persons under Crown authority (officers, tenants, and others owing rents). The remissions for these people were particular and limited: none included relief for debt servitude or for goods sold on credit as such;[34] and, more to the point, those eligible for relief of private debts were not relieved of taxes, duties, or rents, and those eligible for the relief of taxes and duties were not (necessarily) eligible for the relief of private debts. Ethnicity in no case formed a basis for inclusion or exclusion from legal protection in the Edicts,[35] and neither am I aware of any Old Babylonian legal proceeding in which a person's ethnicity was of legal consequence, either.

Why was there relief for people from Idamaraṣ but not from Ur? Why were citizens of Numḫâ exempted, but not of Nippur?

The enumerated cities were all ones which had come into the Babylonian kingdom on specific terms: that is, either they were royal cities like Larsa and Uruk (also Isin, Idamaraṣ, Malgium, Kisurra) defeated by Babylon whose thrones Babylon notionally occupied and continued.[36] Suḫûm and Mankisum had likely also been negotiated into the Babylonian kingdom at some later date;[37] contingents

---

[33] Cf. AbB XIV 130 on a *mīšarum*; it is unclear, if *muškēnu* means "commoners," why the term "Amorite and Akkadian" was not used (see discussion in Richardson 2017: 47 n. 35). Given the broad absence of non-Babylonian persons from loan documents (see above), it is likely that even if the term "Amorites and Akkadians" *did* mean "all people" and not just "all Babylonians," non-Babylonians would have been functionally excluded anyway, since neither credit markets nor their relief were open to them.

[34] It is not clear whether or not such conditions were anticipated by or included as extensions of the provisions related to interest, forced collection, etc., but at least they are not specified.

[35] Suhûm (§14) should probably be understood as the name of a geographic province, and not to stand for "Suhaeans." Although Suhûm is not mentioned in the Prologue to LH, a governor (*šāpir* Suhûm) is attested at least once, in CT 4 1.

[36] Richardson 2018: 169–171.

[37] Part of Suhûm came under Ḫammurabi's control by negotiation with Mari (Charpin 2004: 163), but the territory was only substantially attached to Babylon in the middle of Samsuiluna's reign (Charpin 2004: 370; 2010: 39). Babylon's earlier 19th-century claims on Mankisum (as van Koppen – Lacambre 2008–2009: 152–153 and n. 15 now convincingly argue) were probably not revived until after Ḫammurabi's conquest of Ešnunna. Van De Mieroop 2005: 45–46 writes that Babylon "received Mankisum [in] an arrangement certainly imposed by the *sukkal* of Elam" as an attempt to balance power between Mari, Babylon, and Ešnunna.

from tribal centers like Numḫâ had been hired as mercenaries.[38] These groups all had pre-existing *contracts* of some sort with Babylon, reflected by the Edicts.

At an abstract level, it seems significant that there were differences both *between* people we might otherwise suppose were "native citizens"; *and between* people we might all label alike as foreigners. Neither all "natives" nor all "foreigners" were counted as equals. The Edicts in fact *created* these special classes: whether the Crown considered them to be people subject to law (i.e., as legal subjects, citizens) or to command (i.e., as dependents of a domain)—their status was *made* and maintained as different. One effect of this distribution was that so many different levels of belonging, privilege, and exemption prevented easy dyads of insiders vs. outsiders from emerging in the first place.

Story 3: Exiles and floating royals

Low-status mercenaries and workers were not the only out-of-place people populating the Late Old Babylonian landscape, as we find temple and civil officers from the southern Babylonian cities now resident in the north. On the one hand, the appearance of so many southern exiled elites in the north had more to do with a royal program to emulate and artificially reconstruct the cultic and cultural Sumerian south in the Amorite north than with actual exiles.[39] Their presence was put in a spotlight because Babylon took an active interest in "looking southern/ Sumerian." One particularly intriguing effort was the cultic veneration of thrones for "faraway places." A certain image of the Sumerian south—now effectively a semi-foreign place—was conceptually valorized as an ideal place and past, while other places had no grip on Babylon's cultural imagination.

On the other hand, the textual attestations undeniably involved some flesh-and-blood elite southern exiles, instrumental to a Babylonian plan to claim kingship over a south that had been lost after the revolts against Samsuiluna, probably against the slowly-encroaching Sealand Dynasty. So among the many people crowded into the little cowpen of the Late OB state, and afforded an outsized share of ideological attention, were persons who were (or purported to be) officials and clergy resettled from the southern cities—mostly of Uruk, Isin, and Larsa, but also of Nippur, Ur, and elsewhere.

One is tempted to wonder how many of the resident aliens or "runaways" (*munnabtu*) from Elam, Subartu, Suhûm, etc., were also formerly landed, titled, or important persons in their homelands, and what the relationship was between invited, accepted, and uninvited visitors. This leads me to speculate on the question of whether or how many non-Babylonian persons living in Late OB Babylon were exiles, whether high (i.e., from foreign courts or even descendants of foreign rulers) or low (e.g., members of outcast populations) as a consequence of the wars of the previous century.

---

[38] See Charpin 2001 on the connection between *maḫanum* and Numḫâ.
[39] See Richardson 2018.

The speculation is hardly an unlikely one. Exile and banishment are both dealt with in Old Babylonian Laws (LE §30, LH §154),[40] and deportees, runaways, and refugees from all levels of society are well attested in letters and omens.[41] Political exiles are well-known from the Mari letters, with princelets, out-of-favor viziers, and pretenders scattered across the "Amorite world" of the 18th century. Dominique Charpin has written on extradition and rights of asylum, and Adam Miglio on the refugees called *kaltū* who were aspirants to thrones, and the family members (*mādarū*) whom might become *kaltū* in turn.[42] If it seems like an unlikely fairy tale to imagine a Mesopotamian world with princes and pretenders floating around all over the place, one might try the following thought exercise. First, consider how many petty kings, luckless second sons, diplomats, pretenders, and generals were turned out by war and intrigue all over the Syro-Mesopotamian world between 1770 and 1720, including the (ex-)royals called *mādarū* or *pirḫu*. Then wonder: did these people really all just melt back into the social landscape and go back to being local landlords or farmers without a backward glance? Maybe. But it seems unlikely that such pasts could be sloughed away like so much snakeskin: even the private letters of Babylonian families commonly invoked the generational histories that remembered lost farms and cities, evoking a historical horizon of about a century. Given the unlikeliness of forgetting, it is not that hard to imagine that either southern elites or third-generation royals nursed memories of former family greatness. It seems equally unlikely that some non-Babylonian families digging canals in Sippar or staffing some fort on the Tigris, loosely referred to as "Gutians"[43] or "Numḫâ", did not have their own stories of lost homes and dreams of return. There is no evidence for this, and I doubt there ever will be.[44] But it seems ridiculous to pretend that outsiders themselves, marked separate for so long, did not think about home, making only two-dimensional social comparisons to the Babylonians among whom they lived.

Story 4: The mercenary landscape

The next story concerns the reception of a radically different *Gastarbeiter* population: the many ethnic mercenary contingents populating the Late OB landscape. Their presence at this time has been long noted, but somewhat underrated; newly-published texts from the fortress of Dūr-Abi-ešuḫ (CUSAS 8 and 29) now give us substantially new insight to the issue. Foreign soldiers have been identified in

---

[40] These are briefly noted by Westbrook 2008: 317–318, 321 in his article on personal exile; cf. below on various forms of household banishment and compare to e.g., CAD N/1 s.v. *nakāru* v. 8d, "to move away."

[41] E.g. referenced by/as *naparšudu*, *ḫabirūtim*, *ṭardu*/*ṭarīdu*/*ṭaridūtu*, *kuššudu*, etc.

[42] See esp. Miglio 2014 and 2016: 302–304 on the *kaltū* and *mādarū* from the Mari letters; also Charpin 2004: 197 n. 943.

[43] Pongratz-Leisten 2000: 218: "Already by the end of the Old Babylonian period, the term 'Gutian' was of little more than vague geographic or ethnic significance."

[44] One might compare the large literature on modern myths of homeland and return in disaporic communities. If applied to ancient contexts, the twelve questions posed by Safran 1991: 95–97 about the social and political effects of diaspora could yet be enormously fruitful.

many individual texts and circumstances; and certain groups, such as Numhaeans and Kassites, have been particularly linked to the mercenary function for this time. These observations, however, have not extended much farther than to position foreign mercenaries as a particular kind of worker in a particular line of work. The question has not been asked as a socio-political issue: what did it mean that there were large numbers of foreign men-at-arms, perhaps even a majority of the Crown's soldiers, living in Babylonia?

These were not groups who had just been hired yesterday; they had been present in Babylonia for a century or more, during which time it would have been unavoidable that mercenary groups developed and maintained group identity, especially labelled by ethnonym for so long.[45] There is only limited evidence for primary production at Ḫaradum[46] and Abi-ešuḫ,[47] but what there is is concentrated in the period after Ad 20, with allied evidence for local economic activity[48] (including herding[49]), and traces of civic,[50] cult,[51] family,[52] and community identities.[53] One notes as well the many mentions of other

45 See Richardson (2019c and 2019d) for mercenaries and *ḫabbātu* in 18th- and 17th-century Babylonia.

46 There is evidence for primary production in the texts excavated from Ḫaradum (Joannès 2006), including sales of arable land there (nos. 2 and 32) and various small loans and accounts of barley (e.g., nos. 16 and 17). It is less clear that local production accounted for larger quantities of grain such as the 70+ še.gur (21,000+ liters) of barley in nos. 24 (igi-sá?) and 105.

47 At Dūr-Abi-ešuḫ, the barley disbursed to soldiers in CUSAS 29 1–41 seems clearly to have been shipped in from the outside during the years Ae 13(?) through Ad 16, though there is also evidence for substantial reserves kept on-site (e.g., CUSAS 29 131, with over 400 še.gur in stock; see also no. 137). However, the consignments of plowblades documented in the same corpus (CUSAS 29 118–124) date to a later point (Ad 21–24), with no overlap, and memoranda about barley and other comestibles *not* clearly from elsewhere cluster in an even later time periods (CUSAS 8 54–89, Aṣ 2–Sd 11), again with no overlap. Though the non-overlapping evidence may reflect an accident of discovery, it is curious that the central disbursal of barley to fortresses here coincides with the fortress-provisioning texts of TLOB 1: 16–20, which span the years Ad 11–23. On the strength of the temporal restriction of the evidence we have, I have proposed a change from the provisioning of fortresses to their independent primary production after ca. Ad 23 (Richardson 2002: 320–324).

48 Ten contracts from Dūr-Abi-ešuḫ in CUSAS 29 are attested, dating from Ae 4 (no. 175) through Ad 31 (nos. 138 and 187), including also 126, 127, 188, 178, 173, 179, and 185. The 35 contracts from CUSAS 8 fall in a later time, from Ad 29 (no. 1) through Sd 13 (no. 53), including also nos. 2–22 and 41–52. Note commercial ties with Arrapḫa, suggested by CUSAS 8 51, 53, and perhaps 82.

49 E.g., CUSAS 8 41–43.

50 CUSAS 29 188 (Ad 8) documents silver paid as *šubultum*-dues of Dūr-Abi-ešuḫ to Babylon.

51 Note the references to the shrines of Nabium, Adad, and Inanna of Agade in CUSAS 29 162–163; it is not at all clear that these were disbursements to shrines in Nippur rather than in Dūr-Abi-ešuḫ itself. Further, note the many divination and other rituals carried out there (e.g. CUSAS 29 44ff., esp. 206), and the temple personnel rations of CUSAS 8 59 and 60, the latter of which is for the Mišārum temple.

52 Some texts suggest that soldiers received rations for families as well as themselves, when we find phrases of the type erén *ù aḫītim*, "soldiers and their dependents" (e.g., TLOB 1 20, CUSAS 8 39, AbB II 54; see CAD A/1 s.v. *aḫītu* s. 5). But this is probably to be distinguished from phrases of the type erén *ù* erén *aḫītim*, "soldiers and other workers" (CUSAS 29, passim). At least one private household is acknowledged in CUSAS 8 56–57 (Aṣ 1 and 14) and 29 125 (Ae 21), and multiple sons of one father are mentioned in, e.g., CUSAS 8 87 and 88 (i.e., dumu.meš PN).

53 Richardson 2005: 282–283: "[F]or many such soldiers, these towns were not merely billets, but rather the hometowns in which entire families had grown up." Compare with Pruzsinszky 2019, this volume, on "semi-autonomous settlements."

fortresses in the Dūr-Abi-ešuḫ texts, and the frequent communication between them.[54]

None of this is to suggest that Dūr-Abi-ešuḫ functioned at the institutional level as a Babylonian city; we should note in particular the virtual absence of civic officers like a *ḫazannu* or *rabi sikkatim*,[55] with mostly Crown and temple titles alongside professional names (lúlunga, šitim, etc.). But at Ḫaradum, we find at least a *rabiānum* and a council of elders (*šibūt ālim*).[56] The features of emergent communities are there, at least, and it is against these new identities, cohering over several generations, that we might consider that their loyalties to the kingdom continued to be contingent on the satisfactory continuation of their contract terms (principally, in the payment of rations), usually on a monthly basis. As Michael Heltzer said of the Sutaeans in Babylonia, "they were more like military colonists, with certain rights in their dwelling-place, than simple mercenaries."[57]

The instability of the situation is clear: the Crown relied on groups which were armed, differently denominated, and with an increasing sense of their separate identity. Little suggests that any single group was instrumental to the state's eventual collapse. Rather, the problem to explore here is how the phenomenon of warlord*ism* affected the larger political sense of who belonged to the state and why. In this environment, to a person from Sippar or Kiš, a Kassite soldier here or an Elamite mercenary there was not just a soldier who happened to be a foreigner. To their point of view, that person was not only defined by what he was (i.e., someone belonging to a larger class of armed, foreign mercenaries), but by what he wasn't: a city-dweller, stakeholder in property, or invested with a title. Camped out in fortresses and the countryside, mercenaries were people who properly belonged to the Palace household rather than to state society as citizens understood it.

The number, diversity, and durability of foreign mercenary groups in northern Babylonia at this time astonishing. We know of at least 23 foreign mercenary troops operating in Late OB Babylonia,[58] with other non-Babylonian troops called

---

54 CUSAS 29, including the fortresses at Baganna (nos. 39 and 40), Dūr-Akšak-iddinam (nos. 35 and 189), Dūr-šarrim (nos. 67 and 68), and many others. Note in this connection the text from Ḫaradum mentioning silver given to fund a journey to Dūr-Abi-ešuḫ (Joannès 2006 no. 18).

55 One lonely *rabi sikkatim* appears in CUSAS 29 139.

56 Joannès 2006: nos. 1, 15, 20, 23, and 29; nos. 23 and 24 also mention the *šibūt ālim* of Yabliya.

57 Michael Heltzer (1981), apud Pientka 1998: 265 n. 47.

58 See Richardson 2019d: 230–233 and passim. For a list of places-of-origins and ethnonyms for troops of erén, with exemplary texts cited: Aḫlamu (Joannès 2006 nos. 65 and 104), Aleppo (CUSAS 29 5), Arameans (CUSAS 29 40), Arrapḫa (CUSAS 29 40), Bimatî (CUSAS 29 6), Elam (TLOB 1 44), Gutium (CUSAS 29 40, TLOB 1 55), Hana (TLOB 1 44), Hanigalbat (BM 96955), Idamaraṣ (CUSAS 29 32), Jamutbal (TLOB 1 44), Kassite (TLOB 1 44), nu.kárki (CUSAS 29 71), Numḫâ (AbB VI 190; see also CUSAS 29 12–13), Qaṭana (CUSAS 29 30; probably for Qatanum [i.e., Qaṭna]), Rababî (TLOB 1 17), Šadlaši (VS 18 18), Širamaḫ (TLOB 1 50), Sutû (CUSAS 29 28), Tukriš (MHET II 6 908), Turukku (TÉA 34; see also Béranger 2018 n. 7), Yabliya (Joannès 2006: no. 24), and Yaḫruru (TLOB 1 16). Šubartu appears to designate a single soldier only in CUSAS 29 16 (cf. AbB VI 17); the erén Kuṣṣari of BM 96955 are of undetermined origin. I do not take the designation erén mar.tu to indicate a meaningful ethnonym by this late date (see e.g., TLOB 1 44, where the "mar.tu" are Ḫanaean, Jamutbal, Kassite, etc.). The contingents were often multi-ethnic: note BM 81624, with Elamites and Sutaeans together in the Tigris fortress; and TLOB 1 50, with Širamaḫites, Elamites, and *ba'īrū* in the Bāṣum fortress.

ḫāpiru,[59] *ḫabbātu*,[60] or "men of the land."[61] Conversely, one generally searches in vain for references to troops of Babylon,[62] Dilbat, Kiš,[63] or Sippar (i.e., as erén GN, in clearly military contexts).[64] Importantly, we are aware that ethnically non-Babylonian troops were called on to defend the kingdom from *other* troops of outsiders—e.g., troops of Ešnunna, the Sealand and Samḫarû Kassites—with whom they may have had more in common than the urban Babylonians they were defending. From monthly ration texts, most individual non-Babylonian contingents seem to have been relatively small units of under a hundred men,[65] but some texts reveal that there could be dozens of contingents in single fortresses at the same time (e.g., CUSAS 29 39–40, which each list between thirty and forty individual platoons), with staffing running up to the brigade level of around 4,000 men.[66] There were at least 28 (and perhaps as many as 43) actively staffed fortresses in the kingdom, at a moment when the state had shrunk to only four cities.[67] And these were just the armed groups employed the Crown; there were also other unaffiliated troops, tribes, and "enemies" camped out in the land who were making travel and herding difficult at this time. Altogether, we are looking at a sizeable and diverse non-urban population which was a product of the state and interstate system at war in the previous century.

The mercenaries had many of the characteristics of the 18th century groups called *ḫabbātū*, literally "robbers", though this word itself was rarely used in the 17th century (only sometimes *ḫāpiru*); in what follows, I use the word descriptively with respect to the later time. As Jesper Eidem has written, the *ḫabbātū* were a new phenomenon in northern Mesopotamia in the 1770s and '60s, in the wake of the interstate wars between Mari, Ekallatum, Babylon, Ešnunna, etc. What is the difference between the *ḫabbātū* of 1760 and 1660? Though the *ḫabbātū* may originally have belonged to independent polities, by the 1600s these polities were long gone

---

[59] CUSAS 29 39 and 62.

[60] YOS 13 205 (Ad 4) lists an ugula *ḫa-ba-ti*. Cf. CUSAS 29 191:2, reading erén *ḫa-°-ab-bi-tu* (not, as the editors have it, *ú-ḫa-x-ab-bi-tu*); best explained as a writing for *ḫabbātu*. See also Richardson 2019c.

[61] CUSAS 29 40 and 120.

[62] Cf. CUSAS 29 25:7.

[63] Cf. CUSAS 29 39 rev. 1′.

[64] Note a few troops from Babylonian cities not under the rule of Babylon at this time: of Isin, Maškan-šāpir, and Uruk (e.g., CUSAS 29 8 and 39–40).

[65] Ration texts which give both total amounts of grain and rates per man include CUSAS 29 5 (the amount and rate reflect 35 erén Ḫalaba), 19 (54 erén Kaššî), 31 (5 erén Kaššî), 33 (15 erén Maškan-šāpir), etc. The difficulty in reconstructing contingent sizes when rates are not given within a text lies in the wide range of rates attested, ranging from 10–60 sìla per man per month, but the size of the individual troops seems relatively small, safely under 100 men.

[66] See e.g. TLOB 1 18–20, which list 71,640+, 5,163, and 23,666 liters of grain, respectively; the first is, however, not a ration text, strictly speaking, but an account of an (annual?) reserve for one fortress. The largest disbursal for soldiers in one place of which I'm aware is CUSAS 29 40's disbursal to the erén *birti* nibru^{ki} as monthly rations (rev. 22′) of 74,190 liters of barley (obv. 1-27 and rev. 1′–9′; restorable by subtracting the 24.2.0 še.gur given to two other fortresses rev. 10′–14′ from the total on rev. 15′ of 271.3.3 še.gur, leaving 247.1.3). At the range of rates given above in n. 65, this would provender anywhere from ca. 1,235–7,419 men; while the range is large, the numbers attest to brigade-level staffing in some fortresses.

[67] See Richardson 2019b.

or otherwise unreachable. The *ḫabbātu* had not only preserved group identity across that time, but identifiable leaders and officers, responsible for the receipt and distribution of their rations.[68] These were surely administrative rather than political relationships—the officers were in position as receivers (šuti.a) and distributors of rations to their troops—but the political potential of patronage needs little explanation. Warlord status would translate smoothly to independent leadership, such as for Araḫab, "man of the lands" (*a-ra-ḫa-ab* lú ma-da, in year-name Ad 17), the Agum *bukāšum* of AbB VI 24, or the Tiggil lugal erén Kaššî of OLA 21 20. The path from platoon-leader to prince should be no less imaginable to us than that of the foundation of a "legitimate" dynasty (of Kassites, or the Sealand) through some originally non-royal lineage.[69]

Thus we have separate groups, living in distinctive places, with their own leaders; we should not find it difficult to imagine they might have developed independent goals. These were not just ephemeral bands of mercenaries anymore, but permanent and institutional social units, developing a warlord culture which came to characterize the age. The mercenary groups had routine and regular rationing, dependents, landholding regimes, religious practices, living in fortresses (*birtū*), encampments (*bitāti*), and bivouacs (*karāšu*) which were not attached to the cities of the Babylonian state, and this in a context where the term "the land" already had a distinct legal and administrative meaning. These are all the stable socio-economic ingredients of an identifiable society—jobs, families, and communities. Neither quite migrants nor Babylonians, the mercenaries conform to the phenomenon of the "coalescence of remnant populations", typically as low-status guest workers with local mobility.[70] As McGeough (2019, this volume) puts it, they were at best only "administrative subjects", belonging to the state on a qualitatively different basis than those who understood their subjectivity in terms of shared language, soil, cult, and blood. The political loyalty to the state of these separate groups, fully armed, was entirely contingent on getting paid their monthly wage.

Two other contributions to this volume elaborate the separateness of military communities: Candelora (2019) points out that mercenaries formed the durable social bonds that can only be forged between people who depend on each other for their lives; Mushett Cole (2019) writes that enclaves tend towards a military nature, forming counter-identities to surrounding host societies, such as the Gurkhas or Cossacks. These ties seem intuitive, and it is not hard to imagine why this was an unstable setup in political-military terms.

But what did it mean culturally? The normalization of foreign mercenaries as the main part of the military changed the relationship between civil society and the Crown, because they increasingly became the king's troops, and not necessar-

[68] Noting the nomenclature of *ḫabbātū*-bands by the names of their leaders (Eidem 2011), one observes the administrative language of erén X níg.šu PN; erén X *itti* PN {title}; etc. See also Richardson 2019c: 17–20 and 2019d: 233.

[69] If the latter is not already circular reasoning, since every founding member of a dynasty was not originally a king himself.

[70] See especially Cameron 2013: 219, 223–224, 226–227.

ily the state's—because the separateness marked *by* the state distinguished them from other subjects. Thus the presence of these populations not only reflected the different status of those foreigners, but further changed the relation of native citizens to the king. This distinction seems enshrined in a later Assyrian *tamītu* oracle, which describes exactly this three-way tension between city, king, and troops in the Late Old Babylonian period:

> "Or, the senior resident man who lives in the city will not go out of his mind, will not lose his reason, will not confer with the enemy army, will not open the bridge of the city gate, and will not expel the troops (under the authority) of Marduk and Samsuditana, son of Ammiṣaduqa, king of Babylon, will not allow the enemy army into the city, will he?"[71]

The stark separateness of these groups reflected a framing of primarily ethnic rather than political identities as separate and dangerous, since they were denominated in ethnic terms most of the time.[72] If we compare this to the granting of legal privileges by the Edicts which had the purpose of bringing people within the legal circle of the state, we find that (to some degree) social *membership* and *togetherness* was almost always contingent upon *political* identity.[73] Conversely, when we look the mercenaries (as well as workers and slaves) as they were marked by administrative texts, their separateness was almost always framed in *ethnic* terms. Political identity was a form of or avenue to partial legal personhood, while ethnic identity consistently marked separateness. Without making a Frankenstein monster from this distinction, it remains fair to say that in the Late OB context, one can begin to think that political identity and origin was something that worked to domesticate the foreign, as a matter of essential similarity, whereas (mere) ethnic identity remained a qualitatively different way to mark relations.

Inside Out: The Strangers Next Door

As complicated as outsiderness could be, we oversimplify it when we compare it to a supposedly stable benchmark of insiderness; to assume that the perception of outsiderness took place from a fixed vantage point. In fact, both categories of "inside" and "outside" were moving targets. Practices of differentiation cannot be taken as acts of objective denomination, but ones *instrumental* to maintaining or altering specific relations; they do not describe, but rather aim to get something done.

---

[71] Lambert 2007: 27 (BOQ 1:78–84). See Richardson 2019d for a historical interpretation of this magico-literary text.

[72] The 23 units listed in n. 58 include only three terms which are necessarily political rather than ethnic: Arrapḫa, Qaṭana, and Širamaḫ, though many terms are fundamentally ambivalent on this point (e.g., Elam); see below n. 73 on Idaramaraṣ and Numḫâ.

[73] Idamaraṣ and Numḫâ are the rare cases of overlap between the political communities recognized legally and the ethnic communities recognized administratively.

I will tell three stories about "insiders", about the precarious and negotiable terms of belonging to Babylonian household and society, even if one seemed undoubtedly to belong in the cultural sense. These stories may be told more briefly for having been described, in part, by work published elsewhere. The stories do not have directly to do with foreigners, but tell us much about the potential of falling out of position, in relative if not absolute terms, and about the central role that anxiety played in the social maneouvers necessary to maintain or acquire insider status. The much-feared possibility of becoming marginalized in the home society is, I argue, a crucial countervalent force against which the reception of culturally or geographically alien persons was produced: not a single tension between two stable polarities, but a systemic tension organized around two attractors; more like the interface between two weather systems, each with its own internal dynamics, than like a rubber band stretched between two points.

To put this in more concrete and relevant language, I describe the difference in the reception of foreign people between a host culture which is economically and socially well-to-do, and one which has serious domestic problems of economic insecurity, homelessness, and political division. It seems meaningless to evaluate a society's sense of who "outsiders" are without also thinking about expressed types and problems of alienation *within* that host culture. Looking at such conditions of belonging thus allows us to contextualize or triangulate the forces affecting the two arenas of social tension. This seems all the more necessary for the study of a society which begins by being as subtle about marking outsiderness in ethnic-political-geographic-linguistic terms as Babylonia is. My first story is about merchants; the second is about women; the third and last is about the alienation of the government itself.

Story 5: Nervous *awīlū*

By the 18th century in Babylonia, a class of well-to-do landowners, titled officials, and merchants come into historical view through the large corpus of letters they shared. Referring to one another as "gentlemen" (*awīlū*), in contrast to others, they constructed, phrase by phrase, a community imagined in terms of the following characteristics: friendly conduct, concern for well-being, personal favor, kinship metaphors, pity, reputation, gentlemanliness, collegiality, and piety.[74] The evidence I gather for the *awīlū* is virtually identical to that gathered so exhaustively by Walther Sallaberger twenty years ago, characterizing it as the functional lexicon or sociolect of an in-group whose identity was bound together via social ethics of fraternalism and friendship (he did not use the word "class").[75]

What I want to highlight in my telling of the same evidence is how contingent and precarious this sense of shared experience really was. Despite the clear existence of a shared discourse about who did and didn't qualify as an *awīlu*, where

---

[74] Cf. Jursa – Häckl 2014, using a four-fold typology of rational, emotional, and personal(ized) arguments, and the "invocation of higher authorities."

[75] Sallaberger 1999.

Sallaberger sees the expressions as descriptions of accomplished social facts and evidence for a well-established class, I see them as typically invoked to rebuke the *failure* of such expected behavior, to describe insufficient performance of its ethos, or, at most, to plead for and encourage future behavior.[76] Rather than reading phrases like "You are my friend!" and "You are my brother!" and "We are gentlemen!", we read instead, over and over, "Why were you *not* friendly to me?" and "Why do you *not* act as my brother?" and "Your behavior is *not* the behavior of a gentleman!" Once one begins to hear it in this voice, it seems impossible to un-hear.

At best, the letters speak of the precarious process of class formation, where every membership was contingent on that day's performance, and not the easy, confident expression of the satisfaction of an accomplished group. Most of the energy spent in the expression of *awīlu*-hood was directed towards policing its boundaries: for making sure once one got in, one stayed in, didn't fall out, and helped to keep out the *hoi polloi*. Just as Fredrik Barth argues that it is the boundary-construction of ethnicity "that defines the group, [and] not the cultural stuff that it encloses" (see Streit's excellent paper on this theme, Streit 2019, this volume), so too it is the case for groups of insiders, too: every class feels like a precariat to its members.

In this respect, we may note a tenth topos that appears in the letters alongside the class-building language of the *awīlu*: the frequent defense by the letter-writer that a third person unknown to the recipient, being introduced as a business colleague, is "not a stranger" (*ūla nakru*): "The man is a man of my household, not a stranger", etc.[77] This term *nakru*, "stranger", is fundamentally exclusive, the same one which means foreign, alien, or hostile. Where the characterization is elaborated,[78] the letters show that the criteria for being a "stranger" or not primarily have to do with whether they were part of an identifiable household or not,[79] or secondarily whether or not the writer had personal knowledge (*idû*) of him.[80] In no letter is "strangeness" a consequence of ethnicity or place of origin. When we look for a place in Old Babylonian thought where people were consistently evaluating others as "outsiders" and "insiders", it is in this context of household membership and personal knowledge. The search for a secure semantic base for Babylonian "insiderness" returns us again and again to the level of the household rather than of the city or the nation; where the closest terms we have for

---

76 For the full analysis of this corpus, see Richardson (in preparation B).

77 See the OB exs. s.v. CAD N/1 *nakru* adj. 1 (in at least two separate cited clusters of OB attestations).

78 Letters which do not explain why or how someone is or is not (*) a "stranger" (*nakru*) include AbB I 49*, II 81, VI 76, XIII 143. AbB X 1 elaborates only that PN is not a stranger because he is a "man of/in my hand" (*awīl qātija*). I do not include mentions of *aḫītu*, *ajābu*, or *bēl lemuti* (e.g. XI 94) here, which more explicitly invoke the idea of an "enemy"; or *šanû* (e.g. XII 172), which is relatively ambiguous as to the judgement of an "other."

79 Letters which define "strangers" with reference to household relations include AbB II 154, VI 69, VIII 134, X 3 ("He and I suckled together at the breast!"), XI 148, XII 144. Cf. ETCSL 4.27.07:106, lú.kúr a-a-na, a "stranger to his father."

80 Letters which define "strangers" with reference to personal knowledge include AbB IV 56 and XII 76. See further CAD I/J s.v. *idû* v. 1b)-2′-a′+c′ for instances of persons vouched for in terms of being known. Cf. ETCSL 2.2.6:67.

"natives" or "citizens" were also very local terms of household status, DUMU and DUMU.MUNUS, lit. "son" and "daughter", and the non-"stranger" was defined by a lack of household status.

So, alongside the pervasive anxiety about who counted as an *awīlum* and who did not, we find that even the few outright distinctions about being a "stranger" that *were* being made had no relation to ethnic or geographic foreignness, but only to who was known to whom among prominent families. All of the relevant distinctions being made by the caste or class of mercantile letter-writers, even when they used the explicit terms we expect, were internal to their ranks, with no hint that any concern for foreignness existed.

Women without households

The second story has to do with women living outside of paternal households. Almost thirty years ago, Caroline Janssen edited a literary letter of King Samsuiluna of Babylon to several of his officials.[81] The text is known from several school copies,[82] datable to the last third of Samsuiluna's reign. The king says in the letter that women living in the temple cloister of Sippar-Jaḫrūrum, called *nadītums*, had complained of hunger, and that the Sippar officials had to see to it that the women's families met their promises to provide those women with food. The letter stipulated that women's families were to sign contracts promising to provision the *nadītums* in the future, and that the cloister was not to accept any woman without such a written agreement. Moreover, her property was not subject to seizure for the debts of her father's household (l. 52, *bīt abiša*).[83] The protections were supposed to be double, from a socio-legal standpoint. On the one hand, a *nadītum* was to be guaranteed support from her *bīt abiša*, even though she resided in another household: she had been "entered" (*šūrubu*, l. 10) into the Cloister, after which point she "lived" there (*ina* gá.gi$_4$.a *wašbat*, l. 20), and not liable to the debt-and-seizure rules of another household—all of which implicated household membership beyond mere residence. On the other hand, she was simultaneously to be supported by her father's household (and/or that of her brothers, if need be). Notwithstanding, the entire arrangement was founded on principles of household belonging, for which the simple preposition *ina* (i.e., to be "inside" a house(hold)) was what subtly marked membership.

The *loss* of household membership, by contrast, was marked in much more lexically diverse ways in OB Akkadian, but no less clearly for being so: one could be "put out" of a household (*šūṣû*),[84] "turned out" (*sakāpu*),[85] "rejected" (*nasāḫu*

[81] Janssen 1991.

[82] Ibid.: 15–21: The letter had an archival afterlife, known from multiple copies late into the 17th century, which attests to an ongoing interest in its themes and perhaps even legal stipulations.

[83] Ibid.: 9: any creditor who seized her property for this reason was someone the King ordered to be called "an enemy (*ajābu*) of the god Šamaš."

[84] See esp. CAD A/2 s.v. *aṣû* v. 6c and 8a, citing CH §172, to be "put out" of the house.

[85] See CAD S s.v. *sakāpu* A v. 2c-1′ and the relevant difficult passages in AbB I 29 and 36, VI 148 and 190, XI 45 (cf. CAD S p. 73).

1a–2′, especially of a child[86]; *zêru* 1a–1′[87]), "driven away" (*ṭarādu* A 2c), or be the subject of various declarations, best known from legal texts, that "You are not my daughter / son / wife / husband."[88] The contingent reality that one might not be ejected from a household, and all the protections that it afforded, brings us to the stark realization of how imperiled the hungry *nadītums* of the royal letter really were: although in a perfect world one might understand it to mean they had the support of both the Cloister and their natal families (with obligations to neither), it is clear that in practice the situation left them *between* two households rather than members of both.

As Jannsen wrote, we cannot know if poor *nadītums* were a new phenomenon in the 1720s; this is simply when it becomes visible in the record. Jannsen connected their appearance to the near-*dis*appearance of Cloister officials from the texts after this time, and also of sales of houses in the Cloister, previously a fairly common transaction. Finally, she questioned whether or not the Cloister itself even existed anymore in the 17th century, abandoned by the *nadītums* for some unknown reason.[89]

To be clear, however, it was only the physical Cloister building and enclosure that apparently disappeared, and not the *nadītums* or even the officials: we know of dozens and dozens of these women living and doing business all the way down through the 17th century.[90] Through a prosopographical analysis, I have shown the 17th century *nadītums* differed from their 18th century predecessors in at least two important respects. First, whereas both centuries give us lots of *nadītum* documents *grosso modo*, the earlier corpus documents the business and landholding of a relatively small number of women with many texts each, the later record is composed out of the one or two texts of many women. Second, the earlier, wealthier *nadītums* were attended, perhaps even served, by a less-wealthy cadre of other (junior?) *nadītums*; in the later period, this two-tiered hierarchy is no longer in evidence.

The personal names of the later *nadītums* became more heterodox, as did the titles of the officials. Their business changed, too: the *nadītum* dealings in real estate dwindled to almost nothing, especially for purchases of houses and land (entirely in keeping with the general absence of purchases for the Late OB as a whole), while their best-attested activity becomes the extension of small amounts of credit in silver and grain (also in keeping with the activity of the later period), and receiving rations. The Cloister itself was no longer mentioned, even as a location for private houses, and so just how and where these poorer *nadītums* were living is a question we cannot answer on present evidence. We are looking, in sum, at a larger number of women engaged in smaller and fewer transactions

---

86 With *aplūtu*, "to disinherit."

87 Often preceding divorce, leaving the household (in which case the common verb *alāku* often appears, simply "to go"), etc.

88 See various negative statements s.v. CAD M *mārtu* 1a-3′, *māru* 1a-3′, etc.; perhaps also in some senses from *abāku* A, *našû* A with *idātu*.

89 Jannsen 1991: 11–13.

90 See Richardson 2010a on the issues discussed in this and the next paragraph.

based in the credit market, rather than a powerful few holding real property and exploiting it for primary production. In sociological terms, the *nadītum* class as a whole was transformed from a closed-rank group to an open-rank one, a scattering of the group which seems to mirror the dispersal of the Cloister as a physical household.

I take note, then, of eight tabular-format texts for dependent women probably living in the temple of Annunītum in Sippar-Amnānum.[91] These texts seem clearly to derive from a single deposition: they are all burned and broken, and dated between 1636 and 1629 BC (i.e., Aṣ 10–17), up until the year before Sippar-Amnānum was burned. About 200 names are listed in these texts, virtually all women, many with children in tow, and only a handful of them identified as the wives of anyone. The women are all classed as *aštapīrū*, "household servants". The women receive from 10–40 liters of barley per month, barely enough to live on; in at least one instance, the grain is said to be stale (BM 80067 iv 5, *šê labīri*). We can imagine that their situation was not improved in the following year when the city was abandoned or destroyed.

I do not suggest that there is a relationship between these women and the hungry *nadītums* of the century before, at least not a direct one. I mean only to begin a sketch of the poverty that afflicted women whose household status was insecure. A sizeable precariat of such women was a feature of the era, and the question of their household belonging was implicated in their economic disadvantage. I do not propose to explain this situation here, or even to insist that it was historically unique—only that it was uniquely forefronted by the cuneiform evidence of the time. But it is curious that we see collectives of unmarried poor women in the cities just at the same time that we observe large bands of male mercenaries in the countryside, a coincidence difficult to ignore. Such a coincidence is surely indirect, but perhaps descended from a common historical context: that the 17th century, following the warfare of the 18th century, was a time in which many households had been broken by hardship and loss, perhaps into the third and fourth generations, and that some of the broken households we see are the sequelae of that time; indeed, it must follow that broken households simply are a more prominent feature of this time than they were previously. Whatever the explanation, we must as a ground condition recognize this large population of (female) persons (and their dependents) in the Late OB who were excluded from traditional membership structures—another class of "outsiders" on the inside.

Story 7: The gerontocracy

My third and final story about "outsider insiders" concerns an unexpected group: the class of top officials. This, of course, ought to be a group of the most thor-

[91] Richardson 2002 I 184–188 and II 239–254 (cf. CUSAS 29 181). These texts will be re-edited and published in a future installment of TLOB 2. The probably associated ration list BM 79785: 35 (Richardson 2002: II 246–248), as well as BM 78881:17, mention Šarrat-Sippar, most likely referring to Annunītum; both texts, however, also mention the *gagûm* (of Sippar-Jaḫrūrum?) in ll. 48 and 16, respectively.

oughly "insider" elites of the entire culture. But by the end of the OB, it had become isolated from the society it claimed to rule.[92] If the "hungry women" episode speaks to a sense of precarious belonging for insiders towards the bottom of the socio-economic food chain, and the nervous merchants story speaks to the same at its middle, this episode indicates how even the very top of the power structures of Babylon were not immune from the contingent sense that they were at the margins rather than the center of the culture.

A prosopographic analysis of all the official classes at the end of the kingdom began from a study of all the personal names of the period 1683–1595 BC.[93] Among its several findings is the identification of two sociologically distinct classes of official titles. The first is an "open-rank" group, characterized by many title-holders with a few attestations apiece—widely-distributed but shallowly-attested titles within the institutions of state society:[94] these include the Crown office of the ugula mar.tu; the priestly offices of gala, $gudu_4$, lukur ^{d}Utu, and sanga; and the civil offices of PA.PA, šu.i, and *rabiānum*. The second contrasts with this starkly, a "closed-rank" group characterized by fewer title-holders with more associated texts per person—narrowly-distributed but deeply attested titles: these include the civic offices of $di.ku_5$ and *rabi sikkatim*; the temple office of *ērib bītim*;[95] and the Crown offices of *abi ṣābim*, dub.sar, ensí, gal.ukkin.na, sipa, ugula dam.gàr, and people calling themselves "servant of the king."[96]

The existence of two "pools" of officials is not in itself problematic or surprising. I would expect that it is a normal for large organizations to accommodate multiple power bases and status systems—meritocracies, oligarchies, bureaucracies—for both structure and flexibility. The hybridization of ranking systems allows for both achieved and ascribed power to be channeled and controlled by the state authority.

But difficulties arise for the closed-rank offices in the last half-century of the state. First, we may note that the Crown offices are categorically more often "closed" than "open" rank: palace power was characterized by a relatively small number of men who stayed in office for many years. Second, the entire superclass of closed-rank officials for the Crown is sharply reduced: the ensí, gal.ukkin.na, sipa, and ugula dam.gàr titles virtually fade away entirely at the beginning of Samsuditana's reign. Third, and against this, at least two classes of titles show

---

[92] The following account is drawn from an extended prosopographic analysis of the LOB-PNI Personal Names database; its findings were presented at the March, 2011 meeting of the American Oriental Society in Chicago in a paper entitled "The Collapse of the First Dynasty of Babylon: From Prosopography to Politics."

[93] The working database on which this analysis is based accounts for 14,392 names from about 3,700 texts of the period as of September 2019.

[94] I characterize titles here as "Crown," "civic," and "temple/priestly" for strictly heuristic purposes; they are not exclusive categorizations.

[95] Also the diviner (máš.šu.gíd.gíd) was a "closed-rank" office at this time, but it is difficult to assign it either as strictly a "priestly" or "Crown" office (though I incline to the latter), or even necessarily an office at all (perhaps better called a professional name). For these reasons, I omit it from this discussion for the sake of clarity.

[96] Many of the last class, of course, overlap with the preceding Crown office title-holders.

that their holders had tenures which deviated greatly from the patterns exhibited for other titles: judges and "servants of the king" largely survived the otherwise (professionally, at least) devastating statistical transition event from the reign of Ammiṣaduqa to that of Samsuditana, unlike their peer office(r)s. But more than this, their tenures often began much earlier in Ammiṣaduqa's reign; lasted deep into Samsuditana's, giving them thirty, forty, or even fifty-year tenures in their offices; and (most importantly), their ranks were not replenished with new titleholders. In plain language, the entire superclass of "closed-rank" officialdom shrank radically after Ammiṣaduqa, and what was left was characterized by a finite number of increasingly aged officers who were not replaced with new blood. I refer to this larger development in the state apparatus as its "recession."

Importantly, this development was somewhat at odds with what we find, statistically speaking, for the pattern of new actors coming into and going out of the textual record in Samsuditana's reign. Without doubt, this is an administrative and economic landscape reduced overall from Ammiṣaduqa's time, but not without life and movement in the larger sense. Despite an overall downturn in text production and all kinds of established actors falling out of the textual record, there was a healthy counteractive rate of new actors coming into that same record right up until the very end of Samsuditana's reign. Palace and city administration shrank away from the society they claimed to run, alienated from it in professional and practical terms.

When we consider this larger trend against the fact that Crown power, at least, was increasingly associated with the mercenaries it fed in the fortresses of the countryside, one wonders exactly what the concept of "outsider" meant, from the perspective of the King and his men? Or what it meant to a state subject, if one trusted one's leaders and their soldiers not much more than "enemies" from outside the state? It is this blurring of the boundaries rather than any clear change in the "content" of what they enclosed which should concern us here; where the acts of distinction, difference-marking, or "othering" were complicated to the extent that the usefulness of those categories was called into question, their function exposed, their discourse power emptied.

Conclusion

I start my conclusion with some self-criticism: if ethnicity presents us with a kaleidoscope of status and function which cannot—*should* not—be reduced into single social identities, the multiple, divided, and shifting conditions under which "natives" make judgements and distinctions about foreigners makes the idea of stable relational categories almost impossible to pin down. These are irrevocably historically unique dynamics. It thus reads as a giant mess to propose a scholarly consideration of Subarian slaves, Gutian mercenaries, and Elamite landholders armed with hoes, swords, and tablets, respectively, *in the same picture* that includes hungry women, high-status exiles, metic citizens with legal privileges, nervous merchants, and an isolated government, all in the context of a world without a meaningful international structure. This seems a hopelessly incoherent social map, even if it faithfully reproduces the messiness of a culture's subjective experience of "the foreign." What could a history of *all* such things hope to achieve?

It is unreasonable and unworkable, to paraphrase the anthropologist Richard Blanton, to take on entire societies as analytic categories. Especially to the points I make about fracture lines within societies, it is not so enlightening to simply point out that vertical distinctions existed within them, since every culture has elites, subalterns, and the people in between. There is nothing new in this. To insist, then, that the mere existence of internal divisions—that problems in defining "insiderness" qualitatively or experientially—recursively shapes the reception and discourse of "outsiderness" come out as a banal truism. Where and when would this *not* be true?

But (luckily) I am writing a historical study and not an anthropological one, and my contention is quantitative rather than qualitative: there can be greater and lesser degrees of difference within and between the two dynamic arenas in which difference-making takes place. Put plainly, I see the Late OB as having greater degrees of difference within and between the two arenas than in other periods of Mesopotamian history. The fault lines between "in" and "out" were drawn more emphatically in this time than in others, *within* the host culture as well as between it and other ethnic, linguistic, regional, or political cultures. The range of judgements and distinctions necessary to produce social recognition of any kind cuts across more levels of society—from the canal ditches to the Palace—then before or after. I emphasize not so much any conflict between the two arenas, but the new, serious, and open questions within the host society about belonging *altogether*.

I will close by pointing to a unique aspect of the OB period: the possibility of becoming alienated from one's god. It is, of course, not uncommon to find evidence in sources of almost every period that kings or other people could have "enemies", or for individuals to be "strangers" to each other. But in contracts of the early OB (i.e., not after the mid-19th century), it could be stipulated that a consequence for the breaking of an oath was to become an "enemy" of a god;[97] it was thus possible that one could become the enemy of any god to whom one had sworn an oath and then broken it, a situation to be "feared" (*palāḫu*).[98] The verb used to describe the denial of an oath or the contestation of an agreement was (since Old Akkadian, in fact) *nakāru*, the root from which *nakru* derives: "strange, hostile, alien." Presumably, formulae in later contracts

[97] See further OB exs. CAD L s.v. *lemnu* s. a-1', especially in the context of one who raises a claim (<*ragāmu*) against an executed contract as an enemy "of DN and RN": e.g., CT 6 36a: 15 (the gift of a "temple," probably from early in the Babylonian dynasty), CT 8 28c: 22 (reign of Sumu-la-el) and 38b: 9 (Ilumma-ila), and Waterman Bus. Doc. 14 r. 3 (Immerum). Given the pairing of god and king, it seems likely that becoming a *lemnu* in this context refers to the breaking of an oath.

[98] See esp. AbB VII 25: 4–7: "Is there no one but me who fears Šamaš and (therefore) has sent you silver?" Note further the phenomenon of contracts witnessed by the gods, the use of various weights and measures named for gods, judicial decisions about property in the presence of divine emblems, and references to being under a (financial?) "obligation to Šamaš" (esp. with *gimillam eli … rašû* [A]: AbB I 132: 15–16, II 87: 16–17, V:173 II:17–19, IX 184: 26–29, and XII 59: 29; cf. VI 32, XII 57, XIV 139, and XIV 201[?]) and other (non-judicial) decisions of Šamaš about business (often obscure: AbB I 135:35, V 232:26–27 [with Marduk], VI 8: 18–19, VI 71: 10, VIII 18: 11, IX 239: 5–6, XII 52: 11 and 13, XII 53: 9, XII 55: 20, XIV 15: 10, and XIV 64: 41).

forbidding the revocation of an oath (e.g. inim nu.um.gá.gá) immediately preceding oaths to gods encapsulated these concepts of alienation from the divine as consequential to such reversals. Such oaths seem limited to the sales of houses, and not of fields;[99] where the further implication of disaffection from a god was alienation from a particular *household*. If we cannot find such prohibitory phrases in the Late OB evidence, it is surely because no house sales are preserved from this period at all.[100] Note that oaths like *aššum Šamaš* lent emphasis to asseverative statements in letters and literary texts, i.e., outside of contractual language.[101] Letters, too, emphasized the importance of the good favor of the gods in their greetings. In this wider context, it is not difficult to imagine that a failure to secure that favor implied the potential hostility of the gods to their "enemies".

The possibility of becoming alienated from a god is further seen in the proliferation of so-called "letters to gods" in the OB, wherein personal appeals from individuals to deities spoke of their "estrangement" from them (*aḫû*, AbB IX 141), asking "What have I done to you?" (AbB V 140 + XIV 9), or implying the gods' negligence in allowing enemies and demons to afflict them (AbB XII 99 and XIII 164).[102] Although such letters cannot be counted as literary forerunners to late second-millennium compositions where these themes of abandonment are critical and sustained, they nevertheless anticipate the trope of personal alienation from a god.[103] And then in the Late OB, we find a few appearances of the unusual phrase "enemy of the god"—i.e., an enemy of Marduk or Šamaš[104]—or of some other supernatural power[105]—in contracts, epithets, and cautionary notes in letters,[106] as well as personal names like Nakarum, "stranger", and Ubārum, "foreigner", (including Ubār-DN) well-attested.[107]

---

[99] A few early exceptions may be noted, e.g. MHET II 1 9, 10, 12, etc. (reign of Immerum).

[100] See e.g. MHET II 4, where the only apparent "sale" texts are either rescripts or inheritances.

[101] See especially Veenhof 1978: esp. 188: "In this context these words imply that Šamaš will act when lies are told. This type of oath or asseveration underscores the importance of Šamaš in social life, in which doing 'what pleases Šamaš' and abstaining from 'what is not pleasing to Šamaš' is wise." On oaths and their breaking, see Veenhof's related note in AbB XIV p. 213 s.v. *nīšu*, specifically pointing to *lemnu* as outcome of a broken oath.

[102] Addressed to "the god, my father," Ninsianna, Amurrum, and Ninmug, respectively. See Foster's editions of two of these as BTM II.37 and .38 (pp. 158–59).

[103] E.g., "The Righteous Sufferer" or "A Sufferer's Salvation" (BTM III.14–.15). Cf. the opinion of Lambert 1996 [1960]: 10–11 (who traces the development to the Ur III period): "The most common complaint is virtually about a broken contract. A man served his god faithfully, but did not secure health and prosperity in return."

[104] AbB IX 20, "I will treat you like an enemy of Marduk (*kīma lemun* ᵈMarduk)!"; Jannsen 1991: 8–9, "Such a man will be the enemy of Šamaš (*ajābu ša* ᵈUtu)."

[105] AbB XII 99.

[106] Note AbB XI 114, warning "Be aware of the god," using the verb *idû*, one of the two semantic bases of non-estrangement cited above (just as well: "Know god!").

[107] CAD U s.v. *ubārum* s. 1h declines to translate PN forms with Ubār-, which is difficult because the range of meanings for *ubārum* runs from "stranger" to "guest-friend," and because the term is rare outside of PN forms in the OB. In the context of this discussion, however, I think it is clear that even if Ubār-PN means something essentially positive like "metic citizen under the protection of DN" (rather than "Stranger to DN"), as it is likely to, it still marks difference at the personal level.

The evidence is modest, but points to the sense that, over the course of the OB, it became thinkable for individuals to be enemies or strangers *to their god*.[108] Altogether, the language in which one might be alienated in social, legal, and even religious senses was here internalized: it was possible to be a friend or an enemy *to a god* and *as a personal matter*, to take it on as an individual identity. The locutions of alienation could now be found in the legal language of contracts, the status language of the social realm, and the spiritual language of prayer. The alienation of the individual became denominated and diffuse throughout the range of idiomatic speech, given a name as someone estranged from god. The social force of these clues requires a good deal more thought, but one cannot help but think of this range of signals and think next about the theodicies and prayers in Akkadian literature of the following ages. "As I went through the streets", laments the *Righteous Sufferer*, "I was pointed at … My city glowered at me like an enemy … My family set me down as an outsider."[109] The possibilities for being a "stranger" would change yet again, this time as an internalized and individual existential condition, as someone foreign even to one's household. The language of the alien and alienation had shifted ground once again, and with it came an entirely different discourse of difference-making.

References

Abraham, K. – K. van Lerberghe, 2017. *A Late Old Babylonian Temple Archive from Dūr-Abiešuḫ: The Sequel*, with the assistance of Gabriella Voet and Hendrik Hameeuw. CUSAS 29. Bethesda, MD: CDL Press.

Beckman, G., 2013. Foreigners in the Ancient Near East. *JAOS* 133/2, 203–216.

Cameron, C.M., 2013. How People Moved among Ancient Societies: Broadening the View. *American Anthropologist* 115/2, 218–231.

Candelora, D., 2019. Hybrid Military Communities of Practice: The Integration of Immigrants as the Catalyst for Egyptian Social Transformation in the 2nd Millennium BC. In J. Mynářová – M. Kilani – S. Alivernini, eds., *A Stranger in the House – the Crossroads III. Proceedings of an International Conference on Foreigners in Ancient Egyptian and Near Eastern Societies of the Bronze Age held in Prague, September 10–13, 2018*. Prague: Charles University, 25–47.

Charpin, D., 1987. Les décrets royaux à l'époque paléo-babylonienne à propos d'un ouvrage récent. *AfO* 34, 36–44.

Charpin, D., 2001. Des Numhéens originaires de Mahanum montaient la garde à Sippar sous Ammi-ṣaduqa. *N.A.B.U.* 2001/2 no. 37.

Charpin, D., 2004. Histoire politique du Proche-Orient amorrite (2002–1595). In D. Charpin – D.O. Edzard – M. Stol, *Mesopotamien: Die altbabylonische Zeit*. OBO 160/4. Fribourg: Academic Press, 25–480.

[108] From Sumerian literature, we find parallel epithets in Šulgi D and Q and Nergal C (ETCSL 2.4.2.04:28 and 136, 2.4.2.17:13, and 4.15.3:42), but these refer to collective foreign enemies, not to Babylonian individuals.

[109] BTM III.14 p. 311 (I: 82f.).

Charpin, D., 2010. Un édit du roi Ammiditana de Babylone. In D. Shehata – F. Weierhäuser – K.V. Zand, eds., *Von Göttern und Menschen: Beiträge zu Literatur und Geschichte des Altens Orients* (FS Groneberg). CM 41. Leiden: Brill, 17–46.

De Graef, K., 1999a. Les étrangers dans les textes paléobabyloniens tardifs de Sippar (première partie). *Akkadica* 111, 1–48.

De Graef, K., 1999b. Les étrangers dans les textes paléobabyloniens tardifs de Sippar (deuxième partie). *Akkadica* 112, 1–17.

Dekiere, L., 1994–1997. *Old Babylonian Real Estate Documents*, Parts 1–6. MHET II. Ghent: University of Ghent.

Eidem, J., 2011. *The Royal Archives from Tell Leilan: Old Babylonian Letters and Treaties from the Lower Town Palace East*. PIHANS 117. Leiden: Nederlands Historisch-Archaeologisch Instituut in het Nabije Oosten.

Fales, M., 2018. The Composition and Structure of the Neo-Assyrian Empire: Ethnicity, Language and Identities. In S. Fink – R. Rollinger, eds., *Conceptualizing Past, Present and Future*. Melammu Symposia 9. Münster: Ugarit-Verlag.

Foster, B., 1996. *Before the Muses: An Anthology of Akkadian Literature*. Winona Lake, IN: Eisenbrauns.

Heltzer, M., 1981. *The Suteans*. Naples: Tipografia Don Bosco.

Janssen, C., 1991. Samsu-iluna and the hungry *naditums*. *Northern Akkad Project Reports* 5, 3–21.

Joannès, F., 2006. *Haradum II: Les textes de la période paléo-babylonienne (Samsu-iluna—Ammi-ṣaduqa)*. Paris: Éditions Recherche sur les Civilisations.

Jursa, M. – J. Häckl, 2014. *Spätbabylonische Privatbriefe*. Spätbabylonische Briefe Bd. 1. AOAT 414/1. Münster: Ugarit-Verlag.

Lambert, W.G., 1996 [1960]. *Babylonian Wisdom Literature*. Winona Lake, IN: Eisenbrauns.

Lambert, W.G., 2007. *Babylonian Oracle Questions*. MC 13. Winona Lake, IN: Eisenbrauns.

Miglio, A., 2014. A Comparative Political History: Israel, Geshur and the "Amurrite Age." *JSOT* 38/4, 439–451.

Miglio, A., 2016. "Amurrite Age" Politics and an Intelligence Report about a Potential Rival to Zimrī-Līm. *Aram* 26/1–2, 301–308.

McGeough, K., 2019. "The Men of Ura are a Heavy Burden Upon Your Subject!": The Administration and Management of Strangers and Foreigners in Ugarit. In J. Mynářová – M. Kilani – S. Alivernini, eds., *A Stranger in the House – the Crossroads III. Proceedings of an International Conference on Foreigners in Ancient Egyptian and Near Eastern Societies of the Bronze Age held in Prague, September 10–13, 2018*. Prague: Charles University, 197–220.

Mushett Cole, E., 2019. Ethnic Enclaves: A Modern Understanding of How Migratory Groups Preserve Ethnic Identity as a Potential Explanation for the Libyan's Retention of a Non-Egyptian Identity in the Late New Kingdom and Third Intermediate Period. In J. Mynářová – M. Kilani – S. Alivernini, eds., *A Stranger in the House – the Crossroads III. Proceedings of an International Conference on Foreigners in Ancient Egyptian and Near Eastern Societies of the Bronze Age held in Prague, September 10–13, 2018*. Prague: Charles University, 221–238.

Mynářová, J., 2019. Are you an Egyptian? Are you a Stranger? Egyptians in the Levant in the Bronze Age. In J. Mynářová – M. Kilani – S. Alivernini, eds., *A Stranger in the House – the Crossroads III. Proceedings of an International Conference on Foreigners in Ancient Egyptian and Near Eastern Societies of the Bronze Age held in Prague, September 10–13, 2018.* Prague: Charles University, 239–255.

Orum, A.M., 2005. Circles of Influence and Chains of Command: The Social Processes Whereby Ethnic Communities Influence Host Societies. *Social Forces* 84/2, 921–939.

Pientka, R., 1998. *Die spätaltbabylonische Zeit: Abiešuḫ bis Samsuditana: Quellen, Jahresdaten, Geschichte* (2 vols.). Münster: Rhema Verlag.

Pongratz-Leisten, B., 2000. The Other and the Enemy in the Mesopotamian Conception of the World. In: R.M. Whiting, ed., *Mythology and Mythologies: Methodological Approaches to Intercultural Influences*. Melammu Symposia 2. Helsinki: The Neo-Assyrian Text Corpus Project.

Pruzsinszky, R., 2019. The Contact Zone along the Middle Euphrates: Interaction, Transaction and Movement. In J. Mynářová – M. Kilani – S. Alivernini, eds., *A Stranger in the House - the Crossroads III. Proceedings of an International Conference on Foreigners in Ancient Egyptian and Near Eastern Societies of the Bronze Age held in Prague, September 10–13, 2018.* Prague: Charles University, 269–284.

Reitz, J.G., 2002. Host Societies and the Reception of Immigrants: Research Themes, Emerging Theories and Methodological Issues. *International Migration Review* 36/4, 1005–1019.

Richardson, S., 2002. *The Collapse of a Complex State: A Reappraisal of the End of the First Dynasty of Babylon, 1683-1597 B.C.* Ph.D. Dissertation, Columbia University, New York.

Richardson, S., 2005. Trouble in the Countryside *ana tarṣi* Samsuditana. In: W.H. van Soldt – R. Kalvelagen – D. Katz, eds., *Ethnicity in Ancient Mesopotamia. Papers read at the 48th Rencontre Assyriologique Internationale, Leiden, 1–4 July 2002.* PIHANS 102. Leiden: Nederlands Instituut voor het Nabije Oosten, 273–289.

Richardson, S., 2010a. A Light in the *gagûm* Window: The Sippar Cloister in the Late Old Babylonian period. In: S. Melville – A.L. Slotsky, eds., *Opening the Tablet Box: Near Eastern Studies in Honor of Benjamin R. Foster*. CHANE 42. Leiden: Brill, 329–346.

Richardson, S., 2010b. *Texts from the Late Old Babylonian Period*. Journal of Cuneiform Studies Supplemental Series 2. Boston: ASOR.

Richardson, S., 2017. Before Things Worked: A 'Low-Power' Model of Early Mesopotamia. In: C. Ando – S. Richardson, eds., *Ancient States and Infrastructural Power: Europe, Asia, and America*. Philadelphia: University of Pennsylvania Press, 17–62.

Richardson, S., 2018. Sumer and Stereotype: Re-forging "Sumerian" kingship in the Late Old Babylonian Period. In S. Fink – R. Rollinger, eds., *Conceptualizing Past, Present and Future*. Melammu Symposia 9. Münster: Ugarit-Verlag, 145–186.

Richardson, S., 2019a. Walking Capital: The Economic Function and Social Location of Babylonian Servitude. *The Journal of Global Slavery* 4, 285–342.

Richardson, S., 2019b. Updating the list of Late OB Babylonian fortresses. *N.A.B.U.* 2019/1 no. 21.

Richardson, S., 2019c. By the Hand of a Robber: States, mercenaries and bandits in Middle Bronze Age Mesopotamia. In: R. Evans – M. De Marre, eds., *Piracy, Pillage and Plunder Antiquity: Appropriation and the Ancient World.* London: Routledge, 9–26.

Richardson, S. 2019d. The Oracle BOQ 1, "Trouble," and the Dūr-Abiešuḫ Texts: The End of Babylon I. JNES 78/2, 215–237.

Richardson, S., in preparation A. *Texts from the Late Old Babylonian Period* 2.1: Sales of Slaves and Cattle.

Richardson, S., in preparation B. Exercising Sympathy: Social Proximity in Mesopotamian Letters.

Roth, M., 1995. *Law Collections from Mesopotamia and Asia Minor*. WAW 6. Atlanta, GA: Scholars Press.

Safran, W., 1991. Diasporas in Modern Societies: Myths of Homeland and Return. *Diaspora: A Journal of Transnational Studies* 1/1, 83–99.

Sallaberger, W., 1999. *"Wenn Du mein Bruder bist, …": Interaktion und Textgestaltung in altbabylonischen Alltagsbriefen*. CM 16. Groningen: Styx Publications.

Streit, K., 2019. The Stranger on the Mound: Tracing Cultural Identity at Tel Lachish during the Late Bronze Age. In J. Mynářová – M. Kilani – S. Alivernini, eds., *A Stranger in the House – the Crossroads III. Proceedings of an International Conference on Foreigners in Ancient Egyptian and Near Eastern Societies of the Bronze Age held in Prague, September 10–13, 2018*. Prague: Charles University, 355–370.

Van De Mieroop, M., 2005. *King Hammurabi of Babylon: A Biography*. Oxford: Blackwell.

van Koppen, F. – D. Lacambre, 2008–2009. Sippar and the Frontier between Esnunna and Babylon. *JEOL* 41, 151–177.

Van Lerberghe, K. – G. Voet, 2009. *A Late Old Babylonian Temple Archive from Dūr-Abiešuḫ*, with the assistance of Hendrik Hameeuw. CUSAS 8. Bethesda, MD: CDL Press.

van Oudenhoven, J.P. et al., 2006. Patterns of Relations between Immigrants and Host Societies. *International Journal of Intercultural Relations* 30, 637–651.

Veenhof, K.R., 1978. Aššum Šamaš, "By Šamaš!", and Similar Formulas. *JCS* 30/3, 186–188.

Veenhof, K.R., 2001. The Relation between Royal Decrees and Law Collections in the Old Babylonian Period. *JEOL* 35–36, 49–84.

Waldinger, R., 2003. The Sociology of Immigration: Second Thoughts and Reconsiderations. In J.G. Reitz, ed., *Host Societies and the Reception of Immigrants*. La Jolla, CA: Center for Comparative Immigration Studies, 21–43.

Westbrook, R., 2008. Personal Exile in the Ancient Near East. *JAOS* 128/2, 317–323.

Westbrook, R., 2009 [1995]. Slave and Master in Ancient Near Eastern Law. In *Law from the Tigris to the Tiber: The Writings of Raymond Westbrook*. Volume 1: The Shared Tradition. Winona Lake, IN: Eisenbrauns, 161–216.

THE PHARAOH'S FIGHTERS: EARLY MERCENARIES IN EGYPT

Hannah L. Ringheim (University of Edinburgh)

Conflict was an integral part of Egyptian society. To display one's prowess and dominance over neighbouring communities on the peripheries of Egypt was an essential domain for the pharaohs, as delineated diachronically in texts and wall iconography. Persisting conflicts during the third to second millennium evinced the confrontations between the Egyptians and outside groups. Such conflicts revealed that manpower was inevitably a necessity. Concomitantly, hand-in-hand with these encounters are the foreign fighters that the Egyptian military relied heavily upon to augment the numbers in their armies.

Past scholarship refers to these foreign contingents as mercenaries; however, this identification frequently proves problematic, especially since the contingents must be differentiated from auxiliary soldiers, captured prisoners or forced migrants (Langer 2017: 41). Additionally, there is a lack of explicit terminology to distinguish a foreign mercenary in the ancient sources and therefore much interpretation relies on context. This paper seeks to trace the origins of mercenary warfare in Egypt and the initial interactions between the Egyptians and the "other" that instigated the use of foreigners in military capacities. To limit this scope, the discussion focuses on specific examples from varying interactions with the Nubians in comparison to the subsequent relations with the Shardana. The contexts and evidence illuminate the roles of external contingents in Egypt and which characteristics in particular attest to mercenaries (Ringheim 2018: 94–106); likewise, it is useful to trace the interactions that do not evince military employment.

Defining a mercenary posits ambiguous perceptions of the term. The modern understanding of a mercenary typically encompasses a negative connotation; they represent fighters in a conflict outside their homeland, where they have no connections or stakes in the outcome of the conflict, and they work primarily for financial motivation (Roberts – Guelff 1982: 387). It is debatable whether these same characteristics apply to foreign fighters in antiquity. Groups considered foreign to an ancient community are, for the most part, ambiguous, as societal boundaries are dynamic and constantly changing. The concept of payment is, therefore, an essential prerogative for the development of this profession. This, alongside a perceived foreign identity, is what plausibly defines a mercenary in antiquity, among other facets as discussed below.

Nubians as Mercenaries

The interactions between the Egyptians and the Nubians span centuries and encompass a variety of complex, culturally entangled contact (Smith 2003). As early as the third millennium, the political and economic stability of Egypt was heavily reliant on the use of outside forces to consolidate the region and to conquer foreign enemies from Upper Egypt (Bard 2007: 161–163; Liszka 2012). As a way of explaining the Egyptian expansionist approach towards Upper Egypt and the use of Nubians in Egyptian armies, Nubians are typically denoted as mercenaries in the majority of contexts in which they appear. As a result, scholars have advocated that the Nubians acted as substantial additions to Egyptian warfare tactics from the Old Kingdom until the end of the 13th century BC, and that the addition of the Nubians was an essential part of Egyptian military success (Moreno García 2010: 26).

Early epigraphic sources from tomb inscriptions present the complex levels of interactions with the Nubians. One of the earliest examples of recruiting Nubian soldiers comes from the well-known 6th Dynasty tomb of Harkhuf, an Egyptian merchant and expedition leader, located in the rock cut tombs of Qubbet el-Hawa in Aswan (Goedicke 1981: 1–20). The inscriptions recount a journey to Nubia, in which the purpose of the expedition was to expand trade connections and to seek those willing to work for the Egyptians in military or administrative capacities (Vischak 2015: 97). As the inscription relates the life of Harkhuf, one particular aspect highlights his interactions with foreigners. The inscriptions mention Harkhuf's subordinates who accompanied him to Nubia, and his official Sabni is distinguished with the title, the "Overseer of Mercenaries" (Kadish 1966: 24; Edel 1955: 51–75; Sethe 1903: Urk. I, 124, 17–25, 11). The interpretation of this title is tenuous, as there have been other suggestions for the transliteration of the title, *ꜥꜣw*, alongside mercenary. For instance, this has been translated to "Caravan Leader" (Faulkner 1953: 34), "Overseer of the Foreigners" (Strudwick 2005: 354), and "Head of the Foreign Language" ("Vorsteher der Fremdsprachigen" in Hannig 1995: 141). Holistically the term indeed connects to complex interactions between Egyptians and foreigners. The context, however, does not differentiate between the collective activities of the Nubians.

Nevertheless, the inscription typifies important aspects of Egyptian exchanges with foreigners during the Old Kingdom. It is clear that Harkhuf's primary aim was to acquire locals to assist with Egyptian objectives, and evidently using foreigners for various jobs was considered an essential task. In this light, it is interesting that Harkhuf elaborated on these roles to such an extent in his funerary autobiography; this duty was significant enough to be part of his eternal tomb inscription. Moreover, the purpose of overseeing the foreigners reflects a significant political encounter. Such interactions with non-Egyptians were described with specific actions, such as "to make peace" or "to appease", suggesting an element of negotiation and creation of alliances (Goedicke 1981: 12). The individuals in charge of negotiating with non-Egyptians, such as Harkhuf and Sabni, had strategic roles to interact with local communities; however, such exchanges do not clearly identify them as hired soldiers fighting for personal gain and remuneration, especially since there is a dearth of evidence to suggest that the Nubians received any type of payment. Rather, the Nubians in the Egyptian military exemplify the consequences of investigating new territory and creating alliances with foreigners in new lands.

Following the initial political and imperialist interactions between Egypt and the communities in Upper Nubia, such relations were not unilateral, with only the Egyptians capitalising on Nubian participation in the military. In some circumstances, the practice was reciprocal. Subsequent exchanges during the Second Intermediate Period evince this change. At a time when localised rule prevailed in Upper Egypt and the pharaohs no longer controlled the fortresses of the Middle Kingdom, autonomous communities, mixed with Egyptians and Nubians, maintained political control. In this environment, Egyptians appear in the service of the Nubian kinglet. The stele of Ha'ankef from Edfu, dating between 1650–1550 BC, provides evidence for Egyptians who fought for the Nubian king for payment before returning to Egypt:

> "I was a valiant warrior, an "Enterer" of Edfu. I transported wife and children and my property from the south of Kush in thirteen days. I brought back gold, 26 (*deben*) and the handmaid [...] I bought two cubits of land [...] I was rewarded for six years (of service in Nubia, whence came the gold with which, presumably, the land was bought)" (translation by Gunn 1929: 5; Säve-Söderbergh 1949: 56).

The stele indicates that fighting for the Nubian kings was a lucrative opportunity, where one could receive payment in land and gold for service. It presents a further consequence of the Egyptian hegemony in Nubia; as Egyptian interests expanded to the south, there were independent followers in pursuit of profit who fought for the Kushite Kingdom. By this point, centuries after the documentation of Harkhuf's initial alliances with the foreigners, the concept of foreign employment for one's own pursuit of remuneration transforms into a conventional endeavour. In this instance, it is feasible to consider this as an act of a mercenary.

Later examples of Nubians in the New Kingdom illuminate alternative roles of Nubians in the Egyptian military. In particular, the Amarna letters document Nubians in four distinct instances. In each of these letters, EA 127, 131, 133 and 187, a sovereign local leader in the Levant sent a request to the Pharaoh Akhenaten, asking him to send specific contingents of soldiers to assist with various military and political situations. These contingents typically encompassed a specified quantity of Egyptian soldiers, Nubians and charioteers (Moran 1992: EA 127, 131, 133 and 287; Vidal 2010: 112). For instance, EA 131 from Rib-Ḫadda of Byblos is addressed to the Pharaoh Akhenaten and asks for new troops; he specifically requests 300 Egyptians, 100 Nubians and 30 charioteers, to stop an insurrection by the sons of Abdi-Aširta (Moran 1992: 212–214). This explicit request for Nubian contingents alongside the Egyptians suggests that the Nubians likely gained a renowned reputation after centuries of fighting for the Egyptians, either as allies or auxiliary soldiers. They were considered a fundamental faction alongside the regular army. In this case, it is likely that the term Nubian over time came to represent a standard profession, rather than a designation of origin.

These glimpses into Nubians in military capacities exemplify a novel way to envision their roles in the Egyptian military. Expeditions in the third millennium indicate attempts to create alliances and to negotiate with the local communities in Upper Egypt. Whether they were initially hired as mercenaries is ambiguous, as there are no records of paments for the Nubian contingents. This is not to state that the concept of the mercenary did not exist; it is evident with the stele of Ha᾿ankef that some independent men sought out lucrative opportunities as a consequence of Egyptian movement in Upper Nubia. It is important to clarify that the notion of being a mercenary is not a static identity; it is possible that Nubians could have begun as mercenaries recruited in the third to second millennium, and by the end of 15th century, they had become regular hires within the Egyptian army. In these latter cases, they do not act as mercenaries, but rather as a standard part of the military.

Shardana Mercenaries

In comparison to the interactions with the Nubians, assessing how the Egyptians confronted foreigners is indeed discernible with the Shardana, one of the contingents of the Sea Peoples. Their emergence corresponded with the demise of the Bronze Age civilizations, including that of the Mycenaean palaces, the culmination of the Hittite empire, among numerous other destructions in the Eastern Mediterranean (Nur – Cline 2000: 44; Cline 2014). It has been suggested that the Sea Peoples engendered these calamities, as well as the contrary, that the Sea Peoples were consequences of the tumultuous environment (Cline – O'Connor 2003: 108–138; Roberts 2008: 15–19).

The initial manifestation of the Sea Peoples groups comes from three specific historical events and texts in Egypt: firstly, from the Battle of Qadesh in 1274 BC against the Hittites, where Sea Peoples groups were depicted as participants in the battle (Roberts 2008: 50). Later, during the fifth year of reign of the Pharaoh Merneptah (either 1208 BC or 1219), the Libyan king attacked Egypt, together with his northern warriors (Kopanias 2017: 115; Cline 2009: 192). The Shardana are mentioned as one of the five contingents, i.e. the "northerners coming from all lands", (Barnett 1960: 10–15) and Merneptah concluded his defeat of these invaders. A third confrontation involving the Shardana and the other Sea Peoples cohorts occurred in 1177 BC, as is represented in the mortuary temple of Ramesses III at Medinet Habu, and again, the Egyptians claimed to overcome the invasion. The sources testify to the perceived, hostile nature of the Sea Peoples. From these interactions, is it possible to identify mercenary employment? What specific traits pinpoint mercenary activity, and how helpful are the sources? From the surviving inscriptions, a reconstruction of the Shardana's mercenary-like characteristics materialises.

Autonomous Cohorts

Firstly, the initial image of the Sea Peoples is that of venturing, independent cohorts that established their presence as hostile enemies against Egypt. Their autonomy is reflected in the renowned inscription of the Battle of Qadesh against the Hittites in 1274 BC, where the events of this battle were recorded in contemporaneous temples at Abu Simbel, Luxor, Karnak, Abydos and the Ramesseum

(Roberts 2008: 50). In particular, the Lukka were recorded in the battle as constituents of a larger body of military contingents that were in alliance against the Egyptians: "The Chief of the Khatti [has] come together with the many foreign countries who are with him, whom he has brought with him as allies", (Gardiner 1960: 29, B40–B50).

The pharaoh was even critical of the manner in which the Hittite king Muwatalli gave all the riches and silver he had in order to recruit fighters, such as the Lukka, from foreign lands (Roberts 2008: 51). Such a statement indicates that, although the pharaoh himself used foreigners for military purposes, as is evident with the Nubians, in this context it was considered a point of weakness to pay foreign fighters. King Muwatalli did not have the manpower to support his army and had to look elsewhere in order to compete with the pharaoh. The subsequent part of the inscription then shows the Lukka as part of the list of prisoners taken by the pharaoh and brought back to Egypt (Adams – Cohen 2013: 646). The pharaohs were clearly accustomed to confronting these hostile military groups and they made a point to record the victories over them.

Likewise, other Sea Peoples cohorts committed similar acts of military alliance against the Egyptians decades after the Battle of Qadesh, while still demonstrating their autonomous behaviour. Looking at the Karnak inscription of the Pharaoh Merneptah (1208 or 1219 BC), the "northerners who came from all lands" were employed by the Libyan king Merey:

> "[…] the wretched chief of the enemies of Rebu, Merey, son of Dedy, has descended upon the foreign land of Tjehenu together with his bowman [...] [Sh]erden, Shekelesh, Akawasha, Lukka, and Tursha, consisting of the seizure of the best of every fighter and every runner of his foreign land […]" (translation by Breasted 1906: 241–252).

The Libyan king was planning to attack the Egyptians from the west and needed military assistance from the foreigners from the north to do so. The inscription emphasises the fact that the Libyan king needed to hire foreigners for the invasion and lists contingents that must have been well-known fighters, since they included the "best of every fighter" from these lands. The motive for the Libyans and northern warriors is also reflected further in the inscription, where they are described in the following way: "[…] to fill their bellies daily do they spend the day wandering and fighting. To seek the necessities of their mouths do they come to the land of Egypt", (Breasted 1906: 241–252, lines 21–23). This description emphasises the warlike nature of the contingents and that they only know how to fight in order to live, which would certainly be a significant trait of a mercenary (Kopanias 2017: 125). It also indicates a level of autonomy and instability of these groups, since they relied heavily on fighting for survival and were willing to invade Egypt for their own prerogatives.

Sea-raiders

In light of the autonomous nature of these groups, a second notable characteristic in Egyptian texts is their role as sea-raiders, conducting acts of piracy. As early as the 14th century, the Amarna tablets recorded raids from the sea on the Egyptian coastline by Lukkan pirates. These seaborne attacks were by no means a new phenomenon. In his letter to the King of Alašiya, Akhenaten accused the king of supporting the Lukka, to which the King of Alašiya responded by stating that the Lukka invaded his own towns as well (EA 38:7–12; Moran 1992: 111–112). Additionally, later Tanis II inscriptions from the reign of Ramesses II suggest that these raids occurred so frequently that the Egyptians devised a novel title for the word "warship" to describe these events, which roughly translated to "ships-of-the-warriors-on-the-sea" (Emanuel 2013: 15). The newly created term suggests the lack of previous experience with these particular war ships and that the phenomenon over time was momentous enough for a renewed description in the Egyptian records.

From the 14th until the 12th century, the seaborne attacks incorporated the Shardana as well (Bietak – Jung 2007: 220). The ubiquity of this group in the sources in comparison to other Sea Peoples contingents is particularly revealing of military interactions with Egypt. The references in the Tanis Stele of Ramesses II to the piratic activities of the Shardana attested to these attacks, almost with admiration:

> "The unruly Shardana whom no one had ever known how to combat, they came boldly sailing in their warships from the midst of the sea, none being able to withstand them" (translation by Kitchen 1982: 40).

This inscription typified the triumphs the cohort had in previous seaborne endeavours and their reputation as invaders. The Shardana appeared on multiple occasions in the sources as a disruptive sea power, as evinced in the iconography of the Battle of Qadesh at Karnak, when they are identifiable primarily by their weapons and ships (Wachsmann 1998). Their unique attire, including the horned helmet with a disc on top and the short sword with round shields, is analogous on various depictions (Fig. 1, from Medinet Habu). The Tanis Stele further illuminated the connection of the Shardana warships and attacks on Egypt: "The rebellious-hearted Shardana […] mighty ships of war are in the midst of the sea", (Bates 1914: 214). In this instance, the Tanis Stele refers to the capture of the Shardana, where declaring such a feat reveals how substantial of a victory it was for Egypt to overcome the Shardana attacks.

Capture and Employment

In response to such attacks, there are recorded instances when the Egyptians captured the Shardana and transported them to Egypt. The sources then demonstrated that some of these prisoners transitioned from captured enemies to paid fighters in the Egyptian army and were stationed in fortresses. The Shardana in

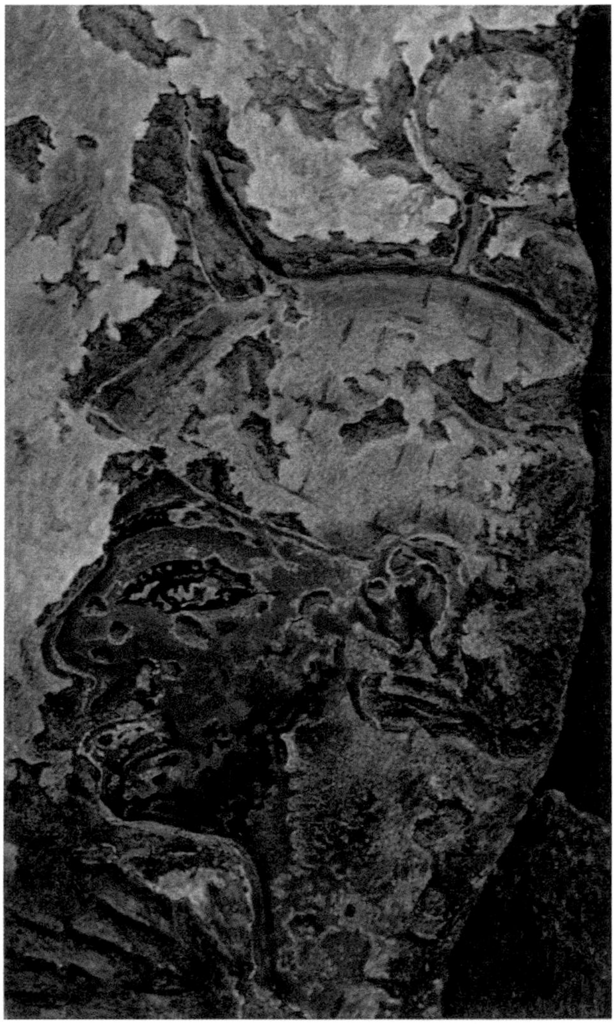

Fig. 1.
A Sherden soldier (Nelson 1932: pl. 65C. Courtesy of the Oriental Institute of the University of Chicago).

particular exemplified this transformation. While monumentalizing his victory at the Battle of Qadesh, Ramesses II described the Shardana in the following way:

> "Now, his person equipped his army and chariotry, and the Shardana of his person's capturing whom he had carried off through the victories of his strong arm, and who had been supplied with all their weapons and given instructions for battle" (Hassan 1929: pls. 10–12).

The pharaoh wanted it to be known that Egypt had captured this group explicitly, and that he was able to integrate them into his army. In another text, the group initially was listed as captives in the Athribis Stele during Merneptah's reign, where they were included amongst the contingents captured during the Libyan campaign (Adams – Cohen 2013: 649, no. 2.1.5). Merneptah subsequently incorporated the "Shardana of the Sea" into his army as well (Gardiner 1947: 15.1–2). In addition, during the reign of Ramesses III, the tradition was continued and he brought the Shardana to Egypt as captives and stationed them in his fortresses as part of his army, according to the Papyrus Harris and to the Lion Hunt scene from Medinet Habu (Adams – Cohen 2013: 649, 2.1.9; Erichsen 1933: 92.1).

Other texts emphasised further assimilation into the pharaoh's army; the Stele of Setemhebu recorded a "fortress of the Shardana", where the pharaoh equipped this group, as well as Nubians, with Egyptian weapons (Adams – Cohen 2013: 649). The Tanis II inscription reiterated this point: "Sherden of the Great Green that are captives of his majesty, they are equipped with all their weapons in the court, service to the crown", (Grandet 1994: Papyrus Harris I, lines 76.5–7, 75.1, 78.10). The clear divisions within the Egyptian military included the factions of foreigners, as was evident in the inscription accompanying the Medinet Habu reliefs. Alongside the fighters in horned helmets serving Ramesses III, the men were divided as follows: "the infantry, the chariotry, the troops, the Shardana and the Nubians", (Edgerton – Wilson 1936: pl. 29). These troops continued to appear in Egyptian sources for more than a century as an integral part of the army.

Payment and Status

During the transition from captives to soldiers, what explicitly separates the Shardana as mercenaries in some instances rather than auxiliary soldiers, such as those who were forced to fight for another hegemony, was that they received forms of payment for their employment. The captured groups received remuneration in the form of land grants from the Egyptians, and this act defined them as a reliable, paid military force fighting for an external cause. The Papyrus Wilbour, dated to the reign of Ramesses V (1149–1145 BC), referred to 59 land plots assigned to Shardana landowners who were mentioned individually by name (D'Amato – Salimbeti 2015: 30). During the tumultuous events of the Late Bronze Age, it is not surprising that land would act as prime payment. Arable land would be in demand and was likely scarce, as evident from the Libyan invasion during Merneptah's reign, where the foreign invaders were described as seeking the "necessities of their mouths do they come to the land of Egypt", (Breasted 1906: 241–252, lines 21–23). Land, as well as food, was clearly essential and one can envision the Shardana as contingents fighting in part to find a place to settle.

Over time, the Shardana became an assimilated group in the country with their own towns. The Papyrus Harris illuminated the Shardana as settlers and soldiers, when Ramesses III declared that "those under his command were able to put their weapons aside, enjoy the company of their families, and sleep soundly in their towns", (Emanuel 2013: 18; Breasted 1906: 504, P. Harris I. 78:9–10). Later texts also refer to the Shardana in the Egyptian domain as landowners. As late as the 9th century BC, the Stele of Donation from Helwan included a donation of lands labelled the Shardana fields, which demonstrated the extent to which these once captured prisoners of war were now assimilated into Egyptian society during later centuries (D'Amato – Selimbeti 2015: 30). A similar transformation from enemy to employed mercenary paid with land grants manifested in the 7th and 6th centuries BC with the Ionian and Carian mercenaries. According to Herodotus, these "men of bronze" landed on the shores of Egypt, most likely for raiding purposes, and the Pharaoh

Fig. 2.
Sherden personal guards of Ramesses II on a relief at Abu Simbel (Breasted 1908: 2, fig. 1. Courtesy of the Oriental Institute of the University of Chicago).

Fig. 3.
Ramses III Lion Hunt scene at Medinet Habu with Shardana soldiers on the lower band. Personal photograph from Medinet Habu. Drawing of relief found in Nelson 1930: pl. 34.

Psamtik proceeded just as his predecessors did; he hired the foreigners as mercenaries in his fortresses and paid them in *stratopeda*, or land grants (Hdt. 2.152).

Another facet of the Shardana is the acquired social status they attain in certain circumstances as hired soldiers. In addition to the texts that indicate their assimilation into the army and subsequent land ownership, their unique social status is also identifiable from the wall iconography at Abu Simbel as soldiers of Ramesses II. In these reliefs, they are depicted with their conventional armour, including round shields, long swords and horned helmets, as special guards stationed outside of the tent of Ramesses II (Fig. 2). Notably these guards are adorned with typical Egyptian kilts, while holding their Shardana weapons. No other foreign contingent of the Sea Peoples is depicted in such a manner, with an amalgamation of Egyptian and foreign traits. The blend of traits is exceptional, as Egyptian iconography uses physical characteristics to separate Egyptians from the "other;" in this instance, the Shardana become assimilated with the Egyptian contingent, suggesting that they began to have a similar status to Egyptians, rather than as the inferior stranger.

In other reliefs, such as the Lion Hunt of Ramesses III at Medinet Habu, their manner of placement as deliberately guarding the pharaoh during a lion hunt suggests the established role the Shardana maintained (Fig. 3). The creator of these battle scenes portrayed them in the centre of the composition as the leading unit for the pharaoh, further communicating their importance. Some insight into the status of the Shardana comes from the Papyrus Wilbour, dated to the reign of Ramesses V (1149–1145 BC). The text refers to 59 land plots that were assigned to Shardana landowners, who were mentioned individually by name (D'Amato – Selimbeti 2015: 30). The size of the land plots was informative of the Shardana's social status; 42 of the land plots were 5 *arouras* in size, similar to other individuals of higher rank, whereas the standard soldier in the Egyptian army would typically receive 3 *arouras* (Emanuel 2013: 19). Likewise, the Papyrus Harris testified to their elevated social status. Ramesses III addressed the "officials and the leaders of the land, the infantry, the chariotry, the Shardana, the many bowmen, and all the souls of Egypt", (Grandet 1994: P. Harris I 75, lines 1–2). Here it is clear that the Shardana act as a substantial part of the Egyptian military and they were recorded alongside military occupations, like infantry, the chariotry and bowmen. This suggests that the Shardana became standardized in the Egyptian army, and by this point the term began to represent a contingent of mercenaries.

Mercenaries in the Egyptian Army

Based on the array of Egyptian texts about the Shardana, a clear narrative of mercenary behaviour emerges. Initially, the Sea Peoples contingents ventured as independent cohorts, conducting sea-raids and piratic activities, and they were considered hostile enemies to the Egyptians. After their eventual capture by the Egyptians, certain factions were settled into military strongholds within the region. In this context, the transition to becoming a hired force is clearly demonstrated by the Shardana. The sources do not reveal a similar pattern of military employment for other captured groups. As payment for this employment, the Shardana received land grants. The final phase of their roles in the military is manifested through social status, where some contingents of the Shardana likely became the personal elite guards for Ramesses II. After over a century of their employment and receiving land grants, it is probable that the Shardana assimilated into Egyptian society, thus becoming indistinguishable in the archaeological and literary record. One example of clear assimilation into society includes a donation stele from the 22nd Dynasty, where the Shardana Padjesef was depicted on the stele as dedicating an offering to the Egyptian gods, Khnum and Hathor (Petrie 1905: 22). A few centuries after the initial interactions between the Egyptians and the Shardana, the Shardana were participating in local ritual practices.

The interactions with the Shardana are exemplary of how the term mercenary could be applied to societies in the third and second millennia. This is not to say that every instance the Shardana appear in Egyptian records, they should be considered mercenaries—the evidence should indeed be contextualised within the wider historical and archaeological narrative. Stemming from exchanges between the Egyptians, as an organised society with avid records, and outsiders, i.e. those on the peripheries of the Egyptian world, the concept of hiring foreigners for pay was constructed. The examples with the Nubians, on the other hand, evince that from the earliest interactions between the Egyptians and their neighbours in the south, bringing Nubians to fight for the Egyptians was a way of establishing alliances and security with outside communities, as well as capitalising on Egyptian expansion for lucrative opportunities. The array of evidence from Egypt provides some of the first, and earliest, glimpses into the use of foreigners in armies, whether hired, captured or acting as allies. Such instances indeed act as the precursor for the mercenary profession that subsequently circulates throughout antiquity.

References

Adams, M.J. – M.E. Cohen, 2013. The "Sea Peoples" in Primary Sources. In A.E. Killebrew – G. Lehmann, eds., *The Philistines and Other "Sea Peoples" in Text and Archaeology*. Atlanta, GA: Society of Biblical Literature, 645–644.

Bard, K., 2007. *Ancient Egypt*. Oxford: Blackwell Publishing Ltd.

Barnett, R.D., 1969. *The Sea Peoples*. Cambridge: Cambridge University Press.

Bates, O., 1914. *The Eastern Libyans*. Oxford: Frank Cass and Co. Ltd.

Bietak, M. – R. Jung, 2007. Swords, Pharaohs and Sea Peoples. In H. Charaf, ed., *Inside the Levantine Maze: Archaeological and Historical Studies Presented to Jean-Paul Thalmann. Archaeology and History in the Lebanon 26-27*. London: Lebanese British Friends of the National Museum, 212–233.

Breasted, J.H., 1906. *Ancient Records of Egypt, Historical Documents from the Earliest Times to the Persian Conquest*. Chicago: Chicago & Co.

Breasted, J.H., 1908. The Monuments of Sudanese Nubia, report of the work of the Egyptian Expedition, Season of 1906–1907. *AJSSL* 23(1), 1–64.

Cline, E.H., 2009. The Sea Peoples' Possible Role in the Israelite Conquest of Canaan. In D. Danilidoued, ed., Δώρον: τιμητικός τόμος για τον Σπύρο Ιακωβίδη. Athens: Academy of Athens.

Cline, E.H., 2014. *1177 BC: The Year Civilization Collapsed*. Princeton: Princeton University Press.

Cline, E.H. – D. O'Connor, 2003. The Mystery of the 'Sea Peoples.' In D. O'Connor, ed., *Mysterious Lands. Encounters with Ancient Egypt*. London: UCL Institute of Archaeology, 107–138.

D'Amato, R. – A. Salimbeti, 2015. *Sea Peoples of the Bronze Age Mediterranean c. 1400 BC – 1000 BC*. Oxford: Osprey.

Dietrich, M. – O. Loretz – J. Sanmartín – H.-W. Kisker, 1976. *Die keilalphabetischen Texte aus Ugarit: einschliesslich der keilalphabetischen Texte ausserhalb Ugarits*. Kevelaer: Butzon und Bercker.

Edel, E., 1955. Inschriften des Alten Reiches V: Die Reiseberichte des *Hrw-hwiff* (herchuf). In O. Firchow, ed., *Ägyptologische Studien: Fetschrift Hermann Grapow*. Berlin: Akademie Verlag, 51–75.

Edgerton, W.F. – J.-A. Wilson, 1936. *Historical Records of Ramses III: The Texts in Medinet Habu*. Chicago: University of Chicago Press.

Emanuel, J.P., 2013. 'Srdn From the Sea': The Arrival, Integration, and Acculturation of a 'Sea People.' *JAEI* 5(1), 14–27.

Erichsen, W., 1933. *Papyrus Harris I: Hieroglyphische Transkripton*. Bruxelles: Édition de la Fondation Égyptologique Reine Élisabeth.

Faulkner, R.O., 1953. Egyptian Military Organization. *JEA* 39, 32–47.

Gardiner, A., 1947. *Ancient Egyptian Onomastica*. Oxford: Oxford University Press.

Goedicke, H., 1981. Harkhuf's Travels. *JNES* 40(1), 1–20.

Grandet, P., 1994. *Le Papyrus Harris I (BM 9999)*. 2 vols. BdÉ 109 / 1–2. Le Caire: Institut français d'archéologie orientale.

Gunn, B., 1929. A Middle Kingdom Stela from Edfu. *ASAE* 29, 5.

Hannig, R., 1995. *Großes Handwörterbuch Ägyptisch-Deutsch. Die Sprache der Pharaonen (2800-950 v. Chr.)*. Mainz: Philipp von Zabern.

Kitchen, K.A., 1982. *Ramesside Inscriptions Historical and Biographical*, IV. Oxford: Blackwell Publishing Ltd.

Kopanias, K., 2017. Mercenaries or Refugees? The Evidence from the Inscriptions of Merneptah on the 'Sea Peoples.' *JGA* 2, 119–134.

Langer, C., 2017. Forced Migration in New Kingdom Egypt: Remarks on the Applicability of Forced Migration Studies Theory in Egyptology. In C. Langer, ed., *Global Egyptology. Negotiations in the Production of Knowledges on Ancient Egypt in Global Contexts*. London: Golden House Publications, 39–52.

Liszka, K., 2012. *"We have come to serve Pharaoh:" A Study of the Medjay and Pangrave as an ethnic group and as mercenaries from c. 2300 BCE until c. 1050 BCE*. PhD Dissertation. Philadelphia: University of Pennsylvania.

Morena García, J.C., 2010. War in Old Kingdom Egypt (2686-2125 BCE). In J. Vidal, ed., *Studies on War in the Ancient Near East*. AOAT 372. Münster: Ugarit-Verlag, 5–42.

Nelson, H.H., 1930. *Earlier Historical Records of Ramses III. Medinet Habu*, Volume 1. Chicago: University of Chicago Press.

Nelson, H.H., 1932. *Later Historical Records of Ramses III by the Epigraphic Survey. Medinet Habu*, Volume II. Chicago: University of Chicago Press.

Nur, A. – E.H. Cline, 2000. Poseidon's Horses: Plate Tectonics and Earthquake Storms in the Late Bronze Age and Eastern Mediterranean. *JAS* 27(1), 43–63.

Petrie, W.M.F., 1905. *A History of Egypt from the XIXth to the XXXth Dynasties*. London: Methuen.

Ringheim, H.L., 2018. *Mercenaries in the Eastern Mediterranean from the Late Bronze Age to the Iron Age*. PhD Dissertation. Oxford: University of Oxford.

Roberts, G.R., 2008. *The Sea Peoples and Egypt*. PhD Dissertation. Oxford: University of Oxford.

Roberts, A. – R. Guelff, 1982. *Documents on the Laws of War*. Oxford: Clarendon Press.

Säve-Söderbergh, T., 1949. A Buhen Stela from the Second Intermediate Period (Khartum No. 18). *JEA* 35, 50–58.

Sethe, K., 1903. *Urkunden des Alten Reichs*, I. Leipzig: J. C. Hinrichs' Buchandlung.

Smith, S.T., 2003. *Wretched Kush: Ethnic Identities and Boundaries in Egypt's Nubian Empire*. Routledge: London – New York.

Strudwick, N.C., 2005. *Texts from the Pyramid Age*. Leiden – Boston: Brill.

Wachsmann, S., 1998. *Seagoing Ships and Seamanship in the Bronze Age Levant*. Texas: Texas A&M University Press.

THE STRANGER ON THE MOUND: TRACING CULTURAL IDENTITY AT TEL LACHISH DURING THE LATE BRONZE AGE

Katharina Streit (Hebrew University of Jerusalem)

Introduction

Reconstructing the cultural identities of past populations is a very complex and at times dissatisfying task, which is nevertheless highly attractive for archaeologists and historians alike. It is often only once the researcher succeeds in adding this additional layer to the data that the research truly "speaks" to us. This holds particularly true for periods of strong transregional interaction, in which different identities face, interact with, or even challenge one another. The Late Bronze Age in the Eastern Mediterranean is frequently envisaged as such an interactive period. By the end of the 12th Dynasty, Canaanites from the southern Levant had migrated into the Delta region, established a political powerbase and subsequently became known as the Hyksos. This so-called Second Intermediate Period came to an end with the conquest of the Hyksos capital, Avaris, and the establishment of the New Kingdom by Ahmose. Egypt thus re-established its political power, and during the 18th, 19th, and 20th Dynasties showed increased economic and military interest in the Levant. This interest is evident in both written sources and material culture (Redford 1992; Bunimovitz 1995; Hasel 1998; Higginbotham 2000; Martin 2011).

Several studies have attempted to characterize the Egyptian involvement in the southern Levant, and to assess whether this period witnessed some movement of individuals there from Egypt. Their results range from the conclusion that quite substantial numbers of Egyptians emigrated to the southern Levant, and controlled administrative and strategic nodes (Weinstein 1981), to that there was no significant presence of Egyptian individuals in the area (Higginbotham 2000). It should be noted that these studies have tended to examine the entire region, by compiling disparate historical sources and the results of numerous excavations. The fact that they reached such contrasting conclusions based on comparable datasets speak to the complexity of the research question.

While wide-reaching studies provide larger amounts of data, their resolution is often decreased, and detailed examinations of specific sites are essential if the aim is to reconstruct the migration of individuals or small groups. Tel Lachish figures prominently in written sources (Epstein 1963; Na'aman 1988; 2011), and its Late Bronze Age layers have been extensively excavated (Tufnell – Inge – Harding 1940; Tufnell 1958; Barkay – Ussishkin 2004; Ussishkin 2004b; 2004c; 2004d). The presence of Egyptians and even their control of the site has been suggested in the past (Singer 1988: 5) but has not been examined in detail. This paper aims to assess whether it is possible to identify Egyptians in the southern Levant with a high degree of certainty, using Tel Lachish as a test case.

Who is a foreigner?

The terminology employed in earlier studies was often arbitrary. Terms such as "Egyptians" and "Canaanites" are used as identifiers without considering the full variability of such ascriptions. However, whether one is arguing for (Weinstein 1981) or against (Higginbotham 2000) the presence of members of a specific cultural group in an area, it is necessary to understand what one is actually searching for. How, for example, should one address an individual born in Country A but raised in Country B? What is the cultural ascription of individuals born to "foreign" parents in a certain country? Into which category should one place the child of parents from different cultural backgrounds? While earlier studies (e.g. Killebrew 2005) have focused on ethnicity, as one aspect of the cultural identity of individuals and groups, which is perceived as an amalgamation of shared ancestry, heritage, language and religion. However, additional aspects of cultural identity such as economic status, subsistence and occupation also define the cultural identity of individuals. The distinction of these aspects is limited for past populations. In this study, cultural identity is therefore applied as an overarching category, composed of many different, and partly unknown, components. While many of these aspects remain elusive, a reconstruction of the cultural identity of past populations adds a further layer to the understanding of historical processes. This study aims to shed light on some aspects of cultural identity, drawing both on archaeological and anthropological data. Ethnicity, for example, a well-studied key aspect in the cultural identity of present populations has been partly oversimplified in past populations, not considering the wide range of variations known from anthropological studies. Archaeological studies have rarely considered fluid models for ethnicity, even though these are well-established in the anthropological discourse. It is therefore critical to first review possible constellations of individual aspects of identity, as observed by anthropologists in more recent populations, before drawing conclusions about past groups.

The anthropological perspective

In 1969, Fredrik Barth edited a volume entitled *Ethnic groups and boundaries. The social organization of culture difference* which constituted probably the most encompassing study of ethnicity at its time. In the introductory chapter (Barth 1969a), Barth constructed a theoretical framework for the study of ethnicity, proposing that ethnicity is not an *a priori* existent condition, but rather is socially constructed. He argued that it is the "ethnic *boundary* that defines the group, not the cultural stuff that it encloses" (Barth's emphasis: Barth 1969a: 15). Ethnicity should be therefore considered as an aspect of a relationship between two groups, rather than a property of one group. Anthropological studies attest to the full range of fluidities of ethnicity, three of which have been discussed in ethnographic research.

The first ethnic fluidity could be labelled "acquired ethnicity". Numerous studies report free and habitual transgression of ethnic boundaries without any devaluation in the ethnic distinctiveness of the respective groups. Gunnar Haaland (Haaland 1969) presented the case of two ethnic groups in Sudan: the Fur and the Baggara. While the former were agriculturalists, the latter led a predominantly pastoral lifestyle. Fluctuations between these two groups were common, including the complete absorption of an individual into a new group, and the adoption of a new lifestyle. No correlation with economic needs caused, for example, by land depletion or the restriction of pasture land was observed, and repeated movements between the groups were reported. Similar free and frequent movements between two groups had already observed by Edmund Leach (Leach 1954) in Burma (Myanmar), where two ethnic groups (Kachin and Shan) oscillated freely. It appears evident that ethnicity is not a fixed category for an individual, but can, at least in some cases, be completely changed and newly acquired.

As a second fluidity we might consider "segmentary ethnicity" (Jenkins 2008: 42–45). Ethnic groups are not homogenous, but frequently have many subgroups that add another layer to the ethnic profiles of their members. A well-studied example is the subdivision of the Pashtun (Afghans) into numerous distinct subtribes, who nonetheless still identify with an overarching ethnic scheme (Barth 1969b). A prominent example of such segmentary ethnicity from the Ancient Near East is the tribal system of the Israelites described in the Biblical account. While the shared ethnic identity of the individual subgroups is evident, so are their distinctive characters.

A third ethnic fluidity is "situational ethnicity", which frequently occurs when people display multiple ethnicities (Okamura 1981; Jenkins 2008: 46–50). Ethnicity in such cases is displayed or concealed depending on a given situation. Examples of ethnographic studies that show pronounced situational ethnicities include those of North Indian Brahmins in English cities (Mitchell 1966), or Sami groups in Norway (Eidheim 1971). The way that an ethnicity is portrayed in a given datum is necessarily situational, and thus necessarily influences our perception of that past ethnicity.

It is evident from the anthropological studies mentioned above that ethnicity is a highly fluid concept. Most nuances can only be perceived when informants are able provide a detailed account of their own or another's ethnic profile. Acquired ethnicity is impossible to track in the archaeological record, and can thus only be observed in written sources, and even then with reservations. Segmentary ethnicities are likely to be subtle, and cannot be expected to be evident in the archaeological record, or rather are likely to be obscured by additional factors. As no informant from the Late Bronze Age is able to directly report on his or her cultural identity, it is virtually impossible to reconstruct multiple- or situational ethnicities and to distinguish them vis-à-vis other aspects. The rather grim implication of this survey is that a large and important portion of ethnicity will forever remain concealed, and our reconstructions will be incomplete. However, despite these limitations, reconstructions should not be considered futile. Material culture and historical sources can provide at least some clues to the identity of individuals, and informed approximations can provide suitable backgrounds upon which to interpret the dynamics, developments, and interactions of Bronze Age societies.

How to identify a foreigner in antiquity

The vast majority of our knowledge about the past is based on data such as settlement layers or historic archives, which have accumulated over many generations. While our options to reconstruct specific individuals are restricted, it is possible to identify the actions of individuals in few instances. In written records, the names of individuals might indicate their (acquired) cultural background, at least so some extent (Hess 1993), but some texts also preserve the identity of the scribe through the act of writing (Devecchi 2012; Mynářová 2015; Vita 2015; Mynářová 2016). Similarly, the creation of a ceramic vessel might follow the aesthetic rules of the collective, but its production is usually performed by one individual, who will (involuntarily) imprint his or her identity into the clay (Branigan – Papadatos – Wynn 2002; Sanders 2015). When searching for individuals, burials might come to mind as the ultimate preservation of the individual. While this is certainly true at least on the level of physical anthropology, the cultural package that shapes a given funerary rite is more complex, as it is difficult to decide whether the burial primarily reflects the identity of the deceased individual or of the society that performed the interment (Stutz – Tarlow 2013).

One key assumption, that cultural backgrounds shape material culture, long stood at the core of archaeological studies. It was not until the early 2000s that the long-accepted "pots = people" equation was seriously questioned in Near Eastern Archaeology, also on the basis of ethnographic studies that disapproved of such a simplistic approach (Bunimovitz – Faust 2001). Nevertheless, material culture is doubtlessly influenced and shaped through the interactions of individuals and groups. For this study I propose a more nuanced view of how humans shape material culture. Two pathways can be distinguished: "embodied cultural automatism"; and "conscious cultural choice".

Embodied cultural automatism includes the full range of unconsciously acquired technical skills, work processes, and aesthetic preferences that are normally transmitted or acquired (embodied) *en passant*. They are thereafter performed automatically without any conscious decision making. Examples of this can frequently be found in the construction methods of domestic houses, or the ceramic production of local wares. As many actions are performed unconsciously and habitually, they are likely to reflect the cultural traditions (and thus potentially the cultural background) in which the respective skill was acquired.

Conscious cultural choice involves active decision making. The choice might reflect the cultural identity of another group and can serve a specific purpose. Examples would be the architectural outline of civic buildings, or the adoption of certain stylistic elements in decorative arts or table wares (either imported or locally imitated). Such conscious cultural choices are often made to transmit social messages, such as status or cultural connections.

An understanding of the distinction between these two pathways can help to dissect foreign influences observed in the data from a site, and to assess whether a datum should be ascribed to individual immigrants, or rather to someone emulating material culture of a different group. While the more complex cultural profiles observed in anthropological studies remain concealed, it will sometimes be possible to distinguish whether a locally- or non-locally socialized individual should be connected to a specific material culture set.

Case study: Tel Lachish in the Late Bronze Age

Tel Lachish (Tell ed-Duweir), which covers twelve hectares, is among the largest tell-sites in the southern Levant (Fig. 1). The site was a major settlement in the Shephelah region during both the Bronze and Iron Ages. This is reflected in written sources, such as Papyrus Hermitage 1116A (Golénischeff 1913; Epstein 1963) and the Amarna correspondence (Rainey 2015), in the Biblical account (e.g. Joshua 10:31–33; 2 Kings 18:13–14; 2 Chronicles 32:9; Isaiah 36:1–2; Jeremiah 34:7; Nehemiah 11:30), and on the wall reliefs of his palace in Nineveh (Ussishkin 1982). The site has been extensively excavated, beginning in the 1930s. Three of these excavation projects unearthed substantial remains from the Late Bronze Age (Fig. 2). The British excavation directed by James L. Starkey (1932 to 1938) uncovered Late Bronze Age features such as the Fosse Temple (Tufnell – Inge – Harding 1940), a number of burials dating to the same period (Tufnell 1958), and substantial wall remains presumably dating to the Late Bronze Age that were uncovered on the summit of the tell (Tufnell 1953: 78, fig.4; Ussishkin 2004b). The project ended with Starkey's murder in 1938, and was subsequently published by Olga Tufnell (Tufnell – Inge – Harding 1940; Tufnell 1953; 1958; Garfinkel 2016). The next major excavation project to uncover remains from the Late Bronze Age was directed by David Ussishkin on behalf of Tel Aviv University (1973 to 1994). Areas P (Ussishkin 2004c), D (Ussishkin 2004b), and S (Barkay – Ussishkin 2004) were particularly fruitful in the architectural remains and stratified archaeological contexts they yielded. A short project, from 2013 to 2017 focusing on the Iron Age, was conducted by Yosef Garfinkel on behalf of Hebrew University of Jerusalem, together with Michael Hasel and Martin Klingbeil on behalf of Southern Adventist University. A Late Bronze Age temple structure was uncovered in the course of this excavation, of which selected results have been presented (Sass – Garfinkel *et al.* 2015; Weissbein 2017). Since 2017, a new Austro-Israeli expedition has been focused on the Middle and Late Bronze Age strata (Streit – Webster *et al.* 2018).[1]

The written evidence

Lachish is mentioned briefly in Papyrus Hermitage 1116A (Golénischeff 1913; Epstein 1963). On the *verso* of this papyrus is an administrative text dated to the reign of either Tuthmose III or Amenhotep II, which describes the passage of a *maryannu* envoy from northern Canaan on their way to Egypt, stopping at several key sites of the southern Levant (Megiddo, Kinnereth, Achshaph, Shimron, Taanach, Mishal, Ḫazor, and Ashkelon). A separate envoy from Lachish was provisioned

[1] The Austro-Israeli Expedition to Lachish is part of the project *Tracing Transformations*, funded by the Austrian Science Fund (FWF) START-grant Y-932, and directed by Felix Höflmayer.

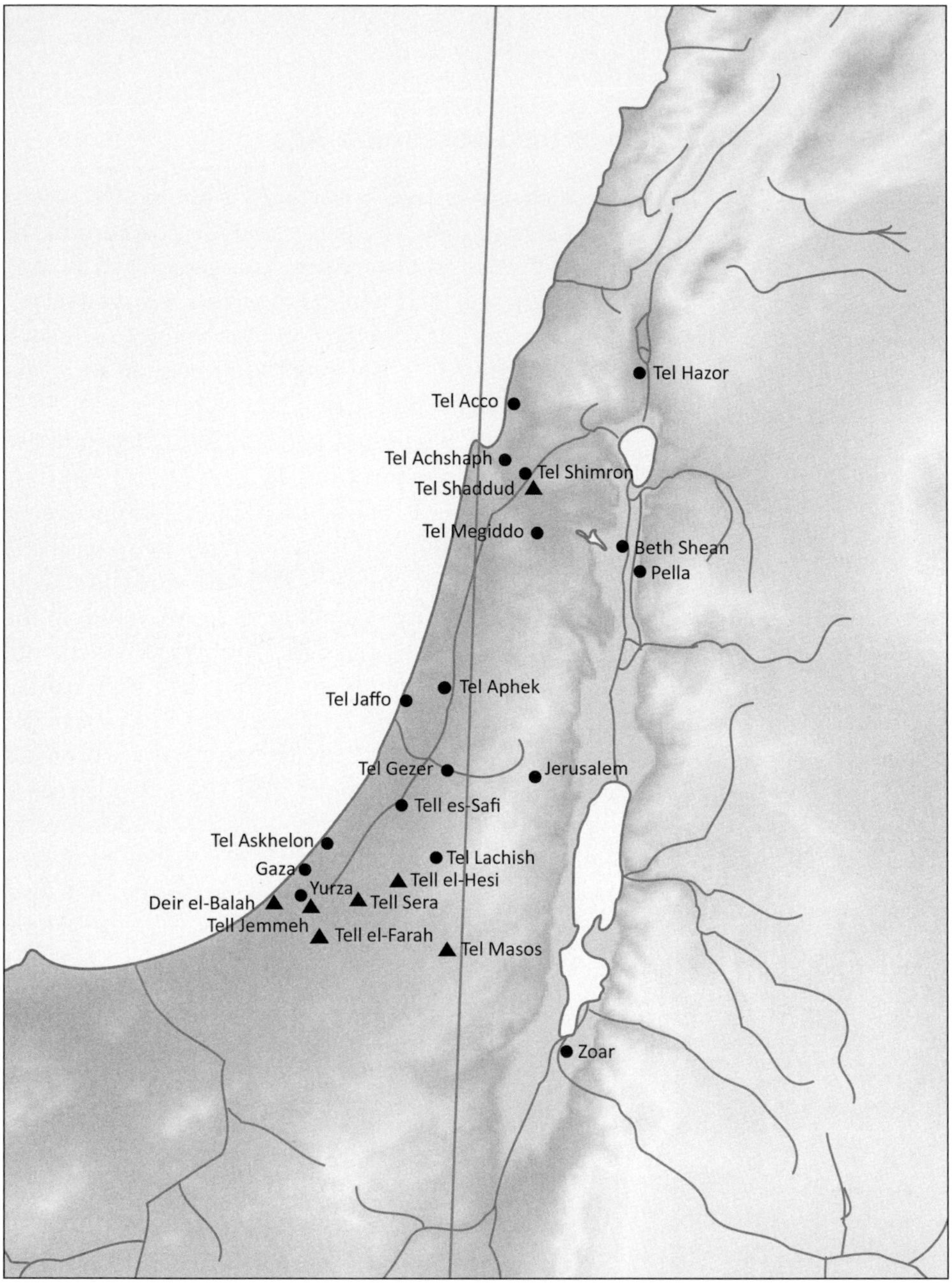

Fig. 1.
Key sites in the southern Levant (● – sites mentioned in the Amarna correspondence; ▲– other key sites with major Late Bronze Age remains).

at the court in Thebes. The mention of Lachish in the time of Amenhotep II has caused some confusion, as no substantial archaeological remains at Tel Lachish have been dated to his reign (Ussishkin 2004a: 58). However, new radiocarbon dating shows that quite substantial architectural remains of Stratum S-3 date into the second half of the 15th century BC (Webster – Streit *et al.* 2019), and thus supports the notion that Lachish was an important centre in the LB IB, as suggested by Papyrus Hermitage 1116A.

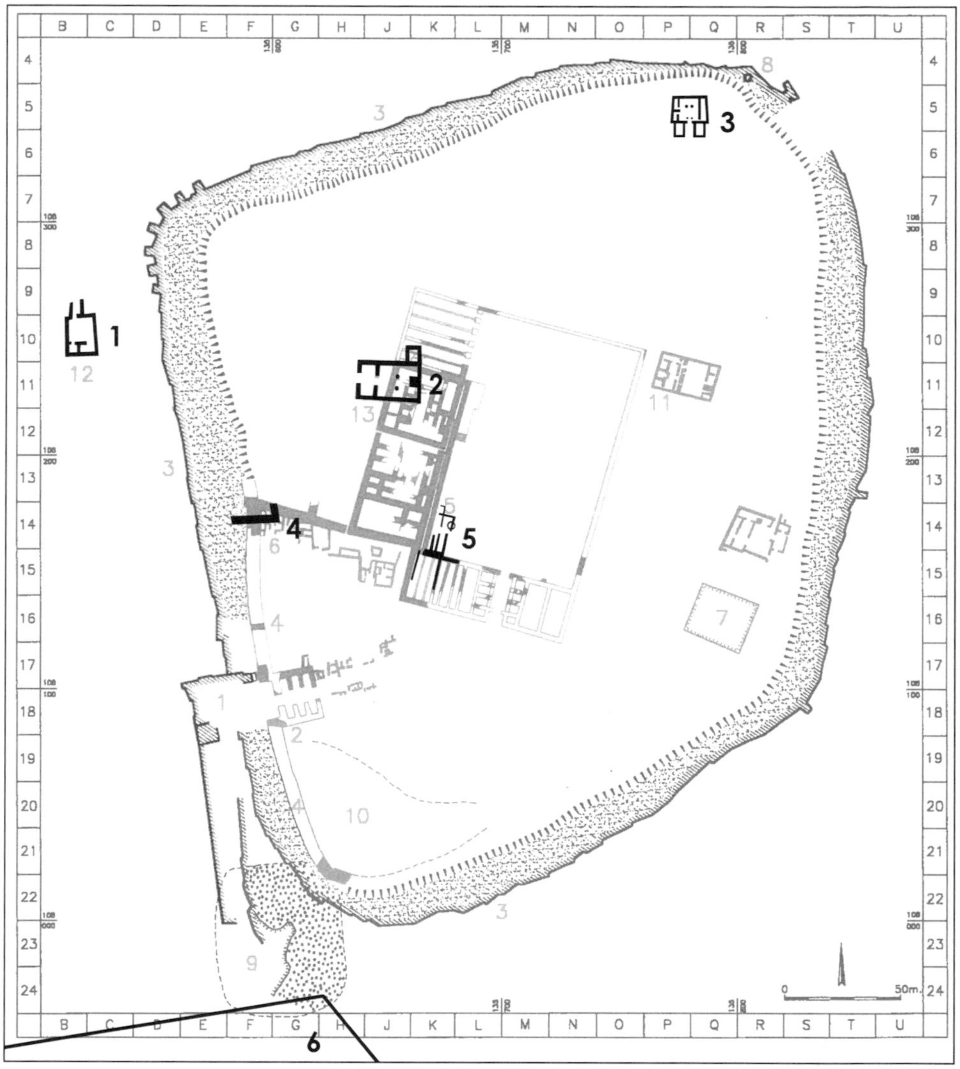

Fig. 2.
Main Late Bronze Age features at Tel Lachish (modified from Ussishkin 2004c: fig. 2.9:
1 – Fosse Temple,
2 – Acropolis Temple,
3 – "North Temple",
4 – "Great Building",
5 – mudbrick walls and silo,
6 – Cemetery 500).

Tel Lachish also figures prominently in the Amarna correspondence. The site is mentioned in six letters (EA 287, 288, 328, 329, 332, 335; Rainey 2015), and three rulers of the city are known by name: Zimreddi (EA 288:43, EA 329), Šipṭi-Baʿlu (EA 330; EA 331; EA 332), and Yabni-Ilu (EA 328). All three names have been described as (North)west-semitic (Hess 1993: 200–221). The Amarna letters also provide some information regarding the role of Lachish in the diplomatic network of the time. According to a letter from Abdi-Ḫeba, ruler of Urusalim (EA 287), Lachish played part in the so-called Qiltu Affair (Na'aman 2011: 289–292), a rebellion (apparently against Egyptian rulership) near the city of Qiltu (probably modern Khirbet Qila), which was supported with food rations by the cities of Gezer, Askhelon, and Lachish. The hostility of Lachish towards Egyptian authority is also expressed in EA 335, a letter from Abdi-Aštarti, ruler of Gath, who claimed that "Lakisu is hostile" (EA 335:10). This stands in stark contrast to the letters sent by the rulers of Lachish themselves, who assert their obedience to Egyptian authority (e.g. Yabni-Ilu in EA 328 and Zimreddi in EA 329). It is impossible to decide whether the accusations of other rulers or claims of loyalty by the rulers of Lachish themselves can be trusted, but it is evident that Lachish was an active participant in the diplomatic network, and that scribes who were well-acquainted with the appropriate diplomatic language and format must have been present at Lachish when the letters were composed, and probably for much longer.

The archaeological evidence

A range of finds from Tel Lachish has been connected to a hypothetical Egyptian presence. In this survey, the most prominent will be discussed and evaluated to determine whether they can be used as cultural identifiers.

Three temples have so far been uncovered at Tel Lachish, two of which, the Fosse Temple (Tufnell – Inge – Harding 1940) and the Acropolis temple (Ussishkin 2004d) have been published. A third is still awaiting full publication, with only selected aspects having been made available (Weissbein 2017). The Fosse Temple (Fig. 3) was uncovered by the British expedition at the western foot of the mound, and has had a profound impact on the chronology of the Late Bronze Age. Three phases of the structure have been identified, and its ground plan was substantially remodelled between the first and the second phases. Imported objects bearing the names of Egyptian kings allowed an absolute chronology to be established, which subsequently defined the now-standard tripartite division of the Late Bronze Age (Martin 2011: 216). The structure is characterised by a square room furnished with benches along its walls. Its location at the foot of the tell, its outline, and its inventory have raised questions regarding the function of the building. Suggestions have included a pottery workshop (Ottosson 1980: 81–92), a temple serving the lower classes (Tufnell – Inge – Harding 1940: 10) or pastoral nomads (Finkelstein 1988: 343), and as a house dedicated for funerary banqueting, a so called "Beit Marzeah" (Bietak 2002). Egyptian influences on the ground plan, and its similarity with New Kingdom Egyptian houses, have been stressed by Manfred Bietak (Bietak 2002). Recently, the cult has been connected to reforms under Amenhotep III, defining Hathor as new focus of religious practice (Koch 2017), yet this interpretation is solely based on a handful of iconographic pieces. While Egyptian influences are clearly visible in both architecture and inventory of the Fosse Temple, no unequivocal evidence has been found there regarding the involvement of actual Egyptians. If Bietak is correct, and Egyptian elements were part of the architectural style of the period, then their incorporation into the structure would likely have been a conscious cultural choice.

The Acropolis Temple (Fig. 4) was excavated by the Tel Aviv expedition in Area P, on the top of the mound (Ussishkin 2004d). As with the Fosse Temple, the Acropolis Temple displays Egyptian architectural features, such as its ground plan, its faceted columns, staircase, and columnated niches (Ussishkin 2004d: 261–267). The cult has, however, been identified as Canaanite, based on the iconographic motifs found in the temple (Ussishkin 2004d: 267). Like the Fosse Temple, its architectural elements seem to have been adopted as a conscious aesthetic choice by local Canaanites, possibly emulating an Egyptian style.

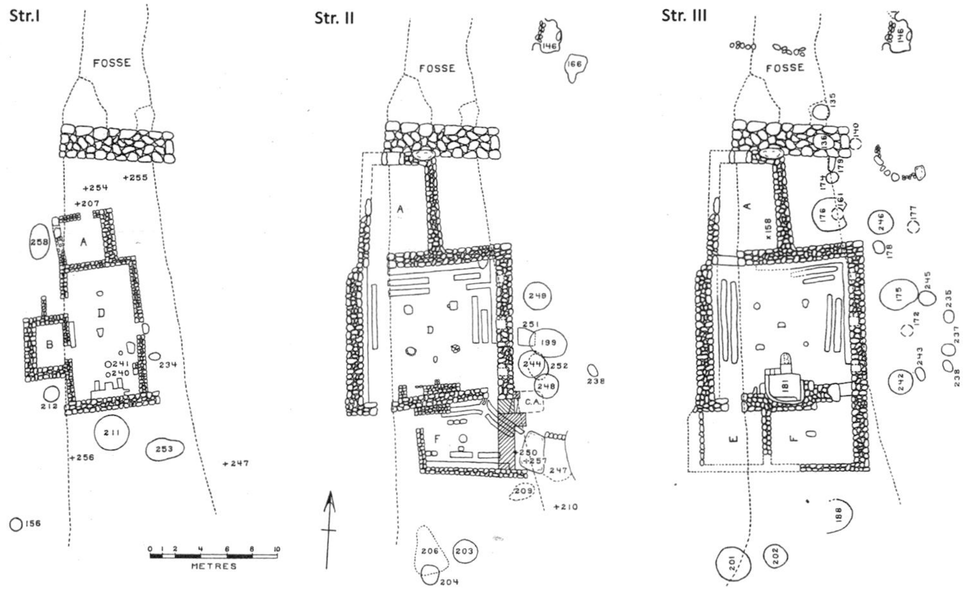

Fig. 3.
Fosse Temple (Str. I: Tufnell – Inge – Harding 1940: pl. LXVI; Str. II: Tufnell – Inge – Harding 1940: pl. LXVII; Str. III: Tufnell – Inge – Harding 1940: pl. LXXIII).

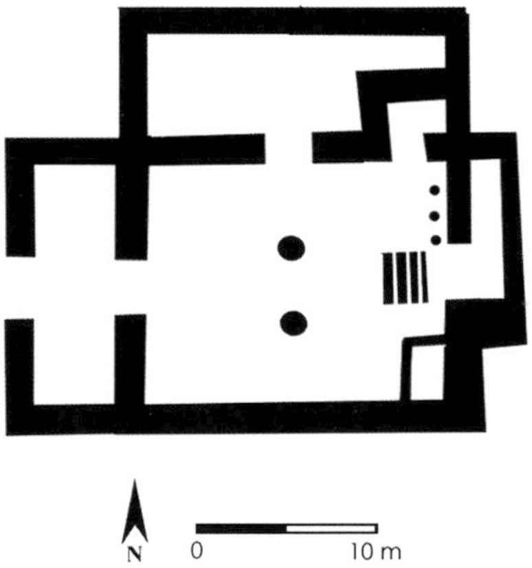

Fig. 4.
Acropolis Temple (with reconstructions, based on Ussishkin 2004b: 217, fig. 6.1).

At the south-western foot of the tell, one tomb (Tomb 570: Tufnell 1958: 131–132, 248–249, pls. 45–46) excavated by the British expedition yielded two anthropomorphic coffins (Fig. 5). This type of coffin has been found at several sites of the southern Levant, such as Tell el-Farah south, Pella, Tell Shadud and, famously, Deir el-Balah (van den Brink – Beeri *et al*. 2017 and references therein). One of the coffins was inscribed with a hieroglyphic inscription, which was however poorly executed and difficult to decipher. It was therefore concluded the inscription was not written by an Egyptian, but rather by a local Canaanite scribe (Tufnell 1958: 132).

The ceramic assemblage of Tel Lachish has been intensely studied by all expeditions to the site. An additional examination was undertaken by Mario Martin specifically to search for Egyptian and Egyptianizing ceramics (Martin 2011: 215–

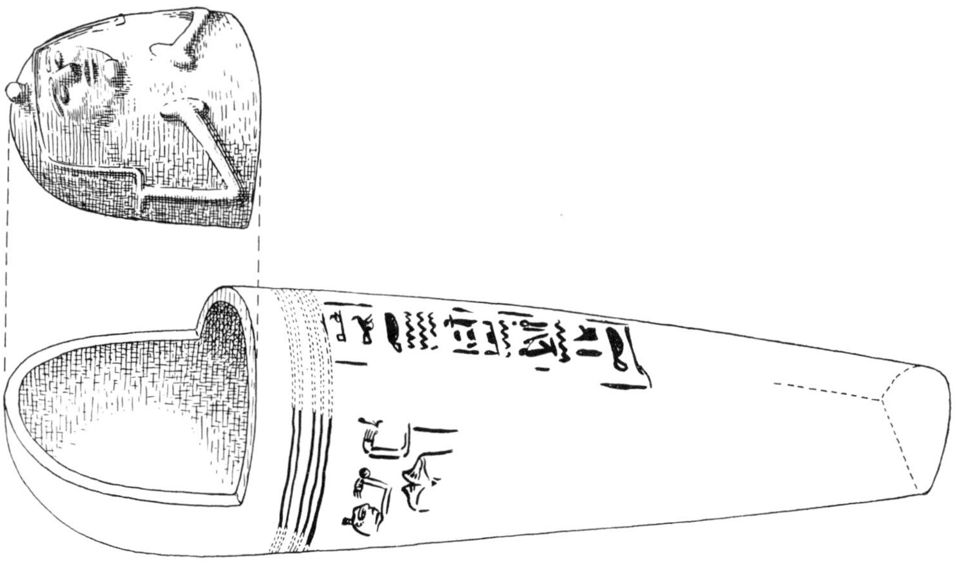

Fig. 5.
Slipper coffin from Tomb 570 (Tufnell 1958: pl. 46).

221). Alongside two or three vessels imported from Egypt (Martin 2011: 219), he also identifies a number of locally produced, Egyptianizing shapes, such as a specific type of flaring-rim bowl (Martin 2011: 218–219) that follows an Egyptian tradition (Fig. 6), but points out that very common Egyptian shapes, such as beer jars or spinning bowls, are completely absent from the assemblage (Martin 2011: 229). The production of Egyptian-style common ware open bowls either points towards the presence of an Egyptian potter or potters producing ceramics for a few individuals or even a small community, or to a local pottery producing the foreign shape, possibly adding local elements such as the preference for ring-bases. Additionally, flaring-rim bowls (and only these) were occasionally inscribed in hieratic script (Fig. 6). In total, 18 Egyptian hieratic inscriptions have been found at Lachish (Tufnell 1958: 132–133; Gilula 1976; Goldwasser 1991; Sweeny 2004). Most inscribed texts are related to a taxation system, which was apparently introduced by the Egyptian authorities. Orly Goldwasser argued, based on epigraphic analysis of sherd No.1, that this scribe "had a trained hand, and was well acquainted with the rules of the Late Egyptian language." She therefore suggested that this scribe must have been Egyptian-trained, and therefore, possibly, Egyptian (Goldwasser 1991: 250–252).

One inconspicuous archaeological context might provide clues regarding the cultural ascription of some inhabitants of Lachish: in Area D, on the summit of the mound, a circular silo of ca 4.2 m in diameter was uncovered in Stratum IV (Ussishkin 2004b: 297–300). The silo (Fig. 7) was built of mudbricks and an above-ground, dome-shaped structure, a building method that stands in stark contrast to other silos in the southern Levant, which are usually sunken into the ground and stone lined (Kempinski – Reich 1992). This style of dome-shaped mudbrick silo is however the most common type in Egypt, and has ample parallels from different sites (Moeller 2010: 89–100 and references therein). As silos rarely fall

Fig. 6.
Hieratic inscriptions
(Tufnell 1958: pl. 44: 3–4).

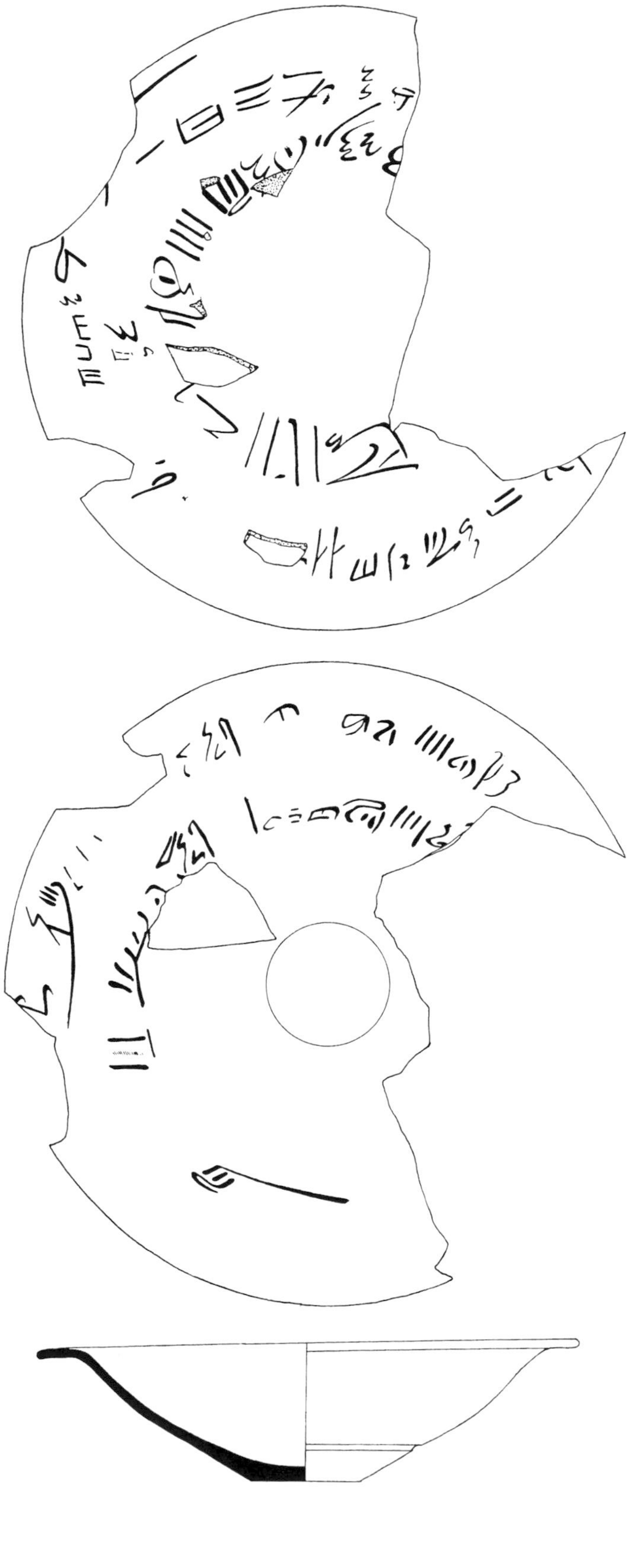

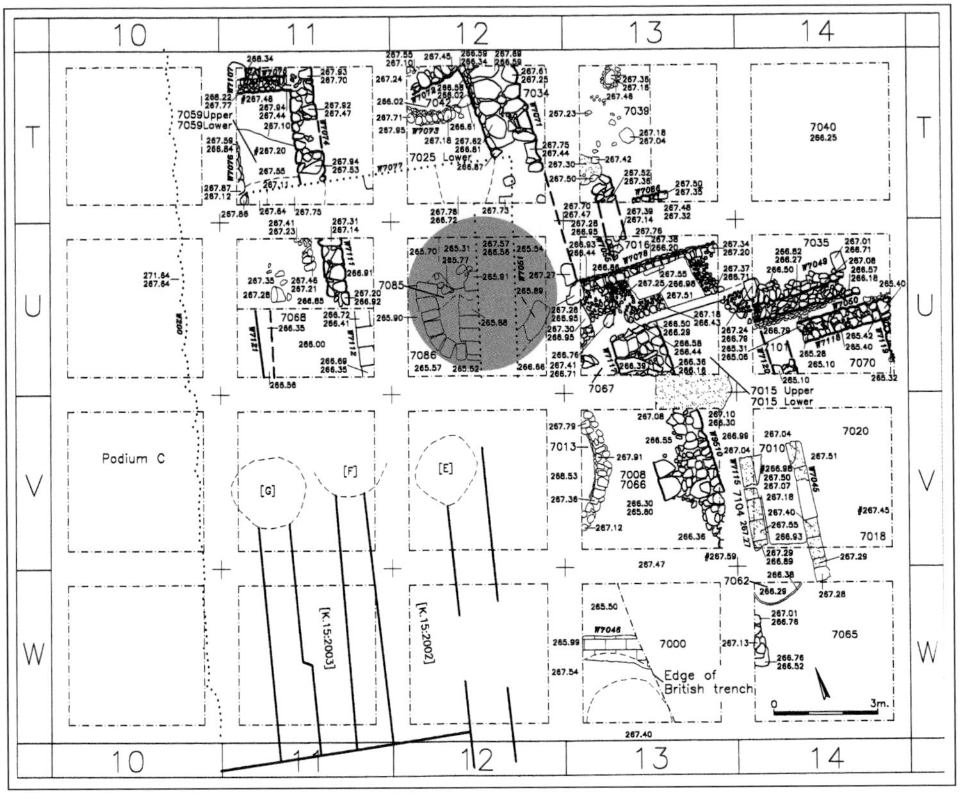

Fig. 7.

Egyptian-style silo Area D (Ussishkin 2004a: fig. 7.2).

into the category of representative buildings, it is unlikely that any conscious decision was made to deviate from the local silo building tradition. It is thus likely that this is an example of embodied cultural automatism, and that the silo was built by one or more individuals socialized in Egypt.

Summary and conclusions

This paper highlights the possibilities and limitations of identifying cultural identities in archaeological and historical contexts. The survey of anthropological studies indicates that there are a wide range of fluid identities, which are virtually impossible to discern in the record, while the complex field of multiple ethnicities complicates the picture and limits the validity of cultural reconstructions. Material culture can nevertheless provide valuable information regarding the cultural background of the population that created it. Two pathways have been distinguished, embodied cultural automatism and conscious cultural choice. While the former represents individuals, who have been culturally shaped in a specific background, the latter can also reflect the cultural preferences of a different, emulated cultural group. This model was tested on the case study of Tel Lachish in the Late Bronze Age in an attempt to identify Egyptians at the site, based on historical sources and archaeological remains. Evidence of conscious cultural choice can be discerned in the culture activity and architecture of the Fosse Temple and the Acropolis Temple, and possibly the burial tradition of anthropomorphic coffins. This evidence matches well with local Canaanites emulating Egyptian material culture and should be understood in the framework of the multitude of imported Egyptian objects, which would also include commonly-found items like scarabs and jewellery. Embodied cultural automatism manifested itself mainly in the ceramic tradition, hieratic inscriptions on flaring-rim bowls, and in the construction of a silo using an Egyptian technique and style. This should be understood as firm evidence for the presence of at least few individuals socialized in Egypt at the site of Lachish.

The West Semitic names of the rulers of Lachish mentioned in the Amarna correspondence, and a burial in Egyptian style an anthropoid sarcophagus that was inscribed by a non-Egyptian scribe, point towards a Canaanite rulership that emulated Egyptians, as suggested by Higginbotham (2000). However, there is sufficient evidence to reconstruct that at least several culturally Egyptian individuals must have lived, more-or-less permanently, at Lachish. It is imaginable that their function was connected to the taxation system, which would fit the evidence of both the hieratic writing tradition and grain storage facilities.

References

Barkay, G. – D. Ussishkin, 2004. Area S. The Late Bronze Age strata. In D. Ussishkin, ed., *The renewed archaeological excavations at Lachish (1973–1994).* Tel Aviv: Emery and Claire Yass Publications in Archaeology, 316–407.

Barth, F., 1969a. Introduction. In F. Barth, ed., *Ethnic groups and boundaries. The social organization of culture difference.* Oslo: Universitetsforlaget, 9–38.

Barth, F., 1969b. Pathan identity and its maintenance. In F. Barth, ed., *Ethnic groups and boundaries. The social organization of culture difference.* Oslo: Universitetsforlaget, 117–134.

Bietak, M., 2002. The function and some architectural roots of the Fosse Temple at Lachish. In S. Aḥituv – E.D. Oren, ed., *Aharon Kempinski memorial volume. Studies in archaeology and related disciplines.* Beer Sheva 15. Beer Sheva: Ben-Gurion University of the Negev Press, 56–85.

Branigan, K. – Y. Papadatos – D. Wynn, 2002. Fingerprints on early Minoan pottery. A pilot study. *ABSA* 97, 49–53.

Bunimovitz, S., 1995. On the edge of empires—Late Bronze Age (1500–1200 BCE). In T.E. Levy, ed., *The archaeology of society in the Holy Land.* London: Leicester University Press, 320–331.

Bunimovitz, S. – A. Faust, 2001. Chronological separation, geographical segregation, or ethnic demarcation? Ethnography and the Iron Age low chronology. *BASOR* 322, 1–10.

Devecchi, E., ed., 2012. *Palaeography and scribal practices in Syro-Palestine and Anatolia in the Late Bronze Age. Papers read at a symposium in Leiden, 17–18 December 2009.* PIHANS 119. Leiden: Nederlands Instituut voor het Nabije Oosten.

Eidheim, H., 1971. *Aspects of the Lappish minority situation.* Oslo: Scandinavian University Press.

Epstein, C., 1963. A new appraisal of some lines from a long-known papyrus. *JEA* 49, 49–56.

Finkelstein, I., 1988. *The archaeology of the Israelite settlement.* Jerusalem: Israel Exploration Society.

Garfinkel, Y., 2016. The murder of James Leslie Starkey near Lachish. *PEQ* 148(2), 84–109.

Gilula, M., 1976. An inscription in Egyptian hieratic from Lachish. *TA* 3, 77–93.

Goldwasser, O., 1991. An Egyptian scribe from Lachish and the hieratic tradition of the Hebrew Kingdom. *TA* 18, 248–253.

Golénischeff, W., 1913. *Les Papyrus Nos. 1115, 1116A et 1116B de l'Ermitage Impériale à St. Pétersbourg.* Saint Petersburg: Ermitage Imperial.

Haaland, G., 1969. Economic determinants in ethnic processes. In F. Barth, ed., *Ethnic groups and boundaries. The social organization of culture difference.* Oslo: Universitetsforlaget, 49–73.

Hasel, M.G., 1998. *Domination and Resistance. Egyptian Military Activity in the Southern Levant, ca. 1300–1185 B.C.* PdÄ 10. Leiden – Boston – Köln: Brill.

Hess, R.S., 1993. *Amarna Personal Names.* ASOR Dissertation Series 9. Winona Lake, IN: Eisenbrauns.

Higginbotham, C.R., 2000. *Egyptianization and elite emulation in Ramesside Palestine. Governance and accommodation on the imperial periphery.* CHANE 2. Leiden – Boston: Brill.

Jenkins, R., 2008. *Rethinking ethnicity. Arguments and explorations.* London: SAGE Publications.

Kempinski, A. – R. Reich, eds., 1992. *The architecture of Ancient Israel. From the prehistoric to the Persian Periods. In memory of Immanuel (Munya) Dunayevsky.* Jerusalem: Israel Exploration Society.

Killebrew, A.E., 2005. *Biblical peoples and ethnicity. An archaeological study of Egyptians, Canaanites, Philistines and early Israel 1300–1100.* Archaeology and Biblical Studies 9. Atlanta, GA: Society of Biblical Literature.

Koch, I., 2017. Revisiting the Fosse Temple at Tel Lachish. *JANER* 17, 64–75.

Leach, E.R., 1954. *Political systems of highland Burma. A study of Kachin social structure.* London: Bell.

Martin, M.A.S., 2011. *Egyptian-type pottery in the Late Bronze Age southern Levant.* CChEM 29. Wien: Verlag der Österreichischen Akademie der Wissenschaften.

Mitchell, J.C., 1966. Theoretical orientations in African urban studies. In M. Banton, ed., *The social anthropology of complex societies.* London: Tavistock, 37–68.

Moeller, N., 2010. Tell Edfu. Preliminary report on seasons 2005–2009. *JARCE* 46, 81–111.

Mynářová, J., 2015. Amarna Palaeography Project. The current state of research. In J. Mynářová – P. Onderka – P. Pavúk, eds., *There and Back Again – the Crossroads II. Proceedings of an international conference held in Prague, September 15–18, 2014.* Prague: Charles University in Prague, 409–421.

Mynářová, J., 2016. Handbook of Amarna Cuneiform Palaeography. A project update. *JAEI* 11, 15–16.

Na'aman, N., 1988. The southern Shefelah during the Late Bronze Age according to the cuneiform documents. In E. Stern – D. Urman, eds., *Man and environment in the southern Shefelah. Studies in regional geography and history.* Giv'ataim: Masada, 93–98.

Na'aman, N., 2011. The Shephelah according to the Amarna letters. In I. Finkelstein – N. Na'aman, eds., *The Fire Signals of Lachish. Studies in the Archaeology and History of Israel in the Late Bronze Age, Iron Age, and Persian Period in Honor of David Ussishkin.* Winona Lake, IN: Eisenbrauns, 281–299.

Okamura, J.Y., 1981. Situational ethnicity. *Ethnic and racial studies* 4(4), 452–465.

Ottosson, M., 1980. *Temples and Cult Places in Palestine.* Boreas. Acta Universitatis Upsaliensis 12. Uppsala: Almqvist & Wiksell.

Rainey, A.F., 2015. *The El-Amarna Correspondence. A New Edition of the Cuneiform Letters from the Site of El-Amarna Based on Collations of All Extant Tablets.* Edited by William Schniedewind and Zipora Cochavi-Rainey. HdO I/10. Leiden – Boston: Brill.

Redford, D.B., 1992. *Egypt, Canaan, and Israel in Ancient Times.* Princeton: Princeton University Press.

Sanders, A., 2015. Fingerprints, sex, state, and the organization of the Tell Leilan ceramic industry. *JAS* 57, 223–238.

Sass, B. – Y. Garfinkel – M.G. Hasel – M.G. Klingbeil, 2015. The Lachish jar sherd. An early alphabetic inscription discovered in 2014. *BASOR* 374, 233–245.

Singer, I., 1988. Merneptah's Campaign to Canaan and the Egyptian Occupation of the Southern Coastal Plain of Palestine in the Ramesside Period. *BASOR* 269, 1–10.

Streit, K. – L.C. Webster – V. Becker – A.-K. Jeske – H. Misgav – F. Höflmayer, 2018. Between destruction and diplomacy in Canaan. The Austrian-Israeli Expedition to Tel Lachish. *NEA* 81/4, 259–268.

Stutz, L.N. – S. Tarlow, eds., 2013. *The Oxford Handbook of the Archaeology of Death and Burial.* Oxford: Oxford University Press.

Sweeny, D., 2004. Section B. The hieratic inscriptions. In D. Ussishkin, ed., *The renewed archaeological excavations at Lachish (1973–1994).* Tel Aviv: Emery and Claire Yass Publications in Archaeology, 1601–1617.

Tufnell, O., 1953. *Lachish III (Tell ed-Duweir). The Iron Age.* The Wellcome-Marston Archaeological Research Expedition to the Near East 3. London – New York – Toronto: Oxford University Press.

Tufnell, O., 1958. *Lachish IV (Tell ed-Duweir). The Bronze Age.* The Wellcome-Marston Archaeological Research Expedition to the Near East 4. London – New York – Toronto: Oxford University Press.

Tufnell, O. – C.H. Inge – G.L. Harding, 1940. *Lachish II (Tell ed-Duweir). The Fosse Temple.* The Wellcome-Marston Archaeological Research Expedition to the Near East 2. London – New York – Toronto: Oxford University Press.

Ussishkin, D., 1982. *The Conquest of Lachish by Sennacherib.* Publications of the Institute of Archaeology, Tel Aviv University 6. Tel Aviv: Tel Aviv University.

Ussishkin, D., 2004a. A synopsis of the stratigraphical, chronological and historical issues. In D. Ussishkin, ed., *The renewed archaeological excavations at Lachish (1973–1994).* Tel Aviv: Emery and Claire Yass Publications in Archaeology, 50–119.

Ussishkin, D., 2004b. Area D. The Bronze Age strata. In D. Ussishkin, ed., *The renewed archaeological excavations at Lachish (1973–1994).* Tel Aviv: Emery and Claire Yass Publications in Archaeology, 282–315.

Ussishkin, D., 2004c. Area P. The Late Bronze Age strata. In D. Ussishkin, ed., *The renewed archaeological excavations at Lachish (1973–1994).* Tel Aviv: Emery and Claire Yass Publications in Archaeology, 188–214.

Ussishkin, D., 2004d. Area P. The Level VI temple. In D. Ussishkin, ed., *The renewed archaeological excavations at Lachish (1973–1994).* Tel Aviv: Emery and Claire Yass Publications in Archaeology, 215–281.

van den Brink, E. – R. Beeri – D. Kirzner – E. Bron – A. Cohen-Weinberger – E. Kamaisky – T. Gonen – L. Gershuny – Y. Nagar – D. Ben-Tor – T. Sukenik – O. Shamir – E.F. Maher – D. Reich, eds., 2017. A Late Bronze Age II clay coffin from Tel Shaddud in the central Jezreel Valley, Israel. Context and historical implications. *Levant* 49(2), 105–135.

Vita, J.-P., 2015. *Canaanite Scribes in the Amarna Letters.* AOAT 406. Münster: Ugarit-Verlag.

Webster, L.C. – K. Streit – M.W. Dee – I. Hajdas – F. Höflmayer, 2019. Identifying the Lachish of Papyrus Hermitage 1116A verso and the Amarna Letters: Implications of New Radiocarbon Dating. *JAEI* 21, 88–99.

Weinstein, J.M., 1981. The Egyptian Empire in Palestine. A Reassessment. *BASOR* 241, 1–28.

Weissbein, I., 2017. Goddesses of Canaanite Lachish. *Strata. Bulletin of the Anglo-Israel Archaeological Society* 34, 41–55.

THE EGYPTIANS' AMBIVALENT RELATIONSHIP WITH FOREIGNERS: THE CASE OF THE PRISONERS OF WAR IN THE NEW KINGDOM

Marta Valerio (Université Paul Valéry Montpellier 3)

My PhD thesis focused on the treatment of prisoners of war in the New Kingdom. Drawing on iconographic and written sources, it reconstructed the destiny of subjugated foreigners, from capture to settling in Egypt[1]. While working on my research, I began to notice some possible signs of the varying attitudes of Egyptians towards foreigners, especially when they stopped being enemies and became residents and, at least to a certain extent, members of Egyptian society.

The presence of foreigners in Egypt was a phenomenon that lasted throughout the Pharaonic period and whose characteristics changed over time. Between the 12th and 14th Dynasties, there was a significant influx of foreign workers, a phenomenon that is attested by various sources, including the papyri from Kahun (Luft 1998: 138–142; Griffith 1898). These sources show the presence of a large community of Asiatics working in fields such as agriculture, tending livestock or handicrafts in cities (Menu 2004b: 35–39; Kasparian 2000). Later, during the New Kingdom, the forced settling of prisoners of war contributed massively to the presence of foreigners in the country (Helck 1971: 342–347; Sauneron – Yoyotte 1950: 67–70).

Building on the results of my doctoral research, this paper investigates the mutable concept of "otherness" held by the Egyptians of the New Kingdom, using iconographical and written sources on prisoners of war as case studies to analyse the relationship between Egyptians and foreigners. In Pharaonic ideology, foreigners represented the Nine Bows against which Egyptians fought to maintain the order of the *maat* (Assmann 1989: 115ff.; Valbelle 1990), the cosmic order, a mission entrusted to the Pharaoh by the deity. The relationship between Egyptians and these foreigners was regulated by a dualism that Antonio Loprieno (1988), in his analysis of Egyptian literature, has described using two antithetical concepts: *topos* and *mimesis*. *Topos* regards Egyptians as superior to "others"; *mimesis* expresses the daily practice of dealing with foreigners that goes beyond the violent relations underlying the *topos*. This paper provides a number of examples of how prisoners of war were treated. It aims to shed light on some possible elements of what Egyptians regarded as "otherness". The evidence presented suggests that Egyptians saw this "otherness" as something that it was possible to eliminate or at least bring under control. In this way, the distance between them and outsiders

[1] *Le traitement des prisonniers de guerre en Égypte sous le Nouvel Empire*, unpublished thesis supervised by Prof. Marc Gabolde (Université Paul Valéry-Montpellier 3) and Paolo Gallo (Università degli Studi di Torino) defended in December 2017.

could be reduced, if not completely cancelled. Foreigners could become workers and also join the Egyptian administration, sometimes reaching high levels. How was this possible? This paper will seek to give some insight into this process.

1. How did Egyptians describe themselves and "others"?

Religious texts of the New Kingdom, such as the hymns to Amun-Re of the pBoulaq 17, the hymns to the Aten and the 4th hour of the Book of Gates, demonstrate that Egyptians viewed foreigners as a component of the created world. However, in Egyptian ideology the description of this world set up an opposition between negative stereotypes of "others" and the positive elements of "Egyptianness", and this opposition helped to define Egyptian identity (Assmann 1996: 80, 84; Schneider 2010: 154; Smith 2007: 218). Egyptians described themselves as *rmṯ*, a word used to mean "human beings". At times, they used this word to create a distinction between themselves, who were deemed worthy of being called human beings, and everyone else outside Egypt, who did not deserve this label (Gardiner 1947: 100). This use of the word *rmṯ* is evident in the description of the chaotic situation in Egypt after the end of the Old Kingdom, set out in the 12th Dynasty text known as the Ipuwer Lamentations (Loprieno 1988: 26–29): "Foreigners have become people (*rmṯ*) everywhere… there are no people (*rmṯ*) everywhere" (Lichtheim 1973: 150)[2].

Groups of foreigners were differentiated according to some stereotyped criteria mostly based on skin colour and clothing. We can see this very clearly in the representation of the "four populations of the world" in the tomb of Seti I and Ramesses III (Smith 2003: 19–29; Yurko 1996), and the same elements were also used in standardised representations of foreigners in rhetorical and historical sources to make them easily and instantly recognisable (Schneider 2010: 154; Ritner 1993: 111–136; Roth 2015: 156–160, 167–171).

Egyptians labelled their enemies (whether Asiatic, Nubian, Libyan) as *ẖsy* "vile, wretched", and the treatment inflicted on them in the propagandistic texts and images was extremely violent. In these sources, the mission of the Pharaoh was to "abolish" or "annihilate" their enemies (to mention some of the terms used). However, it goes without saying that the reality was not as simple as the one sketched in the propaganda sources, and annihilation of the enemy could also take the form of subjugation and pacification.

In texts and images Egyptians willingly equated their foreign enemies to animals, to underline some negative aspects of their behaviour (El-Magd 2016). A very good example of this parallelism is the Tutankhamun box,[3] where the king is represented on his chariot in the act of defeating Nubians and Asiatics, but also while hunting wild animals. This is also connected to the pharaoh's mission

[2] pLeiden 344 *rs.* 1,9. See also the first complete edition of this text: Gardiner 1909: 21–22. Cf. with another passage of the same text: "A foreign tribe from abroad has come to Egypt […] There are no Egyptians anywhere"(Gardiner 1909: 30–31).

[3] Cairo JE 62119; Carter 211.

of warding off disorder (*isft*) (Gardiner 1962; Smith 2003: 26–27; Smith 2007: 226–228).

Difference of language between Egyptians and other neighbouring populations is clearly another sign of otherness and distance. This opposition can already be noted in Egyptian sources from the end of the third millennium, when a stele mentions a "speech interpreter of all foreign countries" (*ꜣꜥꜥ mdw ḫꜣswt nbwt*) (Lange – Schäfer 1902: 398).[4]

On a wall of the tomb of Kheruef (TT 192), Amenhotep III is represented celebrating his jubilee. In the inscription on the base of the pharaoh's kiosk, where images of subjugated enemies were usually represented, mention is made of the "chiefs of faraway countries that ignored Egypt" but also the "chiefs of foreign lands of unknown language (literally 'hidden language')" (Epigraphic Survey 1980: 24, 26; Galán 1997: 37).[5]

Since Thoth had the role of creator of languages, language differences occur in several hymns dedicated to this god (Černy 1948).[6] However, the first mention of the separation of languages by a god is attested in the Great Hymn to Aten, preserved in the tomb of Ay (AT 25) (Davies 1908: 30, pl. 27; Sandman 1938: 94–95). Here, Aten plays the role of demiurge:

> "O Sole God beside whom there is none! You made the earth as you wished, you alone [...] The lands of Khor (Syria) and Kush (Nubia), the land of Egypt. You set every man in his place, you supply their needs; everyone has his food, his lifetime is counted. Their tongues differ in speech, their characters likewise their skins are distinct. For you distinguished the peoples (*rmṯ*)" (Lichtheim 1976: 98).[7]

All these listed features (appearance, chaotic attitude, and language spoken) help to distinguish foreigners from Egyptians. The following examples show how the perception of these features could change when foreigners were captured and taken to Egypt.

2. "Domesticating" the foreigner

2.1. The Sea Peoples in the Medinet Habu reliefs

The impressive reliefs carved under Ramesses III on the outside north wall of his mortuary temple at Medinet Habu give us some insight into the entire process involving foreign prisoners and their attitude. These reliefs depict the battle and the

---

4 CCG 20765.

5 Urk. IV 1866,11–18.

6 Černý considers that the mention of the title of "Lord of foreign countries" attested as early as the 5th Dynasty for the god Thoth, is to be seen as a proof of this role of creator of languages, before that of Aten. Regarding the role of the demiurge in the initial differentiation of human languages, Sauneron (1960: 33–39) collected several attestations in hymns between the Persian and Roman times.

7 See also Mathieu 2008: 62; Grandet 1995: 110–111.

subsequent scenes of capture, deportation and registration of prisoners of war that followed on from the campaign of year 8 of Ramesses III against the Sea Peoples (MH I 36, 37, 42).[8] These scenes make immediately visible the opposition between disorder (the battle) and order (deportation and subsequent scenes): this opposition was a principle very dear to the hearts of Egyptians, who made it explicit in the contrast between *maat* and *isfet*. Below the scene where prisoners are presented to the Pharaoh, the two lower registers show different groups of scribes busy recording the number of hands of the killed enemies as well as the numerous prisoners brought back from the battlefield (MH I 42).

In her analysis of the scenes of these registers, French scholar Bernadette Menu (2004a: 196–198, figs. 1–11) identified ten narrative segments that contained information on the social integration of prisoners.[9] She observed how the prisoners passed from a state of disorder to one of order, a change which was fostered at first by the army and later by scribes. At the beginning of the scene, the prisoners are tied up and brought in by the soldiers. They show an unruly attitude and a level of submission that becomes more and more evident as the representation unfolds. Indeed, some of them, next to the scribes in charge of their registration, have been freed from ropes and march neatly towards the Egyptian officers who put a mark on their shoulders using a kind of calamus (Menu 2004a: 199; Keimer 1948: 65). They are then recorded by other scribes on documents kept in file boxes just behind them (MH I 42).

This recording of former prisoners and their subsequent attitude indicate their integration into the Egyptian system: they sit in groups behind two standing compatriots (who possibly have the status of chiefs) and seem to be receiving orders. Menu interprets the final phase of the representation as the last passage in their journey towards integration: education. This interpretation suggests two reflections on the institutional message conveyed by these images. Firstly, the fact that the prisoners, once integrated into the Egyptian order, no longer need to be kept shackled, because they behave differently, conforming to the local way of life. Secondly, the importance of the "gesture of writing" as a means of order management is evident, either in the scribes' registration or in the marking of prisoners (Menu 2004a: 197–199).

2.2. The Nubian prisoners of General Horemheb's tomb reliefs

The tomb of General Horemheb, the future pharaoh, presents another (earlier) example of the progressively changing attitude of foreign prisoners of war. The scene (Martin 1989: 78–83, pls. 78–93; Martin 2016: 72–76, pls. 33–37, 163–168)[10] is visible on a series of blocks found *in situ* on the south side of the eastern wall,

[8] In fact, it is not the same battle, since the pHarris I 77,3–6 refers to the battle of the year 11 against the Libyans, but the management methods described are very similar.

[9] Her analysis is based solely on iconography, since the inscriptions that accompany the scene are limited to extolling the success of Ramesses III and his power. Cf. KRI V 32,4–33,16.

[10] In another scene depicted on the tomb several groups of prisoners were presented to the pharaoh Tutankhamun, while Horemheb is receiving the gold of valour. Cf. Martin 1989: pls. 105, 107, 108; and Martin 2016: pls. 41–42; 135–141.

completed by a block kept in the Archeological Museum of Bologna (Bologna 1887; PM III^2.2, 656; Morigi – Pernigotti 1994: 32)[11] and by the so-called "Zizinia Block" (PM III2.2, 661; Wiedemann 1889: 424).[12] The action probably takes place on the battlefield, perhaps immediately after the fighting: all the peoples (Nubians, Asiatics and Libyans) traditionally subjected to Egypt are brought to Horemheb by Egyptian soldiers. Meanwhile, the general receives them, standing on the right-hand side of the relief. As Gilroy (2002: 35–44) has pointed out, the representations of foreigners in this context were intentionally caricatured.

Even if this scene has great symbolic value (over and above its purely historical value), what attracts our attention in this context are the scribes at the centre of the scene, positioned between the prisoners' group and Horemheb. They were probably responsible for recording information about foreigners,[13] and the importance of this activity is reflected in the care taken in representing their writing instruments and the baskets used to store them with the documents (Martin 1989: 79; Martin 2016: 73). In addition, they play a hinge role between deportees and the Nubians represented sitting behind the great figure of Horemheb. In the light of what I have argued so far, the recording phase should be considered as preliminary and necessary to integration: a Nubian (perhaps a leader?) is led before Horemheb by a soldier and he then joins one of the two groups of his compatriots seated on the ground. Along the way, he has been beaten or at least threatened by another Egyptian soldier. We may perhaps consider this sequence as a metaphor for the pacification and "training" of these Nubians, a first step in their education. The seated Nubians have therefore already been registered and are awaiting instructions about their fate once they have been sent to Egypt, and this is perhaps what the scribe depicted on the block kept in the Bologna Archeological Museum is dealing with. Even if the Nubians seated without manacles are being threatened by one soldier, they (and also the above-mentioned Sea Peoples in the Ramesside reliefs at Medinet Habu) are similar to the conscripts waiting for a military role depicted in the tomb of another Horemheb (TT 78), who was born under Tuthmosis III and lived until the reign of Amenhotep III (Brack – Brack 1980: pl. 38a).

Some of the practices illustrated in these reliefs can indeed be juxtaposed with content in the pHarris I, a text from the reign of Ramesses IV that lists all the endowments, including people, granted by Ramesses III to each temple or institution in the country (pBM 9999; Grandet 1994). Many times, the papyrus says, they are the result of battles and victories against enemies. The text provides a significant

---

[11] According to Hari (1965: 71–73), this block could not be attributed to the tomb of Horemheb, given the very different style of the depiction (especially the hairstyles), but Martin (1989: 82), was able to demonstrate the opposite using archaeological data.

[12] This block was part of the collection belonging to Count Zizinia, former consul of Belgium in Alexandria. It is still in Egypt, probably in a private collection. See Martin (1978: 9). Hari (1965: 64–68) regarded this block as a stele commemorating one of Horemheb's successors and not as a block from his grave. His hypothesis should be rejected.

[13] As suggested by Menu (2010: 171–183), the presence of several scribes, side by side, can be interpreted as an illustration of the technique of simultaneous recording of data, attested by Middle Kingdom documents concerning the enlistment of workers.

amount of useful information to reconstruct the management practices when dealing with prisoners of war (such as, for example, the practice of marking) and their subsequent treatment, in other words their transformation into manpower depending on private individuals, temples or the army. When the prisoners became workers (farmers, weavers, shepherds, masons, etc.), they were generically referred to as *ḥmw* (Menu 2004: 187–209; Menu 2010: 171–183; Moreno García 2008: 133–138). This word is used in the Egyptian language to indicate people in a state of dependency that may be public or private, which may regard foreigners (not necessarily former prisoners of war) but also Egyptians and its definition was a cause of debate among contemporary authors because it relates to a condition that is sometimes compared to the concept of ancient slavery (Bakir 1952; Loprieno 2012; Poole 2012).

Moreover, in this tomb we find (as in the above-mentioned tomb of Kheruef) the idea of "not knowing Egypt" used in relation to foreigners begging general Horemheb to intercede for peace with the pharaoh (Martin 2016: pls. 44–46, 143–146). This same expression would later be used in the Seti I war reliefs at Karnak (RIK IV 26,12, pls. 8, 26, 18–20, pl. 8; 43,27, pl. 14) and could be interpreted as a way of pointing up the lack of Egyptian *Maat* in their native country. As emphasised by Vanessa Davies, the association between this expression and some scenes of deportation shows how prisoners went on to adopt a more orderly attitude once they became acquainted with Egypt (Davies 2012: 84).

3. Removing elements of "otherness": education, language and dress

The sources analysed so far afford some insight into aspects of the Egyptian concept of "otherness" which, according to royal propaganda, could easily be removed once foreigners had come into contact with Egyptian power. Disorganisation and chaos were transformed into order. Enemies became part of the productive workforce of Egypt, receiving training and even possibly changing their spoken language. By adding new sources to the ones we have just analysed, we will try to complete the picture of what the documentation suggests about the treatment of prisoners of war (but also of foreigners living in Egypt) and their consequent Egyptianisation.

In several passages of the above-mentioned pHarris I (4,5; 5,9; 8,10; 26,2; 28,5; 59,5; 60,3), the Pharaoh claims to have "trained, educated" (and he uses the verb *sḫpr* in this context) the workforce (*ḥmw*) and the "young people"(*ḏ3mw*) he assigned to the temples[14] and in several cases (pHarris I 4,5; 8,10; 59,5; 60,3) this workforce was certainly made up of former prisoners of war. This training will also have involved specific work-related duties, and may even have included teaching spoken and written Egyptian.

[14] This aspect, according to Menu (2008: 815), relates to the education of the prisoners represented in Medinet Habu. For *sḫpr* in the sense of "educate, train" for a job cf. Grandet (1994: II, 19, n. 77) and also Edwards (1960: I 9, n. 13).

The importance of training *ḥmw* is attested already in the twelfth dynasty by pKahun VIII.1 (Griffith 1898: I, 79; II, pl. XXV), in a letter in which the sender asks permission to teach the royal dependent (*ḥm nsw*) Wadjahau to write in order to stop him escaping. Learning to write will enable him to become a scribe: so social promotion in exchange for his loyalty (Menu 2004: 199–200). And as a matter of fact many Asiatic (*ꜥꜣm.w*) names appear in the Kahun archives and often in high functions (Borchardt 1899: 89–103; Scharff 1924: 20–72).

Language is, as we have seen, one of the elements that mark the difference between populations. In the New Kingdom, an example of this is found in the "Israel stele" of Merenptah. In a passage describing restored peace, mention is made of the tranquility of a border fortress: the fear that during the night one might hear the announcement of someone arriving "with a foreign language" (*m rꜥ kꜣwy*) has disappeared (CGC 34025 verso; Breasted 1906: 263–264, §616–617; Fecht 1983: 113, 120, 135–136).

> "The Medjauyu-militia lie fast asleep, the Niau and Tjukten scouts are out in the meadows as they wish [...] There is no shout or call by night: 'Stop! See, who comes with foreign speech!'" (KRI IV 18,13–14).

The question of the different languages spoken by foreigners, in this case by a Nubian, is also raised in a letter addressed to an unproductive scribe, attested by the pSallier I 8,1 (Gardiner 1937: 85).

> "You are with me as a gibbering (*ꜣꜥꜥwty*) Nehsy who has been brought with the tribute" (Caminos 1954: 320).[15]

If, then, language is one of the elements that differentiates Egyptians from other neighbouring peoples, true assimilation must necessarily involve learning Egyptian.

In the above-mentioned scene of "domestication" of the Sea Peoples at Medinet Habu, we witness the progressive integration of the former prisoners, a process that also involves, as suggested by Menu (2004a: 198–201), learning Egyptian. More explicit information on this point can be found on the stele from the temple of Mert Seger at Deir el-Medina. It is from the reign of Ramesses III and relates to Libyan prisoners who have become integrated into the Egyptian army:

> "[...] they hear the language of (Egypt's) people, in serving the King. He abolished their language, he changed their tongues (*p[n]ꜥ.f nsw.sn*), they went on the way that they had not descended (before)" (KRI V 91,6–7).

[15] The verb *ꜣꜥꜥ* "to speak a foreign language" (Wb. I 3,1–2) was used to describe foreign people (especially those living in Egypt) who had not to be acculturated or Egyptians speaking a foreign language. It is sometime understood to mean "interpreter". On this point, see Gardiner (1915: 119–122), Gardiner (1941: 25, n. 4), and Bell (1976: 63).

This text expresses the concept of changing language through the use of the verb *pn*ᶜ "to turn upside down" (Wb. I 508,11–509,9) which seems to suggest the physical change in the position of the tongue (*ns*) necessary to produce the new sounds (Sauneron 1960: 40–41).

The practice of teaching Egyptian and its importance in domestication are also attested by a passage from the Instruction of Ani,[16] written during the New Kingdom:

> "One teaches the Nubian to speak Egyptian, the Syrian and other strangers too" (Lichtheim 1976: 144).

In this didactic text, a father uses this example to show his son how animals can be trained to do things against their nature and even foreigners can learn a language other than their own.

As already pointed out, in figurative reliefs manner of dress is a way of distinguishing foreigners from Egyptians. On the walls of Rekhmire's tomb the former prisoners who had become integrated into productive activities were represented as dressed in the Egyptian manner (Davies 1943: 47–48, pl. LVII -row 2-), whereas in the same tomb the prisoners on their arrival or while receiving some products as remuneration were generally dressed in the (stereo)typical clothes of their country of origin (Davies 1943: pls. LVII - row 1- and XXI–XXIII). It is also interesting to note that the female prisoners were represented with their breasts exposed, in a way that would never have been adopted by Egyptian women (Asher-Greve – Sweeney 2006: 125–126).

The clothing of prisoners (or, in general, of ethnically characterised foreigners) was previously represented in a stereotypical way designed to aid immediate identification of certain individuals or groups as foreigners. From an iconographic point of view, the decision to conform them to Egyptians can be regarded as a way of emphasising their assimilation into local culture and thus their full integration. It would appear, that representing them as foreigners was no longer necessary.

4. What was real integration like?

Apart from the "institutional" representation of the integration of foreigners through forced actions on the part of the state, real assimilation occurred mainly through social relations and the acquisition of an Egyptian way of life, which also gave foreigners the opportunity to climb the social ladder (Panagiotopoulos 2006: 403–404; Schneider 2010: 144–146).

The features I have described can guide our research into the way Egyptians (or rather, Egyptian institutional propaganda) represented these foreigners, and in particular former prisoners of war. But what can we find in sources regarding the way in which foreigners living in Egypt represented themselves? And what can we infer from this about the attitude Egyptians took towards them?

---

[16] This text is known from many sources, the most complete of which is pBoulaq IV (CGC 58042). Cf. Quack 1994.

Living in Egypt required a certain degree of adaptation to its cultural and social system, and foreigners had to become "Egyptians" very quickly, as assimilation was considered a form of domestication in its own right. It is possible to find traces in textual sources that show the presence of foreigners in certain places as agricultural workers, craftsmen, administrative officers and members of the army. Their presence is mostly revealed by their names (Tallet 2000: 135–144; Menéndez 2015: 791–804).

The question is, however, more complicated. As Schneider has pointed out in his studies (Schneider 2003a: 15),[17] we cannot solely rely on the name criterion as a way of recognising foreigners living in Egypt. Further "foreignness" factors need to be established, such as, other members of the family bearing foreign names, foreign elements in burial assemblages or ethnic markers in the representation of individuals. According to certain scholars, some former prisoners of war received a new name upon their arrival in Egypt, as can be seen in the list of prisoners given to Ahmose, son of Ibana (Urk. IV 11,4–14) as a reward for his prowess on the battlefield. These names, which sounded more "Egyptian", might have been based on the name of the pharaoh or the officer who captured them, as well as on other factors, such as geography or religion (Posener 1937: 187; Morris 2014: 374).

However, in terms of material culture, there are few archaeological data attesting to the presence of facilities for foreigners. For this reason, various scholars argue that the presence of foreigners, however considerable their numbers, hardly ever manifested itself in a material culture that is completely Egyptianized (Kemp 1991: 37–39; Kemp 1997: 128; Sparks 2004: 28–29, 47–50; Wachsmann 2013: 163).

It has been suggested that the Egyptian practice of creating colonies of foreigner prisoners in some specific places,[18] far away from borders and from their original place of origin was a way to foster the process of "Egyptianisation" and to limit the numbers of those who fled (Morris 2005: 732–733, 820–821).

As for the self-representation of foreigners (we cannot say if they were ex-prisoners, immigrants or naturalized individuals), we emphasise the existence of stelae and other funerary documents where Nubians or Asiatic individuals are shown wearing Egyptian clothing and bearing their foreign name. This is a difficult subject to deal with as, depending on the social situations, a person could choose to stress a particular aspect of his or her identity. Recently, increasing attention has been paid to this topic also in light of our improved awareness of how to study such phenomena (Liszka 2018: 187; Jones 1997; Schneider 2010; Hagen 2007; Wendrich 2010; Smith 2018).

Conclusions

As we have seen, the elements of "otherness" that Egyptians saw as distinguishing them from foreigners were: language, skin colour, clothing and the disorderly attitude shown by the "others".

[17] See Liszka (2012: 88) for further literature.
[18] This question is in dispute with regard to soldiers.

However, it is true to say that foreigners could be referred to as enemies but could also become part of Egyptian society if they played by the rules.

By way of a preliminary conclusion, we can thus say that Egyptians referred to foreigners using negative adjectives when they were considered enemies and when they placed themselves outside Egyptian law and order (the *maat*) (Assmann 1989). Once captured and deported, they were quickly converted into something economically productive and positive: they became workers (soldiers, artisans, peasants, masons, etc.). At this point, as a group they are no longer referred to with the collective name of foreigners (*ḫ3styw*), which is "exclusively reserved for foreigners outside Egypt who are devoid of any opportunity of acculturation" (Schneider 2010: 144). In most cases they became *ḥmw* or *mrt* (Allam 2004; Moreno García 1998; Andrássy 2005), and these words were used in the Egyptian language to indicate people in a state of dependency which could apply to both foreigners and Egyptians. The fact that sources refer to these people using an inclusive word has to mean something.

To come back to the two antithetical concepts expressed by Loprieno: there is a difference between the view of "foreigners" as a group and "foreigners" as individuals. In practice, Egyptians showed negative attitudes towards groups and positive (or at least tolerant) attitudes towards individuals. This ambivalent approach is evidenced by the presumption that foreigners were inferiors and useful only to serve Egypt, and the parallel possibility that existed for a few of them to hold prominent positions in the Egyptian administration and society (Gordon 2001: 547). Conversely, as maintained by Schneider (2010: 147), the situation was actually more complex as "the ideological pattern of the foreigner *topos* assigned political and ritual roles on the basis of a strict model of inclusion and exclusion which combined the existence or lack of acculturation with the notion of territorial authority and power hierarchy". Social status and profession were the most important factors defining the identity of people living in Egypt during the New Kingdom, and were more important than ethnicity. For this reason, it is possible to assume that foreigners were fully accepted by Egyptian society, and probably simply regarded as Egyptians of foreign origin (Schulman 1986: 193, n. 2; Schneider 2003a; 2006; 2010:148).

Lastly, then, this study has investigated some ways in which the order/disorder dichotomy examined by Bernadette Menu can be substantiated in practice. For foreigners, the passage from disorder to order meant—wearing different clothes, acculturation, learning the language, perhaps a change of name and possible social integration and improvement. If we focus on these aspects, we see ideology turning into real life, even if the reading of sources can hardly ever tell us the ways in which these mechanisms functioned.

Yet more needs to be done in order to understand the level of acculturation that was necessary for foreigners to be integrated into Egyptian society. I would tentatively suggest that investigations into the material culture connected with some place-names based on ethnic group names and on onomastica could help improve our knowledge of the real degree of acculturation of foreigners. Moreover, further investigations of written, iconographic but also archaeological sources will inform us more fully about the way the "new Egyptians" saw themselves, as ethnic identities are fluctuating and determined by economic, social, and political relations (Smith 2003:16; Smith 2018: 140).

Furthermore, as pointed out by Mario Liverani (1990: 144–146): "Peace relationships are the result of an agreement, but a one-directional agreement …The foreigner / rebel has to submit, changing his mind and attitude from rebellion to obeisance". Thus, if this was valid for international relations, it will certainly also have applied to captive people entering Egypt.

References

Allam, S., 2004. Une classe ouvrière: *merit*. In B. Menu, ed., *La dépendance rurale dans l'Antiquité égyptienne et proche-orientale*. Colloque AIDEA Banyuls-sur-mer 2001, Le Caire: Institut français d'archéologie orientale, 135–155.

Andrássy, P., 2005. Die *mrt*-Leute. Überlegungen zur Sozialstruktur des Alten Reiches. In J. Seidlmayer, ed., *Texte und Denkmäler des ägyptischen Alten Reiches, TLA* 3, Berlin: Brandenburgische Akademie der Wissenschaften, 27–68.

Asher-Greve, J.M. – D. Sweeney, 2006. On nakedness, nudity, and gender in Egyptian and Mesopotamian art. In S. Schroer, ed., *Images and gender. Contributions to the hermeneutics of reading ancient art*. OBO 220. Fribourg – Göttingen: Academic Press – Vandenhoeck & Ruprecht, 111–162.

Assmann, J., 1989. *Maât, l'Égypte pharaonique et l'idée de justice sociale*. Paris: Julliard.

Assmann, J., 1996. Zum Konzept der Fremdheit im alten Ägypten. In M. Schuster, ed., *Die Begegnung mit dem Fremden. Wertungen und Wirkungen in Hochkulturen vom Altertum bis zur Gegenwart. Colloquium Rauricum* 4. Stuttgart, Leipzig: Teubner, 77–99.

Bakir, A.M., 1952 *Slavery in Pharaonic Egypt*. CASAE 18. Le Caire: Institut français d'archéologie orientale.

Bell, L.D., 1976. *Interpreters and Egyptianized Nubians in Ancient Egyptian foreign policy: aspects of the history of Egypt and Nubia*. PhD Dissertation. Philadelphia: University of Pennsylvania.

Borchardt, L., 1899. Der zweite Papyrusfund von Kahun und die zeitliche Festlegung des mittleren Reiches der ägyptischen Geschichte. *ZÄS* 37, 89–103.

Brack, A. – A. Brack, 1980. Das Grab des Haremhab, Theben Nr. 78. AV 35. Mainz am Rhein: von Zabern.

Breasted, J.H., 1906. *Ancient Records of Egypt*, III. Chicago: The University of Chicago Press.

Caminos, R.A., 1954. *Late Egyptian Miscellanies*. BES 1. London: Oxford University Press.

Černý, J., 1948. Thot as a Creator of Languages. *JEA* 34, 121–122.

Davies, N. De G., 1908. *The Rock tombs of El Amarna*, Part VI, *Tombs of Parennefer, Tutu, and Aÿ*. ASE 18. London: Egypt Exploration Fund.

Davies, N. De G., 1943. *The Tomb of Rekh-mi-rē' at Thebes* II. PMMAEE 11. New York: The Plantin Press.

Davies, V., 2012. The Treatment of Foreigners in Seti's Battle Reliefs. *JEA* 98, 73–85.

Edwards, I.E.S., 1960. *Hieratic Papyri in the British Museum*, I. IV Series. London: Trustees of the British Museum.

El-Magd, A., 2016. Dehumanization of the 'other': Animal metaphors of defeated enemies in the New Kingdom military texts. *JARCE* 52, 329–341.

Epigraphic Survey, 1980. *The Tomb of Kheruef. Theban Tomb 192*. OIP 102. Chicago: The Oriental Institute of the University of Chicago.

Fecht, G., 1983. Die Israelstele, Gestalt und Aussage. In M. Görg, ed., *Fontes atque pontes. Eine Festgabe für Hellmut Brunner*. ÄAT 5. Wiesbaden: Harrassowitz, 103–138.

Galán, J.M., 1997. The Use of *šalāmu* and *barāka* in Ancient Egyptian Texts. *ZÄS* 124, 37–44.

Gardiner, A.H., 1909. *The Admonitions of an Egyptian Sage from a Hieratic Papyrus in Leiden (Pap. Leiden 344 recto)*. Leipzig: J. C. Hinrichs.

Gardiner, A.H., 1915. The Egyptian word for dragoman. *PSBA* 37, 117–125.

Gardiner, A.H., 1937. *Late-Egyptian Miscellanies*. BiAeg 7. Bruxelles: Fondation Égyptologique Reine Élisabeth.

Gardiner, A.H., 1941. Ramesside Texts Relating to the Taxation and Transport of Corn. *JEA* 27, 19–73.

Gardiner, A.H., 1947. *Ancient Egyptian Onomastica*, I. London: Oxford University Press.

Gardiner, A.H., 1962. *Tutankhamun's Painted Box: Reproduced from the original in the Cairo Museum by Nina M. Davies*. Oxford: Griffith Institute.

Gilroy, T.D., 2002. Outlandish Outlanders: foreigners and caricature in Egyptian Art. *GM* 191, 35–52.

Gordon, A., 2001. Foreigners. In D.B. Redford, ed., *The Oxford Encyclopedia of Ancient Egypt*, I. Oxford: Oxford University Press, 544–548.

Grandet, P., 1994. *Le papyrus Harris I*, I–II. BdÉ 109. Le Caire: Institut français d'archéologie orientale.

Grandet, P., 1995. *Hymnes de la religion d'Aton. Hymnes du XIVe siècle avant J.-C.* Paris: Ed. du Seuil.

Griffith, F.Ll., 1898. *Hieratic Papyri from Kahun and Gurob. Principally of the Middle Kingdom*. London: Quaritch.

Hagen, F., 2007. Local Identities. In T. Wilkinson, ed., *The Egyptian World*. London – New York: Routledge, 242–251.

Hari, R., 1965. *Horemheb et la reine Moutnedjemet ou la fin d'une dynastie*. Genève 20. Genève: Éditions des Belles-Lettres.

Helck, W., 1971. *Die Beziehungen Ägyptens zu Vorderasien im 3. und 2. Jahrtausend v. Chr.* ÄA 5. Wiesbaden: Harrassowitz.

Jones, S., 1997. *The Archaeology of Ethnicity. Constructing identities in the past and present.* London – New York, NY: Routledge – Kegan Paul.

Kasparian, B., 2000. Famille et cosmopolitisme dans l'Égypte ancienne. *Méditerranées* 24, 113–133.

Keimer, L., 1948. *Remarques sur le tatouage dans l'Égypte ancienne*. MIE 53. Le Caire: Imprimerie de l'Institut français d'archéologie orientale.

Kemp, B.J., 1997. Why Empire Rises? Rewiew of *Askut in Nubia: the Economics and Ideology of Egyptian Imperialism in the Second Millennium BC*, by Stuart Tyson Smith. *CAJ* 7, 123–137.

Kemp, B.J., 2006. *Ancient Egypt. Anatomy of a Civilization*. London: Routledge (2nd edition).

Lange, H.O. – H. Schäfer, 1902. *Grab- und Denksteine des Mittleren Reiches*, II. Berlin: Reichsdruckerei.

Lichtheim, M., 1973. *Ancient Egyptian Literature*, I. Berkeley – Los Angeles – London: University of California Press.

1976 *Ancient Egyptian Literature*, II. Berkeley – Los Angeles – London: University of California Press.

Liszka, K., 2012.*"We have come to serve the pharaoh". A Study of the Medjay and Pangrave as an Ethnic group and as mercenaries from C.2300 BCE until C. 1050 BCE*. PhD Dissertation. Philadelphia: University of Pennsylvania.

Liszka, K., 2018. Discerning Ancient Identity: The Case of Aashyet's Sarcophagus (JE 47267). *JEH* 11, 185–207.

Liverani, M., 1990. *Prestige and interest. International Relations in the Near East ca. 1600-1100 B.C.* HANE/S 1. Padova: Sargon.

Loprieno, A., 1988. *Topos und Mimesis. Zum Ausländer in der ägyptischen Literatur.* ÄA 48. Wiesbaden: Harrassowitz.

Loprieno, A., 2012. Slavery and Servitude. In E. Frood – W. Wendrich, eds., *UCLA Encyclopedia of Egyptology*, Los Angeles. http://digital2.library.ucla.edu/viewItem.do?ark=21198/zz002djg3j (accessed on September 30, 2018).

Luft, U., 1998. The Ancient Town of El-Lahun. In S. Quirke, ed., *Lahun Studies*. Reigate, Surrey: SIA Publ., 138–142.

Martin, G.T., 1978. Excavations at the Memphite Tomb of Ḥoremḥeb, 1977. Preliminary Report. *JEA* 64, 5–9.

Martin, G.T., 1989. *The Memphite tomb of Ḥoremḥeb, commander-in-chief of Tutʿankhamūn, I: the reliefs, inscriptions, and commentary*. EES EM 55. London: Egypt Exploration Society.

Martin, G.T., 2016. *Tutankhamun's Regent. Scenes and Texts from the Memphite Tomb of Horemheb*. EES EM 111. London: Egypt Exploration Society.

Mathieu, B., 2008. Le 'Grand Hymne à Aton' (Nouvel Empire, XVIIIe dynastie, vers 1350 av. J.-C.). In J.-L. Chappaz, ed., *Akhénaton et Néfertiti. Soleil et ombres des pharaons*. Milan: Silvana Editoriale, 57–65.

Menéndez, G., 2015. Foreigners in Deir el-Medina during the 18th and 19th Dynasties. In P. Kousoulis – N. Lazaridis, eds., *Proceedings of the Tenth International Congress of Egyptologists, University of the Aegean, Rhodes 22-29 May 2008*. OLA 241. Leuven – Paris – Bristol: Peeters, 791–804.

Menu, B., 2004a. Captifs de guerre et dépendance rurale dans l'Égypte du Nouvel Empire. In B. Menu, ed., *La dépendance rurale dans l'Antiquité égyptienne et proche-orientale.* Colloque Aidea, Banyuls-sur-Mer 2001. Le Caire: Institut français d'archéologie orientale, 187–209.

Menu, B., 2004b. Le contrôle des passages à la frontière égypto-palestinienne sous les XIe à XIVe dynasties. In C. Moatti, ed., *La mobilité des personnes en Méditerranée de l'antiquité à l'époque moderne. Procédures de contrôle et documents d'identification*. Collection de l'École Française de Rome 341. Rome: École française de Rome, 35–39.

Menu, B., 2008. Organisation du travail et gestion des ressources humaines dans l'Égypte du IIe millénaire av. J.-C. In Institut de préparation aux affaires (Toulouse), ed., *Mélanges offerts à Pierre Spiteri* II. Toulouse: Presses de l'Université des sciences sociales de Toulouse, 799–815.

Menu, B., 2010. Quelques aspects du recrutement des travailleurs dans l'Égypte du deuxième millénaire av. J.-C. In B. Menu, ed., *L'organisation du travail en Égypte ancienne et en Mésopotamie. Colloque AIDEA Nice 4–5 Octobre 2004*. Le Caire: Institut français d'archéologie orientale, 171–183.

Moreno García, J.-C., 1998. La population *mrt*: une approche du problème de la servitude dans l'Égypte du III e millénaire (I), *JEA* 84, 71–83.

Moreno García, J.-C., 2008. Review Article: La dépendance rurale en Égypte ancienne. *JESHO* 51, 99–150.

Morigi Govi, C. – S. Pernigotti, 1994. *La collezione egiziana. Museo Civico Archeologico di Bologna*. Milano: Leonardo Arte.

Morris, E.F., 2005. *Architecture of Imperialism. Military Bases and the Evolution of Foreign Policy in Egypt's New Kingdom*. PdÄ 22, Leiden: Brill.

Morris, E.F., 2014. Mitanni Enslaved: Prisoners of War, Pride, and Productivity in a New Imperial Regime. In J.M. Galán – B.M. Bryan – P.F. Dorman, eds., *Creativity and Innovation in the Reign of Hatshepsut, Papers from the Theban Workshop 2010*. SAOC 69. Chicago: The Oriental Institute of the University of Chicago, 361–379.

Panagiotopoulos, D., 2006. Foreigners in Egypt in the Time of Hatshepsut and Thutmose III. In E. Cline – D. O'Connor, eds., *Thutmose III. A New Biography*. Ann Arbor: University of Michigan Press, 370–412.

Poole, F., 2012. La schiavitù nell'antico Egitto: alla ricerca di un paradigma per lo studio dei rapporti di dipendenza. *RSO* 85, 457–481.

Posener, G., 1937. Una liste de noms propres étrangers sur deux ostraca hiératiques du Nouvel Empire. *Syria* 18, 183–197.

Quack, J.F., 1994. *Die Lehren des Ani, Ein neuägyptischer Weisheitstext in seinem kulturellen Umfeld*. OBO 141. Freiburg – Göttingen: Universitätsverlag – Vandenhoeck & Ruprecht.

Ritner, R.K., 1993. *The Mechanics of Ancient Egyptian Magical Practice*. SAOC 54. Chicago: The Oriental Institute of the University of Chicago.

Roth, A.M., 2015. Representing the Other: Non-Egyptians in Pharaonic Iconography. In M. Hartwig, ed., *A Companion to Ancient Egyptian Art*. Chichester: Wiley-Blackwell, 155–174.

Sandman, M., 1938. *Texts from the Time of Akhenaton*. BiAe 8. Bruxelles: Fondation Égyptologique Reine Élisabeth.

Sauneron, S., 1960. La différenciation des langages d'après la tradition égyptienne. *BIFAO* 60, 31–40.

Sauneron, S. – J. Yoyotte, 1950. Traces d'établissements asiatiques en moyenne Egypte sous Ramsès II. *RdÉ* 7, 67–70.

Scharff, A., 1924. Briefe aus Illahun. *ZÄS* 59, 20–72.

Schneider, T., 2003a. *Ausländer in Ägypten während des Mittleren Reiches und der Hyksoszeit. Teil 2: Die ausländische Bevölkerung*. ÄAT 42. Wiesbaden: Harrassowitz.

Schneider, T., 2003b. Foreign Egypt. Egyptology and the Concept of Cultural Appropriation. *ÄuL* 13, 155–161.

Schneider, T., 2006. Akkulturation – Identität – Elitekultur: Eine Positionsbestimmung zur Frage der Existenz und des Status von Ausländern in der Elite des Neuen Reiches. In R. Gundlach – A. Klug, eds., *Der ägyptische Hof des Neuen Reiches: Seine Gesellschaft und Kultur im Spannungsfeld zwischen Innen – und Außenpolitik*. KSG 2. Wiesbaden: Harrassowitz, 201–216.

Schneider, T., 2010. Foreigners in Egypt. Archaeological Evidence and Cultural Context. In W. Wendrich, ed., *Egyptian Archaeology*. Blackwell Studies in Global Archaeology. Chichester: Wiley-Blackwell, 143–163.

Schulman, A.R., 1986. The Royal Butler Ramessessami'on. *CdÉ* 122, 187–202.

Smith, S.T., 2003. *Wretched Kush. Ethnic identities and boundaries in Egypt's Nubian Empire*. London – New York: Routledge.

Smith, S.T., 2007. Ethnicity and Culture. In T. Wilkinson, ed., *The Egyptian World*. London – New York: Routledge, 218–241.

Smith, S.T., 2018. Ethnicity: Constructions of Self and Other in Ancient Egypt. *JEH* 11, 113–146.

Sparks, R.S., 2004. Canaan in Egypt: Archaeological Evidence for a Social Phenomenon. In J. Bourriau – J.S. Phillip, eds., *Invention and Innovation: The social Context of Technological Change*. Vol. II: *Egypt, the Aegean, and the Near East, 1650-1150 BC*. Oxford: Oxbow Books, 25–54.

Tallet, P., 2000. Des étrangers dans les campagnes d'Égypte au Nouvel Empire. *Mediterranées* 24, 135–144.

Valbelle, D., 1990. *Les Neuf Arcs. L'Égyptien et les Étrangers de la Préhistoire à la conquête d'Alexandre*. Paris: Armand Colin.

Wachsmann, S., 2013. *The Gurob ship-cart model and its Mediterranean context*. Ed Rachal Foundation nautical archaeology series. College Station: Texas A&M University Press.

Wendrich, W., 2010. Identity and Personhood. In W. Wendrich, ed., *Egyptian Archaeology*. Oxford: Wiley-Blackwell, 200–219.

Wiedemann, A., 1889. Texts of the 2nd part of the XVIII Dynasty. *PSBA* 11, 422–425.

Yurko, F., 1996. Two Tomb-wall painted reliefs of Ramesses III and Sety I and ancient Nile Valley population diversity. In T. Celenko, ed., *Egypt in Africa*. Indianapolis: Indianapolis Museum of Art, 109–111.

THE FOREIGN TRADE OF TELL EL-DABʿA DURING THE SECOND INTERMEDIATE PERIOD: ANOTHER GLANCE AT IMPORTED CERAMICS UNDER HYKSOS RULE

Sarah Vilain (The ERC Advanced Grant Project
"The Enigma of the Hyksos", Austrian Academy of Sciences)*

Introduction

The archaeological site of Tell el-Dabʿa is strategically located on the Pelusiac branch of the Nile, at the intersection of crucial communication roads. Thanks to the Nile route, it benefited from direct access to the Mediterranean Sea to the north and to Upper Egypt to the south. The Way of Horus, which linked Egypt with the Levantine area (Bietak 1997: 87), was easily reachable eastwards. As a result, excavations established that the city sheltered Near Eastern populations from the late 12th Dynasty until the end of the Second Intermediate Period. However, even if these populations were mostly integrated among the city's inhabitants, the takeover of a dynasty of Asiatics is a unique phenomenon that had a lasting influence on Egyptian's culture. These kings called themselves *Heqau Khasut*—"rulers of the foreign lands"—which was transmitted by Greek sources as *Hyksos*. At Tell el-Dabʿa, the beginning of the Hyksos period was identified in Phase E/2 thanks to modifications in the settlement and in the material culture (Bietak – Forstner-Müller – Mlinar 2001).

The takeover of the Hyksos had an important impact at a local scale, but not exclusively. The presence of foreign imports from Phase G/1–3 onwards suggests that Tell el-Dabʿa was already implied in international trading connections when the Hyksos came to power. However, the establishment of long-distance exchanges necessitates a certain degree of political stability, especially in Egypt, where they occur under royal control. Thus, if one of the partner changes due to political circumstances, as it happened with the takeover of the Hyksos, what becomes of the already established trading connections? Several logical scenarios could be considered: the contacts could be terminated, altered, continue unchanged or be re-oriented, with the introduction of new partners. With this question, this paper proposes an overview of the evolution of connections during the Second Intermediate Period between Tell el-Dabʿa and four different areas: the Levant, Cyprus, Middle Egypt and Nubia. Due to its limited scope, it focusses on the examination of imported ceramics, as the study of their development through-

* This project has received funding from the European Research Council (ERC) under the European Union's Horizon 2020 research and innovation programme (grant agreement No. 668640).

out the stratigraphy of the site should reveal the nature of contacts and whether changes occurred as the political situation was altered.

The Levant

The Second Stela of Kamose, discovered in 1954 in Karnak, relates a campaign of the Theban king against the northern territories controlled by the Hyksos. Even if the veracity of the narration is questionable, it is noteworthy that Avaris is depicted as an important trading centre. According to Habachi's translation (Habachi 1972; Redford 1997: 14, no. 69), the stela's inscription evokes "all the fine products from Retjenu", suggesting that the Levant was one of the trading partners of the Hyksos. More important, raw materials as well as perishable goods are mentioned among the products which originate from this area. Consequently, we have to keep in mind that an unassessed part of the commodities did not leave any traces in the archaeological records.

Relationships between Tell el-Dabʿa and the Levant were investigated by K. Kopetzky, who studied the evolution of Levantine imports in domestic contexts (Kopetzky 2010: fig. 52). She showed that they were reaching a culminating point in Phase F, before declining until the end of the Second Intermediate Period. According to her study, Levantine imports constitute 28.7% of domestic ceramics at their climax, in Phase F, against 13.9% in Phase E/3 and only 5.6% in Phase D/2. The ongoing examination by the author of the evolution of imports in funerary contexts confirms the pattern that was previously observed. Thus, in Area A/II, Levantine imports constitute 24.7% of the vessels of funerary assemblages in Phase F, against 14% in Phase E/3 and 6.7% in Phase D/2 (Bietak 1991; Förstner-Müller 2008).[1] It is noteworthy that, in Area A/II, the lowest quantity of Levantine imports is reached in Phase E/1, shortly after the takeover of the Hyksos. They are then less than 2% of the funerary offerings.

Another specificity of the ceramic assemblage of Tell el-Dabʿa is the presence of locally made vases imitating Middle Bronze shapes already from the late 12th Dynasty. Most of them are made from a fine Nile clay with limestone inclusions (Nile I-d). According to Kopetzky (2010: fig. 52), both imports and local Middle Bronze shapes increased until Phase F in domestic contexts. Middle Bronze shapes then constitute 39.2% of the assemblage, before dropping to around 22% in Phase E/3 and 16.4% in Phase D/2. However, they still supplant imports until the end of the Second Intermediate Period. It is notable that from Phase E/2, imitations of Middle Bronze shapes are occasionally produced in Nile clay I-b-2, a clay usually used for indigenous shapes, recognisable by its sand and chaff inclusions.

In funerary contexts of Area A/II, locally made Middle Bronze shapes reach their climax at the beginning of the Hyksos period, in Phase E/1, where the lowest rate of imports is observed. Local Middle Bronze shapes then constitute almost

[1] These percentages as well as those in the following paragraphs rely on published material. Only vases from graves securely attributed to one of the site's Phases were taken into consideration. These results could evolve in regards to future discoveries.

70% of the ceramics of funerary assemblages. The number of local imitations decreases to about 24% in Phase D/2, but these productions are still more numerous than genuine imported pottery. This diminution at the end of the Second Intermediate Period could be due to the fact that the funerary assemblage of these two phases gives a more important place to the indigenous pottery tradition of the Delta. This specific production develops by its own under Hyksos rule and borrows from both Egyptian and Middle Bonze Age characteristics (Aston 2004: 185).

The decrease of Levantine imports is also accompanied by a progressive change in the repertoire of shapes during the Hyksos period. Indeed, according to our current data, Phases D/3 and D/2 witness a diminution of the part of imported tableware in favour of transport jars, a shift which could be observed both in domestic and funerary contexts. As a result, at the end of the Second Intermediate Period, Levantine imports are almost exclusively limited to Canaanite Jars.

Therefore, the consistency of the presence of Canaanite Jars in all phases of the site make them a good candidate to investigate issues related to the identification of trading partners of the Hyksos. This was addressed by both Neutron Activation Analysis (McGovern – Harbottle 1997; McGovern 2000) and petrography (Cohen-Weinberger – Goren 2004: 69–100) studies that delivered contradictory results. The discrepancies have been explained by methodological issues related to the Neutron Activation Analysis sampling and the database referencing (Goren 2003). The petrographic analyses of forty–six Canaanite Jars from Phases E/2 to D/2 by Cohen-Weinberger and Goren (2004) suggested that most of them belong to Group B2, which coincides with the general northern Levant, and to Group B3, attributed to the north of Israel and the Lebanese coast (Cohen-Weinberger – Goren 2004: fig. 3). These two groups are also best represented among the analysed Canaanite Jars from Phases G/1-3 and F-E/3, showing a remarkable continuity in contacts.

It is noteworthy that group D, which originates from the region between Beirut and Byblos, constitutes 21% of Canaanites Jars during the late 12th and early 13th Dynasties and only 6% during the Hyksos period (Cohen-Weinberger – Goren 2004: tab. 1). In our view, it reflects the increase in importance of other Northern Levantine centres during the Middle Bronze IIB, like Sidon or the Akkar Plain. Complementary petrographic analyses conducted on Canaanite Jars from Memphis and Kom el-Khilgan showed that the northern Levant was the most probable place of origin of a large part of them (Ownby – Bourriau 2009; Ownby 2012: 36–37). Therefore, it seems likely that the content of the jars produced in the area was particularly valued in the Delta.

As the Nile Delta constituted the main gate of entrance of Levantine commodities to Egypt, the study of the distribution of Canaanite Jars would give us an insight on the evolution of contacts between Tell el-Dabʿa and other Egyptian sites during the Second Intermediate Period. As shown in Fig. 1, these productions are concentrated in the Delta and the Memphite area. In the vicinity of Tell el-Dabʿa, at Tell el-Maskhuta, they were identified in domestic and funerary contexts of all levels of the site (Redmount 1995: 186). A newborn was buried in an imported Canaanite Jar in Phase 3 of the site, outside House B in Area R7/R8, a custom also observed at Tell el-Dabʿa (Redmount 1989: tab. 39, fig. 178). Another

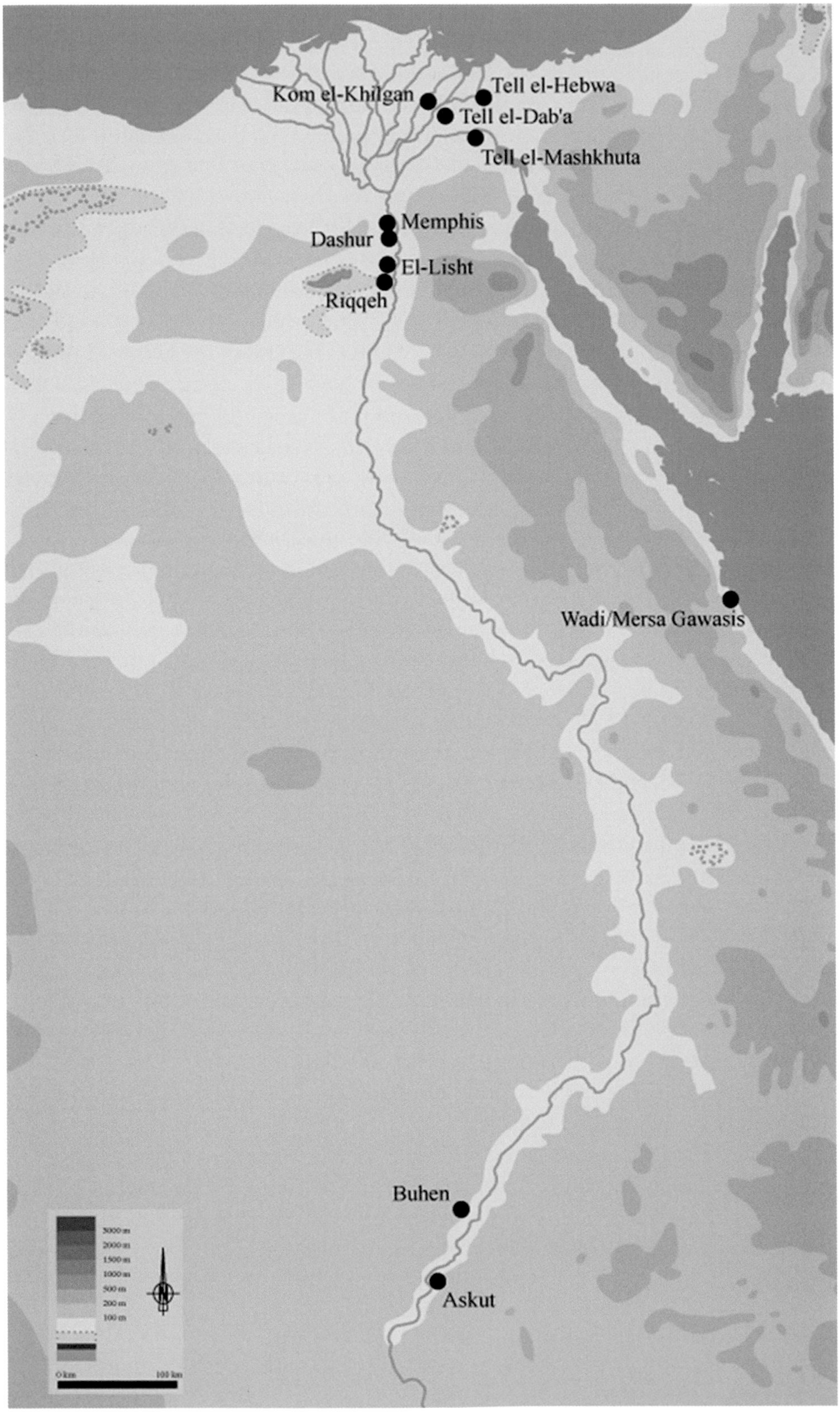

Fig. 1.
The distribution of Canaanite jars in Egypt (S. Vilain, map background: H. David-Cuny).

newborn burial in a jar, possibly of Levantine fabric, was encountered in Phase 5 (Redmount 1989: tab. 39, fig. 178). Further north, excavations at Tell el-Hebwa, delivered one Canaanite Jar which finds close parallels in Phases E/1-D/3 of Tell el-Dabʿa (Abd el-Maksoud 1998: pl. XXVIIId, 243, fig. 37). Eight other examples are dating from the end of the Second Intermediate Period or the beginning of the New Kingdom (Abd el-Maksoud 1998: pls. XXVIIIa, e, f, i, j, k, l, r, 243–245, figs. 36–37).

The presence of Canaanite Jars at Mersa/Wadi Gawasis, a harbour site on the Red Sea, is noteworthy. In the beach area above the site (WG 47) fragments of these jars were discovered associated with a large cooking pot of Nile E fabric, the type of which is well attested at Tell el-Dabʿa (Bard – Fattovich 2010: pls. 11–12). This association suggests that some contacts occurred between the two harbours.

Just south of the Delta, at Memphis, Canaanite Jars constitute the bulk of imported ceramics. According to Bader (2009: Abb. 366), they reach their *floruit* in Phase VII, where they constitute 1% of the whole ceramic assemblage. Interestingly, they almost disappear after Phase VId, correlated to Tell el-Dabʿa's Phases E/2–1 (Bader 2009: Abb 96). At Lisht, the occurrence of Middle Bronze jars can be explained by the presence of Levantines in the royal residence of the 13th Dynasty, as reported in the Illahun papyri (Arnold *et al.* 1995: 20–29). Two fragments of bases and a rim fragment of Middle Bronze IIA Canaanite Jars were found in the pyramid complex of Amenemhat III at Dahshur. The cemetery has been attributed to the 12th Dynasty but was still in use during the 13th Dynasty (Arnold 1982: 41–42). A possible intrusive example was uncovered at Riqqeh in a plundered tomb attributed to the 18th to 19th Dynasty (Engelbach 1915: 10, 21, pls. XXXVII, XLIV).

Occasional fragments of these productions were discovered as far as Buhen and Askut. The examples from Buhen are dated from the late Middle Kingdom (Randall-MacIver – Woolley 1911: 185–186, 195–196, pl. 94). These fragments as well as the ones from Askut may have arrived due to royal acquisition of imported goods which were then sent to the forts near the Second Cataract (Smith 2002: 51). In the current state of research, the most southern sites seem to have received Canaanite Jars before Hyksos rule.

This overview of the evolution of Levantine imports at Tell el-Dabʿa showed that their decline is a phenomenon that precedes the takeover of the Hyksos, as it began already in Phase E/3. One of the factors could be the dislocation of the Middle Kingdom as the power of the Levantine groups in the Eastern Delta rose (Kopetzky 2009: 154). This collapse of the central Egyptian administration and the division of Egypt into different entities had consequences on the organisation of trade. The situation of both political instability and economic weakness more likely facilitated the takeover of the 15th Dynasty. Surprisingly, the Hyksos rulers did not seem to get the possibility or the will to reinforce this ceramic trade with the Levant. Indeed, the gap between the proportion of imitations and imports continues to widen under Hyksos rule, the latest being mostly reduced to Canaanite Jars at the end of the Second Intermediate Period. Despite the decrease of imports, the results of petrographic analyses on these jars suggest a continuity of contacts between the Delta and the Northern Levantine area. However, the limited distribution of these containers in the rest of Egypt after the takeover of the Hyksos is noteworthy. Their drastic decrease at Memphis after Phase VII supports the hypothesis of a rupture of contacts between the two areas. Therefore, it is plausible that the growing isolation of the Delta and the ability of local potters to imitate Middle Bronze shapes made unnecessary the importation of Levantine ceramics at a larger scale. This process could explain why, at the end of the Hyksos period, Levantine imports are mostly limited to Canaanite Jars, still looked for their content.

Cyprus

The island of Cyprus occupies a central position in the Eastern Mediterranean. Its southern coast lies at a distance of about 120 km from the northern Levant and 420 km from Egypt. A direct crossing from Cyprus to Egypt was possible at least during the Late Bronze Age and maybe even earlier (Karageorghis 1995: 73). However, during the Middle Bronze Age the easiest way for Cypriot merchants to reach Egypt was to sail first to a northern Levantine port, such as Ugarit, and then to follow the coast southwards.

The earliest clues of interactions between Cyprus and Tell el-Dabʿa were uncovered from the end of Phase G/1–3. At this time, imports are quite scarce and limited to White Painted Pendent Line Style and Cross Line Style jugs and juglets characteristic of Eastern Cyprus. However, even if Cypriot imports are rare in the early phases of the site, interactions with the island are suggested by the discovery of Tell el-Yahudiya juglets of Nile clay (Nile I-d) made according to the Cypriot tradition (Maguire 2009: 21–24, fig. 3; Aston – Bietak 2012: 302). These juglets testify to the presence at Tell el-Dabʿa of potters who were either Cypriots or at least familiar with Cypriot technics (Vilain 2018).

As shown in Fig. 2, the presence of Cypriot imports increased in Phase F, which also delivered the largest corpus of Levantine imports. However, these vessels are almost absent from Phases E/3 and E/2. We noticed above a concomitant decline of Levantine imports from Phase E/3, which precedes Hyksos rule. Thus, complementary information about this period at Tell el-Dabʿa are brought by discoveries from Area F/II. Excavations of this area yielded the remains of a large complex dated to the end of Phase E/3 or the beginning of Phase E/2 according to the local sequence. This complex was intended for storage as evident by its dimensions, the organisation of space and the materials that were discovered, such as lumps of quartz, obsidian, ochre, or Egyptian blue (Math 2012–2013: 32). On the preserved part of the floor of Locus 1421 was a group of vessels. Their shape and decoration are characteristic of Cypriot White Painted Pendent Line Style juglets. However, all of them are wheel-made, the fabric is Egyptian (Nile I-d) and the handles are not inserted through the walls of the vessels, contrary to the Cypriot tradition. The presence of imitations in this context, where one would have expected genuine imports, could indicate disturbances in supply (Vilain 2018). A large burnt layer was also identified, suggesting destruction by a major conflagration. This discovery raises the possibility of internal troubles, which would have had a further impact on trade. One may speculate whether this conflagration was caused by the establishment of Hyksos rule.

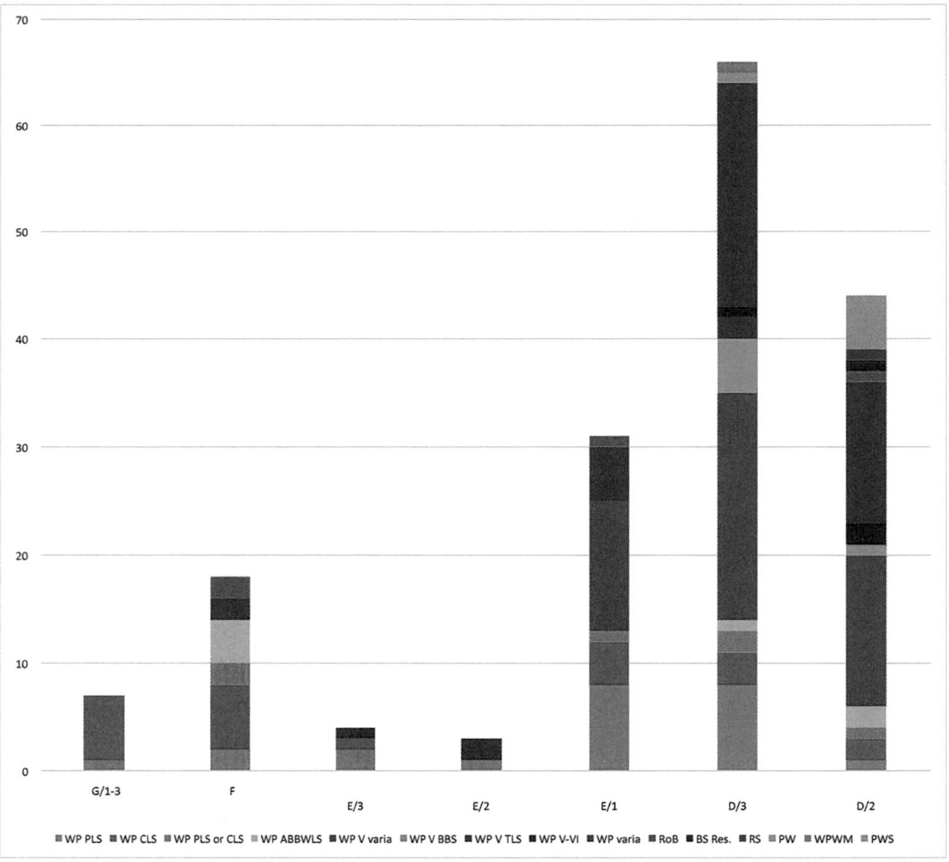

Fig. 2.
The Cypriot pottery at Tell el-Dabʿa, minimum number of individuals from Phases G/1-3-D/2, Areas A/I, A/II, A/III, A/IV, A/V and F/I (Graphic: S. Vilain).

From Phase E/1, Cypriot imports show a different pattern: their frequency is increasing, with a growing presence of the White Painted V. This new increase of Cypriot pottery, while Levantine ceramics are still declining, is not only the result of different trading patterns but also of different consumption modes, as Cypriot vases were likely of different purpose. Indeed, the corpus of Cypriot vessels discovered at Tell el-Dabʿa is mainly composed of jugs or juglets valued for their contents. Open shapes are uncommon but, when attested, consist of painted vessels of high quality. They were mostly considered as luxury items, at least in the earliest phases, and were not imported to such a large extent as Levantine pottery.

Interestingly, the rise of Cypriot pottery from Phase E/1 at Tell el-Dabʿa is mirrored by the presence of Tell el-Yahudiya juglets characteristic of the Hyksos period in Cyprus (Fig. 3). Two poles can be distinguished: 1) the area of Kalopsidha and Enkomi, from where the White Painted Pendent Line Style and Cross Line Style discovered at Tell el-Dabʿa mostly originate; and 2) Central Cyprus at sites located close to the Troodos mining areas. The presence of Tell el-Yahudiya at Klavdhia-Tremithos is noteworthy. The material culture of this site shows connections with Central Cyprus (Malmgren 2003: 113). It belongs to a series of new settlements which were established at the end of the Middle Cypriot period, like Hala Sultan Tekke or Maroni. One hypothesis for its creation is that individuals

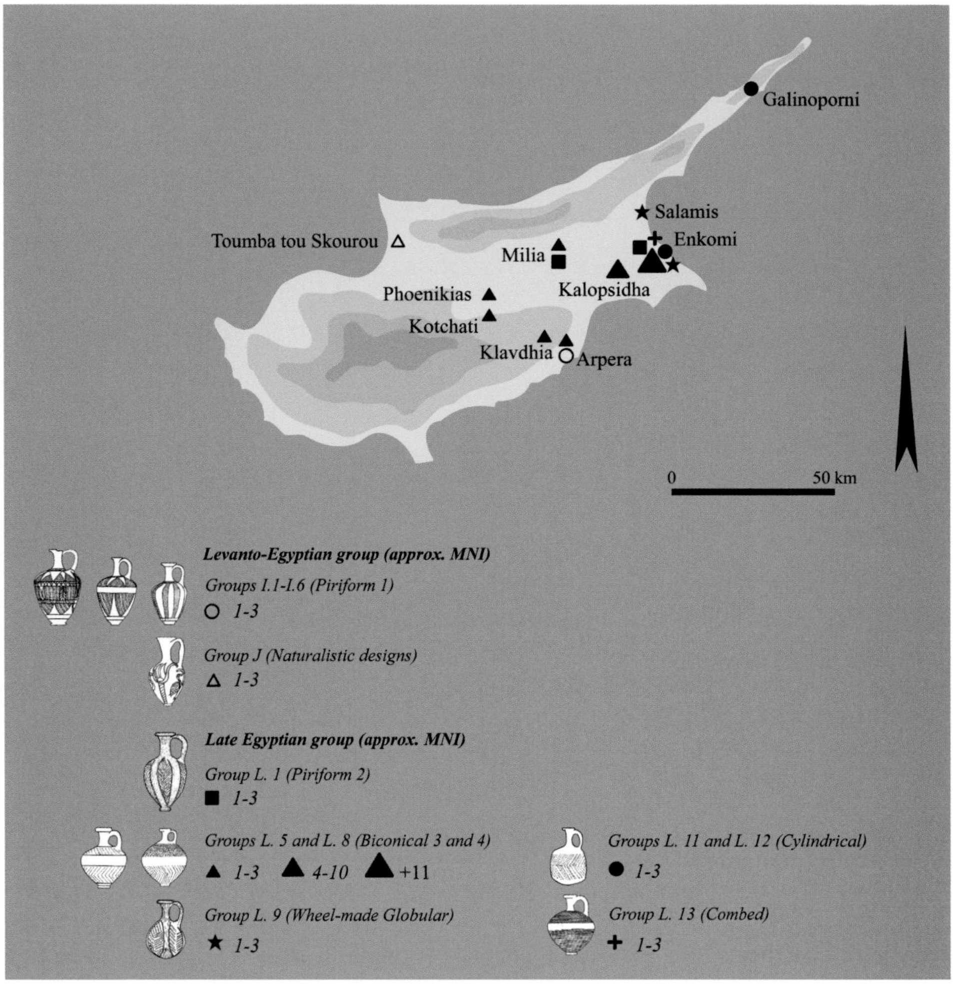

Fig. 3.

The distribution of Tell el-Yahudiya juglets in Cyprus (S. Vilain / P. Aprent, map background: H. David-Cuny).

from the central parts of the island, who were already familiar with the production of copper, were moving down to the coastal area to come closer to the Eastern Mediterranean with its increasing demand for this metal. It is likely that, at least at first, Cypriot ceramics could have been added as complementary cargo to other valuable commodities, such as raw materials. They were progressively valued for themselves, explaining their growing popularity. Therefore, the intensification of contacts, either direct or indirect, is witnessed both by the presence of foreign wares, such as the Tell el-Yahudia vessels in Cyprus, and by the increase of Cypriot ceramics both along the Levantine coast and in the Nile Delta.

Thus, the Cypriot pottery is rarely encountered outside Tell el-Dabʿa. The scarcity of White Painted Pendent Line Style and Cross Line Style productions, which reach their climax at the beginning of the Hyksos period, is remarkable (Fig. 4). Best represented outside the Delta is the White Painted VI, present at Tell el-Dabʿa from Phase D/2 to Phase C/2 i.e. from the end of the Second Intermediate Period to the 18th Dynasty. The vases from Deshasha and Abydos mostly belong to the second half of the Second Intermediate Period according to Merrillees

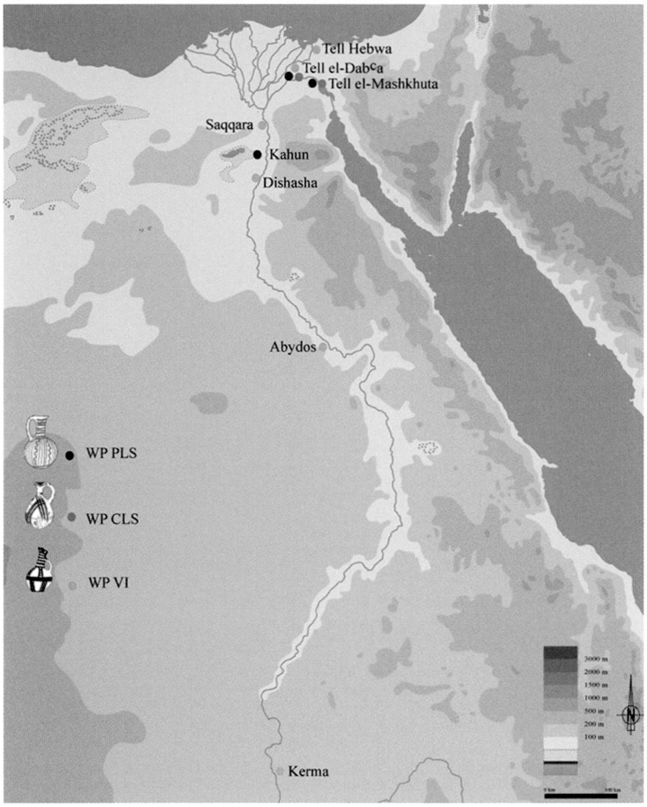

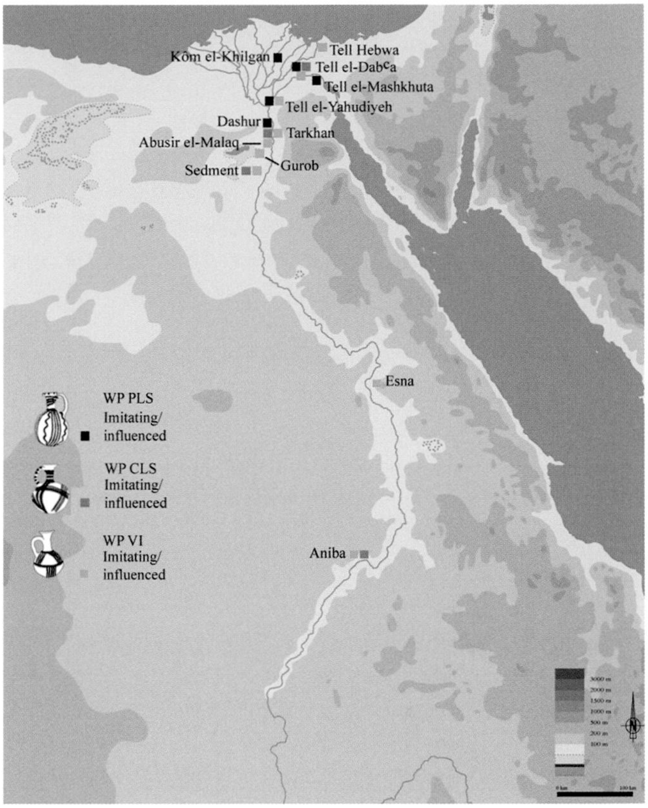

Fig. 4.
The distribution of WP PLS, CLS and WP VI in Egypt (S. Vilain, map background: H. David-Cuny).

Fig. 5.
The distribution of imitations and vases influenced by WP PLS, CLS and WP VI in Egypt (S. Vilain, map background: H. David-Cuny).

(1968: 146). The contexts of other attestations of this ware are more questionable and could be dated to the beginning of the 18th Dynasty. A large part of a White Painted juglet with a pinched mouth was identified as far as Kerma in Nubia. It was published as a White Painted IV (Lecovara 1997: fig. 3.7) but its shape and decoration are typical of White Painted VI (Åström 1972: pl. XLI: 2–3). It was discovered in a Classic Kerma context, correlated with both the Second Intermediate Period and the beginning of the 18th Dynasty. It is noteworthy that no White Painted V, the best represented Cypriot Ware at Tell el-Dabʿa under Hyksos rule (Phases E/1–D/2) has been identified yet outside this site.

Imitations were also occasionally encountered, as shown by Fig. 5. But, once again, they are concentrated around the Delta and are mostly related to the White Painted VI. A superior part of an imitation of White Painted VI juglet was discovered at Abydos, in a context dated from the end of Ahmose's reign by the excavator.[2] The findings from Aniba (Cemetery S, Tomb S69, S71) could come from the end of the Second Intermediate Period or the beginning of the 18th Dynasty (Merrillees 1968: 146). The vases from Gurob (Point Q, Tomb 26) and Tell el-Yahudiya, Tomb 47, 52, 59 (Merrillees 1968) are later and more likely date to the beginning

[2] Unpublished material. I am indebted to S. Harvey, director of the Oriental Institute Ahmose and Tetisheri Project, Abydos, for this information.

of the 18th Dynasty. One could speculate if these imitations were intended in order to compensate a restricted access to genuine imports.

Thus, this brief overview of the development of Cypriot imports throughout the stratigraphy of the site showed that connections with Cyprus were likely re-inforced under the 15th Dynasty. The creation of imitations of White Painted Pendent Line Style jugs from Phase E/3 could have been stimulated by the lack of imports which was observed in this phase and Phase E/2 as well (Vilain 2018). However, Cypriot imports increase again from Phase E/1, suggesting a new development of this trade under Hyksos rule. This development manifests in both a diversification of Cypriot wares and an increase of their quantity between Phases E/1 to D/2. This phenomenon is however limited Tell el-Dabʿa and its area. Outside the Delta, the scarcity of Cypriot imports, especially of White Painted V, could suggest that the rest of Egypt had a difficult access to these specific productions. We are interpreting this phenomenon as another element in favour of the hypothesis of a growing isolation of the Delta under Hyksos rule.

Middle Egypt

Because of its political implications, the takeover of the Hyksos had a strong impact on connections between the Delta and other entities in Egyptian territory. Even if the extent of this impact is difficult to assess, the Marl C pottery is a helpful tool to investigate this situation.

Marl C clays probably originate from the Memphis-Fayum area (Arnold 1981) even if the presence of at least another source in the south cannot be discounted (Bader 2002: 39). This production was studied in detail by Bader (2001). The author highlighted that Marl C vessels, which were attested at Tell el-Dabʿa from Phase H, were suddenly becoming scarce in the assemblage of this site in the late Hyksos period (Bader 2001: 231). The repertoire of shapes also changed: jars with a corrugated neck are not attested at Tell el-Dabʿa after Phase E/1. Still, this type occurs until the late Second Intermediate Period at Memphis (Bader 2002: 41; 2009).

According to Bader (2002: 41), the discrepancy between the Marl C assemblages of Tell el-Dabʿa and Memphis could suggest that contacts between the Eastern Delta and the Memphis-Fayum area could have been restricted after Phase E/1. This perspective is also supported by the scarcity of Canaanite Jars at Memphis after the takeover of the Hyksos. Moreover, by Phase D/2, most of the open shapes of the Marl C repertoire are no longer present in Tell el-Dabʿa's repertoire, except for specific types of bowls (Bader 2002: 50, types 17, 20 and 23). This reduction of the part of imported open shapes at the end of the Hyksos period is a phenomenon that has also been observed with Levantine imports.

In addition, the study by Kopetzky (2010) of Marl clay ceramics discovered at Tell el-Dabʿa in domestic contexts revealed that from Phase D/3, Marl II-c-2/3 vessels[3] were supplanted by Marl II-f productions, a fabric group that likely orig-

[3] The Marl II-c-2 and II-c-3 groups of Tell el-Dabʿa's pottery classification are respectively correlated with Marl C1 and Marl C2 groups of the Viennese System (Kopetzky 2010: 44).

inates near the Eastern Delta (Kopetzky 2010: fig. 44). We are interpreting this shift as another sign of disturbances in contacts with the area from where these vases originate. The loss of access to the southern Memphis-Fayum area at this time and the lack of communication between politically separated territories in Egypt could be an explanation for this phenomenon.

Nubia

The existence of interactions between Egypt and Nubia is already documented in the Old Kingdom. Semi-precious stones, incense, electrum, yellow ochre, oils, spices, wood, ebony, bows and arrows are some of the commodities from Nubia mentioned in the Annals of Amenemhat II (Gratien 2004: 80). At the beginning of the 12th Dynasty, the Egyptians built a series of frontier fortresses to act as a rear guard against the Nubian populations, but they were also stations for trading caravans. The forts served as installations for washing and processing of gold as well as posting expeditions to mine it (Lacovara 1997: 72). The Nubian Kingdom of Kush, with its capital at Kerma, was the main rival of Egypt for the control of the gold deposits of the Eastern Desert (Dirminti 2004). According to Ryholt (1997: 252–253), relations between the two polities culminated in the dynastic marriage between a Nubian queen and a 14th Dynasty pharaoh, parents of the future king Nehesy. Then, long-going diplomatic relations between Egypt and Nubia were already established before the fall of the Middle Kingdom and the takeover of the Hyksos.

Excavations at Tell el-Dabʿa yielded a peculiar corpus of Nubian pottery, essentially composed of open shapes discovered in domestic contexts. Some of these vessels could have been produced locally in the Delta, speaking in favour of a presence of Nubians (Forstner-Müller – Rose 2012: 200; Aston – Bietak 2017: 507). At this stage of the excavation, Nubian pottery has been identified in three main areas, at ʿEzbet Helmi (H/I–H/V), in Area F/II, and in Area R/III (Hein 2001; Fuscaldo 2002; 2004; 2008; Forstner-Müller – Rose 2012; Aston – Bietak 2017). Among the earliest fragments of Nubian pottery identified on the site are two beakers belonging to the Kerma culture, attributed to Phase E/3 (Aston – Bietak 2017: 496). They were discovered in one of the burnt magazines of the Palace of Area F/II, the same area which also delivered the imitations of Cypriot pottery mentioned above.

During the Hyksos period, the Nubian ceramic material is ambiguous. Rose – Forstner-Müller (2012: 7) already highlighted how delicate was the attribution of the findings to a specific Nubian culture, except for the well-known Kerma beakers. However, none of these beakers have been retrieved from the Hyksos period. According to a recent study by Aston – Bietak (2017: 506), even if a few sherds were identified as deriving from the Kerma Culture, they may also relate to another Nubian group. Some fragments of Nubian vessels from L81, in Area F/II, which were previously considered as "Kerman" (Aston – Bader 2009: 63) were lately re-evaluated as "Pan-Grave related" (Aston 2012: 164, n. 41). Thus, at the possible exception of one sherd (Fuscaldo 2008: 110, no. 1), no secure example of Kerma pottery have been recognised at Tell el-Dabʿa under Hyksos rule

(Aston – Bietak 2017: 501). Even if, following the well-known adage, "the absence of evidence is not evidence of absence", this lack of typical Kerma vessels challenges our expectations about Nubian cultures with which Tell el-Dabʿa was in contact.

A well commented section of the Second Stela of Kamose relates how the Theban king captured a messenger with a letter from the Hyksos ruler Apophis in the Oasis of Djesdjes, nowadays known as Baharia (Redford 1997: 14; Colin 2005: 36–38). In this letter, Apophis urges the King of Kush to attack the Thebans from the south, suggesting that the Kingdom of Kush was an ally of Avaris, at least at the end of the Hyksos period. However, this situation is not reflected in the archaeological record, as contacts with the Kerma culture are poorly attested at Tell el-Dabʿa under Hyksos rule.

One hypothesis raised by Aston – Bietak (2017: 508) is that in Upper Egypt the 17th Dynasty acted as a barrier between the two major political and military powers at that time, the Hyksos and the Kingdom of Kush. It seems reasonable to assume that the kings of the 15th Dynasty were intending to benefit from the Nubian resources of gold and ivory. This situation would have been a disadvantage for the 17th Dynasty, both politically and economically (Forstner-Müller – Rose 2010: 181; Colin 2005: 62). Indeed, the abundant Egyptian pottery discovered in Nubia during the Hyksos period comes from Upper Egypt, suggesting that trade was occurring mainly through Thebes at this time (Bourriau 1993: 130; O'Connor 1997: 62).

The hypothesis of the isolationist politics of the Theban Kingdom against the Hyksos is coherent with the scarcity of Levantine and Cypriot imports outside the Delta under Hyksos rule, the decrease of Marl C pottery and the lack of attestations of Kerma pottery during the same period at Tell el-Dabʿa. However, the examination of the distribution of other commodities, such as Tell el-Yahudiya juglets, suggests that connections were much more complex and multi-faceted. At the stage of our research, it is still difficult to assess if all contacts ceased between the separated political entities or if some indirect connections could have still occurred, at least during certain periods. More elements of reflection can be brought by the study of the distribution of Tell el-Yahudiya juglets of Late Egyptian Group (Fig. 6) belonging to categories Piriform 2, Biconical 3 and 4, Wheel-made globular and Combed Ware (Bietak – Aston 2012: groups L.1, L.5, L.8–9, L.11–12, L.13).

Type Piriform 2 developed shortly before Hyksos rule, it is attested between Phases E/3 and D/2 at Tell el-Dabʿa (Aston – Bietak 2012: fig. 253). This type is the most widely spread and was discovered as far south as Kerma in Nubia (Aston – Bietak 2012: fig. 141). Juglets of Biconical 3 and 4 types are encountered at Tell el-Dabʿa from Phases E/2 to D/2 (Aston – Bietak 2012: fig. 253). They are attested in minute quantities on sites along the Nile, in the areas of Memphis, Abydos, Rifa, and in the south at Buhen and Aniba (Aston – Bietak 2012: figs. 167, 182). Sites which yielded Biconical 3 and 4 juglets often delivered Piriform 2 juglets as well. Wheel-made globular juglets and Cylindrical types are only attested under Hyksos rule. They are present at Tell el-Dabʿa from Phases E/1 to D/2 (Aston – Bietak 2012: fig. 253). Their distribution is more limited than the previous types outside the Delta. However, they are still occasionally encountered in the

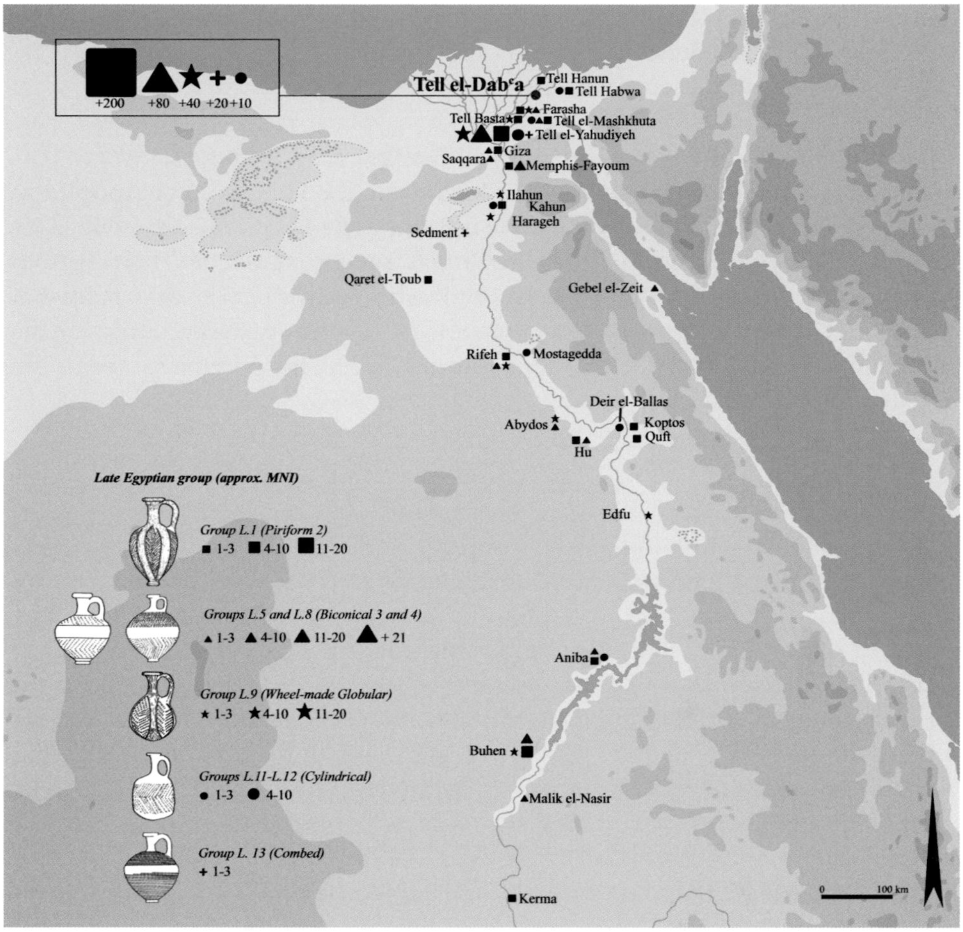

Fig. 6.
The distribution of Tell el-Yahudiya juglets of Late Egyptian Group in Egypt (S. Vilain/P. Aprent, map background: H. David-Cuny).

south at Aniba and Buhen (Aston – Bietak 2012: figs. 189, 201). It is noteworthy that the latest category of Tell el-Yahudiya juglets of the Late Egyptian Group, the Combed Ware, which is a characteristic of the end of the Hyksos period (Phase D/2), is not attested more southwards than Sedment (Aston – Bietak 2012: fig. 206). A detailed study of the distribution and discovery contexts of Tell el-Yahudiya juglets in Egypt is currently in preparation.[4] This first overview suggests that not all communication routes were disrupted, or at least not during the whole Hyksos rule. However, the restrictions in the distribution of the latest types of Tell el-Yahudiya could suggest a more pronounced rupture in contacts towards the end of the Hyksos period.

Of great interest is the discovery of a Tell el-Yahudiya juglet of type Piriform 2 at Qaret el-Toub, located in the oasis of Baharia. This juglet testifies to contacts

[4] This study is a part of the research track "Trade and Crisis Analysis" investigated in the framework of the ERC Advanced Grand Project "The Enigma of the Hyksos" directed by M. Bietak, Austrian Academy of Sciences, Vienna, Austria.

between Baharia and the Delta as suggested by the episode of the messenger depicted in the Second Stela of Kamose (Redford 1997: 14; Colin 2005: 36–38). The role of the Western Desert Oases during the Second Intermediate Period is still difficult to assess. Excavations at Dakhleh showed an expansion of the oasis back then, while the Middle Kingdom and New Kingdom layers only delivered poor archaeological remains (Gratien 2006: 128). Thus, we are interpreting the presence of Tell el-Yahudiya at Baharia as well as the development of Dakhleh during the Second Intermediate Period as signs of a new interest for the oases route under Hyksos rule. At some point, a part of trading connections could have been conducted by nomads, who had free movement through the desert and could interact with both Nubia and the Delta (Aston – Bietak 2017: 508). A better picture of the situation would request further investigations in the Oases area.

Conclusion

The diachronic study of imported ceramics discovered at Tell el-Dabʿa is a useful tool to investigate the nature of the foreign relations of the Hyksos. This overview showed that their takeover had a different impact on already established connections. Trade with the Levant was already weakened by the fall of the Middle Kingdom and the separation of Egypt into different entities when the Hyksos came to power. However, the ongoing decline of Levantine imports continued and even amplified under Hyksos rule. As a result, at the end of the Second Intermediate Period, imitations of Middle Bronze shapes were favoured and imports were mainly limited to specific commodities, such as Canaanite Jars. Further investigations will be necessary to determine if these shifts reflect a voluntary choice instigated by a reduced need for imports, or if they constituted a necessary response to external constraints.

Compared to these shifts in Levantine imports, the examination of the evolution of Cypriot wares at Tell el-Dabʿa revealed a different pattern. Their presence increased under Hyksos rule and, even if imitations occurred, their number never supplanted the quantity of genuine imports. Cypriot vessels were mostly luxury commodities and were responding to specific needs. Consequently, we have to keep in mind that Cypriot imports, even at their climax, constitute only a minor part of the overall assemblage of the ceramics of each phase at Tell el-Dabʿa. Still, their increase under Hyksos rule could be interpreted as a sign of the will to develop connections with the Eastern Mediterranean, as the political situation surely affected the way that the Hyksos could interact with other parts of Egypt.

In regards to these interactions, the decrease of Marl C pottery at Tell el-Dabʿa as well as the decrease of Canaanite Jars at Memphis after Phase VId could reflect disturbances in contacts between the Hyksos and the Memphite-Fayum area. The progressive isolation of the Delta, which seems stronger at the end of the Hyksos period, would have affected not only connections with the rest of Egypt but also with Nubia. One of the consequences would have been a reinforcement of the role of the Oases and nomads in the Western Desert.

Such observations highlight the varying interactions of the Hyksos with different powers across the region. The takeover of the Delta by the Hyksos dynasty was an unprecedented event in Egypt. Therefore, their reign, as well as their fall, is closely linked to the way they interacted not only politically but also economically with both the rest of Egypt as well as the Eastern Mediterranean.

References

Abd el-Maksoud, M., 1998. *Tell Heboua, 1981–1991: enquête archéologique sur la Deuxième période intermédiaire et le Nouvel Empire à l'extrémité orientale du Delta*. Paris: ÉRC.

Arnold, Do., 1981. Ägyptische Mergeltone („Wüstentone") und die Herkunft einer Mergeltonware des Mittleren Reiches aus der Gegend von Memphis. In Do. Arnold, ed., *Studien zur altägyptischen Keramik*. SDAIK 9. Mainz: Philipp von Zabern, 167–191.

Arnold, Do., 1982. Keramikbearbeitung in Dahschur 1976–1981. *MDAIK* 38, 25–65.

Arnold, Do. – F. Arnold – S.J. Allen, 1995. Canaanite Imports at Lisht, the Middle Kingdom Capital of Egypt. *ÄuL* 5, 13–32.

Aston, D., 2004. *Tell el-Dab'a XII. A Corpus of Late Middle Kingdom and Second Intermediate Period Pottery*. Wien: Verlag der Österreischichen Akademie der Wissenchaften.

Aston, D. – B. Bader, 2009. Fishes, Ringstands, Nudes and Hippos – A Preliminary Report on the Hyksos Palace Pit Complex L81, *ÄuL* 19, 19–89.

Aston, D. – M. Bietak, 2012. *Tell el-Dab'a VIII. The Classification and Chronology of Tell el-Yahudiya Ware*. Wien: Verlag der Österreischichen Akademie der Wissenchaften.

Aston, D. – M. Bietak, 2017. Nubians in the Nile Delta: à propos Avaris and Peru-Nefer. In N. Spencer – A. Stevens, eds., *The New Kingdom in Nubia: Lived Experience, Pharaonic Control and Indigenous Traditions*. BMPES 3. Leuven: Peeters, 489–522.

Åström, P., 1972. *The Swedish Cyprus Expedition. Vol. IV. Part. 1C. The Late Cypriote Bronze Age: Architecture and Pottery*. Lund: The Swedish Cyprus Expedition.

Bader, B., 2001. *Tell el-Dab'a XIII. Typologie und Chronologie der Mergel-C-Ton-Keramik. Materialien zum Binnenhandel des Mittleren Reiches und der Zweiten Zwischenzeit*. Untersuchungen der Zweigstelle Kairo des Österreichischen Archäologischen Instituts 19. Wien: Verlag der Österreischichen Akademie der Wissenchaften.

Bader, B., 2002. A Concise Guide to Marl C Pottery. *ÄuL* 12, 29–54.

Bader, B., 2009. *Tell el-Dab'a XIX. Auaris und Memphis im Mittleren Reich und in der Hyksoszeit, Vergleichsanalyse der materiellen Kultur*. Untersuchungen der Zweigstelle Kairo 31. Wien: Verlag der Österreichischen Akademie der Wissenschaften.

Bard, K.A. – R. Fattovich, 2010. Spatial Use of the Twelfth Dynasty Harbor at Mersa/Wadi Gawasis for the Seafaring Expeditions to Punt. *JAEI* 2/3, 1–13.

Bietak, M., 1991. *Tell el-Dab'a V. Ein Friedhofsbezirk der Mittleren Bronzezeit-kultur mit Totentempel und Siedlungsschichten, unter Mittarbeit von Christa Mlinar und Angela Schwab*, Denkschriften der Gesamtakademie, UZK9. Wien: Verlag der Österreichischen Akademie der Wissenschaften.

Bietak, M., 1997. The Center of Hyksos Rule: Avaris (Tell el-Dab'a). In E.D. Oren, ed., *The Hyksos: New Historical and Archaeological Perspectives*. UMM 96. Philadelphia: University Museum, University of Pennsylvania, 87–139.

Bietak, M. – I. Forstner-Müller – C. Mlinar, 2001. The Beginning of the Hyksos Period at Tell el-Dab'a: A Subtle Change in Material Culture. In P.M. Fischer, ed., *Contributions to the Archaeology and History of the Bronze and Iron Ages in the Eastern Mediterranean. Studies in Honour of Paul Åström*. Österreichisches Archäologisches Institut Sonderschriften 39. Wien: Österreichisches Archäologisches Institut, 171–181.

Bourriau, J., 1991. Relations between Egypt and Kerma during the Middle and New Kingdoms. In W. Davies, ed., *Egypt and Africa: Nubia from Prehistory to Islam*. London: British Museum Press, 129–144.

Bourriau, J., 1997. Beyond Avaris: The Second Intermediate Period in Egypt Outside the Eastern Delta. In E.D. Oren, ed., *The Hyksos: New Historical and Archaeological Perspectives*. UMM 96. Philadelphia: University Museum, University of Pennsylvania, 159–182.

Cohen-Weinberger, A. – Y. Goren, 2004. Levantine-Egyptian Interactions during the 12th to the 15th Dynasties based on the Petrography of the Canaanite Pottery from Tell el-Dabʿa. *ÄuL* 14, 69–100.

Colin, F., 2005. Kamosé et les Hyksos dans l'oasis de Djesdjes. *BIFAO*, 35–47.

Dirminti, E., 2014. Between Kerma and Avaris: The First Kingdom of Kush and Egypt during the Second Intermediate Period. In J. Anderson – D. Welsby, eds., *The Fourth Cataract and Beyond. Proceedings of the 12th International Conference for Nubian Studies.* BMPES 1. Leuven – Paris – Walpole: Peeters, 337–345.

Engelbach, R., 1915. *Riqqeh and Memphis VI.* London: B. Quaritch.

Fischer, P.M. – M. Sadeq, 2000. Tell el-Ajjul 1999. A Joint Palestinian-Swedish Field Project: First Season Preliminary Report. *ÄuL* 10, 211–226.

Förstner-Müller, I., 2008. *Tell el-Dabʿa XVI. Die Gräber des Areals A/II von Tell el-Dabʿa.* Wien: Verlag der Österreischischen Akademie der Wissenchaften.

Forstner-Müller, I. – P. Rose, 2012. Nubian Pottery at Avaris in the Second Intermediate Period and the New Kingdom: Some Remarks. In I. Forstner-Müller – P. Rose, eds., *Nubian Pottery from Egyptian Cultural Contexts of the Middle and Early New Kingdom. Proceedings of a Workshop held at the Austrian Archaeological Institute at Cairo, 1–12 December 2010.* Wien: Österreichisches Archäologisches Institut, 181–212.

Fuscaldo, P., 2002. The Nubian pottery from the Palace District of Avaris at ʿEzbet Helmi, Areas H/III and H/VI, Part I: The "Classic" Kerma pottery of the 18th Dynasty. *ÄuL* 12, 167–186.

Fuscaldo, P., 2004. The Nubian pottery from the Palace District of Avaris at ʿEzbet Helmi, Areas H/III and H/VI, Part II: The "Classic" Kerma pottery from the Second Intermediate Period and the 18th Dynasty. *ÄuL* 14, 111–119.

Fuscaldo, P., 2008. The Nubian pottery from the Palace District of Avaris at ʿEzbet Helmi, Areas H/III and H/VI, Part III: The "Classic" Kerma pottery from the Second Intermediate Period and the 18th Dynasty. *ÄuL* 18, 107–127.

Goren, Y., 2003. Review of McGovern P. E., *The Foreign Relations of the "Hyksos"*. BAR International Series 888 (Oxford, 2000). *BiOr* 60/1–2, 105–109.

Gratien, B., 2004. From Egypt to Kush: Administrative Practices and Movements of Goods during the Middle Kingdom and the second Intermediate Period. In T. Kendall, ed., *Proceedings of the Ninth Conference of the International Society of Nubian Studies.* Boston: Department of African-American Studies, Northeastern University, 74–82.

Gratien, B., 2006. Kerma people in Egypt (Middle and Classic Kerma). In K. Kroeper – M. Chlodnicki – M. Kobusiewicz, eds., *Archaeology of Early Northeastern Africa*. Studies in African Archaeology 9. Poznań: Poznań Archaeological Museum, 119–134.

Habachi, L., 1972. *The Second Stela of Kamose and his Struggle against the Hyksos Ruler and his Capital.* ADAIK 9. Glückstadt: J.J. Augustin.

Hein, I., 2001. Kerma in Auaris. In C.-B. Arnst – I. Hafemann – A. Lohwasser, eds., *Begegnungen, Festgabe für E. Endesfelder, K.-H. Priese, W. F. Reineke u. S. Wenig.* Leipzig: Wodtke und Stegbauer, 199–212.

Hein, I. – P. Jánosi, 2004. *Tell el-Dabʿa XI. Areal A/V: Siedlungsrelikte der späten 2. Zwischenzeit.* Wien: Österreichische Akademie der Wissenschaften.

Karageorghis, V., 1995. Relations between Cyprus and Egypt, Second Intermediate Period and XVIIIth Dynasty. *ÄuL* 5, 73–79.

Kopetzky, K., 2009. Egypt and Lebanon: New Evidence for Cultural Exchanges in the first half of the 2nd Millennium B. C. In A.-M. Maila-Afeiche, ed., *Interconnections in the Eastern Mediterranean: Lebanon in the Bronze and Iron Ages. Proceedings of the International Symposium, Beirut 2008.* BAAL Hors-Série VI. Beyrouth: Ministère de la Culture, Direction Générale des Antiquités, 143–157.

Kopetzky, K., 2010. *Tell el-Dabʿa XX. Die Chronologie der Siedlungskeramik der Zweiten Zwischenzeit aus Tell el-Dabʿa.* Untersuchungen der Zweigstelle Kairo des Österreichischen Archäologischen Instituts 32. Wien: Verlag der Österreischichen Akademie der Wissenchaften.

Lacovara, P., 1997. Egypt and Nubia During the Second Intermediate Period. In E.D. Oren, ed., *The Hyksos: New Historical and Archaeological Perspectives.* UMM 96. Philadelphia: University Museum, University of Pennsylvania, 69–82.

Maguire, L., 2009. *Tell el-Dabʿa XXI. The Cypriot pottery and its circulation in the Levant.* Wien: Verlag der Österreichischen Akademie der Wissenschaften.

Math, N., 2012–2013. Remains of an Older Palace (Str. d). In M. Bietak *et al.*, Report on the excavations of a Hyksos Palace at Tell el-Dabʿa / Avaris (23rd August – 15th November 2011). *ÄuL* 22 / 23, 17–53.

Malmgren, K., 2003. *Klavdhia Tremithos: A Middle and Late Cypriote Bronze Age Site.* Jonsered: Paul Åströms Förlag.

McGovern, P., 2000. *The Foreign Relations of the "Hyksos". A Neutron Activation Study of the Middle Bronze Age Pottery from the Eastern Mediterranean.* BAR International Series 888. Oxford: Archaeopress.

McGovern, P. – G. Harbottle, 1997. "Hyksos" Trade Connections between Tell el Dabʿa (Avaris) and the Levant: A Neutron Activation Study of the Canaanite jar. In E.D. Oren, ed., 1997. *The Hyksos: New Historical and Archaeological Perspectives.* UMM 96. Philadelphia: University Museum, University of Pennsylvania, 141–157.

O'Connor, D., 1997. The Hyksos period in Egypt. In E.D. Oren, ed., *The Hyksos: New Historical and Archaeological Perspectives.* UMM 96. Philadelphia: University Museum, University of Pennsylvania, 45–68.

Oren, E.D., ed., 1997. *The Hyksos: New Historical and Archaeological Perspectives.* UMM 96. Philadelphia: University Museum, University of Pennsylvania.

Ownby, M.F., 2012. Les relations économiques entre l'Égypte et le Levant. *ÉAO* 65, 33–38.

Ownby, M.F. – J. Bourriau, 2009. The Movement of Middle Bronze Age Transport Jars. A Provenance Study Based on Petrographic and Chemical Analysis of Canaanite Jars from Memphis, Egypt. In P.S. Quinn, ed., *Interpreting Silent Artefacts. Petrographic Approaches to Archaeological Ceramics.* Oxford: Archaeopress, 173–189.

Randall-MacIver, D. – L. Woolley, 1911. *Buhen.* Philadelphia: University Museum.

Redford, D.B., 1997. Textual Sources from the Hyksos Period. In E.D. Oren, ed., *The Hyksos: New Historical and Archaeological Perspectives*. UMM 96. Philadelphia: University Museum, University of Pennsylvania, 1–45.

Redmount, C.A., 1989. *On an Egyptian/Asiatic Frontier: An Archaeological History of the Wadi Tumilat*. PhD Dissertation. Chicago: University of Chicago.

Redmount, C.A., 1995. Ethnicity, Pottery and the Hyksos at Tell el-Mashkhuta in the Egyptian Delta. *BA* 58/4, 182–190.

Ryholt, K.S.B., 1997. *The Political Situation in Egypt during the Second Intermediate Period c. 1800-1550 BC*. CNIP 20. Copenhagen: Museum Tusculanum Press.

Schneider, T., 2003. *Ausländer in Ägypten während des Mittleren Reiches und der Hyksoszeit*. ÄAT 42. Wiesbaden: Harrassowitz.

Smith, S.T., 2002. Pots and Politics: Ceramics from Askut and Egyptian Colonialism during the Middle through New Kingdoms. In C.A. Redmount – Ch. Köhler, eds., *Egyptian Pottery. Proceedings of the 1990 Pottery Symposium at the University of California*. Berkeley: Archaeological Research Facility, University of California at Berkeley, 43–79.

Vilain, S., 2018. Imitations et productions locales influencées par la céramique chypriote *White Painted Pendent Line Style* à Tell el-Dabʿa. *ÄuL* 28, 487–505.

FOREIGN-INDIGENOUS INTERACTIONS IN THE LATE BRONZE AGE LEVANT: TUTHMOSID IMPERIALISM AND THE ORIGIN OF THE AMARNA DIPLOMATIC SYSTEM

Federico Zangani (Brown University)

The prelude to the diplomatic system of the Amarna letters represents a primary case-study on foreign-indigenous interactions in Syria-Palestine during the Late Bronze Age, since it may be investigated diachronically as the Egyptian political, military, and economic engagement with the local, sociopolitical communities of the northern Levant from the first phase of New Kingdom imperialism to the fully developed geopolitical systems of the time of the Amarna archive. The development of this set of interactions between a foreign power and the sociopolitical communities of Syria-Palestine ranges from Kamose's and Ahmose's operations against the Hyksos in the Levant in the 16th century BC, to the unprecedented territorial expansion of the Egyptian realm under the Tuthmosid kings (ca. 1504–1390 BC), and eventually the establishment of a sophisticated diplomatic system and a geopolitical status quo under Amenhotep III (ca. 1390–1352 BC). In particular, it has never been questioned how the world of the Amarna letters originated in the first place: these are often considered representative of the entire Near Eastern and Eastern Mediterranean world of the second half of the second millennium BC, but such an assumption ignores the fact that the time span of the archive did not exceed a maximum of two or three decades (Mynářová 2015: 150), corresponding to the reigns of Amenhotep III, Akhenaten, and one or more of his successors. In fact, the geopolitical situation in the Levant in the 15th century BC at the time of Tuthmose III was radically different from a century later at the time of Amenhotep III: while the former campaigned systematically between Canaan and the Middle Euphrates region as far north as Carchemish, the latter no longer had this necessity, and military activity was limited to a few, targeted operations.

The geographic focus of this study is the imperial periphery and semi-periphery, i.e. the northernmost territories under Egyptian domination and the area which was still within the Egyptian sphere of influence, but beyond stable political and military control: the province of Upi, in the Syrian heartland, which included the Damascene region, and Amqu (the Beqaᶜ Valley), with the Egyptian provincial centre of Kumidi; the upper valley of the Orontes River, with the cities of Tunip, Qaṭna, and Qadesh; the West Semitic kingdoms of the Lebanese coast and the territory of Amurru, where the Egyptians maintained a provincial base at Ṣumur and military garrisons in Ullaza; and the Syrian coast as far north as the realm of Ugarit. Being at the intersection of at least three different geopolitical spheres (Egypt, Mittani, and Ḫatti), the northern Levant is particularly well-suited to the study of foreign-indigenous interactions throughout the Late Bronze Age, and its distinct status with respect to the southern Levant seems to be reflected in the textual and epigraphic record as well. Moran (1992: xx–xxii) distinguished between a northern and a southern linguistic tradition within the Amarna corpus, divided along a line from Ṣumur to Qaṭna, whereas Liverani (1998: 40–41, 47, 62) pointed out differences in content between letters from the southern vassals—more normal and administrative in character—and letters from the northern Levant, which deal with more specific historical events and more pressing military issues[1]. In fact, the sociopolitical matrix of Syria-Palestine differed significantly from north to south: while southern Canaan had traditionally been within the Egyptian sphere of influence, the northern Levant had a significant Hurrian cultural presence, as well as some Indo-European elements[2] (Mynářová 2007: 42). Therefore, the Amarna diplomatic system should be understood as the result of foreign-indigenous interactions in an area of high sociopolitical complexity and shifting boundaries, and its systematic, analytical study is situated at the intersection of two fields of inquiry: Egyptian imperialism during the 18th Dynasty, and the political and economic history of the northern Levant during the Late Bronze Age.

Unravelling foreign-indigenous interactions in the Late Bronze Age Levant: evidence and approaches

The Late Bronze Age and New Kingdom Egypt have traditionally attracted much scholarly attention due to the wealth of textual and archaeological material preserved, but several aspects of this international age still lack systematic and analytical studies, or new sets of evidence still have to be investigated within the wider geopolitical and cultural context. The latter is the case particularly when the textual and archaeological evidence ranges over more than one discipline within Near Eastern studies. Alternatively, the opposite trend is visible: different sets of evidence have been forced together in order to formulate overarching interpretive models that greatly simplify the complexity and the plurality of systems of the Late Bronze Age. In fact, complexity and plurality both at the local and at the international level are key factors in understanding foreign-indigenous interactions in Syria-Palestine, and the imperial strategy of the 18th Dynasty should not be envisaged as the unilateral product of pharaonic policy-making at the centre of the world-system, but as being influenced to a great extent by the geopolit-

[1] A recent study by Levy (2017) has highlighted a north-south divide in the distribution of Ramesside epigraphic material across the Levant centred around the site of Beth Shean: hieratic inscriptions and architectural elements—attesting to administrative activities and long-term occupation—originate from Palestine, whereas royal stelae documenting military campaigns concentrate in the region north of Beth Shean. Although these data pertain to the 19th and 20th Dynasties, they could reflect the varying extent of Egyptian control over the southern and the northern Levant following the territorial expansion of the 18th Dynasty. Moreover, Levy (2017: 15) aptly points out how Byblos does not conform to this general pattern, and this is probably due to the city's exceptional relationship with Egypt, which dated back to at least as early as the Old Kingdom.

[2] In addition to the Indo-European influences from Hittite Anatolia (Mynářová 2007: 42), some clearly Indo-Aryan elements in the language, religion, and culture of Mittani have attracted much scholarly debate. For a review of the evidence and the dismissal of the Indo-Aryan hypothesis, see von Dassow 2008: 77–90. See also Freu 2003: 21–23; von Dassow 2014: 12–14; and de Martino 2014: 68–69.

ical and economic dynamics of the periphery and semi-periphery. The complexity and diversity of the Levant may be easily explained in light of its geographical characteristics, geopolitical location, and sociolinguistic composition: a region characterised by a diversity of environments, serving as an interface between the Egyptian, Mesopotamian, Anatolian, and Mediterranean worlds, inhabited by various ethnic groups speaking and writing several Semitic and non-Semitic languages. In their study on Mediterranean history, Horden and Purcell (2000) have proposed the two concepts of "microecology" and "connectivity" to characterise the complexity of the Mediterranean world throughout several millennia, and some of their observations could provide valuable insight into the Late Bronze Age Levant. They indicated the Beqaʿ Valley as a region of extraordinary ecological complexity, featuring a dense pattern of local environments, and functioning as a point of transition between the Mediterranean and the semi-arid regions of the Near East (Horden – Purcell 2000: 58). Moreover, the same degree of "connectivity" characterises the Orontes Valley, which constitutes a gateway into the Syrian heartland, as well as the coastal enclaves which are part of the Mediterranean world but also interact with the hinterland to a significant extent (Horden – Purcell 2000: 133). This approach based on microecology has two advantages, according to Horden and Purcell (2000: 80): flexibility over time, which allows for changes in the system; and spatial indeterminacy, which accounts for the fluidity and permeability of boundaries. These two variables are instrumental in approaching the Late Bronze Age Levant, and the negotiations between imperial Egypt and the local Syro-Palestinian rulers in the Amarna correspondence are dictated by strategies to come to terms with this flexibility in time and fluidity in space.

The systematic analysis of foreign-indigenous interactions between 18th Dynasty Egypt and the northern Levant may be conceptualized as the integration of three sets of textual evidence (Fig. 1): Egyptian royal and private inscriptions, which reflect the imperial perspective; texts from Syrian archives, chiefly Kumidi (Kāmid el-Lōz, Lebanon) and Qaṭna (Tell Mishrifeh, Syria)[3], as well as miscellaneous materials from other archives, which may shed light on the local, northern Levantine geopolitical and economic situation; and the Amarna letters, which are the product of the imperial-local, Egyptian-Syrian interactions in the 14th century BC. As far as the archaeological evidence is concerned, it is problematic to formulate hypotheses about foreign-indigenous interactions based on material culture: not only is it difficult to distinguish between foreign imports and local imitations, but objects could also move between different socio-economic contexts as gift exchanges and / or trade in commodities (see Aswani – Sheppard 2003). An example of this phenomenon is the gold scarab of Nefertiti from the Uluburun shipwreck, which was probably issued by the royal family in Amarna in the first place, then donated to a local Levantine ruler, and finally traded as a mere piece of gold, having lost its original sociopolitical value (Zangani 2016: 238). Therefore, a case-by-case assessment is advisable in examining the Egyptian and Egyptianizing

[3] For an overview of the epistolary tradition at Kumidi and Qaṭna as compared to the Amarna letters, see Mynářová 2007: 74–80.

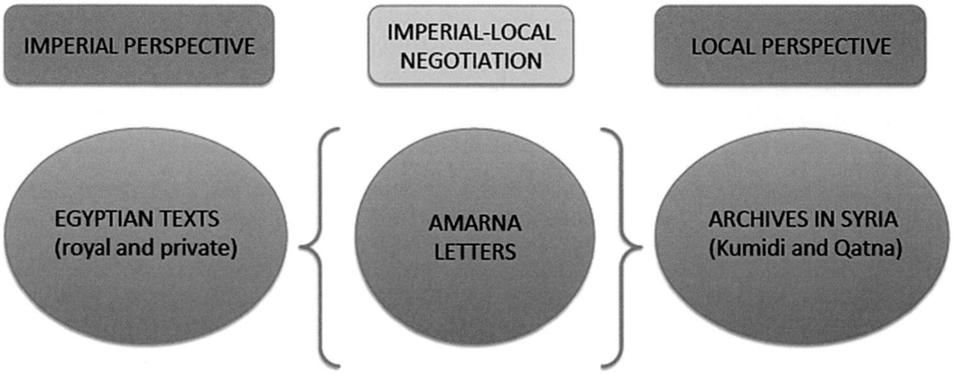

Fig. 1.
Integration of three sets of textual evidence for the study of foreign-indigenous interactions in the northern Levant during the 18th Dynasty.

material culture in the northern Levant, since it presents a series of methodological issues which make it problematic for the study of foreign-indigenous interactions in the Late Bronze Age.

The Egyptian textual record seems to reflect three historical phases in the foreign policies of the 18th Dynasty towards the Levant. The first is the aftermath of the Hyksos rule in Lower Egypt and the initial phase of Egyptian imperialism in Syria-Palestine, corresponding to the reigns of Ahmose through Tuthmose II. Following Ahmose's operations against the Hyksos bases in southern Canaan, Tuthmose I carried out at least one major offensive into northern Syria, in the territory of Naharin, as is witnessed by the biographies of Ahmose son of Ibana and Ahmose Pennekhbet at El-Kab, as well as a fragmentary inscription from Deir el-Bahri (Urk. IV, 103–105), which reports, amongst other things, the first occasion of an elephant-hunt at Niy[4]. The second phase corresponds to the systematic military campaigning and far-flungerritorial expansionism in Syria-Palestine which took place under Tuthmose III and Amenhotep II. The former conducted at least 16 campaigns into the Levant between his 22nd and 42nd regnal year, as attested by his annals behind the 6th Pylon in the temple of Amun at Karnak (Urk. IV, 645–756), as well as many other royal inscriptions and several private texts from his reign. The focus of Tuthmose III's imperial policies was the Levantine coast north of Byblos and the Syrian heartland controlled by Mittani, which was Egypt's main competitor in the northern Levant in this period. It is also worth noting that Qadesh played an important role as a centre of anti-Egyptian resistance in the Orontes Valley, and this characterises the entire New Kingdom, as early as the battle of Megiddo in Tuthmose III's 22nd/23rd regnal year, through the Amarna age, and until the Egyptian-Hittite conflict between Ramesses II and Muwatalli II. As regards the reign of Amenhotep II, this seems to represent a turning point in the 18th Dynasty imperial policies. On the one hand, the king continued the far-flung conflict between Egypt and Mittani in central and northern Syria; on the other, this appears to be the last wave of Egyptian territorial expansion in the

[4] Generally identified with present-day Qala'at el-Mudiq, Syria, next to the Hellenistic and Roman city of Apamea on the Orontes.

Levant, since no large-scale campaigns are attested following his 9th regnal year[5]. In fact, the third and final phase in the 18th Dynasty imperial strategy witnesses a sharp decrease in expansionist policies in the Levant after Amenhotep II, followed by the diplomatic correspondence of the Amarna archive starting from the reign of Amenhotep III. Royal inscriptions contain remarkably little reference to the pharaoh's power over Syria-Palestine beyond a few, common epithets, and no large-scale military campaigns are celebrated. In fact, most of the evidence for the Egyptian involvement in Syria-Palestine during this period stems from the Amarna letters. This is significant, since Egyptian written records in general are not scarce for the late 18th Dynasty, and this lack of references to the Levant does not seem to be due to an accident of preservation.

As far as the second set of evidence is concerned, many texts from Syrian archives are adequately published and accessible, but they have never been considered of Egyptological interest. Their potential, however, could be high, since they provide first-hand evidence for the local, geopolitical and economic dynamics which the Egyptian imperial policies attempted to interfere with and control, and they complement the official record in the study of foreign-indigenous interactions in the Late Bronze Age Levant. The site of Kumidi, in particular, may be considered one of the most important sites in the Beqaᶜ Valley (see Heinz 2005), located as it was at the crossroads of important military and trade routes, on a north-south axis along the Beqaᶜ and on a east-west axis between Sidon on the coast and Damascus in the hinterland (Morris 2005: 238). Kumidi functioned as a major Egyptian provincial centre during the reigns of Amenhotep III and Akhenaten, as attested by several Amarna letters, and was designed to serve Egyptian political, economic, and military interests at this junction between the northern and southern Levant. In addition to Egyptian and Egyptianizing material culture, a total of nine cuneiform tablets in Akkadian (see Edzard et al. 1970 and, for a comprehensive overview of the corpus, Hachmann 2012) originated from the site to this day, and they belong to the archive of the local Egyptian administrator (*rabû*) at the time of Amenhotep III and / or Akhenaten[6]. The Kumidi letters, therefore, could be instrumental in shedding light both on the local governance of the northernmost territories of the Egyptian empire, and on the negotiations between the Egyptian court and the Levantine rulers at the time of the Amarna diplomatic archive.

[5] In fact, two passages in the textual record dating to the reign of Amenhotep II seem to provide indirect evidence for peaceful relations between Egypt and Mittani: the concluding section of the Memphis stela (Urk. IV, 1309.13–1309.20; Badawi 1943; Edel 1953), in which Mittani, Ḫatti, and Babylonia bring diplomatic gifts (*ḥnkw*) and revenues (*bꜣkw*) in order to request the "breath of life" (*ṯꜣw n ꜥnḫ*) (see Klengel 1965: 39–40; Bryan 1980: 423–4); and Amenhotep II's column inscriptions at Karnak, which mention the rulers of Mittani bearing tribute (*jnw*) and begging for the "breath of life" (Urk. IV, 1326.1–1326.10; see Bryan 1980: 423). However, Manuelian (1987: 78) maintains that the lack of Egyptian campaigns after Amenhotep II's regnal year is based solely upon an argument from silence.

[6] Although it is possible that two of the letters (KL 69:277 and KL 69:279, in Edzard et al. 1970) may have been sent by Amenhotep III, Huehnergard (1996) published a letter found on the art market which is likely to have come from Kāmid el-Lōz, and whose sender seems to have been Ili-rapiḫ, Rib-Ḫadda's successor on the throne of Byblos. Therefore, in light of Huehnergard's analysis, this tablet would move—or extend—the date of the archive into the reign of Akhenaten.

Qaṭna, on the other hand, is a different type of political player from Kumidi. It was an important Syrian kingdom situated within the orbit of Hurrian culture (Richter 2005), and a local dynasty of rulers with Hurrian names is known, the most notorious of whom are Idadda / Idanda and Akizzi—the latter featuring in a series of Amarna letters addressed probably to Akhenaten. Archaeological excavations at Qaṭna have yielded not only a substantial quantity of Egyptian and Egyptianizing material culture, but also a significant number of cuneiform tablets, including the archive of king Idadda (see Richter – Lange 2012), which dates to the 14th century BC and is therefore roughly contemporary with the Amarna letters. A study of this corpus could, in fact, generate first-hand evidence for the geopolitical and economic dynamics specific to the region, as well as contribute significantly to an understanding of foreign-indigenous interactions between 18th Dynasty Egypt and the local, culturally Hurrian communities of Syria.

Indirect evidence for interactions between 18th Dynasty Egypt and the northern Levant may originate also from other sites in Syria, such as Alalaḫ and Ugarit. The former was located north of the Egyptian sphere of influence, and was under first Hurrian, and later Hittite hegemony. However, texts from the archaeological stratum known as Alalaḫ IV[7] span a period of roughly 50 years from the mid-15th century to ca. 1400 BC, when the city was in the orbit of Mittani, and may provide valuable insight into the sociopolitical situation of the northern Levant at the time of the Tuthmosid phase of Egyptian imperialism. Ugarit, on the other hand, is a more controversial case: while it is tempting to avail oneself of its extraordinary wealth of epigraphic material, most of the texts are of uncertain date, or they may be dated to the final stages of Late Bronze Age, from the post-Amarna, Ramesside period until the final capitulation of the city in the 12th century BC. An example of the former case is the so-called General's letter (RS 20.33, Ug. 5 20)[8], which is usually dated to the Ramesside period, but which could also be contemporary with the reign of Amenhotep III. Alternatively, texts from the later periods, such as Merneptah's letter (RS 88.2158)[9], could be used as indirect evidence to extrapolate political, social, and economic patterns which may be applicable to the pre-Amarna and Amarna phases. A case-by-case assessment is therefore necessary when dealing with textual evidence from Ugarit.

Many studies have already been dedicated to the Amarna letters, since they are a never-ending source of information for foreign-indigenous interactions in the Late Bronze Age, and, more specifically, for the negotiations between imperial projects and local interests. As has been already discussed above, these texts should not be considered representative of the entire Late Bronze Age, since they represent only the culmination of certain geopolitical processes which started

[7] For the Alalaḫ IV texts, see Wiseman 1953; 1954; and 1959; von Dassow 2005 and 2008.

[8] In the General's letter an unknown sender, termed "the General", after having besieged Ardat, south of Ṣumur, is stationed on the Syrian coast, where his task is to stop any advancing Egyptian troops, and complains about the lack of military supplies. See Izre'el 1988; Izre'el – Singer 1990.

[9] This letter, sent by Merneptah to a king of Ugarit whose name is not preserved, discusses the despatch of craftsmen for the erection of a colossal statue of the Egyptian king the temple of Baʿl at Ugarit. See Yon – Arnaud 2001: 239–248; Morris 2015.

already at the beginning of the 18th Dynasty, reached an apex under Tuthmose III and Amenhotep II, and eventually resulted in a delicate equilibrium at the time of Tuthmose IV and Amenhotep III. An innovative approach, therefore, should take into account the diachronic sequence of these processes and focus on *how*, *when*, and *why* they took place in order to understand *what* the world of the Amarna letters was really like. Galán (1994) made an important contribution in approaching the Amarna correspondence in its historical perspective: since Egyptian royal inscriptions traditionally focused on the king's personal feats, compositions such as the annals of Tuthmose III found no place in the later 18th Dynasty, whereas the vassals' letters in Akkadian were the only form of imperial-local interactions (Galán 1994: 100). Galán ultimately argued for a continuity in the pharaonic imperial policies, pointing out how certain practices such as the collection of tribute by Egyptian military contingents and the reappointment of hostages from the local ruling families in Syro-Palestinian cities, have clear antecedents in Tuthmosid times. Liverani (1998: 33–34), on the other hand, distinguished between different phases in the imperial policies of the 18th Dynasty, and claimed that the local rulers of the northern Levant were forced to submit to the Egyptian domination following the peace treaty between Egypt and Mittani, which in turn made the pharaoh's military presence in Syria rarely necessary. The local geopolitical situation in the northern Levant at the time of the Amarna archive seems to have been characterised by a balance of power which was stable in the long term, but occasionally disturbed by small-scale imbalances which the Syro-Palestinian rulers were ready to report in their letters to the pharaoh (Liverani 1998: 32). However, it has never been thoroughly analysed how and why this overall balance was maintained, and especially how the Egyptian imperial strategy had to—or failed to—deal with these local imbalances, as well as adapt to the sociopolitical mosaic of the Levant in the Late Bronze Age. Innovative research on the Amarna letters, therefore, should be aimed at elucidating not simply macroeconomics and large-scale politics, but also the specific dynamics and events that took place at the local, indigenous level and that contributed to shaping the Egyptian policies towards this region. A "bottom-up"—instead of "top down"—reading of the Amarna letters is therefore advisable to unravel foreign-indigenous interactions in the context of 18th Dynasty imperialism in the northern Levant.

The Hyksos aftermath: Egyptian cultural memory and pre-emptive warfare

As has been already hinted at above, it seems quite logical to suggest that Egyptian territorial expansionism in the Levant during the New Kingdom may have originated from pre-emptive operations against the Hyksos strongholds in southern Canaan[10]. Despite the existence of some epigraphic evidence attesting to

[10] For further discussion on the start of New Kingdom imperialism and pre-emptive strikes against the Hyksos, see Redford 1979: 273ff., Weinstein 1981: 7–10, and, most recently, Morris 2018: 117–120.

Egyptian military activity in the Levant during the Old and Middle Kingdoms[11], Kamose's and Ahmose's struggle against the Hyksos domination in Lower Egypt represents the first, documented case of a large-scale conflict between the Egyptians and Syro-Palestinian peoples, and may thus be instrumental in shedding light on how the Egyptian state developed a long-term interest in and strategy for the geopolitical affairs of the wider region[12].

The Second Kamose stela (Habachi 1972; Helck 1975: 82–97) is particularly interesting in this regard, since it demonstrates an understanding of political terminology and an awareness of diplomatic etiquette well in advance of the Amarna correspondence. Kamose laments the fact that the Hyksos king Apophis (15th Dynasty) considers him a mere "chieftain" (l. 1, *wr*), as opposed to a proper ruler (l. 1, *ḥqꜣ*), thereby implying the same distinction that New Kingdom official inscriptions make between the heads of individual cities in the Levant (*wr*) and the king of Egypt (*ḥqꜣ*)[13]. The conflict is portrayed as a personal issue between Kamose and Apophis, who is designated as a "ruler of Retjenu" (l. 4, *wr nw rṯnw*): this is worth noting not simply because of the *wr*/*ḥqꜣ* distinction, but because it indicates that the Egyptians viewed the Hyksos as a problem originating from Syria-Palestine in the first place. Moreover, the second half of the stela reports a letter sent by Apophis to the king of Kush and eventually intercepted by Kamose, in which the Hyksos ruler seeks Nubian support against the Egyptian offensive (ll. 20–24):

> *ꜥꜣ-wsr-rꜥ zꜣ rꜥ j-p-pj ḥr nḏ-ḫrt nt zꜣ=j ḥqꜣ n kšj ḥr-m ꜥḥꜥ=k m ḥqꜣ nn rdt rḫ=j jn-jw gmḥ=k jrt.n kmt r=j ḥqꜣ ntj m-ḫnw=s kꜣ-ms dj ꜥnḫ ḥr thm=j ḥr jṯnw=j nj pḥ=j-sw mj qj n jrt.n=f-nbt r=k stp=f pꜣ tꜣ 2 r jꜣd=s pꜣy=j tꜣ ḥnꜥ pꜣy=k ḫb.n=f-st mj ḫd m ꜣꜥ mk-sw ꜥꜣ m-ꜥ=j nn ntj ꜥḥꜥ-n=k ḥr tꜣ kmt mk nn dj=j-n=f wꜣt r-sprt=k kꜣ pzš=n nꜣ n dmjw n tꜣ kmt wnn ḫnt-ḥn-nfr ḫr ršwt*
>
> "Aauserre, son of Ra, Apophis, is greeting my son, the ruler of Kush. Why do you stand as a ruler, without letting me know? Do you see what Egypt has done against me? The ruler who is inside it, Kamose, given life, is perforating me on my soil. I have not attacked him like the manner of all that he has done against you. He cut the land in two parts to make it suffer, my land and yours, and he has damaged them. Come downstream, and

[11] The earliest attestation of military confrontations between Egyptians and "Asiatics" is in the biography of Weni, found at Abydos and dating to the 6th Dynasty (Cairo Museum N. 1435; Tresson 1919; Urk. I, 98–110), in which Weni claims to have led an army against the "Asiatic Sand-dwellers" (*ꜥꜣmw ḥrw šꜥ*). As far as the Middle Kingdom is concerned, the stela of Khusobek from Abydos (Peet 1914) mentions a campaign in the southern Levant under Senusret III, and the fragmentary inscription from the mastaba of Khnumhotep at Dahshur (Allen 2008) reports the Egyptian intervention in a local conflict between Byblos and Ullaza also at the time of Senusret III.

[12] Mynářová (2007: 43–44) suggested that it was not until the reign of Tuthmose III that Egypt developed a long-term strategy for the Levant, and that the kings of the early 18th Dynasty were still more interested in Nubia, a region of economic importance due to its gold mines.

[13] For a discussion of the *wr*/*ḥqꜣ* distinction and the use of *wr* to designate foreign rulers following the Hyksos period, see Lorton 1974: 61–63. For the *wr*/*ḥqꜣ* distinction in the Egyptian version of the peace treaty between Ḫattusili III and Ramesses II, see Langdon – Gardiner 1920: 184–185.

Fig. 2.
The king as a sphinx "who tramples all foreign lands" (*ptpt ḫ3swt-nb*), on an arm panel from a ceremonial chair of Tuthmose IV (KV 43, Valley of the Kings; Theodore M. Davis Collection, Metropolitan Museum of Art, New York; accession number: 30.8.45a-c).

do not hesitate! Look, he is here with me: there is no one who will stand up to you in Egypt. Look, I will not give him way until you arrive. Then we will divide the towns of Egypt, and Khenthennefer will be in joy."

The content and tone of the letter are highly reminiscent of the Amarna letters and, in general, of the Akkadian epistolary traditions: the ruler of Kush is addressed as "my son" (*z3=j*), which implies a subordinate position, and substantiates his obligation to provide political and military assistance to Apophis, to whom he owes allegiance. Thus, the letter quoted in this inscription may be considered the Egyptian version of a standard diplomatic letter of the Late Bronze Age, exchanged between a supra-regional power and a subordinate polity, and it might imply the existence of a well-established diplomatic code already at the inception of the Late Bronze Age, roughly two centuries prior to the Amarna correspondence. In fact, the findings of a fragment of an Old Babylonian cuneiform letter (Bietak et al. 2009: 108, 115–118; Bietak 2010: 986–990) and of a Mesopotamian cuneiform seal impression (Lehmann 2011: 63; van Koppen – Lehmann 2013) at the site of Tell el-Dabʿa (ancient Avaris) further suggest that the Near Eastern epistolary tradition was not alien to the Hyksos[14].

Texts from later in the New Kingdom indicate that the Hyksos domination permeated Egyptian political ideology and cultural memory as the antithesis to the correct exercise of kingship and as a dark era of chaos and distress for Egypt. Hatshepsut's inscription inside the rock-cut shrine known as the Speos Artemidos (Urk. IV, 383–391; Allen 2002; Goedicke 2004), near Beni Hasan, details works for towns and temples in Middle Egypt, including the reconstruction of abandoned sanctuaries, and the final part of the inscription presents Hatshepsut as the legitimate king who restored order in Egypt after the widespread destruction caused by the Hyksos. The veracity of this statement is debatable, since almost a century separates Ahmose's reunification of the country and Hatshepsut's reign, and, as Goedicke (2004: 101) noted, it is unlikely that her predecessors left Middle Egypt in such a state of disarray. However, this passage clearly indicates that the Hyksos occupation had a significant impact upon royal ideology, and this in turn suggests that a political and military threat from Syria-Palestine may have occupied an important place in a king's agenda. This historical and geopolitical awareness extended into the cultural memory and the intellectual milieu of Ramesside society, as is the case of the Late Egyptian literary text known as the Quarrel of Apophis and Seqenenre (British Museum EA 10185: Papyrus Sallier I, recto), which portrays Egypt as a land vexed by Hyksos taxation and where the cult of Seth has been imposed to the exclusion of all other deities. This papyrus is dated to the 10th regnal year of Merneptah (19th Dynasty), and almost three and a half centuries separate the scribe Pentaweret from the events narrated (Manassa 2013: 30, 32).

On the one hand, the scarce textual evidence for the conflict between the Egyptian state based in Thebes and the Hyksos polity in Lower Egypt does not permit a clear reconstruction of the Near Eastern geopolitical scenario at the time of Ahmose's reunification of the country; on the other, it is clear that Egypt was affected by the Hyksos, "Asiatic" domination to an unprecedented extent, which resulted in the perception of a constant threat from Syria-Palestine. In fact, the Hyksos rule was probably the first occasion in Egyptian history in which the Levant represented a potential threat to the stability of the country, as opposed to a source of precious items and commodities or the location of small-scale military intervention. This historical phase, therefore, seems to represent a turning point in the foreign policy of the Egyptian state, which would now have to develop a proper imperial strategy in order to maintain a more significant presence in the Levant, guarantee political stability, and safeguard economic interests as well as the internal security of the country.

---

[14] In fact, Egyptian envoys travelling in the Levant are already mentioned in the *Tale of Sinuhe*, in connection with the protagonist's sojourn in Syria: *wptj ḫdd ḫnt r ẖnw ꜣb=f ḥr=j jw sꜣb=j rmṯ-nbt* (B 94–95), "The messenger who would come north or go south to the residence, he would stop by me, for I made every person stop".

This Egyptian perception of the Levant as a potential, ever-present threat finds a surprisingly close parallel in the earlier stages of Roman imperialism. Brizzi (Brizzi – Cairo 2015; Brizzi 2016) has argued, quite convincingly, that Hannibal's invasion of Italy during the second Punic war, culminating with the defeat of the Roman army at the battle of Cannae in 216 BC, had a profound impact upon Rome and her perception of the surrounding world. According to the Roman censuses, the Hannibalic war resulted in 200,000 dead among the forces of the Italian confederation, i.e. almost a third of Italy's male population, upon which Rome depended for both agriculture and military defense (Brizzi – Cairo 2015: 382). Moreover, such a large-scale enemy offensive into the heartland of the Republic led Rome to question the internal stability and cohesion of the Italian peninsula, upon which her very survival depended (Brizzi 2016: 156–158), and this resulted in the adoption of a new policy: pre-emptive warfare, initially through naval disarmament, and later through the annexation of troublesome territories, aimed at preventing another invasion of Italy (Brizzi – Cairo 2015: 386). Brizzi, therefore, identifies the *metus Punicus* ("Punic fear", "fear of Africa"), as the real catalyst of Roman imperialism at its earliest stage, and points out how this issue characterized both sides of the debate over the final destruction of Carthage: on the one hand, Cato the Elder claimed that no enemy power so close to Italy could be tolerated; on the other, Publius Scipio Nasica believed that the fear of Carthage corroborated the Roman military and moral integrity (Brizzi – Cairo 2015: 390; Brizzi 2016: 170).

The second Macedonian war is a prime example of how pre-emptive warfare characterised the early stages of Roman imperialism in the Mediterranean. When Ptolemy IV Philopator, king of Egypt, died in 204 BC and was succeeded by Ptolemy V, a child under regency, Philip V of Macedon and Antiochus III of Syria reached a secret agreement to take advantage of Egypt's weakness and divide between themselves the Ptolemies' non-Egyptian dominions. Although this conflict was confined within the Eastern Mediterranean world and had no anti-Roman intent, this geopolitical instability was perceived as enough of a threat for Rome (Brizzi – Cairo 2015: 383; Brizzi 2016: 160–161). The fear of another invasion of the Italian peninsula appears clearly in the speech delivered by consul Sulpicius Galba to justify the Roman campaign against Macedon, as quoted by Livy in book 31 of *Ab Urbe condita* (see Brizzi 2016: 161–162, 175 fn. 1–2): *'ignorare' inquit 'mihi videmini, Quirites, non, utrum bellum an pacem habeatis, vos consuli—neque enim liberum id vobis Philippus permittet, qui terra marique ingens bellum molitur—, sed, utrum in Macedoniam legiones transportetis, an hostes in Italiam accipiatis'*. (Livy XXXI, 7.2), "He said: 'Quirites, you seem to me to ignore that you have to decide not whether you have war or peace—in fact, Philip, who endeavours to do a major war by land and sea, will not leave it free for you—but whether you transport the legions into Macedon, or you receive the enemies into Italy'". According to Galba, there should be no doubt as to the correct decision: *Macedonia potius quam Italia bellum habeat* (Livy XXXI, 7.13), "Let Macedonia rather than Italy have war".

Latin historiography clearly indicates that a fear of military threats across the Mediterranean played a major role in the earlier stages of Roman imperialism. In fact, Brizzi (personal communication) believes that this was not aimed at territorial expansion initially, but began as a gradual subjugation of all territories and peoples who posed a threat to the security of Rome and Italy. This observation could be applicable cross-culturally and throughout history, and if the *metus Punicus* was indeed the catalyst of Roman imperialism, something similar—a *metus Asiaticus*—could be envisaged for the Egyptian 18th Dynasty, at least at the beginning of its territorial expansion into the Levant. The biographies of Ahmose son of Ibana (Loret 1910; Urk. IV, 1–11) and Ahmose Pennekhbet (Urk. IV, 32–39) at El-Kab indicate that the war of liberation against the Hyksos extended beyond the traditional borders of Egypt and continued into Canaan with the elimination of enemy strongholds such as Sharuhen. Following the reign of Ahmose, the whole New Kingdom witnesses the development of a proper, unprecedented geopolitical strategy for the Levant, whether it consists of territorial expansionism and warfare (especially under Tuthmose III, Amenhotep II, and Ramesses II), or phases of diplomacy and balance of power (the Amarna period and the *Pax Hethitica* following the Egyptian-Hittite peace treaty). Moreover, the Speos Artemidos inscription and the Quarrel of Apophis and Seqenenre indicate that the Hyksos domination in Lower Egypt was an integral part of the royal ideology and the cultural memory of the country. These three observations, therefore, point to clear similarities between the beginning of Egyptian and Roman large-scale imperialism, and suggest that the issue of a *metus Asiaticus* is instrumental in understanding Egyptian-foreign interactions in the Late Bronze Age.

Political realism in the Late Bronze Age: perspectives from Thucydides' Melian dialogue and Machiavelli's *Prince*

The concept of fear is an integral component of the philosophical doctrine known as political realism. In fact, amongst the various theoretical models from the fields of political theory and anthropology, the philosophical debate between realism and constructivism in international relations is particularly valuable, and David (2000) proposed its application to the study of Amarna politics. According to realism, it is the reality of the material world that determines political actions: human nature is seen as fixed and flawed, and the absence of an overarching regulating authority causes a state of anarchy, whose constant features are competition among states and the threat of armed conflict (David 2000: 55–56). Constructivism, on the other hand, inverts this causal relationship: it is how the political actors behave in each situation that determines the reality of the world, and its fundamental structures are social rather than material (David 2000: 56). According to David, therefore, the world of the Amarna correspondence should be regarded as a product of political realism, determined by the will of the Near Eastern states to survive in the system, their struggle for power, a constant threat of war, and a desire to maintain a balance of power. These elements may constitute a key to understand how the world of the Amarna letters originated in the first place, as well as useful parameters in the analytical study of foreign-indigenous interactions in the Late Bronze Age Levant. In fact, the two founding fathers of political realism, Thucydides of Athens (ca. 460–400 BC) and Niccolò Machiavelli (AD 1469–1527), both belonged to two politically fragmented cultures—the world of the Greek city-states and Renaissance Italy respectively—in which boundaries and spheres of influence would shift constantly and abruptly. This undoubtedly offers a clear parallel with the Late Bronze Age Levant, and I suggest that geopolitical and foreign-indigenous interactions were conceived in comparable ways. In book 5 of the *Peloponnesian War*, Thucydides reports a dialogue between the ambassadors (πρέσβεις) of Athens and the inhabitants of the island of Melos immediately prior to the Athenian siege of Melos in 416 BC, as part of the conflict between Athens and Sparta for the supremacy over the Hellenic peninsula and the Aegean. In this dialogue, the Athenians seek to persuade the Melians to surrender and enter the Athenian sphere of influence, and they provide an eloquent definition of political realism: δίκαια μὲν ἐν τῷ ἀνθρωπείῳ λόγῳ ἀπὸ τῆς ἴσης ἀνάγκης κρίνεται, δυνατὰ δὲ οἱ προύχοντες πράσσουσι καὶ οἱ ἀσθενεῖς ξυγχωροῦσιν. (Thuc. 5.89), "...in human reasoning, justice is given from the standpoint of equal constraint, whereas those who are superior do what is possible and those who are weaker have to agree". The Melians easily understand this distinction between justice and realism: ἐπειδὴ ὑμεῖς οὕτω παρὰ τὸ δίκαιον τὸ ξυμφέρον λέγειν ὑπέθεσθε (Thuc. 5.90), "...since you thus decided to speak of what is profitable instead of what is just". The Melian dialogue constitutes a digression in political theory which describes foreign-indigenous interactions in pre-modern societies through language and concepts that are semantically and culturally more comprehensible to modern scholars than any of the textual sources from the Late Bronze Age Near East, and may therefore prove valuable in reconstructing how the Egyptian imperial envoys of the 18th Dynasty and the local, Syro-Palestinian rulers adhered to analogous concepts. According to the Athenian ambassadors, the submission of the island of Melos is in its inhabitants' interests: ὡς δὲ ἐπ᾽ ὠφελίᾳ τε πάρεσμεν τῆς ἡμετέρας ἀρχῆς καὶ ἐπὶ σωτηρίᾳ νῦν τοὺς λόγους ἐροῦμεν τῆς ὑμετέρας πόλεως, ταῦτα δηλώσομεν, βουλόμενοι ἀπόνως μὲν ὑμῶν ἄρξαι, χρησίμως δ᾽ ὑμᾶς ἀμφοτέροις σωθῆναι. (Thuc. 5.91), "We will show this, that we are here in the interest of our sovereignty, and now we make proposals concerning the safety of your city, since we want to dominate you without trouble, and that you survive to the advantage of both of us". The Melians dissent: καὶ πῶς χρήσιμον ἂν ξυμβαίη ἡμῖν δουλεῦσαι, ὥσπερ καὶ ὑμῖν ἄρξαι; (Thuc. 5.92), "And how could it happen to be useful for us to be enslaved, as it is for you to rule?". The Athenians' reply explains one of the most basic underpinnings of imperialism: ὅτι ὑμῖν μὲν πρὸ τοῦ τὰ δεινότατα παθεῖν ὑπακοῦσαι ἂν γένοιτο, ἡμεῖς δὲ μὴ διαφθείραντες ὑμᾶς κερδαίνοιμεν ἄν. (Thuc. 5.93) "Because you would manage to submit before suffering the most terrible things, and we would make profit if we did not destroy you". The geopolitical imbalance between Athens and the island of Melos is comparable to the one between Egypt and the centres of Syria-Palestine during the Late Bronze Age, and, as the Athenian ambassadors point out, ideology has to reach a compromise with reality: οὐ γὰρ περὶ ἀνδραγαθίας ὁ ἀγὼν ἀπὸ τοῦ ἴσου ὑμῖν, μὴ αἰσχύνην ὀφλεῖν, περὶ δὲ σωτηρίας μᾶλλον ἡ βουλή, πρὸς τοὺς κρείσσονας πολλῷ μὴ ἀνθίστασθαι. (Thuc. 5.101), "In fact, the struggle for you is not about valour, from a position of equal power, so as not to incur dishonour, but the decision is rather about safety, so as not to resist those who are much stronger". In their defense, the Athenians claim that this geopolitical law characterizes human history, long before the Peloponnesian war: καὶ ἡμεῖς οὔτε θέντες τὸν νόμον οὔτε κειμένῳ πρῶτοι χρησάμενοι, ὄντα δὲ παραλαβόντες καὶ ἐσόμενον ἐς αἰεὶ καταλείψοντες χρώμεθα αὐτῷ, εἰδότες καὶ ὑμᾶς ἂν καὶ ἄλλους ἐν τῇ αὐτῇ δυνάμει ἡμῖν γενομένους δρῶντας ἂν ταὐτό. (Thuc. 5.105), "And we, who neither established the law nor were the first ones to use it once it was established, but who have received it already in existence and have left it to exist forever, we make use of it knowing that you or others would do the same thing if you were in the same position of power as us". The Amarna letters prove the Athenian ambassadors right in this regard, since the logic behind the doctrine of political realism is the one that characterises foreign-indigenous interactions in the Late Bronze Age Levant as well. Particularly informative in this regard is EA 162, sent from the pharaoh's chancellery to Aziru of Amurru, in which subordination is presented as beneficial to the subordinate (ll. 33-41):

> *ù šum-ma te-ep-pu-uš ardūta*(ÌR^{tá}) *a-na šarri*(LUGAL) *bēlī*(EN)*-ka ù mi-na-a ša ú-ul ip-pu-ša-ak-ku šarru*(LUGAL) *a-na kà-a-ša šum-ma aš-šum mi-im-ma tá-ra-am e-pé-ši an-mu-ut-ti ù šum-ma tá-ša-ak-kà-an an-mu-ut-ti a-˹wa˺-te*^{meš} *sà-ar-ru-ut-ti i-na lìb-bi-ka ù i-na ḫa-˹aṣ˺-ṣí-in-ni ša šarri*(LUGAL) *tá-ma-at qa-du gáb-˹bi˺ ki-im-ti-ka ù e-pu-uš ardūta*(ÌR^{tá}) *a-na šarri*(LUGAL) *bēlī*(EN)*-ka ù bal-ṭa-tá ù ti*$_7$*-i-de*$_9$ *at-tá ki-i šarri*(LUGAL) *la-a ḫa-ši-iḫ a-na māt*(KUR) *ki-na-aḫ-ḫi gá-bá-ša ki-i i-ra-ú-ub*

> "And if you perform servitude for the king, your lord, then what is it that the king will not do for you? But if for any reason you prefer to do these things and if you set these treacherous words in your heart, then you will die by the king's axe together with your entire family. So perform servitude for the king, your lord, and you will stay alive. And you know that the king does not desire (to go) to the entire land of Canaan when he is angry."

The pharaoh's tone is so reminiscent of the Athenian ambassadors' as to justify the reading of the Amarna correspondence in light of Thucydides' Melian dialogue, since imperial power does not simply imply subordination, but also authority, protection, and stability, the absence of which would be particularly problematic in the world periphery and semi-periphery (see Doyle 1986: 56–57). Almost three millennia separate the Amarna geopolitical and diplomatic world from Machiavelli's *Il Principe*, but this treatise is of great relevance to the study of imperialism and foreign-indigenous interactions in the Late Bronze Age Levant[15]. Chapter 5, in particular, deals with the topic: "How to govern cities or states that, before being conquered, used to live according to their own laws"[16]. According to Machiavelli, there are three possible strategies of controlling newly conquered

[15] For a recent study on the Machiavellian aspects of the ancient Egyptian political thought, see Langer 2015.

[16] Original title: *Quomodo administrandae sunt civitates vel principatus, qui, antequam occuparentur, suis legibus vivebant.* [In che modo si debbino governare le città o principati li quali, innanzi fussino occupati, si vivevano con le loro legge.]

states: outright destruction; occupation, with men from the conquering state going there and living there themselves; and a maintenance of the previous form of government, accompanied by taxation and / or tribute, and the establishment of a local elite who is loyal to the foreign conqueror. Of these three strategies, destruction is always the safest option according to Machiavelli, so as to avoid any potential rebellion, while the Egyptian sources indicate that all three were real possibilities in the imperial policies of the 18th Dynasty. In Chapter 10 ("How to measure the strengths of all the states")[17], Machiavelli distinguishes between two types of states in the geopolitical arena: self-sufficient states, whose rulers have enough men and enough financial resources to levy a strong army, that can face any type of enemy; and states that need protection from others, whose rulers cannot face an enemy in open confrontation. This distinction is perfectly applicable to the Late Bronze Age Levant, since the "Great Kings" (*šarrū rabûtu*) of the Amarna correspondence constitute the former category, whereas the local rulers of Syria-Palestine—most famously Rib-Ḫadda of Byblos—undoubtedly belong to the latter. The relationship between the ruler and his subordinates is the subject of Chapter 17 ("On cruelty and clemency, and whether it is better to be loved than to be feared, or vice versa")[18], in which Machiavelli debates whether it is better for a ruler to be loved or feared: a combination of fear and love is desirable in political realism, but whenever this is not possible, fear is a safer strategy, because people are by their very nature ungrateful, unreliable, and constantly crave power and profit. Fear becomes a viable *instrumentum regni* in Machiavelli's political thought, and this aptly describes power relationships throughout history. In fact, Egyptian inscriptions, especially from the New Kingdom, often employ words for fear, awe, and respect for the king (such as *snḏ, šfšft, ḥryt*) to describe his omnipresence in the foreign territories under Egyptian control.

Machiavelli's political realism reaches its apotheosis in Chapter 18 ("How princes should keep faith")[19], in which the Florentine thinker devises the famous metaphor of the ruler as a centaur, half human, half beast. There are two ways of fighting, one by law, and one by force, the former pertaining to mankind, the latter to wild beasts. Whenever law is not sufficient, however, it is necessary to resort to brutal force. The ideal ruler, therefore, should be able to make effective use of both his human nature and his beastly side, hence the metaphor of the centaur. In fact, this Machiavellian concept is not unprecedented: the Egyptians themselves conceived of kingly rule as dual in nature, half human and half beastly, and devised the icon of the sphinx trampling the foreign enemies. Not only does this image occur on some masterpieces of New Kingdom art, such as the wooden chariot and the ceremonial chair (Fig. 2) of Tuthmose IV and the painted chest of Tutankhamun, but also the ritualized language of royal inscriptions includes several

---

[17] Original title: *Quomodo omnium principatuum vires perpendi debeant.* [In che modo si debbino misurare le forze di tutti i principati.]

[18] Original title: *De crudelitate et pietate; et an sit melius amari quam timeri, vel e contra.* [Della crudeltà e pietà e s'elli è meglio esser amato che temuto, o più tosto temuto che amato.]

[19] Original title: *Quomodo fides a principibus sit servanda.* [In che modo e' principi abbino a mantenere la fede.]

verbs for "trampling" (*ptpt, tjtj*), and in the Poetical stela of Tuthmose III (Urk. IV, 610-619) Amun-Re reminds the king of his own mission precisely in these terms: *jj.n=j dj=j tjtj=k* "I have come to let you trample...". It appears, therefore, that several of Machiavelli's principles of political realism were an integral part of the Egyptian conception of kingship and international relations, and this provides valuable insight into how foreign-indigenous interactions were understood in the Late Bronze Age.

Conclusion

The Egyptian imperial strategy in the northern Levant at the time of the 18th Dynasty is a remarkable case-study for foreign-indigenous interactions in the Late Bronze Age Levant, and this paper has offered a few new perspectives and discussed potentially innovative avenues for further research. The remarkable level of complexity and diversity of this region contributed to the evolution of the foreign, imperial policies of the Egyptian monarchy from a phase of territorial expansionism to the attainment of a balance of power and the establishment of the diplomatic system known from the Amarna archive. The letters, therefore, represent only the culmination of this interplay between the pharaonic imperial interests and the indigenous, sociopolitical communities of Syria-Palestine, and should be investigated in both a diachronic and synchronic perspective through a combined analysis with the 18th Dynasty royal and non-royal inscriptions and, most interestingly, contemporary cuneiform archives from Syria, especially those from Kumidi and Qaṭna. Future research on the latter should prove particularly valuable, since they offer a synchronic perspective on the sociopolitical and economic dynamics at the local, indigenous level, and therefore complement the narrative of the other two sets of textual evidence. Moreover, the inclusion of archival documents from Kumidi and Qaṭna would break a rigid methodological boundary between Egyptology and Assyriology, which appears even more unjustified as far as the Late Bronze Age is concerned: Akkadian cuneiform texts from Syria-Palestine should not be the preserve of the latter discipline, but should be treated as first-hand evidence by Egyptologists as well. As regards the diachronic development of these geopolitical trends, the impact of the Hyksos domination upon the royal ideology and the cultural memory of the New Kingdom suggests that the first wave of Egyptian imperialism in the Levant may have originated as preemptive warfare, with a view to preventing another form of foreign rule in the Nile Valley. A much better-documented parallel to this phenomenon may be found in Roman history: following Hannibal's invasion of Italy and the battle of Cannae in 216 BC, the Roman Republic initiated a strategy to annihilate any potential military and political threat across the Mediterranean, which included not only the outright destruction of enemy powers such as Carthage, but also the annexation of unstable territories, as was the case for Greece. Finally, the principles of political realism are particularly applicable to the development of the geopolitical systems of the Late Bronze Age, and demonstrate how certain trends and phenomena may be witnessed cross-culturally and throughout history. The much better understood Attic Greek language of the Melian dialogue in Thucydides'

History of the Peloponnesian War highlights the power imbalance which governs foreign-indigenous interactions whenever an imperial state actor seeks to extend its sphere of influence in the geopolitical system, and the dialogue between the Athenian ambassadors and the inhabitants of Melos closely parallels the Amarna vassal correspondence in modes of communication and negotiation of status. Similarly, an analysis of Machiavelli's *Il Principe* shows how parts of this treatise on political realism could be a quite apt description of the dynamics between the foreign, imperial power of the pharaonic monarchy and the complex sociopolitical communities of the Levant.

References

Allen, J.P., 2002. The Speos Artemidos Inscription of Hatshepsut. *BES* 16, 1–17, pls. 1–2.

Allen, J.P., 2008. The Historical Inscription of Khnumhotep at Dahshur: Preliminary Report. *BASOR* 352, 29–39.

Aswani, S. – P. Sheppard, 2003. The Archaeology and Ethnohistory of Exchange in Precolonial and Colonial Roviana: Gifts, Commodities, and Inalienable Possessions. *Current Anthropology* 44 (S5), S51–78.

Badawi, A.M., 1943. Die neue historische stele Amenophis' II. *ASAE* 42, 1–23.

Bietak, M., 2010. Le Hyksôs Khayan, son palais, et une lettre cunéiforme. *CRAIBL* 154(2), 973–990.

Bietak, M. – I. Forstner-Müller – F. van Koppen – K. Radner, 2009. Der Hyksos-palast bei Tell el-Dabʿa: zweite und dritte Grabungskampagne (Frühling 2008 und Frühling 2009). *ÄuL* 19, 91–119.

Brizzi, G., 2016. *Canne. La sconfitta che fece vincere Roma*. Bologna: il Mulino.

Brizzi, G. – G. Cairo, 2015. Livy: Overseas Wars. In B. Mineo, ed., *A Companion to Livy*. Malden – Oxford: Wiley Blackwell, 382–393.

Bryan, B.M., 1980. *The Reign of Tuthmosis IV*. Ph.D. Dissertation, The Johns Hopkins University.

David, S.R., 2000. Realism, Constructivism, and the Amarna Letters. In R. Cohen – R. Westbrook, eds., *Amarna Diplomacy. The Beginnings of International Relations*. Baltimore – London: The Johns Hopkins University Press, 54–67.

de Martino, S., 2014. The Mittani State: The Formation of the Kingdom of Mittani. In E. Cancik-Kirschbaum – N. Brisch – J. Eidem, eds., *Constituent, Confederate, and Conquered Space. The Emergence of the Mittani State*. Topoi – Berlin Studies of the Ancient World 17. Berlin: De Gruyter, 61–74.

Doyle, M.W., 1986. *Empires*. Ithaca – London: Cornell University Press.

Edel, E., 1953. Die Stelen Amenophis' II. aus Karnak und Memphis mit dem Bericht über die asiatischen Feldzüge des Königs. *ZDPV* 69 (2), 97–176.

Edzard, D.O. – R. Hachmann – P. Maiberger – G. Mansfeld, 1970. *Kāmid el-Lōz – Kumidi. Schriftdokumente aus Kāmid el-Lōz*. SBA 7. Bonn: Dr. Rudolf Habelt GmbH.

Freu, J., 2003. *Histoire du Mitanni*. Collection Kubaba, Série Antiquité 3. Paris: L'Harmattan.

Galán, J.M., 1994. The Heritage of Thutmosis III's Campaigns in the Amarna Age. In B.M. Bryan – D. Lorton, eds., *Essays in Egyptology in honor of Hans Goedicke*. San Antonio: Van Siclen Books, 91–102.

Goedicke, H., 2004. *The Speos Artemidos Inscription of Hatshepsut and Related Discussions*. Oakville, CT: Halgo, Inc.

Habachi, L., 1972. *The Second Stela of Kamose and His Struggle against the Hyksos Ruler and His Capital*. ÄA 8. Glückstadt: J.J. Augustin.

Hachmann, R., mit einem Beitrag von G. Wilhelm, 2012. *Kāmid el-Lōz 20. Die Keilschriftbriefe und der Horizont von el-Amarna*. SAB 87. Bonn: Dr. Rudolf Habelt GmbH.

Heinz, M., 2005. *Kamid el-Loz: Intermediary between Cultures. More than 10 years of Archaeological Research in Kamid el-Loz (1997-2007)*. BAAL Hors-Série VII. Beyrouth: Ministère de la Culture, Direction Générale des Antiquités.

Helck, W., 1975. *Historisch-Biographische Texte der 2. Zwischenzeit und Neue Texte der 18. Dynastie*. Kleine ägyptische Texte. Wiesbaden: Harrassowitz.

Horden, P. – N. Purcell, 2000. *The Corrupting Sea. A Study of Mediterranean History*. Oxford – Malden: Blackwell.

Huehnergard, J., 1996. A Byblos Letter, Probably from Kāmid el-Lōz. *ZA* 86, 97–113.

Izre'el, S., 1988. When Was the "General's Letter" from Ugarit Written? In M. Heltzer – E. Lipiński, eds., *Society and Economy in the Eastern Mediterranean (c. 1500-1000 B.C.). Proceedings of the International Symposium held at the University of Haifa from the 28th of April to the 2nd of May 1985*. OLA 23. Leuven: Peeters, 160–175.

Izre'el, S. – I. Singer, 1990. *The General's Letter from Ugarit. A Linguistic and Historical Reevaluation of RS 20.33 (*Ugaritica *V, No. 20)*. Tel Aviv: Tel Aviv University, Chaim Rosenberg School of Jewish Studies.

Klengel, H., 1965. *Geschichte Syriens im 2. Jahrtausend v. u. Z., Teil 1 – Nordsyrien*. Berlin: Akademie-Verlag.

Langer, C., 2015. The Political Realism of the Egyptian Elite: A Comparison between *The Teaching for Merikare* and Niccolò Machiavelli's *Il Principe*. *JEH* 8, 49–79.

Langdon, S. – A.H. Gardiner, 1920. The Treaty of Alliance between Ḫattušili, King of the Hittites, and the Pharaoh Ramesses II of Egypt. *JEA* 6 (3), 179–205.

Lehmann, M., 2011. Vorbericht über die Grabungstätigkeiten der Herbstkampagne 2009 im Areal A/II von Tell el-Dabʿa. *ÄuL* 21, 47–65.

Levy, E., 2017. A Note on the Geographical Distribution of New Kingdom Egyptian Inscriptions from the Levant. *JAEI* 14, 14–21.

Loret, V., 1910. *L'inscription d'Ahmès fils d'Abana*. BdÉ 3. Le Caire: Institut français d'archéologie orientale.

Lorton, D., 1974. *The Juridical Terminology of International Relations in Egyptian Texts through Dyn. XVIII*. Baltimore: Johns Hopkins University Press.

Liverani, M., 1998–1999. *Le lettere di el-Amarna*. 2 vols. TVOA 2: Letterature mesopotamiche 3 (1-2), Brescia: Paideia.

Manassa, C., 2013. *Imagining the Past. Historical Fiction in New Kingdom Egypt*. Oxford – New York: Oxford University Press.

Manuelian, P.D., 1987. *Studies in the Reign of Amenophis II*. HÄB 26. Hildesheim: Gerstenberg.

Moran, W.L., 1992. *The Amarna Letters*. Baltimore – London: Johns Hopkins University Press.

Morris, E.F., 2005. *The Architecture of Imperialism. Military Bases and the Evolution of Foreign Policy in Egypt's New Kingdom*. PdÄ 22. Leiden – Boston: Brill.

Morris, E.F., 2015. Egypt, Ugarit, the God Baʿal, and the Puzzle of a Royal Rebuff. In J. Mynářová – P. Onderka – P. Pavúk, eds., *There and Back Again – The Crossroads II. Proceedings of an International Conference Held in Prague, September 15–18, 2014*. Prague: Charles University in Prague, Faculty of Arts, 315–351.

Morris, E.F., 2018. *Ancient Egyptian Imperialism*. Hoboken: Wiley Blackwell.

Mynářová, J., 2007. *Language of Amarna – Language of Diplomacy. Perspectives on the Amarna Letters*. Prague: Charles University in Prague, Faculty of Arts.

Mynářová, J., 2015. Communicating the Empire, or How to Deliver a Message of a King. In J. Mynářová – P. Onderka – P. Pavúk, eds., *There and Back Again – The Crossroads II. Proceedings of an International Conference Held in Prague, September 15–18, 2014*. Prague: Charles University in Prague, Faculty of Arts, 149–161.

Richter, T., 2005. Qaṭna in the Late Bronze Age: Preliminary Remarks. In D.I. Owen – G. Wilhelm, eds., *General Studies and Excavations at Nuzi 11/1*. SCCNH 15. Bethesda, MD: CDL Press, 109–116.

Richter, T. – S. Lange, 2012. *Das Archiv des Idadda. Die Keilschrifttexte aus den deutsch-syrischen Ausgrabungen 2001-2003 im Königspalast von Qaṭna*. QS 3. Wiesbaden: Harrassowitz.

Peet, T.E., 1914. *The Stela of Sebek-khu. The Earliest Record of an Egyptian Campaign in Asia*. Manchester – London: Sherratt and Hughes.

Redford, D.B., 1979. A Gate Inscription from Karnak and Egyptian Involvement in Western Asia during the Early 18th Dynasty. *JAOS* 99 (2), 270–287.

Tresson, P., 1919. *L'inscription d'Ouni*. BdÉ 8. Le Caire: Institut français d'archéologie orientale.

van Koppen, F. – M. Lehmann, 2012–2013. A Cuneiform Sealing from Tell el-Dabʿa and Its Historical Context. *ÄuL* 22–23, 91–94.

von Dassow, E., 2005. Archives of Alalaḫ IV in Archaeological Context. *BASOR* 338, 1–69.

von Dassow, 2008. *State and Society in the Late Bronze Age: Alalaḫ under the Mittani Empire*. SCCNH 17. Bethesda, MD: CDL Press.

von Dassow, E., 2014. Levantine Polities under Mittanian Hegemony. In E. Cancik-Kirschbaum – N. Brisch – J. Eidem, eds., *Constituent, Confederate, and Conquered Space. The Emergence of the Mittani State*. Topoi – Berlin Studies of the Ancient World 17. Berlin: De Gruyter, 11–32.

Weinstein, J.M., 1981. The Egyptian Empire in Palestine: A Reassessment. *BASOR* 241, 1–28.

Wiseman, D.J., 1953. *The Alalakh Tablets*. Occasional Publications of the British Institute of Archaeology at Ankara 2. London: British Institute of Archaeology at Ankara.

Wiseman, D.J., 1954. Supplementary Copies of Alalakh Tablets. *JCS* 8, 1–30.

Wiseman, D.J., 1959. Ration Lists from Alalaḫ IV. *JCS* 13, 50–62.

Yon, M. – D. Arnaud, eds., 2001. *Études ougaritiques I. Travaux 1985-1995*. RSO 14. Paris: Éditions Recherche sur les Civilisations.

Zangani, F., 2016. Amarna and Uluburun: Reconsidering Patterns of Exchange in the Late Bronze Age. *PEQ* 148(4), 230–244.

INDICES

Geographical Names

T

Personal Names

Divine Names

A

Adad 323
Amun 31, 33, 42, 43, 61, 69, 223, 408
Amun-Re 372, 420
Amurrum 151, 336
Aten 372, 373

B

Baba 151
Baʿl 204, 274, 410
Baʿlaka 277

D

Dagān 204, 274, 277, 278

E

Ea 274
Enki 290
Enkidu 286
Enlil 140, 142, 150, 151, 154, 288–290

G

Geb 191

H

Hathor 351, 362
Humbaba 286

K

Khnum 351

I

Inanna 288–290, 323
Inšušinak 102–106, 110–113
Iškur 145, 146, 290
Išme-kārab 102, 106
Ištar 121, 150

L

Lamma 300

M

Marduk 274, 275, 280, 327, 335, 336

N

Nabium 323
Napiriša 111–113
Nergal 337
Nin-Nibru 152
Ningirgilu 151
Ninlil 141, 142, 151
Ninmug 336
Ninšubur 152
Ninsianna 336
Ninurta 142, 149, 151, 152, 290
Nisaba 290
Nuska 141, 142, 151, 290

P

Pabilsaĝ 151
Ptah 229

R

Ruḫurater 111
Ra 412

S

Seth 414
Sîn 274, 290
Šamaš 330, 335, 336
Šauška 261
Šimut 113

T

Thoth 60, 373

U

Utu 290

A Stranger in the House – the Crossroads III.

Proceedings of an International Conference on Foreigners
in Ancient Egyptian and Near Eastern Societies
of the Bronze Age held in Prague, September 10–13, 2018

edited by Jana Mynářová, Marwan Kilani, Sergio Alivernini

Vydala: Univerzita Karlova v Praze, Filozofická fakulta,
nám. J. Palacha 2, 116 38 Praha 1

Obálka (s použitím ilustrací A.-K. Jeske a C. Hamiltona):
AGAMA® polygrafický ateliér, s.r.o., Praha

Ilustrace: P. Aprent, S. Cohen, H. David-Cuny, A. Goddeeris, C. Hamilton, A.-K. Jeske, C. Reichel, U. Seidl, K. Streit, S. Vilain, W. Więckowski

Fotografie: Archive of the Czech Institute of Egyptology, N.R. Brown, D. Candelora, J. Galczynski, Metropolitan Museum of Art, Oriental Institute of the University of Chicago, H.L. Ringheim

Vydání první, Praha 2019

Grafická úprava: AGAMA® polygrafický ateliér, s.r.o., Praha

Tisk: TNM print, Chlumec nad Cidlinou

ISBN: 978-80-7308-928-3